Of Hawaii

Big Island
of Hawai'i

9th Edition

The Most Complete
Guide to Family Fun
and Adventure!

Catherine Bridges Tarleton

Ulysses Press

Published by: Ulysses Press
            P.O. Box 3440
            Berkeley, CA 94703
            www.ulyssespress.com

ISSN 1042-8062
ISBN 1-56975-501-9

Printed in Canada by Transcontinental Printing

10 9 8 7 6 5 4 3 2

Managing Editor: Claire Chun
Editor: Lily Chou
Copy Editor: Steven Zah Schwartz
Editorial and Production: Lisa Kester, Matt Orendorff,
    Tamara Kowalski, Barbara Schultz, Kathryn Brooks,
    Sara Pflantzer, Nicholas Denton-Brown
Cartography: Pease Press
Cover Design: Leslie Henriques, Sarah Levin
Indexer: Sayre Van Young
Front Cover Photography: Gettyimages/Photodisc Blue (large image);
all other photos from photos.com

Distributed by Publishers Group West

The author and publisher have made every effort to ensure the accuracy of information contained in *Paradise Family Guides: Big Island of Hawai'i*, but can accept no liability for any loss, injury, or inconvenience sustained by any traveler as a result of information or advice contained in this guide.

Write to Us!

If in your travels you discover a spot that captures the spirit of the Big Island, or if you live in the region and have a favorite place to share, or if you just feel like expressing your views, write to us and we'll pass your note along to the author.

Ulysses Press
P.O. Box 3440
Berkeley, CA 94703
E-mail: readermail@ulyssespress.com

Table of Contents

MAPS

★ indicates personal favorites and listings
that are highly recommended

 indicates child-friendly amusements,
locations and businesses

indicates shops and malls

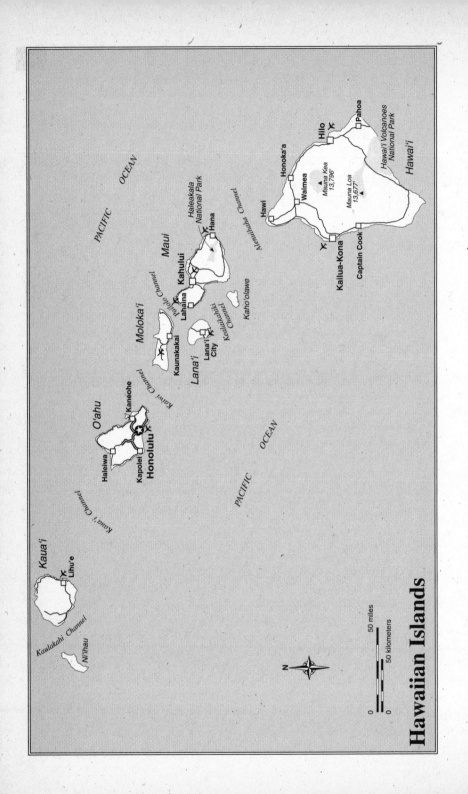

Hawaiian Islands

Preface

There's one thing that everyone brings back from vacation, no matter who they are and no matter where they go: stories. One size fits all, two or three will do for everybody you know—they're unbreakable, un-losable, and they're free. The Big Island is full of stories.

As we prepare to go to print on the 9th edition of *Paradise Family Guide: Big Island of Hawai'i*, it strikes me as important to talk about this as a living, growing thing, a continuing story. Like many places on the planet, we have seen a lot of change in recent years and months, many since the last edition of this book. First-time visitors will find more things that are familiar from their world, and fewer things that are strange to them. Returning guests may be surprised.

Yet there is still adventure. It is still possible to find a place of solitude, a long stretch of unaccountable time, a new taste or experience that can only happen here. There are still secret stories in quiet valleys, forest walks and forgotten beaches. There are legends in the vast ocean, volcanic mysteries and towering sagas of mountains with nothing between you and the stars.

To me, the best adventure and the greatest stories will always be about the people here. This book is only a rough outline, a few examples of what we have to offer. To really learn what that is, you'll have to get to know us a little better. I urge you to open your ears and listen, open your heart, open your mind. Talk story with us and take away something you may not expect but cannot refuse. We call it *aloha*, and no matter what changes around us, that abides. That's our story.

Catherine Bridges Tarleton
November 2005

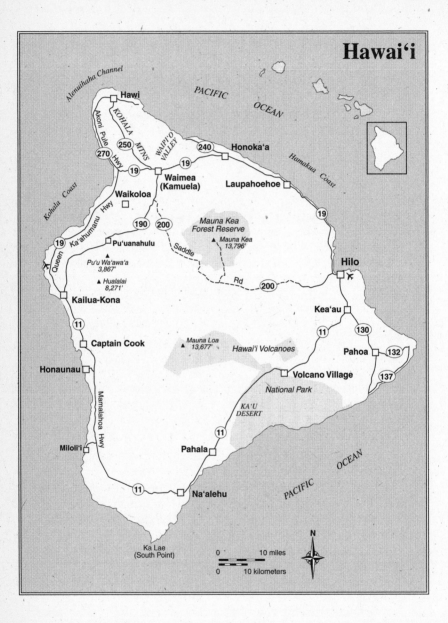

Hawai'i

CHAPTER 1

General Information

The Big Island's Best Bets

Attraction   Unless you have an active volcano in your own back yard, Volcanoes National Park is a rare and awesome experience. In addition to the active eruption, there are exploration hikes and nature trails, a cool museum on the rim of Halema'uma'u Crater, Hawaiian cultural performances and programs at Volcano Art Center and a Junior Ranger Program for kids 5–12

Best Way to See the Volcano on a Tight Schedule   A helicopter flightseeing tour

Best Attraction #2   The Beach. Isn't this why you come to Hawai'i? For almost any kind of beach-goer, from sun worshipper to windsurfer, we recommend Hapuna Beach State Park on the Kohala Coast. Wide white sand, reliable conditions, picnic pavilions, ample parking, restrooms, showers and a snack bar make this the Best Bet for Big Island beaches

Best Sunset Cocktails   The Gazebo Bar, Mauna Kea Beach Hotel. OK, this guide certainly does not promote drinking as a pastime, especially drinking and driving and especially with kids along, *but* just in case your Hawaiian fantasy is to sip one of those fancy libations in the tall glass with a paper umbrella, while waiting for the elusive green flash on the horizon just as the sun sinks into it ... you've come to the right place. In Kona, it's Kalanikai Bar & Grill at the Outrigger Keauhou Beach Resort

Best Ocean Activity   Whale watching, seasonal. Swim, sail, snorkel, scuba, snuba, surf, swim with the dolphins, kayak, boogie board, fish or frolic anytime

Best Ocean Activity without Getting Wet   A voyage with Atlantis Submarines.

Best Free (or Nearly Free) Things to Do • Volcanoes National Park • Beach • Lapakahi State Park and Puʻukohola Heiau National Historic Site • Puʻuhonua o Honaunau Place of Refuge • Petroglyph trail at ʻAnaehoʻomalu • Hula show at the Kings' Shops, Waikoloa • A stroll through Liliuokalani Park and along Banyan Drive in Hilo • Hilo Farmers' Market • ʻAkaka Falls State Park • Amy B.H. Greenwell Ethnobotanical Garden in Kona • Ahuena Heiau, Mokuaikaua Church and Huliheʻe Palace in Kona

Most Beautiful Beach   Kaunaʻoa Bay Beach (Mauna Kea Beach)

Scenic Views   Pololu Valley Overlook at the end of the road in North Kohala, and the Waipiʻo Valley Overlook at the opposite end in the Hamakua District

VOLCANOES FROM THE SKY

It's a long drive to Volcanoes National Park, two hours from either Kona along the southern route or the Kohala Coast resorts along the northern route. Once you enter the park and make stops at the visitors' center and interesting sites along the way, it's another hour before you reach the eruption itself. Don't get us wrong, this is a most worthwhile trip, but if time is limited and you want to do it all, spend the extra dollars and take the flightseeing tour. This is absolutely the best way to see the Big Island's most spectacular show.

Most "birds" take up to six passengers in comfortable, air-conditioned cabins, some with stereo headsets and music synchronized with the flight path. The ride is smooth and the view is awesome. Skilled pilots can position you just above the most current lava flow activity, where you may see red lava emerge from the earth's core and flow seaward, where its encounter with the ocean forms a giant column of steam. You'll soar over inaccessible waterfalls and Eden-like valleys, across lush tropical forests and remote rocky terrain. It's like being in a movie. Everything depends on the weather, and conditions change constantly. Several local helicopter companies offer similar trips at competitive prices. Ask your hotel or condo concierge.

A word about photographs. If you're a fanatic or a pro, by all means, put the lens up to your face and click away. If not, put the camera down and take in everything with your own two eyes. A photograph can barely capture the dramatic experience you're about to undertake, and too much time looking through the lens could make you nauseous. Some of the companies offer multi-camera videos of your flight, starring you and your family. Take 'em up on it.

Place for Hikes and Explorations   Volcanoes National Park

Easy Hike   Thurston Lava Tube in Volcanoes National Park or the forest trail at 'Akaka Falls State Park

Moderate Hike   Kipuka Puaulu/Bird Park just outside Volcanoes National Park, or Kilauea Iki Crater trail inside

Challenging Hike for Experienced Backpackers   1) Mauna Loa Summit Trail, Hawai'i Volcanoes National Park, a strenuous 36.6-mile, 4-day hike to mountain summit; 2) Waipi'o and Waimanu Valley Trail (Muliwai), Hamakua Coast, a difficult two- to three-day wilderness backpacking trip

Family Adventures on Land   "Flumin' Da Ditch," Kohala Mountain Kayak Cruise through the canals, flumes and caves of the irrigation ditch system of North Kohala's old sugar plantations; or a trail ride skirting the scenic ridge of Pololu Valley on mule-back, with Hawai'i Forest & Trail Outfitters

Way to See the Stars   Weekly (free!) star-gazing astronomy program at the Onizuka Center for International Astronomy at 9,200-foot level of Mauna Kea

Must-see Cultural Tour   A self-guided walking tour through Pu'uhonua o Honaunau Place of Refuge, South Kona Coast

Cultural Events   1) The annual spring Merrie Monarch Hula Festival, Hilo (tickets are hard to get but the town is jam-packed with related cultural festivities); 2) any of the series of Na Mea Hawai'i Hula Kahiko performances, free to the public, Volcano Art Center, Hawai'i Volcanoes National Park; 3) the myriad food events, parades, concerts, hula performances and many other happenings islandwide, annually during Aloha Festivals in September and the Kona Coffee Festival in November

Scenic Drives   1) Kawaihae to North Kohala (Hawi and Kapa'au), to Pololu Lookout, back via the Mountain Road to Waimea. Then, Waimea to Honoka'a, Kukuihaele and Waipi'o Valley Overlook; 2) Kona Coffee Country, including Pu'uhonua o Honaunau Place of Refuge; 3) Hamakua Coastline to Hilo, stopping at Laupahoehoe Beach Park, 'Akaka Falls and Onomea Scenic Drive

Golf Course   A toss-up between the Mauna Kea Golf course, Mauna Kea Resort, ranked among "America's 100 Greatest" and "Hawai'i's Finest" by *Golf Digest*, or the Francis I'i Brown South Course at Mauna Lani Resort, equally acclaimed by the same magazine for its 17th hole, which it ranks as a "Pearl of the Pacific"

Golf Course on a Budget   The Robert Trent Jones, Jr., course in Waikoloa Village

Best Resort for Kid Stuff   Hilton Waikoloa Village, Kohala Coast

Chocolate   Big Island Candies in Hilo or Kona; Kailua Candy Company in Kona

Family-friendly Restaurants Denny's in Kona; Don's Grill or Ken's Pancake House in Hilo; Paniolo Country Inn in Waimea
Best Way to Rent a Condo Visit www.sunquest-hawaii.com
Macadamia Nuts and Confections Mauna Loa Macadamia Nut Farms in Hilo; Mac Pie in Kona

The Big Island

If you've ever had a cup of Kona coffee, you've tasted the Big Island. Robust, fortifying, indulgent, luxurious, warm, fragrant, complex, comforting. Once you've taken it in, your concept of coffee changes. Your expectations are greater, your tastes are more experienced and your life is a little richer.

The Big Island is all those things. The Big Island is the Big Island because it's big. Too big, too diverse to be characterized by only one name. Officially, it is "Hawai'i," the same name as the state. And despite the best efforts of PR persons and tourism bureaucrats to put a more glamorous spin on the name (the Orchid Island, the Volcano Island and, most recently, the Healing Island), "Big Island" is the one that stuck and stayed over the years—just like a lot of folks who live here. Today we say we're "FBI," from Big Island.

The Big Island is home to the rainiest city in the U.S. (Hilo), its highest mountain (Mauna Kea, 13,796 feet measured from sea level, over 35,000 from the ocean floor) and the country's southernmost point at Ka Lae. It grows the only American coffee, has the largest non–long distance calling area, the most ethnically diverse population per capita, and is the largest consumer of Spam. It is the biggest of Hawai'i's main islands, bigger than O'ahu, Maui, Kaua'i, Moloka'i, Lana'i, Kaho'olawe and Ni'ihau put together. It is also the youngest geologically, with new land still under construction thanks to ongoing volcanic activity. In fact it is the *hanai* (adopted) mother of Hawai'i's newest island, Lo'ihi Seamount, forming underwater off the southern coastline.

Historically, it was the first island sighted by Polynesian explorers, who perhaps were guided by the steam clouds from Mauna Loa's eruption at the time. It is the birthplace and the final (secret) resting place of King Kamehameha the Great, the first *ali'i* (chief) to conquer, unite and rule all the main islands as one kingdom. This is the place where Captain Cook landed in 1778 and where he was killed. This is where missionaries built their first commissioned church in the islands, and where Queen Ka'ahumanu first broke the ancient *kapu* (taboo) system. These events forever changed the course of Hawai'i's history.

The Big Island is internationally known for Kona coffee, thanks to the caffeine wars of the 1990s, and also in the last century it was reportedly the *pakalolo* (marijuana) capitol of the state. Kilauea Volcano, Hawai'i's first big attraction, is located in a remote and desolate area, miles from anything that looks like tourism. The expensive mega-resorts and vacation residences for the rich and famous are set along the Kohala Coast, surrounded by inhospitably bleak lava rock. Gray, rainy Hilo hosts the world's brightest hula talents during the annual Merrie Monarch Festival. In Kona, modern athletes compete in the Ironman Triathlon World Championship, while down the coast at the restored village of Pu'uhonua o Honaunau, stone-age crafts are taught and practiced. Cowboys ride and rope on horseback in Waimea while soldiers maneuver tanks at Pohakuloa. Chefs prepare Maine lobsters from Kona and Japanese Kobe-style beef from Kohala. In hospitals, advanced medical machines treat patients side by side with "healing touch" practitioners, acupuncturists and *lomi lomi* massage therapists. On the same night, a scientist studies the constellations from the international astronomy community at Mauna Kea's summit, while far below a navigator charts the course for his canoe with ancient stellar navigation. The Big Island is a place that brings contradictions together, a place of amazing change.

But to truly take it in and appreciate the scope of the Big Island, you have to let go of your preconceptions. As your plane approaches Kona International Airport, close your eyes and picture Hawai'i. Palm trees, white beaches, tropical flowers, mai tais and hula dancers. Now open your eyes. Oops, what happened? There's nothing here that resembles the common vision of Hawai'i. As far as you can see, it's rock—black, empty, lifeless lava rock, like a gigantic parking lot half-bulldozed by Godzilla then abandoned. Take heart, this is just a tease, and it's just the beginning. The Big Island is good at teasing. It's never what you expect, but it always exceeds your expectations in some way. We suggest you approach your Big Island vacation with a plan, but not an itinerary, and allow some time to be swept away by your fantasy. Whatever you're looking for, whether it's beach time, great golf, ocean adventures, hiking, biking, history or just something new to eat, you'll find it.

Island History

Most quick histories of Hawai'i begin with first contact by outside influences: Captain James Cook's "discovery" of the islands in 1778. But the Hawaiian Islands, although still *keiki* in geological terms, are many thousands of years old, with a unique ecosystem developed seren-dipitously at Mother Nature's whim.

One of the most readable histories is a novel, James Michener's *Hawaii*. He begins with a single bird, blown off its migratory route by a storm, soaring over the most isolated land mass on earth and depositing a seed. Many generations later, the islands were home to diverse species of plant and animal life who for the most part accidentally found their way to a temperate, nurturing climate for growing things.

The islands themselves are living, growing things. Tectonic shift, movement of the great plates on which the continents are formed, allows magma to escape upward from cracks in the ocean floor. This volcanic action transports lava to the surface where it cools and hardens. Layer upon layer over time builds mountains of rock. Even as they build, the ocean erodes away the circumference, turning stone into sand and coastline into reefs.

Rainwater runs into cracks and crevices, percolating through the porous lava to create a lens of fresh water beneath the island, which pressure forces back to the surface as freshwater springs. Seeds carried by birds, wind or ocean waves find a niche to sprout in. Coconuts and other plants wash up on shore. Insects and spiders arrive in storms or as "stowaways" on other creatures, and evolve into species found nowhere else.

Thousands of miles away from any other land mass, tiny com-pared to the continents, far off course from established shipping lanes, Hawai'i might have happily remained an isolated Eden. But people in other places had the idea to explore. Far to the west and south, the essentially Stone Age people of Tahiti, Java, the Marquesas and Society Islands and others were masters of celestial navigation. Their ocean-going double-hulled sailing canoes carried a good crew long distances over many days at sea. Legends told of a new country to the east, and for reasons perhaps of their own, brave explorers set sail to find it. They took provisions for the trip as well as plants and animals to begin their new life on arrival: coconut, taro, breadfruit, sweet potatoes, bananas, *ti* and other medicinal plants, dogs, pigs and chickens. They also brought their oral history, traditions, government, polytheistic religion and high hopes. Couples traveled together, fully intending to find their new home, raise a family and make it last.

After the long voyage, it is believed the first land sighted was Hawai'i Island, where a volcanic eruption may have flashed like a beacon, or a towering steam cloud pointed the way. The voyagers made landfall near Ka Lae, South Point, and began the colony where the first Hawaiians were born.

People built a society from what they found, what they brought with them and what they could grow. All sustenance came from nature: not just food but building materials, clothing, medicine, transportation, toys, art and music. For example, the coconut gave food and water; its shell was carved into bowls and cooking implements; fronds thatched into roofing, woven into baskets, shoes, mats and other useful things; the tree trunk carved into drums. In a few growing seasons, life and culture were established.

Over the generations an elaborate, well-balanced system of fishing and farming developed and thrived. *Ali'i,* chiefs, ruled over *maka'ainana,* commoners, living on triangular reaches of land called *ahupua'a,* with their long bases spanning the ocean coast and high points stretching up into the mountains. At the ocean, people fished, gathered seaweed and shellfish and made salt from seawater. They trapped the *keiki* of more desirable fish in ponds along the shore and raised them to eating-size. Up *mauka,* at higher, wetter elevations, they farmed taro for their staple food, *poi,* and grew sweet potatoes and other vegetables that they traded with the community *makai,* by the ocean.

Ceremonial occasions like the *makahiki* to honor the deity Lono at the beginning of the new lunar year marked the seasons. Celebrated with a *lu'au* feast, ancestral chant and *hula,* these festivals gave *ali'i* and *maka'ainana* the necessary ritual and order to the year. A third class, the *kahuna,* served as priests and experts in the arts and sciences. It was their responsibility to bless any event—planting, canoe launch, childbirth or death—and to pass on the cumulative knowledge of the people through spoken-only language. The *kahuna* advised the *ali'i* and guided the *maka'ainana* with education, religious ritual, healing practices and counsel.

During this time, the stories of the elders grew into fabulous myths: mischievous Maui who roped the rays of the sun to slow its race across the sky; Pele, the volcano goddess, who created the islands one by one with her *o'o,* digging stick; the industrious little-folk, the *menehune,* who built great stone structures unseen in the dark of night; the great god Lono, whose symbol was a white cloth draped over crossed sticks. Passed down in chant and *hula,* the stories grew into a mythology with an elaborate pantheon of gods and goddesses.

Social order was maintained by the swift and decisive justice of the *kapu* system of complex law. The rules were strict, enforced by *ali'i* warriors and punishable by death. Men and women ate in separate *hale,* houses, and women were prohibited from eating certain foods. Various fish could only be taken in season, and the schedule of planting and harvesting was rigid. Commoners, the *maka'ainana,* worked; *ali'i* ruled. Often they warred violently with other *ali'i*; powerful armies feuded over land boundaries, with negligible effect on the work of *maka'ainana*. Their worlds were very different and there was no crossing over. If even the shadow of an *ali'i* fell across a *maka'ainana*, the commoner might be killed. In addition, the gods made harsh demands, including human sacrifice.

The *kapu* system bonded the people with fear and force, but it insured the culture would remain in place and unchanged, and that *ali'i* rule would stand unchallenged. It is believed this may have been the status quo for up to a thousand years.

In 1758 Halley's Comet passed over Hawaiian skies as it did elsewhere in the world. It marked the birth of Kamehameha, an *ali'i* child born in a secret place on the Big Island. He was raised into manhood and took his place as ruler of his father's *ahupua'a*, an enormous man full of *mana,* spiritual power, strength and ambition. One of his *kahuna* prophesied that if he rebuilt the great *heiau,* temple, at Pu'ukohola, one day he would unite and rule all the islands as one kingdom. Kamehameha gave the order and the *heiau* was constructed.

Into this world, in January 1778, sailed English sea captain James Cook with his two ships, the *Discovery* and the *Resolution.* Cook was a well-known explorer, en route from Tahiti, searching for the Strait of Anian, a passageway through North America. He located the Hawaiian islands quite by accident and made first landfall on Kauai, where he named his find the Sandwich Islands in honor of his sponsor, the Earl of Sandwich, First Lord of the British Admiralty. He explored the islands for eight months, stopping at O'ahu and Maui to interact with the natives, and along the way met the lesser *ali'i* Kamehameha of the Big Island, 20 years old.

A year later, after unsuccessfully searching northern waters for his passageway, Cook's ships sailed into Kealakekua Bay on the south Kona coast, January 17, 1779. It was during *makahiki;* the people were feasting in celebration of Lono, when they looked up and beheld his symbol drifting toward them from the sea. Cook was honored as the incarnation of Lono and welcomed with offerings, food, and women. After a few weeks to repair and re-provision his ships, trade with the natives and allow his sailors shoreleave, Cook departed on February 4 to continue his voyage.

Bad luck and bad weather forced Cook back a few days later, with a broken mast on the *Resolution*, but this time his welcome was very different. Perhaps believing he had cursed them, possibly doubting his divinity, *maka'ainana* treated Cook and his men with hostility. On February 14, after various small incursions, the ship's cutter was stolen from the *Discovery*. When Cook confronted the thieves with arms, they met him with their own weapons. The conflict escalated quickly; Cook was slain; his surviving crew sailed away. Cook was gone, but he changed Hawai'i forever; his ships left behind rats, mosquitoes, bacteria, venereal disease. As it had brought life thousands of years before, serendipity now brought death.

And more ships would come, their captains willing to trade weapons for food, firewood, salt and fresh water. By 1791, Kamehameha was a strong, shrewd military leader. He coveted the *malihini,* strangers', tools of war, as did other feudal *ali'i.* When an English schooner, the *Fair American* sailed into Big Island waters, warriors boarded and took control, killing the crew except for one man, Isaac Davis. At the same time, another English ship, the *Eleanora,* was anchored off Kealakekua Bay and one of her sailors, John Young, went to shore and was captured by Kamehameha. With exciting new war technology and the knowledge of these two men, Kamehameha would be undefeatable. Young and Davis were ordered to train Kamehameha's warriors for a new kind of battle.

The ensuing years saw much warfare and bloodshed as Kamehameha's armies, with the help of English cannons and muskets, conquered neighboring *ali'i* on Maui and Hawai'i. On O'ahu he drove opposing warriors over the steep *pali*, cliffs, at Nu'uanu. Kauai was never conquered but eventually capitulated. The prophesy was fulfilled. Hawai'i was one nation with one ruler responsible for all.

But the islands were no longer secret. Many more ships came, trading weapons for the fragrant sandalwood that brought good profit in China. Whaling ships from America exchanged trinkets and rum for provisions and female company and dominated the wharves of Lahaina and Kona with their raucous lifestyle. With one leader to negotiate for all, it was easy for power-hungry *ali'i* to sell out until the land was denuded. They dressed in European costume and looked at themselves in fancy mirrors, while their people became sicker and began to die by the thousands. It is believed that from Cook's first contact in 1778 to the first recorded census, Hawai'i's population decreased by more than 300,000 people.

Into these disastrous times sailed different traders, in search of pagan souls. The first shipful of Christian missionaries from New England landed on the Big Island in 1820, two years after Kamehameha's death. They clothed the nearly naked "heathen" women, scorned what they considered lascivious behavior such as *hula* and refused to deviate from a strictly Protestant path. They warred with the hard-drinking, promiscuous whalers and curtailed their licentious activities. They constructed Hawai'i's first church building and set about their work of spreading the Word. To their credit, they devised a written Hawaiian language, translated the Bible, and taught the people to read and write. Without this, much of the culture would have been lost forever. Many of the missionaries died and many more left in the first years, when their stubborn adherence to mainland ways failed them in the hot climate of this different world, but they gained a foothold which became a cultural coup. Once converted, re-organized by the church, Hawaiian life changed; governing power shifted and a new authority was established.

Queen Ka'ahumanu, favored wife of Kamehameha the Great, listened to the Gospel, saw a spiritual void where it seemed the old gods had abandoned her, and sought redemption from the new religion. It was she and her son, Liholiho, Kamehameha II, who brought down the *kapu* system in one day by publicly eating together. *Heiau* were destroyed, ritual and *hula* prohibited and the *kahuna* shunned. The people turned to the Cross.

They learned what money was, and how missionary men with money could purchase land to call their own, even from the *ali'i*. In a relatively short time, island real estate was a disaster, the rational, neat boundaries of *ahupua'a* carved into plots and traded like goods. In an effort to organize the debacle once and for all, or possibly tilt the scale in *malihini* favor, the Great Mahele, a "legal" motion begun in 1841, allotted lands between the King, various *ali'i* chiefs and the *maka'ainana* by making salable portions and rules of exchange. To a people with no concept of "land ownership," this arbitrary division was meaningless. Many found themselves ousted from homesteads generations old.

One who profited well from the land exchange was a seaman named Samuel Palmer Parker, a former sailor who found favor with Kamehameha and married his granddaughter. As a wedding gift he received a few acres, to which he strategically added many more. But there was a problem; the land was overrun by wild cattle. In 1794, Kamehameha had been presented with a few head of beef cattle by British explorer George Vancouver (in exchange for "ceding" the Island to Great Britain). He immediately placed a *kapu* on the cows and allowed them to range freely over the island, where they thrived and reproduced in great numbers. These cattle were devastating Parker's land and he petitioned the King for permission to contain them. It was granted, but the job was too much for Parker and his crew of *maka'ainana*. He hired imported Mexican *vaqueros* to help.

Although horses had been introduced years earlier, it was the *paniolo* (Spanish, Español) who taught the locals to ride, rope and ranch cowboy-style, before the American Wild West existed. Fresh beef was a profitable, welcome commodity for ships; Parker Ranch grew into one of the world's largest cattle operations and created an entire *paniolo* culture. It dominated central Hawai'i for over 150 years, providing not just food, but employment, schools, housing and a strong sense of community to the Waimea area (also called "Kamuela," Samuel, in honor of Parker's son).

At the same time, agriculture hit the Big Island in a big way. Thanks to creative real estate practices, former missionary families and other business people accumulated large parcels of land in the greener *mauka* regions and began plantations. Many crops were tried with varying degrees of success, and coffee became a major product of the Kona area. A variety of Arabica beans were first planted in 1813 by King Kamehameha the Great's consultant Don Francisco de Paula y Marin (who is responsible for bringing in many of the plants, trees and flowers we take for granted as "Hawaiian"). In 1828, an American missionary transplanted a *Coffea arabica* bush to Kona, and began to cultivate it commercially. Coffee flourished in the higher elevations' rich volcanic soil and its quality rivaled the best from Africa or South America. Tended and harvested by local workers, burlap sacks of coffee berries were hauled down the slopes on donkeys, dubbed "Kona nightingales" for their braying song. Coffee roasteries thrived and the process was perfected to an art form—but it was sugar cane that drove the island's economy for nearly a century.

Sugar is a labor-intensive process to grow, harvest, refine and export, and all the jobs were not filled by Hawaiians. To take up the slack, plantation owners hired groups of people in immigration "waves" from China, Japan, Korea, the Philippines and Portugal. Slavery was not a practice; the basically "indentured" workers lived in camps delineated by ethnic group and were provided a wage, food, housing, education for their children, church and social life in exchange for long hours of hard work. In a short time, the "lunch pail" social system, where everyone shared something of their own culture, melded into a colorful yet more or less unified local population. From this grew a special language called "pidgin." Some linguists say it originated with children at play, quickly learning to communicate with various words from Hawaiian, English, Spanish and other languages.

A narrow-gauge railroad was built to transport cane from plantation to factory, and a network of water flumes crossed the Hamakua hills. Hilo became prosperous as a commercial harbor town and in the remote, unknown district of Puna, a new industry was born: tourism. This is where Pele still lived, luring the curious to view her spectacular works. A small thatched hut near Halema'uma'u Crater, at times a caldron of red lava, became known as Volcano House, the first hotel on the island.

In a very short time, the course of Hawai'i turned 180 degrees. The *maka'ainana*, instead of working the land for *ali'i* chiefs, now worked for *haole* (Caucasian) plantation owners, on vast tracts of farmland, raising cattle, growing coffee and sugar cane. When Kamehameha died in 1820, only 42 years after Cook's arrival, his heirs ruled a radically different kingdom. Most died as young, fairly ineffective leaders without a vision for their people, and the bloodline ended with the death of Lot, Kamehameha V, in 1874.

The elected king, David Kalakaua, for whom the Merrie Monarch *hula* festival is named, helped preserve the precious culture by restoring the art of *hula* to prominence and returning to the people some of what was lost. He also brought electricity to Hawai'i, magically lighting the palace after meeting Thomas Edison in America. In 1887 O'ahu businessmen saw the popular Kalakaua as a threat to their interests and manipulated him into signing a new constitution, decreasing the monarchy's power and the rights of Hawaiians in a major way. When he died in 1891, his sister Liliuokalani became Queen of a troubled monarchy.

On January 16, 1893, a group of American businessmen, with the assistance of U.S. marines, staged a secret coup. They deposed the Queen and placed her under house arrest in her Honolulu home. The Territory of Hawai'i was proclaimed a protectorate of the United States. Although Liliuokalani petitioned presidents Harrison and Cleveland to restore the Hawaiian Kingdom, and in spite of outraged resistance, this act nailed the coffin closed on Hawai'i's past; it was now irreversibly part of the modern world.

After the chaos at the end of the 19th century, the Islands enjoyed a time of relative peace in the early 20th century, until December 7, 1941, when Japanese planes attacked Pearl Harbor. Even though it was not one of the United States, Hawai'i went to war. At once, most of O'ahu's population was at work rebuilding the Pacific Fleet. Hundreds of men, among them the highly-decorated 100th battalion made up of Americans of Japanese ancestry, became heroes on international battlefields.

On the Big Island, the quiet *paniolo* town of Waimea exploded almost overnight, when 55,000 marines arrived, following the disastrous loss in Tarawa, Japan. Parker Ranch manager Hartwell Carter leased acreage to Uncle Sam, whose troops pitched tents in the field of "Camp Tarawa" and began training for a joint-services attack on a place called Iwo Jima. Parker School became the USO Club; local kitchens turned into hamburger stands; soldiers from Montana and Texas challenged *paniolo* to Hawai'i's first rodeo.

The war years introduced Americans to Hawai'i, where they discovered an idyllic vacation destination, with alluring beaches, exotic food, culture and tropical romance. Honolulu expanded immediately to welcome thousands of visitors by ship and commercial airlines. On the Big Island, seaside accommodations began to grow up along the peaceful Kona coastline, which became known as a vacation spot for adventurers, away from Waikiki. It was the place for deep-sea fishermen, explorers, beachcombers, scuba divers, stargazers, game hunters and cowboys.

In 1959, Hawai'i became the 50th star on the American flag and took the final step into the 20th century. In 1960, forward-looking Governor William Quinn was aware of Hawai'i's dependency on the floundering sugar cane industry. As cheaper sources became more viable in the international market, something would have to replace that income in the islands. He believed the future was in tourism and invited noted conservationist Laurance S. Rockefeller to visit and view some Big Island beach properties. Rockefeller took a swim in Kauna'oa Bay, a recreation area of Parker Ranch, and sealed the deal. He built the most expensive resort in the world at the time, Mauna Kea Beach Hotel, with a Robert Trent Jones, Sr., golf course, the island's first. Forty years later, what was a craggy scrabble of black rock and *kiawe* trees is the luxurious Kohala Coast, "golf capitol of Hawai'i," and playground for the world's affluent, with eight world-class resorts and an explosion of top-flight residences.

But all play and no work does not sustain a growing community, and the Big Island hosts amazing works in progress. Mauna Kea's summit, 33,500 feet above the ocean floor (a towering 13,796 feet above sea level), is home to the world's premier international astronomy community, with thirteen telescopes gazing heavenward nightly. The ongoing research at Volcanoes National Park surpasses any location worldwide. Experiments in aquaculture and deep-ocean energy resources are making real progress at Kona's Natural Energy Labs Hawai'i. High up on the Saddle Road, Pohakuloa Training Area exercises state-of-the-art military equipment for the Stryker Brigade. In Waimea, hi-tech medicine works side-by-side with traditional cultural practices in the small but ground-breaking North Hawai'i Community Hospital setting.

In less scholarly matters, Kona is recognized as the "Napa" of coffee-lovers; the annual Merrie Monarch Festival welcomes *hula's* best; the original Ironman fields thousands of world-class triathletes in the sport's spotlight event; the Kona International Billfish Tournament is at the top of its game. More and more Hollywood film and TV studios choose the Big Island for quality locations.

Hawaiian Language

One of the more positive things the early missionaries
did for Hawai'i was to standardize the ancient spoken
language into an alphabet and system of writing. Until
then, Hawaiian was a spoken language only. A member of
the Polynesian language family, Hawaiian is very similar to Tahitian
and other Pacific Island languages and dialects.

The written Hawaiian language has an alphabet of twelve letters:
five vowels (a, e, i, o, u) and seven consonants (h, k, l, m, n, p, w).
Syllables are made up of one, two or three letters. Every syllable in
a word is pronounced. Every syllable ends in a vowel, so every word
ends in a vowel. For example, look at the word "Ho/no/lu/lu." Each
syllable contains two letters, a consonant and a vowel. Each syllable
is pronounced and each ends with a vowel sound.

The vowels are pronounced as follows:

a—Say "ah" (aloha)
e—Hey (lei)
i—See (Waikiki)
o—Oh no (aloha)
u—Ooo la la (luau)

Some vowel combinations resemble diphthongs and are pronounced as combination sounds:

ai and *ae*—Aye aye sir—Waikiki, Kawaihae (kah-wye-high)
ao and *au*—Powwow (luau)
ei—hay (lei)
oe—boy (aloha oe)

The accent generally falls on the next to last syllable (as in
"Honolulu"), although some words are evenly accented (as in
"Waikiki"). The *okina* (') is used to indicate a glottal stop, or pause,
between sounds. This may have been an indicator that a *k* sound
found in other Polynesian dialects has disappeared in Hawaiian
usage. Where this mark appears, the accent falls on the preceding
vowel, as in the following: *pu'u* (poo-oo; hill), *ali'i* (ah-lee-ee; chief)
or *a'a* (ah-ah; rough lava).

The consonants are pronounced as they are in English, except
for *w,* which is sounded as a *v* if it introduces the last syllable of a
word. Examples are the famous Polynesian ceremonial drink, *awa*
(actually pronounced "ava"), and the area on O'ahu called Ewa (pronounced "Ehva").

The name "Hawai'i" is still under debate. Although it introduces
the next-to-last syllable, many people insist that the v sound pre-
vails. Likewise, the glottal stop is often glossed over. (Don't be con-

cerned with perfect pronunciation on this word because someone is going to disagree with you no matter what you say. However, you can avoid sounding too much like a *malihini* (stranger) by avoiding the pronunciation "hah-wye-yah." That just doesn't work.)

It's going to be easy for you to learn and try using a few words of Hawaiian on your visit. Almost all place names are Hawaiian words, so that's a good starting point. Remember that new words, like new tastes and sights, add dimension to your travel experience and your memories afterward. Here is a very brief glossary to get you started, and we'd recommend you also purchase a pocket Hawaiian language dictionary.

GLOSSARY

a'a—(ah-ah)—rough, clinky lava

aina—(eye-nah)—land

akamai—(ah-ka-MYE)—smart

ali'i—(ah-lee-ee)—chief

aloha—(ah-loh-hah)—greetings

a'ole—(ah-OH-lay)—no

auwe—(ow-way)—oh no!

hale—(hah-lay)—house

hana hou—(ha-nah HO)—to do it again, encore

hanai—(hah-NYE)—adopted

haole—(how-lee)—a Caucasian, foreigner

hapa—(hah-pah)—half

hauoli—(how-OH-lee)—happy

heiau—(heh-ow)—temple

holoholo—(just like it looks)—to travel

hui—(hoo-ee)—group, union, club, etc., most often referred to business groups who pool their money for investment purposes

hula—(hoo-lah)—dance

imu—(ee-moo)—underground oven to roast luau food

kai—(kye)—ocean

kahuna—(kah-HOO-nah)—teacher, priest

kalo—(kah-loh)—taro, poi is made from its root

kama'aina—(kah-mah-AI-nuh)—native born

kane—(kah-nay)—man

kapu—(kah-poo)—keep out, forbidden

keiki—(kay-kee)—child

kokua—(koh-KOO-ah)—help

lanai—(lah-NAH-ee)—porch or patio

lei—(lay)—garland of flowers

lomi lomi—(loh-mee LOH-mee)—to rub or massage

A FEW WORDS ABOUT PIDGIN

Pidgin is one of those great, eclectic "chop suey" languages that includes a little bit of everything—perfect for the Big Island. It contains a colorful mingle mangle of Hawaiian with some English, Spanish, Portuguese, Japanese, Chinese, Korean and Filipino words thrown in for good measure. Some linguists believe it was invented by sugar cane plantation children while they were playing together. You'll hear pidgin words and phrases at the beach, the gas station, local stores and restaurants, although you might not recognize them as a separate language. Pidgin has been commonly used by enough people for enough years that it's a trend among Hawai'i's contemporary writers to use Pidgin exclusively in novels, periodicals and some non-fiction works.

Here is a short course on common Pidgin phrases you may hear, with the polite suggestion that you use this to develop your skills in listening to pidgin, not speaking it.

any kine—anything
ass why—that's the reason, that's why
brah, bruddah—brother, good friend
buggah—guy, friend, also a pest or nuisance
bumbye—soon enough
chicken skin—goose bumps, when your skin gets the chills
chop suey—all mixed up
cockaroach—to steal or sneak away with something
da kine—a generally used term referring to everything, as in the right thing

lu'au—(loo-ow)—party with entertainment and *imu*-cooked food

mahalo—(mah-HA-low)—praise, thanks

makai—(mah-KYE)—toward the ocean

malihini—(mah-lee-HEE-nee)—a newcomer or visitor

mana—(mah-nah)—supernatural or divine power

mauka—(mau-*rhymes with cow*-kah)—toward the mountain

mauna—(mau-nah)—mountain

menehune—(may-nay-HOO-nee)—a hardworking mythical Hawaiian dwarf or elf

nani—(nah-nee)—beautiful

okole—(oh-KOH-lay)—bottom (butt)

ono—(oh-no)—delicious

pali—(pah-lee)—cliff, precipice

paniolo—(pah-nee-O-low)—Hawaiian cowboy

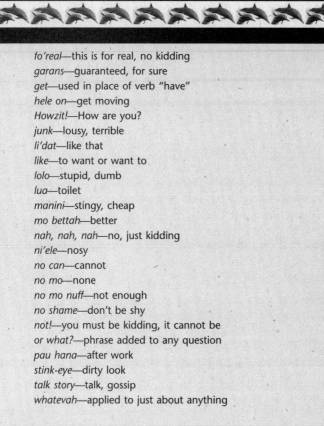

fo'real—this is for real, no kidding
garans—guaranteed, for sure
get—used in place of verb "have"
hele on—get moving
Howzit!—How are you?
junk—lousy, terrible
li'dat—like that
like—to want or want to
lolo—stupid, dumb
lua—toilet
manini—stingy, cheap
mo bettah—better
nah, nah, nah—no, just kidding
ni'ele—nosy
no can—cannot
no mo—none
no mo nuff—not enough
no shame—don't be shy
not!—you must be kidding, it cannot be
or what?—phrase added to any question
pau hana—after work
stink-eye—dirty look
talk story—talk, gossip
whatevah—applied to just about anything

pau—(pow)—finished
poi—(poy)—a paste made from the taro root
pua—(poo-ah)—flower
puka—(poo-ka)—a hole
pupu—(poo-poo)—appetizers
wahine—(wah-HEE-nay)—woman
wiki wiki—(WEE-kee WEE-kee)—hurry

BIG ISLAND PLACE NAMES

Halema'uma'u—crater, fire pit
Hilo—first night of new moon
Holualoa—long sled course
Honoka'a—rolling bay
Ka Lae—south point
Kailua—two seas

Kapaʻau—elevated portion of a *heiau*

Kawaihae—water of wrath; refers to people who fought over water supply in this arid area

Kealakekua—pathway of the god

Kona—leeward side

Mauna Kea—white mountain

Mauna Loa—long mountain

Naʻalehu—volcanic ashes

Pahoa—dagger

Puʻukohola—hill of the whale

Waiakea—broad water

Waikoloa—water for ducks

Waimea—red water

Waipiʻo—curved water

Island Ecology

FAUNA

MONGOOSE No, it's not a rat. That sneaky brown animal with the long tail is a mongoose, brought in by farmers during the last century to eat the cane toad (which did not work since the toads are nocturnal and mongoose are not). Mongoose are harmless, ferret-like animals that populate most of the island. You'll see them hopping out of rubbish cans or patrolling empty lots.

GOATS Small families of wild goats are often seen grazing along roadsides, even in the drier areas. These are descendants of "escapees" and are very shy.

DONKEYS The "Kona nightingales" came to the island many years ago to help haul coffee beans down from the mountains. Now their great-great grandchildren range the *mauka* (mountain) areas unrestrained. You'll see the donkey-crossing signs along the highway, and you may see the donkeys themselves, particularly at dusk.

CATS Feral cats are everywhere on the island. You'll see them roaming beach parks and campsites at night, sometimes in groups. Animal activist organizations are making various efforts to control the population and care for the colonies appropriately. For the most part these cats have been living wild for generations and are not domestic animals. They are wary of humans, but if you're camping, do be sure to secure your food. And if you choose to feed them, be aware that you may draw large numbers.

GECKOS Geckos are amusingly animated little "lizards" that find homes in the most unlikely places around the island. You find

CREATURES TO WATCH OUT FOR

Campers and hikers should be aware that the Big Island hosts both centipedes and small scorpions. While neither is deadly poisonous, both have nasty stings. Scorpions hide under rocks in dry areas, and centipedes turn up almost anywhere. If you have a close encounter, treat it like a bee sting and watch for unusual swelling, redness or signs of allergic reaction. Consult a doctor if you are concerned. There are also various species of spiders, bees and wasps, including ground-dwelling bees. The good news is—no snakes!

them in plants and trees, on window screens and picnic tables, in trunks of cars and sometimes suitcases. They are harmless bug-eaters and there are many species, including a bright green-to-brown chameleon, a putty-colored house gecko that chirps in the evening and a recent addition, the Madagascar gecko, vivid chartreuse with blue toes and splashes of red on his back. Visiting kids will enjoy a gecko hunt, but be sure to let them go.

COQUI FROGS Our newest neighbors are small tree frogs, who take up residence in forests and gardens, schoolyards, resort landscapes and public parks, especially in the wetter areas. Listen for their loud, bird-like chirping after dark. With a benevolent environment, no natural enemies and almost unlimited food supply, these noisy little guys have become serious problems to Hawai'i's ecology. An eradication program using caffeine (believe it or not) is underway.

BIRDS The Big Island is home to many indigenous birds such as the 'elepaio, 'i'iwi, and various species of honeycreeper that only experienced birders are likely to spot. However, birdlife is plentiful and the more common bird species are fun to watch as you make your way around the island. It might surprise you to see cardinals, English sparrows, mockingbirds and other "stowaway" species that came to the island on ships. Although seagulls are rare, you might see a Hawaiian stilt as he trips along the beach at dinnertime, or the large white frigate bird soaring overhead.

The common mynah is a robin-size black bird with a bright yellow beak and, yes, he's related to the talking mynahs in pet stores. He loves to steal rubbish or leftover food, and his raucous cries and animated behavior are unmistakable.

Majiro are tiny green birds that have white circles around their black eyes, and are often seen in papaya trees, enjoying the fruit for breakfast.

FORAGING

Now, before we go any further, we are *not* suggesting that any visitor break the law by stealing fruit, coffee, nuts or flowers from a farmer's land just because they happen to grow close to the roadside. What we *are* saying is that the Big Island is a huge garden, and someone—especially someone from a city—hiking or casually driving along might enjoy the unique experience of picking and eating something wonderful. Here, then is a very brief guide to "free-range" foods you might find at random. As always, if you're not sure, do what your mother told you, "Don't eat that!"

Avocado   Avocados fall to the ground when they are ripe. However, avocados generally turn to baby food once they hit the ground and you really need a long-handled picker to bother with them. In season they are plentiful and cheap, but if you're lucky enough to find a short enough tree, look for fruit that pulls off the stem easily, and don't take more than you can eat.

Bananas   If they're completely green, don't bother; they will not ripen once picked. They'll begin to turn yellow from the top of the bunch. Take a few and leave the rest, being careful not to pull down the tree.

Coconuts   Now this is fun. Find a brown, dry coconut that is lightweight. Break the stem end off, decorate it with aloha motif, and address it to a friend back home. The post office is still happy to handle these Hawaiian postcards. Perfect for anyone who thinks they have everything. If you want to eat one, find one that is golden brown in color, with no cracks. You'll need a machete to whack the outer husk off and get to the round, woody nut inside. Once you've extracted that, you should be able to punch holes through the "eyes," drain the juice out, crack the shell and scrape out the white coconut meat. Unless you happened to pack your machete, visit a local craft show for a coconut demonstration.

Coffee   Do not pick coffee beans. This is a serious cash crop that should be left untouched, and there are plenty of free samples available on the Kona side. Enjoy looking at the trees—and

If a loud, musical bird call or a persistent knocking on the roof wakes you up in the morning, it's a francolin. These quail-like ground birds live in family groups and patrol their neighborhood like clockwork, announcing sunrise and sunset to anyone within earshot.

If you're lucky enough to spot the Hawaiian *pu'eo*, it's said to be a good omen for your travels. This small, brown and white owl

smelling the flowers if you're lucky enough to find them in bloom (coffee is a relative of gardenia).

Flowers   Local custom says unless you're making a lei, or plucking one blossom for behind your ear, leave the flowers for everyone to enjoy. (Note: Oleanders are toxic.) It is particularly uncool to disturb the fuzzy bright red *lehua* flowers on an *ohia* tree. These are favorites of volcano goddess Pele.

Guava   Don't climb the scrubby trees; the fruits fall when they're ripe. Examine the fruit and don't take any with holes as they will have bugs. Cut them in half and suck the delicious pulp off the seeds. Some people eat the skin, seeds and all.

Macadamia nuts   Leave them on the trees. Trust us, you do not have anything that can crack one. And farmers take trespassers very seriously. The trees are beautiful and can be identified usually by a sign that says "Somebody's Mac Nut Farms," or something to that effect.

Mango   The trees are tall, but again the fruit falls to the ground when ripe. Pick up unbruised green fruit with a yellow-pinkish tinge, check for bug holes, then peel and eat the orange flesh around the large central seed. Start slowly, as some people have an adverse reaction that produces cracks around their lips. Mangoes are so delicious it's almost worth the risk.

Papaya   Growing from umbrella-like trees, the fruit is suspended from the very top, which is usually hard to reach, and the trunk is not strong enough to support a climber. If you find one with reachable fruit, select one or two with a some yellow showing. Fully yellow fruit will be too ripe and fully green fruit will not ripen off the tree. Slice the papaya in half, discard the black seeds and enjoy with a spritz of lime juice.

Sugar cane   Look for the white tufted stalks, resembling pampas grass. You can peel a piece of the cane and suck the sweet pulp.

might be seen silently gliding over the fields at dusk as he hunts for dinner.

The i'o, or Hawaiian hawk, is a rare sight, too, but you might see one soaring over higher elevations, or patiently watching the road from a telephone line.

A distant relative of the Canadian goose, the *nene* is a protected species of ground-dwelling bird. You may see them in Volcanoes

National Park or other remote areas and will recognize them by their size and distinctive black markings. Please don't approach them.

FLORA

As you cruise along Big Island roads, take a look at the veritable Garden of Eden growing all around you. Especially in rainier areas, worlds of flowers, fruit trees and tropical plants decorate the landscape with lush color and a thousand shades of green.

Banana trees grow wild in wetter areas. They are broadleafed stalks that grow in patches and a ripe bunch will hang away from the tree, "upside down" to what you may expect, with the bananas pointing upward.

Guava are small, about lemon-sized, yellow fruits that grow on scrubby trees in the gulches and along backroads.

In season, *mangoes* are abundant in the island's rainier neighborhoods. Look for a long stem hanging from the branches, and a green to gold and crimson, almond-shaped fruit.

Coffee trees are short shrubs with long sprays of white flowers that become red "cherries," which are picked, dried, husked, roasted and brewed into extraordinary coffee.

Once most of the Big Island was devoted to *sugar cane*. This beautiful crop spread tall, green tufted grass across acre after hilly acre, waving and singing in the tradewinds. Although the industry has gone, sugar cane plants continue to grow wild in most wet areas.

Avocados, like mangoes, grow wild in many areas. There are many species of both. Look for ripe ones in Hilo Farmers' Market, roadside stands or local grocery stores.

Local farms have grown into specialists, producing not only excellent-quality tropical fruits, but also chocolate, vanilla bean, edible flowers, exotic mushrooms, gourmet tomatoes and salad greens, baby vegetables and much, much more. **Hawaii AgVentures**, a new enterprise of the Big Island Farm Bureau, offers farm tours and gourmet dining experiences in some out-of-the-way places foodies won't want to miss. Private tours to coffee and chocolate factories, cattle ranches, herb farms and flower producers start at $95 (13-person minimum). A particularly special excursion takes place every Tuesday with Peter Merriman, one of the first chefs to popularize Hawaii Regional cuisine. He offers a behind-the-scenes farm tour and prix-fixe dinner at Merriman's Restaurant in Waimea ($115). 800-660-6011; www.hawaiiagventures.com.

Papayas grow on funny-looking trees that resemble green umbrellas—long, pale trunks with fan-shaped leaves; they grow wild in many areas.

Eucalyptus trees have grown into abundant forests all along the Hamakua Coast during the last five years. These tall, straight trees with unusual flaky-looking bark were planted on former sugar cane land as part of a planned paper pulp industry. A snafu in the system has left us with plenty of raw material but no processing plant. While alternatives are being considered, we have to wonder if Koala farming has a future here.

"Wild" flowers—many of them escapees from island gardens— bloom along roadsides and trails. Look for the tiny purple-white bamboo orchids peeking above their tall, grassy stalks; red, white and fragrant yellow ginger with their shiny oval leaves growing among shade trees; trailing vines of yellow flowers that become "wood roses" when dry; the large trumpets of belladonna, multicolored nasturtiums, impatiens; yellow, red, white or pink hibiscus; and many others in Big Island forests, roadsides and parks.

It's hard to distinguish "native" Hawaiian plants since so many varieties have been imported for agriculture and landscaping. Ancient Polynesian settlers arrived with taro plants, whose cooked root becomes the food staple *poi*, breadfruit (*ulu*), coconut and ti plants, and found creative ways to use the plantlife they found. If you're interested in learning more, we'd suggest a visit to the Amy B. H. Greenwell Ethnobotanical Garden in Captain Cook, or one of the other botanical gardens islandwide.

Traveling with Children

BEFORE YOU GO Involve the whole family in planning the trip. Brief the little kids on what it's like to fly on a plane, what good travel manners are, what to expect at the airport, including security checks ("Tommy, they're only going to borrow your blankie and put it through the machine. They'll give it back.") You might even play airport together and practice. Come up with a family plan on what to do in case someone gets lost. Some travel advisors suggest mild sedatives or sleep aids to keep kids calm while traveling; ASK YOUR DOCTOR before you drug your children. If you need kid-proofing items like outlet covers or folding gates, request them from your hotel or condo in advance, or bring them with you. This tip is worth repeating: get everyone (especially teens) involved in the planning process and there may be fewer complaints on the trip. Help supervise luggage and carry-on packing and keep an open mind for adventure. If you're traveling with a larger family group, have a conversation about money and agree on a few rules about who pays for what. This will save a lot of vacation time and prevent hard feelings later.

WHAT TO CARRY ON Get everyone to wear shoes that are easy to slip off and on, and make sure everyone has socks because airplane floors can get very cold. Those with a photo ID might want to display it in a clip-on badge holder or neck lanyard (such as conventioneers wear) so it stays visible and does not get lost. Keep in mind everything you carry on will have to be X-rayed, including strollers, baby seats and kids' backpacks. Include absolutely everything you need for infants; don't count on the airline for supplies. Moms of young kids may want to pack an apron or smock for themselves (and bibs for the kids), wet wipes and ziplock bags for dirty clothes, to arrive looking reasonably fresh and clean. Some experts advise carrying a change of clothes for everyone in case you get stranded overnight (or at least swimsuits and shades so you can go ahead and hit the beach even if luggage is delayed). If you're coming from a cold climate, stash winter coats in your checked luggage after you get inside the airport. Dress in light layers you can remove when you reach warmer weather. Some travellers carry a bright, tropical shirt

PLANNING YOUR FAMILY VACATION

It's good to get everyone involved in the planning process by visiting a library or bookstore together for some background information, reading, music and movies about Hawai'i (suggestions provided at the end of this book). Or, spend some time exploring the internet for an amazing amount of interesting information, and great geography or science report material (see "Communications: Websites" later in this chapter). Try www.gohawaii.com, the Hawai'i Visitors and Convention Bureau site; www.nps.gov/havo, Volcanoes National Park site; or www.ifa.hawaii.edu/mok/about_maunakea.htm, the Center for International Astronomy site, just as jumping-off points.

We've discovered a collection of websites geared to traveling with kids. Check out www.thetravelmom.com, www.familytravel guides.com or www.family.com. The Travel Channel's family travel expert Tracy Gallagher has frequent pieces on the air and on the site: www.travel.discovery.com. Of course much more information is available with a little surfing, including sites focused on single-parent travel or same-sex parent travel, blended families, multi-generational families and everything you can think of. If you have questions, answers are out there.

or accessory to lift their energies and get in the mood just before arrival. DO be certain to carry on everyone's prescription medications, enough for at least 24 hours. And, since kids have an excellent knack for getting sick at inopportune times, carry baby aspirin, cough medicine and other over-the-counter remedies you normally have at home, along with wet wipes, band-aids and tissues. Split the cash, credit cards and travelers checks between Mom and Dad and make sure you have a recent photo of each child. The experts advise carrying snacks and juice (not milk) for the flight, since kids might not be hungry or interested when the meal is served. Some also advise a series of little gifts and quiet activities to disperse at intervals throughout the travel day and keep kids entertained. You'll be a hero if you have extra batteries when the Gameboy or CD player dies.

AT THE AIRPORT . Arrive earlier when you're traveling with kids to allow plenty of time to check in and get everybody through security checkpoints. Attach the free elastic luggage tags to toddlers with their name, address, flight numbers and parents' cell phone numbers in case you get separated in the airport. Reconfirm your seat assignments before you reach the gate. (It's best to request seating assignments when you make your reservations, and double-check before the flight.) If you haven't done so already, request bulkhead seats (front row) with more room for the kids to move around. Large families should request seats on the same side of the aisle, since it's easier to keep tabs on the row in front or behind, and impossible to move across the aisle during meal service. If you have a long wait, find an empty gate area and let the kids run off some energy before they have to fly again. If you have smokers in the family, cut them a little slack and let them board last and disembark first on your connecting flights. It takes time to reach a smoking area (in many cases outside the airport) and get back to the gate. For tips on finding airport smoking areas, visit www.smokingsection.com/air port.html and individual airport websites.

ON THE PLANE Be sure your seat has airsick bags, which can be also used for dirty diapers (dispose of them; don't leave in the seat-pocket or pass them to flight attendants). Kids are especially sensitive to ear pain when cabin pressure changes. Some things that help: sucking on a straw, lollipop or bottle, big yawns and wide open-mouth funny faces, swallowing, chewing gum. Ask the flight attendants. We've heard that it helps to put warm, moist paper towels in two styrofoam cups and hold one over each ear. Keep in mind that the best-laid plans of moms and dads are unfortunately likely to fall apart in real life. Your kids may not be perfect little travelers, but it will be a lot easier on everybody if you've included in your own

ON THE PLANE WITH KIDS

Awareness is important all around. Please know if your kid is kicking the seat in front of him, or wandering around the plane, or otherwise being a nuisance. We know for a fact that the most important thing you can give a kid on a plane is *attention*, your positive attention, before things get out of hand. We've seen a little attention go a long, long way with the most difficult children. Parents who talk to their boys and girls, who watch what they're doing and show interest, have a much better flight than those who just say no or ignore them. Play with them. Read to them (we'd much rather listen to a storybook than you saying "no" and them saying "I want"). We've seen kids, already bored with the Gameboy and the in-flight movie, respond to simple games like tic tac toe, hangman or go fish, especially if Mommy or Daddy plays too. (Of course, the time to do this is before they're out of control.) Every kid wants attention. Give them some. You might enjoy it. (P.S. This works in restaurants too.)

carry-on a good supply of patience, a great big positive attitude and a lot of extra attention to share with your kids. Contrary to what it feels like above the ocean (to all of us) the flight does not last forever. You will be here soon, and you're going to have a great time.

AT THE HOTEL OR CONDO Make sure your kids know their room number, and show them how to dial the front desk if they need help. Practice walking to the emergency exit in case of fire. Talk about good hotel manners (refraining from bed-jumping, floor-stomping, balcony screeching), and be sure they understand the costs for video gaming, movies, minibar items, etc. Hotels will put parental blocks on the TV and remove the minibar on request. Establish rules with older kids for room service orders, room charges and phone calls. (Hotels charge a service fee for local calls and a hefty surcharge for long distance, even with calling cards. Use your cell.)

OUT AND ABOUT Don't leave valuables in the car. Take turns watching your stuff on the beach. Use the buddy system in the water or on a hike. Have a family plan for what to do in case you get separated. Tag each toddler with their name, parents' cell phone numbers and the name and number of your hotel or condo.

Don't be a slave to your schedule. Take time to explore the unexpected places you encounter serendipitously. Relax. Talk to each other. Halfway through your stay, have an "evaluation" meeting and check in with everyone on how things are going. Try to make sure everyone is included and no important element is left out as time compresses closer to the end of your stay. When it's time to go you might want to make a family scrapbook and have everyone contribute something to its pages.

TRAVELING IN THE ISLAND WITH KIDS

BABYSITTING Most hotels and condos have a babysitting service or list of available babysitters and will help you with arrangements. Fees usually run from about $12 to $15 per hour and up. Certified babysitters are also available in some areas through People Attentive To Children Hawai'i (PATCH) at Malihini Keiki Care (808-331-2909; fax 808-331-2810; e-mail: mkcare@hawaii.rr.com).

BABY EQUIPMENT RENTAL Aloha Baby Rentals has everything you can think of, including rocking chairs, room monitors and duo strollers. P.O. Box 40, Kailua-Kona, HI 96743; 866-478-2229; 808-326-1700; www.alohababyrental.com.

Another source is **Baby's Away**, a nationwide company with Big Island locations. 800-996-9030; 808-987-9236; www.babysaway.com.

In Waikoloa, **A-1 Rentals** offers a full line of baby equipment, including cribs and highchairs, strollers, carseats, swings and all kinds of toys. 808-883-3675; e-mail: info@dorkelsrentals.com.

CAR SEATS Car seats are required by Hawai'i state law for children ages three and under at all times when riding in an automobile. Most car rental companies have child car seats available but charge a $10 to $15 daily fee. Also, during peak travel seasons, demand may be high and reservations for car seats may not be completely reliable. You may want to consider bringing your own, and possibly use it on the plane. Check with your travel agent or airline. If you check the car seat as baggage, put it in a box or use a large plastic bag and be sure to label it clearly.

CRIBS Cribs can be provided by most hotels and condos for a fee of $15 to $25 per night. Local rental shops also have them available for a few dollars per night if you opt to not bring your own portable crib.

DINING Most restaurants provide a special *keiki* (children's) menu, and you'll find McDonald's, Burger King and other familiar eateries around the island, some with a playground area. Check the menus at fast food stores for interesting local items you can't get anywhere else.

FOR EMERGENCIES Call 911, just like at home. See also "Medical Information" later in this chapter.

BEACHES—POOLS

Always be attentive to keiki *near the water.*

Even at the calmest of beaches, an occasional large wave can roll in by surprise. Currents can be strong and shallow water can be

·deceiving. A children's flotation device is strongly recommended in all cases. Apply a good sunscreen before beachtime, and don't let the kids stay out in the sun for too long. Several short periods are better in Hawai'i's strong sunshine. (The same goes for mom and dad.)

When you arrive, we suggest you pick up a copy of the free *Big Island Beach & Activity Guide* (www.beachactivityguide.com) for maps, tips and the most current information on Big Island beaches and beach parks. For photos of island beach parks, visit www.hawaii web.com.

On the west side of the island, **Spencer Beach Park** at Kawaihae provides one of the calmest beaches on the Big Island. Its small beach and sparkling clear water are perfect for the small ones. **Hapuna Beach State Park,** just south of Kawaihae below the Hapuna Beach Prince Hotel on the Kohala Coast, is a large expanse of open sand, great for the kids to run and play. The water is shallow and the surf moderate but adults must be vigilant with youngsters in the water. Continuing south, '**Anaeho'omalu Beach Park**, fronting the Waikoloa Beach Marriott on the Kohala Coast, is a large sweeping crescent with moderate surf and shallow water. In Kona, **Kamakahonu Beach**, fronting the King Kamehameha Kona Beach Hotel next to the Kailua-Kona Pier, is also a fine small beach with gentle water that seems to have been made just for *keiki*.

On the east or Hilo side of the island, one of the better beaches for kids is **Onekahaka Beach Park**, with nice sandy-bottom pools created by the large breakwater and retaining walls. **Coconut Island** is another fun place to play, just off Banyan Drive, and connected to the shore by a long footbridge. This is a good spot for picnicking, fishing and playing in the shallow, sandy pools. Conditions at **Hilo Bayfront Park** are not the best for swimming, but it's a popular fishing spot, and a good place to watch canoe races on the weekends.

Most kids (and parents too) are fascinated with exploring the beach and shores for bits of coral, seashells and the interesting creatures who live in ocean tidepools. A good place to see and feed the myriad schools of Hawai'i's colorful reef fish is at **Kahalu'u Beach Park**, in Keauhou just south of Kailua-Kona. At the beach park next to the Keauhou Beach Hotel, schools of colorful fish swarm about in the shallow calm waters. It is a perfect place to view and handfeed the fish. Children will enjoy the experience of seeing the marine life up close. If they are old enough, they can use a mask and snorkel to gain an underwater view of the colorful reef life. (Be sure to check for a perfect fit.)

Check with your hotel or condo desk, visitor publications and the local newspapers for additional children's activities around the

Big Island. It's a busy, community-minded place, and almost any weekend, almost everywhere on the island you'll find an interesting cultural festival, concert, charity fun run or walk, ball game, ice cream social, food event or arts-and-crafts fair. These are well worth looking into, and can be great opportunities to experience some of the Big Island's many diverse aspects.

CHILDCARE PROGRAMS

Kohala Coast resorts have supervised kids' activity programs with swimming, shoreline explorations, Hawaiian arts and crafts like lei making, *hula* dancing and other fun things.

The **Fairmont Orchid Hawai'i's** "Keiki Aloha" program offered to kids 5-12 features Hawaiian sandcastle building, lei making, petroglyph, tidepool and cave explorations and other fun things. Full-day program, 9 a.m.-4 p.m. is $60 including lunch, half-day morning or afternoon is $40, Friday or Saturday evening dinner and a movie program is also $40. Other activities include arts and crafts, swimming and snorkeling, video games, beach volleyball, basketball, scavenger hunts, kayaking, shell hunts and rock graffiti. The Fairmont is also home to "the Orchid Beachboys," to meet and greet older kids or whole families and introduce ocean adventures like shoreline fishing, surf lessons, canoe paddling or kayaking. 808-885-2000.

The **Four Seasons Resort Hualalai's** "Kids for All Seasons" is for children 5-12 years old, 8 a.m.-5 p.m. and is complimentary to resort guests year-round. Fun activities include volcano building and gecko hunts. The "Hale Kula" activities center for teens and families has a 54-inch surround-sound TV, six video game stations, a grassy area for organized outdoor games and access to family fun like canoe paddling, hiking, surfing lessons and horseback riding. They also offer a family dinner on the beach, complete with tiki torches and a bonfire for s'mores. True to form, Four Seasons goes quite the dis-

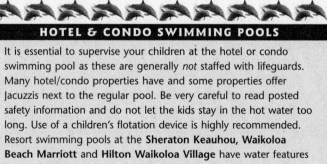

HOTEL & CONDO SWIMMING POOLS

It is essential to supervise your children at the hotel or condo swimming pool as these are generally *not* staffed with lifeguards. Many hotel/condo properties have and some properties offer Jacuzzis next to the regular pool. Be very careful to read posted safety information and do not let the kids stay in the hot water too long. Use of a children's flotation device is highly recommended. Resort swimming pools at the **Sheraton Keauhou, Waikoloa Beach Marriott** and **Hilton Waikoloa Village** have water features and slides (Hilton's is giant and resembles a water theme park).

tance to welcome "younger guests" with special child-size robes, milk and cookies on arrival, a video library and more. 808-325-8000; www.fourseasons.com.

The **Hapuna Beach Prince Hotel**'s year-round Keiki Camp provides kids with the opportunity to make new friends, play games, explore and learn something about Hawai'i in a fun-filled day. Cost is $50 for the full day, including lunch, $25 for the half-day program. Half price during off-season May through September. 808-880-1111; www.hapunabeachprincehotel.com.

With a nod to the other excellent Kohala Coast resorts, **Hilton Waikoloa Village** really has the most to offer active families, with the biggest variety and largest number of things for kids to see and do. The lobby and public areas are full of tropical birds and the ponds are full of swans, koi fish and waterfowl (even flamingos). Their inter-resort transportation is done by small-gauge railroad train or a mini motorboat. For kids 5-12, there's Camp Menehune, a daily themed program with everything from arts and crafts, games and water activities to *hula* dancing and Hawaiian plays. There's a touch pool in the Discovery Center, a book corner, an art area and much more. Full day is $65 per child; half-day is $50 and both include lunch. For two or more, the first child pays full rate and the second is $15 off. There are creative, well-organized day programs, night programs (including something called Whacky Hula Luau Night) and complimentary drop-in activities. If that's not enough, they also offer Keiki Hour playtime for kids under 5 for only $15, and some of the most extensive family activities on the island, including nature tours, countless ocean activities and the on-site Dolphin Quest programs. And they permit outside guest children for $75 on a space-available basis. 808-886-1234; www.hiltonwaikoloavillage.com/camp/about.asp.

"Na Keiki in Paradise" at the **Kona Village Resort** is a complimentary drop-in activities program primarily for kids 6-12, with tours and explorations, fishing, *hula* classes, coconut painting and Hawaiian crafts, net throwing, games and more. There is also a kid's dinner program from 5:30 p.m. to 8:30 p.m., allowing Mom and Dad some time to themselves. After-dinner activities include a marshmallow roast on the beach, stargazing and storytelling. A complimentary program for teens offers more adventurous fun like snorkeling, sailing, kayak and tennis lessons, softball and volleyball games. 808-325-5555; www.konavillage.com/kids.

At the **Mauna Kea Beach Hotel**, Keiki Camp is available for $50 full day, including lunch, and $25 half day. Kids enjoy supervised activities at the beach and around the grounds, games, Hawaiian crafts and making new friends. Half-price during the "shoulder season," May through September. 808-882-7222; www.maunakeabeach hotel.com.

For *keiki* 5-12, "Hui Na Keiki O Mauna Lani" at **Mauna Lani Bay Hotel and Bungalows** offers activities, games, snacks and Hawaiian crafts year-round. The cost is $50 per day for the first child 5-12 years old and $35 for other children in the same family; the program runs 9:30 a.m. to 3:30 p.m., and includes explorations and activities, snacks and a camp T-shirt. Lunch or dinner is additional. Ask about their new half-day program for kids 3-4 years old. 808-885-6622; www.maunalani.com.

KONA AREA The Sheraton Keauhou Bay Resort & Spa (a shiny new incarnation of the old Kona Surf, which opened in 2004)

SELF-SERVICE LAUNDRIES

Most hotels and condo units have a laundry service available, either the commercial send-out type or in-house coin-operated machines. Check with your front desk. For those in need of self-service laundries, there are a few located around the island. Hours of operation may vary.

Ed's Laundromat, open daily 6 a.m. to 10 p.m. Na'alehu Shopping Center, Na'alehu, Ka'u District, just off Highway 11 in town center.

Hale Haloi, open daily 6 a.m. to 10 p.m. Kealakekua Shopping complex, Highway 11, next to Cap's Drive In.

Hele Mai Laundromat, open daily 6 a.m. to 10 p.m. Kailua-Kona, Palani Road and Kuakini Highway a block above the King Kamehameha Hotel, North Kona Shopping Center; 808-329-3494.

Hilo Quality Washerette, open daily 6 a.m. to 10 p.m. 210 Hoku, Hilo; 808-961-6490.

KC Washerette, open daily 5 a.m. to 9 p.m. In the village of Kainaliu, Kona; 808-322-2929.

Suds n' Duds Laundromat, open daily 7:30 a.m. to 8:30 p.m., Sunday until 7:30 p.m. Kea'au Town Center, Kea'au; 808-965-2621.

The Wash Laundromat, open daily 6 a.m. to 8 p.m. Hawaiian Ranchos Center, Hawaiian Oceanview Estates, South Kona; 808-929-7072.

Tyke's Laundromat, open daily 6:30 a.m. to 9 p.m., 74-5583 Pawai Place, Kailua-Kona, 808-326-1515; and open 6 a.m. to 10 p.m. at 1454 Kilauea Avenue, Hilo; 808-935-1093.

Volcano Wash & Dry, open daily 7 a.m. to 9 p.m., 19-4084 Old Volcano Road, behind Thai Thai Restaurant in Volcano Village.

has "Keiki Club Keauhou" for kids 4 years and 8 months to 12 years old, 9 a.m.-4 p.m. daily, and night camp 6:30-9 p.m. two nights per week. There's also a special program for *keiki* 2-4 years old, and an activities center. Other facilities on the resort include hands-on culture programs, Moʻolelo storytelling in the gardens, a sandy-bottomed pool, and the soon-to-be famous Manta Ray Super Pool & Slide— multi-level pools with waterfalls, hidden grottoes, bridges, bubbling whirlpools, a 200-foot long lava-tube waterslide and awesome interactive children's fountains. As a very special service, Sheraton offers themed "Keiki Birthday" (Hawaiian, King or Queen for the Day, Sports Mania, Water Extravaganza and Wild Animal Safari) reasonably package-priced from $145 for hotel guests/$175 off-property. Coming soon: the "Manta Ray Experience," with observation areas, high definition underwater cameras fed into guest rooms, expert lectures and snorkel/scuba excursions. 866-500-8313; 808-930-4900; www.sheratonkeauhou.com.

Especially for Seniors

The Big Island is big on *ohana* (family), particularly the multi-generational extended family that seems to embrace everyone. The families, from grandparents to babies, like to do things together—whether it's spending time at the beach, eating in a restaurant or touring around the island telling stories. Maybe that's why multi-generational family groups choose the Big Island as a vacation destination. There's something for everyone, and plenty of room for even the larger family to spread out in different directions, or gather together and enjoy the company. In general seniors are treated respectfully, perhaps more so than in other vacation areas.

SENIOR DISCOUNTS Seniors traveling to and around the Big Island are advised to inquire with all airline, car rental firms, hotels, restaurants and paid attractions/activities as to whether any senior discounts are available. Your travel agent can be helpful on this also but don't hesitate to ask if you make your own reservations. Be ready to provide a valid driver's license or photo I.D. To help you get around if you don't drive, the County of Hawaiʻi offers seniors a discount of a third off the regular bus fares on its Hele On bus system. The bus system covers the entire Big Island with regularly scheduled services. For complete information and the latest fares, contact the Hele On Bus, County of Hawaiʻi Transit Agency, 25 Aupuni Street, Hilo, HI 96720; 808-961-8744 or 808-961-8343.

ELDERHOSTEL PROGRAMS The national Elderhostel program conducts courses, workshops, seminars and activities of various types throughout the country specifically for seniors. For details, information and costs on Hawai'i programs, contact Elderhostel, 11 Avenue de Lafayette, Boston, MA 02111; 617-426-8506; 877-426-8056; fax 877-426-2166; www.elderhostel.org. On the Big Island, the following groups/organizations host various Elderhostel courses and activities. Contact them directly for schedule and information.

The **University of Hawai'i at Hilo** participates in the Elderhostel program, offering seniors the opportunity to spend one or two weeks on campus or nearby areas in various programs such as Hawai'i-Pacific culture, history, language, astronomy, vulcanology, oceanography, marine science and more. Fees cover tuition, room and board. Inquire with Elderhostel Program Director, University of Hawai'i at Hilo, 200 West Kawili Street, Hilo, HI 96720-4091; 808-974-7555; fax 808-974-7684.

The **Lyman Museum and Mission House** also coordinates and hosts one- or two-week annual Elderhostel program seminars, workshops and cultural activities for seniors. 276 Haili Street, Hilo, HI 96720; 808-935-5021.

The **Volcano Art Center** presents an annual schedule of two-week Elderhostel courses and activities. These programs are geared toward active participants, including nature hikes through volcano craters and rainforests, Hawaiian culture and natural history lectures, demonstrations and snorkel excursions. Program price includes all lodging, food, field trips and instruction. P.O. Box 104, Hawai'i National Park, HI 96718; 808-967-8222; fax 808-967-8512; e-mail: vaceh@gte.net; www.bishop.hawaii.org/vac/home.html.

Travel Tips for the Physically Impaired

When making your travel plans it is best to do so well in advance and to inform the hotels and airlines that you have special needs that require specific services. A good travel agent should also be able to assist, and visitor industry facilities in Hawai'i can accommodate you. It would be wise to bring along your medical records in case of an emergency, and it is recommended that you bring your own wheelchair and inform the airlines accordingly.

ARRIVAL AND DEPARTURE Both the Hilo and Kona airports on the Big Island are accessible for mobility impaired persons. Parking stalls are available at both terminals for the disabled. Restrooms with wheelchair-accessible stalls are also found in both terminals. The local airlines are very conscientious in accommodating those with special needs. Special lifts to the aircraft are provided for wheelchair passengers at Kona airport but the Hilo airport has jetway ramps available for boarding and exiting planes.

TRANSPORTATION Check with **Accessible Vans of Hawai'i** for information/rates and arrangements on renting a wheelchair-accessible van. They rent special vans throughout the Hawaiian Islands. 800-303-3750; www.accessiblevanshawaii.com.

The Hawai'i County Hele On bus system provides a demand-response transportation service with lift-equipped vans within the Hilo and Kona areas only to accommodate individuals unable to utilize the standard transit buses. This curb to curb service is available 7 a.m. to 4:30 p.m. Monday through Friday except county holidays. Requests for service must be made at least a day in advance. For information, call the Transit Agency's Hele On Bus Office at 808-961-8343; for county bus schedule information call 808-961-8744.

MEDICAL SERVICES AND EQUIPMENT For a list of medical centers and hospitals, see "Medical Information" later in this chapter. Some agencies can assist in providing personal care attendants, companions and nursing aides while on your visit. One is the **Center for Independent Living-East Hawai'i** in Hilo at 808-935-3777 and in West Hawai'i/Kona at 808-323-2221.

The following companies provide medical equipment rentals: **Big Island Medical Equipment**, Kona, 808-323-3313; **Rainbow Medical Supply**, 180 Kinoole Street, Hilo, 808-935-9393, or 67-1185 Mamalahoa Highway in Waimea, 808-885-7688, www.rainbowmedicalsupply.com; **Ban-Nix Home Medical Equipment**, Waimea, 808-885-1925. **Kona Rent All**, 74-5603 Pawai Place, Kailua-Kona, 808-329-1644, has a large line of rental equipment.

ACCOMMODATIONS Big Island hotels and condominiums in general provide accessible rooms and facilities. Because these are subject to availability, request reservations well in advance and be specific about your needs. Inform the reservationist if you need an accessible bathroom, shower stall, grab bars or special toilet seat. If you have oxygen equipment in your room, it is important to inform your hotel for fire safety reasons. If you are hearing-impaired you should inform your hotel so that you can be assisted in case of emergency. Most hotel accommodations can also provide flashing-light telephones and doorbell indicator lights.

GUIDE DOGS AND SERVICE DOGS The State of Hawai'i has recently revised its strict 120-day quarantine for dogs and cats; however, bringing pets along on your Hawai'i vacation is not a recommended practice. Guide dogs for the blind and service dogs for hearing-impaired persons may be admitted into the state under a specific set of quarantine regulations. All arrivals must enter the state through Honolulu International Airport only; the Animal Quarantine Branch (808-837-8092; fax 808-483-7161) must receive notification at least 24 hours in advance, and a series of very detailed requirements must be met. Please plan well in advance. For more information contact Hawai'i Department of Agriculture, Animal Quarantine Station, 99-951 Halawa Valley Street, Aiea, HI 96701-5602; 808-483-7151; fax 808-483-7161; e-mail: eqs.rabies@gte.net; www.hawaiiag.org/hdoa/ai_aqs_guidedog.htm.

What to Pack

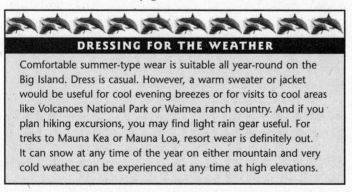

It's easy to pack for a Big Island vacation. Bring your favorite, most comfortable summer clothes, walking shoes and a swimsuit. Dress is very casual here; shorts, T-shirts and sandals are perfectly acceptable almost everywhere, day and night. If you're a jeans person, that's fine too. What that doesn't cover, the following will: slacks and an aloha shirt for gentlemen, a muumuu or casual dress for ladies. Even in the fancier restaurants, ladies never need hose or heels; gentlemen never need ties. Some places recommend jackets, but it's not required generally. Other than that, pack for what you like to do. Resorts expect proper golf or tennis attire (collared shirt and appropriate shoes) and beach cover-ups in public areas. If you're touring, plan on dressing in light layers. A big shirt over a tank top protects you from sunburn as well as a chilly tropical breeze or air conditioning. Your swimsuit can serve double duty with a pareau wrap or cover-up. (It's not customary on the Big Island for people to be "out" in swimwear.)

For the kids, bring plenty of play clothes to cut down on laundry time, and a couple of swimsuits to let one dry while the other's in use. We've noticed *keiki* (kids) tend to over-pack toys and games, then want more when they get here. For them, a lesson in focus

DRESSING FOR THE WEATHER

Comfortable summer-type wear is suitable all year-round on the Big Island. Dress is casual. However, a warm sweater or jacket would be useful for cool evening breezes or for visits to cool areas like Volcanoes National Park or Waimea ranch country. And if you plan hiking excursions, you may find light rain gear useful. For treks to Mauna Kea or Mauna Loa, resort wear is definitely out. It can snow at any time of the year on either mountain and very cold weather can be experienced at any time at high elevations.

might be helpful, but you know the stuff they absolutely cannot live without. If that rotten-looking "bankie" has to come along, it has to come along. Don't worry about what people will think; they had bankies too.

Speaking of living without, a word about electronics. We almost guarantee that if you can live without your cell phone and laptop on vacation, you're going to have a better time (and so will the people around you). Unless you're a roving reporter on assignment, please consider leaving these symbols of the outside world behind and allow yourself the freedom to enjoy a totally detached, complete retreat. It will be good for you. (You might even take your watch off.) If you can't stand to be disconnected, you'll find most hotels have in-room internet access, some have dataports, and even in the more remote areas of the island you can find the occasional internet café or business center with computer time for rent. (See "Internet Cafes" later in the book.)

If you dress comfortably in light layers for the flight, you'll be ready to go when you reach the Big Island. Your carry-on luggage should include necessary medications, toilet articles, and a change of underwear (if not a complete change of clothes) in case your luggage is misdirected or a delayed flight causes an overnight at another airport. We'd also suggest that you include your swimsuit and sunglasses so you can hit the beach immediately, luggage or not. And a good book will get you through the longest wait, no matter where you are. It might be smart to equally distribute important items and even clothing in everyone's luggage so the delay of one bag won't be traumatic for one individual. Use the buddy system to keep up with carry-ons.

Sunscreen, shades, hats, towels, batteries, beach toys and other necessities are readily available in shops almost everywhere. We recommend you double-check any prescription medication you take on a regular basis so you don't waste vacation time getting a refill, and pack a second pair of reading glasses in a different place from the first, just in case. (Our only other packing tip is this: Don't buy new shoes for the trip. Bring your most comfortable pair of sandals or walking shoes and sneakers as a backup. Don't let bad shoes and sore feet hold you back!)

Weddings & Honeymoons

The Big Island is very big on *aloha*. Of course, that means love, and there are very few places left on the planet where there is so much love in the air. If you dream of a

Hawaiian honeymoon, you can make it come true here. Surrounded by natural beauty, blessed with nearly perfect weather every day of the year, this is the kind of place where people remember how to relax, get to know each other on a different level, and return home in some way transformed. The Big Island loves honeymooners. It also loves to welcome couples for their weddings—from grand celebrations at the best resorts to barefoot ceremonies on the beach. Here you can step across the Japanese bridges of Liliuokalani Park in Hilo, exchange vows at sea aboard a sleek catamaran, walk down the aisle of a 200-year-old stone church or a tiny country chapel overlooking the ocean. The selection of settings is limited only by your fantasy.

REGULATIONS   Obtaining a marriage license is easy. Just visit www.hawaii.gov/health/vital-records/vital-records/marriage. There is a bride-friendly list of requirements and procedures; you can even download a license application on the spot. Or call 808-586-4545 or e-mail vr-info@mail.health.state.hi.us.

Basically, this is all there is to it. You do not have to be a resident of Hawaii, or a U.S. citizen, and you don't need a blood test. Legal age to marry is 18 and proof of age is required. If you're 18, you'll need a certified copy of your birth certificate. Those over 18 may present a driver's license, passport or other valid photo I.D. When you arrive in Hawaii, you need to appear together in person before a marriage license agent. You'll need the completed application, proof of age (written consent from both parents if you're under 18) and a $60 fee. There is no waiting period and the license is valid for 30 days. Your marriage must be officiated by a licensed performer, and a copy of the marriage certificate will be mailed to you within 60 to 120 days after the ceremony. For contact information on marriage license agents, you may write to the Marriage License Section, Department of Health, State of Hawai'i, 1250 Punchbowl Street, Honolulu, HI 96813, or call 808-586-4545. On the Big Island, call the Department of Health at 808-974-6008. Resort wedding coordinators and independent wedding planners will also be able to assist with marriage license agents and officiants.

One small note about a controversial subject. At present the State of Hawai'i does not recognize same-sex marriage, nor does that appear to be on the political agenda in the near future. There are, however, special celebrations and ceremonies performed for any couple who wishes to publicly affirm their commitment to each other in a discreet fashion. Wedding planners can assist. And something new, a "Reciprocal Beneficiary Relationship" legal partnership. See www.hawaii.gov/health/vital-records/vital-records/marriage/vital-records/reciprocal/index.html.

GENERAL INFORMATION

WEDDING SERVICES

The following wedding coordinators and planning services can provide everything you need, down to the last detail, for a flawless Hawaiian wedding from simple to spectacular. Various packages are available and may include such extras as flowers, photography, video, music, champagne, wedding cake and limousine. Once again, with the Big Island's diverse culture and mid-Pacific location, our professional wedding planners are experienced in wedding customs from just about everywhere. Priests and ministers of practically every religious persuasion are available, as are non-denominational and lay celebrants. If your perfect wedding includes a kosher menu or a Buddhist blessing, it is only necessary to ask.

Paradise Weddings Hawai'i—This full-service wedding coordinator can arrange everything on the Big Island including location, minister, music, flowers and leis, photographer, video service, champagne and wedding cake. Complete wedding packages start at $495. Custom arrangements, from intimate to outrageous, are Debbie Cravatta's specialty. Get married on a beach at sunset, in a quaint chapel by the sea, aboard a sailboat, on a cliff-top golf tee, in a quiet garden near the sacred ponds of King Kamehameha the Great, or any resort location. This is a very reputable service, highly recommended. P.O. Box 383433, Waikoloa, HI 96738; 808-883-9067; 800-428-5844; fax 808-883-8479; e-mail: wwwed@aloha.net; www.paradiseweddings hawaii.com.

Romantic Beach Weddings—Beautiful, romantic and original ceremonies with a soulful intent are performed on the Big Island by Rev. Lona Lyons, a licensed, non-denominational minister since 1993, and include Hawaiian traditions. Full-service coordination and planning services include weddings, renewals of vows, commitment ceremonies and rites of passage. Unique budget and luxury packages are tailored to your needs and include a barefoot beach ceremony, a sunrise ceremony, weddings at sea, a two-day divine marriage, rainforest waterfall eco-tours, and a five-star marriage and wedding feast. Rev. Lona creates an atmosphere with warmth and gentleness that deepens your experience of love. 808-896-6666; fax 808-326-1513; e-mail: lonalyons@aol.com; www.romanticbeachweddings.com.

Parker Ranch opens up a host of possibilities for romantic weddings *paniolo*-style, in their 150-year old historic homes and gardens. Select from poetic settings such as a gardenia, lavender or rose garden or Mana Hale, "House of the Spirit," with interiors of treasured Hawaiian *koa* wood. "Romance at the Ranch" wedding services begin at $500 and can be customized with catering, flowers, photography, decorating, entertainment and a horsedrawn white wedding carriage. 808-885-2303; www.parkerranch.com

Most Big Island hotels and resorts love to host weddings, renewals of vows, honeymoons, anniversaries and other special celebrations. They may also have a full-time wedding coordinator on staff to assist with all the arrangements and fine details. If they do not, a professional wedding planner (see above) can easily work with your hotel to help sort out all the options available and arrange your wedding, reception and honeymoon requirements. This is especially helpful if you live elsewhere and are trying to make plans long-distance. A wedding planner can also be a more economical choice, but this is not always the case. The hotels and resorts have been

CREATIVE CEREMONIES

Many reputable Big Island planners are at your service. **Watabe Wedding Corporation** (http://hnl.watabe.com) specializes in welcoming wedding parties from Japan. Companies like **Aloha Weddings in Paradise** (www.aloha-weddings.com) and **A Fairy Tale Wedding** (www.getmarriedinhawaii.com) offer package or comprehensive à la carte service at your choice of locations island-wide. There are many others to choose from. Pick your fantasy and go from there.

But you don't have to get married to celebrate a special day for the two of you. Marriage vow renewals are becoming more and more popular as anniversary ceremonies, easy to plan and wonderfully romantic. A planner can help dress up the occasion to your heart's desire at poetic sites, land or sea, as island-style as you care to go. They'll help you find formal aloha wear, elaborate bridal *pikake* or traditional open *maile* lei, a *kulolo* cake, a Hawaiian-language ceremony, handcrafted *lauhala* favors and many other wonderful things.

For example, **Hawaiian Butterflys** offers the fun, surprising new tradition of a Monarch butterfly release during your ceremony. Available on all islands, prices range from $98 to $700. www.hawaiianbutterflys.com.

An attractive resource to help start dreaming is *Pacific Rim Weddings* magazine. Beautiful photography, inspiring ideas, and "only in Hawai'i" tradition to make your special day everything you've dreamed. www.pacificweddings.com.

Or keep it simple. The good captains of the catamaran *Alala* will perform a wedding vow renewal for $25 per couple (in addition to regular excursion rates) which includes fresh flower lei for both of you, a shipboard ceremony at sea and customized certificate signed by the captain. Weddings, receptions and other special occasions are welcomed, limited only by your imagination. www.hawaiioceansports.com.

hosting wedding couples for a long time, and it is a big part of the hospitality business. Various packages are offered to suit your needs, and many couples choose to have the resort staff take care of everything—wedding site and ceremony, reception menu and wedding cake, a block of rooms for guests, and the honeymoon suite. As always, do your homework, and keep in mind that this is an island. Things tend to move more slowly over here, and it may take a little extra time to bring in a particular flower, bottle of wine or other essential touch for your special day—but hardly anything is impossible. Remember: Rates are subject to change.

Fairmont Orchid Hawaii—Offers a 14,000-square-foot grand ballroom and a clutch of scenic resort settings for lovely garden, estate or beachside weddings. With a reputation for fine service and first-class facilities, Fairmont's conference/catering department ably assists with arrangements for custom weddings. The Orchid Romance packages ($1,559) provide site, officiant, bridal bouquet or lei, groom's boutonnière or lei, wedding cake, champagne, Orchid wedding certificate and keepsake. The Beachboys Ocean Wedding is something unique, a shoreline site with tiki torches, welcome *oli,* Hawaiian chant and *pu*, conch shell, ceremony, Hawaiian music, romantic dinner for two and a conch shell etched with your wedding date. For an over-the-top experience, inquire about the Orchid Exclusive—roundtrip limo from the airport, two nights in the presidential suite, Dom Perignon upon arrival and crystal champagne flutes, a couples oceanside massage, all the features of the Orchid Romance package plus Hawaiian bath crystals with flowers and candles and two Spa Without Walls logo bathrobes. Why not? It's only $18,975. Newlyweds who marry at the Fairmont have at their disposal the Fairmont Platinum Honeymoon service, with special VIP concierge to help plan the honeymoon of your dreams. Or, reserve a Romantic Getaway package, from $559 per night, including luxury accommodations, limo transfers from the airport, a couple's massage at the Spa Without Walls waterfall or oceanfront *hale*, breakfast for two daily and a "Make Room for Romance" amenity: a trail of flower petals from threshold to boudoir, where chilled champagne and chocolate-dipped fruit and other romantic goodies await the new Mr. & Mrs. 1 North Kaniku Drive, Kohala Coast, HI 96743; 808-885-2000; 800-845-9905; fax 808-885-8886; e-mail orchid@fairmont. com; www.fairmont.com/orchid.

Four Seasons Resort Hualalai—Offers its well-known level of excellence to wedding couples who seek a particular style in a romantic Hawaiian setting. Perfectionist wedding services work directly with the couple or their wedding coordinator to polish every detail as befits a Four Seasons experience—creative menus, floral designers, select linens and tabletop decor, custom cakes or whatever you envision. Contact the resort for pricing information. Honeymooners can choose the Romance Package (from $62 to $790 per night), which includes luxurious accommodations, a welcome bottle of champagne upon arrival, his-and-hers waffle-cloth robes and a Hawaiian music CD. Four Seasons also specializes in "memorable interludes" like side-by-side massages, a canoe ride for two or a private, romantic dinner on the beach. P.O. Box 1269, Kailua-Kona, HI 96745; 808-325-8000; fax 808-325-8100; www.fourseasons.com/hualalai.

Hapuna Beach Prince Hotel—A beautiful, contemporary property designed to maximize its picturesque setting overlooking one of Hawai'i's very best beaches. With a grand ballroom to accommodate 850 guests and a selection of open-air tropical settings, this is an excellent choice. As an added benefit, Hapuna is partnered with Mauna Kea Beach Hotel next door in one elegant resort. Wedding parties have access to the entire collection of scenic ceremony sites, luxury guest rooms and reception facilities. The resort's Honeymoon/Romance Package starts at $469 per night and includes a convertible rental car, champagne and chocolates waiting in your oceanview room, buffet breakfast for two each day, one candlelit dinner for two on your private lanai or at the award-winning Coast Grille or Batik restaurants. A three-night minimum stay is required.

A full-time wedding coordinator is on staff to assist couples with every arrangement. Thoughtfully organized wedding packages begin with the essential Lehua Package, $2,400, including your choice of wedding site, clergy, white floral lei or *haku lei po'o* (head lei) for the bride, woven *maile* lei for the groom and photographer. The Maile Package ($3,200) adds to the above a chilled bottle of champagne and two keepsake flutes, wedding cake for two, and a professional solo musician. The Pikake Package, $4,200, enhances the day with salon services for the bride and groom, a Hawaiian wedding certificate, videography package and a special evening amenity. With the Ilima Package you can have it all: everything above plus *lomi lomi* massage and spa treatments for the bride and groom and a night in an oceanfront suite. The resort also offers extra-mile assistance with reception menus, decor and entertainment, rooms for your guests and other personalized arrangements. 62-100 Kauna'oa Drive, Kohala Coast, HI 96743; Wedding Services 808-882-5465; fax 808-880-3200; www.hapunabeachprincehotel.com.

Hilton Waikoloa Village—Hale Aloha (house of love) is the resort's private wedding pavilion overlooking Wailua Bay. The quaint, Hawaiian-style wedding chapel has simple yet elegant *koa* wood, stained glass and custom tile interiors. Hale Aloha is constructed to

RELIGIOUS SERVICES

Respect for Hawaiian mythology and the traditional deities is very much alive here, though subtle and not easy to explain or fully understand. The Big Island contains Pele's home at Halema'uma'u in Kilauea Caldera. She is the goddess of fire, said to take on the aspect of an old woman with a white dog or other forms as she walks through everyday life. People speak of encounters with her, of visions in the glowing lava, a whispery voice, a sense of presence. Pele's story is old; it comes from a time when the world was much simpler, where people lived in partnership with nature in order to survive. To love, respect and actually deify that which gives you life is not that hard to understand. In a way, we are all guests of nature, all guests in Pele's home. It is not a bad idea to be mindful of that, and to behave with courtesy and respect.

Everybody comes to Hawai'i to have a better life—whether traveling by voyaging canoe, American missionary ship, sugar cane or whaling trader, wartime troop carrier, luxury liner or Boeing 747. And almost everyone who comes here feels a special, at least somewhat mystic, connection at some point during their stay. These experiences are commonplace; it is far and away the exceptional person who does not feel "chicken skin," or goosebumps, when he first sees the *pu'eo* (owl) just at dusk, or watches a whale breach and crash back into the ocean surface, or feels primeval steam from deep-earth volcanic vents, or hears the pure and powerful force of Hawaiian chant and drums. Some people, like us, are compelled to come back and stay. Your experience will be uniquely your own, and we invite you to pay attention to that sort of thing without working at it too hard. At the very least, you'll have a great story to tell.

All that being said, the Big Island is a very special place for the spiritually minded with many different disciplines, from established churches to aesthetic retreats, spas and sweat lodges, swims

maximize the natural light and scenic ocean setting for your special day. The Hilton Waikoloa has a large professional banquet and catering and special-function staff that can tailor-make your wedding start to finish. Or you may select from their varying levels of prix-fixe wedding packages, named for Hawaiian flowers. Start with Ginger, $1,100, for use of grounds, non-denominational minister, two leis and roses, bottle of champagne, wedding cake for two and a resort "Just Married" boat ride. Jadeflower, $1,800, adds to the above package a bridal nosegay bouquet, groom's boutonniere, photography package, and a solo guitarist. Orchid, $2,100, takes the next step, with the addi-

with dolphins, readers of tarot, aura, past-life, astrology and other things, and whole realms of intriguing activities to nurture body and soul. These services are not detailed in this guidebook, but we'd like to direct you to the Yellow Pages or local newspapers and visitor publications for more information, with the following advice: If you are looking for a spiritual experience here, you're likely to find it with or without the help of a hired guide. We can also say from experience that most people are more likely to find spirituality in the most unlikely places.

For those who like to include church as part of their vacation, many resorts offer Sunday service on-property, but if yours does not, there is a place for you to go. Visitors are always welcome in local churches, and in resort areas they make up a regular part of the church family. Like everything else on the island, the diverse ethnic makeup and wide range of different lifestyles is reflected in the places of worship. There are Korean, Chinese and Japanese-style Buddhist temples, synagogues, Catholic and Protestant churches of many denominations, Mormon temples, gathering places for Bahai, Jehovah's Witness, Seventh-Day Adventist, Christian Science and many others.

In Kailua-Kona, you can attend Sunday services at Mokuaikaua Church, Hawai'i's first Christian church built by missionaries in 1820. Or visit the remarkable painted churches in Captain Cook or Puna, with vivid, floor-to-ceiling murals of Bible stories. Imiola Congregational Church, the cornerstone of "church row" in Waimea, is a tiny place bursting with aloha (visit them at www.imiola.com). In Puako, the Catholic Church of the Ascension is a beautiful, circular sanctuary decorated with bright tropical flowers from people's yards. A look in the Yellow Pages (between Chocolate and Cigars) will probably tell you everything you need to know, or check with your hotel or condo concierge desk.

tion of a solo guitarist for one hour, salon services for the bride and an upgraded photography package. Maile, $3,700, steps up with a cascading bridal bouquet, more-inclusive photo package and a video package, and Pikake, $4,300, takes your wedding to the next level with upgraded photo and video packages, a Hawaiian duo instead of guitarist, decorations in the Wedding Chapel and chocolate strawberries at turndown. Detailed information is available online for your convenience. www.hiltonwaikoloavillage.com/weddings.

For honeymooners, the Hilton's Romance Package is $509 per night and includes deluxe oceanview guest room, welcome amenity,

Seaside Cabana massage for two, one dinner for two at Kamuela Provision Company or Donatoni's, complimentary *yukata* robes, sunset catamaran sail for two and full American breakfast for two each day (three-night minimum stay required). 425 Waikoloa Beach Resort, Kohala Coast, HI 96743; 808-886-1234; 800-445-8667; fax 808-886-2901; www.hiltonwaikoloavillage.com.

Kona Village Resort—If you want a big fancy wedding to outdo your best friend's, don't get married at Kona Village. If you want a simple, elegant ceremony that focuses on the most essential aspect of marriage (the two of you), this is the place. Kona Village's on-site coordinator sees to music, ministers, marriage licenses and a generous portion of aloha for special weddings at the beach, on a private island in a tropical fishpond or other romantic settings under the rustling palms. For newlyweds, romance is in the air, and everywhere else, here. Guest rooms are secluded individual *hale* (thatched-roof huts), some with a beachside hammock or private jacuzzi, and none with telephone, TV, radio or alarm clock to distract you from each other. There is a weekly sunset reception at the Bora Bora Bar just for honeymooners, and as a special enticement for couples during the months of May and September, children's programs are not offered.

Three-, five- or seven-night Honeymoon/Celebration Packages start at $1,500 and include double accommodations, full American plan (breakfast, lunch and dinner for two daily), beach activities, tennis, fitness center, glass-bottom boat, a bottle of champagne, line art drawing of your *hale*, and a gift basket. The five-night Celebration, from $2,725, adds two *pareau* (Hawaiian beach wraps) and the seven-night Celebration, from $4,035, adds your choice of massage, tennis lesson or sunset catamaran sail for two. P.O. Box 1299, Kaupulehu-Kona, HI 96745; 808-325-5555; 800-367-5290; fax 808-325-5124; www.konavillagehoneymoon.com.

Mauna Kea Beach Hotel—A classic, timeless setting for all manner of celebrations. With its idyllic location along the crescent sands of Kauna'oa Bay and long history of gracious hospitality, Mauna Kea has, since 1965, been the place where traditions begin for happy couples. As an added benefit, Mauna Kea is partnered with Hapuna Beach Prince Hotel next door in one elegant resort. Wedding parties have access to the entire collection of scenic ceremony sites, luxury guest rooms and reception facilities.

The resort's Honeymoon/Romance Package starts at $514 per night and includes a convertible rental car, champagne and chocolates waiting in your beachfront room, buffet breakfast for two each day, one candlelit dinner for two on your private lanai or at the award-winning Coast Grille or Batik restaurants. A three-night minimum stay is required. See the listing for Hapuna Beach Prince Hotel (above) for full details on arrangements ad packages.

Mauna Lani Bay Hotel and Bungalows—Mauna Lani has something nobody else has: a gracious, talented director of weddings and romance, with many years of experience building wonderful weddings—Mrs. Pinkie Crowe, Director of Romance and Weddings. She and her staff preside over the comprehensive details of elaborate-to-barefoot ceremonies and receptions, with music, flowers and lei, photography, video and other special touches. The resort offers "storybook" sites such as the historic Eva Parker Woods Cottage on the beach, and the reflective Hawaiian fishponds and coconut groves of Kalahuipua'a. The essential Aloha Wedding Package is only $500 for site, officiant and witness. The Sunset Wedding Package, $1,950, adds a solo guitarist, bottle of champagne, cake, photographer, bridal bouquet or lei for the bride and boutonniere or lei for the groom, chairs, reception tables and waiter and a flower-bedecked latticework archway. The Intimate Wedding, $2,500, includes limousine transfer to and from the Cottage.

For your honeymoon stay, consider Mauna Lani's special Romantic Interludes five-night package. From $3,075 to $3,395, depending on room category, your Interlude includes double accommodations, champagne on arrival night, breakfast for two daily, one elegant Canoe House dinner for two or a snorkel or sunset sail cruise, two 50-minute spa treatments and complimentary use of the fitness club. 68-1400 Mauna Lani Drive, Kohala Coast, HI 96743; 808-885-6622; 800-367-2323; fax 808-885-1484; e-mail: maunalani@mauna lani.com; www.maunalani.com.

Outrigger Keauhou Beach Resort—Keauhou is Kona's up and coming visitor destination, rapidly adding to the quality accommodations and services available for Big Island visitors. South of Kailua-Kona town on Ali'i Drive, the Outrigger Keauhou offers beautiful seaside sites for wedding ceremonies and receptions and full-service catering staff to make the day stressless. Their Romance Package is $1,095 including three nights of ocean view accommodations, champagne and keepsake flutes on arrival, daily buffet breakfast, Kalona Spa massage for two and a mid-size rental car. 78-6740 Ali'i Drive; Kailua-Kona, HI 96740; 808-322-3441; www.outrigger.com.

Royal Kona Resort—The Royal Kona has two wedding packages, Hawai'i's Orchid Wedding including a marriage license appointment, minister for an oceanfront ceremony, special bridal nosegay bouquet and groom's boutonniere. Hawai'i's Maile Wedding adds a pair of *maile* leis, deluxe wedding cake, and a photography package. Special honeymoon room packages are also available with the wedding packages. 75-5852 Ali'i Drive, Kailua-Kona, HI 96740; 808-329-3111; 800-222-5642; fax 808-329-7230; www.hawaiianhotels andresorts.com.

Sheraton Keauhou Bay Resort & Spa—Keauhou means "a new beginning," a meaningful place for couples to start their life together. Just-refurbished facilities include the "little white church," Bayside Chapel and Reception Lawn, the Hawai'i Lawn above the multi-level swimming pool and other indoor/outdoor settings. Their Director of Romance will help with every detail on an à la carte basis for a totally custom affair. Or select from value-added packages such as the Keauhou, $2,500 including site, clergy, solo guitarist, lei for bride and groom, champagne and chocolate-covered strawberries and a Hawaiian wedding certificate. Hana Aloha $4,800, adds a wedding cake, upgraded florals and photo package. Or go for broke (so to speak) with the $20,000 "Ultimate Luxury and Romance" package including five nights in an oceanview suite, limo airport transfers, welcome floral arrangement, wedding coordination, site, clergy, bridal bouquet, groom's boutonniere, specialty lei for both, the "bridal pathway" scattered with orchid petals, a musical duo, upgraded champagne for the couple and guests, keepsake flutes, a two-tier wedding cake, tuxedo and gown pressing, Hawaiian wedding certificate in a *koa* frame, lady's beach package for the bride and five attendants, men's golf package for the groom and five companions, daily continental breakfast and a privately catered four-course dinner for two on your wedding day.

In case that doesn't cover it, the Sheraton's honeymoon/anniversary package starts at only $390 per night for double room, daily room service or breakfast buffet, a Spa Keauhou couples massage or two rounds of golf, private dinner for two in an oceanside cabana and champagne and chocolate-dipped strawberries on arrival. 78-128 Ehukai Street, Kailua-Kona, HI 96740; 808-930-4900; www.sheraton keauhou.com.

Waikoloa Beach Marriott, Outrigger Resort—With its lovely proximity to 'Anaeho'omalu Bay as well as the excellent array of Waikoloa resort amenities, a wedding coordinator on staff and flexible, reasonably priced packages, this property is an excellent choice. Features include outdoor venues for up to 700 and the Paniolo Ocean Terrace for a breathtaking oceanview gathering place. Hawai'i Calls restaurant offers intimate private dining rooms for wedding parties or elegant banquet facilities for grander receptions. The hotel welcomes your private wedding planner, or will assign a "certified wedding coordinator" to assist personally with details for your special day. Their website at www.marriott.com/meetings/weddings has suggestions and personal stories, plus access to a free wedding resources line at 877-468-7569. 69-275 Waikoloa Beach Drive, Waikoloa, HI 96738-5711; 808-886-6789; 800-922-5533; fax 808-886-1832; www.waikoloabeachmarriott.com.

Helpful Information

BANKS Basic hours are 8:30 a.m. to 3 p.m., but some are open until 4 or 5 p.m. Most will cash U.S. traveler's checks with a picture I.D. ATMs are available in convenient locations islandwide.

CREDIT CARDS A few small condominiums still do not accept any form of credit card payment, but stores, gas stations, restaurants, and hotels consistently do. For lost or stolen credit cards phone: American Express 800-992-3404; VISA 800-847-2911.

SALES TAX A sales tax of 4.167% is added to all purchases made in Hawai'i. There is an additional room-use tax added to your hotel or condominium bill.

HOLIDAYS Holidays unique to the state of Hawai'i: March 26 is Prince Kuhio Day, June 11 is Kamehameha Day and August 21 is Admissions Day.

Communications

TELEVISION Most hotels and condominiums have in-room televisions with cable service and pay-per-view movies. The major networks have Honolulu stations that broadcast to the Big Island. They are KHON-FOX, KGMB-CBS, KHNL-NBC, KHET-PBS and KITV-ABC. Other major TV channels are carried by cable TV companies, and generally most programming is current with what you're used to watching on the mainland. (In some cases, episodes run about a week late.) Sports enthusiasts, please remember the time difference—you may have to get up early to watch your favorite game. Or, some sports events may be shown pre-recorded. Channel numbers can vary from district to district depending on the cable company and from hotel to hotel depending on their arrangements with same. *Big Island Visitor Magazine* does a pretty good job of sorting out the channel numbers, and there's always the TV guide channel on your television.

Tip: **Big Island Television** Channel 9 provides insider tips and special programs about the Big Island 24 hours a day. BITV does an excellent job of presenting a good variety of island culture and history along with suggestions for shopping, dining and recreation. It is a commercial TV station, but the advertising is fairly unobtrusive and the information is presented in entertaining, fun-to-watch shows the whole family will enjoy.

RADIO Because of the massive mountains Mauna Kea and Mauna Loa, radio reception on the Big Island can be tricky when you're on the road. Some of the larger stations are

- KANO, 91.1 FM Hilo, National Public Radio
- KAPA, 99.1 FM Kona, 100.3 FM Hilo, "all Hawaiian all the time"
- KAOY "K-Hawai'i," 101.5 FM Kona, 92.7 FM Hilo, rock from around the world
- KKOA, 107.7 FM, contemporary country-western
- K-BIG, 106.1 FM Kona, 97.9 FM Hilo, Hawaiian music and current hits
- KIPA, 790 AM Kona, 620 AM Hilo, oldies
- KISS, 93.9 FM Kona, 95.9 FM Hilo, contemporary Top 40
- KWYI, 106.9 FM Kona, light contemporary and oldies
- KBGX Lava 105.3 FM, Hawai'i oldies from the '50s, '60s and '70s

PERIODICALS If you're planning your visit far enough in advance, or if you love the island and want to keep informed, you may want to subscribe to one of the daily newspapers. Because the papers will be sent via third-class mail, it can take a week or more to receive your paper, so it might be practical to only subscribe to the Sunday edition. Or, thanks to the internet, online versions of Big Island papers are available to you at a click.

Hawai'i Tribune-Herald is a daily paper published in Hilo, with island, state, national and international news; 355 Kinoole Street, Hilo, HI 96720; 808-935-6621; www.hilohawaiitribune.com. *West Hawai'i Today* is a similar paper published in Kona and includes the weekly *North Hawai'i News* insert; 75-5580 Kuakini Highway, Kailua-Kona, HI 96740; 808-329-9311; www.westhawaiitoday.com. There are also a couple of small press publications with specialized emphasis and coverage. The monthly *Coffee Times* is a magazine format with focus on Kona coffee country and culture; P.O. Box 1092, Captain Cook, HI 96704; 800-750-5662; www.coffeetimes.com. *Hawai'i Island Journal* is a bi-monthly paper that provides an energetic, fresh perspective on island news and events; P.O. Box 227, Captain Cook, HI 96704; 808-328-1880; www.hawaiiislandjournal.com.

VISITOR PUBLICATIONS Many free publications are available at hotel and condo concierge desks, visitor kiosks, the airport, shopping centers and many other spots islandwide. Most of these are very good, targeted to the Big Island visitor and focused on their needs.

They make their money by selling advertising so naturally the pages are full of tourist-related ads; however, the information between those pages can be very interesting and helpful, and is updated on a quarterly or monthly basis. Plus, these publications often have discount coupons on everything from meals to island tours, souvenirs, clothing and film processing.

Some of the best to look for are *Big Island Beach & Activity Guide* (www.beachactivityguide.com), a good quick reference to beaches islandwide; *101 Things to Do on Hawai'i the Big Island* (www.101 things.com); *Kona Views* (www.konaviews.com); *Big Island Visitor Magazine,* a complete cable TV guide (www.bigislandvisitor.com); *This Week Big Island* (www.thisweek.com); and *Spotlight's Big Island Gold* (www.spotlighthawaii.com). Believe it or not, there's also a wealth of information in Big Island phone books.

WEBSITES   If you're a net-surfer you already know there is a limitless world of information on the web. There are thousands of Hawai'i-based websites available, some, of course, better than others. Most provide active, clickable links to other sites that will lead you on a virtual journey through any aspect of travel that suits your fancy.

For travel arrangements, you may already be familiar with the bigger travel sites: Expedia, Travelocity, Orbitz, Hotels.com, Priceline and many others. These offer bargain airfares, cruises, car rentals, hotel accommodations and activities at discounted rates. If your schedule is flexible and you're a web surfer, you may find excellent bargains on the internet. Rates, restrictions and availability change rapidly on the web.

Be sure of what you want before you commit since changes cost money, usually a $100 re-ticketing fee on major air carriers plus any additional ticket cost. If you're putting your own itinerary together, it's usually best to book your airfare first, then go to work on hotel rooms. Check your family's priorities first. If you want particular rooms at a particular place, start with that and work your airfare around it.

Another option to explore is a wholesale company that can offer substantial savings by booking air and hotel accommodations in one package. Try **Classic Custom Vacations**, www.classicvacations.com or **Pleasant Hawaiian Holidays**, www.pleasantholidays.com.

We suggest you start with the following sites, and we encourage the whole family to get involved.

www.gohawaii.com, the Hawai'i Visitors and Convention Bureau site, has hundreds of live links to its members and associates, a good calendar of events, island-by-island guide, historical information and excellent general resources. You can even send your friends an animated *hula* dance message that you compose yourself.

www.alternative-hawaii.com, one of the best calendar sites, with easy-to-use and attractive presentations for all types of island events, things to see and do, and absolutely gorgeous photography.

Visit the Big Island's biggest attraction, Volcanoes National Park, at **www.nps.gov/havo**, an excellent site with a world of information, maps, tips and suggestions. Then go to the stars and see the Center for International Astronomy site at **www.ifa.hawaii.edu/mok/about_ maunakea.htm**.

There are thousands of sites about accommodations. If you're looking for a bed and breakfast, start with Hawai'i Island Bed & Breakfast Association, **www.stayhawaii.com** or Hawaii's Best Bed & Breakfasts, **www.bestbnb.com**. For a condo vacation, one of the best is Sunquest Vacations, with a large, islandwide inventory in every price range, **www.sunquest-hawaii.com**. For Kona specifically, try Kona Hawai'i Vacation Rentals, **www.konahawaii.com**.

www.konaweb.com is a fun, independent site with lots of active links to other pages and all sorts of chatty information on island attractions, restaurants, activities and a calendar of events. It features personal reviews of all kinds of things from visitors and residents as well.

www.virtualguidebooks.com has 360-degree virtual tours of favorite places islandwide, including some of the most remote. And **www.hawaiiweb.com** has still photos of most points of interest, descriptions of and directions to island beach parks and much more.

Other fun sites are **www.alohajoes.com** for Hawaiian music, **www.snorkelbobs.com** for snorkeling tips and other stuff, **www. hawaii-forest.com** for nature and eco-info and **www.hawaiifruit.net** and related links for everything you ever wanted to know about things that grow.

Medical Information

For emergencies call 911.

HOSPITALS

Kona Community Hospital, Kealakekua (808-322-9311)

Hilo Medical Center, 1190 Waianuenue Avenue (808-974-4700)

Ka'u Hospital (808-928-8331)

Kohala Hospital (808-889-6211)

Honoka'a, Hale Ho'ola (808-775-7211)

North Hawai'i Community Hospital, 67-1125 Mamalahoa Highway, Waimea (808-885-4444).

CLINICS

There are also several clinics around the Big Island to handle emergencies or walk-in patients needing urgent care. Your condominium or hotel desk can provide you with suggestions or check the Yellow Pages.

Kona District Kaiser Permanente Medical Care Clinic, 75-184 Hualalai Road (808-334-4400); Keauhou-Kona Medical Clinic, 78-6831 Ali'i Drive, (808-322-2750); Kona-Kohala Medical Associates, 75-137 Hualalai Road, Kailua-Kona (808-329-1346); Hualalai Urgent Care, Crossroads Medical Centre, Henry Street (808-327-4357)

Waikoloa/Kohala Coast Hawai'i Family Medical Center, Waikoloa Highlands Center (808-883-8877)

Waimea Kaiser Permanente Medical Care Clinic, 67-1185A Mamalahoa Highway. (808-881-4500); Lucy Henriques Medical Center, on Highway 19 near Parker Ranch Center (808-885-4451)

Hamakua Coast Hamakua Health Center, 45-549 Plumeria St., Honoka'a (808-775-7204)

Hilo Kaiser Permanente Medical Care Clinic, 1292 Waianuenue Avenue (808-934-4000); Hilo Medical Associates, 73 Pu'uhonu Place (808-934-2000)

See "Helpful Phone Numbers" at the end of the chapter for more numbers. Calling 911 will put you in contact with local police, fire and ambulances.

Getting There

Arrival tips: Before you land, take off aprons and bibs, wash hands and faces with wet wipes, put dirty clothes in ziplock bags, gradually start putting everything away and make sure nothing is lost. To get in the mood, change into a brighter shirt or add a colorful accessory to liven up airport "neutrals." At the airport send one person on the shuttle for the rental car and leave one to pick up luggage. This saves you having to schlep bags twice. If you are missing a bag, make the claim and do the paperwork, then go on with your vacation. It's not worth the extra delay and stress of waiting around the airport—the airline will deliver your bag when it arrives. Wayward bags are almost always found, so try not to worry. Condo vacationers are going to want to shop for kitchen provisions. Stop at a convenience store for everybody's favorite beverage and a snack, then check in, shower, change clothes, relax and make a list for one "designated shopper." Grocery shopping by a committee of tired people can be expensive in time and money. If you're travelling with a large family group, stick to the

SUN SAFETY

The sunshine is stronger in Hawai'i than on the mainland, so a few basic guidelines will ensure that you return home without a burn. Use a good sunscreen (at least SPF30 for kids), reapply after swimming and don't forget the lips. Opaque clothing is even more effective than the best sunscreen, if you can stand to keep covered—and wear a hat to protect your face. Exercise self-control and stay out a limited time the first few days. It is best to avoid being out between the hours of noon and three when it is the hottest. Be cautious of overcast days when it is very easy to become burned unknowingly. Don't forget that the ocean acts as a reflector and time spent in it equals time spent on the beach.

"who pays for what" rules you discussed to avoid hard feelings. Once you arrive at your lodging, take time to unpack; don't live out of suitcases. You'll feel less transient, more "here." If you can, take off your watch. And don't turn on the TV first thing; take a minute to breathe, look at the view, and relax.

Departure tips: Even though the airports are small, you still have to allow the requisite 90 minutes to check in and get through security procedures. If you're returning to a cold climate, pack winter coats on top so you can easily put them on when you reach your destination airport. Again, have one person dropped at the airport with the luggage and another turn in the rental car. Your first luggage check point is the Department of Agriculture station before you go to the airline counter (you do not have to take this step for interisland travel). There are several additional check points for luggage, so be patient. Keep in mind that any fresh fruit or flowers will be confiscated at the gate, so don't carry these on. (Hawai'i's insect population is not allowed to leave the state.) Again, use the free luggage tags to I.D. toddlers with their name, flight number and parents' cellphone numbers. And don't be sad, you'll be back. *A hui hou!*

AIRLINE INFORMATION

There are more ways to plan travel than ever before. Competition is fierce and services are interconnected. You can book room and car packages through your air carrier, earn airline miles from your rental car company, and pay part of your hotel room with your airline miles. Travel planning by internet opens even more options, worlds of information and bargain basement prices at the touch of a button.

Because of the complexities of today's travel universe, we recommend a professional travel agent to help you with your Hawai'i vacation. Travel agents do not charge their traveling clients; they earn commissions from travel providers based on a percentage of the rates (10 to 15 percent in the case of most hotels) or a flat rate (currently $50 per booking from the airlines). Travel agents have access to an enormous amount of information, information that changes constantly. More and more, they are networking with wholesale companies, allying with travel consortia and otherwise working very hard to keep up with the times and provide their clients with the very best possible rates. You can do it yourself; it's easy. However, travel agents book trips for a living and they can almost always save you money. More importantly, they can save you a great deal of time and aggravation. Remember, time is the most valuable commodity you have to spend, particularly on vacation.

This is particularly true if your family is coming together from different cities for a reunion, wedding or other special occasion. Either one lucky person usually gets charged with making the travel arrangements for everybody, or it's every man for himself. Either way, it's difficult to avoid wasted time, hard feelings or inevitable frustrations. Visit a professional, give them your complete itinerary and let them handle it for you.

FLIGHTS TO THE ISLANDS

At present, several airlines fly directly into Kona International Airport from mainland cities, the most convenient way to go, but currently there are no direct mainland flights into Hilo. Both Kona International Airport and Hilo International Airport are modern terminal facilities. Kona airport's runway accommodates international jumbo jet flights and the terminal is undergoing continual upgrades. Hilo's runway can also handle large aircraft, but it remains underutilized, not the second gateway to the Big Island its designers planned. Kona is increasingly busy with more and more flights as the visitor industry develops on the island's sunny west side. In fact, you can start sightseeing right at Kona airport with a visit to the Ellison S. Onizuka Space Center (see Chapter 2 for more information).

Most U.S. and many international airlines fly into Honolulu, from where you can take a short flight on one of several interisland carriers (see below). Hawaiian and Aloha Airlines also provide connections through Kahului Airport on Maui to Hilo or Kona. United Airlines is still the dominant air carrier to Hawai'i with about half of all traffic to and from the islands. United provides direct mainland-to-Kona service (without the Honolulu stopover) from Los Angeles and San Francisco daily (and from Denver, Chicago and other cities seasonally). Their schedule may shift according to seasonal demand

(Christmas–New Year's, for example), when flights are added. If your schedule allows you to book these direct flights, especially traveling with kids, the savings in time and trouble are invaluable.

Please be aware that if your mainland-based carrier does not fly directly into Hilo or Kona, they will book your connecting flight from Honolulu at a substantially discounted rate, and interisland fares have increased significantly in recent years. It is no longer advisable to book only as far as Honolulu and count on a less expensive interisland flight when you arrive. When you check in at the airport, have your luggage checked to your final destination, Hilo or Kona. At the Honolulu International Airport, the mainland terminal is a separate building, about a quarter-mile walk or shuttle ride from the

KONA COFFEE FARMS

The Big Island is big on coffee. Kona coffee is about the best in the world. If you don't believe us, ask Starbucks, or just look at the price tag: $13 to $15 a pound for 100 percent Kona coffee beans. The Kona district has the perfect combination of altitude, sunshine, rainfall and volcanic soil to produce excellent coffee beans, internationally recognized for quality and taste. The first coffee tree was brought to the island in 1813 by King Kamehameha the Great's consultant Don Francisco de Paula y Marin (who is responsible for bringing in many of the plants, trees and flowers we take for granted as "Hawaiian"). In 1828, an American missionary transplanted a *Coffea arabica* tree to Kona, and the rest is history. Today there are over 600 private, largely family-run coffee farms on the island. Coffee is also grown on O'ahu, Kaua'i, Maui and even Moloka'i, but Kona still dominates the market.

A word about buying Kona coffee. The best and most expensive is 100 percent Kona. Regulations permit coffee companies to use the words "Kona Blend" on their packaging if their blend of coffee beans includes at least 10 percent Kona beans. Most flavored coffees will be blends and can be very good. But if you want the real deal, read the label. Kona blends and 100 percent Kona coffees are available at most island grocery stores (hint: look for discount coupons in tourist publications), Hilo Hattie's, K-Mart, Costco and elsewhere. However, genuine coffee lovers will appreciate the chance to visit coffee farms, roasteries and museums for a closer look at their favorite beverage and spend a pleasant day touring the "Napa" of coffee. See "Coffee Farms" in Chapter 6 for more details.

interisland terminal, so it's impractical and unnecessary to retrieve luggage in Honolulu and re-check it on your interisland flight.

The following airlines have direct flights into Kona International Airport (as always, subject to change).

Hawai'i-based Carriers

Aloha Airlines—Aloha Airlines flies into Kona from Oakland, Burbank, San Diego, Sacramento, Orange County, Reno, Las Vegas and Vancouver (some with stops in Honolulu or Maui). 800-367-5250; www.alohaairlines.com.

Hawaiian Airlines—Hawaiian Airlines flies into Kona from Las Vegas, Phoenix, Portland, Seattle, Los Angeles, San Diego and San Francisco (some with stops in Honolulu or Maui).

U.S./International Carriers

American Airlines—800-433-7300; www.aa.com

Japan Airlines—800-525-3663

United Airlines—800-863-8331; www.ual.com

The following American and international airlines have flights into Honolulu International Airport and can arrange your interisland reservations to Kona or Hilo.

Air Canada—888-247-2262; www.aircanada.ca

Air New Zealand—800-262-1234

Aloha Airlines—800-367-5250; www.alohaairlines.com

American Airlines—800-433-7300; www.aa.com

American Trans Air/Pleasant Hawaiian Holidays—800-435-9282

China Airlines—800-227-5118

Continental Airlines—800-523-3273; www.continental.com

Delta Airlines—800-221-1212; www.delta-air.com

Hawaiian Airlines—800-882-8811; www.hawaiianair.com

Japan Airlines—800-525-3663

JTB/Oli Oli—800-839-6636

Korean Air—800-438-5000

Northwest Airlines—800-225-2525; www.nwa.com

Philippines Airlines—800-435-9725

Quantas Airways—800-227-4500

United Airlines—800-864-8331; www.ual.com

INTERISLAND FLIGHTS

Hawaiian and Aloha Airlines are the primary interisland air carriers and offer generally competitive fares. Advance reservations are required and you'll need to check in through several security points, so arrival 90 minutes before your scheduled flight is recommended.

Both airlines also offer promotional discounts, group rates, wedding party specials, internet-only discount rates, and air-room-car packages.

Aloha Airlines—In the U.S. & Canada 800-367-5250, 877-879-2564; in Honolulu 808-484-1111; on the Big Island 808-935-5771; e-mail: aloha@alohaair.com; www.alohaairlines.com.

Hawaiian Airlines—In the U.S. & Canada 800-367-5320; in Honolulu 808-838-1555; on the Big Island 800-882-8811; www.ha waiianair.com.

Island Air—Flights are limited between Kona on the Big Island and Honolulu via Lanai or Kapalua on Maui. In the U.S. 800-323-3345; in Honolulu 808-484-2222; from the Neighbor Islands 800-652-6541; www.islandair.com.

Mokulele Flight Service—This Hawaiian family–owned independent air service offers interisland flights on a regular schedule between Kona and Honolulu, and Kona and Kahului Airport on Maui. 808-326-7070.

Pacific Wings—Pacific Wings is a small commuter air service based on Maui and connects several Hawai'i destinations with Kamuela Airport on the Big Island. The airline provides scheduled air service in and out of Kamuela Airport to Kahului on Maui and to Honolulu with connecting services to other points. The airline provides service to those smaller island airports not as readily serviced by Hawaiian and Aloha Air. Pacific Wings operates twin-engine Cessna 402C aircraft and offers competitive fares with Hawaiian and Aloha. Pacific Wings also offers special air tour packages to specific island destinations/attractions. 808-873-0877, 888-575-4546, fax 808-873-7920; e-mail: info@pacificwings.com.

Cruise Lines

Before the advent of modern jet airlines, most visitors to Hawai'i traveled by elegant ocean liner for a "Titanic" luxury experience (minus the sinking, of course). Today, cruise ships have added a whole new dimension to Hawai'i vacation options. Like self-contained floating resorts, cruise ships now offer indulgent spas and fitness centers with shipboard exercise programs in addition to (perhaps) over-indulgent food service, casinos, professional entertainment and overall party atmosphere. Cruising can be a great way for families to go, with a wide range of kid's games and organized activities. Evening programs allow mom and dad to enjoy dinner and a show by themselves while the kids do their own things with friends (and remember, they can't get off the boat at sea).

The newly-refurbished *Pride of Aloha* (Norwegian Cruise Lines) offers seven-day interisland voyages from Honolulu, with their Freestyle Vacation options in dining, attire and activities (www.ncl.com). Full-day stops in Kona offer opportunities for shore excursions and an evening sail by Kilauea volcano. Distinctive and very colorful island decor is used throughout, including six various tropical-themed restaurants, three lounges and the Kumu Cultural Center. Kid's Crew provides supervised activities for the littler ones while a video arcade and teen disco help entertain teens. The new *Pride of America*, commissioned in June 2005, will add a new dimension to the Hawai'i cruise fleet. Shipboard activities will be extensive: swimming pools and hot tubs, Rascals Kid's Club and Connections Teen Club, sports, spa, shopping, arcades and eight restaurants and ten lounges with diverse American themes from Mardi Gras to Hollywood to Waikiki.

Cruising can be a great way to see more than one island without making separate arrangements for flights, hotels and cars. It does take longer to cruise than to fly, but the convenience may be a good trade-off, depending on how much time you have. Plus, prices are generally inclusive of meals and shipboard activities.

As with every other aspect of planning your Big Island vacation, there are a lot of options to choose from. Once again, we recommend an experienced travel agent (there are cruise specialists) and a little homework. A good site to start with on the internet is www.cruise web.com.

Another benefit of cruising is the warm welcome you receive when the ship docks. With the dramatic increase in cruise ship arrivals into Hilo and Kona, the old "boat days" festivities are making a comeback. Often local visitor industry groups, civic and cultural clubs and craft vendors are on hand to meet and greet arriving passengers at the docks. This is a resurgent and rapidly growing segment of the travel industry, one which we expect to hear more good things about as more ships choose the Big Island for a destination.

Following are cruise lines whose ships presently call at Hilo or Kona ports:

Norwegian Cruise Lines—800-327-7030; www.ncl.com
Holland America—877-724-5425; www.hollandamerica.com
Royal Caribbean—800-398-9819; www.royalcaribbean.com
Carnival Cruise Lines—888-227-6482; www.carnival.com

Driving on the Big Island

Driving on the Big Island is really no different from anywhere else, with one small exception: People are nice. Big Island drivers are generally the most courteous and congenial you're likely to find. The majority drive with *aloha*, which may catch you off guard when they yield to let you make a left turn in front of them, wave you through an intersection and even smile. Unfortunately, like anywhere else, there are, of course, some who don't, so it pays to drive with aloha *and* awareness at the same time. The speed limit is 55, despite long, tempting stretches of nearly empty road on the Kona side. Police do enforce the speed limits; they also enforce the seatbelt law. Don't let a ticket mar your vacation.

Directions are easy. (Remember the *shaka* map in your hand? Make a fist with your right hand. Extend your thumb, north and pinkie, south.) There's basically only one road. Queen Ka'ahumanu Highway, Route 19, covers the northern half of the island from Kailua-

TRAFFIC WOES

The Big Island has recently obtained a new, modern feature in common with most of the rest of the world: traffic. We are sorry to say that the days of careless cruising down empty highways are, for the most part, past. Naturally, traffic to us is nothing compared to where most visitors come from, and a little planning can alleviate most inconvenience.

Following are suggestions to help avoid more bothersome traffic delays:

Remember a little patience goes a long way toward minimizing stress and lowering blood pressure. Allow extra time for your travels, particularly for departing flights.

Tune in to local radio stations for reports of accidents and alternate routing.

Waimea and Kailua-Kona experience regular "rush hour" delays in the afternoons. Travel to/through these areas before 3 p.m. or after 5:30 p.m.

Regular traffic law and common courtesy don't disappear just because you're on vacation. Please don't pass on the shoulders, cross double yellow lines, exceed or fall too far below the speed limit, make U-turns or stop in no-parking areas. If you get lost, pull completely off the road and stop the car, then look at your map. *Mahalo.*

Cars are not the only traffic. Keep alert for pedestrians, bicyclists and animals on the roads. Cyclists, remember to stay on the shoulders or in marked bike lanes wherever possible, stop at stop signs and streetlights, and, please, if you find yourself on a winding road with traffic backing up behind you, use common sense. Pull over and walk your bike to a wider area, consult your map and ride someplace where it's safe.

Kona to Hilo (from your middle finger, under your thumb and over to your wrist). And Hawai'i Belt Road, Route 11, covers the southern half (from your wrist around the top of your pinkie back to your middle finger).

Small, green, numbered signs on the shoulders are mile markers between towns and very often used to give directions. It's also a good idea to use the practical Hawaiian words *mauka* toward the mountains and *makai* toward the ocean. In other words, if somebody tells you the gas station is just past 113-mile marker on the Queen K *mauka* side, you should know exactly where to go. Also keep your eyes open for the bright red and yellow Hawaiian warrior markers, which indicate historic sites.

An excellent road map of the Big Island, *Hawai'i, The Big Island* by cartographer James A. Bier, is highly recommended. It's available at local bookstores or can be ordered from Catalog Order Desk, The University of Hawai'i Press, Honolulu, HI 96822.

Getting Around

FROM THE AIRPORT It's best to arrange your ground transportation at the same time you book airline and hotel reservations. We recommend a rental car, particularly if this is your family's first visit to the island, so you can experience more of what there is to see and do conveniently. If you don't have a rental car, most hotel and condo properties in Hilo, Kona and the Kohala Coast have an airport transfer service available for a fee, and taxi service is available but expensive. The County of Hawai'i regulates that its public Hele On bus system does not service the airports. Some of the local tour bus/limo companies provide airport to hotel service on a pre-arranged basis. Try **Roberts Hawai'i** (800-831-5541, in Kona 808-329-1688, in Hilo, 808-966-5483) or **Luana Limousine Service** (Kona 808-326-5466). Reservations should be made at least a day in advance or through your travel agent.

PUBLIC TRANSPORTATION In the Kailua-Kona and Keauhou areas, you can catch the **Ali'i Shuttle**, which serves the entire length of Ali'i Drive from Kailua-Kona to Keauhou. The shuttle runs Monday through Saturday and takes 45 minutes in each direction. Its turn-around points are the Lanihau Shopping Center in Kailua-Kona and the Kona Surf Resort in Keauhou. The shuttle makes stops along Ali'i Drive at all major hotels and shopping centers. The fare is $2 each way; hours of operation are (northbound) from Kona Surf every 90 minutes 8:30 a.m. to 7 p.m. and (southbound) from Lanihau Center 9:20 a.m. to 6:20 p.m. Look for the white bus and just flag it down. 808-938-1112, 808-775-7121.

The other general transportation alternative is the **HeleOn bus system** operated by the County of Hawai'i. The public buses operate in Hilo and Kailua-Kona as well as offering islandwide service. Standard fare for short distances is 75¢ within Hilo or Kailua-Kona, and gradually increases depending on how far you are going around the island. The around-the-island fare, Hilo to Kona, is a reasonable $6 one way/$12 round trip.

Hele On bus tickets are sold by the sheet at a 10 percent discount from the regular per ticket fare. Ten tickets per sheet cost $6.75. Seniors (60+), the disabled and students can buy ticket sheets for $5. As an example, a one way trip from Hilo to Kona would cost seven tickets. Bus tickets are available at various stores, shops and businesses around the island displaying the Hele On bus poster. There is a $1 per piece charge for luggage and backpacks. For bus schedules and ticket information, contact County of Hawai'i, Mass Transportation Agency, 630 East Lanikaula Street, Hilo, HI 96720; 808-961-8744; e-mail: heleonbus@interpac.net.

LIMOUSINE SERVICES   If you want to splurge on transportation for that special occasion, wedding, honeymoon or for whatever reason, you can arrange for a personalized limousine for everything from airport-hotel service to a complete private around-the-island tour complete with champagne and catered lunch. The cost is obvi-

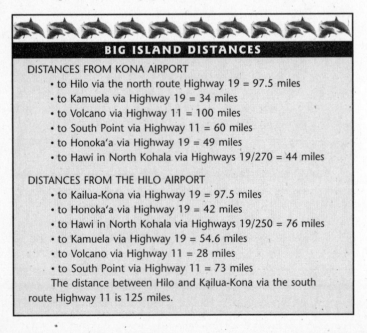

BIG ISLAND DISTANCES

DISTANCES FROM KONA AIRPORT
- to Hilo via the north route Highway 19 = 97.5 miles
- to Kamuela via Highway 19 = 34 miles
- to Volcano via Highway 11 = 100 miles
- to South Point via Highway 11 = 60 miles
- to Honoka'a via Highway 19 = 49 miles
- to Hawi in North Kohala via Highways 19/270 = 44 miles

DISTANCES FROM THE HILO AIRPORT
- to Kailua-Kona via Highway 19 = 97.5 miles
- to Honoka'a via Highway 19 = 42 miles
- to Hawi in North Kohala via Highways 19/250 = 76 miles
- to Kamuela via Highway 19 = 54.6 miles
- to Volcano via Highway 11 = 28 miles
- to South Point via Highway 11 = 73 miles

The distance between Hilo and Kailua-Kona via the south route Highway 11 is 125 miles.

ously expensive but first-class for those who can afford it. Here's a listing of limousine service operators:

Carey Town & Country Limousine (888-563-2888) provides chauffeur-driven luxury sedans, limousines, vans, etc., plus airport/hotel transfer service on all the Hawaiian islands.

Luana Limousine Service (808-326-5466; 800-999-4001) provides full-service limousine service on the Big Island.

Meridian Hawaiian Resorts Transport (808-885-7484 or 808-887-6100) operates out of Mauna Lani Bay Hotel and Bungalows, Kohala Coast.

Resorts Limousines (808-327-9742; fax 808-327-0023; e-mail: resortslimos@aol.com) offers transportation by limo, SUV and multi-passenger vans or airport transfers, hotel pickups, customized tours and more. Special wedding/honeymoon touches available by request include fun things like magnetic "just married" signs, champagne and a red carpet.

TAXIS Big Island taxi service is expensive. Metered fares are standard between companies islandwide, as of June 1, 2005, $3 for pickup plus $2.40 per mile, but miles add up fast in the long distances between airports and hotels, or hotels and island attractions. If you do choose to use taxi service, it's best to pre-arrange transportation and to clarify hours of operation. Unlike mainland taxicabs, some companies in some locations close at night unless a pickup time is pre-arranged. On the other hand, many taxi companies offer sightseeing tours and special service 24 hours a day.

Hilo's taxi services include **A-1 Bob's Taxi** (808-959-4800, 808-963-5470), **AA Marshall's Taxi** (808-936-2654), **Ace One Taxi** (808-935-8303), **Percy's Taxi** (808-969-7060), **Hilo Harry's Taxi** (808-935-7091). Kona/Kohala/Waimea taxi services include **Air Taxi & Tours** (808-883-8262), **Aloha Taxi** (808-325-5448, 808-329-7779), **Alpha Star Taxi** (808-885-4771), **C & C Taxi** (808-329-6388, 808-325-5121), **D & E Taxi** (808-329-4279), **Kona Airport Taxi** (808-329-7779), **Paradise Transportation Inc.** (808-329-1234) and **Triple A-1 Taxi** (808-325-3818).

RENTAL CARS, VANS AND FOUR-WHEEL DRIVES The Big Island has some 1,500 miles of paved county and state roads and highways. And those roads and highways pass through some of the loveliest and most diverse scenery in Hawai'i. The best way to see it all is by hiring your own car. Most standard rental car companies have outlets at Hilo and Kona airports and a few have desks at major hotels and resorts. They offer a variety of cars at a variety of rates, with special low-season, weekly discount, and holiday package deals. You can check out the following list and contact them yourself (most

CIRCLE ISLAND DRIVE

You can drive completely around the Big Island from Hilo to Kona in a day. It's only 225 miles, but it is a long and tiring drive, not really conducive to sightseeing and leisurely exploring. We'd suggest you make a two-day tour of it and give yourself time to see everything. Drive the 100 miles on the northern route from Kona to Hilo through Waimea, spend the night, see the volcano the next day and return along the southern route.

From Kailua-Kona, drive north on Route 19 along the hot, black lava coastline on your right and the sparkling Pacific on your left. About 30 miles pass, then you reach the stop sign at Kawaihae. Turn right and head inland and uphill along a winding road through gradually greener countryside, and be on the lookout for rainbows. In Waimea, it's suddenly cooler and misty. Turn left at the stoplight and continue through a Western-style town surrounded by rolling hills that make you think of Ireland instead of islands. When you leave town, the scene opens up into a vast panoramic pasture land, and you pass between flanks of tall forest.

A few more miles later, past Honoka'a, the sun comes out again and you're back to the ocean on the other side of the island. The road swings southward along beautiful stretches of former sugar cane plantation land, now forested with eucalyptus trees. If you look closely, you can still see sugar cane tufts waving in the breeze, banana trees along the roadside or gardens of tropi-

have toll-free numbers and websites) or you can have your travel agent do it. Do inquire about room and car or air, room and car packages.

Rental cars are your best bargain for transportation since they give you the independence and mobility to come and go as you please and to see and do what you want. Rates vary greatly among the car rental agencies as well as by season so it's wise to shop around. A survey of Big Island car rental agencies revealed the following rates, all with no mileage charges. The daily rate for an economy/compact ranges from $30 to $50. For a mid-size car, the daily rate ranges from $35 to $55. Full-size cars range from $40 to $60. Mini-vans range from $55 to $85. Keep in mind that these figures are only approximate.

Special rates may apply during the "low" season in Hawai'i, usually from Labor Day until about Thanksgiving and again from Easter until about June 1. Hawai'i's peak season from Thanksgiving to Easter or spring break finds demand and prices high on rental cars. The summer season, although not as strong as winter, generates a fair amount of demand and rates seem to fluctuate. Some local events, such as the

cal flowers, wild ginger and bamboo orchids. The road winds through three V-shaped gulches into deep, almost-secret valleys and crosses a series of bridges where a quick look to the right might show you a waterfall. If not, you might visit 'Akaka Falls State Park or the World Botanical Gardens at Umauma before you continue to Hilo. Just outside of town, at the village of Pepe'ekeo, look straight ahead at the horizon. If it's a fairly clear day, you might be able to make out the steam cloud from Kilauea for a moment. Cross the "singing bridge" over the Wailoa River into Hilo and cruise along the shoreline of tranquil Hilo Bay.

Enjoy your time in Hilo, then head to Volcanoes National Park, south on what is now Highway 11, past farm communities and misty *ohia* forest, gradually climbing up to Kilauea.

After your experience in the park, head south on Hawai'i Belt Road, Route 11, towards the southern tip of the island. Cruise along uncluttered highway, through farmland and colorful little towns worth a stop, and long stretches of empty, rainy lava fields before the road reaches the ocean again on the Kona side and turns north. If you're not worn out, take time to explore Pu'uhonua o Honaunau, a "place of refuge" where fugitives found sanctuary and forgiveness. From here the road winds through the upper elevations of Kona coffee country before dropping back down into familiar territory and the flat black lava land of Kona.

Merrie Monarch *hula* competition in Hilo and the Ironman Triathlon in Kona, can deplete the rental car supply and drive the prices up.

One thing that affects car rental rates is the extra charge for insurance coverage. This rate can run anywhere from $15 and up per day. This increases the daily rate drastically and most agencies strongly encourage you to buy the coverage. However, it is suggested that you check with your own insurance company at home to verify exactly what your policy covers. In fact, bring along your insurance company's address and telephone number just in case. Hawai'i is a no-fault state and without the insurance, if there is an accident, you are required to take care of all the damages before leaving the island.

Most of the car rental agencies have similar policies. They require a minimum age of 25 and a major credit card.

Please note: the Saddle Road is off limits to regular rental cars. Driving on it violates the rental car agreement. You'd need a four-wheel-drive vehicle to reach such places as the summit of 14,000-foot Mauna Kea and other inaccessible backcountry or off-road locations, which are also off limits to regular rental cars.

If you pick up your car at one airport, say at Kona, and drop it off at Hilo, most car rental agencies will charge you what is called a "drop" charge. This can run as high as $30 to $40. That's why it is usually best to pick up and return a rental car at the same location.

Warning: Even paradise has its share of thieves so *never* leave your automobile unlocked at the beach, park, scenic site or parking lot. Take personal valuables with you, secure your car and your valuables, and don't leave the keys in your car.

RENTAL CAR LISTINGS   Alamo Rent A Car, 800-327-9633; Kona 808-329-8896; Hilo 808-961-3353

Avis Rent A Car, 800-831-2847; Kona 808-327-3000; Hilo 808-935-1290

Budget Rent A Car, all locations, 800-527-0700.

Dollar Rent A Car, 800-800-4000; Kona 808-329-2744; Hilo 808-961-6059

Enterprise, 800-736-8222; Kona 808-331-2509

Hertz Rent a Car, 800-654-3011; Kona 329-3566; Hilo 808-935-2896; www.hertz.com

National Car Rental, 888-868-6207; Kona 808-329-1674; Hilo 808-935-0891; www.nationalcar.com

Thrifty Car Rental, all locations 866-450-5101; 800-367-5238; Kona 808-329-1339; Hilo 808-961-6698; www.thrifty.com

Aloha Exotic Car Rental has something different. Contact owner/ "Director of Fun" Tim Kuglin for a stylish ride in one of their 1957 Porsche Speedster replicas. This four-speed sportscar is the perfect island cruiser. Hummers also available. Drivers must be at least 30 years old with valid credit card, driver's license and active insurance. Rates: from $299. Kona; 808-331-1997; www.aloha-car.com.

CAMPER/RV RENTALS   In recent years, two companies started offering modern, self-contained RVs for rent, in part due to the increasing demand for alternative vacation experiences. While this is a great opportunity for those who enjoy RV camping, a word of caution is in order. Most of the Big Island campgrounds and state/county parks that allow camping are not really as equipped for RV motorhomes as those on the mainland. Electrical, water and disposal hook-ups for RVs may be hard to find, and we suggest you talk at length with the rental company you choose. However, since the RVs are rented as fully self-contained, including their own water supply, etc., finding a place to park and set up camp for a night shouldn't be much of a problem. As with any other situation on your trip, use common sense, lock up valuables and be aware of what might be private property or otherwise questionable surroundings.

Harper Car and Truck Rentals arranges pick-ups and returns for either Hilo or Kona. They have two- and four-wheel-drive

Winnebago motor homes available that sleep up to five people. The campers have stove, oven, shower, refrigerator, a/c, microwave, sink, generator, propane tank and shade awning. Water tanks hold a two- to three-day supply. Two-day rental minimum. Rates: 2-wheel-drive motorhome $135.95 per day; 4-wheel-drive motorhome, $149.95 per day. 456 Kalanianaole Street, Hilo, HI 96720; 808-969-1478; 800-852-9993; fax 808-961-0423.

Island RV/Safari Activities rents self-contained Tioga motorcoaches. These vehicles are top-of-the-line and comfortable, with all the conveniences including linens, grill, lounge chairs, galley, utensils, cookery equipment, etc., and sleep up to four people. The company also has snorkel gear and beach equipment available for rent, and offers shuttle service and island tours. Rates: Motorhomes begin at $250 per day. 75-5785 Kuakini Highway, Kailua-Kona, HI 96740-3137; 808-334-04640; 800-406-4555; e-mail: info@islandrv.com; www.islandrv.com.

MOTORCYCLE, MOPED, MOTORSCOOTER RENTALS The Big Island is a great place to ride motorcycles—from long stretches of sunny coastline with stark black lava on the one side and the sparkling blue Pacific on the other, to winding mountain lanes under a canopy of trees, through green pastureland, forested highway and breathtaking V-shaped cutaways over forested gulches with distant waterfalls. The list goes on. Unfortunately, the weather can vary as widely as the scenery, and bikers need to be prepared for rain and be aware of wind. There is presently no helmet law in Hawaii, but caution is always advised.

DJ's Rentals rents scooters, mopeds, small bikes and large Harley-Davidsons. Rates: from $150 for 24 hours. 75-5663A Palani Road, Kailua-Kona, across from King Kamehameha's Kona Beach Hotel; 808-329-1700; 800-993-HOGS; e-mail: rent@harleys.com; www.harleys.com.

Kona Harley-Davidson rents and specializes strictly in Harley-Davidson motorcycles. Rates: $120-$150 per day. 74-5615 Luhia Street, Kailua-Kona; 808-326-9887; e-mail: konahd@kona.net; www.konaharleydavidson.com.

BICYCLE RENTALS Hawaii Sports Connection, 75-5699 Kopiko Place, Kailua-Kona; 808-329-3309.

C&S Outfitters, 64-1066 Mamalahoa Highway on east side of Kamuela; 808-885-5005; fax 808-885-5683.

Dave's Bike & Triathlon Shop, 75-5669 Ali'i Drive, Kailua-Kona, behind Atlantis Submarine and Kona Pier; 808-329-4522.

H P Bike Works, 74-5599 Luhia, Kailua-Kona; 808-326-2453.

Hawaiian Pedals, Kona Inn Shopping Village, Ali'i Drive, Kailua-Kona; 808-329-2294.

Hilo Bike Hub, 318 East Kawili Street, Hilo; 808-961-4452.

Mauna Kea Mountain Bikes Inc., P.O. Box 44672, Kamuela, 96743; 808-883-1030.

Mid Pacific Wheels, 1133C Manono Street, Hilo; 808-935-6211.

AIRPLANE RENTALS For those who prefer wings to wheels, Big Island Air Service Hawai'i can help. This company rents Cessna 150 and 172 airplanes for your airborne photo safari, personal circle-island tours and adventures in Big Island skies. Rentals to qualified pilots only; dual-rentals available. Kona International Airport; 808-326-2288.

Grocery Shopping

You can expect to pay quite a bit more on average for groceries on the Big Island compared to what you pay in most areas of the U.S. mainland. Like on the mainland, however, island markets vary in price so it pays to shop around. You'll find a range of grocery stores on the Big Island, from simple mom-and-pop country stores to modern convenient supermarkets like Safeway. Grocery store chains you might not be familiar with are KTA, Sack n' Save, Suresave and Foodland. Most of them advertise in the local newspapers, offering weekly specials and coupons.

On your trips around the island and through the towns, don't hesitate to visit one of the old-fashioned, small town general stores, usually with grandma or grandpa still tending the register, maybe with the help of a younger family member who's returned to take over the business. With their homey country atmosphere, simple furnishings and fixtures and ancient coolers that keep beer and soda chilled, these old town stores allow you to step back into an earlier era of Hawaiian history. You might luck out and get there just as the homemade cookies, fresh sushi, or other country goodies are coming out of the kitchen, or somebody's cranking up the shave ice machine.

Calendar of Events

Following are some of the best cultural, community and sporting events that take place around the Big Island each year. For detailed information and specific dates (which vary annually) see www.gohawaii.com, the Hawai'i Visitors & Convention Bureau site, and While you're here, check out the local Big Island newspapers and visitor periodicals where you are staying.

January
Hauoli Makahiki Hou!—New Year celebrations islandwide

USTA Challenger Tennis Tournament—Hilton Waikoloa Village, Kohala Coast

Senior PGA Mastercard Championship Golf Tournament—Four Seasons Resort Hualalai, Kona

February

Kung Hee Fat Choy!—Chinese New Year celebrations islandwide

Heiva—Tahiti Fete of Hilo Tahitian Dance Extravaganza, Hilo

Waimea Cherry Blossom Heritage Festival—Waimea

Hawai'i Wood Show—Hilo

Portuguese Day in the Park—Hilo

Panaewa Stampede Pro-Am Rodeo—Hilo

Kona Chocolate Festival—Kailua-Kona

Grow Hawaiian Horti/Cultural Festival—Amy Greenwell Ethnobotanical Garden, Captain Cook

March

Kona Stampede Rodeo—Honaunau

Prince Kuhio Day (March 26)—State holiday

Haili Men's Invitational Volleyball Tournament—Hilo

Kona Brewer's Festival—Kailua-Kona

Magic Spectacular—Kainaliu

Ukulele Festival—Kings' Shops in Waikoloa

Spring Dance Concert—Kilauea Military Camp, Hawai'i Volcanoes National Park

Annual Dance & Music Concert—Volcano Art Center, Volcano

Merrie Monarch Hula Festival—and related cultural events including a parade, traditional quilting show and much more, Hilo. Scheduled activities begin on Easter Sunday

April

Hilo Rain Festival

Ka Ulu Lauhala O Kona Festival—Kona–Kohala Coast

Lava Man Triathlon—Kohala Coast

International Nights—University of Hawai'i at Hilo

May

May Day–Lei Day Celebrations—islandwide

Keauhou Kona Triathlon

Visitor Industry Charity Walk—Kona

Memorial Day Observances—islandwide

June

King Kamehameha Day—(June 11) Floral Parade, Kailua-Kona

King Kamehameha Day Celebration—Coconut Island, Hilo Bay

Lei-draping of King Kamehameha statues—(June 11) at the old Kapa'au Courthouse, North Kohala and at Wailoa State Park, Hilo

Annual Forage Field Day Taste of Hawaiian Range—Kamuela

Kona Marathon & Family Fun Runs—Kailua-Kona
Waiki'i Music Festival—Waiki'i Ranch, Kohala
Dolphin Days—Hilton Waikoloa Village, Kohala Coast
The Great Waikoloa Food, Wine & Music Fest—Hilton Waikoloa Village, Kohala Coast
Pu'uhonua o Honaunau Cultural Festival—Honaunau
Kona Classic fishing tournament—Kona
Obon Festival Dances—(June through August) A Japanese tradition practiced islandwide

July

Fourth of July—celebrations islandwide
Parker Ranch Rodeo and Horse Races—Waimea
Turtle Independence Day Celebration—Mauna Lani Bay Hotel & Bungalows
Rubber Duckie Race—Kings' Shops at Waikoloa Beach Resort, Kohala Coast
Annual Big Island Slack Key Guitar Festival—Hilo
Firecracker Fishing Tournament—Kailua-Kona
Hawaiian International Billfish Tournament—Kailua-Kona
Annual Big Island Bonsai Show—Hilo
Big Island Slack Key Guitar Festival—Hilo
Annual Skins Marlin Derby—Kailua-Kona
Kilauea Volcano Wilderness Run—Hawai'i Volcanoes National Park
Kilauea Cultural Festival—Kilauea Military Camp, Volcano
Mango Festival—Pahala, Ka'u District
King's Swim—Kona

August

Aloha Festival Royal Court Investiture—Hawai'i Volcanoes National Park
Pu'ukohola Heiau National Historic Site Hawaiian Cultural Festival—Kawaihae
International Festival of the Pacific—Hilo
Admissions Day Holiday Celebrations—islandwide
Queen Liliuokalani Outrigger Canoe Races—Kona

September

Big Island Aloha Festivals—numerous interesting and fun activities islandwide including the Falsetto and Storytelling Contest, Miss Aloha Nui Contest for great ladies of great stature, Aloha Festivals Poke Contest and the Kupuna Hula Festival
Terry Fox Weekend—Four Seasons Resort Hualalai
Parker Ranch Round-Up Rodeo—Waimea
Kona Marathon—Kona

Waikoloa Open Golf Championship—Waikoloa Village
Queen Liliuokalani Birthday Celebration—Hilo
Annual Hilo Orchid Society Show—Hilo
Mealani "Taste of Hawaiian Range" food festival—Kohala Coast

October

Hamakua Music Festival—Honoka'a, Hamakua Coast
Annual Waimea Powwow–Native American Culture Fest—Waimea
Mauna Loa Macadamia Nut Festival & Parade—Hilo
Ironman Triathlon World Championship—Kailua-Kona

November

Hawai'i International Film Festival—islandwide theaters
Big Island Festival of Fine Food, Wine, Culture and Relaxation—Kohala Coast (www.bigislandfestival.com)
Christmas in the Country—Volcano Art Center, Volcano
Christmas Arts and Crafts Fairs—Hilo, Kona and Kamuela
Kona Coffee Cultural Festival & Parade—and related activities, Kailua-Kona

December

Annual Waimea Christmas Parade—Waimea
Christmas Parades and Holiday Craft Fairs—islandwide
Christmas at Hulihe'e Palace—Kailua-Kona
Christmas Concerts—UH-Hilo Theater, Hilo
Lyman House Museum's "A Christmas Tradition"—Hilo
Christmas Concert in the Park—Hilo
Passport to International Cultures Culinary Show—Waikoloa Beach Resort
Traditional Mochi Rice Pounding—islandwide (808-963-6422)
Mele Kalikimaka!

Weather

The Big Island's weather is a study in variety and extremes. Claiming both the driest locality in the state as well as the wettest population center in the islands, the Big Island lies well within the belt of northeasterly trade winds generated by the semi-permanent Pacific high pressure cell to the northeast. The climate of the island is greatly influenced by terrain. Its outstanding weather features are the marked variations in rainfall by elevation, the persistent northeasterly trade winds and the equable year-round temperatures in localities near sea level.

Over the island's east windward slopes, rainfall occurs principally in the form of showers within the ascending moist trade winds. Mean annual rainfall, except for the semi-sheltered Hamakua district, increases from 100 inches or more along the coasts to a maximum of over 300 inches at elevations of 2,000 to 3,000 feet and declines to about 15 inches at the summits of Mauna Kea and Mauna Loa. In general, the southern and western leeward areas are sheltered from the trades by the high mountains and are therefore drier. Mean annual rainfall may range from 10 to 30 inches along the coasts to 120 inches at elevations of 2,500 to 3,000 feet.

Kohala and Kona: The driest area on the Big Island and the state with an average annual rainfall of less than 10 inches, is the coastal strip just leeward of the southern portion of the Kohala Mountains and of the saddle between the Kohalas and Mauna Kea. This is the area surrounding Kawaihae Bay on the Kohala Coast. The Hawai'i State Planning and Economic Development Department did a "Sunshine Map" study and found that the Kohala Coast has the highest sunshine rating in the state—even higher than such noted resorts as Ka'anapali on Maui and Waikiki on O'ahu. Kohala also maintains a near-constant 78°F year-round. The Kailua-Kona and Keauhou resort areas average about 20 inches of rainfall annually. With such consistent sunny dry weather it is easy to see why the Kona and Kohala areas have become such popular destinations.

Hilo: And then we have Hilo. Poor Hilo! It has been the butt of more jokes about its rain than there are umbrellas to sell. It seems that through the years, people have taken a special delight in maligning Hilo for its rather damp atmosphere. They make up stories about how you don't tan in Hilo, you rust!

All kidding aside, it does rain an awful lot in Hilo, more than any other population center in the Hawaiian archipelago. Within the city of Hilo average rainfall varies from about 130 inches a year near the shore to as much as 200 inches in mountain sections. The wettest part of the island, with a mean annual rainfall exceeding 300 inches, lies about 6 miles up-slope from the city limits. Rain falls about 280 days a year in the Hilo area.

In fact, Hilo is recognized as the rainiest city in the United States by the U.S. Census Bureau's County and City Data Book. Hilo has the highest average annual rainfall, 128.15 inches, of any of the nation's cities with a population of 25,000 or more. Interestingly, Hilo's total rainfall in 1990 surpassed all previous records when 211.22 inches of rain were recorded.

Needless to say, even Hiloans were in awe of nature's abundance that year. With such a soggy reputation, Hilo certainly doesn't need any more detractors. In fact, it really isn't as bad as one would think. Many of the showers are brief passing ones and, according to statistics, three-quarters of Hilo's rain falls at night. Thus it doesn't spoil most daytime visitor activities. Hilo's temperatures remain fairly constant also, averaging a high of 81°F and a low of 66°F year-round.

And like the Kona-Kohala climate that has provided such marvelous conditions for resorts and the visitor industry, Hilo's climate has created special conditions also. Only in Hilo and the surrounding area will you find the lush tropical beauty of the rain forest jungle, breathtaking waterfalls cascading down green gulches, and acres of gorgeous tropical flowers like anthuriums, orchids, birds-of-paradise and ginger. The ample tropical rain makes Hilo and the windward side of the Big Island a real paradise. Even with its sodden reputation as a rainy old town, Hilo indeed is a special place for many people.

Trade Winds Trade winds are an almost constant wind blowing from the northeast through the east, averaging 5 to 5 mph, and caused by the Pacific anti-cyclone, a high pressure area. The cell remains fairly stationary in the summer (May through October), causing the trades to blow steadily 90 percent of the time, bringing cooling relief for the generally warmer temperatures. In winter (November through April), interruptions diminish the winds' constancy and they blow 40 to 60 percent of the time with competing weather fronts and storms.

Kona Weather Hot, humid and muggy weather is called Kona weather and is often due to an interruption of the trade winds. The trades are replaced by light variable winds and are most noticeable during the warmer summer months. Kona winds may also bring storm fronts and rain from the southwest, the opposite direction from which storms generally approach the islands. Kona storms are noted for their ferocity, bringing high winds, surf and rain, and have occasionally caused property damage.

Detailed information on weather-related emergencies and natural disasters is provided in the early pages of the Big Island Verizon Phone Book under a yellow-margined section called "Disaster Preparedness Info." Without becoming anxious, please be aware that island environments are vulnerable to powerful natural events that can occur any time with very little or no warning. Have a family plan of what to do in case of emergency—where to meet, buddy system, cellphone numbers—and turn on the radio for local Civil Defense advisories. Other than that, use common sense: be aware of your environment, don't be afraid to ask questions, pay attention to lifeguards and hotel or condo management instructions, don't take unnecessary risks, stay calm and stick together.

Earthquakes Because of its volcanic origins and ongoing activity, earthquakes are part of Hawai'i's geosystem. Volcanic eruptions on the Big Island are often preceded and accompanied by earthquakes. Few of these are strong enough to be felt or cause any damage. Major earthquakes are the result of fault action. Some of these faults are on the ocean floor while others are volcano-related. Volcanic earthquakes are caused when sections of a volcano's inner works shift prior to erupting. It is usually associated with the inflation or deflation of a lava reservoir beneath the mountain as the lava swells or drains away.

Fire Because much of the Big Island is extremely dry, brush fires are an unfortunate fact of life. Campers, outdoor cooks and smokers must be obsessive about extinguishing every spark. Fire grows fast and moves rapidly in windy areas, causing road closures and traffic delays. Always heed Civil Defense advisories and police roadblocks.

Hurricanes Hawai'i lies in the hurricane belt and is susceptible to these tropical cyclones from June through December. These storms carry severe winds of between 75 and 150 mph and are often marked by rain, thunder and lightning. Most are spawned along the coast of Mexico and follow the trade winds in a westerly direction across the Pacific. Some are born close to the equator and move north. Since 1950, over a hundred hurricanes have been recorded in Hawaiian waters. Of these, only a few have passed nearby or directly struck parts of the Hawaiian islands. Hurricane Iwa in 1982 and Hurricane Iniki in 1992 did extensive damage, mostly confined to the island of Kaua'i and to a lesser extent O'ahu. The Big Island has luckily been avoided by hurricanes most of the time, due to its large mountain masses. However, hurricanes in other locations can bring heavy surf, very high winds and severe rainstorms to the Big Island. Campers near the shoreline need to be particularly vigilant of weather conditions at all times.

Tropical storms Very heavy rainstorms can cause severe flooding, not only in coastal areas but in the higher elevations where streams overrun their banks. Mud, falling rocks and debris make serious driving hazards. Stay off the roads if possible, never try to cross standing or flowing water if you are at all unsure, and always heed Civil Defense advisories and police roadblocks.

Tsunami Hawai'i is susceptible to tsunamis or tidal waves. Over the last century and a half, nine major tsunamis have caused moderate to severe damage and numerous deaths along affected coastlines. Although some tidal waves are locally generated from earthquakes, most of Hawai'i's tidal wave threats originate in South

America or Alaska's Aleutian Islands. On the Big Island, Hilo is particularly vulnerable to tsunamis due to the funnel shape of Hilo Bay, allowing an already speeding tidal wave to concentrate its force upon reaching land. An Aleutian Islands tsunami in 1946 rolled into Hilo, pushing the water to 10 meters above sea level in some places. The death toll reached 83 and property damage was extensive. In 1960, a Chilean-generated tsunami struck Hilo at a speed of 65 kilometers per hour and wreaked havoc along Hilo's bayfront, destroying a major residential and business section. The water rolled in 11 meters high and 61 people were killed. There have been a few tidal waves generated by Big Island earthquakes as well. A statewide Tsunami Warning System is in place and the Hawai'i Civil Defense System also coordinates disaster programs. Warning sirens and TV-radio broadcasts indicate approaching danger around all the islands. If you are on a beach or low-lying coastal area when you receive such a warning, you must immediately seek higher ground as far away from the coast as possible. (Note: The Tsunami Warning System is tested at 12 noon on the first Monday of every month.)

Helpful Phone Numbers

The area code for the entire state is (808). Calls anywhere on the Big Island are considered local calls, and do not require the area code when dialing. If calling off-island from one island to another, it is necessary to dial 1-808 and the number.

  EMERGENCY: Police, Ambulance, Fire, **911**

  Police Non-emergency:
    Hilo 808-935-3311
    Kailua-Kona 808-326-4646
    Waimea 808-887-3080
    Otherwise dial "0" for operator who will assist you
  Poison Control Center: 800-222-1222
  Civil Defense Agency: 935-0031
  Sexual Assault Crisis Line: 808-935-0677
  Missing Child Center Hawai'i Hotline: 800-753-9797
  American Red Cross:
    Hilo 808-935-8305
    Kona 808-326-9488
  Hospitals:
    Hilo Medical Center 808-974-4700
    Kona Hospital 808-322-9311
  Hawai'i Volcanoes National Park Headquarters: 808-985-6000
  Volcano Eruption Message/Information: 808-985-6000

Hawai'i State Parks Division: 808-974-6200
Hawai'i County:
    Parks & Recreation 808-961-8311
    Office of Complaints & Information 808-961-8223
    Research & Development 808-961-8366
U.S. Coast Guard: 808-933-6943
Search & Rescue: 800-552-6458
Weather Forecast:
    Island of Hawai'i 808-961-5582
    Hawaiian Waters 808-935-9883
    NOA weather radio broadcast 808-935-5055

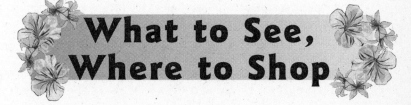

CHAPTER 2

What to See, Where to Shop

To understand the lay of the Big Island, just take a look at a map and keep the weather in mind. The island is roughly shaped like a hand in the "shaka" gesture. (Make a fist with your right hand. Extend your thumb and pinkie. That's a *shaka*, a gesture of greeting and a friendly wave.) Your folded fingers are the west side of the island (Kona side), where it's reliably dry and sunny. Your wrist is the east side (Hilo side), where it's rainy most of the time. Most tourist action is in the west; most government and "real" business takes place in Hilo. The volcano is on the Hilo side; the best beaches are on the Kona side. Your thumb and pinkie are the North Kohala and Kaʻu districts, respectively. North Kohala is a lush, green former sugarcane plantation; Kaʻu is dry and secluded, the southernmost point in the U.S.

On a real map, the Big Island is divided into districts, each with its own personality. Starting with the North Kona District, at about your middle finger, is the Kailua-Kona/Keauhou area. This is tourist territory, full of restaurants and shops and a world of ocean activities. It's a great place for active families to rent a car and go. There are many condo properties in all price ranges and several good hotels here.

About 30 miles north of Kailua-Kona is the South Kohala District, containing the sunny stretch of shoreline called the Kohala Coast, where the most expensive luxury resorts live, along the very best beaches. The Kohala Coast resorts are great places for just about everything—golf, tennis, dining, shopping, spas, ocean activities, luxury accommodations, lush tropical landscaping and, again, truly excellent beaches.

The farther you go from the Kohala Coast, the prices go down, accommodations vary, the weather is less dependable and the beaches less perfect. But that doesn't mean you shouldn't do it. The Big Island is overall a magnificent place to drive, with a huge variety of scenery, climate (23 of the planet's 25 microclimates), elevation and adventure. If you don't like the weather where you are, get in the car and a short drive will put you in a completely different environment—and remember, you can't get more than 26 miles away from the ocean. If you're lucky enough to rent a convertible or a motorcycle, take advantage of it.

Driving up your thumb to North Kohala takes you to an area that is not as rural as it used to be, with new luxury subdivisions developing along the coast. The little towns of Hawi and Kapa'au are growing into interesting art communities surrounded by tropical foliage in the old-fashioned plantation area until you reach the end of the road at Pololu Valley Overlook. The trip to North Kohala is a great scenic drive, and a fun place to shop, stroll around and enjoy. Uncommon historical sites, nearly inaccessible valleys, rugged beaches and remote forests make for good adventures on foot, mule, horseback or ATV.

At the crossroads of your thumb and first finger (the intersection of North and South Kohala districts) is the cool, green *paniolo* (cowboy) town of Waimea/Kamuela (both names apply). A cool, green, upcountry community once home to the largest privately owned cattle ranch in the world, Waimea is now an up-and-coming residential community, rapidly expanding to meet demand. Waimea is full of opportunities to shop and eat, to catch a colorful cultural festival and to experience the countryside on horseback.

Heading east you reach the Hamakua Coast, an absolutely stunning stretch of agricultural property along the ocean *pali* (cliffs), and the idyllic Waipi'o Valley. The Hamakua District also reaches up *mauka* (toward the mountain) to include Pohakuloa Training Area military base and the summits of both Mauna Kea and Mauna Loa. Hamakua's backcountry regions like Waipi'o are perfect avenues for backpackers to retreat from the rest of the world. To the south is the small, wedge-shaped North Hilo district, then the much larger South Hilo District, where Hilo town is located. Hilo is rainy but full of charm, surprises and things to see and do. A place where "real" people live and work, Hilo has its own brand of aloha.

South of Hilo, past your wrist and heading for your pinkie, are the Puna and Ka'u Districts. These two districts share Volcanoes National Park, along with its benefits and dangers. Puna, once a relatively undeveloped area for alternative lifestyles and escapists, is well on its way to becoming a prosperous agricultural community. Ka'u is remote and still fairly empty, holding its own as a rural Big Island retreat. Volcanoes National Park is a great place to hike and to learn about the island's culture as well as its geography.

From your pinkie heading back north to the airport (at about your ring finger) is the South Kona District, home of Kona coffee country and important historical sites at Captain Cook and Puʻuhonua o Honaunau. South Kona is full of history and places to play—kayak, snorkel and play in the water, hike, bike and explore on land.

Now that you have the island "well in hand," we hope you enjoy planning your Big Island vacation, that the information provided here is useful, and that your Big Island visit is more than you hope for. We encourage you to engage all of your senses and take in the Big Island like a cup of Kona coffee, a delicious experience to be tasted and savored, enjoyed and remembered again and again

Kona District

As your plane approaches Kona International Airport, you may be in for a shock. "This is Hawaiʻi? It looks like the moon!" Nothing but flat, black rock as far as you can see. That's Kona. Lava flows from Mauna Kea, Mauna Loa and Hualalai over the last 300 years have created what looks like a gigantic parking lot for rugged SUVs. Don't be alarmed. A short drive north or south brings you to the Hawaiʻi you're looking for, complete with sandy beaches, coconut trees, rainbows over mountain slopes and tropical flowers arrayed along forested country roads.

The Kona Coast has a reputation for fine sunny weather, with daytime temperatures averaging in the high 70s and low 80s year-round. Rainfall varies by elevation but averages from 10 to 40 inches per year, making it the perfect habitat for sun worshippers. Most Kona accommodations are in condominium properties, with a wide range of prices and amenities to choose from. There are also several good hotels and a selection of bed and breakfasts in interesting locations. The full spectrum of restaurant options is available within a few miles, and there is unlimited variety in shopping, unless you're shopping for snowshoes.

Heading south from the airport along Highway 11 (the only road) takes you to Kailua-Kona town (just "Kona" locally), a rapidly growing visitor and kamaʻaina community and active tourist location. One of the most active and energetic locations on the island, Kona is where you go to do things, especially things in the ocean, like snorkel and sightseeing cruises, fishing charters, submarine rides, parasailing, and much, much more. (See Chapter 6 for details.) It's also a good place to shop, eat and stroll, with fascinating historical sites within easy walking distance from downtown hotels and condos.

Above Kailua-Kona, a short stretch of Highway 180 takes you through the interesting art community of Holualoa, then reconnects with Highway 11 heading south as it passes through the greener, cooler Kona coffee country communities Kainaliu, Kealakekua, Captain Cook, Keei and Honaunau. An excellent guide, the *Kona Coffee Country Driving Tour* (available from concierge desks, visitor kiosks or www.konacoffeefest.com) takes aficionados through the "Napa of coffee" for an excellent day of sightseeing, education and tastings.

The South Kona district is an important area in Hawai'i's history. Captain Cook is named after Captain James Cook, who "discovered" Hawai'i in 1778. A memorial just off Kealakekua Bay marks the site of his death some years later. Further south, Pu'uhonua o Honaunau is a painstakingly restored Hawaiian village and *heiau* (temple) where ancient tradition permitted sanctuary to fugitives.

From there, the drive south becomes longer and less populated, with stretches of barren black lava or dry hill country for miles until you cross into the Ka'u District, which contains Ka Lae (South Point), the southernmost point in the U.S.

Kona is diverse and alluring, containing a taste of Hawai'i's favorite things from the mountains to the sea: verdant tropical landscape, quaint little towns with a sense of history, the sparkling blue Pacific and a world of ways to explore it, good accommodations, fine restaurants and a welcoming attitude. When you think about it, where else in the world can you sit at a restaurant and look out at the ocean where your dinner was fished up, and at the same time see the mountains where your coffee came from? There's a lot to like about Kona.

KAILUA-KONA TOWN

Kona is a town that loves change. Over the years it has been the site of Hawai'i's very first commissioned Christian church, and one of the last homes of its reigning monarchy. It has grown from a quiet fishing village to a remote destination for the more adventurous 1930s tourist, and has now earned global recognition for the Hawaiian International Billfish Tournament and the Ironman Triathlon, not to mention the world's greatest cup of coffee (in a town that only got its first Starbucks a couple years ago).

While everything in Kona used to be concentrated along Ali'i Drive, now shops, restaurants and businesses stretch *mauka* to include new shopping centers with mainland chains like Kmart and Wal-Mart, Border's Books & Music, Safeway, Costco, Macy's, Home Depot and many others. Kona now looks more like a modern suburb than a fishing village, with a lot more to offer visiting families.

You're going to want a rental car, but right in town are three of the Big Island's most interesting and important historical sites,

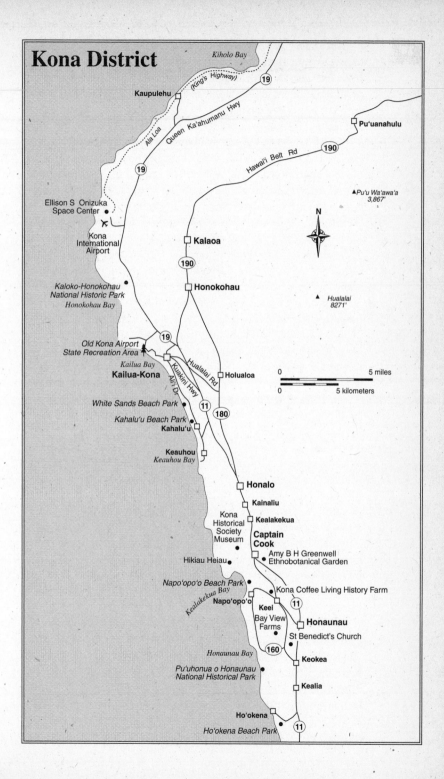

Kona District

Kiholo Bay

(King's Highway)

19

Kaupulehu

Ala Loa

Queen Ka'ahumanu Hwy

Pu'uanahulu

190

Hawai'i Belt Rd

19

▲Pu'u Wa'awa'a
3,867'

Ellison S Onizuka
Space Center

N

Kona
International
Airport

Kalaoa

190

Kaloko-Honokohau
National Historic Park

Honokohau

▲ Hualalai
8271'

Honokohau Bay

19

Old Kona Airport
State Recreation Area

Kailua Bay

Hualalai Rd

Holualoa

Kailua-Kona

Kuakini Hwy

0   5 miles

Ali'i Dr

0   5 kilometers

White Sands Beach Park

11

Kahalu'u Beach Park

180

Kahalu'u

Keauhou
Keauhou Bay

Honalo

Kainaliu

Kona
Historical
Society
Museum

Kealakekua

Captain
Cook

Amy B H Greenwell
Ethnobotanical Garden

Hikiau Heiau

Napo'opo'o Beach Park

Kona Coffee Living History Farm

11

Napo'opo'o

Keei
Bay View
Farms

Honaunau

Kealakekua Bay

St Benedict's Church

160

Keokea

Honaunau Bay

Pu'uhonua o Honaunau
National Historical Park

Kealia

Ho'okena

11

Ho'okena Beach Park

Ahuena Heiau, Mokuaikaua Church and Hulihe'e Palace, all located within walking distance of each other along Ali'i Drive. These three structures may look like simple buildings—a Hawaiian *heiau*, a rustic stone church and a European mansion—but together they represent an amazing timeline for the Big Island, each marking endings and beginnings to an era. Ahuena was King Kamehameha's final residence. Mokuaikaua was the first commissioned Christian church in Hawai'i. Hulihe'e Palace was one of the last homes of Hawai'i's reigning monarchy.

★ **Ahuena Heiau** is located on the grounds of King Kamehameha's Kona Beach Hotel. The ancient *heiau* was reconstructed by Kamehameha I between 1812–1813 after he had achieved his goal or destiny to unite all the Hawaiian islands under his rule. The heiau is dedicated to Lono, god of peace, agriculture and prosperity. The buildings are fully restored with wood-frame and grass-thatched huts and carved tikis with the image of Kalaemoku, a chief deified for his healing powers over disease, according to hotel sources. Other tiki images represent deities respected and honored by Kamehameha the Great for the benefit of his kingdom. In this area Kamehameha I lived out his life and conducted matters of government until his demise on May 8, 1819. A walkway in front of the hotel leads directly to it, and it is open to the public. After your visit, you may enjoy an escape from the heat and a stroll through the hotel lobby to see its many Hawaiian artifacts, including *ahu'ula* (feather cape), *mahi'ole* (feather helmet), *pahu heiau* (temple drum), war weapons, hula implements, dramatic murals by Hawaiian artist Herb Kane and portraits of Hawaiian royalty including King Kamehameha I and his favorite wife Queen Ka'ahumanu. 75-5660 Palani Road. 808-329-2911.

Just south and across Ali'i Drive is ★ **Mokuaikaua Church.** This beautiful old stone edifice was built by missionaries in 1837 and is the first commissioned Christian church in Hawai'i. Constructed of lava rock and crushed-coral mortar, its interiors are fashioned from native *ohia* and **koa** woods. It is open to the public and Sunday services welcome visitors. As Ahuena stands for the end of Kamehameha's rule, Mokuaikaua marks the beginning of the missionary era and its subsequent sweep through Hawaiian culture. One year later, ★ **Hulihe'e Palace** was built as a summer home for Hawaiian royalty, a dramatic symbol of drastic change in less than 50 years. The palace was built by Governor John Adams Kuakini, who was Queen Ka'ahumanu's brother, and used as a vacation residence until the overthrow of the monarchy in 1893. Hulihe'e Palace was purchased by the Daughters of Hawai'i, a cultural preservation and civic society, in 1925 to save it from being auctioned. Their docents maintain stewardship of the building and its manicured grounds, museum and gift shop. The palace boasts fascinating Hawaiian antiques, including a formal dining table carved from a single tree, a steamer trunk used by Queen Kapiolani on her 1887 voyage to England, priceless pre-contact artifacts, tools and jewelry and handmade Hawaiian quilts. Free concerts are performed on the grounds on the last Sunday of each month in honor of Hawaiian monarchy. Open daily 9 a.m. to 4 p.m. Admission $4. 808-329-1877.

Right next door is one of Kona's original hotels, the old **Kona Inn**, originally built in 1929. Now restored as **Kona Inn Shopping Village**, it stretches along the ocean with a variety of shops and eateries. At the far south end is the **Kona Inn Restaurant**, worth stopping by for a look at its collection of "granders" (1,000-pound marlin and other trophy fish) mounted on the walls. You should be thirsty by now, so

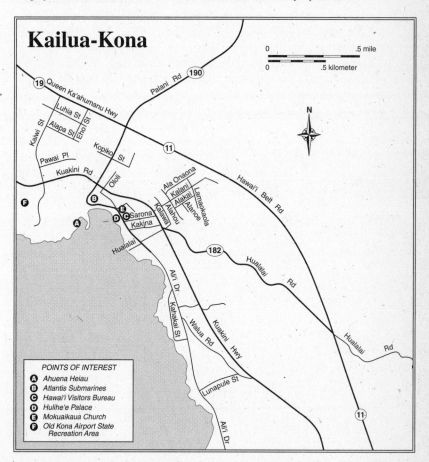

Kailua-Kona

0   .5 mile
0   .5 kilometer

N

19 Queen Ka'ahumanu Hwy
Palani Rd **190**

Luhia St
Alapa St
Eho St
Kaiwi St
Kopiko St
Pawai Pl
Kuakini Rd
Ololi
11
Hawai'i Belt Rd

Ala Onaona
Kalani
Alakai
Lamaokaola
Alahou
Alanoe
Sarona
Kakina
Kalawa
Hualalai
182
Hualalai Rd

Ali'i Dr
Kahakai St
Walua Rd
Kuakini Hwy
Hualalai Rd

Lunapule St
Ali'i Dr
11

F
B
E
C
D
A

POINTS OF INTEREST
- **A** Ahuena Heiau
- **B** Atlantis Submarines
- **C** Hawai'i Visitors Bureau
- **D** Hulihe'e Palace
- **E** Mokuaikaua Church
- **F** Old Kona Airport State Recreation Area

sit down for a cold one. You'll get a kick out of the old-fashioned belt-driven ceiling fans, and the ocean view is lovely. If your visit occurs when the Kona Symphony plays one of its concerts here on the lawn, you're in for a very special treat. And don't miss "Bosco the Amazing One Man Band" performing free Wednesday through Sunday evenings (call 808-322-6604 for updated showtimes).

Kona Inn is a marvelous place to stroll, shop, snack and people-watch (for that matter, so is the entire length of Ali'i Drive from King Kamehameha's Kona Beach Hotel south to the Royal Kona Resort, about 1 mile). Browse through a remarkable collection of funky, fun, fine, functional, fashionable, fabulous shops, galleries and restaurants in the various small, colorful shopping centers: **Seaside Mall, Kona Banyan Court, Kim Chong Complex, Kona Marketplace, Ali'i Sunset Plaza, Coconut Grove Marketplace, Waterfront Row and back to Kona Inn Shopping Village.** But wait—there's more (you may want to get the car): 200 yards up Palani Road is **Kona Coast Shopping Center, Lanihau Center** and **Kopiko Plaza.** And you really owe yourself a stop into **Hilo Hattie's** for a shell lei, a taste of Kona coffee, a video or craft demonstration and the ultimate selection of Hawai'i souvenirs and aloha attire. (If you don't feel like walking there's a free shuttle from most Kona hotels.) Do look for freebies and discount coupons in current visitor publications.

If you continue *mauka* (toward the mountain), turn right on Highway 11 and take the first left, you reach **Crossroads Shopping Center** (Wal-Mart, Border's and Safeway). Look for the cut-through road to **Makalapua Center** (Kmart, Macy's and Makalapua Stadium Cinemas). About 6 miles south down Highway 11 is the turn-off for **Keauhou Shopping Center,** with its great group of restaurants and interesting stores like Paradise Found, the elegant ForDun's for fine gifts, Originals by Oscar, Showcase Gallery, amazing Alapaki's for Hawaiian gifts and handcrafts, plus a large Long's Drugs, Ace Hardware, KTA grocery and Keauhou Stadium Cinemas. Keauhou offers complimentary "Aloha Fridays," with a Polynesian hula show in the evening and during the day, craft demonstrations, ukulele and lei-making lessons and more. Check local newspapers or your hotel/condo concierge desk. Your shopping tour of Kailua-Kona will be also be full of opportunities (sales pitches) to sign up for island tours, ocean activities, luau and all kinds of fun events.

Up *mauka* (toward the mountain), between Kailua-Kona on the upper road (Highway 11) is a short bypass road, Route 180, that takes you through **Holualoa Village.** Route 180 is a twisty country lane, flanked by trees, pastures and tropical greenery. Holualoa, once a sleepy farm town, is now a growing artist community full of interesting galleries, studios and shops. Check out **Kimura Lauhala Shop**

As a word of advice, remember that your time on vacation is the most important thing. Don't overcommit yourself or feel that you absolutely must do everything there is to do or your trip is ruined. Also be aware that kiosks sell deeply discounted activities in exchange for your attendance at a timeshare presentation. (Some will sell activity packages without the presentation; it's good to ask first.) This can be a good savings if you want to spend the time and happen to be in the market for real estate. It might work for your family to hold a little meeting in advance, decide on a few "must-do" things, like a luau, a helicopter ride and a snorkel trip. Divide up into two groups if somebody gets seasick and somebody else is allergic to hula. The more time you spend planning in advance, the less time you spend decision-making on the island. The main thing is: remember, it's your vacation. Relax; don't be pressured; do what you want to do. We're all here to help you have fun in different ways. (By the way, we're finding many of these activity centers have been bought by Expedia.com.)

(808-324-0053) for a fine selection of woven *lauhala* hats (as good as Panama hats), purses and baskets plus other local authentic handicrafts. This tiny, family-run business has been around for a long time. They are happy to answer your questions and help find the perfect remembrance of your visit. Open Monday through Friday 9 a.m.-5 p.m., Saturday 9 a.m.-4 p.m., closed Sunday. Holualoa is one of the stops along the **Kona Coffee Country Driving Tour**, a tour guide brochure published by the County of Hawai'i and the Kona Coffee Cultural Festival (808-326-7820; www.konacoffeefest.com).

Hawaiian Gardens, about three miles above Kailua-Kona town, is a full-service tropical garden center and also has beautifully landscaped tropical gardens and grounds. The garden center is noted for its towering trees, lush landscaped grounds and numerous displays of exotic flowers. A full-service gift shop features cut tropical flowers, potted orchids, bromeliads and bonsai trees plus other Hawaiiana gifts. At the junction of Palani Road and the Mamalahoa Highway (old Route 180); 808-329-5702.

Just outside of town is **Ali'i Gardens Marketplace**, a colorful, fun and funky open-air farmer's market and craft fair open Wednesday through Saturday 9 a.m.-5 p.m., with 50-plus vendors selling their wares—fresh produce, tropical flowers, Kona coffee, fruits and more—plus free ukulele and hula demos daily. Shuttle service from the pier and nearby lodgings. 808-331-1381.

SOUTH KONA DISTRICT

If you were to continue south on Highway 11, you can explore **Kainaliu** town. It's the home of the restored Aloha Theatre, a main street full of interesting shops and galleries old and new and, if you're lucky, some of the best *huli huli* chicken anywhere. Follow your nose—on the weekends there's usually a truck-pulled rotisserie set up on the *makai* side of the road, selling whole or half *kiawe*-roasted chickens for local charities. The next town south is Honalo, home of Teshima's restaurant and the intricate historic edifice of the **Dai Fujiki Soto Buddhist Mission**, built in 1914 and open to the respectful visitor 9 a.m.-4 p.m. daily.

Next stop is just outside of Kealakekua at the ★ **Little Grass Shack** right on the highway. Even if you don't remember the old song, this is a perfect photo-op and the shop has a good collection of Hawaiiana, gifts, a few antiques and local arts and crafts. Open Monday through Saturday 9:30 a.m.-5 p.m., Sunday 10:30 a.m.-5 p.m. 808-323-2877.

Nearby, the ★ **Kona Historical Society Museum** is housed in the historic Greenwell Store located on Highway 11, a half mile south of Kealakekua. The museum has fascinating historic displays featuring early Kona history; it also maintains a growing reference library and archives. The historical society also conducts guided walking tours of historic Kailua Village. The ★ **Greenwell Coffee Farms** (808-323-2275; www.greenwellfarms.com) is next door to the Kona Historical Society Museum. Tour coffee groves and learn about the famed Kona coffee industry while you taste the finished product for yourself. Also operated by the Kona Historical Society is the ★ **D. Uchida Farm** (808-323-2006), Hawai'i's first living history farm. The seven-acre working coffee and macadamia nut farm is listed on both the State and National Registers for Historic Places. The farm was homesteaded in 1900 by a Japanese immigrant family, and its present tours and programs help keep the history of Kona's coffee farming community alive. Historic buildings, authentic artifacts, costumed interpreters and guides, live animals, working machinery and producing orchards give a true sense of place. See "Museums" in Chapter 6 for more information. Kona Historical Society Museum: Open 8 a.m. to 8 p.m. weekdays, closed holidays. P.O. Box 398, 81-6551 Mamalahoa Highway, Captain Cook, HI 96704; 808-323-3222 or 808-323-2006.

In the village of **Captain Cook**, look for the famous old landmark, Manago Hotel, where room rates are reasonable and local-style family meals are still served in the dining room. Captain Cook has its own collection of shops and eateries to explore for gifts, antiques and souvenirs. There are also several coffee farms, as listed on the Kona Coffee Country Driving Tour, and two important historical sites: **Kealakekua Bay** and Hikiau Heiau, relevant to British explorer and navigator Captain James Cook, who "discovered" Hawai'i late in the 18th century.

★ **Hikiau Heiau** is a restored temple site located near the bay in the village of Napo'opo'o. It was here in late 1778 and early 1779 that Captain Cook was initially received with great respect and reverence by the Hawaiians who thought him to be their god, Lono. A monument across the bay, accessible by boat or kayak, marks the exact spot where Captain Cook later fell, mortally wounded in a confrontation with the Hawaiians. Many of the snorkel/dive cruise boats come here to let guests dive in the clear waters of the **Kealakekua Bay Marine Reserve** sanctuary. The Captain Cook monument is also reached by a moderately difficult hiking trail from Highway 11 at Captain Cook town (see "Hiking" in Chapter 6 for more information). The waters of Kealakekua Bay are designated as the Kealakekua Bay State Historical & Underwater Parks and are a wonderful snorkel and dive zone.

★ **Amy B. H. Greenwell Ethnobotanical Garden** is about 12 miles south of Captain Cook. One of the best attractions on the island, this 15-acre botanical garden is a trip back through time, giving visitors a look at Hawaiian plant life before foreign contact. A living museum of Hawaiian ethnobotany (the study of plants and human culture that support each other), the garden hosts 45 kinds of kalo (taro), 35 varieties of sugarcane, 23 banana species and many other endemic plants, medicinal herbs and more. Open 8:30 a.m. to 5 p.m. daily, except Sundays and holidays, for self-guided tours. Docent guided tours given on Wednesday and Friday at 1 p.m. Located at 10-mile marker on Highway 11; 808-323-3318.

★ **St. Benedict's Church**, just off Highway 160, which branches off from Highway 11, is well worth a visit. The church's interior is elaborately painted in colorful, dramatic religious scenes and Bible stories. 84-5140 Painted Church Road.

The **Ellison S. Onizuka Space Center**, located at the Kona airport, is a memorial to the Big Island's own native son and astronaut. Born and raised on a Kona coffee farm, he was lost aboard the Challenger space shuttle in 1986. The museum features memorabilia from Ellison's career in space exploration and includes hands-on displays and a piece of "moon rock" on loan from NASA. Open daily 8:30 a.m. to 4:30 p.m.; adults $3, children $1. For information, contact Onizuka Space Center, P.O. Box 833, Kailua-Kona, HI 96745; 808-329-3441.

Highway 160 leads on down to Honaunau Bay and to the ★ **Puʻuhonua o Honaunau National Historical Park**. This very special place is the best-preserved heiau in the islands. The "City of Refuge" was a designated sanctuary for fugitives who could be taken in with permission of the *kahuna* (priests) if they were able to reach its remote location. It is a must-see for vacationers because it gives a clear picture of Hawaiʻiʻs ancient history and culture, as well as the simple pleasures and challenges of everyday life in a difficult environment. Knowledgeable park rangers provide information and maps for the easy, self-guided walking tour through the complex. The site has a restored village and ancient temple with carved wooden tiki images, thatch-roofed *hale* lining an ancient cultivated fishpond, and canoe and tapa houses, each of which has a story to tell. At various times of the year, local Hawaiian cultural groups put on authentic arts-and-crafts demonstrations, cultural festivals and other educational events. There is ample parking, restrooms, a shop, and a nice beach nearby for a picnic. 808-328-2288.

Kohala Coast

The northwestern edge of the Big Island is divided into two districts, the South Kohala and North Kohala districts. Most of the South Kohala District is a long stretch of rugged black lava coastline on the western side of the Big Island and it is in this district that the Kohala Coast proper, home to the best beaches and fancy resorts, lies. One of the most reliably sunny spots in the state with less than nine inches of rain annually, its dry, scrubby landscape has been made beautiful by expensive resort and residential developments over the last 40 years. The South Kohala District is the "high-rent neighborhood" of the Big Island because it includes the four mega-resorts along the Kohala Coast: Hualalai Resort (Kona Village Resort and Four Seasons Hualalai), Waikoloa Beach Resort (Hilton Waikoloa Village and Waikoloa Beach Marriott), Mauna Lani Resort (Mauna Lani Bay Hotel & Bungalows and the Fairmont Orchid) and Mauna Kea Resort (Mauna Kea Beach Hotel and Hapuna Beach Prince Hotel). (Hualalai is technically in the North Kona District, but the resort is included here for your convenience). While this acclaimed resort area is a world unto itself, the island's South Kohala District also includes the small harbor town at Kawaihae, the uphill subdivision of Waikoloa Village and the cooler, greener pastures of the town with two names: Waimea/Kamuela (same place), 12 miles east of the coastline, inland.

The rest of the district, downslope from Waimea and along the coast to the higher elevations in North Kohala (a separate district about 20 miles away), is virtually desert. Only the resort areas, where irrigation and technology permit the lush tropical landscaping we expect, are green. It's hard to imagine what life was like for early Hawaiian villagers, with very little fresh water and almost no rain or no edible vegetation. A look at the windblown brown coast, carved with old lava flows and studded with stubborn *kiawe* (mesquite) takes a lot of romance out of the image of tropical island living. Dry areas like this had the reputation for producing strong people and fierce warriors. It's easy to see why.

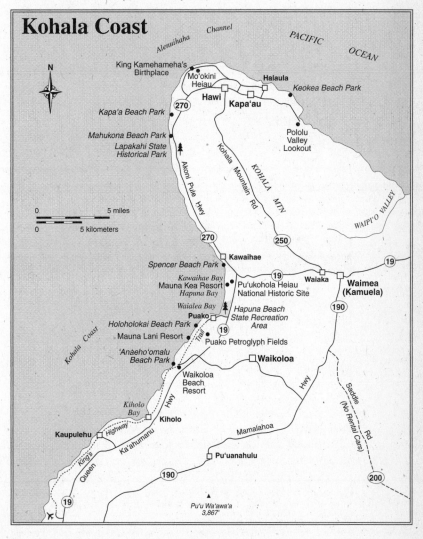

Kohala Coast

For travelers, however, so much sunshine is a blessing. A few years ago, the State of Hawai'i produced a statewide sunshine map that confirmed what Hawaiians knew long ago: the Kohala Coast has the highest sunshine rating in the islands—even higher than such sun resorts as Ka'anapali on Maui and Waikiki on O'ahu. Kohala Coast weather is consistent: average annual rainfall was 8.7 inches over the last 35 years or so that records have been kept. Temperatures average in the mid-60s for lows and mid- to upper 80s for highs, with 78 degrees the average year-round. Once the site of small fishing villages and canoe harbors, the "sunniest coast in Hawai'i" is now an international destination for golfers and beach-lovers, thanks to the weather.

SOUTH KOHALA DISTRICT

This district contains the sunny, upscale Kohala Coast area, along with Waikoloa Village, six miles up *mauka*, the Kawaihae Harbor area and the *paniolo* town of Waimea, twelve miles inland, all connected by Highway 19, Queen Ka'ahumanu Highway. This road was completed in the mid-1970s by the County of Hawai'i, with the aid of resort developers like Laurance S. Rockefeller, to give hotel guests access to and from the Kona Airport, who otherwise traveled the 90-some miles from Hilo Airport. Highway 19 in this area is generally straight, with fairly unobstructed views of the sloping uplands of Kohala and many vast old lava flows on the *mauka* side, and the amazing Pacific ocean on the *makai* side.

BIG ISLAND FARMERS MARKETS

1. ★ **Ali'i Gardens Marketplace**, 75-6129 Ali'i Drive, Kailua-Kona, Wednesday-Saturday
2. ★ **Hilo Farmers Market**, Kamehameha Avenue at Mamo Street, Wednesday-Saturday
3. **Ka'u Farmers Market**, Na'alehu Theater, Saturday 8 a.m.-noon
4. **North Kohala Farmers Market**, across from Hawi Post Office, Saturday 7:30 a.m.-1 p.m.
5. **Panaewa Hawaiian Homelands Farmers Market**, Hilo Wal-Mart sidewalk, daily 8 a.m.
6. **South Kona Fruit Stand**, 84-4770 Mamalahoa Highway, Captain Cook, Monday-Saturday 9 a.m.-6 p.m., Sunday 11 a.m.-5 p.m.
7. **Volcano Farmers Market**, Cooper Center on Wright Road, Volcano, Sunday 6:30-9 a.m.
8. **Waikoloa Village Farmers Market**, Waikoloa Community Church across from the school, Saturday 7:15 a.m.
9. **Waimea Hawaiian Homesteaders Farmers Market**, Kuhio Hale, Saturday 7 a.m.-noon

About 15 miles north of Kailua-Kona on Highway 19, be on the lookout for yellow road signs with the silhouette of a donkey. This area is frequented by the small herds of "Kona Nightingales," the descendants of the donkeys used years ago to pack supplies and goods up and down the old coastal trail. They were also used to carry bags of coffee harvested from the coffee farms on Kona's steep mountain slopes. They now roam wild in this area and can sometimes be seen near the highway, especially at twilight when they are more likely to cross the highway.

Up *mauka*, the old upcountry route, Highway 190, passes through rolling ranch country along the drive between Kailua-Kona and Waimea. Because it is at a higher elevation, it is a much cooler drive than the coastal Highway 19, with beautiful coastline overlooks and winding, tree-lined roads through the country. If you're lucky, the purple jacaranda trees will be in bloom. On either route, the distance between Kailua-Kona and Kamuela is approximately 40 miles or a driving time of one hour.

Back down by the ocean, the *makai* road along the Big Island's noted Kohala Coast takes you past a string of luxury resorts, golf courses and some of Hawai'i's best beaches. The turnoff at **Waikoloa Beach Resort** leads to ★ **'Anaeho'omalu Beach Park**, the Waikoloa Beach Marriott, Outrigger Resort, the Hilton Waikoloa Village, golf courses, and luxury condo complexes. 'Anaeho'omalu Beach is a lovely, sweeping crescent of golden sand fronting a fishpond. The Waikoloa Beach Marriott, an Outrigger Resort, sits behind the beach and fishpond areas with easy access to the beach.

King's Highway is the centuries old footpath that winds along the Kohala Coast and through the Waikoloa Beach Resort. Portions of the old coastal trail wind through the lava fields and golf courses and hiking is allowed. Hawaiian petroglyph fields lie scattered throughout the area.

South Kohala shopping is concentrated in the Kohala Coast resort areas and up in Waimea town. Naturally, the resort-area outlets are more pricey, but the atmosphere is festive and if this is your passion, resort shopping is a perfect way to spend the day. Mauna Kea Resort and Mauna Lani Resort hotels offer their own collections of shops featuring fine art and jewelry, resort wear, gifts and sundries, but Waikoloa Resort is the best bet for a shopping day.

The **Kings' Shops** at Waikoloa Beach Resort are a great way to spend the day and satisfy your need to shop (for all budgets). Indulge in some fast or fine food, absorb a little culture at complimentary afternoon hula shows and sign up for island activities. Among the

SHOPPING FOR ANTIQUES

If you are an antique buff, you'll find all sorts of antiques, collectibles and old attic items like vintage aloha shirts and muumuus, old soda and milk bottles from now-defunct Big Island bottle works, plantation-era items, books, interesting ethnic treasures, Hawaiian implements and artifacts of all manners of eclectic things. Buy them now as the value of these disappearing odd treasures continues to climb rapidly. The following is a list of antique shops worth browsing. If you're planning a stop at a particular shop, you might want to call ahead to check on their hours, as those can vary. We'd like to suggest a stroll down Honoka'a town's Mamane Street, which offers several of the better, funkier and more interesting shops for antiques.

Kona District

    Antiques-Art-And in Kealakekua, across from Chris' Bakery; 808-323-2239

    ★ **Antiques & Orchids** A lovely place for tea. 81-6224 Mamalahoa Highway, Kealakekua; 808-323-9851

    Cinderella's in Holualoa, next to Kona Arts Center; 808-322-2474

    Discovery Antiques 61-6593 Mamalahoa Highway; 808-323-2239

    ★ **Hula Heaven** Kona Inn Shopping Village, 75-5744 Ali'i Drive, Kailua-Kona; 808-329-7885

    Island Lifestyles 74-5563 Kaiwi Street; 808-329-5807

    ★ **Little Grass Shack** Highway 11, Kealakekua; 808-323-2877

    ★ **Once in a Blue Moon Antiques** 74-5598 Luhia Street (Old Industrial Center), Kailua-Kona; 808-334-0022

    Robert Teasley Collection 64-5563 Kaiwi Street, Kailua-Kona; 808-331-8788

    Statements 73-5564 Owalu Street, Kailua-Kona; 808-326-7760

North Kohala District

    Mother's Antiques & Fine Cigars 55-3419 Akoni Pule Highway, Hawi; 808-889-0496

tenants are Endangered Species, Noa Noa, Under the Koa Tree, Island Shells, Indochine, Sgt. Leisure, Crazy Shirts, The Gecko Store, Blue Ginger, DFS Galleria (duty-free), Pacific Rim Collections, Genesis Galleries, Dolphin Galleries, Malia Waikoloa, Kane By Malia, Making Waves, Na Hoku, Paradise Walking Co., Maui Divers, Whalers General Store, Giggles, Haimoff & Haimoff Creations in Gold, Louis Vuitton, Macy's, Royal Gold, Sunglass Hut,

Waimea

★ **Gallery of Great Things**   Parker Square Center, Highway 19, Kawaihae Road in Waimea; 808-885-7706

Mauna Kea Galleries   65-12988 Kawaihae Road, Waimea; 808-887-2244

Silk Road Gallery   Parker Square Center, Highway 19, Kawaihae Road in Waimea; 808-885-7474

Upcountry Connection Gallery   in Waimea; 808-885-0623

Waimea Antiques & Collectibles   65-1290 Kawaihae Road, Waimea; 808-885-0024

Hamakua Coast

★ **Honoka'a Market Place**   45-3586 Mamane Street, Honoka'a; 808-775-8255

★ **Honoka'a Trading Co.**   Mamane Street, Honoka'a; 808-775-0808

Seconds to Go Inc.   in Honoka'a; 808-775-9212

Hilo

Antiques & Coins   191 Kilauea Avenue, Hilo; 808-969-1881

Dragon Mama Futon Shop   266 Kamehameha Avenue, Hilo, 808-934-9081, and also 159 Kalanikoa, Hilo, 808-933-9816; www.dragonmama.com

Ets'ko   35 Waianuenue Avenue, Hilo; 808-961-3778

Glass from the Past   28-1672A Old Mamalahoa Highway, Honomu; 808-963-6449

Home Place   197 Kilauea Avenue, Hilo, below Spencer's Gym; 808-935-7494

Kilohoku Treasures   762 Kanoelehua Avenue, Suite 4; 808-933-2755

Mid Pacific Store   76 Kapiolani Street, Hilo, opposite Lyman Museum; 808-935-3822

Oshima's Art & Collectibles   202 Kamehameha Avenue, Hilo; 808-969-1554

Puna District

Pahala Plantation Cottages & Store   Pahala; 808-928-9811

Zac's Photo and the Ukulele House. There's a Starbucks, several good restaurants for lunch or dinner and a nice food court with a lovely outdoor gazebo overlooking the lake.

Hilton Waikoloa Village also offers options for die-hard shoppers in its a complex of 18 shops, boutiques and galleries: Dancing Dolphins, Discover Waikoloa, Dyansen Gallery, Na Hoku Jewelry, Philip Rickard, Reyn's, Sandal Tree and Kohala Spa Essence and Images.

Waikoloa Village is located on the mountain slopes above the resort about six miles. Waikoloa Road, which leads to the village, intersects Highway 19 (Queen Ka'ahumanu Highway on the Kohala Coast) and connects the old Waimea to Kailua-Kona upcountry road, Highway 190. At Waikoloa Village, there is the **Waikoloa Highlands Center**, a small full-service shopping center with a grocery, **Waikoloa Village Market, B Natural** health food store, **Exclusive Designs** aloha wear, Dorkels video, snorkel and baby-care rentals, **Elegant Flowers & Gifts**, a pharmacy, gas station, beauty salon, real estate and vacation rental offices, a business center, health care clinic, dentist, post office, bank with ATM and a Robert Trent Jones, Jr., golf course, as well as several eateries and a great little coffee shop. Although there are no tourist attractions as such, the village's convenient location near the Kohala Coast resorts makes it a good option for condominium vacation rentals.

Back on Highway 19, **Mauna Lani Resort** has Fairmont Orchid, Mauna Lani Bay Hotel and Bungalows, and The Islands, Mauna Lani Point and Mauna Lani Terrace condos. The ancient fishponds at **Kalahuipua'a** next to the Mauna Lani Bay Hotel have been restored and can be seen on a walk through the hotel grounds. This beautiful site is now operated as a working aquaculture preserve stocked with mullet fish.

★ **Holoholokai Beach Park** is just north of the Fairmont Orchid, where a trail leads to the nearby ★ **Puako Petroglyph Fields**. Petroglyphs are images hand-carved into the rock, as a system of language, historical record or storytelling. The fields at Puako offer some of the best examples of human and mythical figures, easily accessible and fascinating to see.

A mile south of Hapuna Beach on Highway 19 is the Puako Road turnoff, where there is public access to the beach areas of **Puako**. Puako is a very small town, consisting of one road, one store, one apartment-condo building and interesting houses from luxury oceanside mini-resorts to ramshackle shacks. The Catholic Ascension Church is a beautiful, island-style church that welcomes visitors to Sunday mass.

★ **Hapuna Beach State Recreation Area** is one of the best, with good facilities for swimming as well as picnicking, photo-ops and a snack bar.

Mauna Kea Resort comprises the Mauna Kea Beach Hotel and the Hapuna Beach Prince Hotel and surrounding golf courses. The resort covers a large tract of land between and above Kauna'oa Bay and Hapuna Beach and the rolling hills above. Mauna Kea was built by Laurance S. Rockefeller in 1965 and was the first hotel in the area.

Kawaihae is most noted as a fishing and commercial boating harbor port facility, but **Kawaihae Center**, a small shopping complex, houses a number of shops, including the classic Harbor Gallery. Several take-out or dine-in eateries offer a wide range of snacks and spots for sunset cocktails. There is a gas station, convenience store and, most importantly, an ice cream shop.

NORTH KOHALA DISTRICT

North Kohala has changed. Hawi, 18 miles north of Kawaihae on Route 270, used to be an undiscovered treasure, pleasantly distanced from the resorts. Now this former sugar cane plantation town has met the demand of returning visitors for a more genuine Hawai'i experience. Run-down streets with abandoned storefronts have transformed into eclectic little galleries, shops and restaurants—delightfully and colorfully presented in a cozy, funky array, well worth the trip. Or, make a day of it by also taking in often-overlooked historical sites, excellent photo opportunities and a couple of lovely, smaller beach parks. The coastal drive along Route 270 is spectacular, as is the mountain Route 250 in a completely different way.

From the Kohala Coast resorts, head north on Highway 19. Turn left at the stop sign and head up the coast. Start off early in the day because the first two stops get very hot before noon. Almost immediately on the left is a sign for ★ **Pu'ukohola Heiau National Historic Site**. Stop by the recently renovated visitors center, then take the relatively easy hike around this important Hawaiian landmark. If your visit brings you to the island in August, you might be lucky enough to catch part of the annual re-enactment (minus the sacrificial part), when hundreds of islanders dress in authentic *malo*, feather headgear and ti-leaf capes and walk in the footsteps of the ancestors for a day. Pu'ukohola Heiau National Historic Site is on the Kohala Coast at Kawaihae Bay and is well worth a visit. This massive *heiau* was built by Kamehameha the Great in 1791 upon the advice of a priest who told Kamehameha that he would conquer all the islands of Hawai'i if he did so. By 1795, Kamehameha did conquer all the islands of Hawai'i except Kaua'i, which later acceded and recognized him as the ruler of all Hawai'i. At the time Kamehameha built his *heiau*, his main rival was his cousin Keoua Ku'ahu'ula, also a chief. Kamehameha invited Ku'ahu'ula to his temple dedication to make peace and Ku'ahu'ula fatefully accepted. As Ku'ahu'ula and his party landed at the beach below the heiau, Kamehameha's warriors swept down and killed them all. Ku'ahu'ula's body was carried up to the temple and offered as the principal sacrifice to Kamehameha's war god. Thus the *heiau* was dedicated according to ancient Hawaiian religious custom.

Continuing north, on the *makai* (ocean) side of the road, look for the sign for **Lapakahi State Historical Park**. On this site is a restored Hawaiian village, and a fairly easy hike along its rocky paths may change your mind dramatically about the romantic life of a tropical native. As you look around and realize very little has changed in the 200 or so years since Hawaiians populated the spot where you stand, notice that fresh water was a precious commodity, that everything you needed had to come from the land or the ocean. Fish were traded to upcountry farmers for sweet potatoes or taro. Salt was "mined" from sea water in handcarved pockets in the stones near shore. Cloth was made by beating plant fiber into pulp. Coconut trees were the general store of the time, providing food, dishes and utensils, roofing supplies, musical instruments and toys. It was a difficult, physically demanding life, yet one which produced one of the most poetic, spiritual, ecologically sensible, good-humored cultures to evolve on the planet—one which was apparently successful, by standards of population and artistry, until the outside world "discovered" it in the 18th century.

As you continue north, you'll see signs for **Mahukona Beach Park** and **Kapa'a Beach Park**, both of which have parking, restrooms, picnic pavilions and a small stretch of beach for swimming and sunning. At Mahukona, you may see signs of the old railroad that used to serve the sugar cane plantations. After the Japanese attack on Pearl Harbor, the railroad was destroyed and most of the equipment dumped into the ocean, but there are places where you can see the old ties and platforms.

If you're feeling adventurous, you may want to explore King Kamehameha's Birthplace and Mo'okini Heiau, a bit of a drive down a dusty dirt lane just before Upolu Airport at the very north tip of the island. This ancient, remote area is maintained as an important historic site for visitors and residents, featuring a large original *heiau* complex and *kahuna's* (priest's) house arranged on a wide green lawn overlooking the vast ocean, where whales are commonly seen in season. To find them, look for Upolu Airport Road two miles west of Hawi on Route 270. The turn-off leads down two miles to the coast and the tiny airstrip at Upolu Point, the northernmost point on the Big Island. The airport road is a bumpy narrow asphalt single-lane strip through cattle pastures.

King Kamehameha's Birthplace and the adjacent Mo'okini Heiau are just west of the airstrip. A sign points the direction along the coast to the old settlement. The 1.5-mile bumpy, rutted and very dusty road from the airstrip along the coast to the restored birthplace site is unimproved dirt and driving it can be hazardous. There can be several deep ruts and mud bogs that may or may not be passable. Drive at your own risk! If you can't get through, you can always park the car and walk the rest of the way. Kamehameha's birthplace is a large square-shaped rock wall enclosure about 75 yards per side, and encloses various other foundations and structures. It sits about 50 yards from the beach in an open, sloping area. The wind and sun are both strong here.

★ **Mo'okini Heiau** is located just off the same road as the birthplace site. It occupies the summit of a hill and as such dominates the immediate area. The temple is where the *ali'i nui*, the kings and ruling chiefs, fasted, prayed and offered human sacrifices to their gods. The temple was built about 480 A.D. and is one of the largest on the Big Island, measuring 267 feet by 250 feet on the west and east walls, and 135 feet and 112 feet on the north and south walls. The walls are 30 feet high and 15 feet wide, in the shape of an irregular parallelogram.

The stones used in constructing the temple are of smooth, water-worn basalt. Legend has it that the stones come from Pololu Valley on the east side of the Kohala peninsula, 10 to 14 miles away. According to legend, each stone was handed from man to man the entire distance (requiring 15,000 to 18,000 men), to build the temple in a single night, from sunset to sunrise. Mo'okini was constructed under the direction of High Priest Kuamo'o Mo'okini and was dedicated to the battle god, Ku. Throughout its 1,500-year history, members of the Mo'okini family have served as *kahu* (guardian) of the Mo'okini. The latest member of the family to inherit the title of Kahuna Nui (high priestess and councilor to a high chief) is Leimomi Mo'okini Lum, a direct descendant of High Priest Kuamo'o Mo'okini.

Today, the *heiau* and adjoining Kamehameha birthplace are open to visitors to stroll the grounds and learn about the history and culture of old Hawai'i. Various celebrations and cultural days are held here on special occasions such as King Kamehameha Day (June 11).

Just up the road is the former sugar cane town of **Hawi**. There's only one street, so park on the right and enjoy the short walk around. Starting on the right is **Aunty's Place**, a local eatery with a tiny bar (see Chapter 4). Next door is **Sandwich Isle Designs**, an interesting jewelry shop made even more so by floor-to-ceiling murals of oceanscape. Step in the front door and say hello to the mermaid at your feet, dolphins and *honu* (turtles) just under the surface. Fluffy white clouds hang overhead and the horizon traces the circumference of the room.

Other great stops are **Mother's Antiques, Imports & Fine Cigars** for Hawai'i-made smokes, **L. Zeidman Gallery** for finely crafted wooden bowls and sculptures, **Star Light Crystals**, **Kohala Healthfoods** or **Kohala Coffee Mill** for a great selec-

BROWSING FOR BOOKS

Big Island bookstores make up in quality what they might lack in quantity of shops. Each area has at least one good choice for booklovers seeking the latest in contemporary fiction, antique Hawaiiana, a comfortable beach read or island-style children's story. Books are valued *omiyage* (gifts) and make wonderful souvenirs, allowing you to enjoy your vacation again and again. Although you can pick up books at K-Mart, Wal-Mart and Costco, these shops are the kinds of places to take your time, ask questions and enjoy browsing.

Kona District

The sole proprietor of **Island Books**, a classic, jam-packed bookshop, has 30 years in the book business, and the reputation as "the oldest used bookstore in the state." An impressive collection of Hawaiiana from 50 cents to $1,000 includes rare and out-of-print titles on every imaginable island topic. Located one block south of the Aloha Theatre in Kainaliu town, mailing address: 79-7430 Mamalahoa Highway, Kealakekua, HI 96750; 808-322-2006.

Kohala Coast

A must-stop on your visit to Kapa'au, **Kohala Book Shop** is a booklover's paradise—with rooms full of floor-to-ceiling shelves crammed with new, used and out-of-print books, classic Hawaiiana, bestselling fiction and more. Lots of comfortable niches to curl up in, and friendly folks to answer questions or let you browse at leisure. A coffee shop next door completes a perfect rainy-day experience. Open Tuesday through Saturday 11 a.m.-5 p.m. 35-4522 Akoni Pule Highway, Kapa'au town; 808-889-6400.

Hamakua

The **Last Chance Store** in Kukuihaele, on the winding road to Waipi'o Valley, has an excellent selection of Hawaii-based fiction, non-fiction, poetry and picture books for kids and grownups. Also a fine gallery for local artisans, with a long front porch to relax on and sip a cold drink. 808-775-9222.

tion of snacks, *omiyage* (gifts) and ice cream. **As Hawi Turns** is famous for fantastic and funky gifts (check out the "fat mermaid" ornaments) and **Na Pua O Kohala** offers fresh-flower leis and lei-making kits, tropical bouquets and a creative "Frequent Flowers" program to enjoy year-round.

Ahead is the smaller town of **Kapa'au**, with its own interesting selection of arts, eats and history. You can't miss the grand ★ statue of **King Kamehameha I**, as he gestures in welcome from his lofty

Hilo

Basically Books is something special. If you have a question about Hawai'i, the answer is here somewhere, in one of their hundreds of books and maps. Named 2002 Retailer of the Year by the Retail Merchants of Hawai'i, Basically Books is one of the best stops you can make in Hilo town before you begin your special Big Island pursuits. They have books, maps and guides for paddlers, divers, surfers, snorkelers, hikers, campers, bikers and backpackers (and those of us who like to lie on the beach and read). New, used, out-of-print, reference, contemporary fiction, spirituality, children's books and gifts are available along with any kind of map you can think of, nautical charts, globes, compasses and flags. Always friendly, knowledgeable staff can answer your questions. (See "Suggested Reading" at the end of this book.) Open Monday through Saturday 9 a.m.-5 p.m., Sunday 11 a.m.-4 p.m. 160 Kamehameha Avenue, Hilo, HI 96720; 808-961-0144; 800-903-6277; e-mail: bbinfo@basicallybooks.com; www.basicallybooks.com.

Book Gallery is a good source for a wide variety of books about everything to do with Hawai'i, including fiction, nonfiction, spirituality, crafts, cookery, kids' books, maps and gift items. Prince Kuhio Plaza, Hilo; 808-935-4943.

The Big Island version of the national franchise **Waldenbooks** has plenty of Hawai'i-based books to choose from. Open Monday through Friday 10 a.m.-9 p.m., Saturday 9:30 a.m.-7 p.m., Sunday 10 a.m.-6 p.m. Prince Kuhio Plaza, 111 East Puainako, Hilo; 808-959-6468.

The bookstore franchise and coffee shop operation **Borders Books & Music** has an extensive selection of Hawai'i-based books, videos, CDs and gift items. Same great Borders service. Check local newspapers for visiting authors and special community activities. Open 10 a.m.-6 p.m. daily. 301 Maka'ala Street, Hilo (across from Prince Kuhio Plaza on Kanoelehua Avenue/Highway 11); 808-933-1410. There's also a location in Kailua-Kona at 75-1000 Henry Street, Kailua-Kona, at the corner of Henry and Highway 11 just below Wal-Mart; 808-331-1668.

vantage point in front of the old North Kohala Civic Center. Park here and stroll around the quiet grounds, read some interesting history of plantation days, war days and present days posted on the building's aging walls, and take advantage of the photo-op with His Royal Highness.

The statue was originally commissioned as a monument for Honolulu. It was cast in bronze in the 1880s in Paris and, after a rather turbulent history, including being sunk in the South Atlantic

Ocean near Cape Horn at Port Stanley in the Falkland Islands, it ended up here at the Kapaʻau Courthouse in 1912. Before this statue was salvaged from the icy waters of the Atlantic, a duplicate model was cast and that one now stands in front of the Judiciary Building, Aliʻiolani Hale, across from Iolani Palace in Honolulu. Since the original statue was no longer needed in Honolulu, it was placed in North Kohala. Each June 11, Kamehameha Day, local residents drape the statue with beautiful flowing flower leis.

Several years ago the statue was restored by art conservators who painstakingly removed more than 20 coats of paint. When they reached the base bronze, a community meeting was held to see if it should be left "naked," as the original sculptor intended, or to re-apply the paint. After much deliberation, elders elected to give the statue its bright colors back, and the art experts agreed. Since it had never stood as a bronze statue, it was now more of a folk art work, and a part of community tradition. The town fathers found a small piece of an authentic feather cape and showed it to conservators so they could match the exact yellow, and a special high-tech automotive paint was tinted and applied.

There's also a story about Kamehameha's eyes. We're told that most sculptors make eyes by carving deep holes into the metal, where the pupils would be, to give depth to the expression. However, when Kamehameha was first brought to town, one of the townsmen thought he needed actual eyeballs. He found a couple of ball bearings, just the right size, and hammered them in place. This local legend has yet to be verified.

Visit **Sue Swerdlow Gallery** to enjoy her vivid Hawaiian tropicals. One of the Big Island's most popular artists, Sue owns and operates her spacious gallery in the growing art community of Kapaʻau, which she calls "a gem in the jungle." Fine art and smaller gift items feature the vivid, energetic style of an artist in love with Hawaiʻi. Hours can vary, but appointments can be arranged any time. Kapaʻau; 808-889-0002, 808-883-9543; www.sueswerdlowart.com.

Gary Ackerman established his **Ackerman Galleries** over 25 years ago. Today it still offers work by him and other outstanding island artists, and a Gift Gallery featuring fine jewelry including the signature gold plumeria collection. Open daily 9:30 a.m.-6 p.m. Kapaʻau; 808-889-5971; e-mail: ack4art@hialoha.net; www.ackerman galleries.com.

Take time to browse through **Kohala Book Shop**, the "largest used bookstore in Hawaiʻi," for hard-to-find titles, beach reads or antique Hawaiiana (see "Browsing for Books" in this chapter). Enjoy a coffee break at **Nanbu Gallery Espresso Deli** before continuing your drive tour.

From here the road gets more interesting, winding through jungly gulches past an occasional house or fruit stand, climbing up to higher elevations where wild fields and wind-bent trees live. Near the end of the road, you come around one final curve and confront a dramatic view of ★ **Pololu Valley** that will take your breath away. Park in the circle, but watch out for the yellow cats that usually monitor the parking lot. Look down onto a rugged gray-sand beach and watch waves progress from miles out, to boom onshore at the foot of misty green, unspoiled hills. If the weather is clear, you may see entries to the other valleys between here and Waipi'o, where the road picks up again.

The rock islets that stand just off the mouth and beach of the valley are actually chunks of the Big Island, separated at some time in the far past, probably by volcanic activity. This is one of the best photo-ops on the island.

The beach of Pololu Valley is composed of fine black lava sand. However, the dangerous surf and a strong undertow make swimming unadvisable. A trail leads down to the valley floor and the beach for a nice hike, although it can be hazardous in or just after rain. It's only a 15-minute hike down, quite a bit longer back up, and the trail is often wet and muddy in places. Some parts are quite rocky as well, so good footwear and hiking attire is recommended. The black-sand beach is piled high with lava rocks, with a beautiful view of the *pali* along the coast in either direction. A stream flows down from the valley and there are nice views back into its far reaches. Be aware of "No Trespassing" signs and respect private property if you choose to wander back into the valley.

For a different, equally spectacular route home, turn left in Hawi town on Highway 250 and head uphill. This road will lead to Waimea in 21 miles, through gorgeous upcountry ranchland, tree-lined winding roads and vistas from the top of the world. Do stop at the overlook point and look down upon the coastline and tiny beaches in the distance, taking a moment to let it sink in how big the Big Island really is.

If you've started out early enough, you may want to close the loop on this tour by continuing on to Honoka'a and **Waipi'o Valley overlook**, 13 miles east. Turn left at the intersection of Highways 250 and 19, go into town and left again at the stoplight in Honoka'a and turn left into town. (There are three streets going down toward the ocean from the highway and it doesn't matter which one you take.)

At the bottom of the hill, turn left on Highway 240 and head down the woodsy road, through old plantation subdivisions vividly planted with tropical flowers, to the end of the road at the entry to Waipi'o Valley.

Park and walk down the long staircase to the railing overlook. Now you are looking at the opposite end of the series of valleys that began at Pololu. It always strikes us how gray and misty Pololu is compared to green Waipi'o with its turquoise water and white-sand beach. Waipi'o is home to many Big Islanders who make a living with a remote tourist trade, or by farming. Some make the steep 4WD-only commute out every day for hotel jobs or other work. In the old days, it was a busy farm community, and over the years it has been an area for "alternative" lifestyles, a training ground for the Peace Corps (complete with water buffalo) and a beautiful, relatively untouched and timeless place to explore.

Don't take the rental car down. Tours by van, horse-drawn wagon or horseback, ATV, mountain bike and foot are available in nearby Kukuihaele, all of which give you safe transportation, refreshments, a chance to experience the beach, talk story with local experts and really get a sense of place.

Waimea Town

Waimea is home to one of the largest privately owned cattle ranches in the country, Parker Ranch, and has always been a *paniolo* town. Its Western theme is everywhere; even the stop signs at Parker Ranch Center say "Whoa." *Waimea* means "red water," and the town was originally named after seasonal mountain streams with their reddish hue. When the post office was built, it was named after Samuel ("Kamuela") Parker of Parker Ranch, and that's where the confusion began. To make matters even more confusing, there is a Waimea town on each of the other major Hawaiian islands, which may be why the postmaster at the time preferred the name Kamuela for the Big Island's Waimea. Many Big Islanders use the two names interchangeably when talking of the same place, but we're not trying to throw you off, honest.

Waimea town lies at the foot of the Kohala Mountains, on the edge of a vast plateau that stretches to the base of towering Mauna Kea. The plateau slopes gradually to both the east and west, forming a perfect valley for pasture and farmland. Many of the vegetables, herbs, edible flowers and other specialties served in island restaurants are grown right here in Waimea, along with quality beef, veal, lamb and poultry.

★ **Parker Ranch Visitor Center** is located in the back of Parker Ranch Center on Highway 19 in the heart of Waimea town. Those who take the time off from the beach to experience "Old Hawai'i" from the Parker Ranch point of view find it fascinating, time well-spent. Start with the entertaining orientation movie, check out the antique-filled museum, sign up for guided tours of the fabulous historic estates "Mana" and "Pu'uopelu," the latter with an impressive collection of original Impressionist paintings and Chinese antiques. Other intriguing Ranch activities include an old-fashioned horse-drawn carriage ride, *paniolo* trail rides across the greener pastures, ATV excursions, skeet-shooting, hunting excursions, riding and dressage lessons and scheduled rodeos and horseraces. Stop in the Parker Ranch Store for great Western-style clothing, hats, belts, boots, T-shirts, cowboy and cowgirl outfits, great *omiyage* (gifts) and much more. The Ranch is branching out as a visitor destination and welcomes families in search of a truly unique Big Island experience. Group rates are available, as are a variety of indoor and outdoor facilities for meetings, retreats, family reunions, weddings. Adventures can be customized to include riding, hiking, eco-tourist explorations and education opportunities. Open daily except Sunday, 9 a.m. to 4 p.m. (The store is open Sunday.) Museum admission: $6.50 adults, $5.50 seniors, $5 children 4 to 11. Historic Homes admission: $8.50 adults, $7.50 seniors, $6 children 4 to 11. Parker Ranch, P.O. Box 458, Kamuela, HI 96743; 808-885-7655; www.parkerranch.com.

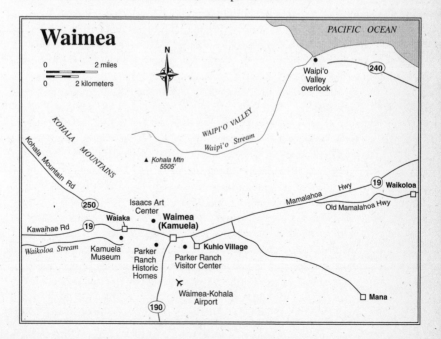

Camp Tarawa Monument is of interest to World War II/Pacific War vets and history buffs. This is a large stone marker and plaque on Highway 190 just outside the entrance of Pu'uopelu. The marker notes the surrounding grounds of Parker Ranch that were used as "Camp Tarawa" from 1943–45 by the 2nd and 5th U.S. Marine Divisions that trained here prior to the invasion of Iwo Jima, Okinawa and other islands in the far west Pacific leading to the end of the war.

Kamuela Museum in Waimea is at the intersection of Routes 19 and 250 (Kohala Mountain Road). It is the largest privately owned museum in Hawai'i with interesting collections of ancient Hawaiian weapons, World War II relics, furniture of Hawaiian royalty, and other antiques and art objects. Open daily, but call ahead for hours. Adults $5, children under age 12 $2. 808-885-4724.

As you drive into town up Kawaihae Road, stop at **Parker Square** on your right. This nice, U-shaped building offers a pleasant stroll through various shops on an old-fashioned wooden plankway that just sounds good as you go. Start at the **Gallery of Great Things** on one end and dig through a collection of Asian and Pacific treasures in all shapes, sizes and budgets, including museum-quality art, Hawai'i-made jewelry, quilts, paintings and sculptures. Do at least pick up and hold one of Jesus Sanchez's hand-bound, *koa*-covered blank books (painstakingly crafted in Hilo) and look at the *netsuke* collectibles right beside the front door. Open Monday through Saturday 9 a.m.-5:30 pm, Sunday 10 a.m.-4 p.m. P.O. Box 6209, Kamuela, HI 96743; 808-885-7706; fax 808-885-0098; e-mail: ggt@ilhawaii.net. Wander through great shops like **Sweetwind Books & Beads, Bentley's, Imagination Toys, Silk Road Gallery, Kamuela Goldsmiths, Waimea Coffee Company** and end up in **Waimea General Store**, before continuing on your way into town.

Across the street is the new **Isaacs Art Center**, home to the Hawaii Preparatory Academy art collection, vintage furniture and works by important Hawaii artists of the last century. A Preservation Honor Award recipient from the Historic Hawaii Foundation, the Center is open Tuesday through Saturday, 10 a.m.-5 p.m. Free admission, 808-885-5884.

Next to Parker Square is the **Quilted Horse** in the High Country Traders building. This is a source for Hawaiian quilts and quilting supplies, gift items and usually friendly conversation. Hawaiian quilts are deceptively expensive, but a real quilter will attest to their value. This folk-art form has been practiced by Hawai'i's women since the late 19th century, when missionary women taught sewing outdoors, under the trees. The bright sunlight made crisp shadows of leaves on the plain white cloth, which inspired cut-work patterns, each cut from one piece of contrasting, bright-colored fabric. It's assumed that Hawaiian women, who made cloth by an arduous process of tapa beating, thought the missionary ladies were nuts to cut up beautiful whole cloth, then sew it back together. However, they excelled at it and passed the tradition on to the present, with its share of *kapu*, taboo and legend. Traditionally, each quilt has a name and a secret name, known only to the quilter. A quilt can decorate the bed, but is never sat upon. And if they become worn or faded, they must be burned. (Please note that some machine-made knock-offs are available at much lower prices, but if you want an authentic quilt, ask questions and be sure of what you're buying.)

Leaving the Quilted Horse and Parker Square, turn right onto the main road, which curves to the right just before a stoplight. Go straight through the intersection and you will see **Parker Ranch Center** on the right. Take a look at the **Ikua Purdy Statue**, a life-sized bronze sculpture of horse and rider working a steer. There is ample parking in the complex, large restrooms, a variety of eateries and plenty of stores to explore. On the west end is **Healthways II**, a nice, big health food store jammed with fresh organic fruits and vegetables, canned and frozen vegetarian meals, vitamins, aromatherapy products and natural cosmetics. In the back is a deli counter, offering veggie sandwiches, smoothies and other fare for the conscientious.

Opposite is the **Parker Ranch Store**, full of *paniolo* souvenirs, cowboy and cowgirl attire and a funky combination of Western-Hawaiian gift items, which leads into a central food court with a great selection of tasty carry-outs: Chinese, Japanese, Korean and the great cross-cultural cuisine of ice cream. (The Little Juice Shack is right around back.) A huge stone fireplace is surrounded by handpainted murals of Waimea countryside; there are ample seating and large comfortable restrooms. Starbucks on the opposite corner, offering a selection of Kona coffees along with its usual menu, and comfortable areas to sit and "talk story." Beyond that are the Foodland grocery store and a Blockbuster Video. You'll also find Giggles, Morning Glory Kamuela, Paniolo Pantry, Reyn's and other interesting shops.

Here too is the **Kahilu Theatre**, built by Parker Ranch heir and New York performer Richard Smart. Kahilu hosts a busy schedule of international music, dance and drama performances, current films and more—including an amazing Circus Camp for kids. 808-885-6868, www.kahilutheatre.org.

Note that both Foodland and KTA (across the street) have competitive prices on popular *omiyage* items like Kona coffee and macadamia nuts. We'd encourage you to read labels and be sure of what you are buying. To be labeled "Kona Coffee," a blend is only required to have 10 percent Kona coffee beans. Most flavored varieties and decafs contain very little actual Kona beans. There are also blends of "Hawai'i Coffee," which include beans from Kaua'i, Maui and Moloka'i farms. These are fine coffees, but if you want 100 percent Kona, it's expensive. And, if you're planning to tour the coffee region, you'll have numerous opportunities to taste some of the best on the planet.

Across the street from Parker Ranch Visitor Center is **Waimea Center**, smaller and funkier, but worth the stop, if just to wander down the sidewalk once and smell the different eateries. Say hello to the cowboy statue and take a look at the beautiful stained-glass landscape in the central courtyard. The entire parking lot is laid out in a one-way traffic pattern, usually enforced by security guards. Pay attention to the arrows on the asphalt, and have a little patience.

Continuing out of town to the east, you pass historic "church row," a pretty strip of five various church buildings fronted by a cherry-tree-covered lawn—a real picture-postcard if you're lucky enough to visit when they're in bloom.

You can do Waimea in half a day. One strategy is to save it for your day-after-sunburn, when you'd most appreciate cooler temperatures. Another is to check the *Waimea Gazette, West Hawai'i Today* or *North Hawai'i News* for festivals, parades and other events happening in town. Waimea is a busy community and takes its holidays and special occasions very seriously. The Cherry Blossom Festival, Aloha Week festivities, Christmas parade, Pow Wow and many others make great excuses to drive into town, do a little shopping and stay for a meal.

Saddle Road

This section is added for informational purposes even though there are no towns or services of any kind along the Saddle Road. It is included because the road winds through some surreal-looking landscape with stark lava flows, cinder cones and volcanic peaks. This is the route to one of the island's primary attractions: the world-renowned telescope observatories at the summit of Mauna Kea mountain and the weather observatory on Mauna Loa.

Caution: Driving on Saddle Road, Highway 200, is prohibited in rental cars due to hazardous driving conditions. It is a violation of car rental contracts. The road is continually being upgraded so be aware of construction and potential delays.

The Saddle Road is so-called because it passes through the plateau adjoining the massive Mauna Kea and Mauna Loa mountains, like a saddle in between. From Waimea to Hilo via the Saddle

Road is a distance of 60 miles and from Kailua-Kona to Hilo it is 87 miles. However, because of the narrow winding road conditions (especially near the Hilo side) and the extreme caution needed when driving it, this route often takes longer to drive than other routes around the island.

The drive does present some different scenery, however. The towering peaks of Mauna Kea and Mauna Loa are seen from a closer perspective along the road in between them. The early-morning hours are generally clear while from midday on into the afternoon, clouds roll upslope from the eastern Hilo and Hamakua districts and tend to fill up the plateau area between the mountains, obscuring the views. Traveling from west to east, the road passes through vast tracts of green ranch pastures, extending down from Mauna Kea's lower slopes. This is generally dry, windy and wide-open country-side. On the Hilo side, the road passes through several miles of heavy rainforest vegetation above the town that gives way to extensive fern and ohia lehua forest of the mountain's mid-elevation slopes. Interspersed here and there are rough and rugged lava flows until at the 3,000-foot level on the central plateau, where it appears to be one huge lava flow.

Midway on the Saddle Road is the turn-off for the Mauna Kea Summit Road, which leads up to the summit of the 13,796-foot mountain (about 1 hour from Hilo, Waikoloa or Waimea and 2 hours from Kailua-Kona).

Caution: Youngsters under 12, pregnant women and anyone with respiratory or cardiac problems are advised not to go to Mauna Kea's summit. The very thin air (60 percent of normal oxygen) can cause altitude sickness and nausea. Even scientists working at this elevation experience difficulties. Mauna Kea's weather can change suddenly and dramatically, especially in winter months. From November to March, it can snow anytime and blizzard conditions are possible. Even the summer months can bring strong winds and below-freezing temperatures at the summit. Warm clothing is essential year-round and warm drinks, food and emergency supplies are essential. There are no services at the summit. We strongly advise you limit your visit to the Onizuka Center and enjoy the stars safely.

At the 9,200-foot elevation level (6.5 miles up the summit road) is the ★ **Onizuka Center for International Astronomy**, named in honor of Astronaut Ellison Onizuka, a native son of the Big Island who died aboard the *Challenger* space shuttle in 1986. This is truly cool. Pack a picnic (coffee, hot chocolate, tea and some snacks are available on-site) and warm clothes and go up in time for sunset, genuinely awesome at this elevation. On a clear night, you can even see the glow of red lava from the flow many miles away. At twilight, watch for satellites and the space station, then at dark, get a glimpse of the rest of the galaxy, up close and personal, through 14-inch Celestron telescopes. See star clusters, double stars, nebulae, supernovas, planets and something called the "Zodiacal light" from the best vantage point on Earth. The Visitor Information Station is open daily 9 a.m.-10 p.m. With interpretive guides to answer questions, displays, videos and computers to view astronomy software. During the day a Celestron telescope with solar filters is set up to view sunspots and solar activity. The First Light bookstore is open 9 a.m.-9:30 p.m. for snacks, books and souvenirs. Summit tours are held Saturday and Sunday 1-5 p.m. and stargazing programs take place 365 nights a year, weather permitting, from 6 to 10 p.m. And they're free. For more information, call the center at 808-961-2180 or 808-974-4273 for a recorded message. For weather updates and snow and road conditions on Mauna Kea: 808-961-5582; www.ifa.hawaii.edu/mko/maunakea.htm. (Commercial tours are also available from various providers like Mauna Kea Summit Adventures, www.maunakea.com.)

The Onizuka Center also serves as the base camp for scientists and astronomers engaged in research projects using the telescopes up at the summit. The center, at 9,200 feet, is a safer and more comfortable elevation for researchers than the extremely thin air at the nearly 14,000-foot peak. Above the Onizuka Center, the John A. Burns Way extends another 6.6 miles to the very top. There are no facilities for the public above the center; 4WD transportation is required, with adequate fuel for the return to Hilo or Waimea. There are no opportunities to look through the telescopes during the day and visitors are not permitted after dark. The road to the summit can be dangerous and is subject to severe weather. The high altitude carries serious health risks.

Mauna Kea's extremely dry climate, high altitude and remote location far away from lighted areas offer some of the consistently best conditions for optical, infrared and radio astronomy of any site on the planet. Here at the summit, above 40 percent of the earth's atmosphere, water vapor in the air is minimal, and the number of cloud-free nights is greater than anywhere else in the world.

There are 13 working telescopes here, 9 for optical and infrared astronomy, 3 for submillimeter wavelength astronomy and 1 for radio astronomy. These amazing instruments represent the leaders of the astronomy community, including the twin W. M. Keck Telescopes, the largest optical/infrared instruments in the world, and the James Clerk Maxwell Telescope, the largest submillimeter instrument. The 82-foot wide, 100-foot tall antenna dish of the Very Long Baseline Array is part of the 5,000-mile-wide radio telescope that stretches from the Virgin Islands to Hawai'i, with dish sites across the mainland.

The **Mauna Loa Access Road** leads off the Saddle Road in the opposite direction of the Mauna Kea Summit Road. This drive of just over 17 miles to the 11,000-foot level of Mauna Loa passes through nothing but stark barren lava flow country. There are sweeping views back across the Saddle Road plateau and to Mauna Kea on cloudless days. But other than that, the 34-mile round trip on this road is a drive across a moonscape rock desert.

At the end of the Mauna Loa Access Road is the **National Oceanic and Atmospheric Administration (NOAA) Mauna Loa Weather Observatory**, which keeps track of developing weather over Hawai'i using sophisticated instruments and satellite communications. A hiking trail from the end of the road here continues on up to Mauna Loa's summit and to a hiker's cabin, then connects to a trail system leading downslope on the other side to Hawai'i Volcanoes National Park. It is a very strenuous hike over rugged terrain, not for novices or unprepared casual hikers. Only experienced backpackers with full supplies should attempt the route. Check "Hiking" in Chapter 6 for details.

Along the Saddle Road is **Pohakuloa Training Area**, a large military base used by the Army for live firing exercises, Stryker Brigade training and military maneuvers. Be on the alert for large, slow-moving military trucks on the Saddle Road and an occasional convoy of military vehicles or even a tank! A continuing road improvement project began in 2003.

Mauna Kea State Recreation Area is also located on the Saddle Road, with picnic areas, restrooms and phone available. The park is on the plateau at the foot of Mauna Kea and the area abounds with introduced wild game birds like pheasant, quail and partridge as well as many species of native Hawaiian bird life. Visitors can enjoy the peace and solitude of this remote area and stroll through the trails and backroads of the park area to gain a perspective of this most unusual part of Hawai'i. Cabins are available by permit in advance, but there is no potable water on site.

Hamakua District

Just north of Hilo, and running the length of the Big Island's east side some 40 miles to Honoka'a and another 10 miles beyond to Waipi'o Valley, is the Hamakua Coast. Up until the early '90s, when the sugar industry finally closed down, this region's vast sugar plantations annually produced thousands of tons of raw cane to feed the sugar mills along the coast. And while the majority of ex-sugar cane land is now planted in eucalyptus forests, there is a growing diversified agriculture economy being developed in macadamia nut orchards, ginger, papaya, bananas, dryland taro and timber throughout the region. The future of this rich agriculture region is still being written.

Along the Hamakua Coast are numerous gulches filled with gushing streams and waterfalls, verdant tropical rainforest vegetation, and weathered old plantation villages hinting at Hawai'i's past. A generation or two ago, most of the Big Island's population lived in such plantation camps.

Driving the Hamakua Coast can be an enjoyable scenic cruise. The route passes through a number of small towns and settlements along the way, each with a melodious Hawaiian name: Papa'ikou, Pepe'ekeo, Honomu, Hakalau, Laupahoehoe, O'okala, Pa'auilo and Pa'auhau.

Like the Hamakua Coast is generally quite wet, receiving well over 100 inches of rainfall annually. However, rainfall varies by elevation and you will notice changes in vegetation and terrain as you travel toward somewhat drier Honoka'a.

Most of the coastline on this eastern side of the island is rugged, marked by high cliffs dropping straight to the pounding ocean surf. There are very few safe beach areas along this entire coast; however, the parks and overlooks along the way provide wonderful scenic vistas. Compared to the Big Island's dry western coastline, the east side is like a lush, green Eden.

★ **Honoka'a** is the largest town on the Hamakua Coast. Since the sugar industry soured, it's started to branch out in different directions, as an art community and a diverse, growing residential neighborhood. You may enjoy a one-street walking tour for a chance to nose through overstuffed antique stores and junk shops, visit the macadamia nut factory, take in the galleries and wonderful smells of fresh coffee, pizza and other good things. Walk by the **People's Theatre**, and appreciate the restoration efforts that went into making a retro classic from a falling-down movie theater, now home of the successful annual Hamakua Music Festival in October. 808-775-3378; www.hamakuamusicfestival.org.

★ **Tex's Drive In** is on Highway 19 above Honoka'a town. Don't miss this Honoka'a institution, famous for fresh hot *malasadas* (deep-fried Portuguese doughnuts, a sheer delight anytime) and other local fast-food items, plate lunches and sit-down meals. Tex's has expanded to include the **Honoka'a Visitors Center**, a large gift shop, restrooms and ample indoor-outdoor seating. Right next door is the huge greenhouse of **Mohala Pua Garden Center**.

★ **Waipi'o Valley** is located at the end of Route 240, about nine miles north of Honoka'a. The road passes through the tiny villages of **Kawela**, **Kapulena** and **Kukuihaele**. **The Last Chance Store** has cold sodas, ice cream and snacks, and a gift gallery including wood-work, paintings and art photography, glass, pottery, jewelry, clothing and a good selection of Hawai'i books for kids and adults. This shop is also the starting station for **Waipi'o Valley Shuttle**, narrated 90-minute 4x4 tours of the magnificent Waipi'o Valley, just a half-mile further on. The tour details the valley's history and culture and the interesting family enterprise of taro farm. The shuttle tour is $37 per person, children under 12 are $15. Shuttles operate daily except Sunday, 9 a.m., 11 a.m., 1 p.m. and 3 p.m. 808-775-7121.

You can also see the Waipi'o Valley via horseback rides with **Waipi'o Na'alapa Trail Rides** (808-775-0419) or **Hawaii Resorts Transportation** (808-775-7291). These are two-and-a-half-hour horseback tours on the floor of Waipi'o Valley.

★ The dramatic overlook at the top of **Waipi'o Valley State Park** is the starting point for the steep winding road leading into the valley. *Caution*: Under no circumstances should you attempt to drive your rental car down the dangerously steep valley road. Only 4x4 vehicles are allowed. In addition to the steep road, there are numerous streams on the valley floor that must be crossed and regular rental cars will not make it.

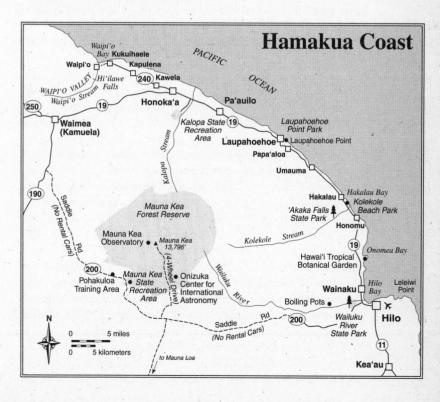

Hamakua Coast

Waipi'o Valley park provides a covered picnic pavilion and restrooms at the top of the valley, and spectacular views of the valley interior with its almost vertical 2,000-foot walls. A freshwater river runs oceanward from the twin waterfalls of Hi'ilawe in back of the valley. The wide black-sand beach and heavy pounding surf are unfortunately not safe for swimming because of hazardous undercurrents, but the beach remains a beautiful retreat for relaxation and contemplation.

★ **Kalopa State Recreation Area** turn-off is about five miles south of Honoka'a town. The park has camping cabins and picnic tables, as well as a nature trail system through stands of reforested lands and native rainforest.

Pa'auilo is located about five miles south along Highway 19. The former plantation manager's residence is set back on the hill next to Earl's Snack Shop in town and workers' camp housing stretches out below the highway. The town has changed little since its heyday as a plantation center. Be sure to stop just south of Pa'auilo at Donna's Cookies for the some of the best homemade cookies on the Big Island.

★ **Laupahoehoe** and **Laupahoehoe Point** are about 11 miles farther south. The old town area has a school, bakery, post office, a police station and the former jail. There is also the old **M. Sakado Store**, another real classic mom-and-pop store survivor from an earlier era.

Just on the north edge of town, there is a scenic overlook alongside the highway before you get to the gulch leading down to Laupahoehoe Point. A short downhill drive takes you to a grassy park with picnic tables, restrooms and scenic views of the Hamakua Coast. A monument stands on the point in memory of the 24 teachers and school children who were swept to sea in a 1946 tidal wave.

The ★ **Laupahoehoe Train Museum** is located at the intersection of main street and the highway. Displays and exhibits, colorful murals, an orientation movie, old documents and train memorabilia donated by area residents keep the Hamakua Coast's railroad heritage alive. There's a small snackbar, restrooms, and friendly docents to answer your questions. P.O. Box 358, Laupahoehoe, HI 96764; 808-962-6300.

Papa'aloa is another old plantation village located just off the highway. This village is a reminder of earlier days when the plantation town was surrounded by workers' camp housing, the mill garage and warehouses, a ball field, and old storefronts—all indications of a once lively and bustling community.

★ **World Botanical Gardens** is located near the 16-mile marker on Highway 19. This 300-acre development on former sugar cane fields has been established as a world-class botanical garden. There are thousands of species of tropical plants and trees, fruit orchards, and native Hawaiian species in a rainforest environment. Nature trails lead to the lookout point of the spectacular 300-foot triple cascades of Umauma Waterfalls. Enjoy free samples of fresh tropical fruit like banana, papaya, guava or pineapple. 808-963-5427.

Honomu is about 11 miles north of Hilo and is a typical old sugar plantation country town whose two-block main street hosts a small group of interesting shops, galleries, diners and churches on the route up to 'Akaka Falls.

To find the beautiful ★ **'Akaka Falls State Park** take Route 22 above Honomu town. The paved road rises sharply through the hilly fields for about 3.6 miles. The 66-acre park is a refreshing stop after the uphill drive and restrooms and picnic tables are available. An easy hike down into the ravines passes mystic stands of bamboo, ginger, and many flowering trees and plants—a breathtaking tropical greenhouse. Walkers are rewarded with inspiring views of the 420-foot cascades of 'Akaka Falls and nearby Kahuna Falls tumbling into deep gorges. This is a good family activity, but don't let the kids run too far ahead as the paved trail is usually damp and can be slippery.

★ **Hawai'i Tropical Botanical Garden** is located along this scenic route just north of Papa'ikou at beautiful, historic Onomea Bay. Nature trails meander through tropical rainforest, cross streams and waterfalls, and follow the rugged coast. There are extensive collections of over 2,000 species of palms, bromeliads, gingers, exotic ornamental and other international tropical plants. Well worth the ticket price when you see what they have created out of former overgrown wild jungle. A garden of joy for nature photographers. Flowers are available for purchase online. Open daily 8 a.m.-5 p.m. Adults $15, children under 16 $5, group/family one-year pass $35. 27-717 Old Mamalahoa Highway, Papa'ikou, HI 96781; 808-954-5233; www.htbg.com.

★ **Old Mamalahoa Highway Scenic Drive** is just five miles north of Hilo at the intersection with Kalanianaole School. Old Highway 19 follows the rugged rainforested Hamakua Coast for four miles before linking back with the newer Highway 19. The scenic route takes in numerous gulches and coves as it winds through lovely coastal country with scenic views of the rugged Hamakua Coast and lush rainforest jungles. Shower trees, royal poinciana, breadfruit, coconut, African tulip, and royal palms line the route much of the way. The old route passes through aged sugar plantation villages with melodious names such as Papa'ikou, Onomea, Pepe'ekeo, and Kawai Nui. It's definitely an easy and scenic drive well worth taking; this was the only route around the island in the pre–World War II days.

Hilo

What we love about visiting Hilo is its special sense of being a "real" place, where real people live and work. Hilo was not invented for the visitor industry; it was an industrial blue-collar town that grew up on its own and is now the seat of county government, and the second largest city in Hawai'i (believe it or not).

Hilo was the government and commercial trade center for the sugar plantations that dominated island industry for most of the last century. The abundant rains still produce a lush green tropical landscape and former cane lands are being planted in macadamia nuts, papayas, bananas, tropical flowers and garden crops that hold more economic promise and are more environmentally sound. With its distinctly tropical climate, Hilo has become the center for the world's largest tropical flower industry. Anthuriums, those heart-shaped long-lasting blooms that fetch upwards of $5 each in mainland winter markets, are sold by the thousands by numerous farmer co-ops and flower farm exporters. The orchid industry features countless varieties of award-winning flowering plants exported worldwide.

Hilo is also gaining recognition as a residential small college town with the growth and expansion of the state-supported University of Hawai'i at Hilo and adjoining Hawai'i Community College. The schools share a lovely campus and a cosmopolitan enrollment of some 4,000 to 5,000 students from around the islands of Hawai'i, the U.S. mainland and all over the Pacific Rim. The University of Hawaii at Hilo's University Research Park is home to the Joint Astronomy Center, which operates two observatories on Mauna Kea and the headquarters of the Caltech Submillimeter Observatory, also on Mauna Kea, operated by the California Institute of Technology.

The last few years have seen much improvement in downtown Hilo, particularly along the bayfront, as new businesses have renovated old shop buildings. Restaurants, gift shops, art galleries, boutiques and other interesting places add new life to the old-fashioned downtown area without taking away from its charm.

Author John Penisten says, "After experiencing the real Hilo and its notorious rain, perhaps you'll come to see that Hilo does indeed have its place in the sun. Some see Hilo as a salve to soothe and comfort those with tortured soul and psyche who seek relief in a definitely slower and perhaps saner pace of life. With its warm showers, lush tropical splendor, and friendly caring folks, Hilo is indeed a balm for troubled souls and aching hearts. You see, the old line about Hilo's rain is really relative. It's all in how you look at it. Hilo's rainy reputation has kept the visitor counts to a minimum, which some folks don't mind. Because of it, Hilo has been slow to change. And perhaps that's good. It has helped Hilo to retain its essential hometown charm and personality, a valuable asset these days. Yes, there is a bright side to Hilo. And you really need to discover it for yourself. Oh, and when you come, bring your umbrella. It looks like a shower today!"

★ **Liliuokalani Park** is located on Banyan Drive neighboring the hotels along the shore of Hilo Bay. This picturesque, authentic Japanese garden park was named in honor of Hawai'i's last reigning monarch, Queen Liliuokalani. It was built in the early 1900s as a memorial to the immigrant Japanese who developed the old Waiakea Sugar Plantation. The park features a collection of Oriental bridges of various styles and materials informally arrayed among the gardens and ponds. We imagine the designer envisioned a meditative walking grounds, where one might consider life's transitions, "bridges," some high, some low, some easy, some more difficult. With or without so much thinking, it is one of Hawai'i's loveliest parks, and it's free—a must-see on your visit to Hilo.

Giant old Banyan trees make a shady canopy over Hilo's hotel row and give it the name ★ **Banyan Drive**. Most of these handsome spreading trees were planted over a 40-year period beginning in 1933 with a tree planted by Mr. & Mrs. Cecil B. DeMille, who were on the island filming *Four Frightened People*. Babe Ruth planted his tree two days later. Other VIP notables included President Franklin D. Roosevelt, Amelia Earhart, Fannie Hurst and King George V. There's even one planted by a then-aspiring politician named Richard Nixon. Each of the 46 trees is marked accordingly and each has a story to tell.

★ **Coconut Island** in Hilo Bay is a small island just offshore from Liliuokalani Park, reached from behind the Hilo Hawaiian Hotel. (Note: Park in the public lot by the bridge, not in the hotel lot, where towing is enforced.) Coconut Island is an entertaining place to watch the local fishermen try their luck, and the kids swim and dive from an old bridge platform. There are picnic tables, public restrooms and rain shelters available. Coconut Island is often used for cultural events, concerts and hula shows by local organizations of all kinds. It's definitely worth a stroll at sunset if you are staying at a nearby hotel, and a fun place to let the kids run and play.

Rainbow Falls and Boiling Pots are above downtown Hilo, just off Waianuenue Avenue at **Wailuku River State Park**. This small park features walking trails, public restrooms and magnificent views of **Rainbow Falls**. Go early in the morning for your best shot at seeing the legendary rainbows when the sun strikes the spray beneath the falls. A little farther up the road, above Hilo Hospital, the Wailuku River is pocked with giant holes and recesses, called **Boiling Pots**, in the lava-rock gorge. The Pots create a series of deep swirling pools, falls and rapids during heavy rain periods. There is no safe swimming in this treacherous and deep gorge but it is a cool natural formation to see for yourself. There are restroom facilities, picnic tables, and a scenic overlook of the Wailuku River Gorge. Still farther up *mauka* are the **Pe'epe'e Falls**, which begin the river's long tumble down to Hilo and out to sea.

Suisan Fish Market is located on Hilo Bay at the mouth of the Wailoa River and within walking distance of the Banyan Drive hotels. Although public fish auctions are no longer conducted, this Hilo institution remains a landmark on visitor maps. 85 Lihiwai Street; 808-935-8051.

★ **Hilo Farmers' Market** is a wonderfully colorful circus of fruits and vegetables, tropical flowers, honey, coffee, fresh-caught fish, hand-sewn lei, *ono* (delicious) baked goods and sometimes baby animals. Across the street is an ever-expanding flea market chock-full of crafts and imports, collectibles, jewelry and eclectic things. Open Wednesday, Saturday and Sunday mornings from early until noon or so at the corner of Mamo Street and Kamehameha Avenue, across from Mo'oheau Park. Rain or shine, this is one of Hilo's most memorable things to do.

★ **Lyman Museum & Mission House** is an old New England–style missionary home built in 1839 for Rev. David and Sarah Lyman, the first Christian missionaries to arrive in Hilo. In addition to the original Lyman House, the museum next door holds a unique collection of memorabilia of early Hilo and Big Island life including numerous artifacts from the diverse ethnic cultures who populated Hawai'i in the 18th and 19th centuries. Museum hours are Monday through Saturday, 9:30 a.m. to 4:30 p.m. Admission $7 adults, $5 seniors, $3 children 6-17. Mission House tours are given several times daily beginning at 9:30 a.m. 276 Haili Street; 808-935-5021; www.lymanmuseum.org.

★ **Pacific Tsunami Museum** is one of Hilo's most unique attractions. Located in the old First Hawaiian Bank on Kamehameha Avenue, the museum is a repository of information and research on global tsunami and tidal wave phenomena and an educational resource for the public. Particularly poignant today, the exhibits not only preserve the local history, but serve as a living memorial to those who lost their lives and loved ones to tsunami. There are guided

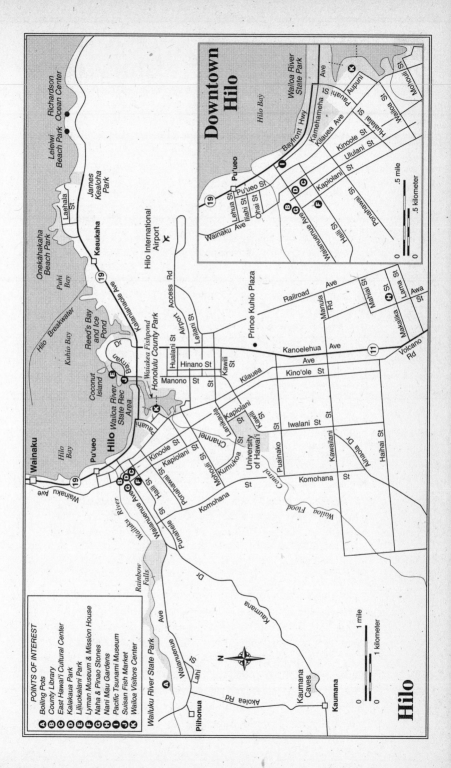

Downtown Hilo

POINTS OF INTEREST
- Ⓐ Boiling Pots
- Ⓑ County Library
- Ⓒ East Hawai'i Cultural Center
- Ⓓ Kalakaua Park
- Ⓔ Liliuokalani Park
- Ⓕ Lyman Museum & Mission House
- Ⓖ Naha & Pinao Stones
- Ⓗ Nani Mau Gardens
- Ⓘ Pacific Tsunami Museum
- Ⓙ Suisan Fish Market
- Ⓚ Wailoa Visitors Center

Hilo

FACTORY TOURS

★ **Mauna Loa Macadamia Nut** Factory is located three miles south of Hilo on the east side of Volcano Highway 11 and back in through the orchards a couple of miles. Look for road signs marking the entrance. A visitors center provides free samples of Hawai'i's popular gourmet nut and a wide variety of macadamia nut products are available for purchase. There is also a free narrated factory tour, a movie, and a chance to take your picture with the world's largest mac nut. Open daily 9 a.m.-5 p.m. 808-955-8612.

★ **Big Island Candies** is straight ahead as you exit the Hilo Airport Road at the main intersection of Kanoelehua Avenue. Go straight through the intersection onto Kekuanaoa Street and go three blocks, turn right on Hinano Street and the factory is on the immediate right. This must-see candy factory is famous for its delectable hand-dipped dark and white chocolate shortbread cookies and many other tempting, tasty treats—now including sugar-free goodies and interesting things like chocolate-dipped *li hing mui* (sour dried fruit), crispy rice and animal crackers in the "Da Kine" section. Browse the gift shop, watch the factory operations through large windows, and sample fresh Kona coffee and chocolates. This will be one stop you won't regret. Open daily 8:30 a.m.-5 p.m. 585 Hinano Street; 808-935-8890; e-mail: contactus@bigislandcandies.com; www.bigislandcandies.com.

Mehana Brewing Company welcomes visitors who stop by the tasting room with free samples of its various microbrews. Sample from Mehana Beer, Volcano Red Ale (won bronze medal in 1998 World Beer Championships), Mehana Mauna Kea Pale Ale, Tsunami Lager and Roy's Private Reserve. Mehana's smooth taste is from the pure Hawaiian water and fresh ingredients used. They also have a gift shop with logo-wear, caps, glasses and gift items. Guided tours throughout the day. Open Monday through Friday 9 a.m. to 5:30 p.m., Saturday 10 a.m. to 4 p.m. 275 East Kawili Street; 808-934-8211; e-mail: karen@mehana.com; www. mehana.com.

tours, movies of tsunami events, interactive computer terminals, and a museum gift shop. Open Monday through Saturday, 9 a.m.-4 p.m. Admission: $5 per person. Corner of Kalakaua and Kamehameha Avenues, downtown Hilo; 808-935-0926; www.tsunami.org.

A block down the street is the new **Mokupapapa Discovery Center**—an exhibition full of ocean information and learning opportunities on bayfront Kamehameha Avenue. Kids of all ages enjoy interactive displays, including a 2,500-gallon reef aquarium and submersible training station. Affiliated with the National Oceanic Atmospheric Administration and National Marine Sanctuaries. Admission free. Open Tuesday through Saturday, 9 a.m.-4 p.m. 308 Kamehameha Avenue, Suite 203; 808-933-8195; e-mail: jeffrey.kuwabara@noaa. gov; http://hawaiireef.noaa.gov.

Around the corner and a block up is **Memories of Hawaii-Big Island**, a new little piece of island history preserved in the old Ebesu Flower Shop on Keawe Street. Memorabilia from sports, plantation days, railroads and day-to-day life of times gone by. Admission: $6 adults, $5 seniors, $3 students. 301 Keawe Street; 808-961-0024; e-mail: mohbi@yahoo.com.

The **Naha Stone** is at the Hilo Public Library, three blocks uphill from the Hilo Bay waterfront. Look for the two large stones on the front lawn. The long horizontal one is called the Naha Stone, which, according to Hawaiian legend, was used to sever the umbilical cords of royal children and to test the claims of royal blood in newborn males. During a ceremony, those who remained silent were recognized as future mighty warriors, while those who cried out were said to lack courage. As a young man, Kamehameha I, not unlike young Arthur, allegedly raised and overturned the large stone, proving his great strength and indisputable courage. As king, Kamehameha went on to conquer and unite the Hawaiian Islands under one kingdom in 1810. The Naha Stone is estimated to weigh three and a half tons and was brought from the island of Kaua'i in a high chief's (apparently unsinkable) canoe. The smaller upright rock is called the **Pinao Stone**, and was supposedly brought from its place as the entrance pillar to an ancient Big Island temple, Pinao Heiau.

★ **Downtown Hilo Walking Tours** are scheduled for the third Saturday of each month at 9 a.m. Sites include **Kalakaua Park**, in the center of downtown Hilo, originally conceived as a civic center by King Kalakaua whose benevolent bronze statue watches the grounds. He holds a taro plant in one hand and a hula percussion instrument, the ipu in the other. Other nearby places of historical interest included in the walking tour are the Old Police Station (see below), Palace Theatre, Lyman Museum and others. Reservations can be made through Lyman Museum. The tours are free and begin at the museum. 276 Haili Street; 808-935-5021. Note: you can download the self-guided Downtown Hilo Walking Tour at www. downtownhilo.com/hilo/tour/guide.

East Hawai'i Cultural Center is located in downtown Hilo, opposite Kalakaua Park and the post office. The center is housed in the old police station, a historic building constructed in 1932 and placed on the National Register of Historic Buildings and Places. The center is dedicated to culture and the arts in East Hawai'i. Ongoing shows at the Mauka and Makai Galleries feature works of local and visiting artists in diverse media. Exhibits are free and open to the public. Community theater performances are sponsored by the center throughout the year as well as concerts, special events and other artistic endeavor such as classes in glassblowing, ukulele, oil and watercolor painting, stained glass and children's art. Open daily except Sunday, 10 a.m. to 4 p.m. 141 Kalakaua Street; 808-951-5711; www.ehcc.org.

★ **Wailoa River State Recreation Area** runs along the banks of Wailoa River (on a fearless site devastated by tsunami in 1946 and 1960). Parking is at the end of Pi'ilani Street and the visitor center access road of Pauahi Street. Peaceful, scenic lawns surround the Wailoa River and Waiakea Fish Pond, with lots of picnic tables and several covered pavilions. A good place for a pleasant picnic and after-lunch stroll over the arching bridges. The Big Island Vietnam Memorial, a memorial to tsunami victims and a permanent tsunami exhibit are on-site, along with a statue of Kamehameha the Great. The Wailoa Center features various free art exhibits, seasonal showings, and cultural displays by local artisans. Check the schedule at the center for current show. Center hours Monday, Tuesday, Thursday and Friday 8:30 a.m.-4:30 p.m., Wednesday noon-4:30 p.m., Saturday 9:30 a.m.-3 p.m., closed Sunday and holidays. 808-933-0416.

University of Hawai'i at Hilo and **Hawai'i Community College Campus** is located between Lanikaula and Kawili streets in Hilo. The university and community college, which share a common campus and have a combined enrollment of some 5,000, offer two- and four-year degree programs. The university utilizes its special geography and resources to offer programs of study in such unique fields as Hawaiian Studies, Pacific Islands Anthropology, Marine Science, Oceanography, Aquaculture, Vulcanology, Geothermal Energy, Astronomy and others. The community college specializes in the liberal arts, business education and vocational-technical trades. The serene campus is landscaped with many species of tropical trees and plants. Its theater hosts numerous public performances, concerts, shows and plays throughout the year and the Campus Center art gallery has ongoing displays. The campus annually hosts several Elderhostel senior citizen courses for U.S. mainland visitors as well as a broad range of summer session offerings. Visitors are welcome. For information, contact the Office of University Relations, 200 West Kawili Street, Hilo, HI 96720-4091 (both colleges at the same address); UH-Hilo 808-933-3567 or HCC Provost's Office 808-933-3611.

★ **Pana'ewa Rainforest Zoo** is one of Hilo's least known and most delightful free attractions. It is the only natural tropical rainforest zoo in the United States. The small facility is operated by the County of Hawai'i and features exotic rainforest species in natural environment enclosures. Visit a celebrity white tiger named Namasté, African pygmy hippopotamus, water buffalo, rainforest monkeys, a tapir, various jungle parrots, and endangered Hawaiian birds like the nene goose, Hawaiian i'o (hawk), pu'eo (owl) and Hawaiian stilt. The zoo is a pleasant walk through natural Hawaiian rainforest with numerous flowering trees and shrubs. Colorful, vociferous peacocks strut openly. The zoo is adjacent to the Pana'ewa Equestrian Center. Open daily 9 a.m. to 4 p.m. except for Christmas and New Year's Day. Petting zoo every Saturday 1:30-2:30 p.m. Located a couple of miles south of Hilo just off the Volcano Highway 11 on Mamaki Street; 808-959-7224; www.hilozoo.com.

★ **Nani Mau Gardens** is just three miles south of town off Volcano Highway. You can't miss the turn off the highway—just look for beautiful floral beds and displays at Makalika Street. From the highway, it's a half-mile to the gardens, where you find 20 acres of artistically landscaped tropical flowers, trees and plants. Nani Mau offers a spectacular orchid garden, rare palms and tropical fruit orchards, ginger and anthurium gardens, and much more. There is an intriguing Japanese-style bell tower crafted from 20,000 boards without a single nail or screw. The gift shop offers handcrafted items and souvenirs and features the unique, fanciful artworks of Kristie Fujiyama (www.ieineverybody.com). Buffet lunch is served in the Garden Court restaurant (only $11), and you can pamper yourself at the new Nani Mau Salon & Spa. An excellent site for garden weddings, with indoor and outdoor facilities for over 300 guests and full-service professional planners. Open daily 9 a.m. to 4:30 p.m. Adults $10 and children 4 to 10 $5. Self-guided tours, narrated tram tours and lunch packages are available, as are group rates and educational school tours. 421 Makalika Street, Hilo; 808-959-3500; www.nanimau.com.

Hilo can be a great place to shop. It has the island's only mall, **Prince Kuhio Plaza**, with your favorite mainland-style brand-name stores like Sears, Macy's, Suncoast Video, Spencer Gifts and Radio Shack, along with surf shops, men's and women's aloha apparel, Hawaiian craft booths, local-style crackseed and penny candy stores and multiplex cinemas (www.princekuhioplaza.com). Across the  street is **Waiakea Center**, with large anchor stores like Ross, Office Max, Wal-Mart (Hilo's favorite store), Hilo Hattie (a must-see), and Borders Books & Music, along with one of the Big Island's best food courts. For less-serious but more engaging shopping, wander around the meandering streets of the old downtown area to discover unassuming little arts-and-crafts shops, eclectic galleries and antique boutiques begging to be explored.

Sugawara Lauhala & Gift Shop is the place to visit if you are looking for authentic Hawaiian handicraft items. Look for genuine locally made Hawaiian *lauhala* woven slippers, hats, baskets, handbags, mats and related goods. 59 Kalakaua Street; 808-935-8071. **Sig Zane Designs** carries a variety of beautiful, locally designed and Hawaiian-motif aloha wear for men and women. And do check out the craft village at **Hilo Farmers' Market** on Saturday. 122 Kamehameha Avenue; 808-935-7077.

★ **Hilo Hattie's** is the original aloha-wear factory. A wonderfully tourist-geared all-in-one-store, Hilo Hattie's features Hawaiian shirts, shorts, dresses and muumuus plus other gift items like jewelry, macadamia nuts, chocolates, souvenirs, books and videos, toys and more. Free samples of Kona coffee, tropical juice, a shell lei and people who go out of their way to make you feel welcome. This is really a must-stop. Open daily 8:30 a.m. to 6 p.m. 111 East Puainako in the Prince Kuhio Plaza; 808-961-3077; www.hilohattie.com.

Other than these, take time to explore Hilo's smorgasbord of multi-cultural shopping options, and discover its many surprises and treasures. Don't miss **Basically Books** for maps, globes and books on everything you ever wanted to know about Hawai'i, from the stars above the mountains to the secrets under the sea. (See "Browsing for Books" in this chapter for more information.) 160 Kamehameha Avenue; www.basicallybooks.com. Check out the beautiful little stores in the restored **S. Hata Building**, with its handsome bell tower out front, and drop by **Two Ladies Kitchen** for a fresh strawberry mochi. 274 Kilauea Avenue; 800-903-6277.

Puna District

The Puna District of Hilo town is a wide open area of lava lands, rugged coasts, and rainforest slopes leading up to Hawai'i Volcanoes National Park, which straddles the Puna–Ka'u border. Within Puna are the country towns of Kea'au, Kurtistown, Mountain View, Pahoa, Volcano and other growing residential subdivisions. The district is noted for orchid, anthurium, papaya, banana, macadamia nut, and other tropical farm products. The combination of adequate rainfall and warm sunny conditions make it ideal for cultivating tropical fruits and flowers. Puna has experienced a lot of growth in recent years. A new highway bypass, agricultural development, construction of a Kamehameha Schools satellite campus and other additions have made what was once a sleepy rural area for those seeking an alternative lifestyle into a busier, more prosperous community. If you haven't visited for a while, you're going to be surprised.

About one-third of Hawai'i Volcanoes National Park is located within the Puna District (and two-thirds in the Ka'u District). Since 1983, Puna, in the "east rift zone," has been the site of ongoing volcanic eruptions and spectacular lava flows from Kilauea Volcano's vents, Pu'u O'o and Kupaianaha. The first three years of the eruption were episodic outbreaks of dramatic lava fountaining and bursts from Pu'u O'o vent, which gradually formed a cinder cone several hundred feet high. More recent eruptive activity comes from the large lava pond and vent called Kupaianaha, located at the 2,200-foot elevation. Both vents are in remote, inaccessible areas and the best view of eruption activity is from a helicopter. (See "Air Tours" in Chapter

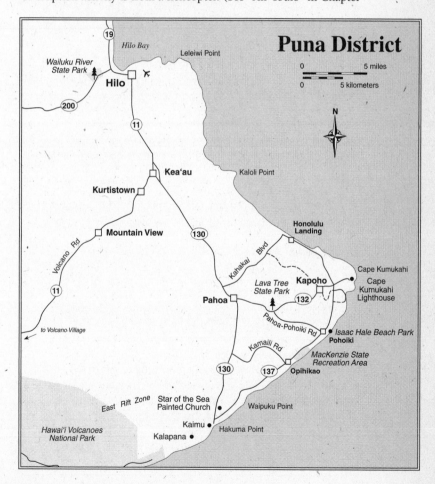

Puna District

6 for information; there's also more information about Volcanoes National Park later in the chapter.)

This almost continuous volcanic eruption is unprecedented in modern history. For more than 20 years the volcano has steadily erupted, sending lava flows rolling downslope toward the sea, in the process causing considerable damage to man-made structures as well as thousands of acres of Hawaiian forests. The entire village and residential areas of Kalapana on the island's southeast coast have been totally destroyed by lava, forcing residents to evacuate their homes and relocate elsewhere. Altogether, almost 200 homes and 25 square miles of land have been covered by lava up to 70 feet deep. However, the destructive force of the volcano is also creative, adding hundreds of acres of new land to the Big Island coastline since 1983. As the molten lava enters the sea it explodes and shatters into fine pumice and cinders, which are carried by the surf along the coast. This volcanic residue accumulates in such great quantities that it creates new black-sand beaches along this rocky shore.

Highway 130, which passed through the Kalapana area and continued around the island, ends here. It is no longer possible to drive through Kalapana and on out the coast to the south entrance of

FLOWER FARMS

For tropical flower aficionados, there are numerous orchid and anthurium farms and nurseries throughout the Puna District, most of which welcome visitors. On the main Highway 11, at the 22.5-mile marker in the Glenwood area, is the award-winning ★ Akatsuka Orchid Gardens (808-967-8234), one of the largest and most notable orchid farms in Hawai'i with many varieties of orchids on display and for sale. Yamamoto Dendrobiums Hawai'i (808-968-6955), Mountain View Orchids (808-968-6644), Hawaii Orchids (808-966-7712), Hilo Orchid Farm (808-968-8801), Hata Farm (808-966-9240) and Bergstrom Orchids (808-982-6047) are but a few of the orchid and anthurium farms in the Kea'au–Mountain View area that welcome visitors. Or visit the Mauna Kea Daylily Garden for something wonderfully different (808-966-6693). In the Pahoa–Puna area, try Hawaiian Greenhouse Inc. (808-965-8351), Puna Flowers & Foliage (808-965-8444), or Puna Ohana Flowers (808-965-8456). In Hilo, visit Orchids of Hawaii on Kilauea Avenue (800-323-1449), and don't miss the weekly Hilo Farmers Market at Kamehameha Avenue and Mamo Street. In addition, as you drive along be on the lookout for farm and nursery signs welcoming visitors to stroll the gardens.

Hawai'i Volcanoes National Park. The black-sand beaches, for which the area was famous, have been covered with lava and no longer exist. Visitors can travel Highway 130, the Chain of Craters Road, from inside Volcanoes National Park, but it dead-ends now just west of the Kalapana area.

In the past, the biggest attraction in Puna was the volcanic activity. However, National Park rangers now operate a mobile visitors center van at the end of the road. The rangers provide maps and information on hiking trails to the current eruption site and lava flows. Check first to be sure conditions are safe for hiking the area, as the east rift zone changes constantly.

To reach the other side of the lava flows, you have to backtrack through Pahoa to the main entrance of Hawai'i Volcanoes National Park. Then follow Highway 130, Chain of Craters Road, to the Kamoamoa area (minimum two-hour drive from Kalapana). If the eruption is still current, you will likely see a vast steam plume rising from the water, glowing cracks in the palisades, and perhaps red lava pouring over the *pali*. There may be monitored trails of varying lengths leading to viewing sites.

Caution: Conditions changes frequently. Check with the visitors center at the park entry first. Listen to and take their advice. There are no restrooms, water, phones or facilities of any kind along the coast and no shade. Volcanic fumes can present health dangers to children, pregnant women, or those with cardiac or respiratory difficulties. If you do any hiking, prepare for a long, hot walk in the sun with adequate water, a hat, sunscreen and good-quality covered shoes for the sharp jagged lava rock trails.

★ **Star of the Sea Painted Church** is one of the Kalapana area's more famous attractions. The historic church was rescued from lava flow destruction in 1990 and moved to a new location alongside Highway 130 just above the Kalapana area. This wooden frame structure dates from the early 1900s and was built by an early Belgian Catholic missionary priest who also did the intricate paintings of religious scenes on the walls and ceiling. It is now a community center.

Highway 132 (Kapoho Road) passes through papaya and orchid fields to the site of the former **Kapoho Village**, which was completely covered by a fiery lava flow in 1960. A historic plaque marks the site. At the end of Kapoho Road you can drive right up to the **Cape Kumukahi Lighthouse**, which, according to local lore, was spared by Madame Pele to protect Hawaiian fishermen at sea. The lava flowed around and past the lighthouse grounds but did not touch the lighthouse itself.

Text continued on page 126.

SHOPPING FOR ART AND HANDICRAFTS

You can bring part of your Big Island vacation home to enjoy year-round, with a piece of expertly crafted work by very talented local artisans in paint, textiles, wood, glass, jewelry and creative mixed media. For detailed current exhibit information, check the bi-weekly newspaper *Hawai'i Island Journal's* "Island Art" section. Below are just a very few suggestions.

North and South Kona Districts

Most Kailua-Kona galleries will be open 7 days, while most Hololualoa and Kainaliu galleries are closed Sunday.

Kailua-Kona

    Hulihe'e Palace Gift Shop 75-5718 Ali'i Drive; 808-329-6558.

    ★ **Kailua Village Artists Galleries Inc.** Artists' co-op with a broad range of artworks, handicrafts and gift items. 75-5660 Palani Road, King Kamehameha's Kona Beach Hotel, 808-329-6653; also in the Keauhou Beach Hotel, 78-6740 Ali'i Drive, Keauhou-Kona, 808-324-7060; www.konaart.com.

    Wyland Galleries Famous paintings of whales, dolphins and other sealife that decorate office interiors and gigantic exterior walls throughout Hawai'i. Waterfront Row, 75-5770 Ali'i Drive; 808-334-0037; www.wyland.com.

Holualoa town

    ★ **Holualoa Ukulele Gallery** in the old post office building; 808-324-1688.

    Ululani Gallery (featuring the art of Herb Kane); 808-322-7373; www.ululani.com.

    Whole in the Wall Gallery 75-5897 Mamalahoa Highway; 808-322-9959.

Captain Cook

    ★ **Big Island Art Farm** Gallery and gift shop including an "affordable art" section. Closed Sunday. Next to Manago Hotel on Highway 11; 808-323-3490.

Kainaliu Town

    Blue Ginger Gallery Mamalahoa Highway; 808-322-3898.

    Eternal Wave Gallery 79-7407 Mamalahoa Highway; 808-322-3203.

    Lavender Moon Mamalahoa Highway; 808-324-7708.

South Kohala District

Most of these galleries are open daily.

    ★ **Dolphin Galleries** A fun place featuring whimsical art such as Dr. Seuss prints, bronze froggie sculptures and dramatic glass waves. The Kings' Shops, Waikoloa; 808-886-5000.

    ★ **Harbor Gallery** Bright tropical landscapes, exquisite wood carvings and other works of island art. Kawaihae Shopping

Center, just north of Kohala Coast resorts; 800-865-0824; 808-882-1510; www.harborgallery.biz.

Waimea

★ **Dan DeLuz Woods Inc.** Elegant, hand-carved bowls, boxes and other beautiful things by master woodworker Dan DeLuz. Artist's workshop in back. 64-1013 Mamalahoa Highway; 808-885-5856.

★ **Gallery of Great Things** Parker Square shopping center, Highway 19; 808-885-7706.

Waimea Arts Council Full season of local artist showings and sales, all media. Friendly conversation included for free. 808-887-1052.

North Kohala District

Ackerman Galleries Closed Sunday. Kapa'au town; 808-889-5837.

Nanbu Gallery 54-3885A Akoni Pule Highway, Kapa'au; 808-889-0997.

★ **Sue Swerdlow Art Gallery** 54-3862 Akoni Pule Highway, Kapa'au town; 808-889-0002.

Without Boundaries/Sushi Rock 55-3435 Akoni Pule Highway, Hawi; 808-889-5900.

Hamakua Coast

Hamakua Artisan Guild Ask about their annual studio tour. 808-775-7715; www.hamakuaartists.com.

Honomu Plantation Gallery Honomu Village; 808-963-5022.

Waipi'o Valley Artworks Kukuihaele; 808-775-0958.

Woodshop Gallery & Cafe Honomu; 808-963-6363.

Hilo

Art in the Iron Works Open Tuesday through Saturday 10 a.m.-4 p.m. 1266 Kamehameha Avenue; 808-935-2300.

Cunningham Gallery Closed Sunday. 794 Pi'ilani Street; 808-935-7223.

Dreams of Paradise South Hata Building, 308 Kamehameha Avenue; 808-935-5670.

Ohana Gallery O Hawaii 46 Waianuenue Avenue; 808-935-8494.

Volcano

★ **Volcano Art Center** 808-967-7511; e-mail: gallery@volcanoartcenter.org; www.volcanoartcenter.org.

Pahoa

Pahoa Art Center 15-2771 Pahoa Village Road; 808-965-8760.

Also on Kapoho Road is ★ **Lava Tree State Park**, where hollow lava impressions of tree stumps are visible. The lava flowed around the living trees and baked them, leaving a hollow lava shell. Tall, ancient trees in the *kipuka* (area untouched by lava) seem to talk to each other as the wind rustles their high canopy. A multitude of birds make their home in the forest, including several protected Hawaiian species.

The end of Kapoho Road near the Cape Kumukahi Lighthouse intersects with Highway 137, known as the Opihikao Road, narrow and winding along the coast south toward Kalapana. There are large orchards of papaya and macadamia nut trees in the area as well as some magnificent views of rugged coastline.

The 32-mile drive from Hilo to Volcano Village near Hawai'i Volcanoes National Park is all uphill, from sea level in Hilo to 4,000 feet at Volcano. Along the way, you pass through the abandoned cane fields of the former Puna Sugar Company and its old mill near **Kea'au**. Further on upslope, the cane fields give way to groves of eucalyptus trees and vegetation of the tropical rainforest. Fields of wild ginger, orchids and other exotic plants fill the roadsides and meadows of the scattered country homesites and small ranches of the area. Finally, stands of rugged and hearty *ohia* trees with their deep red *lehua* blossoms become apparent nearer the Volcano area.

The small towns and villages of the Puna District offer less in the way of shopping opportunities than Hilo, but are still well worth the time to explore. In fact the growing towns of Kea'au and Pahoa have begun reinventing themselves as education communities since welcoming Kamehameha Schools Campus in 2001. In Pahoa Village, enjoy wandering through shops and boutiques, multi-ethnic eateries and colorful galleries. Stop by the restored **Akebono Theater** (Hawaii's oldest theater), see the historic, still-operating **Village Inn** built in 1910, a large new health food store, tobacco and bookshop and others. Godmother's restaurant is noted for good Italian food and music.

In Kurtistown, the tiny trees crafted to perfection will amaze you at the **Fuku-Bonsai Cultural Center & Hawaii State Bonsai Repository** on Olaa Road. Open 8 a.m. to 4 p.m. Monday through Saturday; admission by donation. Workshops, retail shop, free newsletter and extensive online plant store. 808-982-9880; www.fukubonsai.com.

A few miles farther down the road, stop in Mountain View at **Mountain View Bakery** (808-968-6353) for something different, a taste of their famous "stone cookies," perfectly made for coffee-dunking. In the Glenwood area at the 20-mile marker is **Hirano Store** (808-968-6522), where you can buy cold drinks, sandwiches, snacks, gas and general store supplies.

★ **Volcano Village** is along the old Volcano Highway, which is just a mile from the national park entrance. In the village there are several shops and eateries such as the Volcano Store (the "upper store") and Kilauea General Store (the "lower store"), Lava Rock Café and Thai Thai, plus a great Farmer's Market on Sunday, 8 to 10 a.m. A mile and a half past the National Park entrance, on the Ka'u side, turn onto Pi'i Mauna Drive to the Volcano Country Club Golf Course and drive to the ★ **Volcano Vineyards and Winery** (808-967-7772), a must-stop for samples (and cases to ship home) of the award-winning Symphony Dry and Symphony Mele, Volcano Red and Blush, Hawaiian Guava Wine and a remarkable Macadamia Nut Honey Wine. Visit the shop for winery souvenirs, wine accessories, logo products and Hawaii art. www.volcanowinery.com.

Hawai'i Volcanoes National Park

★ **Hawai'i Volcanoes National Park** is the star of the show, as far as Big Island tourist attractions. Where else in the world can you safely get close to an active volcano? On any given day, thousands of visitors pass through the park gates to experience what must be one of the last great wonders of the natural world. In 1982, the United Nations Educational, Scientific and Cultural Organization (UNESCO) declared the Park a World Heritage Site for its natural, historical and cultural importance, having "universal value" for all people. If you've come this far, please don't leave without a visit to Madame Pele's home.

The park is full of otherworldly wonders. There's a "drive-in" steam vent to peer into, a drizzly lava tube cave to walk through, a museum to explore and make your own earthquake, trails to hike past barren wasteland or ancient forests. Then, drive (check with rangers for current conditions) down the long road back to the sunny ocean coastline towards the current eruption site. A towering plume of steam marks the spot where red lava enters the sea. If you're prepared to hike, you can get closer.

In addition to explore-it-yourself natural phenomena, the park offers a regular schedule of cultural and art programs year-round. Events such as the "After Dark in the Park" natural history lectures, *Hula Kahiko* (ancient hula) performance and other special happenings add depth even to a family visit.

For a wealth of fascinating advance information (and great science report material) visit their website. The site is excellent and well-organized, with multiple links to other informative pages. Printed brochures, which are also excellent, should be requested by sending a postcard with your name, address and area of interest to: P.O. Box 52, Hawai'i Volcanoes National Park, Volcano, HI 96718; 808-985-6000; www.nps.gov/havo. (Teachers, look for the "Traveling Trunk" option under Education Programs.)

Kids 5 to 12 can join the Junior Ranger Program, and a new kid-flavored website offers a "virtual field trip" (not affiliated with the Park). Check out www.efieldtrips.org/volcanoes.

Entry fees are $10 per car for a 7-day pass; $20 for a yearly pass; $5 for visitors on bicycle, moped, mule or their own two feet. The 12-month Golden Eagle Passport, Golden Access Passport and Golden Age Passport are valid here. The park is open 24 hours a day year-round.

The recently renovated ★ **Kilauea Visitor Center** is located a mile west of Volcano Village just inside the main entrance. Here visitors will find a natural history museum, current eruption information, and a free 20-minute movie shown on the hour from 9 a.m. to 4 p.m. daily. Park rangers are on duty to answer your questions and give instructions on viewing the eruption site, which you should listen to. Guided walks are offered daily. Open 7:45 a.m. to 5 p.m. daily.

The ★ **Thomas A. Jaggar Museum** is 3 miles inside the park, perched on the very edge of Halema'uma'u Crater. The museum displays lava samples, seismic equipment showing islandwide mini-earthquakes (including make-your-own) and Hawaiian volcano lore. Open daily 8:30 a.m. to 5 p.m. 808-985-6049.

The ★ **Volcano Art Center**, located adjacent to the visitors center, occupies the original Big Island tourist lodging, Volcano House, constructed in 1877 to replace a thatched-roof hut that had accommodated visitors for 31 years. The art center, established in 1977, provides historic information on the park as well as works produced by local potters, painters, woodcarvers and other creative artisans for sale or free appreciation. The center also produces art shows, performances, and art, writing and photography workshops year-round. Some of the programs allow visitors and residents a chance to interact with artists who receive their inspiration from the volcano. Occasionally, a resource artist will lead a walk through some spectacular area of the park to describe and demonstrate the use of natural materials and/or atmosphere of the park environment in creating artwork. The walks focus on protecting and enhancing the fragile national park environment. Open 9 a.m. to 5 p.m. P.O. Box 104, Hawai'i Volcanoes National Park, HI 96718; 808-967-8222; www.volcanoartcenter.org.

The gigantic and still-steaming fire pit **Halema'uma'u**, a 3,000-foot diameter, 1,300-foot-deep lava vent, lies on the floor of **Kilauea**

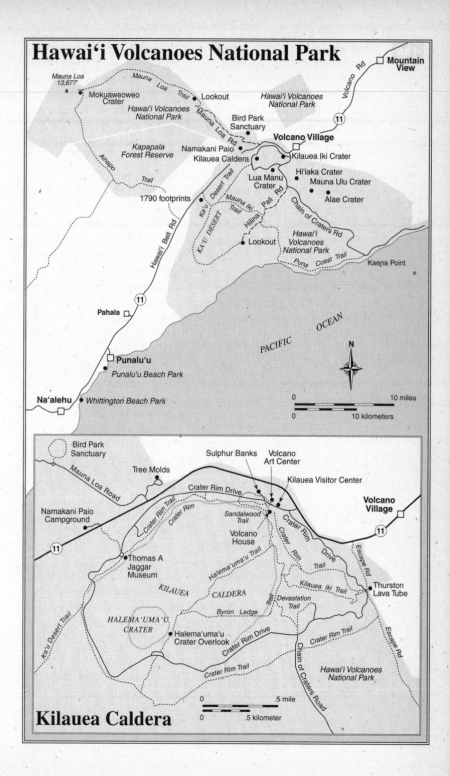

Hawai'i Volcanoes National Park

Mauna Loa
13,677'

Mokuaweoweo
Crater

Mauna Loa Trail

Lookout

Hawai'i Volcanoes
National Park

Hawai'i Volcanoes
National Park

Mauna Loa Rd

Bird Park
Sanctuary

Volcano Rd

Mountain
View

11

Volcano Village

Kapapala
Forest Reserve

Namakani Paio

Kilauea Caldera

Kilauea Iki Crater

Ainapo

Trail

Lua Manu
Crater

Hi'iaka Crater

Mauna Ulu Crater

Alae Crater

1790 footprints

Mauna Iki
Trail

Ka'u Desert Trail

Pali Rd

Chain of Craters Rd

Hawai'i Belt Rd.

Hilina

Hawai'i
Volcanoes
National Park

Ka'u DESERT

Lookout

Puna Coast Trail

Kaena Point

11

Pahala

PACIFIC   OCEAN

N

Punalu'u

Punalu'u Beach Park

Na'alehu   Whittington Beach Park

0   10 miles

0   10 kilometers

Bird Park
Sanctuary

Tree Molds

Sulphur Banks

Volcano
Art Center

Mauna Loa Road

Crater Rim Drive

Kilauea Visitor Center

Namakani Paio
Campground

Crater Rim Trail

Crater Rim

Sandalwood
Trail

Volcano House

Volcano
Village

11

Crater Rim

11

Thomas A
Jaggar
Museum

Halema'uma'u Trail

Escape Rd

KILAUEA   CALDERA

Crater Rim

Drive

Trail

Kilauea Iki Trail

Thurston
Lava Tube

Ka'u Desert Trail

HALEMA'UMA'U
CRATER

Byron Ledge

Devastation
Trail

Halema'uma'u
Crater Overlook

Crater Rim Drive

Crater Rim Trail

Chain of Craters Road

Escape Rd

Crater Rim Trail

Hawai'i Volcanoes
National Park

0   .5 mile

0   .5 kilometer

Kilauea Caldera

Caldera. Kilauea Iki is a huge cinder cone vent that last erupted in 1959. Both of these vents are easily viewed from **Crater Rim Drive** and can be reached on foot by easy hiking trails. There are vast fields of lava, once-molten rivers of liquid rock spewed out from the earth's center. Two types of lava emerge from Hawai'i's volcanoes: *pahoehoe*, with its black and relatively smooth surface, and *'a'a*, which solidifies in a jumble of small clinker-like rocks with sharp edges and rough surfaces.

Kilauea is the legendary home of the Hawaiian fire goddess *Pele 'ai-honua* ("Pele who eats the land"), who is both creator and destroyer. Native Hawaiians have long had a healthy respect for her, and even today ceremonial offerings are cast into Halema'uma'u while chants, songs and dances are performed in her honor. It is said that Pele has a fondness for gin. During the final days of Kalapana, before lava covered what was left of the quiet, coastal community, gin bottles, lei and other gifts lined the edge of the flow.

One of the outstanding features of Hawai'i Volcanoes National Park is its fine system of hiking trails. Beginning at various points along

Park regulations are simple and enforced for your safety and the protection of this fragile, valuable natural area. Backcountry permits are required for overnight stays. They are available at the visitors center at no charge. Climbing on or removing rocks from any archaeological feature is prohibited. No firearms are permitted. Wildfires are a serious threat to the park, so no fires are permitted except in designated pavilion areas. Parking is restricted to parking lots only. Bicycles are only allowed on paved roads and some designated park trails. Pets must be leashed at all times and are only permitted on primary roads and developed sites. Do not feed or disturb the wildlife or exceed the posted speed limit.

What about the rocks? Don't take them with you. Leave them in the park. We remember years ago listening to a local man reassure a curious tourist that the rock thing was an old wives' tale. The hapless *malihini* (stranger) pocketed the stone and walked away, and the local guy laughed like crazy. The park receives hundreds of lava rocks in the mail every year, returned by unfortunate visitors who took them home and experienced extremely hard luck. It may be a coincidence, superstition or something else we don't understand, but it doesn't matter to us. Be respectful; leave the rocks on the island. There are plenty of nice souvenirs in the shops. (For more on this interesting phenomenon, read *Powerstones: Letters to a Goddess* by Linda Ching.)

the Crater Rim Drive and Chain of Craters Road, hikers can choose from routes that offer outstanding close-up views of volcanic craters, steaming lava vents and colorful sulfur banks, to sweeping vistas of Kilauea's lava flows and sloping flanks, and a cool pastoral trail leading through a rare bird sanctuary. For your own safety, use common-sense precautions and listen to ranger advisements. Stay on the trails.

Along other trails of the park, hikers may see some rare and endangered flora and fauna. Among these are the sacred *ohelo* berry, held in high regard as an offering of appeasement to Madame Pele, or the *pukiawe*, used in making leis, and the rare sandalwood tree. Birds likely to be seen are the Hawaiian honeycreeper and the wren-like *'elepaio* that inhabit the **Bird Park Sanctuary**. Visible along some trails are petroglyphs, ancient Hawaiian rock carvings.

Devastation Trail, a raised boardwalk path located behind the cinder cone of Kilauea Iki, winds through the vast fields of lava cinders and pumice that buried and burned off most of the living vegetation. All that is left is a myriad of picturesque tree stumps and stark cinder landscape. ★ **Thurston Lava Tube Trail** is located just off the Crater Rim Drive, two miles from the visitors center. Here one can walk through a giant lava tube much like a cave. The short trail leading to it passes through a pleasantly cool fern forest. Please see "Hiking" in Chapter 6 for more details on these and other trails.

★ **Volcano House** (808-967-7321) is the national park's best lodging. The first Volcano House, now in existence across three different centuries, was built in 1846 as an overnight waystation for visitors who rode on horseback all the way from Hilo to see the splendors of the volcano. It's had a number of distinguished guests down through the years including Mark Twain, Franklin D. Roosevelt and many other celebrities. The original historic structure now houses the Volcano Art Center near the main entrance. (See Chapter 3 for more information on Volcano area accommodations.)

Ka'u District

The southern Ka'u District is the largest geographic district on the Big Island (so large the entire island of O'ahu could fit inside); it's also one of the most remote and least populated. It contains about one-fifth of the island's land, 800-plus square miles, including most of the massive Mauna Loa (13,680 foot) and the western two-thirds of Hawai'i Volcanoes National Park. Ka Lae, South Point, on this coast of the Big Island is the southernmost point in the United States. The district is mostly dry lava desert, windblown grasslands and rugged rocky coastline. Inland, there are cattle pastures and macadamia nut orchards. Ka'u is serviced by the main around-the-island road, Highway 11, which connects it to Volcano and Hilo to the east and Kona to the west. Sparsely populated, Ka'u has only three small towns: Pahala, Na'alehu and Waiohinu.

★ **Hawai'i Volcanoes National Park** is the Ka'u District's biggest attraction. The bulk of the park lies within the district's boundaries (with a small portion in the Puna District to the east). For visitors, the national park headquarters, visitors center, volcano observatory, campgrounds, Volcano House inn, and related sites are centrally located around Kilauea Caldera in the Ka'u District near Volcano Village (see Hawai'i Volcanoes National Park on page 127).

From Hilo drive 35 miles on Highway 11 through the Puna District described in the previous section. From Kailua-Kona travel 96 miles via Highway 11 around the South Point area, a rather long drive through desolate stretches of open lava fields, dry scrub land, and the Ka'u Desert. The road has some short stretches in the South Kona area where it is winding and narrow, but otherwise is excellent. If you have a rental car you should plan at least a day trip to Volcano; an overnight visit is even better.

Allow a minimum of two and a half hours for the drive from Kailua-Kona to the national park, and it's best to get an early start. The drive up to the park passes through South Kona's coffee farms, fruit orchards and flower farm country, gradually turning away from the coast and heading further inland as it turns around Mauna Loa's southernmost slopes. The land here, some eight to ten miles inland from the coast and at 2,000-foot elevation, is damp and cool, a contrast to the drier resort areas of Kona and the lands traversed along the way. The terrain is marked by lush vegetation and stands of tropical forest. Ranch grazing lands appear intermittently along with macadamia nut orchards in an otherwise sparsely populated area.

Manuka State Wayside is along this route. This is a lovely and well-maintained arboretum with a variety of dry upland forest plants and trees. Picnic tables and restrooms are provided and there is a nature trail as well.

Ka Lae, South Point, is reached via South Point Road, which branches off from Highway 11 at the extreme southern tip of the Ka'u District. The narrow road continues 12 miles to the South Point Peninsula, where it terminates. It passes by the **Kamao'a Wind Farm**, a wind-powered electricity-generation facility utilizing huge wind turbines. This stark, windswept, hot, dry and grassy area is the southernmost point geographically in the United States. The first Hawaiians are believed to have landed here and settled the area around 400 A.D. There are old canoe mooring holes and the ruins of a fishermen's *heiau*. Fishermen still use South Point to moor their boats but they must hoist them up and down the high cliffs to the relatively calm waters below. The foundations of an old World War II military camp are also found in the area.

Green Sand Beach, composed of green olivine crystals giving it an "Emerald City" hue, is located five miles east of South Point. Mahana Bay, site of the beach, is accessible only by hiking. The coastal road and trail is extremely rough and rugged over rocky terrain. From the end of the road where a boat launch ramp and a parking area are located, it's a two-mile hike to the beach at the bottom of a steep cliff. The trail down can be hazardous, and there are no facilities of any kind at the beach. The bay is not safe for swimming due to rough surf and strong currents. It is a beautiful and unique sight, but not an easy one to reach (and harder to leave). Hiking permits to Green Sand Beach are required because you must cross private lands under control of the Department of Hawaiian Home Lands. There is no charge for the permit, which can be faxed to your hotel or condominium. Varying procedures may cause padlocks to appear on the gates, but these are usually circumventable. Vehicles are presently restricted from using the coast road. For permit infor-

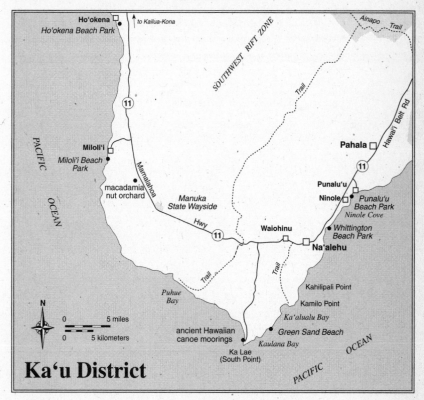

Ka'u District

mation, contact: Department of Hawaiian Home Lands, 160 Baker Avenue, Hilo, HI 96720; 808-974-4250.

Naʻalehu proudly proclaims itself to be "the southernmost town in the USA" and has a large sign stating the fact alongside the town shopping center. At the shopping center, located right on the highway mid-town, there is a coffee shop, grocery store, and snack shop for refreshments. Take time to visit the restored Naʻalehu Theater, built by Hutchinson Sugar Co. in 1940, now a museum and digital media center.

Punaluʻu Bakeshop & Visitor Center, across the road from the shopping center, is home to one of Hawaiʻi's favorite foods. This is a bakery and snack shop that bakes fresh thousands of sweet "Portuguese-style" loaves every week, plus ice cream, cookies, *anpans, malasadas* and other bakery treats. Sweetbread is now available in varieties like taro, mac nut, guava, mango and "Kalakoa," a rainbow blend of several flavors. The Visitor Center offers a picnic area, restrooms, a café, gift shop, free sweetbread samples and the family-friendly atmosphere of its four-acre tropical estate. Open daily except Christmas and New Year's Day 10 a.m. to 5 p.m.; 866-366-3501, 808-929-7343; www.punaluubakeshop.com.

The **Mark Twain Monkeypod Tree** is in the neighboring town of **Waiohinu**. It was planted by the famous author during his 1866 visit to this area. The original tree toppled in a storm several years ago but the roots have sprouted new saplings and the tree lives, sort of like Twain's tall tales. Other American authors of the era, Jack London and Robert Louis Stevenson, enjoyed exotic visits to the Kaʻu District.

The region is also home to **Kapapala Ranch**, a 29,000-acre working cattle operation on the slopes of Mauna Loa. The ranch offers visitors a *paniolo*-style experience, with private guest cottages, horseback riding and ranch activities, plus a "Summer Camp with Donkeys" for kids 7 to 12, for $250 including meals. (Kids must be able to sleep overnight.) 808-968-6585; www.kapapala.com. Passing through these very small Hawaiian country towns will give you a sense of having stepped back into an earlier time, where the fast-paced modern world hasn't quite made inroads yet.

Punaluʻu is about eight miles further on toward the national park. This is the location of **Punaluʻu Beach Park** and Seamountain Golf Course. At Punaluʻu Beach Park, make time to stop and admire one of Hawaii's most dazzling black-sand beaches, a dramatic backdrop for sunbathing sea turtles who make their home in these remote waters. (The turtles are a federally-protected species and must not be touched or disturbed in any way.)

Pahala is five miles further on from here. The Ka'u Sugar Mill just off the main center of town was the last operating mill on the Big Island until it too closed in 1996. Where vast green fields of sugar cane once formed a beautiful background along Highway 11, macadamia nuts and other crops are planted, along with high hopes for a brighter future as a more diversified agriculture center. Pahala Village offers a large public swimming pool, tennis courts, and nearby activities such as horseback riding, hula and ukulele lessons, Hawaiian quiltmaking, yoga and massage. The restored bank building on Maile Street is now **Pahala Plantation Store**, an old-fashioned venue for Hawaiian crafts, 100-percent Ka'u Coffee and local produce. Nearby, explore **Plantation House Antiques** for treasures from another age. An austere meditation cloister lies up *mauka* in the **Wood Valley Temple and Retreat Center**, established in 1974 in the old Nicheren Shu Japanese church. Wood Valley hosted the Dalai Lama and thousands of devotees in 1980 and 1994. In 2003, the Hawai'i Volcanoes National Park and Nature Conservancy completed purchase of 117,000 acres here to enlarge the park and plan for conservation use of the land.

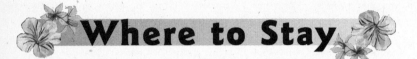

CHAPTER 3

Where to Stay

The Big Island has a wide range of choices for all kinds of vacationers and every travel budget—from a bare-bones camper cabin in the mountains to a $7,000-a-night private beachside suite with butler. As you think about what your family's priorities are and how much you have to spend on them, where to stay will start coming into focus.

Kailua-Kona (just "Kona" locally) is a bustling, active tourist center, perfect for people who like to go places and do things; it's home to most of the island's more energetic, commercial activities. And, since most of Kona's visitors are on the go, it's the perfect setting for condominium vacation rentals. There are only a handful of actual hotels between Kailua-Kona town and five miles down Ali'i Drive in the fast-growing Keauhou area. Although most of Kailua-Kona's accommodations are set along the coastline close to the ocean, few have actual sandy beaches on-site. However, a number of smaller public beaches are close by, and the views from the rugged, rocky shoreline are spectacular from almost anywhere in town.

The Kohala Coast in the South Kohala District is a 30-mile stretch of black lava and dry, *kiawe*-studded hills, from Kawaihae Harbor to Kaupulehu, just north of Kona International Airport. It is dominated by four major resort properties containing luxury hotels, condos and vacation residences, golf, tennis, restaurants and a wide variety of shops and recreation activities. This is the "high-class neighborhood" on the island, and the resorts are excellent and expensive.

Condominium properties, too, are excellent here, with access to the fine facilities of the resorts. Just like in Kona, the condo buildings consist of individually owned vacation rental units, which are handled by various agents on behalf of their owners. For reservations at a particular property, contact one of the agents listed under the property name; they can describe their units at various properties in the Kohala Coast and other island areas. South Kohala's accommodations are easy to distinguish.

Moving away from the ocean decreases the price and increases the range of lodgings. Waimea/Kamuela has a growing network of good-quality B&Bs offering unique settings and a more personal look at the island. Waikoloa Village, six miles up *mauka* from the Waikoloa Beach Resort, has a variety of vacation condo rentals only a few minutes' drive from the Kohala Coast resorts. Accommodations are limited in the North Kohala District, but there's a selection of unique properties in this quiet, rural area.

Particularly for hikers, campers and off-road wanderers, the Hamakua Coast can deliver some wonderfully quiet, naturally peaceful vacation experiences and memories. There is a variety of good B&Bs in unique locations, from restored plantation houses to lofts in the trees.

Most of Hilo's hotels are located along Banyan Drive on the Waiakea Peninsula, which extends out into Hilo Bay. There are no sandy beaches, as the lava-rock coastline is too rough and rugged, although the coast offers lovely views of Hilo town, Hilo Bay and, if the weather permits, the peaks of Mauna Kea and Mauna Loa. Several good B&Bs reside in the Hilo area, as well as condominium properties and private homes for vacation rentals.

There are two hotels in the Volcano area, one inside and one just outside the National Park, and all kinds of interesting B&Bs to choose from. East Hawaii is a different, quieter place, somewhat closer to nature and removed from the busyness of the Kona side. Here and in the southern reaches of Ka'u and South Kona, you'll find a selection of B&Bs in settings by the ocean shore, up in the misty mountain forest or out in wide-open ranch country.

You have a lot of choices, and we hope this chapter will help make it easier to find the perfect spot for you.

THINGS TO KNOW ABOUT USING THIS CHAPTER

Lodgings are organized geographically by district, beginning with the South and North Kona Districts, followed by the Kohala Coast and continuing around the island to North Kohala, Waimea/Kamuela), the Hamakua Coast, Hilo, the Puna District and the Ka'u District (these last two districts share Volcanoes National Park). In each district, accommodations are then broken down into B&Bs, Condominiums and Hotels, Hostels and Homes (not every district offers every category). Listings within these sections are then organized alphabetically.

Rates quoted for the hotels are the most current rack rates available at the time of publication and are, of course, subject to change without notice. However, hotel rack rates have become more of a goal than a reality, since most reservations are booked at various discounted rates in order to compete for your business. (The same may not be true of B&Bs or other smaller, privately owned lodgings.) Rates listed are for double occupancy (2 people) unless otherwise specified. There is generally an extra charge for additional adults, but usually not for children staying in their parents' room if extra bedding is not required. All lodging in Hawai'i will add on an 11.167% tax, which includes a 4.167% sales tax and 7.25% hotel room tax. Gratuities for room maids, restaurant servers, bell and valet parking staff, recreation staff and other personnel are additional at your discretion, but here are general guidelines: porterage, (bellman or luggage attendant) $8 per person roundtrip, or $2 per bag each way; housekeepers, $2 per room per day; waitstaff or bartenders 15% of the check before tax; valet parking attendant $2 when they bring the car to you.

Because of the extreme diversity of accommodations, ratings have not been given to individual properties. However, we have used a ★ to indicate a B&B, hotel, condo or other lodging with a consistent quality in its "niche." Starred properties will offer something special in price value, location, facilities or services, based on personal experience, reputation, longevity, previous editions of this guide and other travel sources. If you see the girl with the hat, you've found an establishment that offers a childcare program. Please see "Traveling with Children: Childcare Programs" in Chapter 1 for more details.

Depending on how and when and where you make reservations, rates can vary as much as 50 percent off rack rates. The most expensive Kohala Coast resorts are traditionally booked solid from Christmas through New Year's Day, with no discounted rates available. Between Thanksgiving and Easter is generally considered "in-season," when rates are higher. The months of May and September and the first two weeks of December are usually the lowest-occupancy times of any year. Rates are much more flexible during these times, with bargains to be had for those who persevere. On the other hand, Kona hotels and condominiums will have availability at Christmas, but will be booked in October during the Ironman Triathlon. For budget tips, see "How to Save Money" below.

Keep in mind the most important thing about your Big Island vacation is *you* and your vacation time. Determine what your family's priorities are and go for it. For example, if you want to sightsee, shop and sign up for activities, you can stay at a Kona condominium for a week for the about same price as one or two nights in a Kohala Coast resort. If you want to spend pampered days soaking up the sun, pay a higher room rate, forego the rental car and enjoy the island's best beaches. It's up to you!

HOW TO SAVE MONEY

Timing

As mentioned above, the Big Island's visitor industry fluctuates seasonally. The peak season, with its consequent highest prices, is generally from mid-December to after Easter. Slower, shoulder periods, where more promotional rates and specials may be offered, are usually from after Easter to Thanksgiving. The real bargain time to visit tends to be from Labor Day through the month of September and then the first two weeks in December each year. Hilo hotels are not as prone to price fluctuations (except during Merrie Monarch week or other local events). Kohala Coast resorts are booked out over the Christmas–New Year holidays, when Kailua-Kona usually has space. And Kona hotels are jammed in October for the Ironman, when other areas may be offering discounts. Travel agents are experts in finding the best accommodations at the best rate for you and your family.

Location

The rule is simple: to find the more expensive accommodations, follow the sun, as the sunniest areas also have the best beaches and the best hotels. The price goes down as the weather gets cloudier. In a nutshell, this is how it works: Kohala Coast = luxury resorts; Kailua/ Keauhou-Kona = mostly condo properties, a few mid-range hotels, and one upscale property; North Kohala and Waimea = mostly B&Bs; Hamakua = B&Bs; Hilo = a few mid-range hotels and B&Bs; South Kona = B&Bs and one condo resort; Ka'u and Puna = B&Bs and a cluster of different accommodations at Volcano Village.

Type of accommodation

B&Bs have some of the most interesting locations, from tree houses to log cabins, coffee farms to rainforest retreats. The prices range generally from about $75-$150 a night. A condo vacation can be a real budget-stretcher, offering the most space for your dollar, from simple studio apartments to luxurious hotel-like suites in resort locations, about $100-$200 average (but the price can go much higher depending on location). Keep in mind that a little distance from the ocean is not necessarily a bad thing. The Big Island is a great place to drive—and in fact you're never more than 26 miles from the ocean. Kailua-Kona's hotels are nicely tourist-geared, set close to the ocean and within walking distance of a lot of fun, from about $150-$250. Hilo's hotels are a good value, about $100-$150, and Kohala Coast resorts are pricey, but have all the deluxe amenities, from about $350 to thousands.

Condo Vacations

A condominium vacation can be perfect for families that need room to spread out and prefer to make most of their own meals and snacks. There can be more freedom and less fuss in a condo and most are far less expensive than hotel accommodations.

GENERAL POLICIES Condominiums usually require a reservation deposit equal to one or two nights' rental to secure a confirmed reservation and possibly an additional security deposit. Generally a 30-day notice of cancellation is needed to receive a full refund, although a cancellation fee may apply at any time. Most condos and agents require a three- to-five-night minimum stay and full prepayment 30 days prior to or upon arrival. Most condos also require a minimum stay of three to five nights or longer in the winter and during peak holiday seasons. The peak winter season brings heavy demand for condo units, and the restrictions, cancellation policies, and payment policies are much more stringent. It is not uncommon to book as much as two years in advance for the Christmas–New Year's season. Most resident managers *do not* handle reservations on site. Contact the rental agents listed for those properties.

Condos may be reserved on-line or by phone from various reputable management companies. These companies handle different units at properties for different owners. One property may deal with five or six management companies for their vacation rentals. It's a bit of a maze, but not impossible to manage. Our best suggestion is this: if you'd like to reserve a condominium (particularly in Kona, but elsewhere on the island as well) contact one of the agencies listed at the end of the chapter by phone or internet. Advise them of your priorities regarding size, location, amenities and price range. They can then recommend a selection of condos available for the dates you request. If you are looking for a particular property, let them know up front.

To further complicate the process, prices vary widely according to the season. The highest rates will be charged during the peak season between Thanksgiving and New Year's; mid-level rates are in effect during spring and fall shoulder seasons and lower rates will likely be available in the summer. In addition, various rental companies offer room and car packages and other special deals, and last-minute internet rates to boost business. Rates will also vary according to view, size, property location, facilities and the number of people in your party. Weekly and monthly rates are also available at some properties. A description and location is provided, with the recom-

BED-AND-BREAKFAST LODGING

B&Bs have become the accommodation of choice for an increasing number of visitors as an alternative to the usual resort condominiums and hotels. They are often less costly and provide a range of interesting accommodations from clean simple rooms to luxurious, well-appointed, fully equipped suites, cottages and vacation homes. On the Big Island, B&Bs offer the chance to experience an overnight in a renovated 1930s sugar plantation estate, a historic missionary home, a log cabin, *paniolo* ranch house, beachside cottage and even a tree house. In most cases, B&Bs provide a more homey, less commercial atmosphere and opportunity to get to know the *kama'aina* (residents) more personally. They usually include a continental-style breakfast of coffee and tea, fresh fruits, juice and pastries or breakfast breads, which may be pre-stocked in the unit as kitchen provisions, or served buffet-style in a common area. A hot, sit-down breakfast is offered in exceptional cases. B&B innkeepers are in general gregarious, knowledgeable about the island and eager to assist with advice, suggestions and referrals to activities, restaurants and other fun things. Many provide island adventures themselves on land or sea, and many get to know their guests as friends, welcoming them back again and again.

B&B Quality and Service   The County of Hawai'i and industry representatives have cooperated to establish standards and guidelines for the operation of B&Bs via the Hawai'i Island Bed & Breakfast Association, www.stayhawaii.com. HIBBA as an industry organization attempts to ensure that members adhere to quality B&B operating standards of cleanliness, service and maintenance and value for lodging dollars. Member B&B operators are identified in listings by: **Member-HIBBA.**

Hawai'i's Best B&B, www.bestbnb.com, is a booking service that handles exclusive upscale B&B operations around the Big Island. Member B&Bs are guaranteed to provide a high-quality B&B experience with overall excellent facilities, amenities and service. Member B&B operators are identified in listings by: **Member-Hawai'i's Best.**

In addition to individual B&B listings, you'll find a list of reservation agencies at the end of the chapter. Because the number of B&Bs has increased markedly in recent years, and because the levels of quality and service can vary widely in privately run lodging, we recommend booking through an agency.

mendation to again, contact the rental agencies, let them know your needs and let them find the perfect place for you and your family. To give you an idea of the rate range, expect 1-bedroom units to average $75-$150 per night; 2-bedroom units, $100-$250. As we've said, the high-end properties and vacation homes will be much higher.

Lodging Best Bets

Best for Active Families on a Budget a condo vacation in Kailua-Kona. Book through an agency such as Sunquest Vacations (www.sunquest-hawaii.com) and let them assist with activity planning too.

Best for Active Families with a Bigger Budget the Hilton Waikoloa Village on the Kohala Coast. Big, busy, energetic and packed with activities for all ages. In Kona, consider the newly refurbished **Sheraton Keauhou Resort & Spa**.

Best for Honeymooners, and Other People Seeking Perfect Privacy **Kona Village Resort**, a cluster of private hale void of phones, TVs, disturbances from the outside world.

Best to Brag to Your Friends About **Four Seasons Resort Hualalai**, ultra-plush and pricey, prized for perfect service.

Best Beach **Mauna Kea Beach Hotel** on the Kohala Coast. Also best tennis and one of the best for golf.

Best for Golf a real toss-up: **Waikoloa**, **Mauna Lani** or **Mauna Kea** resorts. Between the three, six great golf courses with fine clubhouse facilities and excellent accommodations.

Best Hamakua Getaway **Waipi'o Wayside** in Kukuihaele or **Waianuhea** in Ahualoa. Both offer classy, classic accommodations in tranquil tropical settings and friendly personal service.

Best Getaway in the Deep South **Macadamia Meadows Farm Bed & Breakfast** in Na'alehu

Best Spa Retreat This is hard. Probably the Four Seasons, although it's reserved exclusively for use of its guests. The **Mauna Lani Spa** is excellent as is the Fairmont's "Spa Without Walls," but the **Hilton's Kohala Sports Club & Spa** may top them, just for sheer breadth of service and treatment options.

Best in Hilo **Hilo Hawaiian** is our favorite of the hotels along Banyan Drive in Hilo town. **The Shipman House** is something special, a Victorian home in a jungly setting with a lot of class.

Best for Adventure-Seekers on a Budget **Arnott's Lodge** in Hilo, geared to the active vacationer with scheduled hikes, tours and other fun things. In Kona, **Pineapple Park** keeps over 100 kayaks on hand for personalized excursions.

Best for Military   Use the discounts you've earned in the service at **Kilauea Military Camp** in Volcanoes National Park. Private cabins, fun activities, good food and entertainment.

Best for Enlightenment-Seekers   Kalani Oceanside Retreat in Pahoa.

Best in Volcano   **Kilauea Lodge** is classic, with excellent gourmet dining. For romantics, the **Chalet Kilauea Collection's Inn at Volcano** has theme-decorated suites to suit your fantasy. For family get-togethers or perhaps writers on retreat, the well-appointed private vacation residence at **Sugi House.**

Best and Longest History   Volcano House, the Big Island's first, and the oldest continuously operated hotel in Hawaii.

Kona District

SOUTH KONA DISTRICT

BED AND BREAKFASTS

Affordable Hawai'i at Pomaika'i (Lucky) Farm
83-5465 Mamalahoa Highway, Captain Cook, HI 96704. 800-3ALOHAS; 808-328-2112; fax 808-328-2255; e-mail: nitabnb@kona.net; www.lucky farm.com.

This is a working four-acre coffee farm in Captain Cook over-looking Keei Bay from the 1,000-foot level, about 12 miles south of Kailua-Kona. There is one bedroom in this historic 1935 farmhouse with private bath. The Greenhouse has two large rooms with private baths and entrances and is surrounded by tropical plants. These rooms sleep 2-4. The Coffee Barn sleeps up to 5 people and also has a tropical garden setting with a queen bed, couch, half bath and an outdoor shower. Shared lanai with bay view, TV room, library and shared kitchen. Easy access to local beaches, dining, shopping, activities and attractions. French spoken here. Member-HIBBA.

Rates: $60-$85; $10 extra person

Aloha Farm B&B
93-5440 Painted Church Road, Captain Cook, HI 96704. 808-328-0604; e-mail: rdilts@alohafarms.com; www.alohafarms.com.

This is a farm located south of Kailua-Kona town and about two miles from Kealakekua Bay on five acres. It's a peaceful area with nice panoramic ocean and sunset views from a covered lanai. Guest rooms have king or queen beds and private baths. Kitchen privileges, snorkel gear, beach towels, coolers and advice included. Traditional farm breakfast with the farm's own Kona coffee and tropical fruits. Snorkel, swim and scuba dive in nearby bays. Member-HIBBA.

Rates: $65-$100; $15 extra person

Aloha Guest House

84-4780 Mamalahoa Highway, Captain Cook, HI 96704. 800-897-3188; 808-328-8955; fax 808-328-9564; e-mail: vacation@alohaguesthouse.com; www.alohaguesthouse.com.

This home is at the end of a private road, at the 1,500-foot elevation level, and set amid a citrus and macadamia nut plantation alongside a state forest preserve area. It's a very secluded, country atmosphere. The home provides sweeping ocean views of the Kona Coast. Free internet access and use of snorkel gear, mountain bikes and boogie boards included. All rooms have private baths. Traditional island-style breakfast. German and French spoken here. Member-HIBBA.

Rates: $110-$280

Areca Palms Estate B&B

P.O. Box 489, Captain Cook, HI 96704. 800-545-4390; 808-323-2276; fax 808-323-3749; e-mail: arecapalms@konabedandbreakfast.com; www. konabedandbreakfast.com.

This is a comfortable cedar home located in the rural area of Kealakekua, Kona. The four spacious guest rooms are beautifully and comfortably furnished with private bath, cable TV, robes, refrigerators and either ocean or garden view. Large open living room and front-back lanais provide lots of room. Large open yard has lots of tropical fruit trees, plants and greenery plus a garden spa. AAA 3-diamond, Member-HIBBA.

Rates: $95-$130; $25 extra person

Bayview Inn

Box 1237, Captain Cook, HI 96704. 808-328-0406; e-mail: bayviewinn@ hawaii.rr.com; www.konabayviewinn.com.

A tropical garden home up mauka of Kealakekua Bay within a 40-acre mac nut orchard. Private entry and bath, twin or queen beds, fridge and microwave; snorkel gear, beach towels, coolers and boogie boards included. Smoke-free property. Member-HIBBA.

Rates: $90-$125

★ Beautiful Edge of the World B&B

P.O. Box 888, Captain Cook, HI 96704. 800-660-8491; 808-328-7424; fax 808-328-7424; e-mail: weigelt@aloha.net; www.konaedge.com.

This custom-built home features local koa woodwork throughout; private baths, internet access, laundry facilities included. Long, encircling lanais provide lots of room to watch Kona's famous sunsets and meet with new travel friends. Breakfast includes savory traditional, Japanese or vegan specialties along with the farm's own fresh Kona coffee and tropical fruits. Easy access to Kona area attractions. German, Spanish, Japanese and Korean spoken here ("with varying degrees of imperfection"). Member-HIBBA.

Rates: $55-$90

Belle Vue B&B

Captain Cook. 800-772-5044; phone/fax 808-328-9898; www.kona-bed-breakfast.com.

Overlooks Kealakekua Bay with Pacific Ocean view and an expansive panoramic South Kona coastline view. The property is a lush five-acre farm with coffee, avocado, papaya and banana trees. Located in Captain Cook, 20 minutes south of Kailua-Kona. Quiet, serene, yet walking distance to restaurants and shopping, 90 minutes to Volcanoes National Park, 15 minutes to beaches and just minutes to snorkeling, scuba diving and kayaking in Kealakekua Bay.

Rates: $95-$165, $25 additional person

Camp Aloha B&B

84-5210 Painted Church Road, Captain Cook, HI 96704. 808-328-2304; e-mail: konajoan@yahoo.com; www.stayhawaii.com/campaloha.

Separate south wing of a tropical farm residence offers king bed, full private bath and kitchen on the covered lanai. Hot tub, pool and beautiful ocean views. Discounts for longer stays. Member-HIBBA.

Rates: $60-$99

Cedar House B&B and Coffee Farm

P.O. Box 823, Captain Cook, HI 96704. 866-328-8829; phone/fax 808-328-8829; e-mail: cedarhouse@hawaii.rr.com; www.cedarhouse-hawaii.com.

This is a lovely cedar and redwood home located on 4.5 acres of beautifully landscaped tropical grounds. It's located in Captain Cook town above historic Kealakekua Bay and is 12 miles south of Kailua-Kona. Four guest rooms and one cottage have tasteful contemporary decor and garden or ocean view, private entrance, TV, queen or king beds and private or shared baths. Four-night minimum. Member-HIBBA.

Rates: European Room $70; Pacific Room $75; Pikake Rose Room $85; Ulu Room $95; cottage $110; $660 per week, $1,980 per month

Da Third House B&B

85-4585 Mamalahoa Highway, Captain Cook, HI 96704. 808-328-8410; e-mail: dathirdhouse@webtv.co; www.stayhawaii.com/dathird.

Individual studio with ocean view, private bath, king bed and queen futon, fridge, microwave, TV and private continental breakfast. Member-HIBBA.

Rates: $65-$85

Dragonfly Ranch: A Healing Arts Retreat

P.O. Box 675, Honaunau, HI 96726. 800-487-2159; 808-328-9570; e-mail: reservations@dragonflyranch.com; www.dragonflyranch.com.

This private country estate is only three minutes from Honaunau Bay on Highway 160, about 20 miles south of Keahole Airport, Kona. The ranch is situated just above Pu'uhonua o Honaunau and provides an alternative B&B experience. All rooms have private entrances, indoor bath and private outdoor shower. Choose from Honeymoon Suite, Writer's Studio, Lomilomi Suite, the Pele Room or Dolphin room. Features include fireplace, sauna, TV/VCR, kitchenette, sundeck and "spa pamperings." Luxuriously rustic, with beautiful views of the coast. Uniquely appointed with outdoor beds, an organic garden and a labyrinth housed in a "rainbow illuminarium."

Rates: Honeymoon Suite $250; Writer's Studio $175; Lomilomi Suite $175; Pele Room $100; Dolphin room $100; Dragonfly Room $125

Hale Ho'ola B&B

85-4577 Mamalahoa Highway, Captain Cook, HI 96704. 877-628-9117; 808-328-9117; e-mail: tlc@hale-hoola.com; www.hale-hoola.com.

This is a nice two-story plantation-style home overlooking Honaunau Bay from the 800-foot elevation level. There are great ocean views and cool relaxing ocean breezes. Guest rooms have private entrances, baths and lanais. Welcoming hosts serve up island-style breakfast and lots of local lore and information. Member-HIBBA.

Rates: $95-$135

Horizon Guest House

Hawai'i's Best B&Bs, P.O. Box 485, Laupahoehoe, HI 96764. 800-262-9912; 808-962-0100; fax 808-962-6360; e-mail: reservations@bestbnb. com; www.bestbnb.com.

This luxury retreat is located on 40 acres overlooking the Kona Coast, 40 minutes south of Kailua-Kona town and away from the hustle and bustle. Four guest rooms are well-kept and furnished with refrigerator, lanai and antique decor. Colorful Hawaiian quilts cover each bed. Great coast views from the spreading deck where guests enjoy pool, jacuzzi and barbecue. Member-Hawaii's Best.

Rates: $250

Kealakekua Bay B&B

82-6002 Napo'opo'o Road, P.O. Box 1412, Kealakekua, HI 96750. 800-328-8150; 808-328-8150; fax 808-328-8866; e-mail: kbaybb@aloha.net; www.keala.com.

This is a private cottage on five landscaped acres a short walk from Kealakekua Bay. It has two bedrooms (sleeps up to 6), 2.5 baths, full kitchen and great view of the bay from the covered porch. Great for families or couples traveling together. The nearby host home also has a master bedroom with private entry, jacuzzi and nice view of the bay. A garden-level wing has two guest bedrooms, living area and private patio. Two-night minimum stay.

Rates: Pali Room $140; Lehua Room $120; Ali'i Suite $190; Ohana Kai Guest House $250; $25 extra person

Rainbow Plantation B&B

P.O. Box 122, 81-6327B Mamalahoa Highway, Captain Cook, HI 96704. 800-494-2829; 808-323-2393; fax 808-323-9445; e-mail: sunshine@ aloha.net; www.rainbowplantation.com.

This country home is located on seven acres of organic coffee and macadamia nut orchards and forest land. Nature lovers will enjoy watching the birds in the lush gardens and the koi in the ponds. The large rooms have private entrances and baths, TV and refrigerator. Breakfast is enjoyed on the oceanview lanai. There's a gazebo with barbecue. Located at the 1,200-foot elevation level above Kealakekua Bay and 11 miles from Kailua-Kona, just minutes to beach snorkeling, restaurants, shopping and attractions. Free kayak use with a four-night stay. French and German spoken here. Member-HIBBA.

Rates: $79-$99

Tara Cottage

Reservations through Hawai'i's Best B&Bs, P.O. Box 485, Laupahoehoe, HI 96764. 800-262-9912; 808-962-0100; fax 808-962-6360; e-mail: reserva tions@bestbnb.com; www.bestbnb.com.

This is a unique octagon-shaped studio cottage, rare to find in the islands. Located on 10 rural acres above Kona's Kealakekua Bay with nice ocean views. It's a peaceful, unhurried setting, ideal for those seeking to just relax or while away days snorkeling, kayaking, sunning, etc. The cottage can sleep three and has southeast Asian decor, kitchenette, barbecue, laundry facilities, phone, TV/VCR, stereo and an outdoor garden shower. Owner lives in separate cottage on property. Three-night minimum. Breakfast is not provided.

Rates: $185; $25 third person

HOTELS, HOSTELS AND HOMES

Manago Hotel

P.O. Box 145, 82-6155 Mamalahoa Highway, Captain Cook, HI 96704. 808-323-2642; fax 808-323-3451.

This is an old-fashioned family hotel operated by the Manago family since the place was founded in 1917. There are 64 rooms, some with shared bathroom facilities. The hotel features a homey family-type environment and the restaurant is one of the island's best for local family-style meals. Cocktail lounge on grounds. No room telephones. Located right on Highway 11, eight miles from Kailua-Kona in the busy town of Captain Cook at 1,400-foot elevation above the

Kona Coast, overlooking Kealakekua Bay and Puʻuhonua o Honaunau. The Manago Hotel enjoys sunny days and cool, quiet evenings.
Rates: Single 1BR $51, Standard $54, Deluxe $56; $3 extra person

NORTH KONA DISTRICT

BED AND BREAKFASTS

Dolores's 1st Class B&B
77-6504 Kilohana Street, Kailua-Kona, HI
96740. 888-769-1110; 808-329-8778; fax 808-331-
1974; e-mail: firstclassbb@hawaii.rr.com; www.dolbandb.com.

This comfortable home is located on the slopes above Kailua-Kona overlooking Kailua Bay and the Kona Coast. It's 11 miles from Kona International Airport and four miles from Kailua-Kona town, yet near good snorkeling beaches. The separate and private guest cottage is set in a lush tropical garden with lanai views of Kailua Bay and the ocean. The studio and cottage both have private bath and entry, custom contemporary decor and furnishing and TV/VCR. Beach gear is provided along with visitor information from long-term resident-owner.
Rates: Studio (sleeps two) $135, Cottage (sleeps two) $145

Hale Maluhia
76-770 Hualalai Road, Kailua-Kona, HI 96740. 800-559-6627; 808-329-5773; cell 808-345-5955; fax 808-326-5487; e-mail: cottage@hawaii-inns.com; www.hawaii-inns.com/hi/kna/hmh/index.htm.

Located just three miles upslope from Kailua-Kona village, this is a large rambling 5BR home on one acre with outdoor spa, lanai, rec room, VCR and library. The "House of Peace" is wheelchair friendly.
Rates: $90-$125; Cottage from $150; $25 extra person

★ Hawaiian Oasis Bed & Breakfast
74-4958 Kiwi Street, Kailua-Kona, HI 96740. 808-327-1701; e-mail: info@hawaiianoasis.com; www.hawaiianoasis.com.

Really an oasis, this is very upscale lodging, conveniently located minutes from town, yet private and luxuriously appointed. Studio, cottages and suites have private baths and entries, fridge, microwave, cable TV and lanais overlooking the ocean and mature tropical landscaping. Koi ponds, waterfalls, spa, pool, tennis court and workout room on site. Romance and Spa packages available. Resort-style at reasonable prices—one of Kona's best-kept secrets. Member-HIBBA.
Rates: $140-$190

★ Holualoa Inn B&B
P.O. Box 222, 76-5932 Mamalahoa Highway, Holualoa, HI 96725. 800-392-1812; 808-324-1121; fax 808-324-2472; e-mail: inn@aloha.net; www.holualoainn.com.

This attractive cedar home is on a 40-acre former cattle ranch and coffee farm in the village of Holualoa on the cool slopes of Mt. Hualalai. Six spacious guest rooms with private baths; common areas include swimming pool, hot tub, TV room, barbecue area, telescope, billiards table and a rooftop gazebo providing magnificent views of the surrounding countryside and incredible Kona sunsets. Gourmet island breakfast and sunset *pupus*. Member-HIBBA.

Rates: $175-$225; $30 extra person

Nancy's Hideaway Bed & Breakfast

73-1530 Uanani Place, Kailua-Kona, HI 96740. 866-325-3132; 808-325-3132; e-mail: hideaway.kona@verizon.net; www.nancyshideaway.com.

Two individual accommodations, a cottage and a studio, up mauka overlooking the ocean. Each custom-built unit has king bed, private bath, TV/VCR, phone, lanai and continental breakfast provisions. Member-HIBBA.

Rates: $115-$135

Pu'ukala Lodge

72-3998E Mamalahoa Highway; P.O. Box 2967, Kailua-Kona, HI 96745. 888-325-1729; 808-325-1729; e-mail: puukala1@aol.com; www.puukala lodge.com.

This modern expansive home is located at 1,500 feet on the slopes of Mt. Hualalai above the Kona Coast. There are great 180-degree views of the Kona and Kohala coasts. The 1,400-square-foot lanai also provides ample room to enjoy those famous Kona sunsets. Located just five minutes from Kona Airport and seven miles from Kailua-Kona town. Guests choose from well-appointed suites or guest rooms. Pualani Suite has a queen bed, bath, separate sitting room with sofa bed, microwave and fridge. Makai Suite is spacious with two queen beds, bath, lanai. Ohana Suite has two bedrooms, two baths for four people. Aloha Room has queen bed, bath shared with innkeepers, access to lanai. Kamehameha Suite has partial ocean view, microwave and fridge.

Rates: Pualani or Kamehameha Suite, $95; Aloha Room, $100; Makai Suite, $110; Ohana Suite, $165; $25 additional person

★ Silver Oaks Ranch B&B

75-1027 Henry Street #310, Kailua-Kona, HI 96740. 877-325-2300; 808-325-2000; fax 808-325-2200; e-mail: amydecker@hawaii.rr.com; www.silveroaksranch.com.

A 10-acre horse ranch five miles from Kailua-Kona town and Kona airport with a spectacular 40-mile panoramic view of the Kona Coast. Guests enjoy pool and jacuzzi, barbecue, snorkel gear, beach towels, boogie boards, binoculars, coolers, a library of books and videos, Wi-Fi, robes and hairdryers, laundry facilities and the warmth of family service on a working ranch, with horses (for petting, not riding), wild turkeys and a recent addition, Nigerian dwarf goats. Nicely decorated, spacious individual cottages, one with a sleeping loft for children. Additional suites available when extra space is needed. Welcome basket with breakfast provisions. Easy access to Kailua-Kona town activities, shopping, dining, activities and attractions.

Rates: $165; discounts for longer stays

CONDOMINIUMS

Ali'i Villas

75-6016 Ali'i Drive, Kailua-Kona, HI 96740. 808-329-1288. Agents: Sunquest Vacations 800-367-5168; Hawai'i Resort Management 800-622-5348; Knutson & Associates 800-800-6202.

This condo has only ten units in rental programs. It is a beach-front location with palm trees, flowers and a garden setting less than a mile from town. Units are generally clean and well kept, although this is strictly a budget-class operation.

Rates: $95-$175

Casa De Emdeko

75-6082 Ali'i Drive, Kailua-Kona, HI 96740. 808-329-6488. Agents: Sunquest Vacations 800-367-5168; Condo in Hawai'i 888-292-3307; Century 21 800-546-5662; Knutson & Associates 800-800-6202.

This lovely three-story white-washed building is located on the water, although there is no sand beach here. The 40 available units are spacious, comfortable and well-appointed. The central garden courtyard is well maintained with tropical plants. The oceanside swimming pool features a "sandy beach" surrounding the pool.

Rates: $75-$210

Country Club Villas

78-6920 Ali'i Drive, Kailua-Kona, HI 96740. 808-322-9154. Agents: Sunquest Vacations 800-367-5168; Hawai'i Resort Management 800-553-5035, 808-329-9393; Keauhou Property Management 800-745-KONA; Property Network 800-358-7977; Knutson & Associates 800-800-6202; Century 21 800-546-5662.

This condominium is located on the Kona Country Club golf course with easy access to other Keauhou resorts, dining, shopping, etc. Amenities include TV, private lanai on each unit, two tennis courts, and on-request maid service. Available units are 2BR/3BR and have golf course views with Kona Coast beyond. Five-night minimum stay.

Rates: $120-$165

Hale Kona Kai

75-5870 Kahakai Road, Kailua-Kona, HI 96740. 800-421-3696; 808-

329-2155. *Agents: Sunquest Vacations 800-367-5168. Condo in Hawaii 888-292-3307.*

Within walking distance to the village, this 39-unit air-conditioned condo has on-request maid service, TV, barbecue facility. No room telephones. Corner units are larger with bigger lanai area but all units are very nicely furnished. Located right on the water and immediately next door to the Royal Kona Resort, but there is no sand beach. Three-night minimum stay.

Rates: $115-$150

Kahaluu Bay Villas

78-6715A Ali'i Drive, Kailua-Kona, HI 96740. 808-322-0013. Agent: Sunquest Vacations 800-367-5168.

This luxury complex is a short walk along Ali'i Drive to Kahalu'u Beach Park, where there is good snorkeling. Spacious units have separate master bedrooms, full kitchens, ceiling fans, private lanais, pool, gazebo, parking and barbecue area.

Rates: $95-$154

Kailua Village

At the intersection of Hualalai Road and Kuakini Highway near the town center. Agent: Property Network 800-358-7977.

This multi-story complex is one block from the ocean and within easy walking distance of the town center, restaurants, shopping, attractions, Kailua Pier, etc. The 1BR units have ceiling fans, laundry facilities, parking, elevators and access to swimming pool.

Rates: $78-$93

Kalanikai Condominiums

75-5681 Kuakini Highway, Kailua-Kona, HI 96740. 808-329-5241. Agents: Century 21 800-546-5662; Property Network 800-358-7977.

This condominium is located in the heart of the village and within walking distance of resort activities, shopping and restaurants. Amenities include air conditioning and barbecue facilities. Units have mountain views.

Rates: $75-$105

★ Kanaloa at Kona

78-261 Manukai Street, Kailua-Kona, HI 96740. 800-688-7444; 808-322-9625; fax 808-322-3818. Agents: Sunquest Vacations 800-367-5168; Property Network 800-358-7977; Keauhou Property Management 800-745-KONA; West Hawai'i Property Services 800-799-KONA; Century 21 800-546-5662; Outrigger Hotels Hawai'i 800-OUTRIGGER, e-mail: reservations@outrigger.com, www.outrigger.com; Royal Hawai'i Condos 888-722-6284; Hawai'i Condo Exchange 800-442-0404.

One of Kona's best-kept condo secrets, this 120-unit property is tucked away in a private, scenic oceanfront Keauhou location. No sandy beach, but beautiful views and one of the island's most romantic restaurants for dinner. The luxurious units are spacious and fully equipped including lanai wet bar, koa wood interiors, ceiling fans and TV. Kanaloa is bordered on one side by the sparkling blue Pacific with a secluded bay for snorkeling and sunning and on the other by the Kona Country Club golf course. Tennis courts, restaurant, cocktail lounge, barbecue facilities and recreation-meeting room are on the property. A bargain—reserve early.

Rates: $165-$275

Keauhou Akahi

78-7030 Ali'i Drive, Kailua-Kona, HI 96740. 808-322-2590. Agents: Knutson & Associates 800-800-6202; Condo in Hawaii 888-292-3307; Property Network 800-358-7977.

This 48-unit complex is located on the Kona Country Club golf course with ocean views. There are laundry facilities in each unit, full kitchens and an on-property swimming pool. It is 7 miles from Kailua-Kona village but shopping and dining are nearby.

Rates: $105-$135

Keauhou Palena Condominiums

78-7054 Kamehameha III Road, Kailua-Kona, HI 96740. 808-322-3620. Agents: Keauhou Property Management 800-745-KONA; Century 21 800-546-5662; Sunquest Vacations 800-367-5168; West Hawai'i Property Services 800-799-KONA; Knutson & Associates 800-800-6202.

This condo is on the eleventh fairway of the Kona Country Club golf course with easy access for golfing visitors. Units are fully equipped including ceiling fans and TV. The den can be made into an extra bedroom, enabling these units to sleep four comfortably. It's located near the end of Ali'i Drive.

Rates: $86-$110

Keauhou Punahele Condominiums

78-7070 Ali'i Drive, Kailua-Kona, HI 96740. 808-322-6585, reservations 206-742-2440. Agents: Century 21 800-546-5662; West Hawai'i Property Services 800-799-KONA; Sunquest Vacations 800-367-5168; Knutson & Associates 800-800-6202.

This large complex (93 units) has only 2BR/3BR units available in rental programs. It is the last complex at the end of Ali'i Drive in the Keauhou area and on the Kona Country Club with ocean views across golf course. Units are not air-conditioned but are roomy and generally well-appointed, with high ceilings and fans keeping units cool and breezy. The units are clean and well-kept and the grounds are well-groomed. Located 7.25 miles from the village but Keauhou Shopping Center is only half a mile away.

Rates: $115-$185

Keauhou Resort Condominiums

78-7039 Kamehameha III Road, Kailua-Kona, HI 96740. 800-367-5286; 808-322-9122; fax 322-9410; e-mail: english@aloha.net; www.tropweb. com/keauhou.htm. Agents: Sunquest Vacations 800-367-5168; Property Network 800-358-7977; West Hawai'i Property Services 800-799-KONA.

This condo has 48 townhouse units available with TV, two swimming pools and is on the golf course; maid service included. Five-night minimum stay.

Rates: $81-$160

Kona Ali'i Condominiums

75-5782 Kuakini Highway, Kailua-Kona, HI 96740. 808-329-2000. Agents: Hawai'i Resort Management 800-622-5348; Sunquest Vacations 800-367-5168.

Units are fully furnished with private lanai and major appliances. Bedding for up to 4 persons. Tennis court, top-floor sun deck, private sandy beach, barbecue area. Short two-minute walk into Kailua village for shopping, restaurants and resort activities.

Rates: $90-$99

Kona Bali Kai

76-6246 Ali'i Drive, Kailua-Kona, HI 96740. 808-329-9381. Agents: Sunquest Vacations 800-367-5168; Always Sunny Condos 800-479-2173, 360-698-7007; Property Network 800-358-7977; Knutson & Associates 800-800-6202; West Hawai'i Property Services 800-799-KONA; Hawai'i Condo Exchange 800-442-0404; Marc Resorts 800-436-1304.

This condo has 86 units of varying sizes available on Holualoa Bay, Kona, located three miles from town. All units have full kitchen and TV; some have air conditioning. Sauna, jacuzzi, pool, health club, barbecue facilities, convenience store/deli available.

Rates: $84-$295

Kona Billfisher Condominium

75-5841 Ali'i Drive, Kailua-Kona, HI 96740. 808-329-9277. Agents: Sunquest Vacations 800-367-5168; Hawai'i Resort Management 800-553-5035, 808-329-9393.

This condo has 20 units in rental programs, all air-conditioned with TV and barbecue area. It is located across the street from the Royal Kona Resort and is also within easy walking distance of the town center, shopping and several restaurants.

Rates: $80-$94

★ Kona by the Sea

75-6106 Ali'i Drive, Kailua-Kona, HI 96740. 808-327-2300. Agents: Aston Hotels & Resorts 800-922-7866, 800-321-2558; Royal Hawai'i Condos 888-722-6284; Pleasant Hawaiian Holidays 800-672-4587.

This is a well-maintained, quiet, four-story condominium complex with 56 units available for vacation rentals. The bright, nicely appointed and very spacious rooms are air-conditioned with TV and fully equipped kitchen. The complex is located on a rocky beach with swimming pool, jacuzzi, adjoining grass yard for small children, sandy area with barbecue grills and lounge chairs. The shore area attracts lots of surfers because the surf builds and breaks directly in front of the complex, a great place to watch the surfers if you don't take to the board yourself. There is also a public saltwater pool beyond the rock wall at the end of the property, accessed by a public walkway. (On heavy surf days, waves can break up and over the pool's edge, so caution is required.)

Rates: $270-$445

★ Kona Coast Resort/Keauhou Gardens

78-6842 Ali'i Drive, Keauhou-Kona, HI 96740. 808-324-1721; fax 808-322-8217. Agents: Sunquest Vacations 800-367-5168; Property Network 800-358-7977; West Hawai'i Property Services 800-799-KONA; Keauhou Property Management 800-745-KONA.

This lushly landscaped development has a number of rental units available. They are spread out among the complex on a lovely slope surrounded by the fairways of the Kona Country Club, with the ocean just beyond. The units are luxuriously furnished with plush furniture and bedding, and overall are very tastefully appointed. There is a recreation area with tennis, two pools, jacuzzi, gas barbecue area, and wet bar.

Rates: $120-$140

Kona Islander Inn

75-5776 Kuakini Highway, Kailua-Kona, HI 96740. 808-329-3181. Agents: Property Network 800-358-7977.

This condo/hotel has 51 rental units available. Rooms have air conditioning, refrigerator and TV, and there is a pool and jacuzzi, convenience shop with beverages and snacks in the lobby. An older complex (dating from 1969), conveniently located in a narrow strip between Kuakini Highway and Ali'i Drive, within easy walking distance of Kailua-Kona shopping and attractions. A no-frills, no-views, budget property.

Rates: $75-$86

Kona Isle Condominium

75-6100 Ali'i Drive, Kailua-Kona, HI 96740. 808-329-2241; fax 808-326-2401. Agents: Sunquest Vacations 800-367-5168; Hawai'i Resort Manage-

ment 800-622-5348; Knutson & Associates 800-800-6202; Property Network 800-358-7977; West Hawai'i Property Services 800-799-KONA.

This is an oceanfront complex, some units with oceanview. The beautifully manicured grounds are very spacious and pleasant. There are barbecue facilities and tables poolside and lounge chairs near the oceanfront seawall. There is no sand beach here—it is too rocky. Laundry facilities are in each unit. Located 2.5 miles from the village. One-week minimum stay.

Rates: $86-$125

Kona Magic Sands

77-6452 Ali'i Drive, Kailua-Kona, HI 96740. Agents: Property Management Hawai'i 808-329-6488; Sunquest Vacations 800-367-5168; Hawai'i Resort Management 800-553-5035, Hawai'i 808-329-9393.

Located next to famous Magic Sands Beach Park with swimming and body surfing. There are just 10 studio units. Features TV, the notable Jameson's by the Sea restaurant, a cocktail lounge, and on-request maid service. Some rooms have telephones. Three-night minimum stay.

Rates: $95-$140

Kona Makai

75-6026 Ali'i Drive, Kailua-Kona, HI 96740. Agents: Property Management Hawai'i 808-329-6488; Property Network 800-358-7977; Knutson & Associates 800-800-6202; Sunquest Vacations 800-367-5168; West Hawai'i Property Services 800-799-KONA.

This complex has just 15 varying units in rental programs. Amenities include jacuzzi, barbecue, tennis courts, sauna and exercise room. Oceanfront but no sandy beach. Three-night minimum stay.

Rates: $85-$225

Kona Nalu

76-6212 Ali'i Drive, Kailua-Kona, HI 96740. Agents: Property Management Hawai'i 808-329-6488; Sunquest Vacations 800-367-5168.

This small complex is located on the waterfront two miles from Kailua town. Units are completely furnished and well maintained; large lanais, laundry facilities, pool, covered parking, air conditioning.

Rates: $215-$220

Kona Pacific

75-5865 Walua Road, Kailua-Kona, HI 96740. 808-329-6140. Agents: Property Network 800-358-7977; Century 21 800-546-5662; Hawai'i Resort Management 800-622-5348, 808-329-9393; Sunquest Vacations 800-367-5168.

These 1BR and 2BR units provide all the comfort needed for a relaxing vacation experience. They are air-conditioned, have in-unit laundry facilities and a lanai with beautiful ocean view. Complex has elevator and pool. Very close to Royal Kona Resort and within easy walking of the village.

Rates: $85-$145

Kona Plaza Condominiums

75-5719 Ali'i Drive, Kailua-Kona, HI 96740. 808-329-1132. Agents: Century 21 800-546-5662; Knutson & Associates 800-800-6202.

This complex has 75 air-conditioned units in the heart of the village on Ali'i Drive across from the Kona Inn Shopping Village. Restaurants, shopping, Kona Pier, hotels are all within walking distance. Guests have access to a rooftop sundeck.

Rates: $85-$100

Kona Reef

75-5888 Ali'i Drive, Kailua-Kona, HI 96740. Agents: Property Management Hawai'i 808-329-6488; Castle Resorts & Hotels 800-367-5004; Knutson & Associates 800-800-6202; West Hawai'i Property Services 800-799-KONA; Sunquest Vacations 800-367-5168.

This condo has 51 units available as vacation rentals. All rooms are air-conditioned with TV. Facilities include pool, jacuzzi, party pavilion and barbecue. The complex is near shopping and restaurants. Oceanfront location but no sandy beach. Two-night minimum stay.

Rates: $120-$250

Kona Riviera Villa Condominiums

75-6124 Ali'i Drive, Kailua-Kona, HI 96740. 808-329-1996; fax 326-2178. Agent: Knutson & Associates 800-800-6202.

This condo is located on the beach with private lanai on each unit, near tennis courts, golf and snorkeling, plus village shopping and restaurants. There are about 10 units available, accommodating up to four persons. Three-night minimum stay.

Rates: $80-$135

Kona White Sands Village Resort

P.O. Box 594, 77-6469 Ali'i Drive, Kailua-Kona, HI 96745. 808-329-3210; fax 808-326-4137. Agent: Hawai'i Resort Management 800-622-5348, 808-329-9393; Century 21 800-546-5662.

This small 10-unit apartment-hotel has just 5 units available in rental programs. Units have kitchenettes, TV, ceiling fans and private lanais, but no room telephones. This complex is directly across from White Sands Beach. Strictly a no-frills, budget-class lodging. Three-night minimum stay.

Rates: $65-$185

★ Mauna Loa Village

78-7190 Kaleiopapa Road, Keauhou-Kona, HI 96740. Owner: Fairfield Resorts www.efairfield.com; Agent: Tri-West 800-423-6377.

This very attractive complex is in the Keauhou area, located just above Keauhou Bay. The complex is arranged in hexagonal pod-like cluster units. Lovely tropical color schemes accent the tasteful decor and contemporary furnishings of each unit. The grounds are well landscaped with numerous bubbling streams and pools, fountains, gardens and a swimming pool for every 18 units. Ten tennis courts on grounds, golf available next door at the Kona Country Club, and easy access to other resort activities and attractions, shopping and dining.

Rates: $90-$225

Royal Kahili Condominium

78-6283 Ali'i Drive, Kailua-Kona, HI 96740. 808-329-2626. Agents: Property Network 800-358-7977; Century 21 800-546-5662; West Hawai'i Property Services 800-799-KONA.

This complex is across the street from the ocean but has a private oceanfront picnic area and barbecue area. Laundry facilities are in each unit. It is located three miles from the village.

Rates: $95-$140

Sea Village

75-6002 Ali'i Drive, Kailua-Kona, HI 96740. 808-329-6488. Agents: Knutson & Associates 800-800-6202; Property Network 800-358-7977; West Hawai'i Property Services 800-799-KONA; Sunquest Vacations 800-367-5168.

These large spacious units are clean and comfortable and include TV, full kitchen and dishwasher. The central grounds are beautifully maintained and landscaped. Pool area with barbecue facilities is right on water's edge but there is no beach here as it is too rocky. Nice views of Kailua Bay and the village. Three-night minimum stay.

Rates: $118-$190

White Sands Village

74-6469 Ali'i Drive, Kailua-Kona, HI 96740. Agents: Knutson & Associates 800-800-6202; Century 21 800-546-5662; Condo in Hawai'i 888-292-3307; Sunquest Vacations 800-367-5168; West Hawai'i Property Services 800-799-KONA.

This 108-unit condo complex has just a few units available in rental programs. The units are air-conditioned with nicely coordinated furnishings and color schemes. Tennis courts, TV and on-request maid service are available. The central courtyard has a complete kitchen and barbecue area near the pool. The complex is across the street from White Sands Beach Park. Three-night minimum stay.

Rates: $95-$170

★ King Kamehameha's Kona Beach Hotel

75-5660 Palani Road, Kailua-Kona, HI 96740. 808-329-2911; 800-367-6060; fax 808-329-4602; e-mail: reservations@hthcorp.com; www.kona beachhotel.com.

This 458-room hotel is a Kailua-Kona landmark and important historical site. King Kamehameha the Great kept his royal residence here until his death in 1819. During this time he rebuilt the ancient Ahuena Heiau, a temple dedicated to the god Lono, which still stands on the grounds, protected as a National Historic Landmark. The interior spaces of the hotel building are dramatically decorated with Hawaiian artifacts, portraits of Hawaiian royalty and contemporary murals. Cultural tours are provided complimentary to guests. Located on small, sandy Kamakahonu Beach at the head of Ali'i Drive, the hotel offers two restaurants, the popular Billfish Bar by the pool, and the colorful outdoor "Island Breeze" luau. All guest rooms are air-conditioned with TV, lanai, fridge, phone and standard hotel amenities. A variety of facilities includes tennis courts, pool and whirlpool spa, beauty salon, therapeutic massage, lobby shopping mall, Hawaiian Cultural Activity Center and meeting and banquet space. Guest parking $3 per day. Packages are available. No charge for children 18 years and younger occupying room with parents, unless additional bedding is required.

Rates: Town View, $170; Partial Oceanview, $200; Oceanfront, $250; inquire for suite rates; $30 extra person

Kona Hotel

P.O. Box 342, Holualoa Road, Holualoa, HI 96725. 808-324-1155.

Located approximately seven miles from Kailua-Kona town in a prime coffee farming area on the slopes of Mount Hualalai, this rustic 11-room upcountry hotel has been run by the Inaba family for many years. It is one of Kona's original lodgings and is still run with an old-fashioned family atmosphere. Nothing fancy but basic rooming house–style accommodations for guests wanting the bare necessities. Guests share a community bathroom and entertain themselves in the small lobby-TV room. This hotel has a quiet and sedate old-fashioned Hawaiian country ambience.

Rates: $25-$30

Kona Seaside Hotel

75-5646 Palani Road, Kailua-Kona, HI 96740. 808-329-2455. Reservations: Sands & Seaside Hotels 800-560-5558; fax 808-320-6157; e-mail: info@sand-seaside.com; www.sand-seaside.com.

This 200-room property partially fronts Kailua Bay. Most rooms are air-conditioned and all have TV. Restaurant, cocktail lounge, and meeting rooms available. This is in the heart of the village with shopping and restaurants all within walking distance. Kailua Pier is one block away. This is a good budget hotel with clean rooms and simple decor.

Rates: Standard $78-118, Studio Kitchenette $165; $20 extra person

★ Outrigger Keauhou Beach Resort

78-6740 Ali'i Drive, Keauhou-Kona, HI 96740. 808-322-7987; fax 808-322-3117. Agents: Aston Hotels & Resorts 800-922-7866.

The 311-room hotel is located four miles south of Kailua town, right at the water's edge. Lagoons filled with marinelife, mature tropical gardens and flowering trees are part of the historic ten-acre property. The bar terrace has nice open-ocean views, great for watching the surf roll in and whales at play. The Kama'aina Terrace specializes in Hawai'i Regional cuisine; also offers Sunday brunch and a notable Friday night seafood buffet. The Verandah Lounge is a relaxing, open air venue for a continental breakfast in the morning, pupus and beverages throughout the day, and the Kalanikai Bar is one of the top Big Island best places to enjoy a sunset cocktail. Next door is Kahalu'u Beach Park, with good snorkeling and swimming year-round. The grounds contain cultural sites of interest such as a replica of the summer home used by King Kalakaua in the late 1800s, authentic temple foundations and petroglyphs. An Expediafun activities kiosk is located on site, along with a health club and spa services, beautiful swimming pool and more. There is easy access to Kona Coast attractions, dining and activities, plus the hotel has a pool and tennis complex. The hotel is located four miles south of Kailua-Kona town; free parking.

Rates: Garden View $139, Partial Oceanview $154, Oceanview $180, Oceanfront $212, Deluxe Oceanfront $252.

Outrigger Royal Sea Cliff Resort

75-6040 Ali'i Drive, Kailua-Kona, HI 96740. 808-329-8021.

This is a 148-unit condo-hotel about a mile and a half south of Kailua-Kona town. The air-conditioned spacious units are excellent for families and are fully furnished, including kitchen with microwave, small appliances and full in-unit laundry facilities. Guest facilities also include parking, both fresh- and saltwater pools, tennis court and barbecues. The complex is a terrace arrangement, making the lower units closer to the shoreline and very private and quiet. Ask about special deals and discounts for extra nights.

Rates: Garden studio from $150, 1BR from $170, 2BR from $195

Royal Kona Resort

75-5852 Ali'i Drive, Kailua-Kona, HI 96740. Reservations: 800-22-ALOHA; 808-329-3111; fax 808-329-7230; e-mail: info@royalkona.com; www.royalkona.com.

This 450-room hotel is a well-known Kona landmark and one of Kona's original modern tourist hotels. It sits on a rocky precipice jutting into Kailua Bay and affords a commanding view of the town and bay area. Although somewhat dated, the rooms are neat and clean with A/C, TV, refrigerator and complimentary coffee maker. Amenities include Tropics Cafe, cocktail lounge, swimming pool, tennis courts, shops and meeting rooms. The most quiet rooms are in either the village or beach buildings, away from the main building with its noisy-at-night lounge music. Check on their special room-car packages, often cheaper than buying both separately.

Rates: Garden View $210, Part Oceanview $240, Deluxe Oceanview $280, Oceanfront $350, Oceanfront Corner King $385, Suites $500; $20 extra person

Sheraton Keauhou Bay Resort & Spa

78-128 Ehukai Street, Kailua-Kona, HI 96740. www.sheratonkeauhou.com. Starwood reservations 800-325-3589.

Following a $70 million renovation, the old Kona Surf is a star reborn in the up-and-coming Keauhou destination. Their soft opening in October 2004 presented 521 guest rooms and suites featuring "Sheraton Sweet Sleeper" beds, spacious lanai, and contemporary, comfortable amenities. Fun things on the property include a multilevel pool and waterslide complex with whirlpools, river system and waterfall. There's also tennis, golf at the Kona Country Club (two courses), a sand volleyball court, game room, twice-weekly lu'au and luxurious therapies at the Ho'ola Spa. Full-service wedding and meeting planners on-site. As a very special service, Sheraton offers themed "Keiki Birthday" parties (Hawaiian, King or Queen for the Day, Sports Mania, Water Extravaganza and Wild Animal Safari) reasonably package-priced from $145 for hotel guests/$175 off-property. Promising restaurants include the ocean-view Kai, offering a breakfast buffet highlighted by kid-friendly selections and an elaborate Sunday brunch. At dinnertime Kai features creative fish and seafood preparations and other island specialties. Manta Ray Bar & Grill is a casual poolside spot for lighter fare and libations. New in 2005: Crystal Blue sophisticated cocktail lounge, the Keiki Club Keauhou and amazing "Manta Ray Experience," viewing windows, video links, lectures, dive encounters and more.

Rates: Deluxe Mountainview $325, Deluxe Partial Oceanview $375, Deluxe Oceanview $450, Deluxe Oceanfront $500

Uncle Billy's Kona Bay Hotel

75-5739 Aliʻi Drive, Kailua-Kona, HI 96740. 808-329-1393; 800-367-5102; fax 808-935-7903; e-mail: resv@unclebilly.com; www.unclebilly.com.

This older hotel has 145 guest rooms available, all air-conditioned. In-room TV, swimming pool, restaurant, cocktail lounge and shops all available. A no-frills, no views property with a good central location across from the Kona Inn Shopping Village. Good bargain breakfast and dinner buffets with live entertainment in the evenings.

Rates: Standard $94, Superior $99, Superior/kitchen $99; $14 extra person

Kohala Coast

SOUTH KOHALA DISTRICT

BED AND BREAKFASTS

★ **Hale Hoʻonanea**
P.O. Box 6568, Kamuela, HI 96743. 877-882-1653; phone/fax 808-882-1653; e-mail: jroppolo@houseofrelaxation.com; www. houseofrelaxation.com.

Three detached B&B suites located in an exclusive residence at the top of Kohala Estates two miles north of Kawaihae Harbor, Hale Suite, Tranquility Suite and Garden Suite all feature private entrance and bath, kitchenette and lanai. Each suite also includes TV/VCR, library, microwave, coffeemaker, toaster oven and refrigerator. There is lots of privacy in this country neighborhood on the famed Kohala Coast of West Hawaiʻi. The site offers panoramic ocean views, pleasing sunsets and mountain vistas. The hotels, fine dining restaurants, shopping, beaches, activities, golf, historic sites, etc., of the world-class Kohala Coast resorts and Waimea town are just minutes away. Member-HIBBA.

Rates: $100-$130

Makai Hale
Reservations through Hawaiʻi's Best B&Bs, P.O. Box 485, Laupahoehoe, HI 96764. 800-262-9912; 808-962-0100; fax 808-962-6360; e-mail: reservations@bestbnb.com; www.bestbnb.com.

This is a very nice private home just four miles from the best beaches on the Kohala Coast. Noted for consistently fine weather, expansive ocean views from its 500-foot elevation, and pool/jacuzzi deck. Guest wing opens directly to the swimming pool and deck. Whale watching in season (December–May) is excellent. Two-night minimum stay.

Rates: $145; $75 extra person

Puako Vintage Beach Cottage

Reservations through Hawai'i's Best B&Bs, P.O. Box 485, Laupahoehoe, HI 96764. 800-262-9912; 808-962-0100; fax 808-962-6360; e-mail: reservations@bestbnb.com; www.bestbnb.com.

This intimate private beach house made for two features a king bed, a full kitchen, an outdoor shower and a hammock. Puako Beach is across the quiet street.

Rates: from $165

CONDOMINIUMS

The Bay Club

Waikoloa Beach Resort, Waikoloa, Hawai'i. Agent: South Kohala Management 800-822-4252, 808-883-8500, fax 808-883-9818, e-mail: info@ southkohala.com, www.southkohala.com.

Two-bedroom quality condos near the beach at 'Anaeho'omalu Bay and the Kings' Shops. Each air-conditioned unit has two bedrooms and two baths, ceiling fans, washer-dryer, full kitchen, private lanai with wet bar, maid service and upscale furnishings. Common areas include tennis courts, two swimming pools with jacuzzi, barbecue area, exercise room and sauna, plus all the facilities of the Waikoloa Beach Resort.

Rates: $152-$295

Fairway Villas

Waikoloa Beach Resort, Waikoloa, Hawai'i. Agent: Aloha Hawaii Vacations/Aldridge Associates Realtors, 800-66-ALOHA; 808-883-8300; fax 808-883-9102; e-mail: kim@alohahawaiivacations.com; www.aloha hawaiivacations.com.

Located within the Waikoloa Beach Resort area, across the lake from Kings' Shops. This water-view condo offers spacious two-bedroom, two-bath units, tastefully decorated in a tropical plantation style with fully equipped kitchens and large lanai. Discounted rates for condo guests on resort golf courses.

Rates: $102-$190

The Islands at Mauna Lani

68-1050 Mauna Lani Point Drive, Mauna Lani Resort, Kohala Coast, HI 96743-9704. 808-885-5022. Reservations agents: Classic Resorts 800-642-6284, fax 808-661-1025, e-mail: info@classicresorts.com, www.classic resorts.com; South Kohala Management 800-822-4254, 808-883-8500, fax 808-883-9818, www.southkohala.com, e-mail: info@southkohala.com.

This 46-unit super-luxury townhouse complex is surrounded by the lush fairways of the championship Francis I'i Brown Golf Course and five acres of saltwater ponds, streams and waterfalls filled with fish and marine life. The 2BR and 3BR units are incredibly spacious with full kitchen, living room, dining room, bathrooms and private lanais and carports, plus laundry room. They are tastefully furnished with contemporary island-style decor and furniture. These are excellent vacation units for large families or groups wanting lots of space. Amenities include jacuzzi, swimming pool and barbecue areas. Guests have access to Mauna Lani Resort beaches, golf, the Mauna Lani Racquet Club tennis facilities and award-winning restaurants. This condo provides the ultimate in a VIP condo vacation experience; three-night minimum stay. Rates include a full-size car picked up at Kona Airport and a grocery starter package with breakfast items.

Rates: $540-$725

Kolea

Waikoloa Beach Resort, Waikoloa, Hawai'i. Agent: South Kohala Management 800-822-4252; 808-883-8500; fax 808-883-9818; e-mail: info@southkohala.com; www.southkohala.com.

A gated community with direct access to the beach at Anaeho'omalu Bay, the elegant three-bedroom, three-bath villas at Kolea are something special. Air-conditioned, well-appointed units have ceiling fans, laundry room, gourmet kitchen, entertainment lanai with gas grill and wine cooler. Extensive use of natural stone and koa wood throughout. Maid service is provided twice weekly. The Kolea Beach Club welcomes guests with comfortable lounges to enjoy the views or plunge into the infinity pool. Extras include a lava spa with sand bottom, keiki pool with waterfall, picnic pavilion and fitness center.

Rates: $385-$550

★ Mauna Lani Point Condominiums

68-1050 Mauna Lani Point Drive, Mauna Lani Resort, Kohala Coast, HI 96743-9704. Reservations: Classic Resorts 800-642-6284, 808-885-5022, fax 808-661-0125, e-mail: info@classicresorts.com, www.classicresorts. com; Pleasant Hawaiian Holidays 800-672-4587.

This 116-unit complex sits next to the ocean amid the fairways of Mauna Lani's renowned Francis I'i Brown South Golf Course. It is perhaps one of the Big Island's best-kept secrets among luxury vacation rentals. The units have either garden fairway or ocean fairway views. The extra-large units are very well appointed and include large private lanais, living and dining areas, full kitchens, microwave, TV, laundry facilities, air conditioning, double soaking tubs and many other amenities. Each unit has carport parking. These are excellent units for families and groups, plenty of space to spread out; great for youngsters. Easy access to the resort's fine golf, tennis and award-winning restaurants. Guests get preferred tee times at either of the North or South golf courses and reserved court time at the Racquet Club for tennis on hard or grass courts. There is also a private beach club with restaurant at Makaiwa Bay's lovely white-sand beach. Guests have access to a whirlpool, sauna, swimming pool and barbecue pavilion. Three-night minimum stay in high season, none in low season.

Rates: 1BR $340-$445; 2BR $450-$650

Mauna Lani Terrace Condominium

Mauna Lani Resort, Kohala Coast, HI 96743. Agent: South Kohala Management 800-822-4252; 808-883-8500; fax 808-883-9818; e-mail: info@southkohala.com; www.southkohala.com.

These luxury condos are located adjacent to the Mauna Lani Bay Hotel & Bungalows at Mauna Lani Resort. The spacious units are sparkling and well maintained throughout with the tasteful decor and furnishings expected of an upscale vacation residence in the special luxurious ambiance of Mauna Lani. All units are air conditioned with ceiling fan in living room, private lanais, wet bars, and complete laundry facilities. There is easy access to the resort's world-class golf and tennis, health club and water sports. Five-night minimum stay in high season, three nights in low season.

Rates: $284-$580

Puako Beach Condos

3 Puako Beach Drive, Kamuela, HI 96743. Agent: Hawai'i Vacation Rentals 808-882-7000; e-mail: seaside@aloha.net; www.vacationbigisland.com.

This 40-unit condo complex has only a few units available for vacation rentals, so call early. Located in the quiet Puako Beach area near Hapuna Beach State Park on the Kohala Coast, it provides a casual, affordable beach town experience in the heart of expensive resort country. Fully equipped 3-bedroom/2-bath units have TV and kitchen. Great ocean views.

Rates: $140

★ The Shores at Waikoloa

HC02 Box 5460, Waikoloa, HI 96743. 808-885-5001. Agents: South Kohala Management 800-822-4252; 808-883-8500; fax 808-883-9818; e-mail: info@southkohala.com; www.southkohala.com.

There are 64 units available in rental programs. These are 1-2-3 BR, all fully air-conditioned, with full kitchen, TV, washer/dryer, private lanai and wet bar as standard features. The units are very spacious and well furnished with lots of extra room and large bathrooms. Perfect for families. Guests have easy access to pool, barbecue facilities, tennis courts and adjacent Waikoloa Beach and King's Golf Courses. Guests can enjoy dining at any of several resort restaurants at the Waikoloa Beach Marriott or Hilton Waikoloa Village. Golf course fairway location in Waikoloa Beach Resort.

Rates: $148-$236

The Villages at Mauna Lani

Mauna Lani Resort, 68-1400 Mauna Lani Drive, Kohala Coast, HI 96743. Agent: South Kohala Management 800-822-4252; 808-883-8500; fax 808-883-9818; e-mail: info@southkohala.com; www.southkohala.com.

A private townhome property with three models of high-end vacation residences, each with over 2,000 square feet of luxury. Contemporary in design, with zoned air conditioning and ceiling fans, 3 bedrooms, 3.5 bathrooms, gourmet kitchen with center island, decadent baths, great room and dining room. Some units are complete with private pool and spa. Each offers a covered lanai with wet bar, refrigerator and gas grill. Maid service is included twice weekly. The Amenity Center offers a swimming pool and exercise facilities.

Rates: $387-$695

The Vista Waikoloa

69-1010 Keana Place, Waikoloa Beach Resort, Waikoloa, HI 96743. Agents: South Kohala Management 800-822-4252, 808-883-8500, fax 808-883-9818, e-mail: info@southkohala.com; www.southkohala.com; Aloha Hawaii Vacations/Aldridge Associates Realtors, 800-66-ALOHA; 808-883-8300; fax 808-883-9102; e-mail: kim@alohahawaiivacations.com; www.alohahawaiivacations.com.

This luxurious development has 122 units, some in vacation rental programs. The multi-building complex is located right on Waikoloa Beach Drive between the Waikoloa Beach Marriott and Hilton Waikoloa Village and next to the golf course fairways. The spacious units are very nicely furnished with full kitchens, fully air conditioned with access to pool, spa and all resort recreational facilities. Daily maid service is included.

Rates: $140-$395

Waikoloa Colony Villas

Waikoloa Beach Resort, Waikoloa, Hawai'i. Agents: Aloha Hawaii Vacations/Aldridge Associates Realtors, 800-66-ALOHA; 808-883-8300; fax 808-883-9102; e-mail: kim@alohahawaiivacations.com; www.alohahawaiivacations.com; South Kohala Management 800-822-4252; 808-883-8500; fax 808-883-9818; e-mail: info@southkohala.com; www.southkohala.com.

A luxury townhome property with two- and three-bedroom units to accommodate up to eight persons. Each has vaulted ceilings, washer-dryer, central air-conditioning, two baths with shower and soaking tub in the bath, large covered lanai, TV/VCR, full kitchen with dishwasher and microwave. The artfully landscaped grounds contain two swimming pools, tennis courts, a recreation room with kitchen, poolside barbecue area, jacuzzi and fitness center.

Rates: $128-$250

Waikoloa Village

All of the below properties are represented by Aloha Hawaii Vacations/Aldridge Associates Realtors, 800-66-ALOHA; 808-883-8300; fax 808-883-9102; e-mail: kim@alohahawaiivacations.com; www.alohahawaiivacations.com.

Waikoloa Village is a residential subdivision located six miles up *mauka* (toward the mountain) from the Waikoloa Resort area along the Kohala Coast. It is a growing community with a small shopping center, grocery and gas station, three restaurants, snack bars, a new coffee shop and various services including a bank with ATM, post office and Robert Trent, Jr., golf course. Several good condo properties are available at reasonable prices, for families who don't mind a ten-minute drive to the beach. Rates fluctuate widely depending on length of stay (three- to seven-night minimum), size of unit, number of guests and time of year. Generally, Waikoloa Village is a real bargain with all the comforts of home.

Waikoloa Villas   One-, two-, and three-bedroom units with lovely golf course views (and some ocean), two baths, living room

and full kitchen with dishwasher and microwave, ceiling fans, laundry facilities, cable TV/VCR, swimming pool to accommodate one to eight persons.
Rates: $65-$165

The Fairways at Waikoloa Two-bedroom/two-and-a-half-bath units overlooking the third green of the Robert Trent Jones, Sr., golf course. Each has central air conditioning, full kitchen with dishwasher and washer-dryer, jacuzzi tub in the master bath and large wrap-around lanai. Common areas include a swimming pool with barbecue area.
Rates: $95-$180

Waikoloa Village Condominiums One-bedroom/one-bath units with cable TV, lanai and washer-dryer. Full kitchens have dishwasher and microwave.
Rates: $65-$130

Waikoloa Greens Two-bedroom/two-bath units overlooking the golf course, with ceiling fans, washer-dryer, cable TV, full kitchen with dishwasher and microwave. Common areas include swimming pool, barbecue area, workout rooms and kids' playground.
Rates: $81-$130

Paniolo Club Two-bedroom/two-bath units, each with full kitchen including dishwasher and microwave, washer-dryer, living room with cable TV/VCR. Tennis courts and pool nearby.
Rates: $55-$120

HOTELS, RESORTS AND HOMES

★ Fairmont Orchid Hawai'i
1 North Kaniku Drive, Kohala Coast, HI 96743. 800-845-9905;
808-885-2000; fax 808-885-1064; e-mail:
orchid@fairmont.com; www.fairmont.com/orchid.

This lovely 539-room beachside hotel, located at the world-class Mauna Lani Resort, has undergone an extensive renovation, bringing a new dimension to an already-excellent property. Championship golf and tennis courts, professional conference facilities, fine dining and the acclaimed, expanded Spa Without Walls add up to a rewarding resort experience for individuals, families or groups. The guest rooms and suites (54, including 2 presidential suites and its fabled "Gold Floor" with VIP services and lavish appointments) are tastefully decorated and feature mini bar, marble bathrooms, TV with movies and video games, bathrobes, iron and ironing board and other amenities. A daily "resort fee" provides for additional amenities and complimentary use of resort facilities, daily newspaper, spa admission, fitness classes and other special offerings, not the least of which is a complimentary "Kids Eat Free" program.

Restaurants include the well-known Brown's Beach House, the Orchid Court, The Grill and Norio's Sushi Bar and Restaurant for excellent Japanese cuisine. There are also several lounges and bars, including the Kahakai Bar with unbeatable views. The hotel emphasizes recreation, with focus on the attractive white-sand beach and swimming lagoon. A beach equipment and water sports concession provides snorkel, scuba and seasonal whale-watching cruises, sunset sails and many other ocean options. A staff of "beachboys" is on hand to make you feel at home at the ocean, with activities and cultural talk-story sessions and a 35-foot voyaging canoe. There is also a large freshwater pool and jacuzzi, an excellent 10-court tennis pavilion including lighted exhibition courts, and a health and fitness center. Golfers can indulge their passion for the game at the Francis I'i Brown North and South Courses. In addition, you'll find a ballroom, meeting rooms and an outdoor amphitheater. Full-service staff, business center, and theme parties are available, as are settings for picture-perfect weddings and dreamy receptions. Babysitting can be arranged through the concierge. The hotel has received wide acclaim from the media, including Gold Key and Gold Platter Awards from *Meetings and Conventions Magazine*, among others. Value-added packages or "experiences" are offered seasonally. Please inquire when you call for reservations.

Rates: Fairmont Rooms $299-$559, Partial Ocean View $449, Ocean View $559, Deluxe Ocean Front $729, Suites $729-$2,999

★ Four Seasons Resort Hualalai
100 Kaupulehu Drive, Kaupulehu-Kona, HI 96740. 888-332-3442; 808-325-8000; fax 808-325-8053; www.fourseasons.com/locations/hualalai.

Since its opening in 1996, this luxury property has added an element of quality to the Kohala Coast, earning the AAA five-diamond award for excellence in 1999 and every year since. Located on a remote stretch of beachfront land just north of Kona International Airport right next door to Kona Village, the Four Seasons offers 243 rooms and suites arranged in low-rise bungalows along the beachfront or golf course. There are one-, two- and three-bedroom suites, some with private plunge pools. Guests are greeted with welcome lei, tropical juice and cold *oshibori* towels. The large guest rooms (over 600 square feet) are provided with private lanai or garden, TV, fax, refrigerator, large bathrooms with aromatherapy candles and bath salts, and many more high-caliber amenities. Its restaurants are notable for fine food and service, and there are also lounges and more casual eateries. Complimentary beach and ocean recreation includes snorkeling, kayaking, sailing, outrigger canoes and glass-bottom boat rides. Deep-sea fishing and scuba dive room packages are available seasonally. Babysitting can be arranged, and a long list of baby needs like strollers and "child-proofed" rooms are available. Meetings and group events are accommodated in flexible indoor and outdoor function spaces for up to 500 people; the creative staff and wealth of on-site facilities make it easy for planners. There are romantic wedding sites from intimate to grand, with special touches for your special day. Other packages are available except during the "Festive Season" December 19–January 3.

Rates: Golf Oceanview $560, Oceanview $700, Oceanview Prime $725, Oceanfront $800. 1BR and 2BR Suites $1,535-$6,500, Presidential Villa Suite $5,200-$5,950, 3BR Villa Suite, $6,700; $120 third adult in room

★ Hapuna Beach Prince Hotel

62-100 Kauna'oa Drive, Kohala Coast, HI 96743. 866-PRINCE-6; 808-880-1111; fax 808-880-3142; e-mail: mkrres@hapunabeachprincehotel.com; www.hapunabeachprincehotel.com.

This contemporary luxury hotel is named after its breathtaking setting—Hapuna Beach, a long strand of beautiful white sand that's one of the best in the state. Hapuna is part of the legendary Mauna Kea Resort (with neighboring Mauna Kea Beach Hotel), offering two championship golf courses, two picture-perfect natural beaches, thirteen oceanside tennis courts, ten restaurants and unlimited recreation options. Hapuna's 350 ocean-facing guest rooms and suites have private lanai, TV/VCR (with video games), dataports, coffeemaker, refrigerator, bathrobes, slippers and other deluxe amenities. Guests are greeted with tropical juice and chilled oshibori towels. The 4,000-square-foot Hapuna Suite is an exclusive private villa with three bedrooms, kitchen, living room, dining room, den and private swimming pool, jacuzzi and large lanai overlooking the ocean. Attendants serve morning breakfast and evening pupus, and see to your special requests.

The hotel has a large whale-shaped swimming pool, health and fitness center, salon and day spa, resort shops and on-site services such as rental cars, helicopter flight seeing, and ocean activities. There are several restaurants and lounges. Babysitting can be arranged through the concierge. The scenic Hapuna Golf Course was designed by Arnold Palmer and Ed Seay, offering challenging links-style play from sea level to 700-foot elevation. Guests also have access to the famed Mauna Kea Golf Course designed by Robert Trent Jones, Sr., in 1965, and tennis buffs are welcome at the Mauna Kea Tennis Park. Hapuna Ballroom accommodates up to 900 guests for banquets, weddings and other special functions. Excellent conference facilities are available with full-service staff, business center, and dramatic indoor and outdoor locations. Value-added packages and promotional rates are available throughout the year, as well as internet deals. Please inquire when making reservations. Luxurious Vacation Residences are also available, 808-880-3490.

Rates: Terrace View $360, Partial Oceanview $420, Oceanview $470, Premium Oceanview $520, Oceanfront $650, Oceanfront Suite $1,250; Hapuna Suite $7,000

★ Hilton Waikoloa Village

425 Waikoloa Beach Drive, Kohala Coast, HI 96743-9791. 800-HILTONS; 808-886-1234; fax 808-886-2900; e-mail: waikoloa_rooms@hilton.com; www.hiltonwaikoloavillage.com.

At 1,240 rooms (57 are suites), this is the Kohala Coast's largest resort hotel. And, appropriate to the Big Island, everything here is done on a grand scale. The hotel occupies 62 acres lavishly landscaped like a huge oasis in the black lava desert. Water is the theme here, and water features are everywhere. The lush gardens are accented with meandering streams and waterfalls, pools and ponds. Guests travel through the resort via canal boats that cruise over a mile of waterways, or quiet tram trains that shuttle from one end of the resort to the other. Water babies of all ages can indulge in the Ocean Tower pool, the Kohala River Pool with a series of waterslides, or the Kona Pool, complete with waterfalls, whirlpools and a giant 175-foot waterslide. The four-acre ocean-fed lagoon is a giant living aquarium with a rainbow of tropical reef fish and marine life. The famed Dolphin Quest program provides hands-on educational experiences for hotel guests, working and playing with Atlantic bottlenose dolphins. Guests can also stroll the mile-long open-air museum walkway filled with a vast collection of Pacific and Asian artworks. The Hilton hosts 18 boutique and resort shops with everything from sundry items to fine jewelry, original art, handcrafts and fashion resort wear. Additional amenities include several restaurants, a gym and spa, two golf courses and tennis courts.

Other activities that can be arranged by the activities desk include varied in-hotel tours, horseback riding, catamaran sails, snorkel-dive cruises, deep-sea fishing, petroglyph tours, scenic flights and much more. "Legends of the Pacific" luau feast and hula show is presented weekly. With so many guest rooms, Hilton naturally caters to large groups. Meeting facilities include 21 meeting rooms and full-service banquet and convention services staff who specialize in creative theme events. The Hilton is also the only hotel on the island with tele-conference capability. The Hilton's emphasis on attentive aloha-style service in all areas, plus their incredible variety of energetic activities, makes this a family-friendly resort, offering a lot of fun without ever leaving the property. Inquire about value-added packages.

Rates: Garden View $219, Golf View $234, Mountainview $244-$314, Part Oceanview $254-$339, Deluxe Ocean $289-$369. Inquire for current packages and specials, rates on suite accommodations

★ Kona Village Resort

P.O. Box 1299, Kailua-Kona, HI 96745. 800-367-5290; 808-325-5555; fax 808-325-5124; e-mail: kvr@aloha.net; www.konavillage.com.

Kona Village is something special. The first resort to occupy the coast and the only one to remain virtually unchanged since its creation almost 40 years ago, this is the Big Island's most thoughtfully authentic, truly unique resort experience. Situated on the beach at Kahuwai Bay, Kona Village stretches along the coastline in a leisurely fashion. There is no central hotel building; 125 separate thatch-roofed *hale* (houses) are the guest rooms. The *hale* reflect the traditional design and decor of the South Pacific Islands including Hawai'i, Tahiti, Fiji and the Marquesas. All guest *hale* have modern conveniences like a large bathroom, ceiling fan, comfortable, quality tropical furniture, coffeemaker and refrigerator, and lanai with lounges or beach hammocks. What it doesn't have are room phones, TVs or radios to disturb the peace and quiet. The only clock in your hale is on the coffeemaker. We suggest you ignore it, remove your watch and experience what it feels like to live on your own personal schedule. This is a magical, escapist's retreat. Appreciate it.

Excellent food and personable service are offered in the dining rooms. The resort also has cocktails and nightly entertainment. A selection of Honeymoon/Celebration packages are available seasonally and romance is encouraged during May and September, when children's programs and rates are temporarily on hold. A professional wedding coordinator on staff assists with heavenly weddings in a variety of stunning tropical settings. Kona Village has received wide acclaim and recognition from international travel guides and publications such as *Fortune, Travel & Leisure, Condé Nast Traveler, Gourmet Magazine* and many others. It is also winner of the prestigious Kahili

Award for historic preservation from the Hawaii Visitors and Convention Bureau. Three generations of returning guests are testimony to Kona Village's success as a truly unique and valuable destination. Guest room rates include breakfast, lunch and dinner for two.

Rates: One-room *hale*: Standard $530, Moderate $670, Superior $745, Deluxe $830, Royal $940; Two-room *hale*: Garden $875, Superior $965, Deluxe $1,055, Royal $1,160; additional guests infant to two years free, 3 to 5 $38, 6 to 12 $143, 13 and up $193

★ *Mauna Kea Beach Hotel*

62-100 Mauna Kea Beach Drive, Kohala Coast, HI 96743. 866-PRINCE-6; 808-882-7222; fax 808-882-5700; e-mail: mkrres@maunakeabeachhotel.com; www.maunakeabeachhotel.com.

This is the property that started it all and set the bar very high for Big Island hospitality. Created by American conservationist Laurance S. Rockefeller in 1965, its $15 million price tag was the highest ever paid to build a hotel. Today, the Mauna Kea is still one of the best destinations in the world. Guests are still welcomed with a plumeria lei, in the timeless tradition of aloha. Together with its sister property, Hapuna Beach Prince Hotel, Mauna Kea offers two of Hawaii's best beaches, two golf courses, thirteen tennis courts, ten restaurants and unlimited options for recreation, accessible to guests via complimentary inter-resort shuttle.

The 310 guest rooms and suites have ocean, mountain or beachfront views and feature large private lanais, generous closet space, comfortable island furnishings and appointments, coffeemaker, chill box, bottled water, in-room safe, robes and slippers. You can have your TV removed by request and we'd like to suggest that you take a vacation from the TV, too, and rediscover the pleasures of conversation, quiet and the sounds of nature in this very special setting.

The hotel also houses a remarkable collection of museum-quality Pacific and Asian arts and artifacts, which includes 30 handmade Hawaiian quilts, the largest collection in Hawai'i. Complimentary tours are offered weekly, as are tours of the hotel's gardens, mature specimen trees and lush tropical landscaping. Other resort features include elegant locations for celebrations, a full range of salon services and spa therapies, artfully designed freshwater pool with jacuzzi, fitness center, yoga and other exercise classes, a program of Hawaiian arts and crafts, and boutique shops. Babysitting can be arranged with the concierge. The main event is the beach. Proclaimed the nation's #1 beach in 2000 by the "Dr. Beach" annual ratings, Kauna'oa Beach is a crescent of white sand with generally tranquil waters. Packages are available seasonally, as well as internet "hot deals." The holiday period between Christmas and New Year's is traditionally sold out a year in advance. The Mauna Kea is consistently rated among top U.S. resorts in *Condé Nast Traveler, Travel & Leisure* and *Andrew Harper's Hideaway Report.* They enjoy a loyal population of returning guests, who, combined with the genuinely hospitable nature of the staff, create a sense of family, tradition and care. It makes a difference. Luxurious Vacation Residences are also available, 808-880-3490.

Rates: Mountain View $370, Premier Mountain View $390, Beachfront floors two through four $575, Beachfront first floor $620, Deluxe Oceanview $590, Premier Oceanview $650, Suites $975-$1,600

★ Mauna Lani Bay Hotel and Bungalows

68-1400 Mauna Lani Drive, Kohala Coast, HI 96743-9796. 808-885-6622; 800-367-2323; fax 808-885-1484; e-mail: reservations@mauna lani.com; www.maunalani.com.

This sleek, elegant 350-room property sits on 29 lush, oceanfront acres with 36 holes of championship golf, tennis courts, beach activities, luxury spa and fitness center, excellent dining and Hawaiian cultural and archaeological sites. Built in 1983, the Mauna Lani has earned accolades from *Condé Nast Traveler, Travel & Leisure* and other national travel publications. The hotel fronts beautiful Makaiwa Bay Beach at Kalahuipua'a, and all but 27 guest rooms have ocean views thanks to the building's unique shape. The remainder face tropical gardens and Hawaiian fishponds. Guest rooms are very spacious at 550-plus square feet and elegantly appointed with private lanai, TV and VCR, refrigerator, air conditioning, mini-bar, dataports, robes, slippers, coffee, daily newspaper and many other high-end amenities. Fully equipped 1BR, 2BR and 3BR villas are available at Mauna Lani Terrace within the resort, ideal for families. Guests of the villas enjoy full hotel privileges with the exception of room service. Mauna Lani also offers five individual bungalows. These are private, 4,000-square-foot accommodations, each with two master bedroom suites and three baths, attended by round-the-clock butlers who tailor personal service to suit the most discriminating tastes. Babysitting can be arranged through the concierge.

Rates: Mountain View $395, Garden View $475, Oceanview $620, Deluxe Oceanview $660, Oceanfront $710, Deluxe Oceanfront $750, Corner Oceanfront $850, Suites $950, Bungalows from $4,600; The Villas: 1BR $575, 2BR $775, 3BR $1,095, three-night minimum

★ *Waikoloa Beach Marriott, An Outrigger Resort*
69-275 Waikoloa Beach Drive, Kohala Coast, HI 96743. Reservations:
Outrigger Hotels Hawaii 800-688-7444; 808-886-6789; fax 800-622-
4852 or 808-886-7852; www.waikoloabeachmarriott.com.

This elegant 547-room hotel is located just off the beautiful half-mile crescent-shaped 'Anaeho'omalu Bay Beach and lagoon. A dramatic 40-foot mural by noted island artist Herb Kane graces one side of the lobby. The painting shows Captain George Vancouver's ship, *Discovery*, being escorted into 'Anaeho'omalu Bay by a Hawaiian sailing canoe with the imposing Mauna Kea and Kohala Mountains in the background. The mural sits behind the hotel's century-old Hawaiian outrigger canoe, *Kaimalino*. Guest rooms have garden, mountain or ocean views and come with TV, radio, refrigerator, robes, coffee and tea service, dataports and daily maid service. There is also a separate "Voyagers Club," located on the top floor of the Ka'ahumanu Wing, operated as a special concierge section of the hotel with a separate staff and first-class services such as complimentary continental breakfast and sunset cocktails. Other amenities include restaurants and lounges, a ballroom, a salon and spa, and beach activities. With 'Anaeho'omalu Beach and its historic fishponds fronting the hotel, this is one of the loveliest settings along the Kohala Coast. Guests have access to the excellent Waikoloa Beach Resort golf at the Kings' Course, designed by Tom Weiskopf and Jay Morris, and the Beach Course, designed by Robert Trent Jones, Jr. There are six tennis courts and an "action pool" with a 90-foot water slide. Guests of the hotel also have charging privileges at restaurants across the street in the Kings' Shops complex. Complimentary shuttle service is provided. Babysitting can be arranged through the concierge.

Rates: Garden/Mountain View $219, Partial Oceanview $254, Oceanfront $324, Cabana $574. 1BR Suite $975, Royal Suite $3,100

NORTH KOHALA DISTRICT

BED AND BREAKFASTS

Kohala Country Adventures
P.O. Box 703, Kapa'au, HI 96755. 866-892-2484; cell 808-987-7173;
808-889-5663; fax 808-889-6133; e-mail: getaway@pixi.com; www.kcad
ventures.com.

This country guesthouse is set in lovely tropical gardens on a ten-acre farm. Guest rooms have private baths and entrances. The area is noted for a cool, comfortable and breezy climate. Enjoy sunset views of neighboring Maui and easy access to Kohala Coast attractions. Member-HIBBA.

Rates: $75-$160

HOTELS, HOSTELS AND HOMES

Kohala Village Inn

55-514 Hawi Road, Hawi, HI 96719. 808-889-0419; www.kohalavillage inn.com.

The recently refurbished plantation/island-style rooms and suites in this North Kohala Coast inn are clean and simple, all with private bath and some with TV. Easy access to Hawi and Kapa'au towns, which are both growing into colorful art communities with a variety of interesting shops and restaurants. Nearby activities include beautiful Pololu Valley for hiking or horseback riding, explorations of Mo'okini Heiau and King Kamehameha's Birthplace, and seasonal whale watching. The inn has all the country charm of a very small town, and friendly folks. There's also good-quality food in the delightful, family-run dining room for breakfast, lunch and dinner.

Rates: $65-$120

Waimea Town

BED AND BREAKFASTS

Aaah The Views B&B

66-1773 Alaneo Street, P.O. Box 6593, Kamuela, HI 96743. 866-885-3455; fax 808-885-4031; www.aaahtheviews.com.

This charming B&B is set beside a stream with frequent rainbows and a view of Mauna Kea's summit across rolling pasture land. Comfortable, quiet, affordable accommodations near Kohala Coast beaches and resorts and fine dining, shopping and activities in Waimea town. Four individual rooms: The Tree-Top Suite is a whimsical two-bedroom suite perched in the trees, with private bath, TV/VCR, phone, refrigerator, microwave and coffeemaker (sleeps 6). The Dream Room has a jacuzzi, outdoor shower on private deck, king bed and kitchen. The Garden Cottage offers kitchen, private bath, loft and deck, TV/VCR and phone (sleeps 4). The Skylight Room has double bed, stocked bookshelves, computer desk, kitchenette, private bath and cable TV. Member-HIBBA.

Rates: $65-$145

Belle Vue B&B

1351 Konokohau Road, P.O. Box 1295, Kamuela, HI 96743. 800-772-5044; phone/fax 808-885-7732; e-mail: bellvue@aloha.net; www.hawaii bellevue.com. Reservations also through Hawai'i's Best B&Bs, P.O. Box 485, Laupahoehoe, HI 96764, 800-262-9912, 808-962-0100, fax 808-962-6360, e-mail: reservations@bestbnb.com; www.bestbnb.com.

This is a spacious two-story cottage bordering the open pasture-lands of famous Parker Ranch in Waimea. There is a kitchen and cozy fireplace. Upstairs and downstairs units sleep four each. Walking distance to restaurants and shopping. German, French and Italian spoken here. Member-Hawai'i's Best, HIBBA.

Rates: $85-$165; $25 extra person

Ekolu K Ohana Farm

P.O. Box 1621, Kamuela, HI 96743. 808-885-0525; e-mail: ekofarm@gte.net; www.localaccess.com/ekofarm.

We give credit to Ekolu K Ohana Farm for having one of the cuter websites around, with "translations" in English and pidgin. The accommodations are large and comfortable, located on the *mauka* (mountain) side of Waimea town among the fields of a working protea flower farm, with lovely views of Mauna Kea on clear days. A studio, 1BR and 2BR cottage all have private entry and bath (2 in the 2BR), fully equipped kitchens, laundry facilities and welcome basket of baked goods, coffee, fruit and juice and the farm's own *poha* jams and other goodies.

Rates: $60-$170

★ Jacaranda Inn

808-885-8813. Reservations through: Hawai'i's Best B&B, P.O. Box 485, Laupahoehoe, HI 96764, 800-262-9912; 808-962-0100; fax 808-962-6360; e-mail: reservations@bestbnb.com; www.bestbnb.com.

The Jacaranda Inn is one of Waimea's most historic homes and is prominent in the history of Big Island ranching. Built in 1897 as the private residence of an early Parker Ranch manager, the home was purchased by Laurence Rockefeller in 1961 while he built the Mauna Kea Beach Hotel down on the coast. Over the years, the inn welcomed numerous VIPs and celebrities, and was used as the general manager's residence. There are eight spacious and luxurious guest suites in the main house and a separate three-bedroom/three-bath cottage for families or groups. Guests have access to a breakfast room, formal dining room, library/billiard room and lounge. Six of the guest suites feature a sitting room and large bath with whirlpool tub. One room is ADA compliant. The 11-acre site is next to a seasonal stream and waterfall on the west edge of Waimea on Kawaihae Road just minutes away from Kohala Coast resorts, beaches, golf and recreation. Nearby Waimea town offers several fine restaurants, shopping, activities and more. Member-Hawai'i's Best.

Rates: $159-$450

Kamuela's Mauna Kea View Suite and Cottage

P.O. Box 6375, Kamuela, HI 96743. 808-885-8425; e-mail: maunakea view1@webtv.net; www.hawaiibedandbreakfast.org.

This home offers wide open pastoral ranchland views backdropped with Mauna Kea. There is a private suite with 2BRs, living room and kitchen. There is also an attached cottage with chalet-design living room, kitchenette, fireplace, etc. All have queen beds, color TV and phone. Convenient to area attractions and Kohala Coast resorts. Two-night minimum.

Rates: $77-$88; $15 extra person

Merry's Herb Garden

Reservations through Hawai'i's Best B&Bs, P.O. Box 485, Laupahoehoe, HI 96764, 800-262-9912; 808-962-0100; fax 808-962-6360; e-mail: reservations@bestbnb.com; www.bestbnb.com.

This attractive country home reflects the ranching history of Waimea and old Hawai'i. There's an attached 2-bedroom wing with private entrance. It opens to lush green pastures and a distant view of rising Mauna Kea Mountain. The open-beamed ceilings and walls of pane-glass windows accent a spacious living room highlighted by ranch-style furniture and decor. The living room has a dining table plus small refrigerator, microwave, TV/VCR and phone. Two-night minimum. Member-Hawai'i's Best.

Rates: $110; $15 extra person

Waimea Garden Cottages

Reservations through Hawai'i's Best B&Bs, P.O. Box 485, Laupahoehoe, HI 96764, 800-262-9912; 808-962-0100; fax 808-962-6360; e-mail: reservations@bestbnb.com; www.bestbnb.com.

This streamside cottage has three private units on 1.5 acres. The cottage's Kohala and Waimea wings have antique furnishings, patio French doors and decor that lend a pleasant country atmosphere. Three-night minimum stay. Member-Hawai'i's Best.

Rates: $140-$160; $15 extra person

HOTELS, HOSTELS AND HOMES

Kamuela Inn

P.O. Box 1994, Kamuela, HI 96743. 800-555-8968; 808-885-4243; fax 808-885-8857; e-mail: kaminn@aloha.net; www.kamuelainn.com.

This country inn features 31 comfortable standard and kitchenette rooms with TV. The newer Mauna Kea Wing has several spacious, well-decorated rooms, two executive suites and a bright cozy coffee lanai where daily continental breakfast is provided. The original wing's rooms are smaller and simpler but very well kept and clean. Located in a quiet, cool setting across from Edelweiss Restaurant off Highway 19, only 15 miles from Kohala Coast resorts and beaches. Reservations should be made well in advance.

Rates: Standard Single/Double $59, Deluxe $72; Suite (max 3) with kitchen $89, Suite (max 4) with kitchen $99, Penthouse Suite (max 5) $99; Mauna Kea Wing: King Beds $85, Two Twins $79, Executive Suites $185

Waimea Country Lodge

65-1210 Lindsey Road, Kamuela, HI 96743. 808-885-4100; fax 808-885-6711. Agents: Castle Resorts & Hotels 800-367-5004, fax 808-596-0158, www.castleresorts.com.

This small 21-unit country motel features spacious rooms with two king or queen beds. Clean pleasant furnishings, TV and phone with nice meadow and mountain views of Waimea ranch country. Adjacent to Paniolo Country Inn restaurant and nearby shopping, other restaurants and area attractions. It's only a 15-mile drive to the Kohala Coast resorts and beaches.

Rates: Standard $101, Superior $107, Studio Kitchenette $117; $25 extra person

Hamakua District

BED AND BREAKFASTS

★ Akiko's Buddhist Bed & Breakfast

P.O. Box 272, Wailea/Hakalau, HI 96710. 808-963-6422; e-mail: msakiko@aloha.net; www.alternative-hawaii.com/akiko.

Located 15 miles north of Hilo, this peaceful, simple and quiet retreat is hosted by island-born Akiko Masuda. Enjoy walks down main street Wailea town, past green plantation houses with weathered tin roofs, yards bursting in a jubilee of trees, shrubs and flowers of infinite variety in a once-thriving plantation community. Akiko invites her guests to return home to a time when life was simple and gracious. The main house, styled after a rural Japanese monastery with "silent hours," is a 5BR family plantation home. There are also separate rental units on the property: the Banana Patch and Mango Tree Cottages and the Artist Studio. Weekly/monthly rates available.

Rates: $40 single, $55 double; $5 extra person

Hale Kukui Orchard Retreat

P.O. Box 5044, Kukuihaele, HI 96727. 800-444-7130; 808-775-7130; e-mail: retreat@halekukui.com; www.halekukui.com.

There are 2BR and luxury cottage units and a private studio on four acres of high cliff overlooking the Waipi'o Valley and towering coastline bluffs. Located in lush, landscaped grounds with a tropical setting, units have private bath, kitchen and outdoor tubs. Two-night minimum, seventh night free.

Rates: Studio $125, 2BR $160, luxury cottage $175

Kalopa Homestead Guest House

44-2541 Keahua Road, Honoka'a, HI 96727. 877-825-6185; 808-775-7167; e-mail: epe@aloha.net; www.hawaiivacationcottage.com.

A two-bedroom cottage with open view, sleeps two to six people comfortably. Facilities include whirlpool tub/shower, full kitchen, laundry facilities, TV/VCR, free local phone calls. The family shares the homestead with a small herd of dairy goats and invites guests to help bottle-feed the kids. Member-HIBBA.

Rates: $110-$150

The Log Cabin

P.O. Box 1994, Kamuela, HI 96743. 800-555-3963; 808-885-4243; fax 808-885-8857; e-mail: kaminn@aloha.net; www.kamuelainn.com.

This country log house is located a few miles east of Waimea in the upcountry Ahualoa area. The house is at the 2,500-foot elevation level in a cool, lush forest, minutes from Waimea and Honoka'a towns, Waipi'o Valley and other attractions and activities. The lodge-style house has five comfortable and well-appointed guest rooms. The Ekahi and Elima Rooms have private baths; the Elua, Ekolu and Eha Rooms have a shared bath. There is a spacious open-beam-ceiling living room with stone fireplace, library and TV and a large bright kitchen and dining room. Guests share access to an oriental-style gazebo hot tub. Two-night minimum stay.

Rates: Room/shared bath $59, Room/private bath $99, entire log cabin $375

Luana Ola B&B Cottages

P.O. Box 1967, Honoka'a, HI 96727. 800-357-7727; 808-775-1150; www.island-hawaii.com.

A private cottage with full bath, TV, kitchen, laundry, refrigerator, ocean view and convenient walking distance to Honoka'a town's shops and eateries. Member-HIBBA.

Rates: $100-$120 for 2, discounts for longer stays

Mountain Meadow Ranch B&B

46-3895 Kapuna Road, Honoka'a, HI 96727. Phone/fax 808-775-9376; e-mail: bill@mountainmeadowranch.com; www.mountainmeadowranch.com.

Located halfway between Kona and Hilo in romantic Ahualoa, high above the Hamakua Coast, Mountain Meadow is comprised of two separate units, each with its own charm and personality. The Main House B&B is the lower level of a large redwood ranch home, with two bedrooms and a common area with TV/VCR, book and video library, sauna, microwave and refrigerator. The Vacation Home is tucked away in a private part of the Mountain Meadow, with two bedrooms, full kitchen, laundry, TV/VCR and a wood stove. Scenic pastures and majestic trees provide lots of country charm and atmosphere on this seven-acre estate. Enjoy scenic areas like Waipi'o Valley, Parker Ranch, Mauna Kea and Waimea.

Rates: B&B $99 single, extra person $40, Cottage $135

Our Place B&B

P.O. Box 469, 3 Mamalahoa Highway, Papa'ikou, HI 96781. 808-964-5250; e-mail: rplace@aloha.net; www.ourplacebandb.com.

Located four miles north of Hilo off Highway 19, this is a large cedar home with three guest rooms with cable TV. A common lanai, open to each bedroom, overlooks a stream and tropical vegetation; Great Room features a library, fireplace and grand piano. No smoking indoors. Easy access to snorkeling and surfing, botanical gardens, Hawai'i Volcanoes National Park, and shopping and dining in Hilo. Two-night minimum stay.

Rates: $60-$120

★ Palms Cliff House Inn

P.O. Box 189, 28-3514 Mamalahoa Highway, Honomu, HI 96728-0189. 808-963-6076; fax 808-963-6316; e-mail: palmscliffhouse@aol.com; www.palmscliffhouse.com.

Located 15 minutes north of Hilo town, this secluded Victorian-style estate features eight suites with private baths and lanais, and amenities like private jacuzzis with ocean views, gourmet breakfasts, afternoon tea, yoga and cooking classes. Recognized by *Travel & Leisure* and earning a reputation as one of the best, this is a place to relax and enjoy all the advantages of a well-run B&B. Member-HIBBA.

Rates: $225-$375

★ Waianuhea

P.O. Box 185, 45-3505 Kahana Drive, Honoka'a, HI 96727; 888-775-2577; 808-775-1118; fax 888-296-6302; e-mail: info@waianuhea.com; www.waianuhea.com.

This is a special place, offering a more contemporary perspective from a secluded, peaceful *mauka* (mountain) location 2,500 feet above the Hamakua Coast. Waianuhea has five distinctive guest rooms, each with its own Hawaiian name and individual personality. All are complete with private baths, TV/DVD and CD players and internet connection. The bigger accommodations have large soaking tubs and gas or wood stoves. A hot gourmet breakfast is provided daily, or continental breakfast in your room if you prefer. Privacy is their specialty, but your hosts can arrange massage, island tours and other activities to fill your time. A great relaxation room with treatment area and outdoor solar-heated jacuzzi are available in the common area, which also has a snack bar. It's also a nice location for intimate weddings, retreats and exclusive workshops. Member-HIBBA.

Rates: $170-$400

★ Waipi'o Wayside B&B

P.O. Box 840, Honoka'a, HI 96727. 800-833-8849; phone/fax 808-775-0275; e-mail info@waipiowayside.com; www.waipiowayside.com.

This is a refurbished 1932-era sugar plantation home, set on the slopes of Mauna Kea in lush, mysterious Ahualoa, surrounded with colorful flowers and tropical plants. There are five vintage bedrooms, all with private bath: Moon Room with full-size bed and garden view, Plantation Room with double beds, Chinese Room with full-size bed, Bird's Eye Room with queen bed, and Library Room with queen bed and ocean view. Easy access to Waipi'o Valley, Waipi'o Ridge Walk, Kalopa Park, the Hamakua Coast and Waimea town. A lovely spot for family reunions, weddings and retreats. Member-HIBBA.

Rates: $95-$170; $25 extra person

HOTELS, HOSTELS AND HOMES

Hotel Honoka'a Club

P.O. Box 247, Mamane Street, Honoka'a, HI 96727. 800-808-0678; phone/fax 808-775-0678; e-mail: manager@hotelhona.com; www.hotel hono.com.

This rambling old wooden building has been a Honoka'a landmark for years, centrally located on the main street of town off Highway 19. Two different types of accommodations are available: backpacker rooms and hotel rooms. The backpacker rooms are inexpensive, basic lodging in dormitory rooms or private rooms with shared baths. Hotel rooms (all nonsmoking) offer cable TV, private bath, queen-size beds and continental breakfast. Corner guest rooms have ocean views.

Rates: Dorm $15, Backpacker room $25-$35, Standard hotel room $50-$55, Oceanview $60-$70

Waipi'o Lookout Vacation Rentals

P.O. Box 5022, Kukuihaele, HI 96727. 877-924-7464; 808-775-1306; e-mail: contact@waipiohi.net; www.waipiohi.net.

Hale Ono is a one-bedroom country rental on the cliffs overlooking the majestic Waipi'o Valley. Expect gorgeous sweeping coastal vistas, cliffs and cascading waterfalls. Forty acres of pasture with grazing horses complete the view. The rental has a queen bed, living room with full-size futon, a full bathroom, lanai, cable TV and phone; it sleeps up to four. It's a 30-minute walk down to the valley's black-sand beach. The quiet village of Kukuihaele is a short stroll away; larger Honoka'a town is nine miles away and has shopping and dining.

Rates for up to 3 persons: $100/night two-night minimum, $85/per night three-night minimum; $15 extra person; $510/week, up to three persons

Waipi'o Ridge Vacation Rentals

P.O. Box 5039, Kukuihaele, HI 96727. 808-775-0603; e-mail: rlasko 3343@aol.com; www.cyberrentals.com.

A one-bedroom home that sleeps four; fully furnished with refrigerator, microwave oven, coffee maker, fans, television, etc. Located near Waipi'o Valley.

Rates: $75-$85

Hilo

BED AND BREAKFASTS

At the Beach with Friends

369 Nene Street, Hilo, HI 96720. 808-934-8040; e-mail: claud@hilo.net; www.bed-and-breakfast-hilo-hawaii.com.

One of Hilo's best, this intricate, tropical home offers separate quarters with ocean view and a natural pond with koi, ducks and wild birds. Rooms have king bed, private bath, TV/VCR and fridge; common computer room, sitting area and covered lanai perfect for a rainy day. Beautifully decorated rooms are thoughtfully complete for guests, with snorkeling gear, beach towels and a cooler for picnics.

Rates: $120-$150

Bay House

42 Pukihae Street, Hilo, HI 96720. 888-235-8195; 808-961-6311; e-mail: bigbayhouse@excite.com; www.bayhousehawaii.com.

This attractive home overlooks Hilo Bay from a bluff setting. Guests enjoy oceanfront bedrooms with private bayside decks, private baths, TVs, Wi-Fi, continental breakfast with a view and a cliffside hot tub. Historic downtown Hilo is a short five-minute walk away; easy access to east Hawai'i attractions and activities. The home is wheelchair accessible. Each room sleeps two. Member-Hawai'i's Best, HIBBA.

Rates: $105-$120

Hale Kai Hawai'i B&B

Honoli'i Pali, Hilo, HI 96720. 808-935-6330; e-mail: stay@halekai hawaii.com; www.halekaihawaii.com.

This custom home perches on a pali (cliff) above the ocean two miles from downtown Hilo. Three guest rooms and four suites each have ocean views and private baths, king or queen beds, lanai and cable TV. Gourmet breakfast is served daily and the house is decorated with the owner's dramatic photography. Swimming pool and hot tub in the common area. Easy access to area attractions. Smoke-free property. Two-night minimum stay.

Rates: $110-$135; $20 extra person

Hilo Oceanfront B&B

1923 Kalanianaole, Hilo, HI 96720. 800-363-9524; 808-934-9004; fax 808-934-7128; e-mail: stay@hilooceanfront.com; www.hilooceanfront.com.

This beachside home is located in the Keaukaha area of Hilo four miles from the center of town. The two units have private entrance, bath, king bed, kitchenette, TV/VCR and phone. The Dolphin Studio has a private deck overlooking the beachside ponds. The Whale Suite has air conditioning and a large living room and opens onto a deck with hot tub. Easy access to all east Hawai'i attractions and activities, dining, shopping, etc.

Rates: Dolphin Studio $110; Whale Suite $140

Hilo Seaside Retreat

P.O. Box 10960, 1941 Kalanianaole, Hilo, HI 96721. 800-961-9602; fax 310-640-6080; e-mail: info@hiloseasideretreat.com; www.hiloseaside retreat.com.

This is a contemporary three-bedroom home with an adjoining apartment suite on a half-acre of tropical lawns and gardens leading to a private beach and ocean tidal pools; it's located in the Keaukaha area of Hilo just minutes from downtown. The Seaside Suite apartment unit has bedroom, living room, bath and kitchenette with private entrance and sleeps four or five; Master Suite bedroom has private bath, lanai access and ocean view and sleeps two; Lanai Room has lanai access and ocean view and sleeps two. Guests have use of jacuzzi, Japanese furo bath, private beach for swimming and snorkeling, and onsite massage therapy. Enjoy pleasant oceanside environment, listen to the soothing surf, forget the rest of the world for a while. Easy access to all east Hawai'i attractions and activities. Member-HIBBA.

Rates: $125-$165

Holmes' Sweet Home B&B

107 Koula Street, Hilo, HI 96720. 808-961-9089; fax 808-934-0711; e-mail: stay@hilohawaiibandb.com; www.hilohawaiibandb.com.

This island home has two guest units each with private bath, lanai, entrance and queen beds. There are also a sitting room and dining room to enjoy a fresh island breakfast; quiet private location with sweeping views of Hilo Bay. Member-HIBBA.

Rates: $75-$85; $10 extra person

★ The Inn at Kulaniapia Falls

866-935-6789; 808-935-6789, e-mail: waterfall@hilo.net; www.water fall.net.

Custom-built to be what it is: a classic Hawaiian inn. Located four miles from downtown Hilo (on a recently repaved road) with a 120-foot waterfall in its backyard that can be heard like background music throughout the property. Five elegant suites, each with private (marble) bath and lanai, Hawaiian quilts, *lauhala* mats and tropical-style appointments. A separate 3-story, 1.5-bath pagoda accommodates up to 4 adults and 3 children; there's a full kitchen and waterfall views. Common areas include a bamboo garden, hiking trails, barbecue area and swimming in the pond below the falls. They've recently added a licensed massage therapist to the staff.

Rates: $109 inn rooms, $250 pagoda rooms

Maureen's Bed and Breakfast

1896 Kalanianaole, Hilo, HI 96720. 808-935-9018; e-mail: info@maureenbnb.com; www.maureenbnb.com.

This lodging is the old Saiki family mansion (c. 1932) located in the Keaukaha area of Hilo, opposite James Kealoha Beach Park, four miles from town just past the Mauna Loa Shores condo highrise. The home is lovely redwood and cedar finished with a huge open-beam cathedral ceiling in the living room. Arched doorways and windows give this home a touch of New England. Dual staircases wind up to open balconies and guest rooms, with quaint antique furniture pieces, bookcases and artwork to make this inviting lodging seem almost like a gallery. Five guest rooms accommodate two singles and four doubles, a total of ten guests. With the beach right across the street, swimming, snorkeling and sunning are steps away. There is also cable TV/VCR. Children under 7 years old are not allowed due to high stairs and balcony areas.

Rates: $75-$100

Old Hawaiian B&B

1492 Wailuku Drive, Hilo, HI 96720. 877-961-2816; 808-961-2816; e-mail: ironwood@flex.com; www.thebigislandvacation.com.

Located just minutes from Hilo town, overlooking the Wailuku River. Each room has a private bath and entry; breakfast served on the shared lanai. Member-HIBBA.

Rates: $80-$110 for two, additional person $10

★ Shipman House B&B

131 Kai'ulani Street, Hilo, HI 96720. 800-627-8447; phone/fax 808-934-8002; e-mail: bighouse@bigisland.com; hilo-hawaii.com. Reservations through Hawai'i's Best B&Bs, P.O. Box 485, Laupahoehoe, HI 96764, 800-262-9912; 808-962-0100; fax 808-962-6360; e-mail: reservations@bestbnb.com; www.bestbnb.com.

The Shipman House is special. This elegant Victorian-style home dates from 1900 and is currently listed on both the State and National Historic Registers. Now owned by the original Shipmans' great-granddaughter's family, it's one of Hilo's most historic B&Bs. The main home features a wide wraparound lanai and three-story rounded tower with conical roof (which prompts local children to call it "the Castle"). The home is on 5.5 acres including a magnificent rainforest gulch and is landscaped with tropical fruit trees, handsome palms and flowering plants. One guest room in the main house has twin beds; two other upstairs rooms have queens; two guest rooms in the separate 1910 guesthouse have queen beds. All rooms have ceiling fans, private baths, TVs and refrigerators. The historic home is lovingly restored throughout with much original furniture and period pieces, original heirloom china, ceramics and *objets d'art*. Expanded continental breakfast is served on the lanai. The Shipman House is a living early-20th-century museum where you can sleep in the room where Jack London and his wife Charmian stayed for a month while visiting Hilo in 1907. Sit at the same dining table where Queen Liliuokalani, Hawai'i's last monarch, was entertained during Hilo visits in the early 1900s. This is the inn for guests who love an immersion in the local history, culture, charm and authentic hospitality of old Hawai'i. Smoke-free property. Member-Hawai'i's Best, HIBBA.

Rates: from $174-$219; $25 extra person

Waterfalls Inn B&B

240 Kaiulani Street, Hilo, HI 96720. 888-808-HILO; 808-969-3407; e-mail: info@waterfallsinn.com; www.waterfallsinn.com.

A restored 1916 plantation listed on the National Register, this peaceful home overlooks the Wailuku River, half a mile from downtown Hilo. Rooms include private bath with whirlpool or antique soaking tub, TV/VCR/DVD and Wi-Fi. Enjoy breakfast on the verandah and take it easy. Member-HIBBA.

Rates: $130-$190

Wild Ginger Inn
100 Pu'ueo Street, Hilo, HI 96720. 800-882-1887; 808-935-5556; www.wildgingerinnhilo.com.

This quaint old-fashioned inn dates from 1947 and is easily spotted on a rainy Hilo day by its bright tropical pink exterior. The 27 guest rooms provide essential accommodations with private baths (except for two rooms). Good quality breakfasts feature fresh Hawaiian fruits and bakery-delivered organic multigrain breads, Portuguese sweetbreads and more. Occasional on-site barbecue parties offer a chance to meet fellow travelers, backpackers and families. Two blocks from downtown Hilo dining and shopping.

Rates: $55-$90

HOTELS, HOSTELS AND HOMES

★ Arnott's Lodge
Apapane Road, Hilo, HI 96720. 808-969-7097; e-mail: info@arnottslodge.com; www.arnottslodge.com.

These people go the extra mile to provide backpackers and adventurers with a quality, affordable vacation. The lodge is located in the Keaukaha area of Hilo near the beach parks, offering private and bunk rooms with shared bathrooms, a common kitchen and TV room. Some units have private kitchen and bath. They offer added services such as an around-the-island "Big Island Experience," with stops at important historical and cultural sites and daily hiking excursions including Hawai'i Volcanoes National Park, Mauna Kea Summit, Hilo Waterfalls and Puna as well as custom adventure expeditions. Free shuttle service from Hilo International Airport.

Rates: Bunk room $19; Semi-private room $39-$49; Private room $65; 2BR Suite $125; $15 extra person; tenting per person $9

Country Club Condo Hotel
121 Banyan Drive, Hilo, HI 96720. 808-935-7171.

A no-frills lodging with 130 air-conditioned units with phone and TV. Pool, restaurant, cocktail lounge and meeting room are on premises. Located across the street from Naniloa Country Club golf course, within walking distance of Coconut Island and Liliuokalani Park.

Rates: Standard $65, Deluxe $80; $7 extra person

Dolphin Bay Hotel
333 Iliahi Street, Hilo, HI 96720. 808-935-1466; fax 808-935-1523; e-mail: johnhilo@gte.net; www.dolphinbayhilo.com.

This small 18-unit hotel is located in a quiet old residential area of Hilo, four blocks from the downtown area and three blocks from Hilo Bay. There are few amenities other than fans and TV; no room telephones. Kitchen facilities are included in all units. The rooms are bright, airy, spacious and very clean.

Rates: Standard $79, Superior $89, 1BR Suite $109, 2BR Suite $129; $10 extra person

The Falls at Reed's Island

Kaiulau Street, Hilo, HI 96720. www.reedsisland.com.

Just minutes from downtown Hilo, this stunning secluded getaway features 3 bedrooms, 3.5 baths, a full gourmet kitchen, a TV with DVD, an outdoor barbecue, soaking tubs, a computer with DSL and the company of backyard waterfalls. Two-night minimum.

Rates: $325; $25 extra person; $125 cleaning fee

Hawai'i Naniloa Hotel

93 Banyan Drive, Hilo, HI 96720. 808-969-3333; 800-367-5360; fax 808-969-6622; e-mail: hinan@aloha.net; www.planet-hawaii.com/sand/naniloa.

This 325-room tower has long been a Hilo landmark overlooking Hilo Bay. The spacious rooms are air-conditioned with TV, safe, refrigerator and coffeemaker. The hotel features a Chinese and seafood restaurant, meeting facilities, a cocktail lounge, complete health spa/fitness center and resort pool. There is no beach as the shoreline is rugged lava rock, but the bay views are lovely. It is located across from the Naniloa Country Club golf course and in the heart of Banyan Drive hotel row; walking distance to Coconut Island and Liliuokalani Park.

Rates: Standard $100, Partial Oceanview $120, Oceanview $140, Partial Oceanview Suites $120, Oceanview Suites $240; $17 extra person

Hilo Bay Hostel

101 Waianuenue Avenue, Hilo, HI 96720. 808-933-2771; e-mail: hawaii hostel@hawaiihostel.net; www.hawaiihostel.net.

Something new for Hilo, an inexpensive lodging in a convenient location right downtown. Located in what claims to be the oldest surviving wooden structure on the island, the fully restored 1913 hotel provides private and dormitory rooms with ceiling fans, a common area with cable TV, storage lockers, billiards table, high-speed internet access, an outdoor patio garden and a kitchen with free coffee and tea. Island tours can be arranged and it's within walking distance to movies, museums, shopping and restaurants.

Rates: from $18

★ Hilo Hawaiian Hotel

71 Banyan Drive, Hilo, HI 96720. 808-935-9361. Reservations: Castle Resorts & Hotels 800-367-5004, fax 808-596-0158, www.castle resorts.com/HHH.

There's something special about Hilo Hawaiian—quiet, unpretentious but genuinely inviting with a wide, attractive lobby overlooking the bay, and easy strolling distance to the "celebrity" banyan trees, Liliuokalani Gardens and Coconut Island. This is a Hilo classic and favorite gathering place for *kama'aina* (residents) in town for family reunions, weddings, sports events or other special occasions. Time spent in the lounge will guarantee you meet some interesting people. With lovely views of Hilo Bay, Coconut Island and the Hilo waterfront, the 235 spacious, comfortable rooms all have TV with movies on demand, private bath, coffeemaker, standard hotel amenities, room service and maid service. Restaurant, cocktail lounge (with live entertainment and dancing on the weekends), coffee shop, meeting rooms and shops are on-site as well as a swimming pool, massage facility and travel agency. The Naniloa Country Club golf course is across the street. We found the suites to be an exceptional value, particularly for families, including equipped kitchen facilities, living-dining area and two TVs. There is a particular charm (for those of us who live on the "dry side" of the island) in waking up to a gentle rain and having our hot Kona coffee out on the lanai as the sun slowly colors a cloudy Hilo morning.

Rates: Standard $150, Superior $170, Junior Suite $195, 2BR Suite, Oceanview Suite $225; Deluxe Suite $395; $17 extra person

Hilo Seaside Hotel

126 Banyan Drive, Hilo, HI 96720. Reservations: Sand & Seaside Hotels 800-560-5557; 808-935-0821; fax 808-969-9195; e-mail: info@sand-sea side.com; www.sand-seaside.com.

This 150-room hotel is located just opposite Reeds Bay small boat harbor and the Ice Pond swimming hole but there is no good beach here. The rooms are standard but clean and feature ceiling fans and TV. Restaurant, cocktail lounge and meeting rooms are on premises. It is adjacent to the Naniloa Country Club golf course and walking distance to Liliuokalani Park and Coconut Island.

Rates: Standard $88, Deluxe $110, Kitchenette $110; $15 extra person

Uncle Billy's Hilo Bay Hotel

87 Banyan Drive, Hilo, HI 96720. 800-367-5102; 808-935-0861; fax 808-935-7903; e-mail: resv@unclebilly.com; www.unclebilly.com.

This is a 145-room standard hotel located right on Hilo Bay. The rooms have air conditioning and TVs. Uncle Billy's restaurant with nightly entertainment, luau and hula show, cocktail lounge, gift shops and lovely tropical gardens are on grounds. There is no beach as the shoreline is rugged lava rock. It is located across from the

Naniloa Country Club golf course and walking distance to Coconut Island and Liliuokalani Park.

Rates: Standard $84-$92, Superior $94-$102, Oceanfront $104-$112, Superior/kitchen $99-$122; $10 extra person

Puna District

BED AND BREAKFASTS

Aloha Junction Bed & Breakfast
19-4040 Post Office Lane, P.O. Box 91, Volcano, HI 967895. 888-967-72896; 808-967-7289; e-mail: relax@bbvolcano.com; www.bbvolcano.com.

Located close to Volcanoes National Park, Aloha Junction offers rooms with shared baths and suites with private baths. Guest facilities include outdoor jacuzzi, DSL internet service, fireplace and a hearty breakfast. Member-HIBBA.

Rates: $75-$125

Art and Orchids
16-1504 39th Avenue, Kea'au, HI 96749. 877-393-1894; 808-982-8197; e-mail: info@artandorchids.com; www.artandorchids.com.

This 3BR tropical home was recently renovated. Private baths, hot tub with rock wall, lush gardens, koi pond.

Rates: $70-$90

At the End of the Road Bed & Breakfast
Haunani Road, Volcano Village. 808-967-8544; e-mail: haunaniroad@yahoo.com; www.stayhawaii.com/endroad.

A smoke- and alcohol-free Christian-run lodging in a forest setting. Rooms have queen beds and private baths; common area has TV/VCR, CD and woodburning stove. Continental breakfast. Member-HIBBA.

Rates: $60-$65

Bed & Breakfast Mountain View
P.O. Box 963, South Kulani Road, Kurtistown, HI 96704. 888-698-9896; 808-968-6868; fax 808-968-7017; e-mail: info@bbmtview.com; www.bbmtview.com.

This large modern home is located about 15 miles south of Hilo in the rolling farm and forestlands of the Mountain View village area. The home is on a large lot surrounded by forest and lush greenery. The owner/operators are noted Big Island artists and instructors, Linus and Jane Chao, who have an art studio on the lower level where they conduct art classes. Inquire about special art class/room packages. The living and guest quarters are on the upper level. The Cherry Blossom and Heliconia Rooms have king or queen beds and private bath; the Plumeria Room has two twin beds; and the Lehua Room has a queen and shared bath. There is easy access to shopping, dining and attractions of the East Hawai'i–Hilo area and Hawai'i Volcanoes National Park is just minutes away. Smoke free; Chinese spoken here.

Rates: $55-$65 shared bath; $75-$95 private bath

Carson's Kapoho Beach House & Cottage

P.O. Box 1120, Volcano, HI 96785. 800-605-VIEW; 808-985-7377; e-mail: cayenne@aoloha.net; www.carsonscottage.com.

Located on the most eastern tip of the Big Island, the "sun belt" of East Hawaii, this is a great place to relax and listen to the ocean and the wind in the coconut trees. The house has two bedrooms with queen beds that share a bath, beautiful ocean views from every room, light and airy Polynesian decor, fully-equipped kitchen, dishwasher, washer-dryer, jacuzzi and satellite TV. The rustic cottage has two bedrooms (one queen/one twin-bedded) that share a bath, large lanai, full kitchen, nautical decor and large landscaped yard with great moon- and sunrises. Snorkeling and fishing in tidepools and warm ponds nearby.

Rates: $80-$165

Carson's Volcano Cottages B&B

P.O. Box 503, Volcano, HI 96785. 800-845-LAVA; 808-967-7683; e-mail: carsons@aloha.net; www.carsonscottage.com.

Accommodations at this quiet, secluded location include six individually themed guest rooms: Kahaualea, reminiscent of Princess Kaiulani's Hawai'i during the monarchy; Kobayashi, with exotic Japanese motif; Ka'u with bright tropic colors and collectibles from the '40s and '50s; Ginger, Pakalana and Pakaki with treetop views into the rainforest canopy. There are also three romantic "storybook cottages" and two cozy family cottages. Rates include full breakfast served fireside in the dining room and daily maid service. Easy access to national park activities, golf course, restaurants. Deposit required to confirm reservation.

Rates: $105-$165

Country Goose B&B

P.O. Box 597, Volcano, HI 96785. 800-238-7101; 808-967-7759; fax 808-985-8673; e-mail: cgoose@interpac.net; www.countrygoose.com.

This home has two bedrooms with private bath and entry, king or queen bed and double futon quilt. Baseboard heat and electric blankets take the chill out of the crisp Volcano air. Very peaceful and quiet setting. Vacation rental homes also available.

Rates: $90-$150

Fern Forest

Hawaii's Best Bed & Breakfasts, P.O. Box 485, Laupahoehoe, HI 96764. 800-262-9912; 808-962-0100; fax 808-962-6360; e-mail: reservations@ bestbnb.com; www.bestbnb.com.

This little gem is an artistic two-bedroom/one bath house a mile away from Volcanoes National Park in a cool, green forest with giant *hapu'u* ferns. Cozy and inviting with full kitchen, laundry room and handcrafted touches throughout. Member-Hawai'i's Best.

Rates: $135, $20 additional person

Green Goose Lodge

P.O. Box 422, Volcano, HI 96785. 808-985-7172; e-mail: conard@green gooselodge.com; www.greengooselodge.com.

This bed-and-breakfast operation bills itself as "a golfer's dream," located overlooking the fairways of Volcano Golf & Country Club. Individual guest quarters feature TVs and electric blankets, in-room coffee and tea service and golf-course views. Common areas have a large wood-burning fireplace, TV/VCR, library, washer and dryer. Gourmet breakfast and "Tea on the Tee" served daily.

Rates: $80-$175

Hale Makamae Bed & Breakfast

13-3315 Makamae Street, Pahoa, HI 96778. 808-965-7015; e-mail: info@bnb-aloha.com; www.bnb-aloha.com.

Lush gardens surround two private suites and one studio, each with private entrance and bath. Your hosts offer gourmet breakfasts in German or English. Member-HIBBA.

Rates: $65-$110

Hawaiian Retreat

13-3564 Moku Street, Pahoa, Hawaii 96778. 877-965-1279; 808-965-1279; e-mail: eliotrosen@hotmail.com; www.hawaiiantretreat.com.

Three unique, individual units available for romantic, natural getaways to nurture body and soul, located miles from civilization in lush tropical east Hawaii. The main house upstairs is a 1,600-square-foot suite with cedar walls, two bedrooms, kitchen, living and dining rooms, bath and two lanai to accommodate up to four persons. The main house downstairs is a one-bedroom unit with shared kitchen and full bath. "Nature Cottage" is a window-filled octagon space in the garden with private indoor bath, outdoor shower, kitchenette with fridge and lanai. In addition to the therapeutic environment, counseling, classes and private retreats are offered by the resident manager, bestselling author and licensed psychotherapist and holistic health counselor Eliot Jay Rosen (advance appointments are recommended).

Rates: Upstairs lodge, $110-$140 for four people plus $10 each additional person; Garden Room $75-$85 for two; Nature Cottage, $85-$95 for two

Hi'iaka House

Reservations through Hawai'i's Best B&Bs, P.O. Box 520, Kamuela, HI 96743. 800-262-9912; 808-885-4550; fax 808-885-0559; e-mail: reservations@bestbnb.com; www.bestbnb.com.

This is a 1939-era family mountain retreat in Volcano dating from the days when those who were able kept a mountain house to escape to the cooler uplands during warm spells on the coast. Lovely artwork decor in the home, a very comfortable 3BR, one and a half baths, with nicely landscaped grounds. It has a full kitchen, wood stove in living room and a relaxing front porch. Great for families or groups. Two-night minimum stay. Member-Hawai'i's Best.

Rates: $145; $15 extra person

★ The Inn at Volcano

P.O. Box 998, Wright Road, Volcano, HI 96785. 800-937-7786; 808-967-7786; fax 808-967-8660; 800-577-1849; e-mail: reservations@volcano-hawaii.com; www.volcano-hawaii.com.

Part of the Chalet Kilauea Collection of B&Bs, which offers a variety of lodgings in the cool Volcano Village area. The Inn at Volcano is their flagship property and it is a work of art. The luxury-class boutique resort has six distinctive, themed rooms, each with their own intriguing personality. Let your surroundings match your mood with settings such as Out of Africa, Oriental Jade, the Owner's Suite, Continental Lace Suite, Hapu'u Forest Suite or the one-of-a-kind Treehouse Suite. For families or groups wishing for more privacy, there are separate cottages including Ohia Hideaway Cottage, Volcano Country Cottage, Pink Protea Palace, Pele's Plantation House and Hoku Mana House. Relax in the hot tub, enjoy the fireplace and library and wake up to a gourmet breakfast in the art deco dining room. Located at the cool 3,800-foot elevation just minutes from Hawai'i Volcanoes National Park, village store and restaurants. French spoken here.

Rates: $139-$399

Jade Garden Bed & Breakfast

13-1139 Leilani Avenue, Puna, HI 96778. 808-965-0973; e-mail: ajadegarden@earthlink.net; www.stayhawaii.com/jadegarden.

Two remarkable, individually-styled cottages—one with four-poster bed, sleep sofa, full kitchen, private bath and lanai; another

MILITARY RECREATION CENTER

The Big Island is unique among Hawai'i's Neighbor Islands in that it has an official armed forces recreation center. This is the **Kilauea Military Camp** located at Hawai'i Volcanoes National Park. KMC has 55 rental cabins available plus dormitory facilities and the KMC Mess Hall, a military-style cafeteria that serves standard but ample chow. Entertainment and activities are presented in the Lava Lounge. The rustic, well-kept cabins are 1BR, 2BR and 3BR units, fully equipped with fireplace, TV and full bath. Some have kitchen and jacuzzi facilities. The cabins are available only to active-duty regular military personnel, military reserve, national guard or retired personnel or Department of Defense and Foreign Service civilians and their families. The dining hall, like the lodgings, is not open to the general public. Cabin rentals are very reasonable and are based on the rank and grade of the personnel. Reservations are required.

KMC guests enjoy a full range of recreation activities and programs in the national park as well as tours to various scenic attractions around the island. Rental equipment is available, including tennis racquets, bicycles, back packs, sleeping bags for camping and snorkeling gear. KMC also has billiards, ping-pong, video games, mini-golf, a PX and a six-lane bowling alley. There are also Hawaiian music and hula, Hawaiian storytelling, lei making and much more. KMC is only about one mile from the national park visitors center and Volcano House Hotel and restaurant. Volcano Country Club Golf Course is just across the highway. KMC also offers a special "Wild Ginger Tour Package," which is a four-day/three-night stay and includes a meal package, lodging, four island tours of popular attractions and airport transportation. Check with the reservations desk for details. For reservations, contact: Reservations Desk, Armed Forces Recreation Center, Kilauea Military Camp/Lodging, Hawai'i Volcanoes National Park, Hawai'i 96718; 808-967-8333; 808-967-833; fax 808-967-8343. From Honolulu, call 808-438-6707; 24-hour headquarters line 808-967-7315; e-mail: reservations@kmc-volcano.com; www.kmc-volcano.com.

When making reservations, you can also arrange a free shuttle pick-up at the Hilo airport, unless you want to rent your own car for the 45-minute trip to the camp. KMC guests must pay the standard national park one-time entry fee of $10 per vehicle or $5 per person (when using the KMC shuttle) upon entering the park.

Current rates are as follows: 1BR $55-$91; 1BR w/jacuzzi $65-$101; 1BR apartment $52-$88; 1BR apartment w/jacuzzi $62-$98; 2BR cottage $65-$101; 2BR cottage w/kitchen $78-$114; 2BR cottage w/kitchen and jacuzzi $87-$123; 3BR cottage w/kitchen and jacuzzi $99-$133; 3BR apartment $79-$115; extra person $11-$14.

with romantic finds and furnishings from Bali. Gourmet breakfast menu changes daily.

Rates: $85

Kalani Garden Cottages

19-4245 Road B, P.O. Box 698, Volcano, HI 96785. 808-967-8642; e-mail: diane@volcanogetaway.com; www.volcanogetaway.com.

Enjoy the quiet, cool ambiance of Volcano at a 3,600-foot elevation and the privacy of your own island-style cottage just minutes from Volcanoes National Park. Choose the Teahouse Cottage for a touch of the Orient or Lehua Cottage for the feel of old Hawai'i. Surrounded by lush tropical gardens and rainforest, the cottages have kitchenettes and fireplaces to take the chill out of the cool Volcano nights. Generous island-style breakfast included. Complimentary guided hike with three-night stays.

Rates: $115-$130

Kia'i Kai B&B

HC 3 Box 10064, Kea'au, HI 96749. Phone/fax 808-982-9256; 888-542-4524; e-mail: innkeeper@hawaii-ocean-retreat.com; www.hawaii-ocean-retreat.com.

This modern custom-built home has an octagon common area and large windows to see whales, dolphins and seascape views; it's located at the ocean's edge in Hawaiian Paradise Park off Highway 130 south of Hilo and Kaloli Point. The Hawai'i Loa Cottage (sleeps 4) has two bedrooms with king beds, kitchen, private bath and living area. Makali'i Room has ocean view, queen bed, private entrance and private bath; Holomoku Suite has ocean view, queen bed, private entrance, shared bath. Guests share common areas in and around the home. Full continental breakfast each morning plus afternoon refreshments. Easy access to Volcanoes National Park and all other east Hawai'i attractions and activities. Member-HIBBA.

Rates: $95-$155; $10 extra person

★ Kilauea Lodge B&B

P.O. Box 116, Old Volcano Road, Volcano, HI 96785. 808-967-7366; fax 808-967-7367; e-mail: stay@kilauealodge.com; www.kilauealodge.com.

One of the best accommodations on the island, Kilauea Lodge was once a YWCA camping lodge and dormitory built in 1938. It has since been transformed into a romantic, cozy country inn and restaurant and won wide acclaim for comfort, service, quality and fine dining. Set amid the quiet, cool country air of Volcano Village near Hawai'i Volcanoes National Park, there are 14 attractively decorated guest units with private bathrooms and fireplaces. The restaurant offers a full Continental/international dinner menu nightly. Room rates include full American breakfast.

Rates: Hale Maluna Building rooms w/fireplace $145; The Cottage w/fireplace and porch $160; Hale Aloha Building rooms w/garden view $140; Honeymoon Deluxe room w/fireplace and king bed $160; Tutu's Place $165; 2BR cottage with hot tub $175

Lava Tree Tropic Inn

P.O. Box 1824, 14-3555 Puna Road, Pahoa, HI 96778. 808-965-7441; fax 808-965-7410; e-mail: information@lavatreetropicinn.com; www.lava treetropicinn.com.

This is a unique two-story plantation-style inn. It provides several smoke-free comfortable guest rooms decorated with bright, island-style furnishings and artwork from the owner's personal Hawaiiana art collection. Guest clubhouse facilities include a lounge for big-screen TV, a billiard parlor room and large commercial kitchen. Complimentary continental breakfast. Located 25 minutes/ 20 miles southeast from Hilo Airport past Pahoa town on Highway 132 to Kapoho, just past Lava Tree State Park. Lush tropical garden setting, easy access to area attractions.

Rates: $65-$125

Lokahi Lodge

P.O. Box 998, Volcano, HI 96785. 800-937-7786; 808-967-7786; fax 800-577-1849 or 808-967-8660; e-mail: reservations@volcano-hawaii.com; www.volcano-hawaii.com.

This luxury four-room lodge is part of the Chalet Kilauea Collection operation of inns and lodges, combining modern convenience with Volcano country charm. Located one mile from Volcanoes National Park entrance in a plantation-style home that has rooms with private bath, cable TV and VCR.

Rates: $99-$149; $15 extra person

Ma'ukele Lodge

P.O. Box 162, Volcano, HI 96785. 888-507-7421; 808-985-7421; e-mail: volcanobb@hotmail.com; www.volcano-bb.com.

This large country home is located at the 4,000-foot elevation level near Kilauea Volcano. The home has a high open-beam living room with two warm, inviting fireplaces and beautiful woodwork throughout. The three large guest bedrooms have private baths and queen beds. It's in a rainforest setting of towering *ohia* trees and *hapu'u* ferns with lots of birdlife. Easy access to the national park and area activities.

Rates: $95; $25 extra person; house (sleeps 7) $250

★ My Island Bed & Breakfast Inn

P.O. Box 100, Volcano, HI 96785. 808-967-7216; 808-967-7110; fax 808-967-7719; e-mail: myisland@ilhawaii.net; www.myislandinnhawaii.com.

This secluded getaway is located in the pleasant, cool climate of Volcano Village, not far from Hawai'i Volcanoes National Park. The house is a historic, century-old missionary-style home set amid a rambling botanical garden and fern forest jungle. The grounds have a fine collection of exotic plants from around the world. Rooms are neat, comfortable and cozy with various bed arrangements: singles, doubles, triples and families. Color TV and a library of Hawaiiana are available for entertainment. All the mac nuts you can eat. Member-HIBBA.

Rates: $55-$135

Oma's Hapu'u Hideaway

P.O. Box 611, Volcano, HI 96785. 808-985-8959; cell 808-936-3382; e-mail: todd@volcanovillage.net; www.volcanovillage.net.

This forest retreat is located in the heart of Volcano Village surrounded by native *ohia, koa* and *hapu'u* tree ferns, on Hale Ohia Road, within walking distance of village shops, general store, post office and restaurants. The Hapu'u Hideaway is a cedar A-frame cottage with fully equipped kitchen, phone, living room, fireplace, TV/VCR and a loft master bedroom with queen bed and picture-window views. The two bedrooms downstairs have a queen bed and children's bunk beds; sleeps six. Also on the grounds behind the owner's home is the Maid's Quarters cottage, a nicely decorated unit with a bright cheery look and queen bed. There's a fully equipped kitchen and dining area, living room with fireplace, TV/stereo and a gas fireplace in the bedroom. Overlooks nice semi-tropical gardens. The Haunani House has three bedrooms and two baths. The master bedroom has a queen bed and attached bath with shower, the second bedroom has a queen-sized tatami mat bed and the third bedroom has a double bed and shares a large central bath with jacuzzi tub and shower. Gas fireplace, complete kitchen with dining area, living room with phone and cable TV/VCR, CD player. Laundry facilities.

Rates: Hapu'u Hideaway $125, Maid's Quarters $115; Haunani House $135, $15 extra person, fifth night free

Plumeria Hill Bed and Breakfast

13-1265 Opihikao Road, Pahoa, HI 96778. 808-965-8810; www.plumeria hill.com.

This five-acre retreat has ocean views and valley vistas. You'll find peace and quiet, healthful breakfasts and massage therapy.

Rates: $85

★ *Sugi House*

P.O. Box 900, Volcano, HI 96785. 808-967-8674; e-mail: reservations@ sugihouse.com; www.sugi.house.com.

One of Volcano's best-kept secrets, Sugi House may be the perfect hideaway for romantic honeymoons, family reunions or writers and others in search of self-contained solitude. This fully restored 1930s family vacation cottage is obsessively appointed (down to paperclips in the desk drawer); owned and operated by the Chaffin family who take pride in providing extra care, *ohana*-style. Hardwood floors and Hawaiiana furnishings throughout the house's

KALANI OCEANSIDE RETREAT

★ **Kalani Oceanside Retreat** offers a wide selection of interesting seminars, healing retreats, various yoga and dance disciplines, massage and bodywork, guided meditation and other mindful things, in addition to quality lodging and meal services. Special retreats and workshops are scheduled throughout the year and value-added packages are available. Choose from cottages with private baths and ocean vistas, rooms in cedar lodges, triple dorm rooms or orchard campsites. The Tree House has a king bed, private bath, fan, mini fridge, ocean and horse pasture views. The facility has gorgeous acres of botanical and fruit orchards and gardens. Amenities include an Olympic-size swimming pool, two jacuzzis, sauna, massage/wellness gazebo, tennis and volleyball courts and covered meeting/activity space for groups. A separate property, Kalani Kai, is being developed for private, year-round vacation residences. Dining options include the Aloha Café, with wireless internet access and network connectivity, open 7-10 p.m. daily for snacks, ice cream, coffee and a variety of teas. The Dining Lanai serves three healthful meals a day, featuring "Kalani cuisine," focusing on fresh local ingredients, fish, seafood (sometimes chicken) with excellent choices for vegetarians and vegans, along with occasional ethnic feasts. Island tours, stargazing and adventures on land and sea can be arranged separately or packaged with accommodations. Located about 25 miles south of Hilo, past Pahoa town on the coast highway/beach road.

Rates: Tree House $240; Cottage $155; Campsites $20-$30; Lodge room, private bath $135; Lodge room, shared bath $110; $60 extra person. (Inquire about discreet vacations geared to a variety of lifestyles for men, women and families.) Member-Hawai'i Visitors and Convention Bureau, Hawai'i Tourism Authority, Hawai'i Ecotourism Association. RR2 Box 4500, Pahoa, HI 96778, at Ocean Highway, 137-Pahoa Beach Road. 800-800-6886; 808-965-7828; fax 808-965-0527; e-mail: reservations@kalani.com; www.kalani.com.

two bedrooms (with extra quilts/blankets and knit booties for nippy nights), a double futon for extra people, one full bath with a six-inch antique clawfoot tub and "rain drencher" shower head, living room with gas fireplace and window seat with reading lamp, laundry room, fully equipped kitchen, including the spice rack and coffee beans, cappuccino machine, coffee grinder, coffee maker, microwave, toaster, rice cooker, blender, popcorn maker and electric juicer. Other thoughtful touches include a TV/VCR and videotapes (including some for the *keiki*), board games, a library of books for all ages (plus coloring books and crayons), radio, CD player/CDs. And they're probably the only Big Island B&B to advertise a turntable with vintage "records" (remember those?).

Rates: $165 for two, $20 additional persons

★ Volcano B&B

998 Wright Road, Volcano, HI 96785. 800-937-7786; 808-967-7786; fax 800-577-1849 or 808-967-8660; e-mail: reservations@volcano-hawaii. com; www.volcano-hawaii.com.

This B&B is part of the Chalet Kilauea Collection of inns and lodges. The peaceful country home is located in the heart of cool, lush Volcano Village, a mile from the entrance and visitors center of Hawai'i Volcanoes National Park. The house provides six single/double rooms with shared bath. The renovated 1912-vintage three-story home is on a three-quarter-acre landscaped site with fireplace, sun room, reading room, piano, cable TV/VCR and shared kitchen facilities. Access to national park provides year-round hiking, biking, sightseeing and other recreational activities. Near village stores and restaurants.

Rates: $49-$69; $15 extra person

Volcano Cedar Cottage

P.O. Box 629, Volcano, HI 96785. 808-985-9020; e-mail: uilani@volcano cc.com; www.volcanocc.com.

Three accommodations with private entrances and baths in a mountain garden near Volcanoes National Park, and gourmet breakfasts with a local flair. Member-HIBBA.

Rates: $85-$95

Volcano Country Cottages

P.O. Box 545, Volcano, HI 96785. 888-446-3910; phone/fax 808-967-7960; e-mail: aloha@volcanocottages.com; www.volcanocottages.com.

This is one of Volcano Village's oldest family estates, nestled among a stand of large old-growth forest and ferns. Ohelo Berry Cottage is a private studio cottage with kitchenette and sleeps two. Artist's House is a two-bedroom unit with full kitchen and woodstove for cool Volcano nights and sleeps up to eight. Full continental breakfast is provided. Easy access to Volcanoes National Park attractions, fine dining, shopping and activities in the village. Enjoy seclusion and cool Volcano climate. Discounts for extra nights.

Rates: Ohelo Berry Cottage $95, Artist's House $120; $15 extra person

Volcano Inn

P.O. Box 490, Volcano, HI 96785. 800-997-2292; 808-967-7293; fax 808-985-7394; e-mail: volcano@volcanoinn.com; www.volcanoinn.com.

Volcano Inn is actually two separate lodgings, located in the heart of Volcano Village, only a mile from the national park entry. Volcano Inn I is more contemporary, with four guest rooms with private baths, an art gallery, expansive lanai, exercise room and a house full of artworks including the owner's handmade Hawaiian quilts. Volcano Inn II is a lovingly restored 1928 mission-style home, offering three guest rooms and a cottage, each with private bath and decorated with antiques, fine art and other treasures. The common areas hold an elegant library, dining room and lava stone fireplace. Family-style breakfast is served daily, as well as afternoon tea; picnic baskets may be ordered in advance.

Rates: Aloha Room $99.75, Lei Room or Honu Room $123.90, Bird of Paradise Room $126, Guest House at Pali Uli $94.50-$136.50

Volcano Rainforest Retreat

P.O. Box 957, Volcano, HI 96785. 800-550-8696; 808-985-8696; e-mail: volrain@volcanoretreat.com; www.volcanoretreat.com.

This quiet and secluded sanctuary is surrounded by towering fern forest. Designed to emphasize tranquility, the four attractive cottages feature beautiful furniture and woodwork with a handcrafted feel. Each is equipped with full kitchen, living area with wood stove, sleeping loft and private, oversized bathtub open to the forest. Private breakfast, Japanese soaking tubs and forest pavilion jacuzzi. Innkeepers Kathleen and Peter Golden are practitioners of reiki and other natural healing disciplines, and offer counseling and workshops (including couples' retreats) throughout the year. Visit their website for details. Two-night minimum stay. Member-Hawai'i's Best, HIBBA.

Rates: $125-$260; $15 extra person

Volcano Teapot

P.O. Box 511, Volcano, HI 96785. 808-967-7112. Reservations through Hawai'i's Best B&Bs, P.O. Box 485, Laupahoehoe, HI 96764. 800-262-9912, 808-962-0100, fax 808-962-6360, e-mail: reservations@best bnb.com, www.bestbnb.com, also through The Cottages of Volcano, 800-967-7995, e-mail: places@qloha.net, www.alohaweb.com/cottages.

This is a nicely restored turn-of-the-20th-century two-bedroom cottage set on landscaped grounds in Volcano Village. Lovely decorative touches and tea-theme accents are featured throughout. There is a comfy porch and warm wood-burning stove to take the chill out of the crisp Volcano air, and a hot tub pavilion in a romantic garden setting. The cottage sleeps four. Member-Hawai'i's Best.

Rates: $175; $20 extra person

Wild Orchid Bed & Breakfast

P.O. Box 114, Mountain View, HI 96771. 808-968-6969; e-mail: gbwaka@cs.com.

A quiet, upcountry residential neighborhood is the setting for your private accommodations with bath, TV, microwave, fridge; island continental breakfast served daily. Garden suite is wheelchair accessible.

Rates $65

HOTELS, HOSTELS AND HOMES

Hale Ohia Cottages and Hostels

P.O. Box 758, 11-3968 Hale Ohia Road, Volcano, HI 96785. 800-455-3803; 808-967-7986; fax 808-967-8610; e-mail: haleohia@bigisland.com; www.haleohia.com.

This elegant and charming country B&B home (c. 1931) offers various private cottages and suites. Units have kitchens, living rooms and private baths. A large covered deck has table, chairs and barbecue for cookouts. There are well-kept, nicely landscaped grounds and gardens in this exclusive old family estate. Located one mile from national park entrance and visitors center, near hiking trails, picnic areas, golf, restaurants and shopping, Hale Ohia was recently voted #1 B&B in Volcano by Condé Nast Traveler.

Rates: Suites $95-$105, Cottages $110-$165; $20 extra person

Holoholo Inn

19-4036 Kalani Honua Road, P.O. Box 784, Volcano, HI 96785. 808-967-7950; fax 808-967-8025; e-mail: holoholo@interpac.net; www.enable.org/holoholo.

Located in the heart of Volcano Village near the entry to Volcanoes National Park, this hostel operator provides basic dorm lodging and services for budget backpackers. Amenities include kitchen facilities, TV, heated room, laundry facilities, hot showers and sauna. Located off Highway 11 in Volcano Village, just off Haunani Road on Kalani Honua Road near the old Japanese schoolhouse. Japanese spoken here.

Rates: Dorm room $18 (HI-AYH member $15); Private double rooms start at $45

Pineapple Park Hostel

P.O. Box 639, Kurtistown, HI 96760. 877-865-2266; 808-968-8170;
e-mail: ppark@aloha.net; www.pineapple-park.com.

Located about 15 miles south of Hilo in the Fern Acres subdivision on Pikake Road, off Highway 11 and Kulani Road. This large frame country home sits amid nicely landscaped grounds, lots of tropical flowers, palm trees, bamboo groves and tree ferns, a real tropical rainforest environment. Rooms are clean, comfortable and spacious with well-kept furnishings and appointments. Some rooms have private bath while others share. Guests enjoy breakfast, barbecue, game room, pool table, TV/VCR, community kitchen, vending machines and laundromat facilities. Discounts for extra nights. They also have inexpensive hostel accommodations for budget/backpacker travelers. German spoken here. Member-HIBBA.

Rates: Private room with shared bath $65, private room with private bath $85, dorm-style hostel bunks $20

Rainforest Retreat

HCR1 Box 5655, Kea'au, HI 96749. 888-244-8074; 808-961-4410; fax
808-966-6898; e-mail: retreat@bigisland.net; www.rainforestretreat.com.

This private home is surrounded by native *ohia* forest, orchids and horse pastures. A garden studio has private entry and bath, king bed, TV, kitchenette and laundry facilities. Located just off Highway 130 and 20 minutes from Hilo. Member-HIBBA.

Rates: $75-$105; $15 extra person

Ka'u District

BED AND BREAKFASTS

Bougainvillea B&B

P.O. Box 6045, Ocean View, HI 96737. 800-688-1763;
phone/fax 808-929-7089; e-mail: peaceful@interpac.net;
www.bougainvilleabedandbreakfast.com.

This plantation-style home is located on three acres in historic Ka'u, midway between Kona and Hilo. Specializing in "Nights and Breakfasts to Remember," the Bougainvillea offers four romantic guest rooms with private entrance and bath, therapeutic beds and TV/VCR. Pavilion area with barbecue, microwave and kitchen area, pool, hot tub, ping-pong, horseshoe pit, exercise equipment and awesome star-gazing. Massage therapies by appointment.

Rates: $80-$85; $15 extra person

★ Macadamia Meadows Farm B&B

P.O. Box 756, Na'alehu, HI 96772. 888-929-8118; phone/fax 808-929-8097; e-mail: innkeeper@macadamiameadows.com; www.macadamia meadows.com.

This is a contemporary two-story, open-beamed cedar home on an eight-acre working macadamia nut farm near Waiohinu, off South Point Road. The Punalu'u Black Sands Beach Room has both king and queen beds and refrigerator; it connects with the Papakealeo Green Sands Beach Room via a shared bath. They can be rented individually or as a two-bedroom suite. Nice ocean views and footpaths through the macadamia nut orchards to the meadows; superb nighttime star-gazing area. Full continental breakfast provided. Member-HIBBA and HVCB. Often hosting visiting naturalists, astronomers and scientists, the innkeepers have become accidental students in many fields, making their home a fascinating place to meet fascinating people.

Rates: $75-$135

CONDOS, HOTELS AND HOMES

Ohana House

P.O. Box 6351, Ocean View, HI 96737. 888-999-9139; 808-929-9139; www.alternative-hawaii.com/ohana.

This private vacation home includes secluded cottages on four acres of forested land on the Big Island's south end at Hawaiian Ocean View Estates subdivision near historic South Point and remote green- and black-sand beaches, ancient forests and wide open spaces. Quiet, tranquil country atmosphere, generally fine sunny weather at the 4,000-foot elevation level. It's a 40-minute drive from Kona; 90 minutes from Hilo. Steam room, licensed massage therapist available. A mindful, semi-rustic getaway for meetings, workshops and healing retreats, using alternative energy in simple surroundings.

Rates: Cottages $40-$60

Shirakawa Motel

P.O. Box 467, Na'alehu, HI 96772. 808-929-7462.

Advertised as "The Southernmost Motel in the U.S.," this 12-unit country motel offers simple accommodations for relaxation, peace and quiet. It is nestled amid the cool climate of a coffee tree grove and lush vegetation. The Shirakawa family combines the warmth of true old-fashioned Hawaiian hospitality with simple yet modern conveniences; no TV. This is a simple, no-frills getaway for those wanting the solitude of the countryside.

Rates: Standard $45, Kitchenette unit $55, 1BR Suite $65; $10 extra person

Sunterra at Seamountain

P.O. Box 460, Pahala, HI 96777. 800-444-6633; e-mail:
seamount@gte.net; www.sunterra.com.

This condominium/hotel has 35 rental units available to members and non-members of the Sunterra vacation ownership program. Located in the fairly remote Punaluʻu area of Kaʻu, the development is situated at the Seamountain Golf Course and near the ocean front and Punaluʻu Black Sand Beach and Ninole Cove. The nearest town is Pahala, five miles away. Hilo is about 55 miles away, Kona about 65 miles. This is a peaceful rural area, suitable for beach strolling and leisurely golf. All units have full kitchens, TV, laundry facilities, lanai, ceiling fans and standard hotel amenities. Golf clubhouse, cocktail lounge, swimming pool, tennis courts, golf course, barbecue, meeting rooms are on the grounds or nearby. Call for rates and availability.

★ Volcano House

P.O. Box 53, Hawaiʻi Volcanoes National Park, HI 96718. 808-967-7321;
fax 808-967-8429.

Historic, unique Volcano House has been rebuilt several times since its establishment in 1866 (on roots that trace back to Chieftess Kapiolani's grass shack, built in 1824 on the crater rim), with an extensive refurbishment in 1989. It now features 42 comfortable rooms with private bath, traditional koa-wood furnishings and even heat—an unusual feature for hotels in Hawaiʻi. Volcano House has two gift shops, Uncle George's Lounge for cocktails, Ka Ohelo Dining room (possibly the world's only restaurant perched on the edge of an active volcano) and they offer picnic box lunches for your volcano day-tours. A lobby fireplace that has burned continuously for 125 years keeps guests comfortable on misty volcano evenings. The wood paneling and cozy decor create a rustic country lodge atmosphere that gives the Volcano House its special charm.

Rates: Crater View $200, Crater View Deluxe $225, Non-crater View $170, Ohia Wing Garden $125, Ohia Wing standard 495, Namakani Paio Cabins $50, $15 extra person

Rental Agents

BED & BREAKFAST AGENCIES

Following are booking services for bed and breakfasts islandwide that provide a selection of accommodations and price ranges.

All Islands B&B

800-542-0344; 808-263-2342; fax 808-263-0308; e-mail: inquiries@all-islands.com; www.all-islands.com.

Over 1,000 modest to magnificent accommodations on all islands. Reduced rates for interisland air and car rentals.

Alternative Hawai'i Accommodations

e-mail: admin@alternative-hawaii.com; www.alternative-hawaii.com/ accomg.htm.

★ *Chalet Kilauea Collection*

P.O. Box 998, Volcano, HI 96785. 800-937-7786; 808-967-7786; fax 800-577-1849 or 808-967-8660; e-mail: reservations@volcano-hawaii.com; www.volcano-hawaii.com.

★ *Hawai'i's Best B&B*

P.O. Box 485, Laupahoehoe, HI 96764. 800-262-9912; 808-962-0100; fax 808-962-6360; e-mail: reservations@bestbnb.com; www.bestbnb.com.

This booking service caters exclusively to upscale B&Bs on the Big Island. The island's best lodgings, ranging from the most traditional host-home rooms to private country cottages, have been selected for inclusion in the "Hawai'i's Best" collection. Each home or cottage has been chosen for its distinctive personality, inspired attention to detail, and for the warm hospitality offered by its hosts. Each offers a beautiful setting, tasteful and comfortable accommodations, attentive service and a relaxed atmosphere. Host accommodations are available around the island in Kamuela, Hilo, Volcano, Kona and on the Kohala Coast. Rates from $95-$450, with weekly rates available at most properties.

★ *Hawai'i Island B&B Association (HIBBA)*

P.O. Box 1890, Honoka'a, HI 96727. E-mail: hibba@stayhawaii.com; www.stayhawaii.com.

No phone. Their website provides listing descriptions, photos, maps and reservation information for member B&Bs.

Hawai'i Island Bed & Breakfast Inns and Accommodations Index

www.hawaii-inns.com.

This website provides a number of links to bed-and-breakfast operators on the Big Island as well as throughout the Hawaiian islands.

CONDOMINIUM AND HOME RENTAL AGENCIES

The following agencies can assist with rentals of condominiums, private estates and vacation residences, in a wide range of prices and locations islandwide.

Aloha Hawaii Vacations

Aldridge Associates Realtors, P.O.Box 383909, Waikoloa, HI 96738. 800-66-ALOHA; 808-883-8300; fax 808-883-9102; e-mail: kim@alohahawaii

vacations.com; www.alohahawaiivacations.com. An excellent selection of
condo properties in Waikoloa Village, six miles up mauka from the
Waikoloa Resort area along the Kohala Coast.

A Piece of Paradise

P.O. Box 1314, Pahoa, HI 96778-1314. 808-965-6232; fax 808-965-
0814; e-mail: info@apoparadise.com; www.apoparadise.com.

This booking service has vacation homes in the Puna–Kapoho
and Waikoloa areas, as well as Kailua-Kona and Hilo town, ranging
from 1BR to 5BR; varied facilities and amenities; units accommodate
up to 12 people. Rates from $115.

Always Sunny Kona Condos

4887 NW Bryce Court, Silverdale, WA 98383. 360-698-7007; 800-479-
2173; fax 360-613-2858; e-mail: aloha@konacondos.com; www.kona
condos.com.

Aston Hotels & Resorts

2155 Kalakaua Avenue, Suite 500, Honolulu, HI 96815. 877-997-6667;
in Hawai'i 800-321-2558; fax 808-922-8785; e-mail: info@aston
hotels.com; www.aston-hotels.com.

Big Island Vacation Rentals

RE/MAX Properties, Hilo, HI 96720. 808-965-0400; www.bigislandvaca
tionrentals.com.

A stunning collection of individual vacation residences in the
East Hawai'i area, including a glass-brick nautical house, a Balinese
retreat, a waterfall estate and other dream houses.

Century 21

75-5759 Kuakini Highway, Suite 200, Kailua-Kona, HI 96740. 800-546-
5662; 808-326-2121; fax 808-329-6768; e-mail: shelley.spencer@hawaii
moves.com; www.islandsrentals.com.

This full-service realty and property management firm provides
a wide variety of vacation rental condos from $65-$250 and private
homes from $200 on the Big Island's Kona and Kohala coasts.
Weekly rates available.

Castle Resorts & Hotels

3 Waterfront Plaza, Honolulu, HI 96813. 808-545-3510; 800-367-5004;
fax 800-477-2329; e-mail: reservations@castleresorts.com; www.castle
resorts.com.

Condo in Hawai'i

c/o Ron Roddick. 604-943-0085; 888-292-3307; fax 604-943-0056;
e-mail: konacondo@telus.net; www.condoinhawaii.com.

Elite Properties Unlimited

P.O. Box 5273, 505 Front Street #224-2A, Lahaina, HI 96761. 800-448-9222 U.S. & Canada; 808-665-0561; fax 808-669-2417; e-mail: homes@eliteprop.com; www.eliteprop.com.

Family homes and luxury estates with 3-6 bedrooms to accommodate 4-12 people. Big Island vacation homes available at Kohala Coast/Puako, Mauna Kea Resort, Mauna Lani Resort, Kailua-Kona area, and Kealakekua Bay/Honaunau. Weekly and monthly rentals from $425-$2,000 per day with a one-week minimum stay. Maid service, chefs and concierge services available.

Great Hawaii Vacations

800-688-2254; e-mail: info@greathawaiivacations.com; www.greathawaii vacations.com.

This rental listing service has some 620 properties listed for all areas of the Big Island and includes condos and private homes priced $75-$500.

Hawai'i Condo Exchange

1817 El Cerrito Place, Los Angeles, CA 90068. 323-436-0300; 800-442-0404; fax 323-436-0331; www.hawaiicondoexchange.com.

★ Hawai'i's Best B&Bs

P.O. Box 485, Laupahoehoe, HI 96764. 800-262-9912; 808-962-0100; fax 808-962-6360; e-mail: reservations@bestbnb.com; www.bestbnb.com.

This bed-and-breakfast booking service also represents several fully equipped vacation rental homes and cottages in the Puako and Wailea areas of the Kohala Coast. The homes and cottages have oceanfront settings with easy beach access and rent from $105-$225. Facilities and furnishings vary and units sleep up to six people.

Hawai'i Vacation Rentals

7 Puako Beach Drive, Kohala Coast, HI 96743. 808-332-7081; fax 808-882-7607; e-mail: seaside@aloha.net; www.vacationbigisland.com.

This booking service has a variety of condo and home rental units in the Puako Beach area of the Kohala Coast and at Waikoloa Village for $130-$1,200; units accommodate 4-14 people.

Kapoho Tropical Vacation Rentals

Kapoho Beach Lots, RR2 Box 3913, Pahoa, HI 96778. 808-965-8508; e-mail: alohakapoho@aol.com; www.alohakapoho.com.

This booking service has three fully furnished beachside homes available for $70-$165; they accommodate up to six people. Access to swimming pool and oceanfront tide pools.

Keauhou Property Management Company

P.O. Box 390220, Kailua-Kona, HI 96739. 808-326-9075; 800-745-KONA; fax 808-326-2055; e-mail: kona@kpmco.com; www.kpmco.com.

Knutson & Associates

75-6082 Ali'i Drive #8, Kailua-Kona, HI 96740. 808-329-6311; 800-800-6202; fax 808-326-2178; e-mail: knutson@aloha.net; www.kona hawaiirentals.com.

Kona Hawai'i Vacation Rentals

75-5776 Kuakini Highway #105C, Kailua-Kona, HI 96740. 800-244-4752; 808-329-3333; fax 808-326-4137; e-mail: kona@hotmail.com; www.konahawaii.com.

This booking service has several condo and private home rentals for $49-$545, accommodating from three to eight people. Three-night minimum stay.

Kona Oceanfront Rental Homes

P.O. Box 35563, Monte Sereno, CA 95030; 800-464-6038; fax 408-243-4029; e-mail: pearne@ix.netcom.com; www.konaoceanfronthomes.com.

This private home owner has three separate vacation houses available. Two are in the Keauhou area near Kahalu'u Beach Park: Mehina Mele House ($185-$225) sleeps up to five guests, and Sea Breeze House ($275-$450 or $1,925/week) accommodates up to ten. They also offer Dock of the Bay ($250-$400) at Alae Point in Hilo town for up to ten guests. Full facilities and amenities included.

Marc Resorts Hawai'i

810 Richards Street, 2nd floor, Honolulu, HI 96815-2351. 808-922-9700; 800-535-0085; fax 800-633-5085; e-mail: aloha@marcresorts.com; www.marcresorts.com.

Outrigger Hotels Hawai'i

2375 Kuhio Avenue, Honolulu, HI 96815. 800-OUTRIGGER; fax 800-622-4852; e-mail: reservations@outrigger.com; www.outrigger.com.

Island Splendor Vacations

2772 Townsgate Road, Suite B, Westlake Village, CA 91361. 800-877-977-2567; e-mail: sales@islandsplendor.com; www.islandsplendor.com.

Property Network

75-5799 B-3 Ali'i Drive, Kailua-Kona, HI 96740. 808-329-7977; 800-358-7977; fax 808-329-1200; e-mail: vacation@hawaii-kona.com; www.hawaii-kona.com.

Royal Hawai'i Condos

888-722-6284; fax 847-574-8200; e-mail: info@royalhawaii.com; www.royalhawaii.com.

★ South Kohala Management

P.O. Box 384900, Waikoloa, HI 96738. 800-822-4252; 808-883-8500; fax 808-883-9818; e-mail: info@southkohala.com; www.southkohala.com.

One of the best, South Kohala only handles high-end vacation residences ($235-$4,000, average about $1,200) located in the luxurious Kohala Coast resort communities. They are happy to help you choose a home or condo unit to suit your family's particularities and preferences for an ultimate getaway experience. Listings include the Kumulani condominiums at Hapuna, the exclusive homes of The Fairways or Moani Heights at Mauna Kea Resort, and luxury condos of Mauna Lani Terrace, Mauna Lani Point and The Islands at Mauna Lani. They also handle other private homes and villas on the Kona and Kohala coasts. Car rental packages available.

★ Sunquest Vacations

77-6435 Kuakini Highway, Kailua-Kona, HI 96740. 808-329-6438; 800-367-5168; fax 808-329-5480; e-mail: sqvac@sunquest-hawaii.com; www.sunquest-hawaii.com.

Another "best," Sunquest handles a wide variety of condo properties islandwide, in sizes to suit all families and all vacation budgets. Quality service provided to visiting guests by phone or via Sunquest's excellent website, which takes much of the guesswork out of planning a condo vacation. If you don't see exactly what you're looking for, do not hesitate to ask.

Trading Places International

23807 Aliso Creek Road #100, Laguna Niguel, CA 92677. 949-448-5150; 800-365-1048; fax 949-448-5140; e-mail: info@tradingplaces.com; www.tradingplaces.com.

Vacation Rentals By Owner

www.vrbo.com

We've recently found this interesting site filled with fabulous-sounding listings, all for rent through the owners. We have no experience with them but would appreciate hearing yours if you use their service.

West Hawai'i Property Services, Inc.

Keauhou Shopping Village, 78-6831 Ali'i Drive #234-A, Kailua-Kona, HI 96740. 808-322-6696; 800-799-KONA; fax 808-324-0609; e-mail: make reservations@konarentals.com; www.konarentals.com.

CHAPTER 4

Where to Dine

The Big Island is big on food. Every special occasion is a great opportunity to indulge. And, with its diverse ethnic population, fabulous climate for a wide variety of produce and easy access to bountiful fresh fish and seafood, it has something to offer even the pickiest eater. We invite you to make food a part of your Big Island vacation; expand your boundaries a little and discover a new favorite.

We encourage you to leave your prejudices in your suitcases, and get your mind set on trying a few new tastes. We know that memories are made from all five senses, and taste should never be overlooked. Hawai'i as a state and an island is developing excellent chefs and a style of fun, eclectic cuisine that brings together East and West in creative ways, using an amazing palette of local fruits and vegetables, ocean fish and farm-raised seafood, and excellent meats. This is not to say that if you're strictly a meat-and-potatoes kind of person, you're going to be hungry.

Vegetarians too will find plenty to choose from, in eateries from fine hotel dining rooms to corner plate-lunch places islandwide, but to be honest, you're going to have to look a little bit harder. The Big Island is big on meat. However, thanks to Asian influences, vegetable or tofu stir-fry and noodle dishes are common; Italian places offer one or two meatless pastas or pizzas, and it's not at all hard to find fresh salads and fruits. On the plus side, the Big Island is also big on sweets, and if you go a little light on dinner, you can more than make up for it with dessert.

As mentioned, the Big Island has been in the tourist business for a long time. You're going to find whatever you like for breakfast wherever you stay. The larger hotels offer extensive buffet breakfasts for your indulgence and local restaurants serve up eggs and bacon just like home, along with a few more exotic items you might like to try. Lunch is the best time to experiment and explore a few new tastes. Without making a big financial commitment (i.e., wasting a lot of money if you don't like what you order) you can try a *musubi*, bento or bowl of saimin and take it from there. At dinnertime, your choices are practically limitless-just about any kind of food you and your family prefer in a wide range of settings and styles.

If you go to a lu'au you'll have a chance to taste more "Hawaiian" food, and you should. Try some poi; eat it with your fingers. Its mild taste is somewhere between starch and yogurt and it is not at all bad. In fact, it makes a great accompaniment to almost anything, and local households serve it with *lomi* salmon, cream and sugar, even hot dogs. Poi is made by boiling taro root and pounding it smooth with specially carved stone poi pounders. It is probably the most important food in Hawaiian culture, but likely more for nutritional qualities than taste.

For a more familiar, sit-down, semi-fancy dinner, try the good-quality American or European-style restaurants islandwide. The Kohala Coast resorts in particular pride themselves in presenting fresh-caught local fish in a variety of preparations, quality steak (some from the island's Parker Ranch), chicken, pork and pasta, accompanied by salads from abundant local produce with house-made, delectable desserts. We'd like to call your attention to the appetizer, or *pupu* menu, which you'll find almost everywhere, offering smaller portions of house specialties that can make a fun meal when everybody orders something different.

SWEET STUFF

Hawai'i-made ice creams and sorbets are out of this world. For a change of pace try island flavors like guava, mango, Kona coffee, *lilikoi* or, even more unique, lychee, green tea, *haupia, kalolo* and *adzuki* bean. There's Hawaiian vintage chocolate well-worth seeking out, all kinds of macadamia nut delectables, tropical fruit cheesecakes and pies. And then, there are local treats you need to experience: *malasada* (a fresh, warm donut pastry, plain or filled with wonderful things), *manapua* (a stuffed sweet bun), *mochi*, shave ice, *haupia* (an old-fashioned coconut pudding), Portuguese sweetbread and much more. There are exquisite local bakeries in unlikely corners whose empty racks after the lunch hour testify to their reputation.

A word about service. This is a laid-back place. Restaurant service, like the rest of the Big Island lifestyle, can be easygoing and leisurely. In some Big Island restaurants, particularly those with a faithful regular clientele, you may have to wait a bit. While this can be understandably annoying, we invite you to raise your patience threshold a notch, enjoy the atmosphere and relax. With apologies in advance, we promise that in almost every case a smile and a tolerant-to-friendly attitude will win you a lot better service than a demanding demeanor.

For simplicity, the restaurant listings do not include McDonald's, Burger King, Jack in the Box, Kentucky Fried Chicken, Taco Bell, Dairy Queen, Pizza Hut or similar fast-food outlets or 7-Eleven and other convenience stores located around the Big Island. At the end of the chapter are some of the Big Island's popular commercial lu'au offerings and "dinner experiences" on shipboard and an upcountry ranch.

Restaurant listings are first organized geographically as you proceed around the island from Kona to the Kohala and Hamakua coasts, Hilo, Puna and Ka'u. Under each geographic section, restaurants are further broken down into price categories: *Inexpensive* (up to $10 per person prior to adding alcoholic beverages, tax and gratuity), *Moderate* ($10-$30 per person) and *Expensive* (over $30). Primary culinary styles are indicated after each name. Due to changes in menus, management, supplies or other factors, restaurant prices are obviously subject to change at any time. If you are a senior citizen, be sure to ask about a senior citizen discount as more restaurants are extending such a courtesy. Nearly every restaurant offers a *keiki* (children's) menu.

Those restaurants marked with a ★ indicate an exceptional value in quality of food and service, decor and ambiance, unique and unusual cuisine, overall dining experience or a combination of these factors, and not just cost alone. Stars were awarded based on personal experience as well as reputation established by this and other travel references; however, we'd like to remind you that any rating system is subjective. Restaurants go through changes in menu, staff and circumstance, and even the best have a bad night once in a while. Please use these suggestions only as they are intended: a guideline for your own exploration and discovery of the Big Island's smorgasbord of unforgettable tastes.

Our recommendations for best family-dining establishments are indicated with a girl with a hat. While many restaurants offer *keiki* menus, we feel these recommended restaurants have great food, good value (although some are fine-dining establishments and will not be inexpensive) and wonderful atmosphere. If there's no *keiki* menu, most restaurants are happy to down-size standard portions and reduce the cost.

As we've said often, avoid disappointment by calling ahead for specific hours and days of service as some change their hours seasonally based on a variety of factors. Finally, as you travel around the Big Island, you may come across an eatery not listed in this book. It may be new, or one we've missed, and we'd love to hear about it.

Ethnic Foods

The cultural diversity of the Hawaiian islands benefits visitors and residents alike. As immigrants arrived, they brought with them many varied foods from their native lands; some may be familiar while others are new and interesting. little background on some ethnic foods may tempt you to try a few new foods as a part of your dining adventure on the Big Island.

CHINESE FOODS

Bean threads: thin, clear noodles made from mung beans

Char siu: roasted pork with spices

Chow mein: thin noodles prepared with veggies and meat in various combinations, also cake-noodles style

Dim sum: various dumplings and stuffed steamed buns, usually served as appetizers

Egg/Spring/Summer roll: deep-fried or fresh pastry roll with various veggie, meat or shrimp fillings

Kung pao chicken: deep-fried or sauteed spicy chicken pieces

Long rice: clear noodles cooked with chicken and vegetables

Mongolian beef: thinly sliced charbroiled beefsteak

Peking duck: charbroiled duck with *char siu* flavoring

Pot stickers: semisoft pan-fried filled dumplings

Sweet-and-sour sauce: sugar-and-vinegar-based sauce with tomato sauce, salt and garlic flavorings

Szechuan sauce: hot chili–flavored sauce used extensively in beef, chicken, pork, seafood dishes

Wonton: crispy deep-fried dumpling with meat or veggie fillings; also soft style cooked in soups or noodle dishes

FILIPINO FOODS

Adobo: chicken or pork cooked with vinegar and spices

Cascaron: a donut made with rice flour and rolled in sugar

Halo halo: a tropical fruit sundae that is a blend of milk, sugar, fruits and ice

Lumpia: fried pastry filled with vegetables and meats

Pancit: noodles with vegetables or meat

Pinacbet: stir-fry of bitter melon, okra, pork and various seasonings

Pork and peas: traditional entree of pork, peas, flavorings in a tomato paste base

HAWAIIAN FOODS

Haupia: a sweet custard made of coconut milk

Kalua pig: roast pig cooked in an underground *imu* oven, very flavorful

Kulolo: a steamed pudding using coconut milk and grated taro root

Laulau: pieces of pork, beef or chicken, flavored with butterfish, wrapped with luʻau (taro) leaves, then steamed in an outer ti-leaf wrapper

Lomi lomi salmon: diced and salted salmon with tomatoes and green onions

Opihi: saltwater limpets eaten raw and considered a delicacy

Poi: the staple starch of old Hawaiʻi, made from taro root, boiled then pounded into a baby-food consistency

Poke: cut pieces of raw fish or seaweed, usually marinated and mixed with a variety of ingredients: spices and seasonings, seaweed, fruits and vegetables, nuts, seeds and more; for example, ahi *poke* is raw tuna while *tako poke* is marinated octopus

JAPANESE FOODS

Chicken katsu: deep-fried, breaded chicken pieces served with *katsu* sauce

Donburi: chicken, pork or fish entree with veggies and special soy sauce served over steaming rice and topped with egg

Furikake: a seasoning made with *nori* (seaweed) and various ingredients such as sesame seeds, chili pepper flakes and others

Kamaboko: fish cake of white fish and starch steamed together

Miso soup: soup of fermented soy beans

Mochi: a rich sweet dessert made from cooked rice, pounded into a soft dough

Nori: Sheets of dried seaweed used to wrap sushi rolls or as flavoring

Sashimi: very fresh firm raw fish, usually yellowfin tuna (ahi), sliced thin and dipped in wasabi-*shoyu* sauce

Shabu shabu: thinly sliced beef with veggies, noodles and *ponzu* sauce

Shoyu: soy sauce, same thing

Saimin: thin curly noodles, usually served in broth with garnishes like green onion, egg, kamaboko, shrimp and others

Sukiyaki: thinly sliced beef with veggies, noodles and tofu in a broth

Sushi: white rice rolls or cakes with various fish, seafood, seaweed and veggie fillings

Tempura: deep-fried shrimp, fish, seafood and veggies dipped in a light flour batter

Teriyaki: flavorful, savory soy sauce and ginger marinade for beef, chicken, pork and seafood

Tonkatsu: pork cutlet grilled golden brown, served with *tonkatsu* sauce

Udon: noodles served with soup broth, green onions, fish cake slices, and optional meat

Wasabi: very spicy green horseradish root; when mixed with *shoyu* (soy sauce), it is used as a dipping sauce for sushi and sashimi

Wasabi peas: Green peas fried to crunchy, with spicy wasabi coating; sometimes made with peanuts

KOREAN FOODS

Kalbi ribs: flavored similarly to teriyaki, but with chili pepper, sesame oil and green onions

Kim chee: spicy pickled cabbage flavored with ginger and garlic

Mandoo: fried dumplings with meat and vegetable fillings

Mandoo kook, Bi bim kook, yook kae jang: soups served with *mandoo* dumplings, noodles, vegetables, variety of meats

Meat or fish jun: fried or broiled beef or fish with teriyaki-type sauce

LOCAL FAVORITES

Arare: Japanese snack crackers, usually salty and flavored with *nori*, in a variety of shapes and sizes, locally mixed in with hot popcorn

Bento: a box lunch might include tempura shrimp, veggies, scoop of noodles, sushi roll or rice

Chicken lu'au: chicken stewed with coconut milk; also made with squid

Crack seed: a snack made from preserved fruits and seeds—some are sweet, others are sour

Huli huli chicken: Usually half a chicken, rotisseried on an outdoor barbecue; *huli* means "turn over"

Loco moco: traditionally a bowl of rice, topped with a hamburger patty, fried egg, and gravy; now there's Spam *moco*, salmon *moco*, teri chicken and even veggie mocos

Manapua: a large, local-style steamed bun stuffed with *char siu*, curry chicken, sweet bean paste or other good things

Musubi: a kind of sandwich made with rice and Spam or tuna, pressed in a mold and wrapped with *nori* (seaweed)

Ogo: A generic term for the edible seaweed used as an essential ingredient for many seafood dishes

Plate lunches: a traditional favorite might include teriyaki beef or chicken, hamburger with gravy, roast pork, fried fish or any of several other entrees, always served with rice and often a scoop of macaroni salad

Saimin: noodles served in broth with fish cake, veggies

Shave ice: ground ice—mainlanders know it as snowcones, except the ice is more finely shaved—topped with flavored syrups such as strawberry, pineapple, guava, vanilla, mango, root beer, *lilikoi.*

PORTUGUESE FOODS

Malasadas: a kind of doughnut, light, deep-fried and rolled in sugar, sometimes filled

Sweetbread: a dense yeast bread, sometimes flavored with taro or fruit

PUERTO RICAN FOODS

Pasteles: an exterior of grated green banana that is filled with pork and vegetables

THAI/VIETNAMESE FOOD

Fried noodles/fried rice: crispy/soft fried noodles with meat entree and soft rice with meat and vegetables

Green curry: choice of meat entree with peas, string beans, coconut milk and sweet basil

Mein noodles: egg noodle soup with shrimp, seafood or other entree

Musaman curry: curry with onion, peanuts, carrots and potatoes in coconut milk

Pad Thai: Thai-style pan-fried noodles with choice of meat entree or veggies garnished with sprouts

Pho noodle soup: noodle soup with beefsteak, meatball, chicken or combination with veggies

Red curry: choice of meat entree with bamboo shoots in coconut milk and sweet basil

Rice noodle soup: rice stick noodles with shrimp, pork, fish cake, squid or other seafood

Satay sticks: broiled chicken, pork or beef on skewer sticks, served as a side dish

Yellow curry: chicken with coconut milk and potatoes

A FEW WORDS ABOUT FISH

Whether you are dining out or buying fresh fish at the market, Hawaiian fish names can be confusing. Among the more common fish caught commercially and that you'll see at the market and on restaurant menus are ahi (yellowfin tuna) which is most-preferred for *sashimi*, mahimahi (dolphin fish not the mammal) served in many different preparations almost everywhere, and several species of marlin. Other popular table fish include *ono* (wahoo), *opakapaka* (pink snapper) and *onaga* (red snapper) which provide delicate white flaky meat. Here is some background on what you might find on your dinner plate.

A'ama: a small black crab that scurries over rocks at the beach. A delicacy required for a Hawaiian lu'au

Ahi: yellowfin tuna is caught in deep waters and weighs 60 to 280 pounds; pinkish red meat is firm yet flaky and popular for sashimi

Aku: a bluefin tuna that has a stronger taste than ahi

Albacore: a smaller version of the ahi, averages 40 to 50 pounds and is lighter in both texture and color; also called *koshibi*

Ehu: orange snapper

Hapu: Hawaiian sea bass

Mahimahi: called the dolphin fish, but has no relation to Flipper or his friends; caught while trolling and weighs between 10 to 65 pounds; excellent white meat that is moist and light and very good sauteed; a seasonal fish that commands a high price when fresh. **Note:** While excellent fresh, mahimahi is often served in restaurants having arrived from the Philippines frozen, making it far less pleasing. A clue as to whether it's fresh or frozen may be the price tag. If it runs less than $10 to $15 it is probably the frozen variety.

Onaga: caught in holes that are 1,000 feet or deeper, this red snapper has an attractive hot-pink exterior with tender, juicy white meat inside

Ono: also known as *wahoo*; a member of the barracuda family, its white meat is firm and more steaklike. *Ono* means delicious in Hawaiian

'Opae: shrimp

Opah: moonfish; pink to red or orange in color, the meat is rich in flavor

Opakapaka: pink snapper; meat is very light and flaky with a delicate flavor

Papio: a baby *ulua* caught in shallow waters

INTERNET CAFES

Welcome to the 21st century. The Big Island is now home to a handful of places to surf the web, go gaming, work on your digital photos or seek wireless connectivity with the rest of the planet. In Kona look for **Kanaka Kava** (808-327-1600), **Internet Island Lounge** (808-329-8555), **Island Lava Java** (808-327-2161), **Scandinavian Shaved Ice Co.** (808-331-1626), **Surfin' Ass Coffee Co.** (808-329-1276), **Cuz'ns** (808-326-4920) or **Java Net** (808-331-1741). In Honoka'a on the Hamakua Coast, it's **The Virtual Lounge** (808-775-9355). In Hilo, **Bytes & Bites Internet Cafe** (808-935-3520) or **Kope Kope** (808-933-1221) and in Puna, the **Aloha Outpost** (808-965-8333).

Ulua: also known as pompano, this fish is firm and flaky with steak-like, textured white meat

Dining Best Bets

Bakery   O'Keefe & Sons Bread Bakers in Hilo
Burgers   You'll just have to decide for yourself. Try U-Top-It or Lulu's in Kona
Chinese   Royal Jade Garden in Kona; Leung's Chop Suey House in Hilo; Kirin, Hilton Waikoloa Village
Chocolate   The Original Hawaiian Chocolate Factory, Kona
Chocolate Confections   Kailua Candy Co. in Kona; Big Island Candies in Hilo
Coffee   Are you kidding? This is *Kona*!
Filipino   Danicita's Filipino Restaurant in Kona
Food Court   Waiakea Center food court in Hilo; Kings' Shops in Waikoloa Beach Resort
French   La Bourgogne in Kona
German/Continental   Edelweiss in Waimea
Hawai'i Local Style   Big Island Grill in Kona, Teshima's or Manago Hotel south of Kailua town; Ken's Pancake House or Cafe 100 in Hilo (and many other places); Kamuela Deli or Island Style Cafe in Waimea
Health Foods   Evie's Organic Cafe in Kainaliu; Healthways II Deli or Little Juice Shack in Waimea; Island Naturals or Hilo Bay Cafe in Hilo; Aloha Outpost in Puna
Ice Cream   Cold Stone Creamery in Kona; also, Tropical Dreams ice cream brand served in restaurants and snack bars islandwide
Indonesian   Sibu Cafe in Kona

Italian Paolo's Bistro in Pahoa; Pescatore in Hilo; Michaelangelo's in Kona

Japanese Nihon Cultural Center or Miyo's in Hilo

Japanese/Contemporary-Fusion Restaurant Kaikodo in Hilo; Kenichi Pacific in Keauhou

Kids Choice Denny's, Bubba's Burgers or Bubba Gump Shrimp Co. in Kona; Ken's Pancake House or Don's Grill in Hilo; Paniolo Country Inn in Waimea; Kohala Ohana Grill in Hawi, North Kohala

Mac Nut Confections Mac Pie in Kona

Malasadas Tex Drive In in Honoka'a, Baker Tom's just outside Hilo in Papaikou

Mexican Reuben's in Hilo; Tako Taco in Waimea

Mochi Two Ladies Kitchen in Hilo

Pizza Okay, the challenge is on . . . after 15 years on the island, we've not found a pizza that consistently exceeds expectations— we'd love to hear from readers or restaurants willing to prove us wrong.

You might want to explore the web, not just for individual restaurant websites, but for informal forums among visitors and residents, discussing their experiences in Big Island restaurants and attractions. One of the good ones we've found is www.konaweb.com.

Pupus Seafood Bar in Kawaihae

Romantic Evening Italian-style Donatoni's at Hilton Waikoloa Village

Romantic Evening with Ocean View CanoeHouse at Mauna Lani Bay Hotel and Bungalows

Romantic Evening with Volcano Kilauea Lodge in Volcano

Saimin Restaurant Osaka, Nori's Saimin and many others in Hilo

Seafood Seaside Restaurant in Hilo

Steaks on a Budget Outback Steakhouse in Kona

Steaks Not on a Budget The Grill at Fairmont Orchid

Sunday Brunch Mauna Kea Beach Hotel on the Kohala Coast

Sushi (contemporary) Sushi Rock, North Kohala

Sushi (traditional) Nihon Cultural Center in Hilo; Wasabi's in Kona; Norio's in the Fairmont Orchid

Sweetbread Punalu'u Bakery in Punalu'u

Thai Naung Mai in Hilo; Thai Thai in Volcano; Bangkok House in Kona

Top Restaurants For years, it's been assumed that the very best, consistently excellent restaurants were concentrated in the Kohala Coast resorts. However, a "second tier" of excellent dining venues has risen to challenge the status quo. Fine food exquisitely prepared, professionally presented and served in artful settings, surrounded by an atmosphere of gracious hospitality—these qualities are no longer limited to resort dining. Logically, their menus are similar, focused on Hawai'i Regional Cuisine, a fresh-cooking style that features the very best in fresh local fish and produce, creatively prepared. And, naturally, quality comes with a price wherever you choose to eat. Meals at these top restaurants can easily run upwards of $100 per person, but will be a memorable part of your Big Island vacation, and we encourage you to indulge. As a rule, most fine dining rooms here have gone the route of casual dress in recent years; however, please keep in mind that dinner jackets for gentlemen may be recommended. Ask when you call for reservations (strongly recommended)—and *bon appetit*!

Top Resort Fine Dining Venues The Batik (Mauna Kea Beach Hotel); CanoeHouse at The Gallery (Mauna Lani Bay Hotel); The Grill and Brown's Beach House (Fairmont Orchid); Donatoni's and Kamuela Provision Company (Hilton Waikoloa Village); Hale Samoa and Hale Moana (Kona Village Resort); Pahu i'a (Four Seasons)

Top Independent Restaurants *Kona District:* Edward's at Kanaloa, Huggo's, O's Bistro, Aloha Angel Cafe; *Kohala Coast:* Hualalai Club Grille by Alan Wong, Roy's Waikoloa Bar & Grill, Kings' Shops; *North Kohala District:* Bamboo; *Waimea:* Daniel Thiebaut Restaurant, Edelweiss, Merriman's; *Hilo:* Harrington's' Hilo Bay Cafe, Restaurant Kaikodo, Seaside Restaurant; *Puna District:* Kilauea Lodge

Vegetarian Hale Moana at Kona Village Resort

Kona District

Inexpensive-priced Dining

Bad Ass Coffee Co. *(Coffee Shop/Sandwiches/ Snacks)*
Waterfront Row, 75-5770 Ali'i Drive, Kailua-Kona; 808-326-4637.
   Hours: 9 a.m. to 9 p.m. *Sampling:* This small coffee bar features snacks, ice cream, and pastries along with a variety of freshly brewed Kona coffee.

★ **Basil's Pizzaria & Ristorante** *(Pizza/Italian)*
75-5707 Ali'i Drive, right across from Hulihe'e Palace, Kailua-Kona; 808-326-7836.
   Hours: 11 a.m. to 10 p.m. *Sampling:* The all-Italian menu offers pizza, pasta, seafood, eggplant *parmigiana,* chicken *cacciatore,* chicken *marsala,* sausage and peppers, individual gourmet pizzas, New York–style pizzas, sandwiches, soups, salads and more. *Comments:* Nice

atmosphere, open-air views across Ali'i Drive to Kailua Harbor. Good food, good service. Beer and wine are served.

Big Jake's Island BBQ *(American)*
Mile Marker 106, Honaunau; 808-328-1227; second location at the Swing Zone, Kailua, 808-334-1211.

Hours: Tuesday through Friday 11 a.m. to 6 p.m., Saturday 11 a.m. to 5 p.m. *Sampling:* Something new for barbecue lovers, Big Jake offers chicken, pork, and beef brisket barbecue sandwiches or plate meals with coleslaw and baked beans. Catering too.

Bong Brothers Coffee Company *(Coffee/Sandwiches/Snacks/Smoothies)*
84-5227 Mamalahoa Highway, between mile markers 106 and 105, Honaunau; 808-328-9289; fax 808-328-8112.

Hours: 9 a.m. to 6 p.m. *Sampling:* Kona coffee, fruit stand and vegetarian food to go.

★ Buns in the Sun *(Sandwiches/Snacks)*
Lanihau Center, 75-5595 Palani Road, Kailua-Kona; 808-326-2774.

Hours: Monday through Friday 5 a.m. to 4 p.m.; Saturday and Sunday 5 a.m. to 3 p.m. *Sampling:* Expect a full range of fresh baked pastries, breads, rolls, desserts and gourmet sandwiches. Ask about specials including the spicy breakfast sandwich, Kona cheesesteak or Bird of Paradise (sliced turkey, bacon and Swiss cheese on grilled sourdough bread). *Comments:* This small bakery/deli/coffee shop is bright, clean and very popular with residents and visitors alike.

Cactus Bar & Grill *(Mexican)*
75-5711 Kuakini Highway, Kailua-Kona; 808-329-4686.

Hours: Lunch 11 a.m. to 2 p.m. and dinner 5 to 9 p.m.; closed Sunday. *Sampling:* The menu features generous servings of good-quality crab *enchiladas*, chicken *flautas*, chiles rellenos, *chimichangas* and much more—from mild to spicy hot (if you like it really hot, just ask). Beer, wine and cocktails, and margaritas by the pitcher or the glass. Take-out available.

Charley's Thai Cuisine *(Thai)*
Kona Coast Shopping Center, 74-5586 Palani Road, Kailua-Kona; 808-334-0891; second location in Waimea in the KTA Shopping Center, 808-885-5591.

Hours: Lunch 11 a.m. to 4 p.m. and dinner 5 to 9 p.m. *Sampling:* A full menu of authentic Thai dishes includes chicken and beef satays, spring and summer rolls, papaya salad, glass noodle salad, soups, a variety of curries (you can opt to add chicken, beef, pork, shrimp, mahimahi or mussels), noodles, stir-fries and combination dishes.

Coffee Shack *(Breakfast/Sandwiches/Pizza)*
83-5799 Mamalahoa Highway, between mile markers 108 and 109, south of Captain Cook; 808-328-9555.

Hours: 7 a.m. to 4 p.m. *Sampling:* A nice stop on the way south, Coffee Shack has eggs for breakfast, plus a delicious menu of hot (or not) deli sandwiches including vegetarian, salads and fresh-made soups, plus individual gourmet pizzas and a nice selection of desserts, like Kona lime, mac nut and coconut cream pies, cinnamon rolls, chocolate pecan cran bar, carrot cake and more. *Comments:* If you're hungry, don't pass it by.

Cold Stone Creamery *(Ice Cream)*
Crossroads Shopping Center, Kailua-Kona; 808-327-1084; www.coldstone creamery.com.

Hours: 11 a.m. to 10 p.m. Just what we need, a seductive new temptation on the Big Island. *Comments:* Come on, homestyle ice cream made fresh everyday, a list of mix-ins as long as your arm, custom ice cream cakes you can design yourself. There's no way to resist stuff like that. If you don't believe us, take a look at their website. If ice cream were a controlled substance, these people would be in jail.

Cruisin Coffee Kona *(Coffee Shop)*
75-5702 Kuakini Highway, Kailua-Kona; 808-326-9555.

Hours: 5:30 a.m. to 9 p.m. *Sampling:* This coffee house features a variety of espresso, Italian sodas, milkshakes, pastries and snacks. They feature Kona coffee and Seattle's Best coffees.

Cuz'uns Internet Cafe *(Sandwiches/Snacks)*
75-5744 Ali'i Drive, oceanfront in the Kona Inn Shopping Village, Kailua-Kona; 808-326-4920.

Hours: 9 a.m. to 9 p.m. *Sampling:* This small deli snack bar features fresh deli sandwiches, pizza, salads, snacks and beverages. Great smoothies include flavors like mango, guava and pina colada, along with a spirulina energy smoothie and high-protein sports smoothie. Or try Hawaiian-made ice creams, frozen yogurts and sorbets to accompany your high-speed internet, fax and digital photo print service.

Dara's Thai Cuisine *(Thai)*
74-5476 Kaiwi Street, one street north of Palani Road, Kailua-Kona; 808-329-0795.

Hours: 11 a.m. to 9 p.m. *Sampling:* Over 130 items on their exotic menu, featuring complete, reasonably priced lunch and dinner selections of appetizers, soups, salads, hot entrees, noodles and rice dishes. *Comments:* Beer and wine served.

Daylight Donuts & Deli *(Sandwiches/Snacks)*
Keauhou Shopping Center, 78-6831 Ali'i Drive, Keauhou; 808-324-1833.
　　Hours: 6 a.m. to 4 p.m. *Sampling:* This is the only donut shop in Kona, providing a variety of fresh-made-daily donuts, *malasadas* and specialty pastries. They also have fresh deli items like breakfast croissants, deli sandwiches for lunch, salads and a nice selection of smoothies, espresso and coffee drinks, plus Tropical Dreams ice cream.

★ Denny's *(American)*
Crossroads Shopping Center, 75-1027 Henry Street, Kailua-Kona; 808-327-2184.
　　Hours: Open 24 hours. *Sampling:* This is the Big Island's first Denny's, and you'll find pretty much the same menu as the numerous mainland outlets. If you're looking for basic comfort food, egg dishes, burgers and fries, steaks, chicken, spaghetti and pies, this is the place. *Comments:* Service is not Denny's strong point.

Don's Chinese Kitchen *(Chinese)*
Kona Coast Shopping Center, 75-5588 Palani Road, Kailua-Kona; 808-329-3770.
　　Hours: 10 a.m. to 9 p.m. Closed Sunday. *Sampling:* This small lunch counter specializes in a variety of Chinese plate-lunch fare and take-out plus *manapua* (steamed meat-filled buns). *Comments:* This is a popular spot with the shopping center crowds; sidewalk table seating available.

Evie's Organic Cafe *(Health foods)*
Mango Court on Highway 11, Kainaliu; 808-322-0739.
　　Hours: Monday through Friday 9 a.m. to 9 p.m., Saturday and Sunday 9 a.m. to 5 p.m. *Sampling:* Three meals a day of nutritious certified organic food and vegetarian specialties prepared with a personal touch, without GMOs (genetically modified organisms). A recent menu offered homemade soups, sandwiches, wheat-free spelt crust pizzas and waffles, "veggie extravaganzas," juice bar, award-winning desserts (some sugar-free). Retail shop and produce market on-site; live music nightly.

Gomaichi Ramen *(Japanese)*
Corner of Hualalai Road and Kuakini Highway, Kailua-Kona; 808-329-2772.
　　Hours: Open for lunch daily 11:30 a.m. to 2 p.m. and dinner Monday through Thursday 5:30 to 9 p.m. (until 9:30 p.m. on Friday and Saturday). *Sampling:* New eatery with various tasty ramen and other noodle dishes. *Comments:* Moderate prices, friendly service.

Holualoa Cafe Espresso Bar *(Coffee Shop/Sandwiches/Snacks)*
76-5901 Mamalahoa Highway, right in Holualoa Village, five miles above Kailua-Kona; 808-322-2233.

Hours: 6:30 a.m. to 3 p.m. Closed Saturday and Sunday. *Sampling:* This small snack bar offers fresh Kona coffee and local pastries, plus for lunch sandwiches, salad and soup of the day.

Hong Kong Chop Suey *(Chinese)*
Kealakekua Ranch Center, Highway 11, Kealakekua; 808-323-3373.

Hours: 9:30 a.m. to 8:30 p.m. Closed Tuesday. *Sampling:* This simple but clean Chinese kitchen serves up delicious Hong Kong–style food. Many daily plate-lunch and dinner dishes feature chicken, pork, beef and vegetarian choices. House specials include pepper shrimp or calamari, Hong Kong–style crispy duck, and shrimp with black bean sauce. *Comments:* You'll find good Chinese food at reasonable prices. Take-out is available as well as catering.

Island Lava Java *(Sandwiches/Snacks/Coffee Shop/Internet Cafe)*
Ali'i Sunset Plaza, 75-5799 Ali'i Drive, Kailua-Kona; 808-327-2161.

Hours: 6 a.m. to 10 p.m. *Sampling:* This bakery and bistro espresso bar features fine coffees and teas, fresh-baked croissants, muffins, scones, pastries, cakes, fresh sandwiches, snack items and more. *Comments:* Now offering web-surfing service.

Jamba Juice *(Snacks/Smoothies)*
74-5588 Palani Road, Kailua-Kona; 808-327-6900.

Hours: Monday through Friday 5:30 a.m. to 9 p.m., Saturday and Sunday 6:30 p.m. to 10 p.m. Really nice selection of fresh-squeezed fruit and vegetables juices and blends, energy drinks and "enlightened smoothies," plus Jamba breads and pretzels to munch.

Kamuela Deli *(Hawai'i Local Style)*
Kona Coast Shopping Center, 74-5588 Palani Road, Kailua-Kona, 808-334-0017; second location in the Waimea Center, Highway 19, Waimea, 808-885-4147.

Hours: 7:30 a.m. to 9 p.m. *Sampling:* Kamuela Deli is an institution, a museum for all the local dishes everyone loves. Their long, mouth-watering menu truly has something for everyone, from big breakfasts (including a "curry stew omelet") to burgers and sandwiches to generous full dinner plates with various chicken preparations, ribs, teriyaki, roast beef or pork, local fish and seafood. *Pupu* platters and catering available too. Eat in or carry out.

★ Kimo's Family Buffet *(Hawai'i-Pacific Regional Cuisine/Local Style)*
Uncle Billy's Kona Bay Hotel, 75-5739 Ali'i Drive, Kailua-Kona; 808-329-1393.

Hours: Breakfast 7:30 to 10 a.m., dinner 6 to 8 p.m. *Sampling:* The menu changes nightly but usually offers beef, chicken, seafood and other local favorites. *Comments:* One of the last bargains in Kona, especially at breakfast-time, this open-air dining room sits just above busy Ali'i Drive in the heart of town. It has sort of a 1940s South Seas atmosphere and a buffet-only menu heavy in local-style Hawai'i cuisine. There is often evening entertainment and a hula show included. Reservations suggested for dinner.

Kona Cakes & Coffee (Sandwiches/Snacks)
74-5588 Pawai Place, Building A, Kailua Kona; 808-329-6679.
  Hours: 10 a.m. to 3 p.m. Closed Sunday and Monday. *Sampling:* A bakery with a lot to choose from, including cakes for all occasions, baklava, muffins, tortes and tarts and *mochi* specialties. They also offer a "Munchie Menu" of sandwiches, bagels, salads and vegetarian specials.

Kona Natural Foods (Sandwiches/Snacks)
Crossroads Shopping Center, Kailua-Kona; 808-329-2296.
  Hours: Monday through Saturday 8:30 a.m. to 6 p.m., Sunday 8:30 a.m. to 3 p.m. *Sampling:* Nice selection of fresh salads and sandwiches including very good vegetarian options plus hot dishes like Spanish rice and beans or steamed veggies with hummus and brown rice. Juices, smoothies and other good things.

Kanaka Kava Internet Cafe and O$_2$ Bar (Internet Cafe/Hawai'i
Local Style)
75-5803 Ali'i Drive, Coconut Grove Marketplace, Kailua-Kona; 808-327-1660.
  Hours: Sunday through Wednesday 11 a.m. to 10 p.m., Thursday through Saturday 11 a.m. to 11 p.m. *Sampling:* An unusual little place, serving *kava*, a Polynesian beverage with mildly relaxing properties, in coconut shells from a big wooden bowl on the counter. (They offer flavored and juice blends of *kava* as well to enhance the taste.) There's also dinner plates, *pupus*, organic salads and local à la carte items such as *poke*, *opihi* (limpets), steamed taro and squid lu'au. Their new internet services are an interesting contrast and they have an oxygen bar available for $10/15 minutes. *Comments:* In Hawaiian culture, *kava* was a traditional beverage prepared by *kahuna* from the root of the 'awa plant (*Piper methysticum*), and drunk ceremoniously on special occasions. Its flavor is mild with a slightly bitter aftertaste that increases as it "breathes," so best to drink it down. The effects of *kava* are mild too, a slight numbing of the lips and a short-lived feeling of relaxed well-being, not at all like alcohol. If you have any doubts, ask for a taste before you order.

Kona Style Fish & Chips (American)
75-5687 Ali'i Drive, Kailua-Kona; 808-329-4488.
  Hours: 6:30 a.m. to 8:30 p.m. *Sampling:* Hearty American breakfasts with some local-style choices. For lunch and dinner, their no-

table fish—or shrimp, chicken, veggies or mahimahi—and chips are featured, along with several tacos, and specialties like ribs, scampi and lobster tails.

Los Habaneros (Mexican)
Keauhou Shopping Center, 78-6740 Makolea Street; 808-324-4688.

Hours: Monday through Saturday 9 a.m. to 9 p.m. *Sampling:* Serving traditional Mexican cuisine in a bright, sunny atmosphere, Habaneros is a welcome new addition to the Keauhou area.

★ Mac Pie Factory (Bakery/Snacks)
74-5035 Queen Ka'ahumanu Highway, Kailua-Kona; 808-329-7437; 888-622-7437; www.macpie.com.

Hours: 10 a.m. to 6 p.m. Closed Sunday. *Sampling:* OK, this is not actually a restaurant, but the Mac Pie is one of those irresistible things about the Big Island that almost guarantees you'll be back. The shop also has espressos and lattes by the Kona Coffee & Tea Company, smoothies and sweet treats.

Manna Korean BBQ (Korean)
Crossroads Shopping Center, 75-1027 Henry Street, Kailua-Kona; 808-334-0880.

Hours: 10 a.m. to 8:30 p.m. Closed Sunday. *Sampling & Comments:* This is a clean, bright lunch counter operation with a menu board plus steam table of fresh selections. The menu features generous servings of excellent Korean cuisine including *kalbi*, barbecue beef and chicken, chicken *katsu*, fish jun, spicy pork, *man doo*, several soup and noodle dishes and other specials, including "the #1 chicken in Kona." Manna plates let you choose the entree and choice of four veggies and two scoops of rice. It's a lot to eat for $7-$8.

The Nasturtium Cafe (American/Health Foods)
Located in Mango Court, Kealakekua; 808-322-5083.

Hours: Monday through Friday 8 a.m. to 5 p.m. *Sampling:* Their slogan is "Where food feeds body, mind and soul" and this interesting little place offers something for all three. A creative menu features hearty breakfasts, generous organic salads, sandwiches, burgers and wraps and hot entrees including different preparations of free-range chicken, turkey and yes, buffalo. Plenty of vegetarian options (like a yummy eggplant-hummus wrap) and a rather famous flourless chocolate cake.

Oceans Sports Bar & Grill (Burgers/Sandwiches/Hawai'i Local Style)
Located in the Coconut Grove Marketplace between Ali'i Drive and Kuakini Highway, Kailua-Kona; 808-327-9494.

Hours: Monday through Saturday 11 a.m. to 2 a.m., Sunday 7 a.m. to 2 a.m. *Sampling:* A good menu for a sports bar. Oceans has things like *poke* and sashimi, quesadillas, shrimp and chicken for appetizers, wraps, sandwiches, fish tacos and burgers for lunch, and hearty local-style entrees like ribs, steak, roast chicken, island fish and chips, plus a selection of pastas. *Comments:* Sports fans have eight satellites, 11 TVs and 20 beers on tap to choose from and the sign says "Ladies Always Welcome." Pool, foosball, shuffleboard and basketball.

Orchid Thai Cuisine *(Thai)*
74-5563 Kaiwi Street, Kailua-Kona; 808-327-9437.

Hours: Lunch 11 a.m. to 4 p.m. and dinner 5 to 9 p.m. Closed Sunday. *Sampling:* A variety of mild-to-hot spicy Thai cuisine for lunch and dinner, featuring appetizers such as Thai spring rolls and stuffed chicken wings, green papaya, calamari or shrimp salad, Thai soups and entrees like red, green or yellow curry with beef or chicken, cashew chicken, barbecue hen, *pad* tofu, *pad woon sen, pad* Thai, and an assortment of noodle and rice dishes. Many of the entrees come with your choice of fish, seafood, chicken, beef and pork.

Palazzo Aikalima Gelato *(Ice Cream)*
74-5588 Palani Road, Kailua-Kona; 808-328-7375.

Hours: 10:30 a.m. to 9 p.m. *Sampling:* Something different and wonderful for Kona, genuine Italian gelato in a wide world of home-made flavors including local fruits like mango, Waimea strawberries and pineapple. *Comments:* Made fresh with aloha on-site by the family owner-operators, gelato is a refreshing, flavorful alternative to ice cream with less than half the fat.

Paparoni's *(Italian)*
82-6127 Mamalahoa Highway, Captain Cook; 808-323-2661.

Hours: Monday through Saturday 11 a.m. to 9 p.m. and Sunday 4 to 9 p.m. *Sampling:* Deli sandwiches, soups and salads, or heartier fare such as a lasagna or chicken parmesan dinner with salad and garlic bread. *Comments:* A hard-to-miss, friendly stop for great pizza, pasta and more. Daily specials, take-out and pizza by the slice.

Peacock House Restaurant *(Chinese)*
81-6587 Mamalahoa Highway in Kealakekua, across from Kamigaki Market; 808-323-2366.

Hours: Monday through Friday 10 a.m. to 2 p.m. for lunch and 5 to 8 p.m. for dinner; Saturday 11 a.m. to 2 p.m. and 5 to 8 p.m. Closed Sunday. *Sampling:* The menu is Cantonese-Chinese cuisine with dim sum. House specialties include spicy pork ribs, prawns and scallops.

Peaberry & Galette *(Coffee/Sandwiches/Snacks)*
78-6831 Ali'i Drive, Keauhou Shopping Center; 808-322-6020.

Hours: Monday through Thursday 9:30 a.m. to 8 p.m., Friday and Saturday 9:30 a.m. to 10 p.m., Sunday 9:30 a.m. to 6 p.m. *Sampling:* Something new and interesting next to the movie theatres in Keauhou, a coffee cafe and crêperie, offering a large variety of authentic espresso-based drinks (lattes, cappuccino, mocha and more) featuring Illy Caffe beans and Ghirardelli chocolate. Made-to-order crêpes can be hearty and savory for your meal or sweet for a lovely dessert. They also offer sandwiches, salads, cakes and assorted loose teas (brewed and served in pots). *Comments:* There's live music and sidewalk art shows on the weekends.

Philly-Sophical Deli *(Sandwiches/Snacks)*
Across from the Oshima Store, Kainaliu; 808-322-6607.

Hours: Monday through Friday 7 a.m. to 6 p.m., Saturday 7:30 a.m. to 4 p.m. Closed Sunday. *Sampling:* Serving breakfast, lunch and pizza from a little out-of-the-way shop in Kainaliu town, Philly-Sophical Deli invites customers to drop in and "solve the world's problems six times daily." Noted for its Philly cheesesteak, the deli offers indoor-outdoor seating and pizzas to go. *Comments:* Enjoy the story of Pop Pop Cristos Gambone's discovery of the Big Island in 1497.

Pot Belli Deli *(Plate Lunches/Sandwiches/Snacks)*
74-5543 Kaiwi Road, Kailua-Kona; 808-329-9454.

Hours: 8 a.m. to 3 p.m. Closed Saturday and Sunday. *Sampling:* This full deli serves sandwiches, salads, plate lunches, and other deli items. *Comments:* Located in the industrial area and caters to the people working there, the deli can be very busy during lunch. Take-out available.

Quinn's Restaurant *(Seafood)*
75-5655A Palani Road, Kailua-Kona; 808-329-3822.

Hours: 11 a.m. to 11 p.m. *Sampling:* This comfortable eatery and neighborhood pub offers great burgers, sandwiches and sides, plus a nice dinner menu featuring steaks, fresh island fish and seafood. *Comments:* They offer casual late-night dining on the lanai, one of the few Kona dining spots serving late-night dinner.

★ Rocky's Pizza & Deli *(Italian)*
Keauhou Shopping Center, 78-6831 Ali'i Drive, Kailua-Kona; 808-322-3223.

Hours: 11 a.m. to 9 p.m. *Sampling:* The popular menu features excellent pizza (whole or by the slice) with choice of four sizes and 32 toppings. House special pizzas include the Hawaiian, Italian White Pie, Mexican Pizza, "Meatsa" Pizza, Veggie, and Rocky's Combo. They also claim to be home of "Kona's Largest Pizza," a 26-inch party pie for $30.95. There are a variety of calzones, pasta such as spaghetti, lasagna, ravioli, manicotti and eggplant parmesan. And rounding out the menu are barbecue ribs, a variety of sandwiches, salads and sides (ask about their hot wings).

★ **Royal Jade Garden** (Chinese)
Lanihau Center, 75-5595 Palani Road, Kailua-Kona; 808-326-7288.
Hours: 10:30 a.m. to 9 p.m. *Sampling:* This neat family-run restaurant offers a full line of delicious Chinese food. The extensive, varied cuisine features regional hot and spicy dishes and house specialties like Hong Kong honey-garlic shrimp and Mongolian beef, but there's plenty to choose from, with more than 150 selections. House-made soups include egg flower, abalone, pork with watercress and hot and sour. Vegetarians won't go hungry, with vegetable and tofu options on their stir-fries, noodles and chop suey dishes. *Comments:* The food is generally good quality and of ample quantity, served in clean, bright and comfortable surroundings. Take-out, too.

Señor Billy's Cantina (Mexican)
Highway 11, Captain Cook; 808-323-2012.
Hours: 11 a.m. to 9 p.m. *Sampling:* Excellent and varied Mexican food including tacos, burritos, enchiladas, chicken or steak fajitas, fresh fish tacos made with local ahi, *carne asada* and more, including several varieties of house specialty margaritas, tequilas and *cervezas*. *Comments:* Easy-to-find location right off the highway, a longtime favorite in Captain Cook.

Shiono (Japanese)
75-5799 Ali'i Drive, Ali'i Sunset Plaza, Kailua-Kona; 808-326-1696.
A little place with a lot of options for lunch and dinner, including bentos and plate lunches, roll sushi and noodle dishes, plus teppanyaki dinners of beef, chicken seafood or a combination. They also offer a "Fantasy Boat Special" combination dinner with sashimi, sushi, seafood tempura, fruits, salad, miso soup and rice for $23.50 per person.

★ **Sibu Cafe** (Indonesian)
Kona Banyan Court, 75-5695 E Ali'i Drive, Kailua-Kona; 808-329-1112.
Hours: Lunch 11:30 a.m. to 2:30 p.m., dinner 4:30 p.m. to 9 p.m. *Sampling:* A unique menu featuring intriguing Indonesian dishes such as chicken and beef satay, curry and other special exotics. A variety of imported beers is featured. *Comments:* If you like it hot, ask for the extra-spicy version of their Southeast Asian cuisine. Sibu continues to gain notice from mainland and local food writers as one of the most interesting, moderately priced places to eat on the island. Inside and lanai-courtyard dining. Reservations suggested. They now accept Visa and MasterCard for your convenience.

Sunset Grille *(Sandwiches/Snacks)*
Ali'i Sunset Plaza, 75-5799 Ali'i Drive, Kailua-Kona; 808-329-4668.
    Hours: 10:30 a.m. to 3:30 p.m. Closed Sunday. *Sampling:* Made-to-order gourmet deli sandwiches like sunset Reuben, New Yorker, French dip or Philly cheese and creative new combinations like "Seinfeld" (turkey and provolone) or The Vegetarian. There's even a smoked-salmon sandwich with cream cheese, red onions and capers. A good variety of fresh salads includes Caesar, spinach, Greek, chef salad and others.

Tacos El Unico *(Mexican)*
Kona Marketplace shopping center, just off Ali'i Drive, Kailua-Kona; 808-326-4033.
    Hours: 9 a.m. to 10 p.m. *Sampling:* Chef-owner Señora Doña Lupe and her family offer good quality, authentic Mexican specialties. Choose from *carne asada*; burritos of chicken, beef, *lengua* or *cabeza*; *tripas*; and *tortas* of *chorizo*, *carne asada*, *lengua* and chicken. They also offer assorted Mexican bottled waters and sodas. *Comments:* Tacos El Unico means "the only one," and while this little sidewalk cafe is not the only Mexican restaurant in Kona, it's earned a lot of attention among aficionados and has grown into a popular, pleasant and unique eatery.

Taeng-on Thai Cafe *(Thai)*
Kona Inn Shopping Village, 75-5744 Ali'i Drive, Kailua-Kona; 808-329-1994.
    Hours: 11 a.m. to 9 p.m. *Sampling:* The extensive menu is authentic Thai with selections like red or yellow curry, Thai noodles, Thai dumpling soup, sweet and sour veggies, spicy fried rice and many more, with choice of mild, medium or Thai hot seasoning. *Comments:* This airy upstairs dining room has tropical decor combined with touches of Thailand.

Teru's II Restaurant & Bar *(Hawai'i Local Style)*
74-5555 Kaiwi Street, old industrial area of Kailua-Kona; 808-326-7700.
    Hours: Open for breakfast and lunch; Monday through Friday 11 a.m. to 2 p.m., Friday and Saturday 7 a.m. to 2 p.m. *Sampling:* This local-style cafe offers a varied menu including selections like teriyaki chicken and steak, beef stew, liver and onions, fried fish, pork chops, chili and rice, a wide variety of hot and cold sandwiches, soups and salads, plus a number of daily specials.

★ **Teshima's Restaurant** *(Japanese/American)*
79-7251 Mamalahoa Highway, Kealakekua, seven miles south of Kailua-Kona; 808-322-9140.

Hours: Breakfast and lunch 6:30 a.m. to 1:45 p.m., dinner 5 to 10 p.m. *Sampling:* Specialties are Japanese-American cuisine and local favorites and the menu has something for everyone, served in a warm, friendly atmosphere that says "home." *Comments:* This longstanding family restaurant is a popular spot for *kama'aina* and visitors, and has become something of a local landmark. Mrs. Teshima, now an octogenarian, still frequents the kitchen and occasionally drops into the dining room to greet old friends and new customers. Her local-style "comfort food" is as good as ever and we suspect her authentic homestyle recipes have something to do with it. Try the miso soup.

★ *Thai Rin Restaurant* (Thai)
Ali'i Sunset Plaza, 75-5799 Ali'i Drive, Kailua-Kona; 808-329-2929.

Hours: Lunch 11 a.m. to 2:30 p.m., dinner 5 to 9 p.m. *Sampling:* This restaurant turns out great versions of trendy hot and spicy Thai cuisine. The menu features over two dozen items including traditional Thai crispy and fried noodles, chicken satay, five different kinds of curry, spicy soups, Thai garlic shrimp or squid and much more.

Tropics Cafe (Hawai'i Local Style/American)
Royal Kona Resort, 75-5852 Ali'i Drive, Kailua-Kona; 808-329-3111; www.royalkona.com.

Hours: 5:30 a.m. to 9 p.m. *Sampling:* Chef Mike's menu features Hawaiian-style specials and American cuisine including sandwiches and burgers, varied seafood salads (a specialty), omelets and local favorites like saimin noodles, fish and chips, stir-fried beef and chicken, chow mein, fried noodles and more. Breakfast is served a la carte or buffet style. Chef Frank is famous for his generous buffet dinners on holidays or other special occasions. *Comments:* Enjoy the food while overlooking views of Kailua Bay and the village from this edge-of-the-water location.

★ *U-Top-It* (Breakfast/Lunch)
75-5799 Ali'i Drive, Ali'i Sunset Plaza, Kailua-Kona; 808-329-0092.

Hours: Tuesday through Sunday 6:30 a.m. to 2 p.m.; closed Monday. A little place with a big menu. Chef Curtis Masuda apparently took it to heart when his mom said breakfast was the most important meal of the day. Hawaiian Taro PanCrêpes are fresh-made and served with your choices of almost endless toppings and fillings. Or, if you prefer, Chef will customize them for you with house specialties like "Pele's Passion" with raspberry, passionfruit and hazelnut cream, or "Pizzaro" with pepperoni, salami, olives, tomatoes and fresh basil. And you must try one of their custom mimosas—champagne spritzers flavored with mandarin orange, raspberry, strawberry, lime mango, peach or coconut. The lunch menu offers all-day omelets and a mixed selection of American comfort food with smart-carb options and notable burgers. Rapidly becoming a Kona favorite, U-Top-It is a fun way to experience your own creativity, and remember, "you are what you eat."

★ *Wasabi's* (Japanese)
Coconut Grove Marketplace, 75-5815 Ali'i Drive, Kailua-Kona; 808-326-2352.

Hours: Sunday through Thursday 11 a.m. to 9 p.m., Friday 11 a.m. to 10 p.m., Saturday 4 p.m. to 10 p.m. *Sampling:* Traditional Japanese diner specializing in take-out bento box lunches. The varied menu includes *yakisoba*, tempura *udon*, *katsu* chicken, *shabu shabu*, fresh-water eel, teriyaki and chow fun. Their specialty is creative sushi, and they offer a wide variety of excellent individual sushi and sushi rolls to eat there or carry out, including California roll, shrimp tempura roll, dragon roll and crazy roll. Children's portions are available. *Comments:* This small but busy operation is located toward the backside of the Marketplace and is worth seeking out. They've recently expanded to accommodate more sit-down diners and added a sushi bar. Good fresh food, quick service and a new gift shop with a pretty selection of Japanese teapots.

Yaniku Takorea (Chinese)
Ali'i Sunset Plaza, 75-5799 Ali'i Drive #A6, Kailua-Kona; 808-329-7100.

Hours: Lunch 11 a.m. to 2 p.m., dinner 5 p.m. to 9 p.m. *Sampling:* Their extensive menu lists 100 varied items including soups, chicken and duck, beef and pork, seafood, egg-veggie-tofu, noodles and rice dishes, Mandarin cuisine, served family style: chef's shrimp with pineapple, and kung pao with fried noodle. House specialties include a Peking duck dinner. They also offer an all-you-can-eat buffet lunch and Yaniku barbecue-style specialties.

You Make the Roll (Japanese)
75-5725 Ali'i Drive, Kailua-Kona; 808-326-1322.

Hours: Monday through Friday 11 a.m. to 7 p.m. and Saturday 11 a.m. to 4 p.m. *Sampling:* People are raving about this little sushi place in the alley. Lots of choices of freshmade sushi rolls and snacks. Try the Philadelphia Roll with salmon and cream cheese for something good and different.

Moderate-priced Dining

★ *Aloha Angel Cafe* (Hawai'i Regional Cuisine/International)
In the old Aloha Theater Building on Highway 11, Kainaliu; 808-322-3383.

Hours: 7:30 a.m. to 2:30 p.m. for breakfast and lunch; Wednesday through Sunday 5 to 9 p.m. for dinner. *Sampling:* Daily specialties are fresh-baked pastries and cookies, sandwiches, charbroiled burgers, organic salads and fresh local fish. Beer and wine are served (or bring your own wines for a corkage fee) along with fresh juices, Kona espresso and herb teas. Vegetarians have plenty of excellent options, like portobello mushroom pesto pasta or tofu curry. *Comments:* This delightful, funky old building is a treat to visit, even better to stay and eat in. There's a take-out counter in the 1920s theater lobby, but seating winds three-quarters around the building on a rustic, wooden lanai with great views of the countryside. Dinner is served in the nicely restored Hokulai Room. Go early and allow time for an indulgent dessert like Kona lime pie or mac nut turtle bar, then enjoy a selected film at the theater, half-price with your dinner receipt. Breakfast here is a delightful experience.

Ba-le French Sandwich & Bakery *(Sandwiches/Vietnamese)*
Kona Coast Shopping Center, 74-5588 Palani Road #103, Kailua-Kona; 808-327-1212.

Hours: Monday through Saturday 10 a.m. to 9 p.m.; Sunday 11 a.m. to 7 p.m. *Sampling:* A Vietnamese restaurant with a selection of deli sandwiches and house-baked French bread and croissants. The varied menu includes a variety of hot entrees, rice noodle salads, Vietnamese saimin, *manapua*, stir-fries and *pho* noodle soup and much more. "French" deli sandwiches include lemongrass chicken (spicy or not), deli meats, *siu mai* (meatball), and vegetarian options like tofu and veggie. There's also a selection of interesting desserts like homemade taro or mango tapioca, sweet banana *mochi* rice, almond tofu, caramel creme flan and something called "bubble drinks." *Comments:* Eat in or carry out in your picnic basket. For an uncommon restaurant, Ba-Le has stood the test of time in Kona, and continues to offer an intriguing alternative to visitors and *kama'aina.*

★ Bangkok House *(Thai)*
King Kamehameha Mall, 75-5626 Kuakini Highway, Kailua-Kona; 808-329-7764.

Hours: Monday through Friday 11 a.m. to 3 p.m. for lunch; Sunday through Friday 5 to 9 p.m. for dinner. Closed Saturday. *Sampling:* This Thai cuisine restaurant offers a variety of the popular, spicy, hot food of southeast Asia. The extensive menu features 100 selections including beef, chicken, seafood and vegetarian specials. Items like spring rolls, *pad* Thai noodles, beef *panang* curry, sizzling chicken Thai-style and fried rice are excellent. *Comments:* Take-out and delivery available.

★ Big Island Grill *(Hawai'i Local Style)*
75-5702 Kuakini Highway, Kailua-Kona; 808-326-1153.

Hours: Monday through Saturday 6 to 10 a.m. for breakfast, 11 a.m. to 2 p.m. for lunch, 5 to 9 p.m. for dinner. *Sampling:* Rapidly becoming a *kamaʻaina* must-stop in Kona, Big Island Grill offers three meals a day in plentiful portions to satisfy big Big Island appetites. Eggs and things plus *loco mocos* for breakfast, burgers and sandwiches for lunch, tasty salads like coconut shrimp, chicken katsu and chicken salad–stuffed papaya. Their dinner menu includes a variety of local-style "comfort food" like Korean chicken, beef teriyaki, B.I.G. saimin, shrimp or fish tempura and daily specials. There's sweet potato–*haupia* cheesecake for dessert and a lot of other good things. Dine in or get it to go.

★ *Bubba Gump Shrimp Co.* (Seafood/Burgers)
Waterfront Row, 75-5776 Aliʻi Drive, Kailua-Kona; 808-331-8442.

   Hours: Breakfast 7 a.m. to 10:30 a.m., lunch and dinner 11 a.m. to 10 p.m.; Friday and Saturday until 11 p.m. *Samplings:* The breakfast menu is traditional; lunch and dinner menus star shrimp and more shrimp. Choose from New Orleans barbecue shrimp and sausage, drunken shrimp, dumb luck coconut shrimp or fish and chips, Bourbon Street mahimahi, Dixie-style baby back ribs and fresh Northwest salmon. There's also a variety of appetizers, salads, sandwiches, burgers and desserts. *Comments:* Part of the national chain with outlets in California, Florida, New Orleans, and other places, the decor is funky boat dock, shrimp-shack and beach flotsam and jetsam inspired by the movie *Forest Gump.* A fun place to eat for all ages. Some seating outside by the ocean.

Cassandra's (Greek)
75-5669 Aliʻi Drive, Kailua-Kona; 808-326-2840.

   Hours: 11 a.m. to 10 p.m. *Sampling:* For lunch, they offer a good selection of burgers, pizzas, fish and chips and gyros. For dinner, step out of bounds and choose from tempting appetizers like *spanakopita, santorini* shrimp cocktail, *kafteri,* hummus and many more. Then indulge in *moussaka* (eggplant and beef in bechamel sauce), *dolmades* (beef-stuffed grape leaves with *avgolemono* sauce) or *sountzoukia* (spiced meatballs in Cassandra's favorite tomato sauce) along with fresh catch, seafood specialties, lamb, pork and chicken dishes. *Comments:* The Big Island's only Greek restaurant occasionally offers belly dancing on the weekends.

Crystal Blue (Cocktails/Pupus)
Sheraton Keauhou Resort & Spa, 78-125 Ehukai Street, Kailua-Kona; 808-930-4900; www.sheratonkeauhou.com.

Hours: 5 to 11 p.m. *Sampling:* Offers romantic sunset cocktails and a good variety of non-alcoholic selections including blended "virgin" tropicals and fresh fruit smoothies. *Comments:* You'll find comfortable, living-room-style seating for board games and conversation as well as a nearby viewing area to watch the manta rays underwater.

Danicita's Filipino Restaurant *(Filipino)*
Kopiko Plaza, Kailua-Kona; 808-329-3123.

Hours: 5:30 a.m. to 8 p.m. *Sampling:* A long and intriguing menu with a little bit of everything. Pork *adobo*, *sari-sari*, *pinakbet* and pigs feet, seafood *bangus sinigang*, squid *guisado*, shrimp *paria*, *balatong* with *paria*, *sarciado* or *sinigang*, chicken papaya or oxtail soup, *pancit canton* or *bihon* and *binapaitan*. For dessert, banana *lumpia*, *halo halo* and *langka*, mango or *ube* ice cream. *Comments:* We confess unfamiliarity with Filipino cuisine; however, those who know will appreciate the variety and quality here. Take-out, local-style plate lunches, traditional breakfasts and catering available, along with a retail outlet for frozen foods.

★ Drysdale's Two *(Steaks/Burgers)*
Keauhou Shopping Center, 78-6831 Ali'i Drive, Kailua-Kona; 808-322-0070.

Hours: 11 a.m. to 11:30 p.m.; bar closes at midnight. *Sampling:* A great *pupu* menu, plus heavier fare, including prime rib, steak and fresh island fish. *Comments:* An energetic, fun sports bar and island eatery featuring two large-screen TVs for sports events. Indoor/outdoor table seating and a large bar space.

Durty Jake's *(Sandwiches/Snacks/American)*
Coconut Grove Marketplace, 75-5819 Ali`i Drive, Kailua-Kona; 808-329-7366; www.dirtyjakes.com.

Hours: 7 a.m. to 10 p.m.; happy hour 4 to 6 p.m.; bar may be open later. *Sampling:* This indoor/outdoor bar-cafe offers a breakfast menu of waffles, specialty egg dishes, bagels, fresh pastries and other morning items. For lunch and dinner, try their juicy burgers, pastrami burgers, fish tacos, fresh fish, salads, sandwiches, pasta dishes and daily specials plus bar beverages. *Comments:* Live music several nights a week.

★ Harbor House *(American/Seafood)*
74-425 Kealakehe Parkway; Gentry Marina, Honokohau Harbor, Kailua-Kona; 808-326-4166.

Hours: Monday through Saturday 11 a.m. to 7 p.m.; Sunday 11 a.m. to 5:30 p.m. *Sampling:* The menu offers fish or calamari and chips, burgers, clam chowder, a variety of hot and cold sandwiches (including grilled *surimi* crab salad) and local favorites. *Comments:*

This is an old-fashioned bar and grill right on the marina at Hono-kohau. We enjoy this large, airy dining room with its great views of the busy activities of the boat harbor, along with a cold 18-oz. "schooner" of beer.

Hang Loose *(Seafood/Hawai'i Local Style)*
Kona Inn Shopping Village, 75-5744 Ali'i Drive, Kailua-Kona; 808-331-1155.

   Hours: 11 a.m. to 9:30 p.m. *Sampling:* The menu highlights seafood and fresh catch (*ono*, ahi, swordfish, spearfish and mahimahi may be available) prepared singularly or in combination platters, Oriental-style, in salads or creative pasta dishes. *Comments:* Hang Loose occupies a great open-air building overlooking Kailua Bay—great views to complement the food.

★ Hard Rock Cafe Kona *(American)*
Coconut Grove Marketplace, 75-5815 Ali'i Drive, Kailua-Kona; 808-329-8866.

   Hours: 11 a.m. to 11 p.m. *Sampling:* The restaurant's decor, ambiance and menu of American cuisine, burgers and daily specials is much like the other Hard Rocks in this international chain. *Comments:* The Hard Rock Cafe Kona is in a shopping/dining complex and occupies a two-level building with nice views overlooking Kailua Bay. The lower level has the Hard Rock logo shop  while the open-air restaurant is located upstairs. If you're a Hard Rock fan, you'll want the T-shirt.

★ Huggo's on the Rocks *(American/Seafood)*
75-5828 Kahakai Road, Kailua-Kona; 808-329-1493; www.huggos.com.

   Hours: Monday through Friday 11:30 a.m. to 2:30 p.m., dinner 5:30 p.m. to 10 p.m.; Saturday and Sunday 5:30 p.m. to 10 p.m. *Sampling:* Enjoy your favorite beverages along with lunch and dinner. Order from their bar menu of *pupus*, seafood specials, pizza and sandwiches or from Huggo's regular lunch and dinner menus. *Comments:* This is a beach hut bar annex to the popular, award-winning Huggo's main beachside restaurant and is located right next door at water's edge. There's live Hawaiian/reggae music.

Izakawa Kai *(Japanese)*
On Sorona Road, between Kuakini Highway and Ali'i Drive, Kailua-Kona; 808-329-2002.

   Hours: Dinner 5 to 11 p.m. *Sampling:* Billing themselves as a "Japanese restaurant, sushi bar and *sake* club," Izakaya Kai offers a unique menu featuring grill items, stir-fries, noodle dishes, a wide variety of sushi and sashimi, plus "House Favorites" such as *kani korokke,* deep-fried mashed potato and crab patty; *asari sakamushi,* steamed clams in *sake; gyu tataki,* seared beef with ginger; and *chizu age,* deep-fried cheese in a wonton wrap, among others. *Comments:* This is owner Kunihiko Imai's second restaurant, after an award-winning success in Oregon that Zagat ranked 12th in the nation for Japanese food.

Jackie Rey's Ohana Grille *(Hawai'i Local Style/American)*
75-5995A Kuakini Highway, Pottery Terrace, Kailua-Kona (former Lasko's location); 808-327-0209; www.jackiereys.com.

Hours: Monday through Friday 11 a.m. to 2 p.m. for lunch, Monday through Saturday 5 to 9 p.m. for dinner (happy hour 3 to 5 p.m. with half-price *pupus* and drink specials), closed Sunday. *Sampling:* A fun menu with various ethnic contributions, including heavy *pupus* like *poke,* spring rolls and *hoisin* chicken wings, Korean-style short ribs and gazpacho. Lunch features salads, sandwiches and big, half-pound Angus burgers. Dinner highlights a range of family-style selections with fresh catch, pork chops, steaks, ribs and roast chicken, along with pasta and a vegetarian tofu curry with tropical fruit chutney. *Comments:* A friendly, owner-operated family restaurant with a lot of potential. The lunch menu features sandwiches and salads, more elaborate dinner selections. Gaining a following and becoming a good new addition to the Kona restaurant scene.

Kai *(Seafood/Hawai'i Regional Cuisine)*
Sheraton Keauhou Resort & Spa, 78-125 Ehukai Street, Kailua-Kona; 808-930-4900; www.sheratonkeauhou.com.

Hours: Breakfast 6:30 to 10:30 a.m. and dinner 6 to 9:30 p.m. *Sampling:* The recently restored Sheraton Keauhou adds dimension to the Kona area with a selection of new and interesting restaurants just south of Kailua town. Kai's breakfast buffet features "kid-friendly" selections, traditional American favorite hot and cold choices and fresh tropical fruits and juices. For dinner, the name Kai (ocean) is explained as the dining room become a romantic seafood feastery, with a fusion-style menu that honors the cuisines of Hawai'i's many cultures. *Comments:* Keep your eye on Kai. Reservations suggested.

Kama'aina Terrace *(Hawai'i-Pacific Regional Cuisine/International)*
Ohana Keauhou Beach Resort, 78-6740 Ali'i Drive, Keauhou-Kona; 808-322-3441.

Hours: Monday through Saturday for breakfast and lunch 6:30 to 10:30 a.m., dinner 5:30 to 9 p.m.; Sunday 6:30 to 9 a.m. for breakfast, 9:30 a.m. to 1 p.m. for brunch. *Sampling:* The menu here focuses on local-style Hawaiian-Pacific favorites with international accents. Selections range from steaks to hibachi chicken, fresh island fish and seafood. *Comments:* This is a nice open-air dining room with a relaxing ambiance, located near the pool and oceanfront hotel terrace extending over the tidepools.

★ *Keei Cafe* *(Continental/International)*
Highway 11, half-mile south of Kainaliu; 808-322-9992.

Hours: Monday through Friday, 10:30 a.m. to 2 p.m. for lunch, Tuesday through Saturday 5 to 9 p.m. for dinner. *Sampling:* The menu is a mix of Continental and international fare that changes frequently and may include appetizers like black bean soup, eggplant rolls and green papaya salad, entrees such as tofu or chicken fajitas, fettuccine primavera with tofu or chicken, and Hawaiian seafood in a variety of preparations including red Thai curry, pan-seared, or grilled on a bed of baby lettuce with peanut miso dressing. *Comments:* A pleasant surprise in a somewhat out-of-the-way location, worth the drive for a change of taste.

★ *Kona Beach Restaurant* *(Hawai'i-Pacific Regional Cuisine/International)*
King Kamehameha's Kona Beach Hotel, 75-5660 Palani Road, Kailua-Kona; 808-329-2911.

Hours: Breakfast buffet 6:30 a.m. to 10 a.m., dinner 5:30 p.m. to 9 p.m. *Sampling:* The menu features specialties such as Pacific broiled salmon, *kiawe*-smoked prime rib, herbal breast of chicken and more. They also offer buffet dinners on Friday and Saturday, with prime rib and seafood, and on Sunday, the "King Kam's" famous champagne brunch, 9 a.m. to 1 p.m. *Comments:* Their attractive dining room has old-fashioned whaling-ship decor. There are big picture windows providing unbeatable views for each table of Kailua Wharf, Ahu'ena Heiau and Kamakahonu Beach. The service is good, and there are colorful fish tanks to amuse the kids. Reservations suggested for dinner.

Kona Brewing Co. *(Italian/Pizza)*
North Kona Town Center, 75-5629 Kuakini Highway, Kailua-Kona; 808-334-2739; www.konabrewingco.com.

Hours: 11 a.m. to 9 p.m.; Friday and Saturday until 10 p.m. *Sampling:* Their award-winning brews may be worth trying just for their names: Pacific Golden Ale, Longboard Lager, Fire Rock Pale Ale, Lilikoi Wheat Ale, Castaway IPA and Black Sand Porter. You may mix and match for a personalized pint, or order a sampler for your own vertical tasting at the table. The food menu features an interesting variety of creative pizzas such as barbecue chicken, Kona wild mushroom, and Hawaiian lu'au, along with sandwiches, salads, bar snack foods and more. *Comments:* This is Kona's original brew pub, and brewery tours are available. Survivors of the microbrewery craze of recent years, Kona Brewing Company remains a popular, fun and satisfying place to eat and drink, with nice outdoor seating in the garden area and live Hawaiian music on Sunday. The bar closes an hour after dinner. Service has been sporadically off the mark.

★ Kona Inn Restaurant (Seafood)

Kona Inn Shopping Village, 75-5744 Ali'i Drive, Kailua-Kona; 808-329-4455.

Hours: 11:30 a.m. to 10 p.m. (last seating at 8 p.m.) *Sampling:* The menu features fresh island fish, seafood, prime rib, steak and local favorites. *Comments:* There is a pleasant casualness in this open-air veranda restaurant that is the original dining room of the old Kona Inn Hotel. The ceiling fans add to the tropical ambiance and old-fashioned charm. This is one of our favorite places to take visitors, with its beautiful view of Kona Bay, fresh local fish, killer mud pie and other desserts and amicable, consistent service. Dinner reservations suggested.

La Pasta (Italian)

Corner of Hualalai Road and Kuakini Highway, Kailua-Kona; 808-329-9111.

Hours: 5:30 to 9 p.m. *Sampling:* New and worth watching, La Pasta offers nine different pastas including meatless spaghetti *e pepperoncini* or *alla Vongole* with two types of clams. You'll also find appetizers and salads; a couple of dishes have a Japanese flair. *Comments:* Probably best to request an indoor table.

Lulu's (American)

75-5819 Ali'i Drive, Kailua-Kona; 808-331-2633

Hours: 11 a.m. to 10 p.m.; dancing and libations until 2 a.m. *Sampling:* Boasting "red carpet service at shag rug prices," Lulu's offers a colorful, eclectic menu with a little bit of everything for lunch, dinner and *pupus*. Choose from pepper-smoked turkey wings, Cajun cornmeal fried shrimp, Tijuana mahi tacos with chipotle aioli, Fisherman's Bucket, or something from "Big Sweaty's Barbecue Pit," slow-smoked on *kiawe* and guava wood, in small, medium and "sumo" portions. Clever hamburgers claim to be "voted best burger in Tonga 16 years straight." Check out the Bearded Lady, Magnum P.I., Dick Butkus (with peanut butter), or something called "The Slaughterhouse Five" with beef, ham, bacon, pork, pastrami and pepperoni.

★ **Manago Hotel** *(Hawai'i Local Style/American)*
Highway 11, ten miles south of Kailua-Kona at Captain Cook; 808-323-2642; www.managohotel.com.

Hours: Tuesday through Sunday for breakfast 7 a.m. to 9 a.m., lunch 11 a.m. to 2 p.m., dinner 5 p.m. to 7:30 p.m. Closed Monday. *Sampling:* There's no menu; the day's selections are on a board on the wall, but popular items include fried fish, teriyaki and their famous special pork chops. *Comments:* Worth the drive for the good home cooking and Japanese-American specialties, enjoyed by local folks and visitors alike. Call ahead for box picnic lunches to pick up on the way to Volcanoes National Park.

Manta Ray Bar & Grill *(Sandwiches/Snacks/Cocktails)*
Sheraton Keauhou Resort & Spa, 78-125 Ehukai Street, Kailua-Kona; 808-930-4900; www.sheratonkeauhou.com.

Hours: Bar open 10:30 a.m. to 9:30 p.m., food service 11 a.m. to 9:30 p.m. *Sampling:* Lighter fare and cold beverages including good non-alcoholic choices in a refreshing poolside resort setting. *Comments:* Manta Ray has gone out of its way to bring in some of the Big Island's best local entertainers, with music nightly 5:30 to 9:30 p.m. A great place to listen to the music and enjoy your favorite libation.

★ **Michaelangelo's Italian and Seafood Restaurant** *(Italian/Seafood)*
75-5770 Ali'i Drive, Waterfront Row, across from St. Michael's Church, Kailua-Kona; 808-329-4436.

Hours: 11 a.m. to 10 p.m. *Sampling:* A wide selection of Italian fare, including savory appetizers like Marietta escargot in garlic butter, fried calamari and Palermo clam chowder, as well as a house and Caesar salad. Traditional hearty Italian dishes include spaghetti *bolognese,* house-made lasagna, chicken *cacciatora,* and chicken or eggplant *parmigiana.* There is a nice selection of vegetarian pasta dishes like *fettuccine alfredo* or *primavera,* pink penne rigatoni or manicotti *formaggio,* and tempting seafood pastas such as "lava-fire" calamari, macadamia nut sea scallops, *cioppino,* garlic lobster and Trilogy of Fresh Fish. Children's menu available. A dessert tray rounds out the menu. *Comments:* Located on the upper level of the complex, this room has a lovely, open-veranda view of the ocean. Michaelangelo's is one of Kona's few after-hours venues, with dancing 10 p.m. to 2 a.m.

Ocean Seafood Chinese Restaurant *(Seafood/Chinese)*
King Kamehameha Mall, 75-5626 Kuakini Highway, Kailua-Kona; 808-329-3055.

Hours: Monday through Friday 10:30 a.m. to 9 p.m., Saturday and Sunday 11 a.m. to 9 p.m. *Sampling:* The menu features lobster, crab, fresh scallops, shrimp, oysters and traditional Cantonese cuisine like beef, pork, chicken, duck and noodles, plus a generous all-you-can-eat buffet at lunch and dinnertime.

★ Outback Steakhouse *(Steaks)*
Coconut Grove Marketplace, Ali'i Drive, Kailua-Kona; 808-326-2555.

Hours: 4:30 p.m. to 10 p.m. *Sampling:* Big Island version of the popular chain restaurant, featuring their famous steaks, *pupus* like the popular Bloomin' Onion, Shrimp on the Barbie, plus Jackeroo Chops, Botany Bay Fish of the Day and Toowoomba Pasta, side orders, desserts and much more in the signature Australian-style dining room.

Pa Leo *(Seafood/Hawai'i/Regional Cuisine)*
75-4663 Palani Road, Seaside Mall, Kailua-Kona; 808-329-5550.

Hours: Dinner 4:30 to 9 p.m. with bar service until midnight or so. *Sampling:* Pa Leo describes their dinner menu as "Pan-Asian," using fresh catch and local ingredients with an Oriental flair in creative preparation. They also feature a rack of lamb, steaks, chicken dishes and other good things. Soon to be open for lunch too. *Comments:* New and appealing, located where the old Kona Galley used to be overlooking Kona Pier.

Pancho & Lefty's *(Mexican)*
75-5719 Ali'i Drive, across from Kona Inn Shopping Village in the Kona Plaza Condos, upstairs overlooking Ali'i Drive; 808-326-2171.

Hours: 8 a.m. to 10 p.m. *Sampling:* The menu features the usual Mexican fare such as tacos, burritos, enchiladas, chimichangas, tamales, tostadas and varied *pupus. Comments:* Very informal; not particularly family dining.

Restaurant Yokohama *(Japanese)*
Sunset Ali'i Plaza, 75-5799 Ali'i Drive, Kailua-Kona; 808-329-9661.

Hours: Monday through Friday for lunch 11:30 a.m. to 2 p.m., Monday through Saturday for dinner 5 to 9 p.m.; closed Sunday. *Sampling:* This Japanese-style restaurant features teriyaki chicken and beef, *tonkatsu*, tempura, *misoyaki* pork, *sukiyaki, shabu shabu*, sushi, sashimi, noodles and fresh island fish. Bento lunch take-out available.

Rio's Seafood Grill & Bar *(Seafood)*
Upstairs in the Coconut Grove Marketplace, Kailua-Kona; 808-329-8200; www.riosseafood.com.

Hours: Open Tuesday through Friday for lunch, 11:30 a.m. to 2 p.m.; open daily for dinner 5 to 10 p.m. *Sampling:* New and interesting in Kona, Rio's changes their menu frequently to highlight only the freshest local-caught fish from a long list including mahimahi, *hamachi*, swordfish, *opakapaka*, ahi, spearfish, *ono*, marlin, *monchong*, *opah* and others as available, plus lobster, crab, shrimp and scallops. They offer about 20 domestic and imported beers and 25 wines by the glass. *Comments:* The open-air dining room is nicely decorated for a classy tropical evening and has an ocean sunset view to rival more expensive restaurants.

Royal Thai Cafe *(Thai)*
Keauhou Shopping Center, 78-6831 Ali'i Drive, Keauhou-Kona; 808-322-8424.

Hours: Monday through Friday 11 a.m. to 9:30 p.m. *Sampling:* The menu is strictly classic Thai cuisine ranging from pad Thai noodles and jasmine rice to exotic and spicy red, green and yellow curries, to seafood, chicken, beef and pork specialties and chef's special pineapple fried rice or pineapple curry. Diners can choose the degree of spiciness from hot to medium to mild. *Comments:* This small cafe is very clean with an attractive traditional Thai decor. Ample parking.

Sushi Shiolo *(Japanese)*
Ali'i Sunset Plaza, 75-5799 Ali'i Drive, Kailua-Kona; 808-326-1696.

Hours: 11:30 a.m. to 2:30 p.m. for lunch, 5:30 to 9 p.m. for dinner. *Sampling:* The menu here is authentic Japanese sushi including *nigiri*, *unagi*, squid, fish, veggie California-style and chef's special "Kona Wave" with scallop and spicy *tobiko*.

★ Tres Hombres *(Mexican)*
75-5864 Walua Road, at the intersection of Ali'i Drive and Walua Road, across from the Royal Kona Resort, Kailua-Kona; 808-329-2173.

Hours: 11:30 a.m. to 9 p.m. *Sampling:* The menu has tasty Mexican selections like tacos, enchiladas, quesadillas, fajitas and burritos. Other entrees include fresh island fish, chicken and more, plus a nice *pupu* menu. *Comments:* We enjoy visiting this great old building with its long row of open windows overlooking Kona town, and the food is good, too.

Uncle Inbea's Steakhouse *(Steaks)*
81-6372 Mamalahoa Highway, just south of mile marker 111 on Highway 11, Kealakeka; 808-323-2595.

Hours: Open Monday through Friday, 11 a.m. to 3 p.m. for lunch, daily for dinner 3 to 9 p.m. *Sampling:* New and appealing in Kealakekua, Uncle Inbea offers a nice variety of steaks, prime rib, pork chops and daily fresh catch—or try beef or pork barbecue ribs with Uncle's special sauce. Family-owned and -operated.

Expensive-priced Dining

★ *Edward's at Kanaloa* (Continental-International)
Kanaloa at Kona Condominium, 78-261 Manukai Street, Keauhou; 808-324-1434.

Hours: 8 a.m. to 10 p.m. (last seating 8:30 p.m.) *Sampling:* European-trained Chef Walter Mares takes pride in his creative preparations and innovative style. A recent menu featured appetizers of soft shell crab in a pommery mustard sauce, baked oysters with spinach and artichoke, brandy-cured salmon with bowfin caviar and grilled quail. Dinner entrees are again uncommon, such as mussels Provençal, *coq au vin* with cornish game hen, chicken and artichoke strudel, steaks, lamb, lobster and seafood orzo pesto. An excellent wine list is available by the glass or bottle. The lunch menu is equally intriguing, with interesting dishes such as a barbecue-salmon salad with field greens, bleu cheese, walnuts, dried apricots and raspberry vinaigrette, a portobello mushroom sandwich with goat cheese or low-fat ostrich burger. *Comments:* Edward's has long been considered one of Kona's most romantic restaurants, with an awesome oceanside setting that makes the already-excellent food taste even better. Located within the Kanaloa resort complex, Edward's is not easy to find on your own, but more than worth the trouble. Call in advance for directions and reservations.

★ *Huggo's* (Seafood/Continental-International)
75-5828 Kahakai Road, Kailua-Kona; 808-329-1493; www.huggos.com.

Hours: Monday through Friday 11:30 a.m. to 2:30 p.m. for lunch, 2:30 p.m. to 4:30 p.m. for late lunch. Open nightly for dinner 5:30 p.m. until closing. *Sampling:* The menu features a variety of appetizers like island sashimi, seared ahi, Kona *poke* and *kalua* chicken quesadilla plus varied soups and salads. Among the creative entrees are shrimp scampi Provençal, seafood linguine, fresh Kona catch, New York steak, black Angus prime rib, sweet chili chicken, wild mushroom pasta and others. Cocktails and beverages at the bar. *Comments:* A Kona tradition and favorite of *kama'aina* (residents) for over 35 years, this award-winning, family-owned-and-operated oceanside restaurant sits over the water's edge next door to the Royal Kona Resort, with picture-postcard views of Kailua Bay's romantic sunsets. Huggo's has for years offered diners the perfect combination of ambience, cuisine and service that build a great restaurant.

★ *Jameson's by the Sea* (Continental-International/Seafood)
77-6452 Ali'i Drive next to Magic Sands Beach, Kailua-Kona; 808-329-3195.

Hours: Monday through Friday for lunch 11:30 a.m. to 2:30 p.m., dinner nightly 5 p.m. to 9 p.m. *Sampling:* The menu highlights fresh fish and also features varied American-Continental selections such as pasta, beef, veal, lamb, chicken and fresh island fish. Specialties include veal piccata, filet mignon, lobster, calamari and rack of lamb. *Comments:* A *kama'aina* favorite, the oceanfront setting at Magic Sands Beach makes for a romantic atmosphere to enjoy an excellent meal. Smooth, soothing Hawaiian background music, white tablecloths, candlelight, fine service and cheerful bright surroundings add a gracious touch. Beautiful sunsets complimentary with dinner.

★ *Kenichi Pacific* (Japanese/Sushi)
78-6831 Ali'i Drive, D-125, Keauhou Shopping Center; 808-322-6400.

Hours: Tuesday through Friday 11:30 a.m. to 1:30 p.m. for lunch, daily for dinner, 5 to 9 p.m. Kenichi describes their menu as "sushi and fusion cuisine," with artful presentations and graceful service in a subdued, elegant setting. *Sampling:* Creative appetizers include "Total Raw & Local" salad of organic vegetables, sprouted grains and buckwheat with a miso Caesar dressing, Dungeness crab cakes and lobster summer rolls. A recent dinner menu offered creative presentations of local table fish such as ahi, *ono* and mahimahi, as well as macadamia-crusted lamb chops, duck with Chinese five spice, organic New York steak and "Wafu Pasta," *spaghettini* with Japanese mushrooms. *Comments:* Very nice sushi bar and an intriguing dessert menu too. Not inexpensive, but well-worth checking out.

★ *La Bourgogne French Restaurant* (French)
Kuakini Plaza South Center, 77-6400 Nalani, off Kuakini Highway #11, just three miles south of Kailua-Kona; 808-329-6711; e-mail: burgundy@ hawaii.rr.com.

Hours: 6 p.m. to 10 p.m. Closed Sunday and Monday. *Sampling:* Owner and chef Ron Gallaher is a classically trained French cook who prides himself in offering food with "soul and character." A recent menu tempted us with such intriguing presentations as foie gras and sea scallops in a roasted apple raspberry reduction, house-made lobster bisque, osso buco, filet *de chevreuil*, venison with pomegranate glaze, fresh catch, Maine lobster and 100 percent organic Angus beef. "Les Desserts" include chocolate Grand Marnier soufflé, baked caramel apple with cinnamon ice cream, *mousse au chocolat* and cherries jubilee. *Comments:* La Bourgogne is one of Kona's best-kept secrets, highly rated by this and other travel guides (including Zagat, Fodor and Frommer's). Reservations suggested.

★ *O's Bistro* (Hawai'i Regional Cuisine)
Crossroads Shopping Center, 75-1027 Henry Street, Kailua-Kona; 808-329-9222.

Hours: 8 a.m. to 9 p.m. *Sampling:* Chef Ohta's many years of professional culinary experience ranged from France to Houston before she established herself as a founding mother of Hawai'i Regional

Cuisine from her post at the five-star Hotel Hana Maui. Her new dining room has grown from the Oodles of Noodles outlet into a larger, expanded restaurant with a more varietal menu of fresh ingredients in creative preparations, the HRC signature style. A recent menu tempted us with outstanding fresh catch, a very special "Kona-style" tuna casserole, and a selection of her more-requested noodles dishes such as chow fun, pad Thai and the ancho-chicken fettuccine.

★ **Rooster's the Restaurant** (American)
75-5699 Ali'i Drive, across from the seawall in the Kailua Bay Inn shopping plaza, Kailua-Kona; 808-327-9453.

Hours: Monday through Saturday 11 a.m. to 4 p.m. for lunch, nightly for dinner 5:30 to 9 p.m. Sampling: Rooster's is an interesting, friendly kind of place, with mostly American-style egg dishes, sandwiches and burgers during the day for busy people on the go. Dinnertime brings out the tablecloths and more leisurely service, along with upper-end entrees such as live lobster, baby-back ribs, fresh catch and filet mignon with crab imperial, all served with house salad and "shnizzle bread" (with garlic and cheese). Comments: For something special, Rooster's now presents live jazz Thursday, Friday and Saturday nights 6 to 9 p.m.

★ **The Vista** (Hawai'i-Pacific Regional Cuisine/American)
Kona Country Club, 78-7000 Ali'i Drive, Kailua-Kona; 808-322-3700.

Hours: Breakfast and lunch year-round 8 a.m. to 3 p.m.; open for dinner November through April, Wednesday through Saturday 5:30 p.m. to 9 p.m. Call for directions, as the Vista can be tricky to find, but when you arrive you'll see the view is well worth the trouble. Sampling: A recent menu featured fresh-caught local mahi with a Maui onion crust or in an Asian-style stir fry with noodles and ginger-lime sauce. The pineapple cheesecake is an irresistible dessert choice. Comments: After 30 years as a Kona landmark, the Vista must be doing something right. Famous for generous all-day breakfast, amazing sunset views and friendly service. Live music some nights.

Kohala Coast

SOUTH KOHALA DISTRICT

Inexpensive-priced Dining

Boat Landing Pavilion (Sandwiches/Snacks)
Hilton Waikoloa Village, 425 Waikoloa Beach Drive,
Waikoloa; 808-886-1234.

Hours: 6 a.m. to 11 p.m. Sampling: The food court features on-the-go breakfasts, sandwiches, salads, pizza and many children's favorites. There is also a sushi bar for fresh-made California roll, tempura shrimp roll and more plus a full-service bar. *Comments:* This Hilton dining option is especially for families with youngsters looking for a quick snack, lunch or dinner. It's located at the atrium of the resort's Ocean Tower in front of the Palm Terrace Restaurant.

★ **Nalu's Poolside Bar & Grill** *(Sandwiches/Snacks)*
Waikoloa Beach Marriott, 69-275 Waikoloa Beach Drive, Kohala Coast; 808-886-6789.

Hours: 7 a.m. to 11 a.m. for breakfast, 11 a.m. to 11 p.m. for lunch and dinner. *Sampling:* This poolside bar and grill has a light fare menu. Salads include Caesar, sea breeze fruit salad, Indonesian chicken salad and seafood Cobb salad. Sandwiches range from turkey to tuna salad, mahi burger to crab salad; desserts, too. Tropical beverages round out the menu.

★ **3 Frogs Cafe** *(Sandwiches/Snacks)*
Hapuna Beach State Park, Kohala Coast; 808-882-0459.

Hours: 10 a.m. to 4 p.m. *Sampling:* 3 Frogs features hot dogs and burgers, fish tacos, salads and sandwiches, coffee and cold soft drinks—plus shave ice and smoothies. *Comments:* A great place for lunch, just up from the beach. Reasonably priced. Try their Hawaiian salad of romaine lettuce with pineapple and mango, chicken, toasted mac nuts and coconut, only $7.

Village Burger *(Burgers/Sandwiches/Breakfast)*
Waikoloa Highlands Center; 808-883-3712.

Hours: 7:30 a.m. to 8 p.m. *Sampling:* Take-out or eat at a sunny table in the courtyard. Breakfasts, burgers, sandwiches and wraps, plate lunches, and other good things to go.

Moderate-priced Dining

★ **Anthony's Restaurant & Beat Club** *(Pizzeria/Italian/Irish Pub)*
68-1845 Waikoloa Road, Waikoloa; 808-883-9609.

Hours: 11:30 a.m. to 2 a.m. *Sampling:* Lunch and dinner menus feature good burgers, big salads, English-style fish and chips, steaks, and a selection of pastas and pizzas. Try the calamari sandwich at lunchtime. Vegetarians, it's worth the drive for their Tuscan pasta with artichoke, feta cheese and roasted red pepper cream sauce. Late night menu and pizzas to go. *Comments:* Located in the Waikoloa Highlands Center, Anthony's is a small neighborhood pub with good food and friendly service (and the only place around with Guinness on tap). Waikoloa's best option for after-hours entertainment, Anthony presents live music Friday and Saturday 10 p.m. to 1:30 a.m., Karaoke on Tuesday and Open Mike Night on Thursday. Particularly lucky visitors catch the proprietor's own "Johnny Shot" playing vintage rock and roll plus solid originals.

Arnie's (American)
Hapuna Beach Prince Hotel at Mauna Kea Resort, 62-100 Kauna'oa Drive, Waikoloa; 808-880-3192.

Hours: 11 a.m. to 4:30 p.m. *Sampling:* The menu features truly great cheeseburgers with seasoned waffle-cut fries, a variety of sandwiches, fresh catch, Japanese-style golden curry, ahi sashimi, big salads like their seafood Cobb, daily specials and desserts. Try their enormous bowl of saimin (noodle soup with garnishes). *Comments:* A large, bright clubhouse with small bar overlooking the Hapuna Golf Course, Arnie's is a great spot for a leisurely lunch or late breakfast on Sunday. *Keiki* menu available.

Beach Bar (Sandwiches/Snacks)
Hapuna Beach Prince Hotel at Mauna Kea Resort, 62-100 Kauna'oa Drive, Waikoloa; 808-880-3192.

Hours: 11 a.m. to 4:30 p.m. *Sampling:* Amicably set next to the hotel's attractive, whale-shaped swimming pool, the Beach Bar serves up snacks, sandwiches and salads for lunch and afternoon munchies, plus your favorite libations. *Comments: Keiki* menu available. A short walk up from Hapuna Beach State Park, open air with tropical breezes and ocean views.

★ Beach Grill (American)
1022 Keana Place in the Waikoloa Beach Golf Course Clubhouse at Waikoloa Resort; 808-886-6131.

Hours: Breakfast and lunch 7 a.m. to 4:30 p.m.; dinner 5:30 p.m. to 10 p.m. *Sampling:* The menu features a variety of appetizers, salads and sandwiches for lunch with fresh-baked breads, homemade chutneys, dressings and sauces. Dinner features local produce, steaks, fish and seafood as well as exotic curries with basmati rice and *naan* bread. The menu also has a nice selection of wines. *Comments:* Chefs David Brown and Stephen Tabor have brought the Beach Grill over par—it's not just a golf restaurant anymore.

Beach Tree Bar & Grill (American)
Four Seasons Resort Hualalai, 100 Kaupulehu Drive, Kaupulehu-Kona; 808-325-8000.

Hours: 11:30 a.m. to 6 p.m. *Sampling:* The menu features a variety of light California-style American fare and special selections, plus

fresh-baked breads and an extensive salad bar. The Beach
Tree also offers two theme buffet evenings: "Viva Italia"
on Wednesday and "Surf, Sand & Stars Barbecue" on
Saturday. *Comments:* This oceanside dining spot creates a relaxing and informal atmosphere for lunch,
cocktails, and casual evening dining. Contemporary
island entertainment nightly. Reservations recommended.

Big Island Steak House *(Steaks)*
250 Waikoloa Beach Drive, Suite C1, Waikoloa; 808-886-8805; fax 808-886-0455.

Hours: 7 a.m to 2:30 p.m. for breakfast and lunch,
5 to 10 p.m. for dinner. *Sampling:* The menu features
steaks, of course, plus fresh Big Island produce, local
fish and seafood in a variety of preparations. Start off
with *pupus* like Black & Blue ahi sashimi, spinach and
artichoke dip or prawn cocktail, then select from their
steak menu, or choose rotisserie-roasted Lu'au chicken,
coconut prawns or Thai pasta with stir-fry vegetables and
your choice of chicken, tenderloin or prawns. Top it off with Kona
coffee macadamia nut pie or a Big Island banana split for two.
Comments: Located in the King's Shops at Waikoloa Resort, this large,
interesting dining room has decor reflecting the romantic Polynesian
image of 1950s movies, with nostalgic travel posters and collections
of bric-a-brac from Hawai'i's early days of tourism. Upstairs, the
Merry Wahine Bar provides entertainment and tropical libations.

Blue Dolphin Restaurant *(Burgers/Seafood)*
*61-3616 Kawaihae Harbor Road, Highway 270, one mile from the inter-
section of Routes 270 and 19, on the mauka side of the road across from
the harbor; 808-882-7771.*

Hours: Friday and Saturday 5:30 p.m. to 11:30 p.m.,
Wednesday (Open Mike Night) 6 to 11:30 p.m.
Sampling: The menu, of course, emphasizes fresh fish,
and their signature burgers, along with "world
famous" teriyaki beef strips, plate lunches, pastas, salads and desserts. Kids' menu developed from years as
a drive-in, with simple items like "Noodles & Nothing"
to please pickier eaters. *Comments:* This little place has
evolved from a drive-up carry-out window into a full-fare, open-air
dining and music hall. They serve up great island food and live
entertainment by Big Island musicians.

★ Cafe Pesto-Kawaihae *(Italian/Hawai'i Regional Cuisine)*
Kawaihae Shopping Center, Kawaihae; 808-882-1071; www.cafepesto.com.
Hours: 11 a.m. to 9 p.m.; Friday and Saturday until 10 p.m.
Sampling: Although this busy restaurant is best known for its island-

style gourmet pizzas, they also offer a wide variety of excellent and creative soups and salads, pasta and risottos, hot sandwiches, calzones and house-made desserts. Appetizers include *crostini*, *focaccia*, Pacific crab cakes and salmon pizzette. Dinner entrees include selections like smoked chicken linguini, fresh island fish, Asian-style fettuccine, wok-fired shrimp and scallops, mango-glazed chicken and many more specials. They have an excellent kids' menu. *Comments:* Cafe Pesto continues to win awards and accolades statewide for its fresh, creative cuisine. Recently expanded to accommodate a growing clientele, it turns out a consistently good product to keep its diners happy year after year.

The Clubhouse *(Steaks)*

In the Waikoloa Village Golf Course clubhouse building, off Laie Street, Waikoloa; 808-883-9644.

Hours: 11 a.m. to 9 p.m. *Sampling:* New owners bring a fresh menu to Waikoloa, featuring an interesting combination of local style, Italian and comfort food. Start with sashimi or spinach salad, enjoy homemade pizzas, lasagna, burgers, crabcake sandwiches, fish and chips, and much more. *Comments:* There are two restaurants here: an open-air lunch room and bar catering to golfers and the *pau hana* (after work) crowd, and a more-formal, family-friendly dining room with white tablecloths, fresh flowers and tall glass walls overlooking the golf course. Nice *keiki* menu.

Grand Palace *(Chinese)*

Kings' Shops at Waikoloa Beach Resort, 250 Waikoloa Beach Drive; 808-886-6668.

Hours: 11 a.m. to 9:30 p.m. *Sampling:* The menu is perhaps the Big Island's most extensive offering of Chinese cuisine, listing 151 separate items of primarily Cantonese selections. There are some varied Chinese exotics thrown in for good measure: five-spiced octopus, cold jellyfish, shark's fin soup, squid with pepper salt, and scalded shrimp with dipping sauce. More familiar traditionals for the less-adventurous include chow mein, fried rice, spring rolls, Peking duck and a wide selection of beef, pork, chicken, seafood and vegetable dishes. *Comments:* The Grand Palace features a bright, clean dining room with formal table settings, fine Chinese artwork decor and white tablecloths. Carry-out orders and prix-fixe menus for one to five people are available.

Hama Yu Japanese Restaurant *(Japanese)*

Kings' Shops at Waikoloa Beach Resort, 250 Waikoloa Beach Drive; 808-886-6333.

Hours: Lunch 11:30 a.m. to 2 p.m., dinner 5:30 p.m. to 9 p.m. *Sampling:* The traditional Japanese menu offers such favorites as teriyaki beef, pork *tonkatsu*, shrimp or vegetable tempura, broiled fish, shrimp, *donburi*, noodles and more. A small sushi bar serves a good selection of made-to-order sushi rolls. *Comments:* This small restaurant features bright contemporary Japanese decor.

★ Hau Tree Restaurant & Gazebo Bar *(Sandwiches/Snacks)*
Mauna Kea Beach Hotel, 62-100 Mauna Kea Beach Drive, Kohala Coast; 808-882-5810.

Hours: 11 a.m. to 3 p.m. *Sampling:* It's hard for anything to taste bad with a view this good. Right off the sand at Kauna'oa Bay, the Hau Tree offers salads, sandwiches and other light lunch fare at beach umbrella tables, along with ice cream treats like the old-fashioned Ovaltine Froth. *Comments:* Right next door is the Gazebo Bar, home of the best Big Island barstool for enjoying a libation at sunset; beer and wine, soft drinks and cocktails, cool blended tropicals and "virgin" smoothies. The Hau Tree is also the setting for the resort's Saturday-night Clambake seafood buffet, which is the best seafood feast on the Big Island, featuring crab claws, Keahole-Maine lobsters, shrimp, sashimi, a make-your-own ice cream sundae bar and a whole lot more (including meats and vegetables for the less-seafood-inclined), plus live island entertainment. Reservations recommended for the Clambake.

Honu Bar *(Pupus/Desserts)*
Mauna Lani Bay Hotel, 68-1400 Mauna Lani Drive, Kohala Coast; 808-885-6622.

Hours: 5:30 p.m. to 9 p.m. *Sampling:* The Honu Bar serves a wide selection of after-dinner drinks, coffees, lattes and espresso along with remarkable desserts such as crepes suzette, spumoni *bombe* and tiramisu. A heavy *pupu* or light supper menu features Big Island sashimi, seafood antipasto, and oven-baked focaccia flatbreads with sausage, grilled portobello mushrooms or seafood. *Comments:* This sophisticated cocktail lounge affords a private-club atmosphere just off Mauna Lani's atrium lobby. Nightly live entertainment features jazz on weekends; game room with pool tables, chess and backgammon tables.

★ Kawaihae Harbor Grill *(Seafood)*
Across from the Kawaihae Wharf on Highway 270 in Kawaihae; 808-882-1368.

Hours: Lunch 11:30 a.m. to 2:30 p.m., dinner 5:30 p.m. to 9:30 p.m. *Sampling:* The restaurant is serious about quality fresh fish, but they also have good burgers, a lot of different local-style *pupus* (order several and share), salads, sandwiches and tempting dinner entrees like steamed clams, Thai seafood curry, Asian baby back ribs, Maine lobster, Alaskan king crab and *kiawe*-smoked prime rib, plus daily specials and take-out. *Comments:* This small country-style restaurant has a great setting in the renovated old Chock Hoo general store, built in the early 1900s. It's warmly decorated in a bright, simple style with colorful Big Island paraphernalia. Next door is its sister restaurant, the popular Seafood Bar.

Lagoon Grill *(Sandwiches/Snacks)*
Hilton Waikoloa Village, 425 Waikolod Beach Drive, Waikoloa; 808-886-1234.

Hours: 10:30 a.m. to 5:30 p.m. *Sampling:* This restaurant offers lunch only with a menu of sandwiches, burgers, hot dogs, chili, salads, smoothies and desserts. *Comments:* This casual open-air deck eatery sits next to the famed dolphin lagoons where diners can watch the dolphins frolic and play. The bar serves up exotic drinks.

19th Hole *(Sandwiches/Snacks/American)*
Mauna Kea Beach Hotel, 62-100 Mauna Kea Beach Drive, Kohala Coast; 808-882-5810.

Hours: 11 a.m. to 4:30 p.m. *Sampling:* An indoor-outdoor restaurant right off the first tee at Mauna Kea Golf Course, the 19th Hole offers relaxing country club privacy and a menu of lunch dishes and libations you don't have to be a golfer to enjoy. Thick sandwiches, good burgers and hot dogs, house-made soups and desserts, generous salads and the signature 19th Hole Noodles are served up by the personable waitstaff, making for a satisfying mid-day break. *Comments: Keiki* menu available. After lunch, take a look around the pro shop for your new designer golf togs.

Ocean Grill *(Sandwiches/Snacks/American)*
Mauna Lani Bay Hotel, 68-1400 Mauna Lani Drive, Kohala Coast; 808-885-6622; www.maunalani.com.

Hours: 10:30 a.m. to 6 p.m. *Sampling:* The menu offers snacks and light fare of sandwiches, seafood specials, salads and more. *Comments:* This oceanside cafe provides a bright, breezy location between the hotel pool and the beach. A great spot for sunset libations and tropical cocktails anytime.

★ **Orchid Cafe** *(American)*
Hilton Waikoloa Village, 425 Waikoloa Beach Drive, Waikoloa; 808-886-1234.

Hours: 7 to 11:30 a.m. for breakfast, 11:30 a.m. to 4 p.m. for lunch, soda fountain 11 a.m. to 5 p.m. *Sampling:* The breakfast menu is quite traditional while lunch features specials like soups, salads, a variety of sandwiches, tortilla wraps, pizza and Japanese specialties. Soda fountain has snacks, beverages and ice cream treats. *Comments:* This hotel coffee shop has a pleasant poolside setting with parasol-covered tables surrounded by coconut trees. Kids will enjoy the colorful, raucous parrots and macaws, who squawk and talk a language all their own.

★ *Seafood Bar* (Seafood)
Across from Kawaihae Wharf on Highway 270 in Kawaihae; 808-880-9393.

    Hours: 2:30 p.m. to 10:30 p.m.; Friday and Saturday until 11 p.m. *Sampling:* The menu changes daily, featuring ample *pupu* selections such as oysters Rockefeller, coconut shrimp and nightly pizza specials, plus island *poke* burgers, mussels and various West Coast oysters. Try a local-style *pupu* like *edamame* (boiled soybeans) for something different. *Comments:* The Seafood Bar is run by the same people who made Kawaihae Harbor Grill such a treat. Specializing in heavy *pupus* (appetizers) and cocktails, the place is rapidly growing in popularity with visitors and *kama'aina*. Fun Polynesian decor with coconut thatching and a long, comfortable bar. They don't take reservations, and it can get busy in the evenings with hotel workers stopping by for their *pau hana* (after work) beverage of choice, but that only adds to the fun.

Sharky's (American)
Waikoloa Highlands Center, Waikoloa Village; 808-883-0020.

    Hours: Noon to 2 a.m. *Sampling:* Sharky's offers a full American standard menu with some local flair and an active sports bar attitude. *Comments:* Not particularly family dining.

Tres Hombres Beach Grill (Mexican)
Kawaihae Shopping Center, Kawaihae; 808-882-1031.

    Hours: Sunday through Thursday 11:30 a.m. to 9 p.m.; Friday and Saturday 11:30 a.m. to 9:30 p.m. *Sampling:* An essentially Mexican menu also offers fresh island fish, seafood and other entrees in a colorful island atmosphere highlighted by surfing memorabilia. The Mexican food (tacos, enchiladas, quesadillas, fajitas, tostadas and burritos) is good in quality and quantity and the *pupu* menu is outstanding (nachos grande is a meal and a half). *Comments:* Choose a seat in the comfortable dining room with windows overlooking the harbor, on the outside lanai or at the surfboard-tables in the bar (with an interesting selection of tequilas).

Expensive-priced Dining

★ **The Batik** *(Continental-International)*
Mauna Kea Beach Hotel, 62-100 Mauna Kea Beach Drive, Kohala Coast;
808-882-7222.

Hours: 6 p.m. to 9 p.m., varying seasonally. *Sampling:* A recent menu featured whole roasted garlic and escargots to start, a lobster bisque with caviar, and a salad of artichoke, tomato, avocado and asparagus, along with their creative Euro-Asian cuisine, East Indian and Thai curries, island fish, seafood and local meats, specialty garden-fresh produce and such decadent desserts as signature grand marnier soufflé (order before dinner). *Keiki* menu available. *Comments:* Please make reservations and allow enough time to experience The Batik to the fullest—a three-to-five-course dinner with a recommended wine from their extensive list and perhaps coffee and brandy on the moonlit terrace. The ambiance, service and overall dining experience are superb. The dress code is evening resort attire, with jackets suggested, but not required, for gentlemen. Go ahead, dress everybody up and make a night of it.

Bay Terrace *(American)*
Mauna Lani Bay Hotel, 68-1400 Mauna Lani Drive, Kohala Coast; 808-885-6622; www.maunalani.com.

Hours: 5:30 p.m. to 9:30 p.m. *Sampling:* This open-air garden terrace restaurant provides delightful dining *al fresco*. The a la carte dinner menu features American-style selections of beef, fresh island fish, seafood, chicken, lamb, and many specialties. *Comments:* Reservations recommended.

★ **Brown's Beach House** *(Hawai'i-Pacific Regional Cuisine)*
Fairmont Orchid Hawai'i, 1 North Kaniku Drive, Kohala Coast; 808-885-2000.

Hours: Open daily for lunch 11:30 a.m. to 2:00 p.m., and dinner 6 to 9:30 p.m. *Sampling:* Brown's is one of the best-loved restaurants on the island, with a loyal following of upper-end *kama'aina* and visiting clientele. Its setting is absolutely lovely and really fine Hawaiian music and hula by local entertainers are a treat (especially if you're lucky enough to catch Nino Ka'ai). They have a new Chef de Cuisine, Etsuji Umezu, but the menu is not Japanese. Rather it's described as "innovative, island-inspired cuisine featuring the best ingredients available locally—clean, exciting flavors with an emphasis on super-fresh seafood." You can watch the culinary team at work in the newly renovated exhibition kitchen, and during the day the new Brown's Deli offers upscale picnic basket selections or a "decid-

edly elevated local-style cuisine on the lunch menu." *Comments:*
Occasional imperfections in service and presentation are forgivable
in such a beautiful environment. Watch for new house-made breads
by baker chef Kevin Cabrera. Reservations recommended.

★ **CanoeHouse** *(Hawai'i Regional Cuisine/International)*
Mauna Lani Bay Hotel, 68-1400 Mauna Lani Drive, Kohala Coast; 808-885-6622; www.maunalani.com.
  Hours: 5:30 to 9 p.m. *Sampling:* The dinner menu features exotic
pupus such as sashimi and *poke*, Chinese wontons, and eggplant
curry. Entrees include fresh seared mahimahi, pesto seared scallops,
hibachi salmon, grilled marinated *ono*, New Zealand lamb chops,
and Thai seafood curry. *Comments:* OK, this is personal. We love the
CanoeHouse. It's expensive, the service can be sometimes less than
shiny and the food excellence is more consistent at The Batik. But,
in all fairness to the other fine restaurants along the Kohala Coast,
nobody comes close to CanoeHouse's breathtaking location down by
the ocean, where everything tastes better and you could hardly have
a bad time if you tried. The dining room is a lovely, indoor/outdoor
space and the chef specializes in Pacific Rim cuisine with only the
best local seafood, meat and market produce. The food is wonderfully diverse; the service is genuinely warm-to-superb and the contemporary Hawaiian music is a relaxing and romantic accompaniment to the sounds of surf. Reservations recommended. Request an
outside table if it's not windy.

★ **Coast Grille & Oyster Bar** *(Hawai'i-Pacific Regional Cuisine)*
Hapuna Beach Prince Hotel, 62-100 Kauna'oa Drive, Kohala Coast; 808-880-3192.
  Hours: 6:30 p.m. to 9:30 p.m. *Sampling:* Executive Chef Piet
Wigman's menu presents a wide selection of fresh island fish and
seafood plus prime cuts of lamb, veal and beef in a variety of preparations. Emphasis here is on Hawai'i Regional Cuisine, featuring the
freshest local ingredients in an eclectic meld of "East-meets-West"
flavor sensations, well prepared and served by professional waitstaff.
A recent dinner menu tempted us with Coast Grille Sampler of
seared ahi, tempura lobster sushi roll and baked ginger-crusted oysters, oven-roasted scallops, Honaunau free-range chicken stuffed
with mango and apple, with breadfruit and pumpkin *laulau* and a
dangerous dessert sampler plate *du jour.* There is an extensive wine
list and a *keiki* menu available as well. One of Coast Grille's most
unique features is the international oyster bar, where the chef will
open choice local and imported oysters and present them on the half
shell just for you. The sushi chef visits weekly. *Comments:* The hotel's

signature award-winning restaurant, this spacious, domed dining room overlooks the north end of Hapuna Beach and the whale-shaped hotel swimming pool. Reservations recommended.

★ **Donatoni's** (Italian)
Hilton Waikoloa Village, 425 Waikoloa Beach Drive, Waikoloa; 808-886-1234.

Hours: 6 p.m. to 9:30 p.m. *Sampling:* Chef Valentino Luchin's menu features fine northern Italian cuisine and offers an extensive selection of antipasti, gourmet pastas and pizzas, entrees of veal, seafood, chicken and more, plus cappuccino and international coffees. But let's talk about dessert. Among other things, the pastry chef presents lemon mascarpone cheesecake with *lilikoi* sauce (decorated with a marzipan mouse) and the carnival mask of Venice in white chocolate on a layer of flourless chocolate cake with frangelico sauce and fresh fruit. *Comments:* Donatoni's is something special. About the most romantic restaurant on the island, its Italian palazzo design offers *al fresco* seating along the waterway and four individual dining rooms indoors, accompanied by Italian musicians. Donatoni's has our stamp of approval for both fine food and service, and that in itself is an accomplishment. Popular among locals as well as visitors, the lovely contemporary classic decor provides a lush, pleasant ambiance for those very special occasions. Reservations suggested.

★ **The Gallery Restaurant and Knickers Bar** (Continental-International)
Golf Course Clubhouse, Mauna Lani Resort, 68-1400 Mauna Lani Drive, Kohala Coast; 808-885-7777; www.maunalani.com.

Hours: Open daily for lunch 11 a.m. to 3 p.m.; bar menu until 5 p.m.; Tuesday through Saturday for dinner 5:30 p.m. to 9 p.m. *Sampling:* The dinner menu features American Regional Cuisine with distinctive Mediterranean twists, plus steak, fresh island fish, seafood and pasta. The Gallery's Caesar salad wins our stamp of approval, and that's something special. *Comments:* This award-winning dining room is located adjacent to the resort's golf course clubhouse, and provides an casual-elegant dining option for lunch and dinner. The comfortable bar and dining room have lovely views of the Francis I'i Brown Golf Course, lots of open windows and a warm, private-club feel. The Gallery's food is consistently superb and service attentive and personable. Reservations recommended.

★ **The Grill** (Continental-International/Steaks)
Fairmont Orchid Hawai'i, 1 North Kaniku Drive, Kohala Coast; 808-885-2000.

Hours: 6 p.m. to 9:30 p.m. *Sampling:* This upscale dining room has the atmosphere of a plush manor house club room and offers creative Continental/international cuisine. Emphasis here is on dry-aged, corn-fed prime beef, rubbed with Hawaiian sea salt, extra virgin olive oil and a house blend of organic fresh herbs and roasted garlic. Other menu samplings might include appetizers such as lobster and scallop pot pie, *panko*-crusted crabcake and New Zealand clams; soups and salads include asparagus bisque, Maui onion soup, and Caesar salad; entrees include roasted loin of lamb, veal medallion and crab dumpling, marinated Hawaiian snapper, rosemary and thyme-crusted swordfish steak, and grilled prawns. Top dinner off with some incredible dessert choices. *Comments:* Service, presentation and quality are superb. Live dinner music features Hawai'i celebrity Charles Michael Brotman on guitar. Evening resort attire. Reservations recommended.

Hakone Steakhouse*Sushi Bar *(Steaks/Japanese)*
Hapuna Beach Prince Hotel, 62-100 Kauna'oa Drive, Kohala Coast; 808-880-3192.

Hours: 6 p.m. to 9 p.m. (days vary seasonally). *Sampling:* This excellent restaurant features traditional Japanese cuisine along with a fine selection of beef and veal steaks, chops, lobster and fresh catch. *Comments:* A recent "Hale 'Aina" award-winner, Hakone's atmosphere is tranquil and relaxed, with contemporary Japanese decor. A new Asian garden entryway sets the mood on arrival. On Friday and Saturday, Chef Hideo Kurihara presents an elaborate dinner buffet of Japanese cuisine. *Keiki* menu available. One of the Big Island's best sushi bars. Reservations recommended.

★ Hale Moana *(Continental-International/Hawai'i Regional Cuisine)*
Kona Village Resort, Kaupulehu-Kona; 808-325-5555.

Hours: Breakfast 7:15 a.m. to 9:45 a.m., lunch 12:30 p.m. to 2 p.m., dinner 6 p.m. to 9 p.m. *Sampling:* Their legendary buffet lunch is a magnificent spread of salads, hot and cold entrees, grill items and delectable desserts. Hale Moana's dinner menus change nightly, but the chef's emphasis remains on fish from local waters and island market produce presented with aloha in a sophisticated tropical ambience. Freshest catch of the day is offered in your choice of preparations from broiled with herb butter or pineapple salsa, sauteed with lime-beurre blanc, capers or macadamia nuts, or baked in white wine. But there's more. A recent five-course menu sampling was rather remarkable: chilled lobster and soba noodles or fresh island fruits in a papaya shell, miso soup with tofu, *opakapaka* and chives, Caesar salad or stuffed avocado with crab meat remoulade; *then* a choice of osso buco, grilled chicken, Moana seafood platter, or a trio of ostrich, buffalo and beef medallions with mushroom–port wine sauce, and a selection of desserts to die for. A four-course vegetarian menu is offered nightly. *Comments:* Hale Moana is the pleasant and airy main dining room for this very special South Seas–style resort with its trademark individual thatched *hale* (houses). Tall glass walls overlook the beach for poetically beautiful sunset dinners, and an adjacent outdoor garden area is open daily for an elegant lunch. Reservations required.

★ **Hale Samoa** *(Continental-International/Hawai'i Regional Cuisine)*
Kona Village Resort, Kaupulehu-Kona; 808-325-5555.

Hours: 6 p.m. to 9 p.m. *Sampling:* The menu is surprisingly international, what we might call the best of Hawai'i Regional Cuisine that embraces the rest of the world. Selections vary nightly, but always include freshest catch of the day prepared to your liking and chef's special vegetarian selection. A recent example of Hale Samoa's creative, eclectic dinner menus tempted us with a Duet of Dim Sum or coconut-crusted soft shell crab, clear abalone broth with bok choy or cream of roasted Maui onion soup, house-cured gravlax with organic greens or salad Samoa with Kona mango dressing. For the entrees, crab-stuffed giant prawns with purple sweet potato, Hawaiian spiny lobster tail, rib steak Kaupulehu, rack of lamb and much more. *Comments:* The resort's special style and spirit is re-affirmed in Hale Samoa. This warm, intimate dining room features an interesting Samoan motif complete with decorative crafts and an outrigger canoe suspended from the ceiling. Attentive service in a romantic South Seas atmosphere is the tradition here. The sunsets are gorgeous. Reservations are a must.

★ **Hawai'i Calls** *(Hawai'i-Pacific Regional Cuisine)*
Waikoloa Beach Marriott, An Outrigger Resort, 69-275 Waikoloa Beach Drive, Kohala Coast; 808-886-6789.

Hours: Breakfast 6 to 11 a.m., dinner 5:30 to 9:30 p.m. *Sampling:* The menu is a combination of Hawaiian ingredients teamed with classic Mediterranean recipes, flavors and cookery, sort of a Mediterranean-infused Hawaiian cuisine. Seafood entrees include *moi* fish "thread fin," Kohala Coast *laulau*, Keahole lobster and prawn brochettes; other entrees include New York steak, tournedos of beef Oscar, lamb chop *trois poivre*, pork Manila and some innovative appetizers, salads, soups and desserts. The restaurant serves a traditional breakfast menu with an extensive buffet table as well. *Comments:* This beautiful restaurant is the hotel's signature dining room and evokes the nostalgia of the romantic era of 1930s travel to Hawai'i with matching decor and artwork. The casual dining room is open-air.

★ **Hualalai Grille by Alan Wong** *(American/Hawai'i Regional Cuisine)*
Four Seasons Resort Hualalai, 100 Kaupulehu Drive, Kaupulehu-Kona;
808-325-5000.

Hours: 11:30 a.m. to 2:30 p.m. for lunch, 11:30 a.m. to 9 p.m.
for cocktails, 5:30 to 9 p.m. for dinner. Restyled to suit the expanding Big Island upscale population, Alan Wong offers his signature
Hawai'i Regional Cuisine at the Hualalai Grille, with creative new
approaches to familiar dishes. "Soup & Sandwich" is chilled red and
yellow tomato soup served with foie gras, *kalua* pig and grilled
cheese sandwich. Ginger-crusted *onaga* consists of local red snapper
with miso vinaigrette, shiitake and *enoki* mushrooms and corn. For
dessert, savor chocolate crunch: layers of milk chocolate, macadamia
nut crunch and bittersweet chocolate mousse. The restaurant also
features a coffee menu with some of Kona's finest estate-grown and
-roasted coffees. Alan Wong is making a statement on the Big Island
and people are listening. Reservations recommended.

★ **Imari** *(Japanese)*
*Hilton Waikoloa Village, 425 Waikoloa Beach Drive, Waikoloa; 808-886-
1234.*

Hours: 6 p.m. to 10 p.m. *Sampling:* The menu is traditional Japanese with sushi and sashimi, among a number of appetizers followed
by varied specials of tempura, sukiyaki, *shabu shabu*, teriyaki and other
creative offerings. For those wanting a little more flair, *teppanyaki*
chefs prepare your selections of chicken, steak, shrimp and all manner of Asian vegetables right before your eyes. *Comments:* A visit to
this distinctive Japanese restaurant allows you to step into the quiet
serenity of old Japan. An authentically designed Zen meditation garden, koi ponds, splashing waterfalls, shoji doors, and a background
of gentle Japanese music put you into a tranquil state of mind for an
exotic meal. Evening attire for ladies; dress shirts and slacks for gentlemen. Reservations suggested.

★ **Kamuela Provision Company** *(Hawai'i Regional Cuisine)*
*Hilton Waikoloa Village, 425 Waikoloa Beach Drive, Waikoloa; 808-886-
1234.*

Hours: 5:30 p.m. to 10 p.m. *Sampling:* The menu is very creative
featuring Pacific Fusion–style appetizers like macadamia nut shrimp
with mango chutney and charred volcano-spiced ahi and a variety of
soups and salads. Chef Dayne Tanabei's contemporary entrees include
creative preparations of pork tenderloin, lamb chops, somen noodles
and fresh seafood, *hukilau* pie, fresh island fish and seafood selections,
and certified black Angus beef steaks, ribeyes and filets. They also
feature a special Big Island Lu'au Dinner, a personalized family lu'au
just for you. Exotic desserts, tropical ice creams, sorbets and coffees

complete the menu and a complete list of Old and New World wines is available for tasting in the wine bar. *Comments:* This is a beautiful open-air restaurant situated on a bluff overlooking the Kohala Coast surf and shoreline. Greenery, artwork and ceiling fans provide a pleasant, relaxing ambiance to the multileveled rooms. Live, contemporary island guitar music 6 to 9 p.m. Resort attire, collared shirts for gentlemen. Reservations suggested.

★ Kirin Restaurant *(Chinese)*
Hilton Waikoloa Village, 425 Waikoloa Beach Drive, Waikoloa; 808-886-1234.

Hours: Lunch 11 a.m. to 5 p.m. *Sampling:* This is a stylish authentic Chinese restaurant offering the classic cooking styles of China's four major regions: Hunan, Szechuan, Peking and Canton. The extensive menu has over a hundred fascinating selections. Among the more exotic are such items as five-spiced beef, jelly fish, "eight treasures" tofu soup, Yangtze black cod, Szechuan smoked duck, General Tsao's chicken, *wu xi* ribs, *ma po* tofu, various noodle and fried rice dishes, plus the popular dim sum for lunch. *Comments:* The attractive room has classic Chinese decor accents and is located above Donatoni's Italian Restaurant overlooking the boat canal and gardens of the resort. Reservations suggested.

Malolo Lounge *(Coffee/Cocktails/Sandwiches/Snacks)*
Hilton Waikoloa Village, 425 Waikoloa Beach Drive, Waikoloa; 808-886-1234.

Hours: Espresso Bar and Patisserie, 7 to 11 a.m. gourmet sandwiches and appetizers 11 a.m. to 5 p.m., appetizers and cocktails 5 p.m. to 1 a.m. *Sampling:* Early morning offers freshmade maple pecan scones, chocolate croissants, assorted teas and a coffee bar. Choose from salads and sandwiches (BLT, blackened ahi, smoked salmon club) in the afternoon. Evening features heavy *pupus* such as sashimi, prosciutto-wrapped melon, and *poke* and eggplant dip with potato focaccia. For the sweet tooth there's Chocolate Swan Lake, a chocolate swan and pinot noir–poached pear with macadamia nut biscuit and nougat mousse on a vanilla "lake." *Comments:* Malolo seems to fill in the gaps before and after "normal" mealtimes to accommodate late flights, jet lag and unexpected cravings. A very practical approach to food service, providing creative options for diners on the go or those looking for lighter alternatives. Great live entertainment 9 p.m. to midnight.

★ Merriman's Market Cafe *(Hawai'i Regional Cuisine)*
Kings' Shops at Waikoloa Beach Resort, 250 Waikoloa Beach Drive; 808-886-1700.

Hours: Lunch 11 a.m. to 2 p.m., bar menu 2 to 5 p.m. and dinner 5 to 9:30 p.m. *Sampling*: A more casual reprise of the award-winning Merriman's restaurant in Waimea, this indoor-outdoor eatery offers the upscale lunch and dinner menus from Hawai'i Regional Cuisine, which Chef Peter Merriman helped found. Fresh local produce, fish and meats are creatively combined for vivid flavors and attractive presentations of interesting salads, sandwiches (try the tomato pesto), fresh catch, steaks and much more. Service can be leisurely. They offer a nice selection of beer and wine by the glass, live island music and jazz in the evenings, and a small deli counter offers take-away items for your picnic basket. Request an outdoor table in the evening if it's not windy, indoors at lunch, when it's hot.

★ **Norio's** *(Sushi/Japanese)*
Fairmont Orchid Hawaii, 1 North Kaniku Drive, Kohala Coast; 808-885-2000.
Hours: 6 to 9:30 p.m. *Sampling*: A small sushi bar with table seating just off the Orchid Court restaurant, Norio's welcomes even the uninitiated into the wonderful world of raw fish. Go early for a seat at the bar and don't be shy: ask questions, try something new, watch skilled chefs prepare your selections, or let them surprise you with a choice of their own. Ingredients vary daily and the fish can be served as sushi or sashimi as you prefer. Tempura, stir-fries and other cooked dishes can be ordered at tables. Norio's service is attentive, from waitstaff in traditional attire, and they offer a nice variety of Japanese beers, sake and imported plum wines.

★ **Orchid Court** *(American)*
Fairmont Orchid Hawai'i, 1 North Kaniku Drive, Kohala Coast; 808-885-2000.
Hours: Breakfast 6:30 to 11:30 a.m. *Sampling*: An extensive breakfast buffet with traditional favorites plus made-to-order egg station with omelets and egg substitutes, bagels with lox and capers, chicken apple sausage, crispy applewood-smoked bacon, fresh-baked pastries, muffins and bread, fresh tropical fruits, Japanese miso soup and *tsukemono*, fresh fish of the morning, plus chef's daily specials like crêpes, Belgian waffles or macadamia nut pancakes. À la carte items available as well.

★ **Pahu i'a Restaurant** *(Hawai'i Regional Cuisine)*
Four Seasons Resort Hualalai, 100 Kaupulehu Drive, Kaupulehu-Kona; 808-325-5000.
Hours: Breakfast 6:30 to 11:30 a.m., dinner 6 to 9:30 p.m. *Sampling*: Pahu i'a features the skilled combination of fine Western and Asian cuisine with local Hawaiian accents (coined Contemporary

Pacific cuisine), celebrating the freshest island ingredients in simple, elegant preparations. *Comments:* This is the resort's signature dining room, which earned the AAA five-diamond award in recent years. Those familiar with the Four Seasons level of service and quality know what to expect; those who don't may wish to experience what is considered top of the line. The dramatic beachfront setting creates its own ambience, and terraced indoor-outdoor seating maximizes the breathtaking views. Evening resort wear, trousers for men, reservations required.

★ *Palm Terrace (Buffet)*
Hilton Waikoloa Village, 425 Waikoloa Beach Drive, Waikoloa; 808-886-1234.

Hours: Breakfast 6 a.m. to 11 a.m., dinner 5 p.m. to 9 p.m. *Sampling:* This dining room specializes in buffet dining for breakfast and dinner, with the main attraction the varied international buffets for dinner. It is an attractive pastel peach-pink colored room with lots of greenery and lovely waterfalls and pools with swans drifting by. The varied buffet menus change daily and feature Paniolo Barbecue (Wednesday and Saturday), All-American Prime Rib Buffet (Sunday, Tuesday and Thursday), and Seafood Buffet (Monday and Friday). There is also an à la carte menu. *Comments:* A fun place for hungry people.

★ *Pavilion at Manta Ray Point (American/International/Hawai'i Regional Cuisine)*
Mauna Kea Beach Hotel, 62-100 Mauna Kea Beach Drive, Kohala Coast; 808-882-5810.

Hours: Breakfast 6:30 a.m. to 11 a.m., dinner 6:30 p.m. to 9 p.m. *Sampling:* This beautiful, spacious restaurant is the Mauna Kea's original dining room, serving breakfast and dinner indoors or out, along with spectacular ocean views. For breakfast, choose from the well-provisioned, tempting buffet or order à la carte. For dinner, the chef offers flavorful Hawai'i Regional Cuisine, featuring Big Island beef, fish and chicken dishes prepared with fresh local ingredients, and splendid desserts from the pastry kitchen. A recent menu presented shrimp and dungeness crab saute with Hamakua mushrooms and whiskey butter sauce in a pastry shell, a composed salad of avocado, papaya and Maluhia Farm butter lettuce, pine nuts and balsamic vinaigrette, entrees such as steamed *moi* and pistachio and sage–crusted pork medallions with ginger soy butter mashed potatoes. The desserts are amazing and a complete wine list, by the bottle or the glass, complements the gourmet fare in appropriate style.

Keiki menu available. *Comments:* After dark, stroll down to Manta Ray Point and watch the giant, graceful manta rays careen and seem to dance for their supper. Dinner reservations recommended.

★ **Roy's Waikoloa Bar & Grill** *(Hawai'i-Pacific Regional Cuisine)*
Kings' Shops at Waikoloa Beach Resort, 250 Waikoloa Beach Drive;
808-886-4321.

Hours: Open seasonally for dinner nightly 6:30 to 9:30 p.m. *Sampling:* The emphasis is on combining fresh local products with equally fresh, creative cookery methods. The menu features such items as mac nut–crusted mahimahi, sesame-seared *opakapaka*, lemongrass *shutome* and blackened ahi, Mongolian lamb, garlic herb chicken and many other dishes. *Comments:* This is Hawai'i celebrity chef Roy Yamaguchi's Big Island outlet in his now international chain of Roy's restaurants. The style here is similar to the trendy local regional cuisine and culinary approach of his other restaurants with a sizzling, clattery, action-packed exhibition kitchen, busy dining room and general sharp, professional service. You'll want to dress a little, and we suggest an exterior table where it's easier to converse as you enjoy views of the lake.

★ **The Terrace** *(Sunday Brunch Buffet)*
Mauna Kea Beach Hotel, 62-100 Mauna Kea Beach Drive, Kohala Coast;
808-882-5810.

Hours: Sunday 11 a.m. to 2 p.m. *Sampling:* Chef's specials vary weekly, but there are always selections of sashimi, crab claws and shrimp on the cold table, as well as a bountiful salad bar and fresh fruits. The "hot" line features made-to-order omelets and Belgian waffles, prime rib, fresh catch and other entrees, along with chef's soup *du jour* and a bread table offering muffins, pastries, artisan breads and rolls from the pastry kitchen. If that's not enough, stop at the tempura station for crisp-fried vegetables, or the sushi station for made-to-order specialties. The dessert table requires total abandonment of self-control. One of our favorite places to bring visitors, we recently enjoyed the full array, stuffing our *opu* (tummies) with ahi and *ono* sashimi, fernshoot and marinated mushroom salads, lobster bisque, whole Waimea strawberries, a loaded omelet that was a work of art, and a taste of everything else including a chocolate cake so dense we could hardly lift the fork. *Comments:* This is the home of Mauna Kea's traditionally excellent Sunday brunch buffet. Come hungry and indulge in a leisurely meal of your very favorite things while you enjoy the open-air ocean view and live island music to feast by. Reservations suggested. $39 adults, $20 children.

WHERE TO DINE

NORTH KOHALA DISTRICT
Inexpensive-priced Dining

Hawi Bakery
55-3419 Akoni Pule Highway, Hawi town; 808-889-1444.
· *Hours:* 11 a.m. to 8 p.m. Closed Wednesday. *Sampling:* This welcome addition to the North Kohala district offers daily breads, along with fresh-baked muffins and bagels, homemade soups, salads, sandwiches and pizza with fresh-squeezed juices. A great place to stop for a snack on your North Kohala exploration tour.

★ Hula La's Mexican Kitchen & Salsa Factory (Mexican)
P.O. Box 190585, off Highway 270, Hawi; 808-889-5668; 866-HULA-LAS; e-mail: hulalas@hotmail.com.
Hours: 11 a.m. to 8 p.m. *Sampling:* A carry-out counter with a few tables, the Mexican menu offers fun-sounding burritos like Auntie Bertha's Beans, Pele's Pollo (chicken), and Kamehameha Combo "Fit for a King." Or, try Humu Humu Nuku Nuku Acapulco Salsa or Kick Butt Kilauea Salsa (sold by the pound, too) with your nachos, meat or veggie quesadilla or fresh fish tacos with a tall Kohala Ginger Lemonade Crush. On the weekends 9 a.m. to 11 a.m., your eggs come with Portuguese sausage, Pololu pork or fresh fish, a warm tortilla, Spanish rice and beans. *Comments:* A hole in the wall in Hawi town, Hula La's may be one of North Kohala's best-kept secrets. Check out their selection of logo shirts and souvenirs.

J&R's Place (Sandwiches/Snacks)
One block west of intersection of Highways 250 and 270, Kapa'au town; 808-889-5500.
Hours: 10 a.m. to 7 p.m.; Friday and Saturday until 8 p.m.; closed Sunday. *Sampling:* This small-town country cafe features Italian food, pizza, sandwiches, snacks and plate lunches. *Comments:* Simple decor, reasonable prices.

Kohala Coffee Mill (Coffee Shop)
One block west of intersection of Highways 250 and 270, Hawi town; 808-889-5577.
Hours: Monday through Friday 6:30 a.m. to 6 p.m.; Saturday and Sunday 7 a.m. to 5:30 p.m. *Sampling:* This coffee shop serves up fresh-brewed Kona coffee, espressos, cappuccinos and other coffees and beverages along with special snacks and ice cream. *Comments:* They also have gift bags of various Kona plantation coffees, whole beans or fresh-ground, along with Hawai'i-made jams and jellies, sauces and other food items. Live island music or jazz some evenings.

★ Kohala Ohana Grill (Hawai'i Local Style)
55-514 Hawi Road, Hawi town; 808-889-5748.

Hours: Wednesday through Friday for breakfast 6 a.m. to 11 a.m., lunch 11 a.m. to 2 p.m., dinner 5:30 to 8:30 p.m.; Saturday 8 a.m. to 2 p.m. *Sampling:* This family-run restaurant serves up good quality homestyle food in generous portions for the *kama'aina* appetite, and visitors too. Enjoy saimin, *loco moco*, beef stew, Korean chicken and much more in a friendly atmosphere.

Kohala Rainbow Cafe *(Sandwiches/Snacks)*
Highway 270, right across from the King Kamehameha Statue and the old courthouse, Kapa'au; 808-889-0099.

Hours: Monday through Friday 10 a.m. to 5 p.m., Saturday and Sunday 11 a.m. to 5 p.m. *Sampling:* This is a snack shop/cafe/ice cream parlor featuring sandwiches, salads, daily lunch specials and other snacks and goodies.

Sushi Rock *(Contemporary Sushi)*
Located in the Without Boundaries shop, 55-3435 Akoni Pule Highway, Hawi, 808-889-5900.

Hours: Noon to 3 p.m. and 5:30 to 8:30 p.m. *Sampling:* Known for uncommonly good traditional, "new wave" and vegetarian sushi, they also offer a full dinner menu features broiled fish, chicken and tofu prepared creatively, along with house-made soups and fresh salads. Full bar available and a most unique gift shop. *Comments:* According to instructions, we are not to pass through Hawi without dessert, such as a raspberry-*lilikoi* "twinkie."

Moderate-priced Dining

Aunty's Place *(German/International)*
Above Akoni Pule Highway, across the street from Bamboo, in Hawi town; 808-889-0899.

Hours: Monday through Friday 11 a.m. to 9 p.m., Saturday 2:30 to 9 p.m., Sunday noon to 9 p.m. (*pupus* only 4 to 5 p.m.). *Sampling:* The menu features German foods like imported bratwurst, pork schnitzel, sauerkraut (available by the quart) and other house specialties, with a good selection of local-style dishes like chicken *katsu*, *kalua* pig, *shoyu* chicken, sweet and sour pork and daily specials. They also offer daily fresh catch, Gerda's famous fish and chips and her homemade "soups-from-scratch," like creamy potato with turkey and Hungarian goulash. Her small bar at the restaurant's entry serves cocktails, wines, and 20 brands of domestic and imported beers (including Erdinger and 6 other Germans). On Sundays, check out her prime rib dinner. The three-dollar *keiki* menu is very reasonable and includes four dinner selections and chocolate pudding for dessert. *Comments:* This unassuming little place offers a refreshing change of pace for local and visiting diners in a comfortable homey dining room owned and operated by chef Gerda Medeiros. With all this, Aunty's is a hidden treasure that won't stay hidden for long.

★ **Bamboo Restaurant & Gallery** (Hawai'i-Pacific Regional Cuisine) *Main Street, near the intersection of Highways 250 and 270 in Hawi town; 808-889-5555; fax 808-889-6152; e-mail: bamrest@interpac.net; www.thebamboorestaurant.com.*

Hours: Tuesday through Saturday 11:30 a.m. to 2:30 p.m. for lunch, 6 to 8 p.m. (last seating) for dinner. Sunday brunch 11:30 a.m. to 2:30 p.m. *Sampling:* Their menu is actually three in one. *Mauka* (mountain) features steaks, barbecued ribs, beef tenderloin with coffee brandy cream sauce and a Kohala cordon bleu. *Makai* (ocean) offers fish catch served in various styles like Hawai'i Thai, Margaritaville, macadamia nut-crusted or crispy polenta. And, there's "Da Local Style" with Pacific stir-fried noodles or *kalua* pork and cabbage, to name a few. A *keiki* menu is available, as are fresh-made soups and generous salads, daily dessert specials and a hearty *pupu* selection. Fresh fruit smoothies, tropical margaritas and full bar service. Sundays are special with weekly brunch. *Comments:* This is it, the funky, old-fashioned island-style restaurant with great food and authentic aloha that you hoped would be here. The building was an old hotel for sugar cane workers originally built by the Harada family between 1911 and 1915. In 1926, the Takata Store took over the property and ran it as a mercantile shop until 1991, with the motto "everyone should leave the building smiling!" Everyone does. Bamboo keeps its atmosphere alive with colorful artwork and genuine Fred Savage menus from the Matson Cruise Lines of the 1950s. They call their food "Fresh Island style," borrowing from the best of the best of Hawai'i Regional Cuisine, well-prepared and presented. Live entertainment Friday and Saturday nights.

Waimea Town

Inexpensive-priced Dining

Charley's Thai Cuisine (Thai) *KTA Shopping Center, 65-1158 Mamalahoa Highway, Waimea; 808-885-5591. Second location in the Kona Coast Shopping Center, Kailua-Kona; 808-334-0891.*

Hours: 11 a.m. to 3 p.m. for lunch, 4:30 to 9 p.m. for dinner. *Sampling:* A full menu of authentic Thai dishes for lunch or dinner includes chicken or beef satays, spring and summer rolls, papaya salad, glass noodle salad, soups, a variety of curries you can add chicken, beef, pork, shrimp, mahimahi or mussels to, noodles, stir fries and combination dishes. *Comments:* A spin-off of the popular Kona restaurant.

Don's Chinese Restaurant *(Chinese)*
Highway 19 in the old Fukushima Store building, just east (Honoka'a side) of Waimea; 808-885-2025.

Hours: 10 a.m. to 8:30 p.m. *Sampling:* This smallish Chinese kitchen serves up a varied menu of freshly prepared Cantonese specialties. House specials are *char siu* and roast duck. *Comments:* Look for the old-fashioned gas pump in front. They also have an outlet in the food court in Waimea's Parker Ranch Center Food Court and one in Kailua-Kona.

Great Wall Chop Suey *(Chinese)*
Waimea Center (where McDonald's is), Waimea; 808-885-7252.

Hours: 11 a.m. to 8:30 p.m. *Sampling:* A recent menu featured interesting selections such as seaweed tofu soup or abalone soup, *kung pao* shrimp, eggplant Szechuan style, roast duck, mahi with sweet-sour sauce and spicy chicken cake noodle, along with more than a few chop sueys, chow meins and several versions of fried rice. The no-meat menu includes *mu shu*, almond tofu and curry vegetables. *Comments:* Billing themselves as the place for "healthy Chinese food—low calories," Great Wall has presented a wide variety of Cantonese-style cuisine, excellent in quality and quantity, for years. Take-out available.

★ Hawaiian Style Cafe *(Sandwiches/Plate Lunches)*
Kawaihae Road, Waimea; 808-885-4295.

Hours: Monday through Friday 7:30 a.m. to 12:30 p.m.; Sunday 7:30 to 10:30 a.m. *Sampling:* Everybody loves Hawaiian Style Cafe for breakfast. Big portions, bottomless cups of coffee and fine friendly service in a pleasant neighborhood environment make a great start to your day. They are also open for early lunch, with a varied menu featuring local-style plate-lunch favorites including teriyaki, fried fish, chicken, burgers, sandwiches and more. *Comments:* Not fancy, just a good inexpensive meal. Eat at the counter or carry-out. Very popular with residents—for a good reason.

Kamuela Deli *(Hawai'i Local style)*
Waimea Center, Highway 19, Waimea; 808-885-4147. Second location in the Kona Coast Shopping Center, Kailua-Kona; 808-334-0017.

Hours: 5 a.m. to 9 p.m. *Sampling:* Kamuela Deli is an institution, a museum for all the local dishes everyone loves. Their long, mouth-watering menu truly has something for everyone, from big breakfasts (including a "curry stew omelet") to burgers and sandwiches to generous full dinner plates with various chicken preparations, ribs, teriyaki, roast beef or pork, local fish and seafood. *Pupu* platters and catering available too. *Comments:* Eat in or carry out.

★ **Little Juice Shack** *(Juice-Smoothies/Sandwiches/Snacks)*
Parker Ranch Shopping Center, Waimea; 808-885-1686.
Hours: Monday through Friday 7 a.m. to 4 p.m., Saturday 9 a.m. to 4 p.m., closed Sunday. *Sampling:* A very nice selection of fresh fruit and vegetable juices, wheatgrass, blends and smoothies with energy adds available. Homemade munchies include cinnamon rolls, muffins and pastries plus cookies, cakes and other sweet treats. For lunch, there's soup, salad, chili and a menu of fresh-made sandwiches and topped bagels with plenty of vegetarian choices. *Comments:* Located "around back" near the entry to Parker Ranch Visitors Center; drive behind the main shopping center and there's plenty of parking. One of Waimea's best-kept secrets.

Morelli's Pizza *(Pizza/Sandwiches/Snacks)*
Waimea Center, Waimea; 808-885-8557, delivery 808-885-8664.
Hours: Monday through Saturday 11 a.m. to 8 p.m.; closed Sunday. *Sampling:* A great little place for pizza, whole or by the slice, with a wealth of fresh toppings including a loaded vegetarian combo. Morelli's also features oven-baked sandwiches, salads and cakes for dessert. *Comments:* Delivery available in the Waimea area.

★ **Paniolo Country Inn** *(Hawai'i Local Style/American)*
65-1214 Lindsey Road, next door to Waimea Country Lodge, in the heart of Waimea; 808-885-4377.
Hours: 7 a.m. to 8:45 p.m. *Sampling:* The menu features a variety of burgers and sandwiches, barbecued ribs, chicken, pasta, Mexican food and pizza. We've enjoyed the individual pizzas and half-sandwich and soup of the day combos. Beer and wine is available; coffee is always fresh. *Comments:* This comfortable family cafe has a real country ambience and ranch-style decor, with wide booths and open windows. There is an interesting collection of branding irons from Big Island ranches decorating the walls and a large, beautiful aquarium with Hawaiian reef fish to fascinate the *keiki*. Good food, reasonable prices, friendly service make this a good choice for a casual meal, but it does tend to get busy on the weekends, so bring your patience.

★ **Tako Taco** *(Mexican)*
Cook's Corners, Mamalahoa Highway, Waimea; 808-887-1717.
Hours: 12 p.m. to 8 p.m. Closed Sunday. *Sampling:* Generous burritos, fresh fish tacos, fresh salads and a variety of chef's daily

specials. *Comments:* Decor is a fresh and colorful new look for the old Dairy Queen building. From it's expanded dining room, Tako Taco serves up a delicious menu of fast fresh Mexican food to a growing Waimea clientele. Table seating or take-out available.

Waimea Coffee & Co. *(Sandwiches/Snacks)*
Parker Square, 65-1279 Kawaihae Road, Waimea; 808-885-2100.

Hours: Monday through Friday 7 a.m. to 5 p.m.; Saturday 8 a.m. to 4 p.m. *Sampling:* This small coffee shop offers fresh-baked breakfast fare such as pastries, scones, breads and croissants, along with an assortment of bagels and egg dishes. Nice light lunches, sandwiches, soups, salads and rich, delectable desserts. They specialize in over 20 varieties of Arabica coffee from around the world. Daily beverages include a coffee of the day, espresso, cappuccino, chocolate drinks, fresh juices and more. The servers are friendly, there's a small retail store, and if it's not too rainy, enjoy a seat on the long wooden porch outside.

★ Yong's Kal-bi *(Korean)*
Waimea Center, 65-1158 Mamalahoa Highway, Waimea; 808-885-8440.

Hours: 10 a.m. to 9 p.m. Closed Sunday. *Sampling:* This small family restaurant features local and Asian foods with an emphasis on Korean cuisine. The menu lists *kalbi* ribs, barbecue beef, Korean chicken, chicken *katsu*, *mandoo* (Korean wonton), fish and more. *Comments:* The food is very good with ample portions served platelunch style. Clean, attractive location, simple decor; eat here or take out.

TEA FOR TWO . . . OR MORE

For a special birthday or dress-up tea party, consider **Lisa Rose Doll House & Tea Room** in Waimea. Designed for young ladies 4 through 12 years old, birthday party packages "fit for a princess" include dress-up costumes and fun accessories like feather boas, jewelry, high heels and magic wands. They do fancy hairdos, makeup and nails, then stage a mini fashion show and photo shoot for a picture for everybody. Lunch and birthday cupcakes are served and each guest receives a gift from the treasure chest to take home. Parties are priced according to number of guests and length of service, and can be customized to your preferences. Contact Lisa Zakar, Lisa Rose Doll House & Tea Room, 65-1484 Kawaihae Road, Kamuela, HI 96743; 808-885-7202; www.lisarose hawaii.com.

WHERE TO DINE

Moderate-priced Dining

★ **Aioli's Restaurant** (Continental-International)
*Opelo Plaza, 65-1227 Opelo Road, just off Kawaihae Road, west side of
Waimea; 808-885-6325.*

Hours: Tuesday through Thursday 11 a.m. to 2 p.m. and 5 to 8
p.m.; Friday and Saturday 11 a.m. to 2 p.m. and 5 to 9 p.m.; closed
Sunday and Monday. *Sampling:* The menu features Hawai'i-raised
meats, fresh fish and market produce and is changed by the chef every
three weeks, always offering something special for vegetarians. A
recent dinner sampling included Aioli's "weed salad" (organic spicy
greens), creamy garlic soup and intriguing entrees like herb-crusted
black Angus beef, Frenched rack of lamb, roasted pepper and onion
lasagna Florentine, and fan fillet of ostrich with black raspberry
sauce. Homemade breads, cookies and dessert specials round out the
menu. Breakfast is traditional fare and lunch includes sandwiches,
soups, salads and daily specials. *Comments:* This small country-style
cafe has earned acclaim in recent years for excellent food and fine
service. They do not sell alcoholic beverages on-site, but customers
are invited to bring their own wines at no corkage fee. Kamuela
Liquor Store, just down the street, can suggest wine pairings for
Aioli's menus. Their hours are subject to change; best to call ahead.
(Fresh giant cinnamon rolls are baked Saturday mornings.)

★ **Edelweiss** (Continental-International)
Highway 19, Kawaihae Road, Waimea; 808-885-6800.

Hours: Tuesday through Saturday for lunch 11:30 a.m. to 1:30
p.m., dinner from 5 p.m. until *pau* (closing). Closed the month of
September. *Sampling:* Master Chef Hans-Peter Hager's extensive menu
features varied Continental-international cuisine with European
accents, and is unlike anything you'll find elsewhere on the island.
The well-trained waitstaff begins service with a recitation of intriguing daily specials (if there was a quiz afterward you would not name
them all). His regular menu features hot and cold appetizers such as
melon prosciutto, *croute aux champignons* and escargots, varied
house-made soups of the day and fresh salads. Entrees include roast
pork and sauerkraut, *weiner schnitzel*, roast duck *bigarade*, rack of
lamb, veal cutlet *portofino*, filet mignon and chef's own pasta *al fresco*.
A little lighter for lunch, the Edelweiss bratwurst and sauerkraut is
a highlight, along with sandwich selections, soup, salad and daily
hot plate specials. Ask for smaller portions for *keiki*, or chef can
make plain pasta, burgers, grilled cheese and simpler fare. *Comments:*
This delightful chalet-like village inn seems right at home in the
cool, upcountry climate of Waimea town, where it has been a landmark for over 20 years. The unassuming building flanked by iron-

wood trees opens into a cozy, bright dining room, charmingly arrayed with white tablecloths, fresh flowers and original paintings of the green countryside. Reservations suggested.

★ *Waimea Ranch House* (Steaks/Continental)
65-1144 Mamalahoa Highway, next door to Waimea Center, Waimea; 808-885-2088.

Hours: Lunch 11:30 a.m. to 2:30 p.m., dinner 5:30 p.m. to 9 p.m. Closed Tuesday. *Sampling:* Hearty lunch and dinner menus feature generous market salads, huge Italian-style sandwiches, Big Island beef, fresh catch, local seafood, chicken and pasta dishes and much more. Service is attentive and warm; many of the waitstaff have been with the restaurant for years, so feel free to ask your questions about the area. If you like action, ask for a table near the open exhibition kitchen. *Comments:* This is the most recent incarnation of the landmark Cattleman's Steakhouse where *paniolo* (cowboys) used to tie their horses up to the hitching post and have a few *pau hana* (after work) brews. Now a bright, inviting dining room with rich *koa* wood paneling, lots of windows open to the Waimea countryside and quality island-style, "comfort" and European-inspired food, Waimea Ranch House welcomes visitors to share a little history. Do take time to walk around and look at the original paintings, old photographs and local ranch brands seared into the barroom wall.

Expensive-priced Dining

★ *Daniel Thiebaut Restaurant* (International/Hawai'i Regional Cuisine)
65-1259 Kawaihae Road, Waimea; 808-887-2200; www.danielthiebaut.com.

Hours: Lunch 11:30 to 2 p.m., dinner 5:30 to 9 p.m., Sunday brunch 10 a.m. to 1:30 p.m. *Sampling:* Located in the historic old Chock-In Store in Waimea town, Chef Thiebaut offers finely prepared, elaborately presented lunch and dinner dishes. Local-style *pupu* plates include *lomi* salmon, spring rolls and crabcake; for dinner try bacon-wrapped tenderloin, crab-crusted mahi or select from nightly special entrees. Creative desserts such as Waimea strawberry *mille feuille* or peppered strawberries in red wine sauce with coconut ice cream. Sushi is a recent addition. *Comments:* The quaint dining area winds around and through various restored rooms, with decor reminiscent of the restaurant's previous life as a mercantile store. The small, cozy bar is a fine place to wait for your table and enjoy one of the imported draft beers on tap, good wines or your favorite libation. We've enjoyed an early dinner in the bar, making a meal out of several of Chef Daniel's tempting appetizers. Reservations suggested.

★ **Merriman's** *(Hawai'i-Pacific Regional Cuisine)*
Opelo Plaza, 65-1227 Opelo Road, just off the Kawaihae Road, Kamuela;
808-885-6822; www.merrimanshawaii.com.

Hours: Monday through Friday lunch 11:30 a.m. to 1:30 p.m., dinner 5:30 to 9 p.m. *Sampling:* This menu features island-raised beef, fresh island fish and seafood, veal, lamb and daily specials. (You can order a platter with smaller portions of two items.) Notable specialties include fresh-roasted Loeffler corn and vine-ripened Lokelani tomatoes. An interesting selection of appetizers, soups, salads, house-baked breads and desserts rounds out a fine menu. Attentive, friendly service. *Comments:* This restaurant has won wide acclaim for fine dining specializing in fresh Big Island products expertly prepared. Chef Peter Merriman has established a reputation for excellence and has received wide recognition for his contributions to the Hawai'i Regional Cuisine movement. Reservations suggested.

Hamakua District

Inexpensive-priced Dining

Baker Tom's *(Baked Goods/Plate Lunch)*
Highway 19, a few miles north of Hilo (across the road from Pinkie's bright storefront), Papaikou; 808-964-8444.

Hours: 5:30 a.m. to 6:30 p.m. *Sampling:* Baker Tom's is a bakery and food stand tempting passersby with goodies such as creative cheesecakes and decadent cinnamon rolls. The "coconut wireless" (a.k.a. grapevine) says Baker Tom's has the very best *malasadas* anywhere—light, not too sweet and way too easy to eat more than one. *Comments:* The place is decorated with images from chef/owner Tom Wall's home state, Alaska, and fish specials feature, of course, salmon.

Cafe Il Mondo *(Italian)*
75-3626 Mamane Street, Honoka'a; 808-775-7711.

Hours: 11 a.m. to 7:45 p.m. Closed Sunday and Monday. *Sampling:* Delicious Italian specialties like calzones, pizza, pasta with homemade marinara and tempting desserts. Alcohol is not served, but it's okay to BYOB. *Comments:* A little place for big appetites.

CC Jon's Snack in Shoppe *(Sandwiches/Snacks)*
Honoka'a; 808-775-0414.

Hours: Monday through Friday 6:30 a.m. to 4 p.m.; Saturday until 3 p.m. Closed Sunday. *Sampling:* There's a wide range of local and international foods, short-order items, and snacks at this small deli-cafe.

Earl's Drive In *(Hawai'i Local Style/Plate Lunch)*
Located in the landmark Pa'auilo Store on Highway 19, Pa'auilo.

Hours: Monday through Friday 8:30 a.m. to 7 p.m.; Saturday 8:30 a.m. to 6 p.m.; Sunday 8:30 a.m. to 12:30 p.m. *Sampling:* The menu features local-style fast foods and snacks including sandwiches, teri beef and chicken plates, saimin, chili and rice. *Comments:* Earl's is a landmark along the old Hamakua Coast, providing all kinds of food to all kinds of people. Although it doesn't appear to have changed in years, it's somehow keeping pace with a changing place. If you have time, stop and enjoy a snack at one of the tables on the old wooden front porch and enjoy the genuine country atmosphere here.

★ **Fifties Highway Fountain** *(Burgers/Sandwiches/Snacks/Hawai'i Local Style/Ice Cream)*
35-2074 Gout Main Road, Laupahoehoe; 808-962-0808.

Hours: Tuesday through Saturday 7 a.m. to 7 p.m., Sunday 10:30 a.m. to 7 p.m. *Sampling:* A new discovery, and one of the few stops between Honoka'a and Hilo, this little hideaway just off the highway has a huge truckstop-style menu with almost anything you can think of, from a long list of burgers, shrimp or fish boats, hot dogs, chili, fries and onion rings, *loco mocos* and other "snacks," to generous platters with rice or mashed potatoes to go with your steak, roast pork, fried chicken, roast beef, country fried-steak and other hearty fare. Full breakfasts and soda fountain treats too, all styled around a 1950s theme, worth pulling off the road for.

Jolene's Kau Kau Korner *(American/Hawai'i Local Style)*
Intersection of Lehua and Mamane streets, Honoka'a; 808-775-9498.

Hours: 10 a.m. to 8 p.m. Monday, Wednesday, Friday; 10 a.m. to 3 p.m. Tuesday and Thursday. Closed Saturday and Sunday. *Sampling:* They have a varied menu of mahimahi, shrimp tempura, seafood platter, beef teriyaki, New York steak, captain's plate, chicken *katsu*, plus burgers, sandwiches, salads and desserts. *Comments:* Jolene's is a nicely renovated old shop space, made clean and bright with attractive, simple decor and curtains on the windows.

★ **Tex Drive In & Restaurant** *(Hawai'i Local Style/American)*
45-690 Pakalana, just off Highway 19 above Honoka'a; 808-775-0598.

Hours: 6 a.m. to 8:30 p.m. *Sampling:* The menu is long and features mostly local-style dishes, but their burgers are good and there's a variety of other foods to choose from. If nothing else, Tex's is a must-stop to try their fresh hot *malasadas. Comments:* Listed elsewhere in the guide as a drive-in, Tex's has also grown into a pretty good sit-down restaurant. There is a large indoor-outdoor dining area and souvenir shop, an information center, sometimes weekend entertainment, and sometimes cultural events (including an annual psychic fair). Second location in Pahala.

The Virtual Lounge *(Internet Cafe)*
On Mamane Street in the Hotel Honoka'a Club; 808-775-9355; e-mail: virtuallounge@turquoise.net.

Hours: Monday through Friday 9 a.m. to 6 p.m. *Sampling:* Hamakua coffee (some of the best) and espresso, $6 per hour internet service, plus copy, fax, scan and PC repair service. Ask about their wireless hotspots.

Hilo

Inexpensive-priced Dining

Ahokovi's Kitchen *(Polynesian/Hawai'i Local Style)*
1348-A Kilauea Avenue, Hilo; 800-961-4481.

Hours: Monday through Saturday 8 a.m. to 5 p.m. Closed Sunday. *Sampling:* This small lunch counter features authentic Polynesian food, take-out only. There is a daily menu board but staples include a Polynesian mix plate of cornbeef *lu* or lamb *lu* and beef, chicken chop suey or baked chicken. The regular plate lunch has entree choices of cornbeef *lu*, lamb *lu*, fresh cornbeef and cabbage, lamb curry, New Zealand sausage, *palosami*, and beef or chicken chop suey. All plates served with salad and starch of the day—rice, taro, *ulu* (breadfruit), green banana, sweet potato, *tavioka* root or *ufi* (yam). Side orders include squid, fish in coconut milk and special desserts. *Comments:* This is very good and authentic South Pacific–style Tongan-Samoan cuisine.

Akmal Pakistani & Indian Cuisine *(Pakistani/Indian)*
14 West Lanikaula Street, Hilo; 808-969-7479.

Hours: Lunch Tuesday through Friday 10:30 a.m. to 2 p.m.; dinner Monday through Thursday 5 to 8:30 p.m., until 9 p.m. on Friday and Saturday. Closed Sunday. *Sampling:* Tandoori specialties and vegan dishes. Family recipes prepared with imported Indian spices, mild to tongue-sizzling. *Comments:* There's "something to please everyone."

Arirang Lunch Korean Bar-B-Q *(Korean)*
165 East Kawili Street, across from Hawai'i Community College campus, Hilo; 808-969-7151.

Hours: Monday through Friday 10 a.m. to 2 p.m. for lunch, 4:30 to 7:30 p.m. for dinner. Closed Saturday and Sunday. *Sampling:* The menu features Korean barbecue, plate lunches, spicy soups and special burgers. The best items are *bulgogi* (charbroiled lean beef), *kalbi* ribs, *yukejang* spicy soup, and *bulgogi* kimchee burger (hot!).

Ayuthaya Thai Restaurant *(Thai)*
804 Kilauea Avenue, Hilo; 808-933-2424.

Hours: Monday through Friday for lunch 10:30 a.m. to 2:30 p.m., dinner nightly 5 to 8:30 p.m. *Sampling:* This very small eatery is a popular spot for the hot and spicy Thai cuisine. The menu has an extensive listing of over 60 authentic Thai dishes including such items as golden calamari, royal chicken soup, green papaya salad, Thai curries (red, yellow or green), spicy basil chicken, ong choy beef or chicken, several seafood selections plus noodles, rice, salads, soups and veggie choices. House specialties are the *musaman* curry and something called "Ayuthaya Evil Beef," possibly worth tasting just for the name; it's available spiced mild, medium or hot. *Comments:* Carry-out available.

Bear's Coffee (Sandwiches/Snacks/Coffee)
106 Keawe Street, downtown Hilo; 808-935-0708.

Hours: Monday through Friday 5:30 a.m. to 4 p.m.; Saturday 6 a.m. to 1 p.m.; Sunday 6 a.m. to 12 noon. *Sampling:* Best known for its selection of international coffees, espresso and fresh pastries, the menu also features a variety of salads, sandwiches, individual pizza, and other light lunch specials. *Comments:* This small cafe is a Hilo favorite, perfect for perching under the awning on a rainy morning to people-watch.

Cafe Concerto (Italian)
794-D Kilauea Avenue, Hilo; 808-934-0312.

Hours: Lunch Monday through Friday 10:30 a.m. to 3 p.m. *Sampling:* An engaging little slice of Northern Italy, Chef Lando Landi's Cafe Concerto offers Hilo a high-class luncheon option, reasonably priced and served with a signature Italian family welcome and style. A flexible menu with daily specials, fresh-cooked pasta, homemade sauces (available by the jar), salad with fresh mozzarella and extra-virgin olive oil, *schicciata* (a flat dipping bread, also home baked) and made-from-scratch desserts including the traditional *tiramisu.* Look for a trail of flower petals on the sidewalk out front, and the sign over the door that says "La Dolce Vita." Live music most evenings.

★ *Canoes Cafe* (Sandwiches/Snacks)
14 Furneaux Lane, Hilo; 808-935-4070, www.canoescafe.com.

Hours: Daily 11 a.m. to 3 p.m., Wednesday and Friday 9 a.m. to 3 p.m., Market Saturdays 8 a.m. to 3 p.m. *Sampling:* An excellent stop to shop for a quiet picnic at Queen Liliuokalani Gardens at the edge of Hilo Bay, Canoes' menu includes over 20 sandwich selections, available in your choice of deli-style, in fresh-baked sandwich rolls, grilled panini-style or as a wrap. They have a full menu of fresh salads with two different homemade soups daily and mini lunch pizzas. *Comments:* Free lunch delivery to downtown Hilo businesses.

★ Don's Grill (American)
485 Hinano Street, Hilo; 808-935-9099.

Hours: Tuesday through Thursday 10:30 a.m. to 9 p.m.; Friday until 10 p.m.; Saturday and Sunday 10 a.m. to 9 p.m. Closed Monday. *Sampling:* The menu features beef, chicken, pork chops, fish, sandwiches, burgers, soups and salads, daily specials and many local favorites. The house specialty is an excellent rotisserie chicken. *Comments:* This pleasant family restaurant has proven to be one of Hilo's consistently best inexpensive dining-out options. Should you have to wait in line awhile, it's well worth it. Clean facilities, fast courteous service, generally great food and very reasonable prices.

★ Dotty's Coffee Shop (Filipino)
Prince Kuhio Plaza, 111 East Puainako, Hilo; 808-959-6477.

Hours: Monday through Friday 7 a.m. to 9 p.m.; Saturday 7 p.m. to 8 p.m.; Sunday 7 a.m. to 7 p.m. *Sampling:* The daily dinner menu offers family favorites and several daily specials including one or two Filipino dishes. Homemade cornbread, banana muffins and fruit cream pies are delicious! *Comments:* Generally good food at reasonable prices.

Empire Cafe (Filipino)
29 Haili Street, downtown Hilo; 808-935-1721.

Hours: Tuesday through Sunday 8 a.m. to 3 p.m. Closed Monday. *Sampling:* The menu features standard breakfast items and lunch/dinner selections such as Salisbury steak, teriyaki beef, chicken or beef broccoli, Asian curry and Filipino specials like chicken and pork *adobo*, *sari sari* pork soup, *sari sari* with shrimp, *dinadaraan* (exotic blend of prepared pork blood and meats), *pinacbet* (stir-fry bitter melon, okra, pork and seasonings), pork with peas, and chicken papaya. There are also short-order selections like sandwiches, tacos, enchiladas, fried saimin, fried rice, *loco moco*, and various daily specials. *Comments:* This hole-in-the-wall diner is across the street from the Palace Theater and just up the street from the bayfront Kamehameha Avenue. It's not a fancy place and has several tables packed tightly together plus lunch counter service.

Francine Marie Bakery and Taqueria (Bakery/Mexican)
264 Keawe Street, Hilo; 808-934-9112.

Hours: Tuesday through Saturday 8 a.m. to 3 p.m. *Sampling:* A unique little eatery with fresh-baked treats like cream puffs, macaroons and double chocolate brownies, custom cakes and dessert platters, plus hot and not-hot lunch selections with fresh, homemade, homeground corn tortillas. Vegetarian options; catering available.

Freddy's Restaurant *(Hawai'i Local Style)*
454 Manono at Pi'ilani Street, opposite the Civic Auditorium, Hilo; 808-935-1108.

Hours: The fast-food side is open daily 6:30 a.m. to 9 p.m. The dining room is open daily for breakfast and lunch 6:30 a.m. to 2 p.m., and dinner 5 to 8 p.m. *Sampling:* The menu features such items as teriyaki beef and chicken, beef and noodles, beef stew, island fish, plate lunches, burgers, sandwiches plus daily specials. Their general store/deli next door offers a variety of fresh-made deli-style sandwiches and other goodies. There is sit-down a la carte dining on one side of the restaurant and plate lunch/fast food dining on the other.

Happy Valley Seafood *(Chinese)*
Hilo Shopping Center, 1263 Kilauea Avenue, Hilo; 808-933-1083.

Hours: Monday through Friday 10 a.m. to 9 p.m.; Saturday and Sunday 11 a.m. to 9 p.m. *Sampling:* This clean, bright dining room features a Chinese menu listing some 150 items, not counting a daily hot buffet table of specials. There is plenty of standard Chinese fare along with quite a few unusual selections like cold jellyfish, West Lake soup, sizzling rice soup, Mongolian chicken, capital pork ribs, *mu shu* pork, spinach with garlic sauce, several shrimp, scallop, prawn, lobster, squid, abalone and fresh fish dishes, chop suey, chow mein and other noodle dishes, plus set dinner menus. *Comments:* Good varied Chinese food at reasonable prices in clean surroundings.

Hiro's Place *(Hawai'i Local Style/Japanese)*
KTA Supermarket Center, 50 East Puainako, Hilo; 808-959-6665.

Hours: Monday through Friday 5:30 a.m. to 5 p.m., Saturday and Sunday 5:30 a.m. to 4:30 p.m. *Sampling:* This is a local fast-food operation serving up Oriental-American specialties including teriyaki beef, chicken, fish, plate lunches, sandwiches, sushi rice, noodles, bentos and more. *Comments:* Tables on walkway; eat here or take out.

★ **Island Infusion** *(Hawai'i-Pacific Regional/Hawai'i Local Style/International)*
Waiakea Center food court, next to Wal-Mart and Office Max on Kanoelehua Avenue, Hilo; 808-933-9555.

Hours: Monday through Saturday 9 a.m. to 9 p.m., Sunday 9 a.m. to 8 p.m. *Sampling:* One of the most intriguing eateries to come along in a while, this attractive little food counter serves up a variety of innovative island-style dishes at surprisingly reasonable prices. Check out their panini sandwiches made with poi *focaccia,* interesting boboli pizzas, Waikiki wraps like the Ama Ebi (shrimp and sausage with wild greens, tomatoes and mozzarella). Hot plates include *laulau,* rotisserie chicken, highly touted barbecue pork and beef ribs and more (some sold by the pound). Vegetarians will find plenty of satisfying options, as will dessert lovers like us. *Comments:* Chef Mark

Mattos states his aim is to offer "creative island cuisine infused with the flavors of Hawai'i embraced with the spirit of aloha," and while that may be an ambitious statement, this place earns our stamp of approval, and that's something special. Eat in or carry out; lunch delivery available in Hilo.

★ Jimmy's Drive In (Hawai'i Local Style/American)
362 Kinoole Street, Hilo; 808-935-5571.

Hours: Monday through Saturday 10 a.m. to 8:30 p.m.; closed Sunday. *Sampling:* The menu offers a variety of food favorites including Hawaiian, Japanese, Korean and American dishes. *Comments:* This local-style coffee shop is more of a diner than a drive-in, with sit-down service in booths and tables in a wide, brightly lit dining room. The decor and ambiance are simple, and the food is good local fare with large portions served family style. We like to order different things and share.

Kalbi Express (Korean)
Waiakea Center food court, 315 Makaala Street, Hilo; 808-935-7997.

Hours: 10 a.m. to 9 p.m. *Sampling:* This popular local lunch counter serves up excellent Korean cuisine including *kalbi* ribs, barbecue beef, chicken and pork, spicy squid, meat and fish jun, fried *man doo*, *bi bim bap* and combination plates for a taste of everything. *Comments:* Carry-outs and all-size catering menu available at very reasonable rates.

Kay's Lunch Center (Korean)
684 Kilauea Avenue, Hilo; 808-969-1776.

Hours: Despite its name, Kay's is open for breakfast and lunch 6 a.m. to 2 p.m. (Saturday and Sunday from 5 a.m.) and 5 p.m. to closing. Closed Monday. *Sampling:* This is a real local-style restaurant featuring Korean cuisine including barbecue beef, short ribs, and the original crispy Korean chicken, plus cone and *maki* sushi, *musubi*, *laulau*, bentos and plate lunches. Homestyle dinners include miso soup, *kim chee* and hot vegetable of the day with your choice of chicken, fish, beef or liver with bacon. Homemade cream cheese pies for dessert are special. *Comments:* This sit-down dining spot also provides plate/box lunches to take out. Servings are generous and reasonably priced. The decor and ambiance here are simple, nothing fancy, nothing glitzy.

★ Ken's Pancake House (American/International/Hawai'i Local Style)
1730 Kamehameha Avenue, at the intersection of Kamehameha Avenue and Banyan Drive near Hilo's hotel row; 808-935-8711.

Hours: Open 24 hours a day. *Sampling:* Ken's is one of our favorite places to eat breakfast, 24 hours a day, but the enormous menu of this '50s-style diner offers a taste of absolutely everything for lunch and dinner, too. Try plate-size mac nut, banana or coconut pancakes, or the "Kilauea," stacked with bacon, ham and eggs. Or, consider an omelet from the long list (including snowcrab and shrimp), four different kinds of eggs benedict, waffles, sweet bread French toast and eggs-your-way with just about anything you can think of. For lunch or dinner, Ken's has killer chili, big sandwiches, burgers, local-style stews, various saimin and wonton *min*, and a list of *loco moco* including "Sumo Moco" (6 scoops rice, Spam, hamburger or mahi, and 3 eggs with gravy or chili). They also have a variety of American diner-style plates including beef, chicken and turkey, liver and onions, fish, seafood and spaghetti. They have a good *keiki* menu and, in spite of the heavy-sounding specials, are kind to vegetarians or dieters, offering Egg Beaters, meatless bacon and sausage, tempeh and hearty entrees like veggie *moco*, chili, vegetarian benedict and omelets, sandwiches, salads and homemade desserts including shakes, sundaes and ice cream floats. *Comments:* Check out the celebrity photos at the cash register. Take-out available.

Kope Kope *(Sandwiches/Snacks)*
Hilo Shopping Center, 1261 Kilauea Avenue, Hilo; 808-933-1221; www.kopekope.com.

Hours: Monday through Friday 6:30 a.m. to 6 p.m.; 7:30 a.m. to 3 p.m. Saturday and Sunday. *Sampling:* This bright, attractive coffee shop is a good place to stop for coffee, snacks and desserts. The menu has a wide variety of fresh island and Kona coffees, espresso, cappuccinos and lattes as well as international coffees, teas, sodas and other specialty beverages. There is also a lunch, supper and snack menu of light fare such as soups, sandwiches, wraps, bagels and desserts like fresh-baked brownies, carrot cake, scones and cheesecake. Vegetarians find plenty to choose from, with wide selections of all-day omelets, assorted bagels with all kinds of fillings and spreads, topped baked potatoes, smoothies and more.

Kow's Restaurant *(Chinese)*
87 West Kawailani Street, Hilo; 808-959-3766.

Hours: Sunday through Thursday 10 a.m. to 9 p.m.; Friday and Saturday until 10 p.m.; Monday 3:30 to 9 p.m. *Sampling:* Featuring Cantonese-style food, Kow's serves up a wide range (over 200 items) of delectable dishes such as beef broccoli, chicken and Chinese peas,

Text continued on page 280.

DRIVE-INS, OKAZUYA & PLATE-LUNCH SHOPS

Local-style "fast food" drive-ins, *okazuya* and plate-lunch shops may offer similar fare for breakfast, lunch and dinner, but each has a particular clientele and a personality all its own. The emphasis is on good food, good quantity, reasonable prices and fast service. Drive-ins cook their food in a back kitchen; you order from a menu, generally by the piece (i.e., burger, fries, shake) and it's brought to you ready to eat or carry out. At an *okazuya*, everything is displayed like a buffet; you point to order by the piece or serving, and it's plated or packaged to go. They'll always have *musubi* and more finger- than fork-food. A plate lunch shop is an *okazuya* where you always, always get two scoops rice on the plate, then your choice of hot dishes, usually priced by the plate, not by the piece. Any of the three might sell what they call a bento. A bento differs from a plate lunch in that it's pre-packaged in a bento box, the signature see-through plastic container. With any good lunch outlet, the key to success is *variety*, lots of choices, ready to eat right away.

A couple of popular local lunch items are *musubi* and *loco moco*; you'd buy *musubi* in an *okazuya* and a *loco moco* at a plate lunch shop or drive-in. A *musubi* sounds awful but tastes great: fry up a slice of Spam then press between two layers of cooked rice and wrap with *nori* (seaweed)—it's a funky kind of sandwich that's great when you're on the run. *Loco moco* is two scoops of rice with a hamburger patty and fried egg on top, slathered with brown gravy. Since it originated at Cafe 100 in Hilo years ago, *loco moco* has become a standard menu item statewide. Hilo is the kingdom of the lunch shop—all three kinds—and you'll find one on almost every corner. Below is a very short list of notables island wide.

Blane's Drive In, just off Kanoelehua Avenue in Hilo's industrial area. Check out the "menu hotline" for daily specials. 150 Wiwoole Street, Hilo; 808-935-2259, 808-935-4488 (menu hotline). Second location: 217 Waianuenue Avenue above the post office, Hilo; 808-969-9494, 808-969-6677 (menu hotline). Third location: 45-997 Kika Street, Honoka'a; 808-775-7220, 808-775-0027 (menu hotline).

★ **Cafe 100** has been a Hilo institution for many years, named in honor of the highly decorated 100th Infantry Division of Japanese Americans in WWII. A vast menu offers hot meals along with soda fountain treats to take out or eat at picnic tables. You might catch local vintage car clubs here on the weekends. Open daily except Sunday 6:45 a.m. to 8:30 p.m. 969 Kilauea Avenue, Hilo, across from Kapiolani School; 808-935-8683.

Earl's Drive In Open Monday through Friday 8:30 a.m. to 7 p.m., Saturday 8:30 a.m. to 6 p.m., Sunday 8:30 a.m. to noon. Highway 19 in Pa'auilo, Hamakua Coast.

Hilo Lunch Shop is one of the most popular. Open Tuesday through Friday 5:30 a.m. to 1 p.m.; closed Sunday and Monday. 421 Kalanikoa, Hilo; 808-935-8273.

★ **Kamuela Deli** has two outlets: Waimea Center, Highway 19, Waimea, 808-885-4147, open daily 5 a.m. to 9 p.m.; and in the Kona Coast Center, 74-5588 Palani Road, Kailua-Kona, 808-334-0017, open daily 7:30 a.m. to 9 p.m.

Kawamoto Vegetable Shop is one of the best in town. Open Tuesday through Sunday 6 a.m. to 12:30 p.m.; closed Monday. 784 Kilauea Avenue, Hilo, 808-935-8209.

Kona Mix Plate has an amazingly big menu for a small place: plate lunches, sandwiches, burgers, soups and sides. Open daily 10 a.m. to 8 p.m; Kopiko Plaza, Palani Road, Kailua-Kona, 808-329-8104.

Sandy's Drive In has a good old-fashioned breakfast, lunch and dinner featuring burgers and sandwiches, plate lunches and local favorites. And there's always room for Jell-O. Open daily 7 a.m. to 8 p.m. On Highway 11 at Kainaliu, Kona, about 5 miles south of Kailua-Kona; 808-322-2161.

★ **Tex Drive In** is a must-stop for their fresh hot *malasadas* (local doughnuts). Tex has a large indoor-outdoor dining area, restrooms and souvenir shop-and is just about the only stop on the road between Waimea and Hilo. Open daily 6 a.m. to 8:30 p.m.; 45-690 Pakalana, just off Highway 19 above Honoka'a, 808-775-0598. Second location in Pahala offers the same great stuff. Open Monday through Saturday 7 a.m. to 8 p.m., Sunday 7 a.m. to 6 p.m. 808-928-8200.

Verna's Drive In Open 5 a.m. to 10 p.m. daily. Off Highway 130, Kea'au, across from Kea'au School; 808-966-9288.

Verna's Too Drive In Open daily 6 a.m. to 8 p.m. Highway 11, Mountain View; 808-968-8774.

Verna's III Drive In Open Monday through Thursday 7 a.m. to 9 p.m.; and from Friday 7 a.m. until Sunday 7 p.m. Kamehameha and Kanoelehua Avenues, Hilo; 808-935-2776.

Verna's V Drive In Open daily 10 a.m. to 4:30 p.m. At the end of Highway 137 south of Pahoa, where the lava flows cover the highway at Kalapana; 808-965-8234.

Y's Lunch Shop Open Monday through Thursday 7 a.m. to 1 p.m., closed Friday through Sunday; 263 Keawe Street, Hilo; 808-935-3119.

sweet and sour shrimp, cake noodles and more, including something called "Rainbow Tofu." Depending upon availability they have a nice selection of local fish at market price, including mullet, *menpachi, ehu, opakapaka, akulekule,* mahimahi and ahi.

Kuhio Grille *(Hawai'i Local Style)*
Located at the back of the Prince Kuhio Plaza on Kanoelehua Avenue, Hilo; 808-959-2336.

Hours: Monday through Friday 6 a.m. to 10 p.m.; Saturday and Sunday 6 a.m. to midnight. *Sampling:* This small eatery features a local-style menu of short orders, plate lunch items and light meals. Menu items include corned beef hash, teriyaki beef, chili, homemade biscuits, burgers, sandwiches and daily plate lunch specials and bento take-out. *Comments:* Good food at reasonable prices.

L & L Drive In *(Hawai'i Local Style/American/Chinese)*
348 Kinoole Street, across from Hawai'i-Tribune Herald newspaper building, Hilo, 808-934-0888; and in the Waiakea Center food court, 315 Makaala Street off Kanoelehua Avenue, next to Wal-Mart and Office Max, Hilo, 808-935-3888.

Hours: 10 a.m. to 9 p.m. *Sampling:* L & L says they have the "best plate lunch in Hawai'i," and their broad menu covers all the bases from local favorites like *loco moco* and teriyaki to Chinese combination plates, burgers and hot dogs, chili, saimin, a seafood platter and even prime rib. *Comments:* Small, medium and large party pans available with advance order.

★ Leung's Chop Suey House *(Chinese)*
530 East Lanikaula Street at the intersection of Kanoelehua Avenue, Hilo; 808-935-4066.

Hours: Monday through Saturday 9 a.m. to 8 p.m., closed Sunday. *Sampling:* A range of Cantonese à la carte dishes and a buffet counter to select your own plate lunch/dinner are available. Cake noodles are a must! *Comments:* This small eat-in/take-out Chinese kitchen is popular with folks working in the nearby industrial area of Hilo. Good quality food at good prices in a not-too-fancy place.

Ling's Chop Suey House *(Chinese)*
Puainako Town Center, 2100 Kanoelehua, Hilo; 808-981-1689.

Hours: Monday through Saturday 10 a.m. to 9 p.m., Sunday 10 a.m. to 8 p.m. *Sampling:* This Chinese eatery serves up a number of Cantonese-style dishes including beef, pork, chicken, seafood and more. Special items range from cake noodles to crispy chicken with oyster or lemon sauce, to saimin, wonton *min* and much more. They feature a daily lunch buffet of steam table specials where you create your own plate from several choices.

Lola's Boutique and Cafe *(Health foods)*
101 Aupuni Street, Hilo Lagoon Center, Hilo; 808-933-1331.

    Hours: Monday through Friday 11 a.m. to 2:30 p.m.; Friday reservation only for dinner; Saturday 5 p.m. to 10 p.m. *Sampling:* A surprising, out-of-the-way little place with a tasty menu for lunch and dinner, served on the lanai overlooking koi ponds and a waterfall. Burgers (including Boca Burgers), soup, salad and pastas for lunch, along with coffee drinks, smoothies and shakes. Dinner features light fare, such as shrimp and scallops with angel hair pasta or a spinach and parmesan ravioli, with a nice selection of starters and good desserts. Live "global" music and open mic on Saturday.

Low International Food *(Hawai'i Local Style)*
222 Kilauea at Ponohawai Street, Hilo; 808-969-6652.

    Hours: 9 a.m. to 8 p.m. Closed Wednesday. *Sampling:* Operated by the Low family for many years, this popular Hilo diner has a varied menu of Chinese, Korean and local-style plate lunches, sandwiches and specials. Chicken *tonkatsu*, teriyaki beef, and burgers are popular items here. They also bake a line of unusual and delicious-sounding homemade breads such as sweet potato, taro, pumpkin, passion fruit, mango, coconut, banana, guava and "rainbow." *Comments:* You can eat in—several tables are available on the lanai area—or take out.

★ Miyo's *(Japanese)*
Waiakea Villas shops complex, 400 Hualani Street, Hilo; 808-935-2273.

    Hours: Lunch 11 a.m. to 2 p.m., dinner 5:30 p.m. to 8:30 p.m. Closed Sunday. *Sampling:* This inexpensive family-style restaurant features excellent Japanese cuisine. Sample selections include sashimi, sesame chicken, *tonkatsu*, tempura, teriyaki beef, fish, noodles, and *donburi* soups. *Comments:* The upstairs location makes for nice views, overlooking lovely Waiakea Fish Pond and Wailoa Park.

★ Naung Mai Thai Kitchen *(Thai)*
86 Kilauea Avenue, tucked behind Garden Exchange, Hilo; 808-934-7540.

    Hours: Monday, Tuesday, Thursday, Friday for lunch 11 a.m. to 2 p.m. (no lunch on Saturday), dinner Monday through Saturday 5 p.m. to 8:30 p.m. Closed Sunday. *Sampling:* The interesting, 50-item menu features red, green or yellow *musaman* curry, chicken *rama*, eggplant with Thai basil, spicy basil chicken, garlic shrimp, pad Thai and a selection of various other chicken, beef, pork and seafood dishes, prepared mild-to-hot at your request. The eclectic Thai soups are here, as well as salads and *pupus*, plus daily lunch bargains and dinner specials including quality fresh fish. *Comments:* Everybody's talking about Naung Mai. Called a treasure by its enthusiastic operators, this small cafe has been in business (in Pahoa and Hilo) for over 13 years, earning acclaim from customers for authentic Thai cuisine that's "the best we ever had." The small dining room has an open kitchen area and a few tables. Carry-outs available. Excellent Thai food at reasonable prices (the most expensive item on the menu is steamed salmon at $14.95).

New China Restaurant *(Chinese)*
510 Kilauea Avenue, next to Hawai'i Hardware Company, Hilo; 808-961-5677.

Hours: 10 a.m. to 9 p.m. Closed Monday. *Sampling:* The menu features Cantonese- and Hong Kong–style cuisine with a wide selection of beef, pork, chicken, duck, seafood and noodle dishes. They feature some interesting sizzling platters with fresh seafood and a house special stuffed tofu with pork hash. Consider the more unusual items like abalone soup, squid with green pepper and black beans, and lots more to tempt your exotic palate. Try the potstickers or very reasonable lunch buffet at only $6.95. *Comments:* You'll find good food at reasonable prices here. This is a very clean, bright restaurant with simple, pleasant decor.

★ New Saigon Vietnamese Restaurant *(Vietnamese)*
421 Kalanikoa Street, Hilo; 808-934-9490.

Hours: Monday through Friday 9:30 a.m. to 2 p.m. for lunch, Tuesday through Friday 4:30 to 8 p.m. for dinner, closed Saturday and Sunday. *Sampling:* This small, clean and bright eatery serves up an interesting variety of authentic Vietnamese cuisine. The extensive menu lists appetizers like spring and summer rolls, green papaya shrimp salad and Vietnamese crepes. *Pho* noodle soup is a specialty with several varieties like round beef steak, beef meatball and chicken. There is also mein soup, rice noodle soup and beef stew noodle soup. There are several cold vermicelli noodle dishes like noodles and charbroiled pork and veggies, shrimp and veggies, and spiced beef noodle soup. Rice plates include grilled pork chop and veggies, charbroiled shrimp and veggies, beef stew rice plates and more. They also have several types of fried rice and fried noodles plus special set Chinese five-course meals. *Comments:* Good Southeast Asian cuisine not readily available elsewhere on the Big Island.

New Star Restaurant *(Chinese)*
172 Kilauea Avenue, Hilo; 808-934-8874.

Hours: 10 a.m. to 9 p.m. Closed Tuesday. *Sampling:* New Star's specialties include seafood dishes such as *kung pao* shrimp with cashew, live lobster or crab and "Lover's Shrimp." The hearty lunch buffet offers a wide range of selections at a very reasonable price. *Comments:* Good quality, reasonably priced Chinese food prepared by chefs with over 40 years of experience. Banquet facilities available for larger gatherings.

★ Nori's Saimin (Japanese)

688 Kinoole Street, across from the Hilo Lanes bowling alley, Hilo; 808-935-9133.

Hours: Monday through Saturday 10:30 a.m. to 3 p.m. for lunch, Tuesday through Saturday 4 p.m. to midnight, Sunday 10:30 a.m. to 10 p.m. *Sampling:* This Japanese-American noodle shop promotes itself as having the best saimin in town and is a huge hit, especially with folks from other islands. They also have bento box lunches as well as killer chocolate *mochi*, a rich, gooey, sweet rice dessert, and they're the only place in the state to get green saimin (call first to make sure it's available). *Comments:* The varied hours are a little confusing, but they're worth figuring out.

Ocean Sushi Deli (Japanese)

239 Keawe Street, downtown Hilo; 808-961-6625.

Hours: Monday through Saturday for lunch 10 a.m. to 2 p.m., dinner Saturday 4:30 p.m. to 9 p.m. Closed Sunday. *Sampling:* This small but clean diner has a wide variety of freshly made sushi and daily specials. They specialize in sushi and you can choose from a varied list including *nigiri*, *hosomaki*, jumbo *maki*, and sushi boxes and family platters. They also have seafood *poke*, sashimi, and ready-to-cook meals including *yosenabe*, sukiyaki, *shabu shabu* and *gyoza*. *Comments:* Very good authentic Japanese cuisine for reasonable prices. This place earned our stamp of approval and that's something special.

★ O'Keefe & Sons Bread Bakers (Bakery/Sandwiches/Snacks)

374 Kinoole Street, Hilo; 808-934-9334; fax 808-961-5800.

Hours: Monday through Friday 6 a.m. to 5 p.m.; Saturday 6 a.m. to 3 p.m. Closed Sunday. *Sampling:* A highly rated bakery featuring at least 25 different varieties of artisan breads throughout the month. *Sampling:* French and Italian loaves, almond with apricot, olive rosemary, Swiss sunflower, sourdough and sour poi, New York rye, nine-grain honey, focaccia, garlic sage or mac nut pesto flatbreads, potato bread, stollen, panettone and Hilo *nori* bread. There's also a wonderful pastry selection and fresh homemade soup and sandwich specials. Vegetarians can be satisfied with a spicy curried tofu or veggie cheese sandwich on one of their excellent breads. *Comments:* O'Keefe is one of the top two bakers on the island. Look for his product in the better restaurants.

★ Restaurant Osaka (Japanese)

762 Kanoelehua Avenue, Hilo; 808-961-6699.

Hours: 10 a.m. to 9 p.m. Closed Tuesday. *Sampling:* This restaurant and lounge combination has a good variety of Japanese-

American food, and is a favorite stop of neighbor-islanders for their different kinds of saimin. Complete meals Japanese or American style include beef, pork, chicken, and seafood as well as sandwiches.

★ Reuben's Mexican Food (Mexican)
336 Kamehameha Avenue on the bayfront in old downtown Hilo; 808-961-2552.

Hours: Monday through Friday 11 a.m. to 9 p.m., Saturday noon to 9 p.m., closed Sunday. *Sampling:* They serve warm chips and homemade salsa to start, then offer a good selection of Mexican fare: a variety of enchiladas (try the crab), chicken *flautas*, chiles rellenos, *chimichangas* and *burros* (not donkeys, but the biggest burritos you ever want to eat). *Comments:* Reuben's is one of our all-time favorite places in Hilo. There is nothing like a long, rainy evening spent engrossed in conversation and spicy cheese enchiladas with a couple of Dos Equis. This family-run restaurant is a big, open room made festive with colorful serapes on the tables and an amazing collection of sombreros and hand-painted murals on the block walls. Take-out available. Good in quality, variety and quantity. A full bar with Mexican beers and several margaritas by the pitcher or glass.

Royal Siam (Thai)
70 Mamo Street, downtown Hilo; 808-961-6100.

Hours: Monday through Saturday for lunch 11 a.m. to 2 p.m., dinner 5 p.m. to 9 p.m.; Sunday 5 p.m. to 9 p.m. *Sampling:* The menu features over 50 items including chicken, seafood, beef, pork and veggie dishes and wonderful Thai curries, a selection of appetizers and house special Buddha Rama. Food can be ordered either mild, medium or spicy hot. *Comments:* Popular place. Take-out available.

Ryan's Restaurant Okazu-Ya (Japanese/Hawai'i Local Style)
399 East Kawili Street, Hilo; 808-933-1335.

Hours: Monday through Saturday 5:30 a.m. to 2 p.m.; Sunday 7 a.m. to 2 p.m. *Sampling:* This small local lunch counter has a menu of Asian and American dishes. They offer a traditional breakfast menu, and for lunch they have a variety of local favorite plates such as chopped steak island-style, beef stew, pork tofu, *shoyu* roast pork, teriyaki beef, chicken *katsu*, pork *tonkatsu*, fried fish, *loco moco*, bento box lunches, sandwiches, burgers, saimin and more. *Comments:* They have one small dining side room with a handful of tables. Pleasant, clean and generally good food.

Sum Leung Chinese Kitchen (Chinese)
KTA Supermarket Center, 50 East Puainako Street, Hilo; 808-959-6025.

Hours: Monday through Thursday 9 a.m. to 6:30 p.m.; Friday until 7:30 p.m., Saturday until 6 p.m. and Sunday until 4 p.m.

Sampling: A full range of Chinese plate lunches, noodles, and varied Chinese specialties. Take-out available.

Sunlight Cafe *(Hawai'i Local Style/American)*
Hilo Shopping Center, 1263 Kilauea Avenue, Hilo; 808-934-8833.

Hours: Monday through Friday 7 a.m. to 8 p.m.; Saturday 8 a.m. to 7 p.m.; closed Sunday. *Sampling:* This small shopping center diner offers a menu of standard breakfast, lunch and dinner selections. The menu is a mixture of American-Oriental and local-style favorites, offering selections like steak, teriyaki chicken and beef, pork chops, tropical lemon chicken, *shoyu* mahimahi and roast chicken, plus soups, salads, burgers and sandwiches.

★ Tsunami Grill & Tempura *(Japanese)*
250 Keawe Street, Hilo; 808-961-6789.

Hours: Monday through Saturday for lunch 10 a.m. to 2 p.m., dinner 5 to 9 p.m. Closed Sunday. *Sampling:* Tsunami has a menu of special bento box take-out meals, skewer and tempura plates, several types of *donburi, udon* and soba noodles, *kushikatsu,* Japanese curry, seafood and much more. *Comments:* This is a very popular place. Reservations are suggested.

★ Two Ladies Kitchen *(Japanese/Bakery)*
274 Kilauea Avenue, Hilo; 808-961-4766.

Hours: Wednesday through Saturday 10 a.m. to 6 p.m. Closed Sunday through Tuesday. *Sampling: Mochi* is a sweet Japanese treat, made by pounding rice into a soft, smooth dough, which can be shaped, flavored and filled with a variety of fruits, sweet *adzuki* beans and other goodies and daily surprises. Their varied menu of take-out items also includes delectable pie crust *manju* (a small tart filled with sweet bean paste and other things) and fresh-made apple pies, pumpkin pies and biscuits. Their far-and-away winner is strawberry *mochi,* one whole fresh strawberry covered by sweet bean paste and wrapped in soft *mochi.* It's a unique and delightful taste sensation that you must try. *Comments:* We can't go to Hilo without stopping at Two Ladies. This is not a cafe or restaurant but rather a Japanese-style bakery shop that makes quite possibly the best *mochi* on the planet. The small, unassuming storefront is easy to miss, so watch for it on the right-hand (*mauka*) side of Kilauea Avenue as you head out of town (free parking along the curb). Behind the screen door is an amazing kitchen from which comes handmade delicacies in a wide array of shapes and colors.

★ What's Shakin' *(Sandwiches/Snacks)*
27-999 Old Mamalahoa Highway, four-mile scenic route, Pepeekeo; 808-964-3080.

Hours: 10 a.m. to 5 p.m. *Sampling:* Acclaimed by local folks and national magazines, What's Shakin' is famous for fresh fruit smoothies like their signature Papaya Paradise. They also offer island juices, fruit snacks, sandwiches, daily specials and desserts. *Comments:* This country-style snack bar is located two miles north of the famous Hawai'i Tropical Botanical Gardens on old Highway 19. Carry out or enjoy your meal on the lanai or picnic tables under the shade of the banana patch.

Yum Yum Korean BBQ *(Korean)*
Prince Kuhio Plaza, Kanoelehua Avenue, Hilo; 808-959-9977.

Hours: Monday through Friday 10 a.m. to 9 p.m.; Saturday 9:30 a.m. to 7 p.m.; Sunday 10 a.m. to 6 p.m. *Sampling:* This small diner serves up a variety of Korean specials like *kalbi* ribs, spicy Korean chicken, barbecue beef and several daily specials.

Yichiba Noodle House *(Chinese/Japanese)*
Waiakea Center food court, 315 Makaala Street, Hilo; 808-935-6880.

Hours: Monday through Saturday 9 a.m. to 9 p.m.; Sunday until 8 p.m. *Sampling:* A wide variety of Asian-inspired noodle dishes for lunch and dinner, plus party trays and local-style favorites like teriyaki chicken, beef curry, miso and wonton soup, and tempura. Choose from fried noodles, crispy noodles, chow fun, *udon* or ramen with chicken, beef, shrimp, *char siu*, veggies or tofu.

Moderate-priced Dining

★ Cafe Pesto *(Italian/Hawai'i-Pacific Regional Cuisine)*
308 Kamehameha Avenue, in the S. Hata Building, downtown Hilo; 808-969-6640; www.cafepesto.com.

Hours: Sunday through Thursday 11 a.m. to 9 p.m.; Friday and Saturday 11 a.m. to 10 p.m. *Sampling:* The menu emphasizes Asian–Pacific Rim cuisine, with a variety of creative pastas, appetizers, salads and sandwiches and the house special wood-fired pizzas scented with native *ohia* and guava hardwoods with a variety of creative toppings and ingredients, like eggplant pizza and chile-grill pizza. Interesting regional dishes include grilled beef filet and jumbo shrimp, wok-fired shrimp and scallops, mango-glazed chicken and house special tenderloin with shrimp tempura. Seasonal fresh island fish such as ahi, *opakapaka, ono* and mahimahi are served in a variety of preparations. A nice variety of pastas, risottos and calzones round out the menu. *Comments:* With locations in Hilo and Kawaihae, Cafe Pesto has earned acclaim for good quality fresh food and service on both sides of the island. There is bright contemporary décor in the old-fashioned high-ceiling room with open kitchen area. They have a great kids' menu.

Coconut Grill *(Hawai'i Local Style)*
136 Banyan Way, Hilo; 808-961-3330.
  Hours: 11 a.m. to 3:30 p.m. and 4 to 9 p.m. *Sampling:* From its lobby level setting in the old Hilo Seaside Hotel, Coconut Grill serves three meals a day with breakfast specials starting at $5. Lunch and dinner items start at $8, featuring local and Japanese-style dishes, sandwiches, burgers and yummy desserts like their huge mud pie. Great salad bar. *Comments:* Good location and nice "retro-tropical" atmosphere on the Ice Pond at Reed's Bay.

Henri's On Kapiolani *(Steaks)*
139 Kapiolani Street, Hilo; 808-961-9272.
  Hours: Monday through Saturday 5 to 7:30 p.m. Call before going. *Sampling:* The menu offers two excellent steaks and sometimes prime rib (if enough customers have called in to request it) in a simple, out-of-the-way dining room drawn from another era. Reservations a must; no credit cards. *Comments:* A 25-year local legend, Henri's is a bit of a mystery, not always open, not easy to find, but well worth exploring for a unique dinner experience.

Island Cantina *(Mexican)*
110 Kalakaua Street, Hilo; 808-969-7009.
  Hours: Lunch and dinner 11 a.m. to 9 p.m. *Sampling:* Authentic Mexican and Southwest cuisine served with live music in a nice location "on the park" in downtown Hilo town. Everything here is homemade, including sauces, soups and salad dressings. A recent menu featured tequila lime shrimp, notable chiles rellenos, blackened steak, a sizzling fajita platter and an interesting dessert called "Naughty Hula Cheesecake."

★ **Island Naturals Market and Deli** *(Organic/Health Foods)*
303 Maka'ala Street, Waiakea Center, Hilo; 808-935-5533.
  Hours: Monday through Saturday 8:30 a.m. to 8 p.m., Sunday 9 a.m. to 7p.m. *Sampling:* Large, well-run health food store, organic grocer and deli with good vegetarian fare, frequently voted among the best by local reader polls. Also sells food by the pound. *Comments:* A busy place, worth seeking out.

Nani Mau Garden Restaurant *(American/International/Hawai'i Local Style)*
421 Makalika Street, just south of town off Volcano Highway, Hilo; 808-959-3500.
  Hours: Lunch daily 10:30 a.m. to 1:30 p.m. *Sampling:* Daily buffet luncheon features quality local-style specials served in the Orchid Pavilion. *Comments:* This eatery is part of Nani Mau Gardens, a lush collection of tropical, botanical and flower gardens just outside of Hilo town.

★ Nihon Cultural Center (Japanese)
123 Lihiwai Street, just opposite the Liliuokalani Gardens and Banyan Drive hotels, Hilo; 808-969-1133.

Hours: Lunch 11 a.m. to 1:30 p.m., dinner 5 p.m. to 8 p.m. Closed Sunday. *Sampling:* The menu offers a full range of Japanese cuisine including beef, pork, chicken, fish and seafood, plus noodle dishes and our favorite, red miso soup. Nihon has won our friend Keoki's stamp of approval for its sushi bar, and he's tried almost every one on the menu so that's something special. The sushi chef's special include *poke* roll, mac nut roll and *lomi* salmon roll, but there are many more to choose from (sushi bar closed on Tuesday). *Comments:* The attractive building is Japanese-style architecture, beautifully set overlooking Hilo Bay. The interiors are decorated with elegant Japanese art; diners are greeted with traditional Japanese music and waitresses are costumed in *hapi* coats. Good Japanese food in authentic surroundings with gracious service.

★ Pescatore (Italian)
On the corner of Keawe and Haili streets, downtown Hilo; 808-969-9090.

Hours: Breakfast 7 to 11 a.m., lunch 11 a.m. to 2 p.m., dinner 5:30 to 9 p.m. *Sampling:* The restaurant features genuine Italian cuisine. Tasty soups, salads and appetizers complement creative seafood, chicken, veal, vegetarian and pasta dishes. Melt-in-your-mouth bread and scrumptious desserts begin and end a satisfying lunch or dinner. *Comments:* Warm woodwork decor, great food and pleasant service make this small eatery a real dining-out discovery. Reservations suggested.

Queen's Court (American/Hawai'i Local Style/International)
Hilo Hawaiian Hotel, 71 Banyan Drive, Hilo; 808-935-9361.

Hours: Monday through Saturday for lunch 11:15 a.m. to 1:15 p.m., dinner 5:30 p.m. to 9 p.m.; Sunday 10:30 a.m. to 1:30 p.m. *Sampling:* The weekly à la carte menu features varied Continental, American and local-style items. Weekend buffets on Friday, Saturday and Sunday feature seafood and Hawaiian cuisine and are very popular with local folks and visitors. *Comments:* This is one of Hilo's nicest dining rooms with lovely views of Hilo Bay and Coconut Island. Live musical entertainment with dinner. Reservations recommended, particularly on busy weekends, when it tends to get crowded.

Restaurant Miwa (Japanese)
Hilo Shopping Center, Kekuanaoa and Kilauea avenues, Hilo; 808-961-4454.

Hours: Lunch 11 a.m. to 2 p.m., dinner 5 to 10 p.m. *Sampling:* They offer a menu of varied Japanese/American cuisine. Items include sushi, teriyaki chicken and steak, island fish, *udon* noodles, etc. *Comments:* Reservations suggested.

★ *Seaside Restaurant* (Seafood)

1790 Kalanianaole Street, Keaukaha area of Hilo; 808-935-8825;
www.seasiderestaurant.com.

Hours: Tuesday, Wednesday, Thursday and Sunday 5 to 8:30 p.m.
Friday and Saturday until 9 p.m. Closed Monday. *Sampling:* Local
mullet, rainbow trout, *aholehole*, *menpachi*, tilapia and other fresh
fish selections make up the menu in a variety of creative
preparations. They also have fresh imported salmon,
steak, chicken and more. Food presentation is beautiful, service is genuine and the desserts are to die for.
Now offering a sushi bar 5 to 9 p.m. Wednesday, Friday, Saturday and Sunday. *Comments:* This place is
something special. One of the most unique restaurants
islandwide, the Seaside has been operated by the Naka-
gawa family for over 70 years and is a Hilo institution. It's located in
the middle of Keaukaha's fish ponds area, where seafood can't get
any fresher; they raise their own in the surrounding ponds. Reservations accepted for groups of four or more only, and it does get
crowded because this is a great place for families and groups. Great
food and warm, friendly local-style service have made this is one of
the Big Island's best for many years.

Ting Hao Naniloa Restaurant (Chinese)

Hawai'i Naniloa Hotel lower lobby, 97 Banyan Drive, Hilo; 808-935-8888.

Hours: Lunch 11 a.m. to 2 p.m., dinner 5 p.m. to 9 p.m. Closed
Tuesday. *Sampling:* The menu features Mandarin cuisine, exotic spicy
Szechuan and Hunan specialties, non-spicy gourmet fare from Tai-
wan, Beijing and other regions of China. Selections include soups,
appetizers, pork, beef, chicken, duck, seafood and vegetarian dishes
plus noodles, fried rice, spring rolls and potstickers. Seafood specials
include scallops and veggies, oyster with tofu, lobster with black bean
sauce and many more. *Comments:* This small dining room has hotel
courtyard and Hilo Bay views, and offers standard Chinese cooking.

Uncle Billy's (Seafood)

Uncle Billy's Hilo Bay Hotel, 87 Banyan Drive, Hilo; 808-935-0861.

Hours: Breakfast 7 to 10 a.m., dinner 5:30 to 9 p.m. Sunday
brunch 7 to 11:30 a.m. *Sampling:* An extensive menu features steak
and fresh island seafood. *Comments:* The attraction here is casual dining in a Polynesian atmosphere with island decor. Nightly Hawaiian
hula show and Hawaiian dinner music 6:15 to 9 p.m.

Uncle Mikey's (Hawai'i Local Style/Nightclub)

400 Hualani Street, Hilo, 808-961-9187; www.unclemikeysnightclub.com.

Hours: Monday through Friday 6 a.m. to 2 p.m. for breakfast and
lunch buffets, after-hours dancing and live entertainment until late.

Sampling: Uncle Mikey's seems to have everything: carry-out bakery breads and pastries, extensive Hawaiian, Japanese, Chinese and American buffets, the latest trendy cocktails, *pupus,* function spaces for private parties, live local entertainment and more. The highlight is a rather amazing dance club with something different almost every night, from line dancing to Hawaiian music, oldies night and select concerts. *Comments:* The club has a ten-foot TV screen nine feet above the dance floor, eight 32-inch TVs, sonar lighting, laser lighting and intelligent lighting that moves to the beat of the music, which is played on DVD-MTV video. Probably not a family dining venue, but a Hilo attraction regardless, especially for young singles.

Expensive-priced Dining

★ *Harrington's (American/Hawai'i-Pacific Regional Cuisine)*
135 Kalanianaole Avenue, Hilo; 808-961-4966.

Hours: Monday through Sunday 11 a.m. to 3 p.m., dinner 5:30 to 9:30 p.m. *Sampling:* Lunch features generous salads, a selection of interesting sandwiches including a vegetable pita and spicy Cajun shrimp pita and "Mexi-Shimi," seared ahi with a wasabi salsa in a tortilla wrap. The dinner menu highlights fresh island fish and seafood in interesting preparations such as escargot *en casserole,* seafood Caesar salad, Thai scampi and seafood brochette or linguine. Also steak, prime rib, duck and other specials. Desserts are simply rich and wonderful, like their house bread pudding with butter rum cream sauce. *Comments:* Located right on the water, opposite Banyan Drive. The restaurant features relaxed dining in a great, scenic location, with lots of windows open to the "ice pond" and Reed's Bay. Reservations suggested.

Hilo Bay Cafe (Hawai'i Regional Cuisine)
315 Maka'ala Street, Hilo; 808-935-4939.

Hours: Monday through Saturday 11 a.m. to 2 p.m. for lunch, 2 to 5 p.m. for light lunch, open daily for dinner 5 to 9 p.m. *Sampling:* An award-winning, increasingly popular restaurant, rapidly gaining ground as one of the island's best, Hilo Bay Cafe offers an eclectic mix of cuisine created with emphasis on fresh organic ingredients. Very contemporary, "vegetarian friendly," and romantic-to-sexy in style. The dinner menu focuses on local fish and seafood with a somewhat Asian/Pacific Rim flair, along with good steaks, pastas and a variety of chicken dishes. The creative *pupus* include an interesting coconut-tofu kebab and a "cheese course" with various imported or local cheese selections and fresh fruits. *Comments:* In keeping with their commitment to healthy foods, they've done the right thing by offering Guinness on tap.

★ *Restaurant Kaikodo* *(Japanese)*
60 Kiawe Street, Hilo; 808-961-2558; www.restaurantkaikodo.com.
  Hours: Monday through Saturday for lunch 11 a.m. to 2:30 p.m., dinner 5 to 9 p.m.; Sunday for brunch 10:30 a.m. to 2 p.m., dinner 5 p.m. to 9 p.m. *Sampling:* Try the Kumamoto oysters on the half shell with a pineapple-ginger granita to start. Enjoy creative sushi, sashimi or *poke.* Indulge in Kaikodo bouillabaisse, cedar-plank salmon, a "New Wave" duck *laulau* flavored with Chinese five spice or grilled rib-eye with mango-mustard sauce. *Comments:* This restaurant, located in the historic Toyama building (constructed by the Masonic Order in 1908), continues to gain momentum as one of traditional old Hilo's most exciting gourmet restaurants. A high-end contemporary Japanese and "East meets West" fusion-style cuisine is presented in several elegant private dining rooms tastefully decorated with Chinese and Japanese antiques and artworks. The elegant bar in the lounge was imported in its entirety from England. Already an award-winner with a growing popular following, Restaurant Kaikodo is here to stay.

Sandalwood Room *(American/Continental-International)*
Hawai'i Naniloa Hotel, 93 Banyan Drive, Hilo; 808-969-3333.
  Hours: Breakfast 6:30 to 10 a.m., lunch 11 a.m. to 1:30 p.m., dinner 5:30 to 9 p.m. *Sampling:* The menu features American and Continental selections. Specialties include seafood, steak, local favorites and a Hawaiian plate. *Comments:* Dining is in a tropical garden setting overlooking Hilo Bay. Reservations suggested for dinner.

Puna District

Inexpensive-priced Dining

AK Pizza *(Pizza)*
15-2537 Pahoa Village Road; 808-965-9395.
  Hours: Monday through Thursday 10 a.m. to 9 p.m., until 10 p.m. on Friday and Saturday. *Sampling:* Small to extra-large pizzas, subs, calzones and salads. *Comments:* Free delivery within five miles of Pahoa town.

Aloha Outpost *(Internet Cafe)*
15-2950 Pahoa Village Road; 808-965-8333; www.alohaaoutpost.com.
  Hours: 6 a.m. to 8 p.m. *Sampling:* Only two years old and quickly growing, Aloha Outpost is an interesting place for a lot of reasons. Owner-operator LaMont Carroll offers 12 PCs running Windows XP and two Macs on high-speed Roadrunner, and soon-to-come five TVs for Xbox and Playstation gaming 6 to 8 p.m. Their "non-

virtual" menu features with seven different varieties of Puna (yes, Puna) coffees, O'Keefe artisan breads, Tropical Dreams ice creams and a full menu of good things to eat including panini grilled sandwiches, 20 percent vegetarian specialties, shakes, malts, smoothies and "soul food"—fried chicken, ribs, and Carroll's mom's homemade peach cobbler, sweet potato and rhubarb pies. Just relocated to a new and larger location, the Outpost will soon offer live music and poetry readings in the evenings, daily *LA Times*, *New York Times*, *San Francisco Chronicle* and Honolulu newspaper. Stop by if you're in Pahoa.

Black Rock Cafe *(American)*
Pahoa Village Center, 15-2870 Main Government Road, Pahoa; 808-965-1177.

Hours: 7 a.m. to 9:30 p.m. *Sampling:* This family-style cafe has a basically American menu, varied by several different cuisines and creative dishes. They feature a bunch of burgers and sandwiches plus several hot and cold submarine sandwiches. There are mixed appetizers like mozzarella sticks, cheddar cheese poppers, popcorn chicken, Santa Fe chicken egg roll and fresh salads. Entrees include teriyaki steak, New York strip, filet mignon, *kalbi* ribs, chicken *katsu*, seafood platters, fresh catch, an oriental combo platter, baby back pork ribs, *kiawe*-smoked beef ribs, and several pasta dishes plus pizza.

★ Charley's Bar & Grill *(American)*
Kea'au Town Center, Kea'au; 808-966-7589.

Hours: Sunday through Thursday 11 a.m. to 11 p.m.; Friday and Saturday 11 a.m. to 1 a.m. *Sampling:* The menu is mostly American with a few local-style favorites for variety. Hot and cold sandwiches, burgers, shrimp scampi, pasta, pizza, fajitas, New York steak, soups and salads. *Comments:* This pleasant family eatery is located in a busy small-town shopping center. It combines a bar and grill operation with inside or outdoor sidewalk seating. Nice clean atmosphere, pleasant service, generally good food. All kinds of great live entertainment most nights.

Hiro's Snack Shop *(Sandwiches/Snacks)*
Kea'au Town Center, Kea'au; 808-966-6313.

Hours: Monday through Saturday 6 a.m. to 5 p.m.; Sunday 7 a.m. to 2 p.m. *Sampling:* This small lunch counter operation features varied local favorites including plate-lunch choices like chicken *katsu*, Korean chicken, teri beef and chicken, fish and chips, fried ahi, ahi tempura, mixed plates, *loco moco*, sandwiches, burgers and bentos plus several daily specials.

Kea'au Chop Suey House *(Chinese)*
Kea'au Town Center, Kea'au; 808-966-7573.

Hours: Monday through Saturday 9 a.m. to 7:30 p.m.; closed Sunday. *Sampling:* This Chinese restaurant specializes in Cantonese cuisine and the menu features 60 items. Among the selections are saimin noodles, seaweed soup, beef chow mein, Mongolian beef, lemon chicken, roast duck, hot and spicy chicken, egg foo yong, *mu shu* pork, pork chop suey, and a variety of appetizers. *Comments:* Take-out available.

Koa Shop Kaffee Restaurant *(Hawai'i Local Style)*
Just past the 12-mile marker, Mountain View; 808-968-1129.

Hours: Breakfast 7 a.m. to 9:45 a.m., lunch 10 a.m. to 4:30 p.m., dinner 4:30 p.m. to 7:30 p.m. Closed Tuesday. *Sampling:* Generous breakfasts, plate lunches, burgers and daily specials like teriyaki beef, mahimahi, shrimp, *kalbi* and *katsu. Comments:* Next door is Dan De Luz's Woods, with an amazing selection of carvings and gift items from Hawaiian and exotic woods.

★ Lava Rock Cafe *(American)*
Old Volcano Road, behind Kilauea General Store, Volcano Village; 808-967-8526.

Hours: Sunday 7:30 a.m. to 4 p.m.; Monday 7:30 a.m. to 5 p.m.; Tuesday through Saturday 7:30 a.m. to 9 p.m. *Sampling:* The menu is varied, featuring American breakfast dishes, plate lunches like chili, teriyaki beef and chicken, grilled mahimahi, chow fun noodles, and "Stir-Crazy" stir-fry beef, chicken or veggies. There are also a bunch of burgers, varied sandwiches, fajitas, lasagna, soups and salads. For dinner, choose from steaks, shrimp, fresh catch and other house specialties. Prime Rib Special Saturday night after 6:30 p.m. *Comments:* This popular cafe opened in a renovated area at the back of the general store, and is bright and attractive with interesting woodwork throughout, and table or booth seating. Live local music several nights a week.

Luquin's Mexican Restaurant *(Mexican)*
Highway 130, on the main street in Pahoa; 808-965-9990.

Hours: 7 a.m. to 9 p.m. *Sampling:* The menu features a variety of Mexican dishes like hard or soft tacos, a long list of burritos including half a dozen vegetarian options and a *keiki*-size, enchiladas, quesadillas and five kinds of nachos, *botanas* (appetizers), soups, salads and American specialties such as burgers and sandwiches. The bar serves tropical fruit margaritas by the pitcher, small or large. *Comments:* This place will appeal to the adventurous diner who likes Mexican food. The decor is Mexican and tempers the rough exterior of the old wooden building in which it's located. It's also home to Pahoa Orchid Inn, the only hotel in Pahoa.

Pahoa Chop Suey House (Chinese)
Just off the main highway, across from the 7-11 store, in Pahoa; 808-965-9533.

Hours: 10 a.m. to 8 p.m. *Sampling:* This Chinese eatery offers Cantonese-style cuisine. The full menu features seafood, pork, beef, chicken and duck dishes, fried rice, cake noodle and a variety of chop suey. *Comments:* Set dinners for two to four people are also available.

Moderate-priced Dining

The Dining Lanai at Kalani Oceanside Retreat (Health Food)
RR2 Box 4500, Pahoa, HI 96778, at Ocean Highway, 137-Pahoa Beach Road; 800-800-6886; 808-965-7828; fax 808-965-0527; e-mail: reservations@kalani.com; www.kalani.com.

Hours: Breakfast 7:30 to 8:30 a.m., lunch noon to 1 p.m., dinner 6 to 7:30 p.m. *Sampling:* The Dining Lanai serves three healthful meals a day, featuring "Kalani cuisine," focusing on fresh local ingredients, fish, seafood (sometimes chicken) with excellent choices for vegetarians and vegans, along with occasional ethnic feasts. Open to the public. Dinner reservations suggested.

★ Kilauea Lodge Restaurant (Continental-International)
Highway 11, Volcano Village; 808-967-7366; www.kilauealodge.com.

Hours: 5:30 to 9 p.m. *Sampling:* Kilauea Lodge doesn't have to be this good. Without a lot of competition, Chef Albert Jeyte tempts his guests with inspired cuisine that reflects his German heritage. The menu changes daily, but a recent sampling featured creative entrees like Kilauea pasta, chicken *milanese*, five-pepper steak, medallions of venison, lamb Provençal and seafood Mauna Kea. *Hasenpfeffer* and duck *a l'orange* are some of the house specials. A selection of fine desserts and international coffees complete the evening. *Comments:* This cozy dining room is part of the Kilauea Lodge Bed and Breakfast operation. Fine service in an attractive setting with a cheery dining room fireplace and relaxed country lodge atmosphere.

★ Paolo's Bistro (Italian)
333 Pahoa Road, along the old main street row of town buildings, Pahoa; 808-965-7033.

Hours: Tuesday through Sunday 5:30 to 9 p.m. *Sampling:* The dinner menu changes daily and features authentic Italian-Tuscan cuisine. Start with seared ahi *alla mediterrania* or gnocchi, then enjoy a selection of pastas such as fresh ravioli *bandiero*, *puttanesca* with black olives, anchovies and capers, pesto or seafood *capellini*, the house special *cioppino* or Paolo's "speciale del giorno." There is also espresso, cappuccino, special coffees and desserts (Paolo makes tiramisu and you gotta love him for that). *Comments:* This small restaurant has just a dozen tables and bright simple decor, but dining here is an experience worth tasting.

★ **Thai Thai Restaurant** *(Thai)*
19-4084 Old Volcano Road, Volcano Village; 808-967-7969; e-mail: value@aloha.net.

Hours: 5 p.m. to 9 p.m. *Sampling:* The menu has appetizers like pad Thai rice noodles, Thai spring rolls, deep-fried tofu and chicken satay. Soups include *tom yum* spicy sour soup, *tom kha* soup with coconut milk and Thai herbs, noodle soup and rice soup. Traditional curries include red, green, yellow, *penang* and *musaman*, all with choice of shrimp, chicken, beef or pork and served either hot, medium or mild. There are also stir-fry dishes like ong choy, Chinese broccoli, mixed veggies, shrimp with garlic and pepper, cashew chicken, and chicken with ginger. Salads include papaya salad, long rice salad, and pork, beef or chicken with lemongrass. *Comments:* This restaurant is in the middle of old Volcano Village and has a clean, bright, cheery appearance with contemporary decor and Thai artwork as decorative touches.

Ka'u District

Inexpensive-priced Dining

Adriana's Mexican Food *(Mexican)*
95-5586 Highway 11, Na'alehu; 808-936-8553.

Hours: Monday through Friday 10 a.m. to 5 p.m.; open a little later on Friday. *Sampling:* Tamales, burritos, tacos and quesadillas as well as awesome chiles rellenos, all made by Juanita. *Comments:* The chiles rellenos are worth driving down for.

Desert Rose *(Bakery/American/Sandwiches/Snacks)*
Pohue Plaza, Ocean View; 808-939-7673.

Hours: 7 a.m. to 8 p.m. *Sampling:* A bakery and restaurant in one, Desert Rose says "life is short, eat dessert first." Menu offerings include a variety of sandwiches on homemade breads, fresh-baked pastries and cookies daily, good burgers and plate-lunch specialties with made-from-scratch soups, salsas and salad dressings. For dinner, select from American family-style chicken, beef and fresh fish entrees, along with the full lunch menu. Fridays are prime rib nights. Beer and wine are served.

Hana Hou *(American)*
Across the street from the Na'alehu Shopping Center in the middle of the "southernmost community in the USA"; 808-929-9717.

Hours: Monday through Wednesday 8 a.m. to 3 p.m., Thursday through Sunday 8 a.m. to 8 p.m. *Sampling:* This country coffee shop serves up American-style food including steaks, seafood, fresh island fish, chicken and salads. Notable homemade pies and other desserts.

★ Na'alehu Fruit Stand *(Sandwiches/Snacks)*
Main Street, Highway 11, Na'alehu town; 808-929-9009.

Hours: Monday through Saturday 9 a.m. to 6 p.m., Sunday 9 a.m. to 5 p.m. *Sampling:* This snack shop features a variety of sandwiches, pizza, fresh-baked pastries, macadamia nut treats, and fresh-squeezed juices.

Ocean View Pizzaria *(Italian/Pizza)*
Ocean View Town Center, Highway 11, Hawaiian Ocean View Estates, Ocean View; 808-929-9677.

Hours: Sunday through Thursday 11 a.m. to 7 p.m.; Friday and Saturday until 8 p.m. *Sampling:* This small eatery features pizza, pizza sandwiches, sub sandwiches, hot and cold mixed sandwiches, soups, salads, fresh-baked goods and more.

Shaka's *(American)*
Mile marker 64 off Highway 11, Na'alehu; 808-929-7404; www.shakarestaurant.com.

Hours: 10 a.m. to 8 p.m. *Sampling:* Generous breakfasts, burgers, sandwiches and plate lunches. Steaks, chicken, pork chops, fresh catch, big salads and a great *keiki* dinner menu.

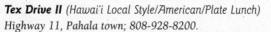

Tex Drive II *(Hawai'i Local Style/American/Plate Lunch)*
Highway 11, Pahala town; 808-928-8200.

Hours: Monday though Saturday 7 a.m. to 8 p.m., Sunday 7 a.m. to 6 p.m. *Sampling:* A sequel to the longstanding favorite in Honoka'a, Tex's boasts a menu of mostly local-style dishes, plate lunches and snacks, but their burgers are good and there's a variety of other foods to choose from. If nothing else, Tex's is a must-stop for their fresh hot Portuguese *malasadas.*

★ Volcano Country Club Restaurant *(Hawai'i Local Style/American)*
Just off Highway 11 on Pi'i Mauna Road, Volcano Country Club Golf Course, at the 30-mile marker from Hilo, across from Kilauea Military Camp, Hawai'i Volcanoes National Park; 808-967-8228; www.volcanogolf andrestaurant.com.

Hours: Monday through Friday 8 a.m. to 3 p.m.; Saturday and Sunday 7 a.m. to 3 p.m. *Sampling:* The menu features a variety of sandwiches, burgers and local-style favorites like saimin, chili and rice, stir-fry veggies, Hawaiian stew, *loco moco,* chow mein, *kalua* pork, oxtail soup (only on Sundays), teri beef and chicken, garlic chicken, and Portuguese bean soup. *Comments:* This rustic dining room is located in the golf course clubhouse. Nice pleasant atmosphere, friendly service and generally good food.

Moderate-priced Dining

★ *Ka Ohelo Room* *(Continental-International)*
Volcano House Hotel, Hawai'i Volcanoes National Park; 808-967-7321.

Hours: Breakfast 7 a.m. to 10:30 a.m., lunch 11 a.m. to 2 p.m., dinner 5:30 to 9 p.m. *Sampling:* The menu features prime rib, steaks, Cornish hen, pork medallions, fresh island fish, several types of pasta and a variety of soups, salads and appetizers. The daily buffet lunch is popular with visitors and features a variety of hot entrees, salads and more. *Comments:* The dining room overlooks majestic Kilauea Caldera and its steaming vents. The rustic country lodge atmosphere makes for a nice ambiance, and dining on the edge of the volcano adds a special charm to the generally good cuisine and pleasant service.

Lu'aus

Many of the Kona and Kohala hotels present a weekly Lu'au for their guests, which is open to the public. Prices vary and commonly include a buffet dinner and hula performance; alcoholic beverages, tax and gratuity are additional. *Keiki* prices are usually available. The buffet will feature traditional lu'au food such as poi (the Hawaiian staple made of taro root), *lomi* salmon (fresh fish salad with diced tomato and green onion), pork roasted in an underground *imu* (oven) and *laulau* (fish and beef steamed in spinach-like taro leaf), along with more familiar foods like steak, chicken, fresh catch, a variety of salads and desserts. After dinner, sit back and enjoy the show. The performances vary; you may see ancient (*kahiko*) and modern (*auwana*) hula, or colorful and energetic dances from New Zealand, Fiji and Samoa, along with the hip-rattling rhythm of Tahiti, or a breathtaking fire dancer. Almost always, the audience is invited to participate, and if you don't actually send your spouse up onstage, you at least find yourself on your feet, swaying and waving to the Hukilau Song.

The traditional lu'au was an ancient celebratory feast, served at *makahiki* (festivities to honor Lono at the beginning of the year) and other special occasions. The menu was likely *imu*-roasted pig, poi, raw fish or *tako* (squid), *opihi* (limpets), *a'ama* crab (small spidery crabs served raw or alive), seaweed, sweet potatoes and some bananas. There was no teriyaki chicken, macaroni salad or dessert table (or mai tais). We don't advocate going back to that kind of a menu, but we do encourage visitors to get out into the community, eat what the local people eat, and attend a hula performance that

NIGHTCLUB/LOUNGE/BAR ENTERTAINMENT

Hawaiian music, in case you haven't heard, is finally entering the spotlight, thanks to the 2005 Grammy Awards, which included the genre for the first time. If you get a chance to hear local entertainers, you'll see why. Consult visitor publications and newspapers to see what entertainers or groups are currently playing what clubs; bi-weekly *Hawai'i Island Journal*'s "On the Town" and "Island Calendar" sections do an exceptional job keeping up with local concerts and entertainment. Except for the Kailua-Kona area and a few clubs in Hilo town, the Big Island is not real big on nightlife. It's a quiet place that appreciates things like the sun going down and the sound of surf on the rocks; most restaurants close early (compared to other tourist destinations). But you can find great bars with dancefloors and DJs spinning hip-hop, pop and disco, or live bands rocking the house. Contemporary local bands run the whole musical spectrum, from country-western, rap, the reggae fusion called "Jawaiian," pop, rock-and-roll to traditional steel guitar and ukulele. More than anything else, island style dominates the evening scene. Almost every hotel lounge features the sweet, laid-back guitar and special energy of local singers, and sometimes hula dancers. These performers are consistently excellent.

KONA DISTRICT Billfish Bar (King Kamehameha's Kona Beach Hotel); Durty Jake's (especially if Joe Conti's playing stick guitar); Evie's Organic Cafe; Hard Rock Cafe; Huggo's on the Rocks (next to Royal Kona Resort); Jackie Ray's Ohana Grill; Kalani Kai Bar (Ohana Keauhou Beach Resort); Kona Brewing Co.; Manta

showcases the artistry and history of the dance culture, not its mylar, commercialized version.

All that being said, the various places that offer lu'au are fun and excellent photo-ops. For authenticity of atmosphere, we suggest Kona Village. Go early for a property tour and a chance to see the whole pig unearthed from the *imu*. Ladies receive a *lei po'o*, head lei, and the menu includes Hawaiian choices along with more familiar options. A colorful hula show follows dinner.

For value, try Royal Kona Resort, on Ali'i Drive in Kona town. There are crafters including coconut tree-climbers, demonstrating their handiwork prior to dinner, artfully set along the oceanfront. There is a good buffet selection of lu'au and familiar food, and a pro-

Ray Bar & Grill (Sheraton Keauhou); Lulu's; Michaelangelo's; Mixx Bistro (Sunday afternoon jazz in the King Kamehameha Mall by Kona Wine Market); Paradise Lounge (above Beachcomber's); Peaberry & Galette (weekend, music and art shows in the Keauhou Shopping Center); Rocky's (Sunday afternoon jazz, Keauhou Shopping Center); Rooster's (Thursday through Saturday jazz); Verandah Lounge (Ohana Keauhou Beach Resort); Windjammer Lounge (Royal Kona Resort). And don't miss "Bosco the Amazing One Man Band" performing free Wednesday through Sunday evenings in the Kona Inn Shopping Village.

SOUTH KOHALA DISTRICT Anthony's Restaurant & Beat Club (Waikoloa Highlands Center); Big Island Steak House (Kings' Shops, Waikoloa Resort); Blue Dolphin Restaurant in Kawaihae; Clipper Lounge (Waikoloa Beach Marriott, An Outrigger Resort); Copper Bar (Mauna Kea Beach Hotel); Honu Bar–Atrium (Mauna Lani Bay Hotel sunset music and hula by the Lim Family); Malolo Lounge (Hilton Waikoloa Village); Nalu's Bar (Waikoloa Beach Marriott, An Outrigger Resort); Reef Lounge (Hapuna Beach Prince Hotel); The Polo Bar and Paniolo Lounge (Fairmont Orchid Hawai'i)

NORTH KOHALA DISTRICT Bamboo in Hawi town

HILO Cafe Pesto (Sunday afternoon jazz); Crown Room (Hawai'i Naniloa Hotel); Kope Kope; Uncle Billy's (Hilo Bay Hotel); Island Cantina, Wai'oli Lounge (Hilo Hawaiian Hotel). For a real experience, visit Uncle Mikey's for a serious dance club and occasional drop-in for local entertainers to *kani ka pila* (jam); www.unclemikeysnightclub.com.

PUNA DISTRICT Charley's Bar & Grill; Lava Rock Cafe; Lava Lounge (Kilauea Military Camp)

fessional hula show by Tihati Productions, featuring dance and music from various Polynesian islands and a chance to get your picture taken with a bevy of hula girls or shirtless men in *malo*, loincloth.

For hula, consider Mauna Kea Beach Hotel's lu'au. The after-dinner entertainment is presented by the skilled dancers of Halau Hula Na Lei o Kaholoku, prestigious Merrie Monarch winners in 2004–2005. The food is good and the oceanside setting is unbeatable.

Whichever you choose—enjoy! And remember that prices are subject to change.

Hilton Waikoloa Village
425 Waikoloa Beach Drive, Kohala Coast; 808-886-1234 ext. 54; www.hiltonwaikokoavillage.com.

The "Legends of the Pacific" Luʻau dinner and hula show takes place at Kamehameha Court on Fridays only at 6 p.m. The bountiful Luʻau buffet, presented in the grand Hilton style, includes traditional foods such as roast pork, poi, island *poke*, sushi, *lomi* salmon, chicken *laulau*, fish, crab, and fresh tropical fruits. More familiar entrees, steamed mahimahi, Parker Ranch ribs, and roasted mango chicken are offered, along with a good selection of fresh salads and desserts like coconut and strawberry *haupia* and warm banana-pineapple cobbler that appeal to the pickiest of eaters and guarantee a full *opu* (tummy). Following dinner is a captivating show of Pacific Rim songs and dances that is one of the most exciting and colorful productions on the Kohala Coast. Reservations required. $72 adults, $36 children 5-12.

King Kamehameha's Kona Beach Hotel

75-5660 Palani Road, Kailua-Kona; 808-329-2911; luʻau reservations 808-326-4969; www.konabeachhotel.com.

The Island Breeze Luʻau is put on each Sunday, Tuesday, Wednesday and Thursday evening from 5:30 p.m. to 8:30 p.m. (You can watch the pig being placed in the *imu* at 10:15 a.m. on luʻau days.) The luʻau begins with the arrival of torch bearers via canoe from Ahuena Heiau, King Kamehameha's temple, fronting Kamaka-honu Beach and the hotel grounds. Conch shells are sounded as the torch bearers land and light the pathway to the luʻau grounds. Visitors can then watch the ceremonial removal of the roast pig from the *imu*, followed by a feast of authentic Hawaiian foods and specialties from Oceania and a Polynesian performance of song and dance, including a Samoan fire-knife dance. Reservations required; aloha attire preferred. $54 adults, $21 children 6-12, free for kids under 5.

The luʻau is definitely not a low-calorie dining option. So eat and enjoy, but just in case you are interested, here is the breakdown! *Kalua* pig 1/2 cup, 150 calories; *lomi lomi* salmon 1/2 cup, 87 calories; poi 1 cup, 161 calories (but who could eat that much!); fried rice 1 cup, 200 calories; fish (depending on type served) 150-250 calories; chicken long rice 283 calories; *haupia* 128 calories; coconut cake 200-350 calories; mai tai 302 calories; pina colada 252 calories; fruit punch 140 calories; blue Hawaiʻi 260 calories; chi chi 190 calories.

★ Kona Village Resort

Queen Kaʻahumanu Highway, six miles north of Kona Airport at Kaupulehu; 808-325-5555.

The Kona Village Resort, with its individual thatched *hale* (houses) in the style of the South Seas, presents its *ahaʻaina* (feast) with an element of authenticity others don't quite match. It has something to do with the magical beachside environment and the faraway sense of place that only Kona Village still provides. Reservations are required to enter the property, and we suggest you arrive by 5:15 p.m. to enjoy a personable tour of this fascinating resort. Ladies are welcomed with fragrant *lei po'o* (head lei) and at 5:30 p.m. the roast pig is removed from its *imu* with some ceremony, followed by cocktails and the lu'au feast. The endless buffet of Hawaiian and Polynesian foods is probably the most nearly authentic lu'au spread on the Big Island (unless you happen to be invited to join someone's family). Feel free to ask your servers' questions about the food or the lu'au; most are very friendly and open to conversation (which could have something to do with them being shirtless, at least the males). An exciting performance of Polynesian chant, song and dance is a stirring end to a memorable evening. Reservations are required; aloha attire preferred. Fridays only, 5:15 p.m. tour, 6:30 p.m. *imu* ceremony. Rates: $84.

Mauna Kea Beach Hotel
62-100 Mauna Kea Beach Drive, Kohala Coast; 808-882-5810.

Mauna Kea Beach Hotel began its Lu'au tradition in the 1960s, when the hotel was new and the coast between it and Kona Village was empty. As a special event for *Time* magazine, the general manager leveled a fancy picnic area along the lava-rock oceanfront, hired the best dancers and musicians on the island, and served up an elaborate spread of the exotic Lu'au food along with the executive chef's more Continental cuisine. Although *Time* never ran the story, that energy began a decades-long tradition which families return to enjoy year after year. Today's lu'au is just as delicious, the setting every bit as romantic. The hula performance is choreographed by Nani Lim Yap, whose hula *halau* (troupe) Na Lei O Kaholoku has won distinguished honors at the prestigious annual Merrie Monarch Festival (the world's best). Reservations required; aloha attire preferred. Tuesdays only. $79 adults, $38 children ages 5-12.

Royal Kona Resort
Ali'i Drive, Kailua-Kona; 808-329-3111; 800-624-7771 75-5852; www.ro yalkona.com.

The "Lava—Legends & Legacies Lu'au" is presented by Tihati Productions four nights weekly in a dramatic, oceanside setting at Royal Kona Resort. The lu'au includes an aloha shell *lei* greeting, traditional opening of the *imu* and removal of the roast pig, torchlighting to the sound of the *pu* (conch shell horn), and *pahu* drum. The lavish buffet with authentic Hawaiian foods includes *imu kalua* pork, turkey, chicken, beef and island fish, poi, Hawaiian sweet potatoes, *lomi* salmon, fried rice, large salad bar, dessert selections. Full open bar with mai tais is included. An elaborate Polynesian revue follows

DINNER WITH A TWIST

For a completely different Hawai'i dinner experience, visit **Kahua Ranch**, which offers weekly *paniolo* (cowboy) barbecues on the grounds of their 8,500-acre working ranch in upcountry Kohala. Transportation is provided from the Kohala Coast up to 3,200 feet above sea level, where the sunset views are spectacular. After a brief welcome reception and introduction to the ranch, enjoy a hearty chuckwagon barbecue featuring Kahua Ranch meats and produce from the Big Island farming community (including Big Island Mac Pie). Then the fun begins. In addition to dance music from island entertainers, you'll have a chance to practice branding, try your hand at roping, horseshoes, pig-petting and other ranch games, have your photo taken with the animals, "talk story" and make s'mores around the campfire, then do a little star-gazing with the ranch's telescope. Evening at Kahua is available Tuesdays and one other day each week, subject to change. Reservations are required. Jeans, sweaters and closed shoes recommended for the cool evening weather. Rates start at $68 and the event is limited to 50 guests. P.O. Box 384598, Waikoloa, HI 96738; 808-987-2108, 808-883-8601; eveningatkahua.com.

Captain Beans' Dinner Cruise   A longstanding Kona tradition, this sunset dinner cruise aboard Capt. Bean's Polynesian-style double-hulled canoe "Tamure" departs Kailua Pier daily at around 5 p.m. (varies with sunset). Cruise along the famous Kona Coast to live island music and entertainment, all-you-can-eat island-style buffet, soft beverages and cash bar (welcome cocktail included in price). Rates: from Kailua-Keauhou hotels $55 adults, $33 children 4 to 11; from Waikoloa/Mauna Lani area $63 adults, $41 children 4 to 11; from Mauna Kea/Hapuna area $66 adults, $44 children. Aloha attire is preferred. Transportation included from select locations; inquire first. 73-4800 Kanalani Street, Suite 200, Kailua-Kona, HI 96740; 808-329-2955; www.robertshawaii.com.

dinner, with colorful performances of song and dance from the South Pacific Islands, including the Samoan fire-knife dance, fast-motion Tahitian and several styles of Hawaiian hula. Reservations are suggested; aloha attire preferred. Monday, Wednesday, Friday, Saturday. $62 adults, free for kids 5 and under.

Sheraton Keauhou Resort & Spa

78-125 Ehukai Street, Kailua-Kona, HI 96740; 808-930-4900; www.sheratonkeauhou.com.

"Origins" is the latest lu'au on the island, Mondays and Thursday nights beginning with a sunset cocktail reception on the Crystal Blue Terrace where guests are treated to Hawaiian cultural demonstrations. For dinner, guests have the option of family-style seating and wait-service in the Ali'i Circle, or the usual buffet configuration. Traditional and expected lu'au dishes are presented along with fresh catch, prime rib, fresh salads, tropical fruits and all kinds of things to suit every taste. The colorful Polynesian after-dinner show features Na Hoku Hano Hano award-winner Danny Couch and his hula troupe. Rates: $65 per person.

Waikoloa Beach Marriott, Outrigger Resort

69-275 Waikoloa Beach Drive, Kohala Coast; 808-886-6789; www.marriott hawaii.com.

The lu'au is temporarily suspended during resort renovation. Call for most current information.

CHAPTER 5

Beaches

Respect the ocean. It is a powerful presence all around us. We've seen it turn from something like a giant turquoise bathtub into a raging gray monster in a matter of hours. It can take away a beach overnight and wreck homes in the blink of an eye, then soothe your soul with its gentle, lapping waves along the shore. It's easy to get engrossed in what you're doing and forget, but a moment's carelessness can change everything. Watch, listen, take a friend, trust your instincts and, when in doubt, get out. Do be aware, but don't be afraid. The experience is well worth it.

The Big Island has over 100 beaches, and they come in white, black, grey and green. The beaches tend to be smaller and some are harder to get to than those on Hawai'i's other islands, but visitors and locals agree they are some of the best anywhere. Many of the beaches are more rocky than smooth, and *tabis* (reef shoes) are recommended. The Big Island is still young geologically speaking and the rocks along its shorelines haven't eroded into the fine, powdery sand you might expect. As you stroll along different beaches, scoop up a handful of sand and observe its composition for tiny shell fragments, green olivine crystals, coral, black and red lava gravel. As the island grows, new beaches are formed from volcanic activity while the ocean transforms the older coastline. It's an amazing process. Some of the most interesting are "storm beaches," made when high surf crashes against the *pali* (cliffs) and leaves enough sand for a beach up there, far above the ocean.

Although every one of Hawai'i's beaches are by law open to the public, some of the beaches you see on the map are not easily accessible by car. For more detailed information on the Big Island's beaches, pick up a copy of the free *Big Island Beach & Activity Guide* (www.beachactivityguide.com) when you arrive.

Beachgoers should also be aware that some of the parks and campgrounds near the beach have become long-term residential locations for local homeless and transient people. This is not necessarily something to fear as much as something to be aware of, with an attitude of "live and let live." However, just like any other vacation destination, do not leave valuables in your car, lock the doors and use common sense. If you feel uncomfortable, trust your instincts and move to another spot.

Hawai'i's residents, wherever you find them, are some of the friendliest, warmest and most compassionate people you'll meet anywhere. Aloha is very real here, and you're likely to experience that directly in some way. And while most people recognize that visitors are a big part of our livelihood, there are some who may look at outsiders as an intrusion on their *aina* (land) whether they own it or not. To put it simply, the Big Island's beach parks are relatively trouble-free, but there's no guarantee even here. We've found it works best to keep a friendly, benign attitude and if confronted by someone who makes us uncomfortable, to walk away. All that being said, don't worry, you're in for some beautiful days at the beach.

Snorkelers will find good areas to explore near some of the more popular and easy-to-reach beaches around the island. A little bit more of a swim leads to better snorkeling over lava rock outcroppings, rocky coves and small bays where the water is usually fairly calm. Good coral patches and beds grow around these areas, which attract varied fish, sea turtles and other marine life. However, because the Big Island is so young geologically, there are no extensive fringing coral reefs that encircle the island or extend out from the shoreline. As in all ocean areas, snorkelers need to be aware of their direction and distance from the shore, and keep alert to currents, surges and surf action especially near rock outcroppings. And don't forget the sunblock!

Along almost any shoreline, tidepools are fascinating mini-worlds to explore. Wear your *tabis* or sneakers and walk up onto the rocks to find a place where the tide has left water behind. Wait quietly for a few minutes and see what life emerges. You might encounter tiny fish, shrimp and crabs, a floating sea cucumber, spiky black sea urchins (don't touch them), the long strands of a spaghetti worms, snails, mysterious cowrie that open their shells when they think you've passed. We once found a moray eel that lifted its head out of the water to have its picture taken. Do keep an eye on the waves; tides can sneak in quickly and cut off your return access, forcing you into an unplanned swim. We'd also suggest that you not take shells from tidepools since creatures might still be living in them.

Beach Precautions

WATER SAFETY

The Big Island's beaches are for the most part, more rugged than those on the neighboring islands of Maui or O'ahu, for example. As mentioned earlier, its beaches are geological "teenagers" that will need much more time to erode into smooth, level strands of soft sand. The western (Kona-side) coasts of the island have reef systems that afford some protection; however, many beaches are gravelly-to-rocky with surf conditions that can change suddenly. Most of the island's beaches are not serviced by lifeguards and many have few or no facilities, including drinking water. Again, we recommend picking up a free copy of the *Big Island Beach & Activity Guide*.

The more remote beaches (Pololu, Waipi'o, Green Sands, for example) we can only recommend to the seasoned hiker and swimmer on their own, or to others via a commercial tour provider. You may see surfers at beaches where we'd suggest you enjoy the view and stay out of the water. Keep in mind that just because there is someone else in the water, it doesn't mean it's safe.

Please, treat the Big Island's wild beaches with respect. Since many have no restroom facilities, try to use the bathroom before you head to the beach. If you must relieve yourself, go well away from the waterline and bury your deposit and any tissue you used. Also, pack out your trash and bring out a little bit that someone else left, too.

Wherever you go to enjoy the beach, do not take undue risks. Others might be visitors just like you, but not as well-informed. Common sense needs to be employed at all beaches.

We don't want to be alarmists, but we'd prefer to report the beaches conservatively. Always, always use good judgment. Here are some basic water safety tips and terms.

A **shorebreak** occurs when the waves break directly on the beach. Small shorebreaks may not be a problem, but waves that are more than a foot or two high may create undertows and hazardous conditions. Conditions are generally more severe in the winter months. Even venturing too close to a shorebreak could be hazardous, as standing on the beachfront you may encounter a stronger, higher wave that could catch you off-guard and sweep you into the water. *Keiki* must be watched carefully even when playing near a shorebreak.

A **rip current** can often be seen from the shore. This is a fast-moving, river-like current that sometimes can be seen carrying sand or sediment. They are common in reef areas that have open channels to the sea. A rip current can pull an unsuspecting swimmer quickly out to sea. Swimming against a strong rip current may be impossible even for the best swimmers. If you find yourself being pulled offshore, relax, signal for help, and try to swim across, rather than against, the current.

Undertows happen when a rip current runs into incoming surf. This accounts for the feeling that you are being pulled down. They are more common on beaches that have steep slopes.

Kona winds generated by southern-hemisphere storms cause southerly swells that affect leeward shores. This usually happens in the summer and lasts several days, and surf may be higher, particularly in winter months. Although it may appear fun to play in these waves, many minor to moderate injuries are recorded at these times. Resorts will post red warning flags along the beach during times of unsafe surf conditions. Most beaches are affected during this time with water turbidity and poor snorkeling conditions. At a few places, such as Kawaihae, these conditions may create good surfing for a few days.

TIPS

Here are some additional beach safety and etiquette tips:

• "Never turn your back to the ocean" is an old Hawaiian saying. Don't be caught off-guard; waves come in sets, with spells of calm in between.

• Use the buddy system; never swim or snorkel alone.

• If you are unsure of your abilities, use flotation devices attached to your body, such as a life vest or inflatable vest. Never rely on an air mattress or similar device from which you may become separated.

• Study the ocean before you enter; look for rocks, shorebreak and rip currents.

• Duck or dive beneath breaking waves before they reach you.

• Never swim against a strong current; swim across it.

THEFT DOES HAPPEN

Never leave anything of importance in your car because theft, especially at some of the more remote locations, is unfortunately high. And be careful of watchful eyes if you stow your valuables in your trunk. There are some unscrupulous folks who may be looking for visitors to do just that. Car rental companies often advise customers to leave nothing in the car and keep the vehicle unlocked to minimize damage in a break-in. In the unhappy event that you do experience a theft, call the police non-emergency number 808-935-3311 or, in an emergency, 911

OCEAN MENACES

The Big Island's ocean playgrounds are among the most benign in the world. There are, however, a few ocean creatures that you should be aware of. We will attempt to include some basic first-aid tips should you encounter one of these. Since some people might have a resulting allergic reaction, we suggest you contact a local physician or medical center if you have an unplanned encounter with one of them.

Portuguese Man-of-War are sea animals seen only rarely but caution is in order. Most resorts and public beaches will post warning signs to help you avoid them. These small creatures, related to the jellyfish, drift in the ocean currents. Sometimes blown on shore by unusual winds, they can cover the beach with their glistening crystal orbs filled with deep blue filament. If they are on the beach, treat them as if they were still in the water—stay away. On rare occasions they will be seen drifting in the ocean during a snorkeling cruise or sea excursion and the crew may change snorkeling destinations. Their long, trailing filaments can cause painful stings. If you are stung, rinse the affected area with sea water or fresh water to remove any tentacles. If you need to pick out the tentacles, do not use your bare fingers; use gloves, a towel or whatever is available to protect yourself. Vinegar, iso-propyl alcohol and human urine, once considered effective reme-dies, are no longer recommended treatments.

As mentioned above, avoid touching **sea urchins** (*wana*). Their long sharp spines are brittle, and easily break off in your fin-gers or toes. If you do encounter one, be sure the entire spine is removed. Soaking the wound in vinegar helps to dissolve the spine; for pain, soak the puncture in hot water for 30 to 90 minutes.

Coral is made up of many tiny living organisms. Coral cuts require thorough disinfecting and can take a long time to heal. If

• Know your limits.

• Small children should be allowed to play near or in the surf *only* with close supervision and should wear flotation devices—and even then, only under extremely calm conditions.

• When exploring tidepools or reefs, always wear protective footwear and keep an eye on the ocean. Also, protect your hands—don't reach anywhere you can't see.

• When swimming around coral, be careful where you put your hands and feet. Urchin stings can be painful and coral cuts can be

an inflamed wound's redness begins to spread, it suggests an infection and requires medical attention. So stay off the coral—and don't touch it.

Cone shells look harmless enough, are conical and come in colors of brown or black. The snails that inhabit these shells have a defense mechanism that they use to protect themselves—and to kill their prey. Their stinger does have venom so it is suggested that you just enjoy looking at them. Cleaning the wound and soaking it in hot water for 30 to 90 minutes will provide relief if you're stung.

Eels live among the coral or in rock crevices and are generally not aggressive. You may have heard of divers who trained an eel to come out and then take food from their hands, but we don't recommend you try to make an eel your pal. While usually non-aggressive, their jaws are extremely powerful and their teeth are sharp. And any sea animal could mistake an approach or sudden movement as an aggressive act. Just keep a comfortable distance—for you and the eel. Also, never reach into the coral or any other place where you can't see your hands. Your fingers might be mistaken for lunch.

Sharks? Yes, there are many varied types of sharks. However, more people are injured by coral than by sharks in Hawai'i every year. Resorts post warning signs if a shark is sighted off the coast. If you should see one, don't move quickly. Swim slowly away while you keep an eye on it. Avoid swimming in murky waters near river mouths after it rains. Also, stay out of the water if you have open cuts and remember, urine or other bodily fluids might attract sharks, so be on the safe side and don't urinate in the water.

dangerous. You can also damage or injure the coral. Coral is living animal which grows very slowly—so don't knock into it or stand on it while snorkeling.

- Respect the yellow and red flag warnings when placed on the developed beaches. They are there to advise you of unsafe conditions.
- After heavy rains, stay out of the ocean until the water clears.
- Avoid swimming in the mouths of rivers or streams or in any areas of murky water.

- Always use fins when boogie boarding.
- Don't feed the fish.
- Keep your distance from pole and net fishermen.
- Remember, it's illegal to do *anything* that causes a dolphin, monk seal, turtle or whale to change its behavior, so do not approach them.

Surface water temperature varies little, with a mean temperature of 73 degrees Fahrenheit in January and 80.2 degrees in August. Minimum and maximum range from 68 to 84 degrees. This is an almost ideal temperature (refreshing, but not cold) for swimming and you'll find most resort pools cooler than the ocean. Of course, if it's windy, it may feel chilly when you get out of the water.

Best Bets

Most Beautiful Beaches   'Anaeho'omalu Beach; Hapuna Beach State Park; Kauna'oa Beach (Mauna Kea Beach)

Safest Playing/Swimming Beaches for *Keiki*   *Kailua-Kona*: Kamakahonu ("King Kam") Beach, Old Kona Airport State Recreation Area, Kaloko-Honokohau National Historic Park; *South Kona District*: Kahalu'u Beach Park, Kamakahonu Beach, Old Kona Airport State Recreation Area, Kaloko-Honokohau National Historic Park; *South Kohala*: 'Anaeho'omalu Beach, Hapuna Beach State Park, Spencer Beach Park, Kauna'oa Beach; *Hilo*: Onekahakaha Beach Park, Leleiwi Beach Park, Coconut Island

There are remarkable sea turtles in the Big Island's waters, and many people report great experiences swimming with them. The bad news is, they do bite. They are also a protected species and should not be disturbed if you find them sunning on the beach. As with all things, treat them with respect.

Shelling/Tidepooling Beaches   *Kailua-Kona*: Old Kona Airport State Recreation Area; *Hilo*: Onekahakaha Beach Park; *South Kohala*: Holoholokai Beach Park

Snorkeling Beaches   *South Kona*: Napo'opo'o Beach Park (Kealakekua Bay State Historical & Underwater Parks), Honaunau Bay, Ho'okena Beach Park; *Keauhou-Kona*: Kahalu'u Beach Park; *Kohala Coast*: 'Anaeho'omalu Beach, Kauna'oa Beach; *Hilo*: Leleiwi Beach Park; *Puna District*: Kapoho Bay

Sunbathing Beaches   White Sands Beach Park, Kailua-Kona; 'Anaeho'omalu Beach, Kohala Coast; Hapuna Beach State Park; Kauna'oa Beach (Mauna Kea Beach)

Using This Chapter

The following listings refer to a variety of beaches and beach parks. The **child icon** indicates beaches that are recommended for family activities. They are more protected and most likely have lifeguards on duty. Also check for ★, which identifies special recommendations.

A close look at the map will reveal many more Big Island beaches than are described here.

And we've found a great website with photos, directions to and descriptions of beach parks: www.hawaiiweb.com. We like to say there's a beach for everybody, and everything you like to do at the beach. Some go by more than one name, with locations pinpointed only by local word-of-mouth. Some are little more than a pocket of sand between craggy lava walls. Some are intimate little gems you might discover for yourself. Some require a 4WD vehicle and a good pair of shoes, but all are waiting for you to explore. We've attempted to include the more-accessible beaches here, and invite you to share your experiences at those we may have omitted. As a note, topless or "clothing-optional" beaches are not at all common and are not legal here, although you may find references to them on some websites or via the "coconut wireless." Big Island beaches are generally family-rated to "PG-13," so not to worry. Of course if you're into that kind of thing, play it safe and book your stay through a clothing-optional vacation provider (and don't forget the sunblock).

Kona District

KAILUA-KONA TOWN

Kona beaches tend to be busy, kind of small, but usually quite nice and equipped for all sorts of watersports and activities. Their proximity to the hotels and resorts of Kailua-Kona make them convenient and easy to find, but parking can be limited on weekends and holidays.

★ *Kahalu'u Beach Park*

This is one of the most popular swimming and snorkeling sites in the Kona area, located next to the Keauhou Beach Hotel, just south of Kailua-Kona. The beach is composed of white sand speckled with black lava pebbles, cobblestones and fragments. Excellent snorkeling and near-shore scuba diving in bay waters protected by a fringing reef, and the area is generally free of strong currents.

Text continued on page 314.

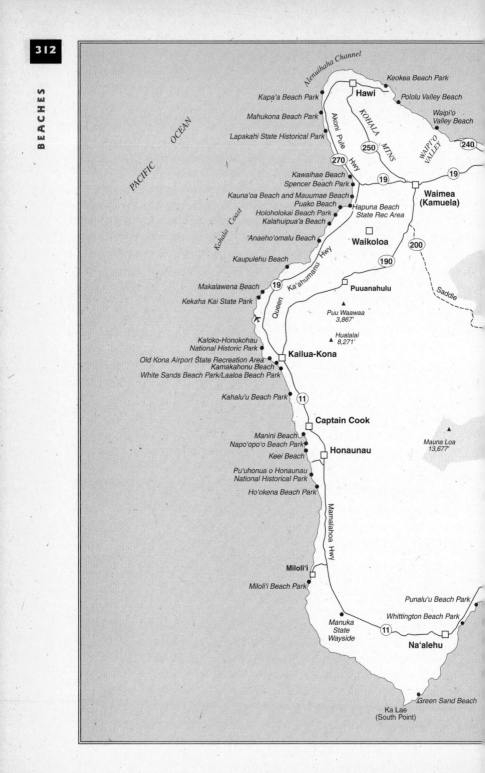

PACIFIC OCEAN

Alenuihaha Channel

Keokea Beach Park

Kapa'a Beach Park

Hawi

Pololu Valley Beach

Mahukona Beach Park

KOHALA MTNS

Waipi'o Valley Beach

Lapakahi State Historical Park

Akoni Pule Hwy

250

WAIPI'O VALLEY

240

270

19

Kawaihae Beach

Spencer Beach Park

Kauna'oa Beach and Mauumae Beach

Puako Beach

Holoholokai Beach Park

Kalahuipua'a Beach

Hapuna Beach State Rec Area

Waimea (Kamuela)

19

'Anaeho'omalu Beach

Kohala Coast

Waikoloa

Kaupulehu Beach

Ka'ahumanu Hwy

200

190

Makalawena Beach

19

Kekaha Kai State Park

Queen

Puuanahulu

Saddle

Puu Waawaa 3,867'

Kaloko-Honokohau National Historic Park

Hualalai 8,271'

Old Kona Airport State Recreation Area

Kamakahonu Beach

White Sands Beach Park/Laaloa Beach Park

Kailua-Kona

Kahalu'u Beach Park

11

Captain Cook

Mauna Loa 13,677'

Manini Beach

Napo'opo'o Beach Park

Keei Beach

Honaunau

Pu'uhonua o Honaunau National Historical Park

Ho'okena Beach Park

Mamalahoa Hwy

Miloli'i

Miloli'i Beach Park

Punalu'u Beach Park

Whittington Beach Park

11

Manuka State Wayside

Na'alehu

Green Sand Beach

Ka Lae (South Point)

Big Island Beaches

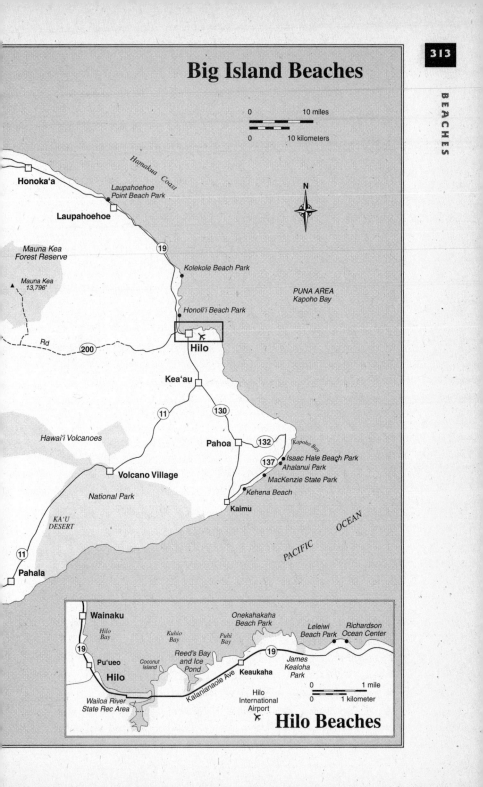

0   10 miles

0   10 kilometers

N

Honoka‘a

Hamakua Coast

Laupahoehoe
Point Beach Park

Laupahoehoe

*Mauna Kea
Forest Reserve*

▲ *Mauna Kea
13,796'*

(19)

Kolekole Beach Park

*PUNA AREA
Kapoho Bay*

Rd

(200)

Honoli‘i Beach Park

✈ Hilo

Kea‘au

(11)

(130)

Hawai‘i Volcanoes

Pahoa

(132)

Kapoho Bay

(137) ● Isaac Hale Beach Park
● Ahalanui Park

Volcano Village

MacKenzie State Park

National Park

● Kehena Beach

Kaimu

*KA‘U
DESERT*

PACIFIC   OCEAN

(11)

Pahala

Hilo Beaches

Wainaku

*Hilo
Bay*

*Kuhio
Bay*

*Onekahakaha
Beach Park*

*Puhi
Bay*

*Leleiwi
Beach Park*

*Richardson
Ocean Center*

(19)

Pu‘ueo

*Coconut
Island*

*Reed's Bay
and Ice
Pond*

(19)

*James
Kealoha
Park*

Hilo

Keaukaha

Kalanianaole Ave

*Wailoa River
State Rec Area*

*Hilo
International
Airport* ✈

0   1 mile

0   1 kilometer

Outside the reef, surfers can find good waves to ride but the rip currents along the reef edge are extremely strong. Caution is advised. Park facilities include picnic pavilions, restrooms, showers, water, lifeguard, parking, campsites and concession stands.

★ White Sands Beach Park/Laaloa Beach Park

Located on Ali'i Drive four miles south of Kailua-Kona town; facilities include showers, picnic area and grills, volleyball, lifeguard and parking along the road. A grove of coconut trees provides some shade and lends a touch of beauty to this small beach park. The lovely white sand and small wave action make this a popular swimming and boogieboarding beach for both residents and visitors. Winter storms often wash the white sand into deeper water, only to carry it back later, hence the park's other names of "Disappearing Sands" and "Magic Sands."

★ Kamakahonu Beach

This is a small cove of sandy beach immediately next to the Kailua Pier and fronting King Kamehameha's Kona Beach Hotel. Extending onto a peninsula in front of the beach is Ahu'ena Heiau, the temple of King Kamehameha the Great. Kamehameha resided here at Kamakahonu during the last years of his life. The beach is very protected and is excellent for sunbathing and swimming, especially good for young children. Also a popular spot for snuba and dive instruction, canoe, paddle boat and snorkel rentals. No public facilities exist on the beach itself but there are public restrooms on the adjacent pier, and the King Kam's shops and snack bars are close by.

Old Kona Airport State Recreation Area

The area consists of a long beach composed of pebbles, rocks and a few pockets of white sand, with safe sand channels for entering the water. Although the coast here tends to be rocky, there are tidepools to explore all along the coastline. The swimming and snorkeling are generally fair to good here, but best on calmer days. Facilities include a jogging trail, picnic pavilions, restrooms, showers, water and plenty of parking. Next to the beach is the old runway, good for skating or rollerblading. Community ball fields are right next door. Part of the Old Kona Airport Marine Life Conservation District.

★ Kaloko-Honokohau National Historic Park

A nice little string of white-sand beaches are a short walk from the Honokohau Small Boat Harbor, within the National Park, just north of Kailua-Kona. This 1,160-acre park spanning a two-mile stretch of coastline was founded to preserve, protect, interpret and demonstrate native Hawaiian activities and culture and to demonstrate historic land use. Archaeological resources include ancient Hawaiian house platforms, fishing shrines, canoe landings, petroglyph rock carvings, religious temples and fishponds, including peaceful, scenic Aimakapa, great for birding. The tidal wetlands are home to many waterbirds, including the Hawaiian black-necked stilt and Hawaiian coot, both endemic to Hawai'i. The park landscape also includes scenic coastlines, sandy beaches, marine tidal pools and native plants. Located three miles north of Kailua-Kona, three miles south of Keahole Airport. There is an unimproved access road just opposite Kaloko Industrial Park open daily 8 a.m. to 3:30 p.m. There is also access to a hiking trail into the park from Honokohau harbor. This is a hot, dry, windy area of open, rough lava flows. Hikers and visitors should come prepared with sunscreen, hats, hiking shoes and water. No water, but toilets are available at the fishpond and beach. A visitor facility is open daily. No camping or fires are allowed. For further information, contact Kaloko-Honokohau NHP, 73-4786 Kanalani Street #14, Kailua-Kona, HI 96740; 808-329-6881; www.nps.gov/kaho.

Kekaha Kai State Park

This beach park is located just a couple of miles north of Kona's Keahole Airport. It is reached off Highway 19 by a narrow, somewhat bumpy road that winds across the lava fields for 1.5 miles. A regular car can make it but drive slowly. The beach is a high sand dune beach with good tidal pools for snorkeling and swimming, but don't go out too far. There's a picnic area, restrooms and parking at the site.

Makalawena Beach

More of a surfing spot than a beach, Makalawena is located north of Kekaha Kai State Park, near Opaeula Pond. It can be reached by a moderately rugged hike along the coastal foot trail. The shoreline is made of intricate caves and is backdropped by sand dunes. Lots of shell-collecting and bird-watching opportunities. No facilities or drinking water at the site.

Kaupulehu Beach

This fronts the Kona Village and Four Seasons Resort north of Kailua-Kona. The white-sand beach is speckled with black lava fragments and pebbles. Kahuwai Bay is good for swimming and snorkeling, although in some areas you need to walk over rock or coral shelf. There is convenient public access (parking is provided by the resort), picnic area, restrooms and showers. According to legend, these waters have healing properties. This is one of those rare places you might see huge sea turtles sunning themselves in the sand.

SOUTH KONA DISTRICT

The beaches of South Kona are fairly isolated, mostly used by local residents. None of these listed are near any resorts, major towns or commercial areas.

Ho'okena Beach Park

Three miles south of Pu'uhonua o Honaunau at the end of a narrow, winding and bumpy paved spur road off Highway 11 is Ho'okena. A small coconut grove with several old Hawaiian homes and beach houses, the park offers campsites, showers, restrooms and picnic tables and some shade trees. Reach the beachfront by a very narrow one-lane roadway between old stone walls. The beach is a combination of black-and-white sand and mixed lava debris, giving the sand a gray cast. The bay is generally calm, and swimming, snorkeling and diving are good, but caution is advised during high surf times.

★ Pu'uhonua o Honaunau National Historical Park

This is one of the Big Island's most popular attractions. In addition to the visitors center, a reconstructed Hawaiian village and impressive, tiki-guarded *heiau*, the park has restrooms, a picnic area, and some of the best near-shore snorkeling and scuba diving on the island at nearby Honaunau Bay. Swimming and sunbathing is not permitted within the park. The generally rocky shoreline has pockets of sandy beach here and there and the shoreline waters teem with marine life. No lifeguards or facilities. For further information, call the visitors center at 808-328-2288.

★ Napo'opo'o Beach Park

Adjoining the village of Napo'opo'o at Kealakekua Bay, the beach consists of pebbles, cobblestones and boulders with only a very narrow strip of sand at the water's edge. The beach attracts many sunbathers and swimmers and some surfers and boogieboarders. Some limited parking, restrooms and a couple of picnic tables. Also next to the park are the ruins of Hikiau Heiau, an old Hawaiian temple. Snorkelers revel in the offshore Kealakekua Bay State Historical & Underwater Parks. The area is full of colorful marine life and offers excellent snorkeling and scuba diving. Many of the commercial boat tours from Kailua-Kona include Kealakekua Bay as part of their route. At the north end, beyond the towering cliffs and on a flat point of land jutting into the bay, is the Captain James Cook Monument, erected to honor the famous British explorer. A plaque

Note: Because of the Big Island's rugged coastlines, finding whole, intact seashells is an uncommon thing. Some tiny shells, however, may be found mixed in the sand on almost any beach.

at the water's edge notes the spot where Cook met his fate in a dispute with the Hawaiians in 1779.

Manini Beach

A very small beach in an out-of the way location just south of Napo'opo'o. Rough water and rocky coast can make swimming a challenge, but offshore diving is decent. Turn toward the coast on Manini Street. At the end of the road, park and take the short walk to the point. No facilities.

Keei Beach

Very shallow water at this quarter-mile-long salt-and-pepper beach allows for safe but limited swimming; good snorkeling due to lots of coral. It's away from the tourist area, with excellent views of Kealakekua Bay and lots of tidepools to explore. In Captain Cook take Napo'opo'o Road down to Kealakekua Bay. At the bottom of the hill, go left toward the Pu'uhonua o Honaunau National Historical Park. Take this road a half-mile, turn right onto a lava-bed road and follow this extremely rough road another half-mile to the beach. No facilities.

Miloli'i Beach Park

Another challenging beach to reach, this one is outside of Miloli'i town, about 33 miles south of Kailua-Kona. Turn off onto a very winding, one-lane, macadam road. It's about a half-hour drive to finish the five miles to the beach. Lots of beautiful tidepools here, as well as reefs that create great swimming and snorkeling spots (but be careful if you venture beyond the reefs). No facilities.

Manuka State Wayside

Located 19 miles west of Na'alehu on Mamalahoa Highway, this lovely botanic garden has stunning ocean views at nearly 2,000 feet above sea level. Native and imported trees dot the grassy, rolling terrain. Restrooms and picnic area available. About five miles off Mamalahoa Highway down a 4WD trail, Manuka Bay and Kaulanamauna Cove are secluded areas, supposed sites of ancient ruins and *heiau*. There are no facilities at the shore.

Kohala Coast

SOUTH KOHALA DISTRICT

South Kohala has the best sandy beaches on the island, perfect for swimming and sunbathing. Some, like Hapuna and Spencer parks, are favorites of local residents and visitors alike. Others, like 'Anaeho'omalu and Kauna'oa beaches, front major resort hotels and are mostly used by their guests. However, as with every other beach in Hawai'i, they are available to the public. Access to the beaches is provided by the resorts (look for the blue "wave" signs), but parking can be limited and a free pass may be required. You may have to wait at the entry if beach parking is crowded, or you might want to visit the property to go shopping, check out a tee time or have lunch before you hit the beach (this is a big hint). Once there, please keep in mind that amenities such as chairs, umbrellas and towels are provided for the resort guests who pay considerably for them. Although it may be tempting to take advantage of same, and may not seem fair, remember that the resorts take the responsibility to clean and maintain these beautiful beaches and their facilities for everyone to enjoy, and they earn their money from their paying guests.

★ 'Anaeho'omalu Beach

This is a beautiful, long, curving, white-sand beach speckled with gravelly grains of black lava, but you might want *tabis* or slippers if you want to walk it. It is a lovely crescent accented with graceful coconut palms and backed by two old fishponds, Ku'uali'i and Kahapapa, which were reserved for Hawaiian royalty in the old days. The beach park fronts the Waikoloa Resort and plenty of free public parking is provided. One of the best places for ocean activities, "A-Bay" offers swimming, snorkeling, scuba diving, windsurfing (best on the island), board surfing and more. A watersports activities concession on the beach provides equipment rentals and instruction for hotel guests and other visitors, as well as sign-ups for sunset sails, glass-bottom boat cruises and more. The beach park facilities include restrooms, showers and picnic tables plus plenty of free parking.

Kalahuipua'a Beach

Located at the Mauna Lani Resort, the beach is adjacent to a series of well-maintained old Hawaiian fishponds that are still used for aquaculture purposes. The beach access is through a historic preserve and public park maintained by the Mauna Lani Resort. The best swimming area of the beach is Nanuku Inlet, a wide, shallow, sandy-bottomed cove enclosed by natural lava rock barriers. This part of the lovely white-and-black-sand speckled beach immediately fronts the Mauna Lani Bay Hotel.

★ Holoholokai Beach Park

This public-access beach park is located just north of the Fairmont Orchid. The park was developed by the Mauna Lani Resort Company and provides restrooms and showers, parking stalls for over 30 cars and barbecue grills on the beach. The beach is not sandy but composed of white coral rocks and some black lava and debris.

There are small pockets of sand here and there. It's a good beach for sunning, tidepool exploring, shelling and snorkeling in the larger tidal pools, but swimming can be hazardous due to rocky shores and rough surf. Great views of the Kohala Coast. A trail from the parking lot leads to the Malama Petroglyph Trail, part of the ancient King's Trail, with over 3,000 well-preserved rock carvings.

Puako Beach

The beach extends along Puako Road in North Kohala south of Hapuna Beach State Park. The shoreline is mostly rocks and pebbles indented by inlets, coves and a great collection of tidepools to explore. Swimmers and snorkelers can find some white-sand beach stretches to enter the water, but Puako's not the best place for swimming and sunbathing. Public access is via the boat ramp at Puako Bay or any of several points along Puako Road, which follows the shoreline homes. Look for the "wave" access signs. Parking may be limited and there are no facilities along these beaches.

Waialea Bay ("Beach 69's")

Finding this popular local beach and surfing spot is a bit of a challenge for the uninitiated, unless the surf's up and you can follow the crowd. Watch for the sign to Puako on the *makai* (ocean) side of Highway 19. Turn in, take the first right onto a narrow unmarked road behind a residential area. Look for parking at 69-mile marker (there may not be a beach-access "wave" sign) and take the short hike across the lava.

★ Hapuna Beach State Recreation Area

Hapuna is undoubtedly one of the best—a beautiful, user-friendly beach with ample, convenient facilities. This is the Big Island's largest expanse of fine white sand. It stretches for over a half mile and provides shallow waters that slope gently to deeper offshore waters. Swimming, snorkeling, body-surfing, windsurfing and near-shore scuba diving are excellent. Shallow, protected coves at the beach's north end provide sandy-bottomed pools that are ideal for little children to splash and play in. The beach facilities are some of the best as well, including private scenic picnic lanai spread along the bluffs, a pavilion for larger groups, restrooms, showers, lifeguards, public phones, great lunch and sweet treats at 3 Frogs snack bar, and plenty of free parking. At the far north end, you will see the grounds of Hapuna Beach Prince Hotel, where nice lunch and libations are served by the swimming pool, just a short walk up from the beach (coverups required). Comments: In all fairness, this beach park's State upkeep is often criticized and tends to have notable ups and downs. Regardless, Hapuna is still the best, even if you find the facilities on a bad day.

★ Kaunaʻoa Beach

One of the most photographed beaches on the island, this is the beach that inspired Laurance S. Rockefeller to build his legendary Mauna Kea Beach Hotel in 1965. It is a long, wide crescent of fine white sand that slopes gently into the deeper off-shore waters and offers excellent swimming, snorkeling and seasonal windsurfing. Surf conditions often permit good bodysurfing and occasional board-surfing; water-sports activity gear is available for rent. Mauna Kea Resort provides public access and some parking (go early, or you may have to wait for a pass at the gate). It also maintains convenient public restrooms and showers near the beach. No cooking is permitted, but there is a good lunch restaurant and bar on the property. Once the playground of *aliʻi* (Hawaiian royalty), Kaunaʻoa Beach is still enjoyed by the elite. In 2000 it was named the #1 beach in the nation by "Dr. Beach" (Stephen Leatherman of Florida International University) and is consistently highly rated by readers of *Condé Nast* and *Travel & Leisure*.

Mauumae Beach

Located just off a private estate parcel within the Mauna Kea Resort, Mauumae is a small, secluded beach with no public facilities. To visit, stop at the security shack at Mauna Kea Beach Hotel and request a beach pass for Mauumae. Parking is very limited and access is via an easy trail from the hotel's support area to the beach. (Note: Despite Mauumae's former reputation as a clothing-optional beach, nude swimming or sunbathing is not legal in Hawaiʻi.)

Spencer Beach Park

The park is located near the port village of Kawaihae and immediately below Puʻukohola Heiau National Historic Park, a famous temple built by Kamehameha the Great. The beach here is a fine white-sand expanse with a very gentle slope to deeper water. The conditions are excellent for swimming, snorkeling and near-shore scuba diving. The protected nature of the bay affords very calm waters with usually gentle surf. It is a good swimming beach for little children. This popular beach can get crowded, especially on weekends and holidays. Keep an eye on the kids in the parking lot, take turns watching valuables on the beach, and do remember to lock the car. Facilities include campsites, picnic tables and grills, lifeguard, restrooms, showers and plenty of parking.

Kawaihae Beach

This is a coral rubble and landfill beach next to the boat harbor that resulted when the harbor was dredged years ago. Many local folks use the area for varied activities such as fishing, canoe paddling, sailing, windsurfing, swimming and picnicking. From the south end of the landfill area is a great view of the nearby Puʻukohola Heiau, and if conditions are right, this can be a good place to hunt for seashells.

NORTH KOHALA DISTRICT

The beaches of North Kohala tend to be of a more rugged variety, often composed of small pockets of coral pebbles and small rocks with an isolated pocket of sand. Often the beach area is lava rock outcropping.

★ Lapakahi State Historical Park

The park is north of Kawaihae Harbor, and although it has no good sandy beach, it does have a rather remarkable restoration of an ancient Hawaiian village along the rugged coastline. Well worth a stop (especially early in the day before the temperature soars) Lapakahi is one of the Big Island's best-kept secrets. As for beachgoers, there are small pockets of coral pebbles and rocky beaches where swimmers and snorkelers can enter the water. At the point where the park trail follows the shoreline and meets a small peninsula of land, there is a small cove with remarkably clear water that slopes gradually before dropping off sharply. Swimmers and snorkelers should not venture out more than 50 yards into the cove, however, due to strong alongshore currents in the area. There are no facilities right on the shore but restrooms are located near the parking lot area and entrance.

Mahukona Beach Park

Between Kawaihae and Hawi on Highway 270 is the site of an old port of the Hawaiʻi Consolidated Railway Company, which transported sugar from the Kohala Mill to boats for trans-ocean shipment. Remnants of the old railway port still exist and old train wheels, parts and related rubble attract snorkelers and divers in the bay's clear waters. There is no real sand beach here, only coral rubble and pebbles, but it's a great place for shoreline fishing, great for snorkeling and pretty good for shoreline diving. Facilities include picnic tables, a pavilion, restrooms, showers, camping area and parking lot.

Kapaʻa Beach Park

Off Highway 11 about 14 miles north of Kawaihae, Kapaʻa is a small, picturesque beach park with a great view of Maui. There's a tiny cove ringed by *kiawe* trees, but it has no sand. Better for snorkeling, shoreline diving or photo-ops than swimming, the beach is a pleasant stop along your drive through North Kohala. Facilities are limited to restrooms and picnic area with barbecue grills; no lifeguard.

Keokea Beach Park

A nice spot for a picnic, with restroom facilities and campsites, but not the best for swimmers. There is a small, cliff-rimmed cove, where the water tends to be rough and the coastline is rugged. Located about six miles east of Hawi off Highway 270; turn at the sign and follow the winding road for one mile.

Pololu Valley Beach

At the end of Highway 270, past the village of Kapa'au, the beach is reached by a difficult trail down to the valley at the end of the highway. The trail is often treacherous if wet, and caution is advised. The beach is a wide expanse of fine black sand with high dunes at the back shore. While swimmers, bodysurfers and surfers use the beach, there are dangerous rip currents that are real hazards. This is a remote, isolated beach, and extreme caution is advised. The flatlands of the valley were once extensively planted in taro farms but are now abandoned. There are no facilities of any kind on the beach.

Hamakua District

The eastern side of the Big Island, the Hamakua Coast, is marked by high vertical *pali* (cliffs). The coastline is rough and rugged, with very few places where coral reefs form and create sandy beaches. Likewise, the North Hilo area has only small pockets of black lava-rock sand in some areas, and no coral-sand beaches, although the area has a special rugged beauty that is captured in places like Laupahoehoe Park.

Waipi'o Valley Beach

This beach is a worthwhile challenge to reach. At the end of Highway 240 is the Waipi'o Valley State Park lookout. Below that, down a hazardous and very steep single lane road carved along the valley wall, is a long black-sand crescent bisected in the middle by the Waipi'o River.

This beautiful, storied valley has an isolated mystique all its own and a visit here makes a special memory. While some swimmers, bodysurfers and surfers ride the often good waves here, the presence of strong rip currents make the beach extremely dangerous for even advanced swimmers. Caution is advised. There are no facilities of any kind on the beach (restrooms at the lookout) and a 4WD vehicle is required. A better plan may be to contact one of the reputable tour providers listed elsewhere in this guide, and visit by car, ATV, or horse-drawn wagon.

★ Laupahoehoe Point Beach Park

This scenic, peaceful park is a lava rock peninsula jutting into the ocean at Laupahoehoe, with steep rugged cliffs and a beach of mostly coral pebbles and rocks. Strong surf and rip currents prevent most water activities, although you might see surfers and fishermen. The rocky shoreline requires extreme caution. Park facilities include picnic pavilions, restrooms, showers, water, parking, camping sites and a small boat launch. It is a pleasant park for picnicking and lots of ironwood trees provide cool shade to enjoy the scenic beauty of the Hamakua Coast. Look for the poignant Tidal Wave Memorial placed in honor of the schoolchildren and teachers lost in the 1946 tsunami.

Hilo

★ Kolekole Beach Park

Despite not having a sandy beach, this is one of the Big Island's loveliest parks. It is fronted by a shoreline of smooth waterworn lava rocks with an adjacent coldwater stream and waterfall. The park grounds and surrounding valley walls are lush and full of tropical vegetation. The stream flows from the beautiful 'Akaka Falls Park located upstream some four miles. While water activities are somewhat limited, the park is an excellent place for a day outing to picnic, explore and enjoy Hawai'i's tropical outdoors. Park facilities include restrooms, pavilions, water, showers and camping areas. Located just off Highway 19, about 12 miles northwest of Hilo.

Honoli'i Beach Park

Located just north of Hilo off Highway 19, on the jungle-y, twisted old scenic route Mamalahoa Highway, this is a local favorite and one of the best surfing beaches in the Hilo area. Restrooms and very limited parking along the roadside are available. A good spot for watching local kids catch the waves on a nice day.

★ Coconut Island

Although there's no beach here, Coconut Island is a great place to stop and play along Hilo Bay, rain or shine. Park beside the Hilo Hawaiian Hotel (in the park's lot—not the hotel's, where towing is enforced) and take the footbridge across to enjoy a picnic lunch, try your hand at fishing, explore the tidepools or relax in the grass. Pavilions, picnic tables, showers and restrooms are available and you might be lucky enough to catch a local concert or cultural festival.

Reed's Bay and Ice Pond

Just off Kalanianaole Avenue on Banyan Drive and across from the Hilo Seaside Hotel, though not exactly a beach area, Ice Pond is a shallow inlet formed by spring-fed stream. You'll sometimes see families playing there, though more often you'll see carloads of teenagers cruising Banyan Drive. While the water is calm and the spot is scenic, there are better places to play.

★ Onekahakaha Beach Park

Located behind Hilo Airport off Highway 137 just outside of Hilo town, this is a favorite spot for visitors and *kama'aina* as well. The park features a breakwater and retaining walls that create protected sandy-bottom swimming areas. Facilities include lifeguard service, pavilions, picnic tables, camp sites and restrooms.

James Kealoha Park

The park has a smooth lava-rock beach, picnic areas and restrooms. Good swimming, surfing and snorkeling are available here. Located east of Hilo along Kalanianaole Avenue.

★ Leleiwi Beach Park

This park also has a smooth lava-rock beach and pavilions, picnic areas and restrooms. Swimming, snorkeling and surfing are good here. Adjacent to the park is the Richardson Ocean Center, a marine education and aquatic display center open to the public; see "Traveling With Children: Entertainment" in Chapter 1 for details on the Richardson Ocean Center.

Puna District

The black-sand beaches of Puna have long been among the Big Island's most dramatic attractions (but please don't be tempted to carry away sand as a souvenir). Although fairly isolated, the beach parks tend to be crowded and their facilities heavily used.

Kapoho Bay

The bay is the backshore area fronting the Kapoho Beach Lots and Vacationland Estates subdivisions in the Kapoho area. While there isn't a sandy beach here, there is a beautiful tidal pond and pool area that is great for snorkeling and swimming. The tidal pools host a variety of marine life and small fish. There are no facilities.

Isaac Hale Beach Park

The park is on Cape Kumikahi, along the Puna Coast, and is the site of a busy boat-launching ramp used by commercial fishermen. The beach here is mostly smooth pebbles and cobblestones and not fine sand, but the bay is good for bodyboarding, swimming and seasonal surf. There are restrooms and showers available. Behind the beach is the Pohoiki Warm Springs, a natural warm-water bath heated by underground geothermal action, used for bathing and soaking.

Kehena Beach

Located on Pohoiki Road between Cape Kumikahi and Kaimu-Kalapana, the beach is a broad expanse of fine black sand below the Kehena Lookout and parking area. Access is via a steep trail down the cliff face. Kehena Beach is popular with swimmers and body-surfers. No facilities available.

★ Ahalanui Park

The area's newest beach park, the three-acre Ahalanui Park was established with a federal grant to replace parks lost at Kalapana to the volcanic lava flows of the 1990s. It's located two and a half miles south of the junction of Highways 132 and 137 on the Kapoho Coast southeast of Pahoa town. You'll find a half-acre pond/pool fed by thermal freshwater springs for a 95-degree natural hot tub experience. Facilities include lifeguard service and shaded picnic areas, restrooms and outdoor showers but no drinking water. There is no real beach here, since it is all lava-rock shoreline, but there is a nice coconut grove surrounding the pool to make for a lovely photo-op.

MacKenzie State Park

Just two miles down Highway 132 from Ahalanui is a whispering pine forest along the ocean coast. Although there is no beach here, soft pine needles, cool breezes and gorgeous views make it a worthwhile stop along the way. There's a picnic area and pit toilets.

Ka'u District

The Ka'u area is most famous for its Green Sand Beach, which is quite remote but accessible via a long, hot hike or commercial ATV excursion. Ka'u is very dry, with long stretches of empty countryside. The South Point area from which Green Sand Beach can be reached is an interesting historical site with old Hawaiian canoe landings and ruins in place.

Punalu'u Beach Park

Located near Pahala, this moderately long black-sand beach is backed by low dunes. The bay has a small boat-launching ramp, a freshwater fish pond and shaded picnic areas with palm trees.

Generally good for sunbathing and swimming, snorkelers should be cautious about venturing beyond the boat ramp because of a powerful rip current that runs out to the boat channel. The current converges with an even stronger shore current outside the bay that makes it more hazardous. Stay inside the ramp area and enjoy the varied sea life here. Hawaiian green sea turtles are quite numerous and easily seen as they surface close in to shore, where they feed on seaweed growing on the rocks and coral. Showers, restrooms and picnic pavilion are available.

Green Sand Beach

Worth the long trip, the beach at Mahana Bay is reached via the end of South Point Road and a very rough four-mile (roundtrip) coastal road, reached only by a four-wheel-drive vehicle or fairly rugged hike. If you hike, just be sure you take enough water and other necessities because there are no facilities or emergency phone (or cell-phone reception) at the beach. The beach is accessed by a steep and hazardous trail down the cliff side, which has loose rocks and cinders that make for slippery footing. Caution is advised. Big grains of olivine crystals from lava give the sand a distinctly green color and glassy luster. The beach, at the base of a huge eroding volcanic cinder cone, is exposed to the sea directly, and heavy surf and storms create dangerous surf conditions. Swimming and snorkeling are advised on only the calmest of days and extreme caution is in order. A permit to cross Hawaiian Home Lands is required for the trip to Green Sands Beach. For details, contact Department of Hawaiian Home Lands, 160 Baker Avenue, Hilo, HI 96720; 808-974-4250. They will mail an application to your home, or fax it to your condo or hotel. A return fax is all that's required at this time; no fees. Apparently some confusion in this procedure causes the gates to be padlocked from time to time, but there is room to drive or hike around the gate. Avoid disappointment and call ahead. Or, book your tour with one of the commercial ATV providers.

Whittington Beach Park

About three miles to the northeast of Na'alehu, Whittington Beach Park is just off Highway 11 on the eastern coast, across from an abandoned sugar mill. A rocky shoreline park with a small black-sand beach, Whittington offers picturesque scenery, picnic tables and pavilions, restrooms and nice tidepools for the kids to explore.

CHAPTER 6

Where to Play

The Big Island is big on fun. There is something to please everyone, from the toes-in-the-water set to the adventure-seeking backpacker determined to explore the most remote areas. Listings marked with ★ indicate particular favorites for fun, value or new and interesting things to check out. Please keep in mind that planned activities are a great way to spend time on vacation, and we encourage visitors to try something they wouldn't have the chance to try at home. However, as we've mentioned before, your time is valuable. Leave yourself some breathing room to explore independently, relax and enjoy the laid-back lifestyle at your own pace.

Best Bets

For Golfers   A round of championship golf at either the Mauna Kea Golf Course or the Francis I'i Brown Course at Mauna Lani Resort, both named among America's top resort courses.

For Golfers on a Budget   The Robert Trent Jones, Jr., course at Waikoloa Village or the 9-hole Hamakua Country Club.

For Ocean-lovers   A snorkeling adventure at Kahalu'u Bay at Keauhou-Kona, Kealakekua Bay State Historical & Underwater Parks in Kona, Anaeho'omalu Bay on the Kohala Coast, or Leleiwi Beach Park in Hilo.

For Ocean-lovers Who Don't Want to Get Wet   A submarine cruise or glass-bottom boat cruise along the Kona or Kohala coast, over spectacular coral gardens alive with tropical fish.

For Dolphin Fans Dolphin Quest encounters for all ages, located at the Hilton Waikoloa Village.

For Volcano-Watchers A helicopter "flightseeing" tour over Hawai'i Volcanoes National Park and the current eruption at Kilauea.

For Extreme Skiers If conditions permit, a ski run down Mauna Kea's fabulous snow-covered slopes.

For Horse Lovers A look at *paniolo* life on a guided trail ride through cool upcountry ranchlands, or a wagon tour through the peaceful valley of Waipi'o.

For Adventurous Anglers Go after a "grander," a 1000-pound marlin off the legendary Kona Coast.

For Hikers A trek through any of Hawai'i Volcanoes National Park trails to experience its unique natural beauty and many wonders, unlike anywhere else on earth. For something different, check out a flight and hike combination excursion into remote Honokane Nui Valley with Island Outfitters.

For Something Different An adventure kayak cruise along the old Kohala Ditch irrigation canal system, or let the whole family explore their artistic nature on a "watercolor safari" to one of the island's picturesque settings (contact Honoka'a artist Janice Gail at Windward Studio; 808-775-0466; e-mail: janicegailart@aol.com).

For RV Road-Warriors Rent a fully equipped 22-foot Tioga motor home and find your own places in the sun.

Activity Booking Services

A word about activity reservations on land and sea. Many timeshare, condominium and new subdivision sales ventures run their own activity-booking services. These offer considerable discounts on island activities (and sometimes free breakfast or lunch) in exchange for your time on a free tour of the property and a (usually heavy) sales pitch. Be aware who you're talking to when you stop by a kiosk or activity desk, and bear in mind that you can purchase activities elsewhere without committing to the property tour. If you're married, both spouses must attend and no-shows are charged full price for their bookings. It's not a bad way to "earn" a good discount, but keep in mind that vacation time is precious, and if you're not really in the market for real estate it might not be the best way to go. On the other hand, these are convenient, one-stop locations to help organize your vacation time with knowledgeable assistants. It's up to you.

Check with your hotel or resort activity desk, or any of the following agencies, to make reservations and arrangements for a full range of ocean sports and activities. They can help you arrange everything from whale watching, diving and snorkeling cruises, fishing charters, sailboat rentals, surfboard, kayak and windsurfing rentals or custom charters just for you. They'll also assist with land tours, hiking, horseback riding, ATV or bike trips and other fun things. Keep in mind that the majority of ocean activities take place in the Kona–Kohala area of the island, although Hilo offers a few charter boat, kayaking and other ocean opportunities.

As a note, many island activities have adopted the friendly custom of cooperative "linking," referrals and cross-selling each other to better serve guests. You can frequently book a helicopter-lu'au package or horseback-sailing combo just by asking. Following are just a few.

Big Island Adventures   Arrangements with numerous land, sea and air tour operators and activity vendors around the Big Island. Free reservation service. *Kona 808-334-1155; Waikoloa 808-883-0100; Hilo 808-935-9063.*

Expedia!fun Attractions   A well-known internet travel service, Expedia has reached out into the "non-virtual" activity business on all the islands, with a Kona kiosk offering adventures like helicopter tours, golf, horseback riding, submarine, fishing or snorkel boat excursions, lu'aus and much more. *800-624-7771; 808-329-7700; www.activityworld.com.*

Kona Marina Sports Activities   This service can arrange a variety of ocean sports activities and specializes in: deep-sea fishing and dive charters. They can arrange full- or half-day as well as share-parties. Japanese language available. *74-425 Kealakehe Parkway, 3rd floor, Honokohau Harbor, Kailua-Kona, HI 96740; 808-329-1115; fax: 808-329-9104; e-mail: uki@ilhawaii.net.*

VIP Activity Services   Some of the island's best. Free reservation service. *877-847-4627; 808-982-8772.*

Adventures and Tours

AIR TOURS

Small-plane Flightseeing
See the Big Island from a bird's-eye view on a scenic flight in a small plane. Flights depart from Hilo or Kona airports and generally include the island's most outstanding features and attractions such as volcano activity, waterfalls and valleys, lava deserts, rainforests and dramatic ocean coastlines.

Big Island Air   This small airline offers complete Big Island Volcano Tour, Big Island Sunset Tour, Circle Big Island/Volcano Tour,

Sunset Volcano Tour and a Super Saver Volcano Tour, plus custom charter flights can be arranged; they fly 9-passenger aircraft. Rates: Circle-island tours $275 per person, $180 for kids 18 and under. *Kailua-Kona; 800-303-8868; 808-329-4868; e-mail: bigisle@ilhawaii.net.*

Hawaii Flight Academy Formerly Sporty's Academy, this FAA Part 141 Certified flight instruction school offers vacation Aviation Adventures from a one-day introduction to a five-day ultimate adventure course. Train with certified instructors in a four-seat modern aircraft, and bring a friend if you like. Priced from $795 to $4,595. Air tours are arranged in cooperation with Island Hoppers. Hawaii Flight Academy provides its Aviation Adventure clients with an activity assistant to help with arrangements for golf, fishing, accommodations and other details of your visit. Their Kona campus, which also offers a four-year aviation degree program for international students. Located at Kona International Airport. *73-300 U'u Street, Kailua-Kona, HI 96740; 800-538-7590; 808-329-0018; e-mail: adventure@ fly-hawaii.com; www.fly-hawaii.com.*

Koa Air Service Hawai'i gives experienced pilots a "dual-rental" experience in their Cessna 150 and 172 airplanes. Enjoy do-it-yourself photo safaris, volcano excursions and island tours with one of their pilots along to assist and enhance the excursion. Rates: $130-$172 per hour. *Kona International Airport, Kailua-Kona, HI 96740; 808-326-2288.*

Island Hoppers A different perspective on island air tours, from a fixed-wing aircraft with 360-degree views from each seat. Flights tour the eruption area at Kilauea and along the rugged cliffs of the North Kohala coastline. Free video memento of the flight with music and narration. *Flights from Hilo or Kona International Airport; 808-969-2000; www.hawaiiislandhoppers.com.*

Mokulele Flight Service This Hawaiian family–owned operator offers airborne photo safaris in high-winged aircraft for unobstructed views of the island's magnificent valleys and waterfalls and the awesome home of Pele at Kilauea. Fully narrated, with two-way communication between passengers and the pilot, guaranteed window seats for all, complimentary video and lots of aloha. 90-minute circle-island air tours begin at $249 per person; 55-minute "Pele's Delight" volcano tours from Hilo start at $149 per person. Military and Senior discounts are available. (Ask about their combo special.) *Kona International Airport, P.O. Box 830, Holualoa, HI 96725; 808-326-7070; www.mokulele.com.*

Helicopter Tours

One of Hawai'i's best, a helicopter "flightseeing" tour is a thrilling way to experience the volcano up close and personal. Although pricey, you get a lot of Big Island for your buck. In general, tours either cover the beautiful and dramatic Hamakua Coast with its tropical rainforests, hidden valleys and countless waterfalls, or they give you the very best (and safest) vantage point to witness the current lava flow at Kilauea, or both. Costs vary accordingly and tours departing from Hilo can be less expensive (keeping in mind the 1.5-hour drive from Kona or Kohala Coast resorts). Tours range from about $100-$410 per person, depending on length of flight, aircraft and departure location. Most require a minimum number of people and advance reservations. Flights always depend on Mother Nature. Also, no scuba diving within 24 hours prior to your flight.

★ **Blue Hawaiian Helicopters**   This tour service offers a full range of island air tours to the volcano areas and all major Big Island attractions, featuring Bose electronic noise-canceling headsets and optional digital video system for a personal movie of your flight. Winner of FAA's Certificate of Excellence since 1998. Flights aboard the A-Star touring helicopters include Circle of Fire/Waterfalls (from Hilo); Big Island Spectacular and Kohala Coast Adventure (from Waikoloa). Rates: $191.13-$228.75 per person from their Waikoloa location, from $165 per person from Hilo. Ask about the exclusive ECO-Star craft ($368-50-$443.75). *P.O. Box 384473, Waikoloa Helipad, Waikoloa, HI 96738; 800-786-BLUE; 808-886-1768 Waikoloa; 808-961-5600 Hilo; www.bluehawaiian.com.*

Island Outfitters   This is something different a 25-minute helicopter flight into almost inaccessible Honokane Nui Valley, and a half- or full-day hike along a streamside trail and the old Kohala Ditch. Tours include day packs, water bottles, weather gear and snacks (lunch on the full-day tour). Experienced owner/guide Tom McAuliffe has backpacked every major trail in Hawai'i and is a UH honors grad in geography. Custom tour packages may be arranged to include hiking, diving, photography, star-gazing and volcano treks, mountain biking, kayaking, scuba, hunting, fishing, birding and, yes, just sightseeing. Rates: morning or afternoon tours, $380; full-day, $650. Charter rates are available. *P.O. Box 4441, Hilo, HI 96720; 808-966-7933; e-mail: islehike@aloha.com; www.islandoutfittershawaii.com.*

Safari Helicopters   This family-owned company has been in business since 1987, with a sturdy reputation for safety and professionalism. Safari's ASTAR birds are state of the art, with two-way radio communication between passengers and pilot, FAA-approved multiple-camera video system, a "Super Mega Window" for superior viewing and New Generation Bose X headsets. They specialize in air tours of the Big Island's volcano country with a special three-video camera system that captures all the scenery of your one-hour Volcano & Waterfalls flight along with the pilot's narration and your

SOMETHING DIFFERENT

Wa'akaulua, a 50-year-old double-hulled Hawaiian sailing canoe, gives six passengers a seldom-seen perspective of the ocean, along with valued lessons in Hawai'i's history, natural sciences and seafaring. Not a "cruise" (you'll be expected to paddle if the wind is lax) and not a whale-watching photo-op, this is an authentic sail with Captain Kiko, an experienced master boat builder and sailor, well-versed in ocean culture and the particular beauty of the Big Island shoreline. He also offers land adventures. The canoe lives in Punalu'u, but voyages depart from Hilo, Kona, Puako or Kawaihae, depending on your interest and Mother Nature. Rates: three-hour sail, $75 per person. Longer and overnight trips available. P.O. Box 490, Pahala, HI 96777; 808-938-5717; e-mail: kiko@waakaulua.com; www.waakaulua.com.

conversation. Rates start at $119 per person. *Hilo International Airport, Hilo, HI 96720; 808-969-1259; 800-326-3356; e-mail: reservations@safarihelicopters.com; www.safariair.com.*

★ **Sunshine Helicopters** Fly the "Black Beauties" with this 30-year veteran helicopter service, offering custom CD music, "sky-cam" five-camera video system and other comforts. Their tour menu offers 45- to 120-minute flights over lush, unspoiled coastal valleys and the ever-changing drama of the volcano. Rates: $170 Kohala/Hamakua Coast, $185 Formations of Pele–Kilauea Volcano, $390 Big Island Volcano Deluxe, $125 half-hour Valley Tour. *21-100 Kauna'oa Drive, Hapuna Heliport–Mauna Kea Resort, Kohala Coast, HI 96743; 800-622-3144; 808-882-1223; fax: 808-882-1100; e-mail: sales@sunshinehelicopters.com; www.sunshinehelicopters.com.*

Tropical Helicopters This pilot-owned and -operated air tour company offers various Big Island adventures from Hilo including Volcano–Rainbow Falls, $138; Volcano Deluxe, $158, and "Feel the Heat" doors-off, up close and personal way to experience eruption, $158-185. From Kona, the two-hour Hawaii Experience in their new Bell 407 is $335; a 90-minute Volcano Tour $280 and one-hour Valley & Waterfall flight is $180. Custom charters are available. *Main Terminal Building, Hilo International Airport, Hilo, HI 96720; 808-961-6810; fax: 808-969-1632; e-mail: info@tropicalhelicopters.com; www.tropicalhelicopters.com.*

Volcano Helicopters They offer a full range of sightseeing tours into Hawai'i Volcanoes National Park and surrounding countryside. *Hilo International Airport, P.O. Box 626, Volcano, HI 96785; 808-961-3355.*

BIKING

The Big Island offers some of the most varied scenery anywhere in the Hawaiian islands. It also has some of the largest expanses and stretches of wide-open uninhabited country in the islands. The geography ranges from desert beaches to tropical rainforests to dry lava deserts. An excellent way to see and experience the changing scenes is by bicycle touring.

Many visitors to the Big Island bring their own bicycles and camping equipment and make up their own itinerary. (Check on your hotel's bike policy first. Some do not permit bicycles, skateboards, roller skates or scooters on-property). The Big Island's highway system is generally good-to-excellent in most areas but often the shoulders are unimproved. Bikers need to exercise caution on the open road, especially in narrow winding sections of highway. If you are an adventurous bicyclist, you may want to plan your own tour of the island. Just keep in mind the long distances between towns in some areas like the Ka'u, South Kona, and the Kohala Coast area and plan accordingly for water, food, lodging and other needs. If you want to opt for an organized commercial bicycle tour you might try the following operators.

Biking Resources

For a look at Hawaii County's "bike plan" including interactive biking maps, visit www.hawaii.gov/dot/highways/bike/bikeplan/index. htm. For more information on biking and trails on the Big Island, the following groups and organizations may be able to assist.

Peoples Advocacy for Trails Hawai'i (PATH) This nonprofit community group advocates the development and improvement of trails around the Big Island for non-motorized multi-use: recreation, fitness and alternative modes of transportation. *P.O. Box 62, Kailua-Kona, HI 96745; 808-326-9495; e-mail: path@aloha.net; www.hialoha.com/path.*

Big Island Mountain Bike Association There are two tour guide/maps available online for Big Island visitors and bikers, containing trail descriptions, maps and safety information on ten featured trails located around the Big Island. Riders at every level, from beginner to advanced, will discover scenic trails along the coastline, through rainforest, rolling open pasture country and perfect picnic spots. Unique points of interest are included along with trail characteristics rated according to trail type, distance, rider level, elevation changes, riding time and more. Their website has the trail guide online. *P.O. Box 6819, Hilo, HI 96720; 808-961-4452; www.interpac. net/~mtbike.*

Bike Tours

Huberbikes Located just off Ali'i Drive in Kailua-Kona, Huberbikes Ironman Service Center offers top-of-the-line equipment, including custom-fit and fabricated frames and bikes by cycling champ Chris Huber. Among other unique services, Chris and his team will handle your bike coming in and departing Kona for triathlon participation (range of service $30-$195). Along with rentals, repairs, sales and accessories, the company offers cycling adventures island-wide and an annual seven-day training camp for the serious. (Chris holds the world record for human-powered vehicle speed, 68.73 mph.) 73-5580 Maiau Street, L, Kailua-Kona, HI 96740; 808-936-3762; e-mail: chris@huberbikes.com.

★ **Kona Coast Cycling Tours** This outfitter and operator offers three- to four-hour half-day and four- to six-hour full-day bike adventures, for all levels of ability and interest from "casual" to "intense," top-of-the-line road bikes or hybrid comfort bikes, with full van and mechanic support, great food and personal service. The Kohala Mountain Downhill is 20 miles, four to five hours; a challenging 56 miles, six to eight hours for bikers 16 and over, costs $155 including snacks and lunch. A shorter bike trek that might be better for families is Coffee Country Express, a 7-mile mostly downhill ride, three-and-a-half to five hours long for $60 adults or kids 12 to 16, including snacks and beverages. Enjoy the changing panorama of the Big Island via the less-traveled and offroad routes of these unique biking adventures. Children must be 2 years old to participate. Rates: 7- or 15-mile Coffee Country Tour, $62.50-$95; 20-mile Old Mamalahoa Highway Tour, $125. Custom and charter rates available. Photos and details of the bikes on their website. P.O. Box 2213, Kailua-Kona HI 96745; 877-592-BIKE; 808-345-3455; e-mail: bikeinfo@cyclekona.com; www.cyclekona.com.

★ **Mauna Kea Mountain Bikes Inc.** This bike outfitter offers private guided tours of rainforest trails, scenic highways and some of the Big Island's best backcountry mountain and ranch areas. Adventures range from 2-4 hours with varied distances, from the easy 2.5-hour Kohala Downhill tour for beginners to increasingly tougher rides along Mana Road or Mud Lane in Waimea hill country. The 3.5-hour Mauna Kea Kamikaze ride is a 13-mile bike trek on steep gravel and paved roadways starting from Mauna Kea's summit, 13,796 feet, and zooming downhill with incredible 360-degree views all the way (if you have time to turn your head). All rides include full equipment and bike. They provide a range of mountain and offroad touring bikes and equipment. Rates: $75-$80 Kohala downhill; $55-$65 Mana Road or Mud Lane; $90-$120 Mauna Kea Kamikaze. Bike rentals start at $25 per day. P.O. Box 44672, Kamuela, HI

Bike Rentals

Aquatic Perceptions Multi-Sports Tours This multi-sport outfitter provides mountain bike rentals and a variety of bike adventures on the east side of the island and the green slopes of North Kohala, from four to eight hours on DiamondBack 21-speed Cross or Comfort-Style mountain bicycles. Tours start at $70 per person and include helmet, gloves, rain gear, beverages and snacks. Bike rentals are $5 per hour, $25 per day, $120 for 7 days. (See their listing under kayaking later in this chapter.) Volcano downhill runs and Coastal Jungle bike treks and excursions around Hilo Bay, the Hamakua Coast and the Puna Coast areas. Instruction also available. *111 Banyan Drive, Hilo, HI 96720; 808-939-9997; 808-938-1228; e-mail: kayak scuba@aol.com; www.multi-sport-hawaii.com.*

Hawaii Sports Connection This shop carries a full line of bikes and equipment and other sporting goods and gear. They also do repairs. Rates: $20-$30 per day. *75-5699 Kopiko Place, Kopiko Plaza, Kailua-Kona, HI 96740; 808-329-3309; 808-329-9718; fax: 808-329-7340; e-mail: sports@ilhawaii.net; www.bibikes.com.*

C&S Outfitters Friendly, experienced outfitter provides full line of bike gear and supplies, plus sun protection, souvenirs, snacks and beverages. Open Monday through Saturday 9 a.m. to 5 p.m. Bikes are $24 per day (5-hour minimum) and $130 per week, including helmet and toolkit if needed. Car racks and padlocks available for rent; $45 delivery charge to local accommodations. C&S suggests bikers bring their own bike shoes and pedals along if they don't want to bring their own bikes. Jogging strollers for rent too. *Located in Waimea at the intersection of Highway 19 and Kamamalu Street; 808-885-5005; fax: 808-885-5683.*

Dave's Bike & Triathlon Shop This shop has a variety of mountain bikes and road bikes to rent by the hour, day or week. They also provide service, repairs, accessories and supplies. Rates: $15 per day for mountain bikes and beach cruisers, $25 per day or $60 per week for road bikes. *75-5669 Ali'i Drive, Kailua-Kona, HI 96740; 808-329-4522.*

★ ***P Bike Works*** They have a full line of bike rentals (daily, weekly, monthly) as well as also equipment sales, rentals and repairs. Rates: from $35 per day for road bikes, $40 for deluxe road bike and $45 for full suspension mountain bike. Multi-day and weekly rates available. *74-5599 Luhia, Kailua-Kona, HI 96740; 808-326-2453.*

Hawaiian Pedals Bike Rentals This shop has a wide range of bike rentals available including mountain bikes, performance bikes and tandem touring bikes. They also have a range of tour excursions available. Call for current rates and availability. *75-5744 Ali'i Drive, Kona Inn Shopping Center, Kailua-Kona, HI 96740; 808-329-2294.*

Hilo Bike Hub This shop specializes in sales and repair of mountain bikes and related equipment. Ask about their special Friday "Fun Rides" through Ku Ali'i Forest. *318 East Kawili Street, Hilo, HI 96720; 808-961-4452; e-mail: hilobke@gte.net.*

Mauna Kea Mountain Bikes Inc. They have a full line of bike and related equipment rentals. *P.O. Box 44672, Kamuela, HI 96743; 888-MTB-TOUR; 808-883-0130; e-mail: mtbtour@aol.com.*

Mid Pacific Wheels This shop offers a full line of rental bikes and equipment. *1133C Manono Street, Hilo, HI 96720; 808-935-6211; www.midpacificwheels.com.*

Bike Trails

There are several bike paths and trails around the Big Island ranging from easy rides to more challenging backcountry, offroad and mountain trails for skilled riders. Regardless of your bike-riding skill level, there's a Big Island bike trail waiting for you to explore. There's everything from a difficult mountain climb to a cruise down a volcano or an easy peddle along a mostly smooth coastal trail. On Big Island bike trails, you'll enjoy the many scenic vistas and unspoiled panoramic views of the island's less traveled offroad backcountry trails and paths that you get only from a bike.

Kona District **Walua Road** off Kuakini Highway is a few miles south of downtown Kailua-Kona. Turn onto Lako Street, just opposite the Kilohana/Komohana housing tract. The paved trail begins above the Chevron gas station; it's a 6.4-mile round-trip, 45-minute ride through housing subdivisions. The trail crosses residential streets so be aware of local traffic; ride climbs uphill gradually, from 400 feet to 1200 feet elevation. There are nice panoramic ocean views and tropical landscaping all along the way. The ride back is downhill all the way.

Pine Trees trail is just north of town, before Kona International Airport, off Highway 19 at the Natural Energy Lab of Hawai'i (NELHA) grounds. Turn into NELHA just before the airport entrance and go about one mile to the coastline. This is a 6.4-mile round-trip, 1.5-hour ride. The trail begins 50 yards north of the parking lot. The lava trail turns to sandy beach road that winds along the coast for 1.2 miles. The trail ends at the Ho'ona Historical Preserve. From the parking lot, the trail heads south, and where the trail curves, veer right and follow the beach trail for 2 miles. This is an easy ride for beginners; warm and windy but nice coastal panoramas.

North Kohala Coast Highway 270 between Kawaihae and Hawi town along the North Kohala coastline is about a 10-mile stretch, a beautiful, scenic run of wide, fairly straight and level highway with bike shoulders and good visibility. Bikers can trek along a portion of the Ironman Triathlon bike route, have lunch in Hawi town and return along the same path, or take the winding mountain road down to Waimea and back to Kawaihae, although some portions of this route are very narrow and weather may be a factor. Use caution and common sense. Although the coastal highway is pretty consistently sunny, the wind can be strong so pay attention and don't forget sunblock and plenty of water.

Pohue Road trail is located in the North Kohala District between Hawi town and Mahukona. There are two access points. From the Kohala Mountain Road (Highway 250), turn onto Pohue Road just past the 17-mile marker. Follow the gravel road 50 yards, turn right on the grassy road and go through the gate. From the Akoni Pule Highway (Highway 270, the coastal route north from Kawaihae), look for the access just past the 18-mile marker and turn inland. This country road maintained by the government features varied terrain and wonderful open views of ranchlands and Maui across the sea. Road surfaces vary from rocky cinder to dirt lanes across ranchlands. Riders have a choice of riding uphill or downhill or both. Either way is 5 miles, round-trip 10 miles. It takes a half-hour to ride down, one hour or more to ride up. Wide open panoramic views in generally warm, breezy conditions.

Kohala Mountain Road (Highway 250) runs 20 miles up and over the Kohala Mountains between Waimea and Hawi. This is perhaps the Big Island's most scenic pastoral route and passes through rolling ranch country, green mountains and pastures, herds of grazing cattle and sheep, and beautiful views of the distant Kohala Coast. This is a narrow, winding road and is lined with ironwood trees that serve as a windbreak along the upper reaches where the Kohala winds can be brisk. Caution is advised; moderate in difficulty.

Highway 270 from Kapa'au to the Pololu Valley in North Kohala is a pleasant, easy, 8-mile, one-way ride through old sugar plantation country and lush open coastal hill country. It's a narrow winding road so caution is advised. The area has several old plantation settlements with a distinct rural Hawaiian charm. Along the way, the road passes by the historic Wo On Store and Wo Tong Chinese Society Building dating from 1886, Keokea Beach Park and several churches and other buildings in this historic area. Other roads branch off and meander in this North Kohala area, providing many miles of exploration and discovery for adventurous bikers.

Saddle Road/Mauna Kea Backcountry Mana Road is one of the Big Island's most scenic and longer backcountry bike trails and passes around the east and north sides of Mauna Kea. Take Saddle

Road up the mountain from either the Hilo or Kona side and follow the Mauna Kea Access Road leading to the summit, opposite a hunter check-in hut. Drive north on this road about 2 miles and turn right (east) on the dirt road leading down and across pasturelands; cross a cattle guard gate. From Waimea, the Mana Road access junction is on Mamalahoa Highway, just across from the Department of Hawaiian Home Lands complex. This upcountry trail links Saddle Road and Waimea. It's a 45-mile trek either way and is an all-day, 6-8-hour ride, taking your time. Elevation changes from 3,000 feet to 6,500 feet. The trek ranges from smooth, level dirt or gravel road through cattle pastures to rough, rugged and rutted trail in dense upland forest. This is also a 4WD vehicle road used by hunters. Unspoiled vistas of mountain slopes and forest overlook distant ranchlands and stands of magnificent old *koa* trees throughout the upcountry pastures. Don't be surprised to come upon herds of cattle, which usually scatter when they see people. There are numerous cattle gates to pass through; be sure to close them all. To bike Mana Road one way, arrange to have someone meet you at the other end. You'll need lots of food and water plus cool weather rain gear. On clear days, there are any number of great picnic spots along the Mana Road to just relax and enjoy Mauna Kea's magnificent upcountry. A couple of cabins are available to campers along the trail; contact State Forestry and Wildlife, 808-974-4221.

Kilohana Trail is accessed via Saddle Road. Look for the Kilohana Hunter Check-in Station sign between the 44- and 45-mile markers and turn onto this gravel road; the trail begins on this northwest side of Mauna Kea. This is a 6.6-mile, one-way ride for experienced riders only, about 1.5 hours each way. The road climbs gradually on gravel then dirt surface, where it gets rough. At 2.2 miles go right at the fork and this takes you to Ahumoa, a cinder cone at 7,042-foot elevation with nice views of surrounding country. The road continues up (you may have to walk part way) for another 3.1 miles to Pu'u La'au and a hunter's cabin surrounded by eucalyptus trees at 7,446-foot elevation. This is a good place to rest, picnic and enjoy the views before heading back down the same route.

Hamakua Coast Highway 240 runs from Honoka'a north to the Waipi'o Valley overlook, a 10-mile, one-way ride through rolling hills and old sugar plantation lands along the Hamakua Coast. The road passes through the old plantation settlements of Kawela, Kapulena and Kukuihaele before reaching the top of Waipi'o Valley. It's a pleasant, easy ride with nice views of the north side of Waipi'o Valley.

Hilo Kulani Trails is just south of Hilo off Highway 11. At 4.2 miles south of Hilo, turn right onto Stainback Highway at the sign for Panaewa Rain Forest Zoo. Continue 2.6 miles and turn right at

Waiakea Arboretum. Take the first left off the highway and the first set of trails begins. This is a challenging, dense forest ride on single-track trails with lots of slippery conditions, roots, rocks, fallen logs and mud but is otherwise a cool forest ride. There are majestic 100-foot-tall eucalyptus trees all around. Distances and times vary; routes wind throughout the Waiakea Forest Reserve area.

Puna District Old Puna Trail runs along the Puna coastline from Hawaiian Paradise Park subdivision north to Haena Beach. Head south from Hilo to the turnoff for Highway 130 at Kea'au. Take Highway 130 about 4.5 miles, turn left on Kaloli Road and go another 4.2 miles to Beach Road. Head left on Beach Road and pick up the trail, which is somewhat rough and rugged. The trail follows the old Puna trail that linked the area with Hilo back in the 1800s. The ride is through lush tropical forest with fruit trees, flowers and bright foliage; 4WD trails branch off to fishing spots on the coast but these are rough trails to be avoided. You'll see Haena Beach nestled in evergreens and Norfolk pines. It is a 10-mile ride one-way, about 3 to 4 hours long.

Puna Coast Beach Road is accessed by heading south on Highway 11 from Hilo to Kea'au. Turn onto Highway 130 for 4.6 miles, then turn left at Kaloli Road in Hawaiian Paradise Park subdivision. Go 4.2 miles downslope to Beach Road at the coast, then turn right on Beach Road for 1.2 miles. The old Puna trail begins here and runs 10.5 miles one way, an hour ride. It is mostly level on a cinder and dirt road through fields of wild orchids and coastal rainforest. There are great views along this isolated and remote rugged coastal area. The dirt road ends at Kapoho but the coastal road, Highway 137, continues 12 miles to the settlements of Pohoiki, Opihikao and Kalapana areas. This would be advised only if you can arrange a pickup at the Kalapana end. Otherwise it's a long ride back the same route or via Pahoa town and Highway 130.

Ka'u District/Volcanoes National Park Volcano Trails are 30 miles south of Hilo and 97 miles south of Kona via Highway 11 at Hawai'i Volcanoes National Park. All paved roads in the park are open to bikers, although some unpaved trails may also be open. Check with park rangers at entrance or visitors center and get a map.

The 11-mile **Crater Rim Drive** circles Kilauea Volcano summit caldera and goes through tropical rain and fern forest, past steaming vents and smoking sulphur banks, craters and cinder cones. There are a number of short walks at places like Devastation Trail and Thurston Lava Tube plus several craters and overlooks. The Chain of Craters Road winds downslope from Crater Rim Drive some 20 miles to the recent eruption sites along the Kalapana Coast. The road terminates where the latest lava flows have crossed it. If eruption activity is still ongoing, it's possible to see steam plumes where the lava enters the ocean. Visitors might also be able to see the lava flows at a close distance if rangers feel it safe enough.

Bikers can take Chain of Craters Road but should be warned it gets a lot of traffic and is a long climb back up from the coastal flats. Distances and times for bike trails vary within the national park.

Ainapo Trail is located south of Hawai'i Volcanoes National Park on Highway 11. At 12.2 miles past the park entrance, turn right on an access road marked by a gravel turnout, a gate and Ainapo Trail Road sign. Hang right for about .1 mile. The ride alternates on a dirt and grass track, gradually climbing through pasture, guava tree thickets and rocky outcroppings. There is a gate one mile in and in another 3.5 miles the road forks; keep right for 4.4 miles to the Ainapo Trailhead. The famed Ainapo Trail is for hikers only and leads to the summit of Mauna Loa. There is a cabin about a 3.5-hour hike up at the 7,750-foot level. To reserve the cabin, call State Forestry & Wildlife, 808-974-4221. Bikers return the same route. This ride is 9 miles long, 3 hours up to trailhead and 1 hour back down.

BOATING

Surrounded by some of the world's most amazing waters, the Big Island offers every opportunity you can think of to enjoy the ocean. An armada of pleasure craft stands ready to help and reputable, experienced operators can introduce you to a world of water sports and fun activity suitable for all age groups and experience levels, from non-swimmers to athletes looking for a new challenge. See separate listings for Fishing, Kayaking, Scuba Diving, Sea Excursions-Sailing-Cruises, Snorkeling, Snuba, Surfing-Windsurfing and Whale Watching. Please keep in mind that many charters and ocean activity companies are extremely flexible, offering multi-sport opportunities and combination tours. Reservationists in these frequently family-run businesses are dependably friendly and well-informed and will be happy to answer your questions. If their company doesn't offer what you're looking for, they know someone who does. Websites of the larger operators like Ocean Sports (www.hawaiiocean sports.com) and Red Sail Sports (www.redsail.com) are good starting points to learn more about the possibilities.

BOWLING

The Big Island has locations on both sides of the island in Hilo and Kona. Both are full-service bowling lanes with equipment rentals and snack bars. They're open daily, except major holidays, but check for specific hours as they may vary from time to time.

Hilo Lanes   *777 Kino'ole Street, Hilo; 808-935-0646*
Kona Bowl   *75-5586 Ololi Road, in the Lanihau Center, Kailua-Kona; 808-326-2695*

CAMPING

The Big Island has numerous county, state and national parks in both inland and coastal locations. Some are designed strictly for those with their own tents and camping gear, and some have basic cabins or shelters for overnight or longer rentals. Facilities vary widely.

County of Hawai'i Parks

The County of Hawai'i maintains 11 parks around the island with designated campgrounds for those with their own tents and camping gear. County parks have no cabins and facilities vary. Some have full restrooms, showers and drinking water; others may have primitive pit latrines and no drinking water. Check ahead on what facilities are available to avoid disappointment. Permits are required for campgrounds and for use of the pavilions. County campsites are on a first-come, first-served basis, with advance reservations required for peak seasons like the winter and summer holidays. Camping permits are issued for one week per park in summer months and two weeks per park in other months. Camping fees at county parks are adults $5 per day, juniors (13-17) $2 per day, children (12 and under) $1 per day. For reservations, permits and complete information regarding any of the County of Hawai'i parks, contact: Department of Parks and Recreation, County of Hawai'i, 25 Aupuni Street, Hilo, HI 96720. 808-961-8311; in Kona 808-327-3560; e-mail: cohparks@hotmail.com; www.hawaii-county.com. Hours are Monday through Friday 7:45 a.m. to 3:45 p.m., closed for lunch 12 to 1 p.m.

Campgrounds are found at the following county parks:

Kona District—Ho'okena Beach Park, Miloli'i Beach Park

Kohala Coast—Keokea Beach Park, Kapa'a Beach Park, Mahukona Beach Park, Spencer Beach Park

Hamakua Coast—Laupahoehoe Point Beach Park, Kolekole Beach Park.

Puna District—Isaac Hale Beach Park

Ka'u District—Punalu'u Beach Park, Whittington Beach Park.

State of Hawai'i Parks & Recreation Areas

The State of Hawai'i maintains a system of parks and recreation areas around the Big Island. Three of them presently are designated for use as campgrounds and two have simple lodging facilities. Parks are equipped with developed campgrounds, camping shelters, and basic housekeeping cabins or barracks-type group accommodations. The condition of these facilities is subject to change, depending on weather and the uncertainties of government maintenance and upkeep. (We've heard stories from fine to deplorable.) Check first with the State Parks office. Campers need to be aware that most state camping cabins and facilities will be very rustic accommodations with few amenities short of the basics. There are no entrance, parking, picnicking or camping fees. However, permits are required for camping and lodging in the parks. The maximum length of stay allowable in any park is five nights. Advance reservations are required for any state park cabin or campground. Keys for reserved cabins are available from the park caretaker or Division of State Parks office in Hilo, 75 Aupuni Street. Check-in time is 2 p.m., check-out time is 10 a.m. For complete information on obtaining a camping and lodging permit, contact: Department of Land & Natural Resources, Division of State Parks, Hawai'i District Office, P.O. Box 936, 75 Aupuni Street #204, Hilo, HI 96721-0936. 808-974-6200. The office is open 8 a.m. to 3:30 p.m. Monday through Friday. Detailed information and a downloadable permit are available at www.hawaii.gov/dlnr/dsp/hawaii.html.

Hapuna Beach State Recreation Area Located on Queen Ka'ahumanu Highway 19, 2.3 miles south of Kawaihae on the Kohala Coast, this is one of best stretches of white-sand beach on the island. Picnic pavilions are available. Six simple four-person A-frame cabins/shelters are available and have a table, wooden platforms for sleeping bags, electrical outlets and shared cooking facilities, showers and toilets. Cabins are $20 per night.

Kalopa State Recreation Area Located at 2,000-feet elevation on Kalopa Road, 3 miles upland of Highway 19 about 5 miles south of Honoka'a on the Hamakua Coast, this site has picnic pavilions, campgrounds, group cabins (for up to 32 people total) and a shared recreation/mess hall.

Group cabins (1-8 people) are $55 per night; $5 per night per extra person

MacKenzie State Recreation Area Located on breezy and warm coastal cliffs in an ironwood grove on Kalapana-Kapoho Road, Highway 137, southeast area of the Big Island. Picnic pavilions available; primitive campground, no drinking water.

Manuka State Wayside Located 19.3 miles west of Na'alehu. A smaller area for picknickers and open shelter camping. No drinking water.

Mauna Kea State Recreation Area   On Saddle Road about 35 miles west of Hilo. Recently reopened in pretty good shape, but there is still no potable water, so bring your own bottles. Cabins and picnic areas with view of Mauna Kea and Mauna Loa. A good spot for hunters. Nights can be cold, so be prepared.

Hawaiʻi Volcanoes National Park

The national park maintains three drive-in campgrounds within Volcanoes National Park for campers with their own tents and gear. Each has pavilion shelters with picnic tables and fireplaces but you need to bring your own wood or fuel. Check the discount stores in Hilo or Kona for camping supplies. No permit is needed and there is no charge for camping. Camping is on a first-come, first-served basis. Stays are limited to seven days per campground per year.

The park service also maintains three simple backcountry cabins for hikers but you must register at park headquarters for overnight stays; cabins are first-come, first-served, but they're not heavily used so hikers can usually be accommodated. It is necessary to check on trail conditions and water supplies before undertaking a backcountry hike. The cabins are located in remote, desolate areas, some at high elevations where severe weather can occur, especially during the winter months. Check with park rangers for information.

One campground, **Namakani Paio**, has simple A-frame cabins that can accommodate four people in one double bed and two single bunks. The cabins all share a central restroom and shower facility. Outside each cabin is a picnic table and a barbecue grill. You must provide your own charcoal and cooking utensils. Cabins include bed linens, towels and blankets (picked up at Volcano House, 3 miles away). It's recommended you bring extra blankets or sleeping bags (especially in winter) as the cabins are not heated and temperatures can drop to the mid-50s. Rates: $40 per night, double. Reservations are recommended and can be made through Volcano House, P.O. Box 53, Hawaiʻi Volcanoes National Park, HI 96718; 808-967-7321; fax: 808-967-7321.

For complete information, contact: Superintendent, Hawaiʻi Volcanoes National Park, Volcano, HI 96718. 808-985-6000; www.nps.gov/havo.

COFFEE FARMS

In November each year, the Kona Coffee Cultural Festival celebrates Kona's prized product with picking contests, cupping competition, parades and all kinds of food, music and arts events from Kona's diverse ethnic population. For more information contact Kona Coffee Cultural, P.O. Box 1112, Kailua-Kona, HI 96745; 808-326-7820;

www.konacoffeefest.com. They also put together an excellent Kona Coffee Country Driving Tour map and brochure (if you take one sip at every stop you're guaranteed to be wired by the time you get back to your hotel). Note: There are hundreds of coffee farms in Kona now, with changing policies for drop-in visitors. Some of them are hard to find. The roads of "Kona Mauka" tend to be narrow, winding, not well-marked and often shoulderless. Visitors must be aware of slow-moving farm vehicles, bicycles and sometimes heavy local traffic. Look at your map first, appoint a navigator, and if you get lost, remember to pull all the way off of the road before you stop to get your bearings. Below is just a sparse sampling of suggested stops.

Bay View Farms This coffee farm is just above Pu'uhonua o Honaunau Place of Refuge on Painted Church Road. Free explanatory tours of the farm and processing plant, award-winning coffee tasting and a retail shop. Their new Coffees 'n Epicurea Patisserie (808-328-0322), located at mile marker 106 on Highway 11 just north of the farm, offers a tempting selection of sweet treats including the chef's special purple *haupia* pie and passionfruit cheesecake. Open 6:30 a.m. to 6 p.m. daily. *P.O. Box 680, Honaunau, HI 96726; 800-662-5880; 808-328-9658; fax: 808-328-8693; www.bayviewfarmcoffees.com.*

Coffee Shack Located just north of 108-mile marker. Enjoy coffee production displays and tasting room with espresso bar overlooking the Kona coast and Kealakekua Bay. *P.O. Box 510, 83-5799 Mamalahoa Highway 11, Captain Cook, HI 96704; 800-800-6267; 808-328-9555; fax: 808-328-9461; www.coffeeshack.com.*

Country Samurai Coffee Company One of the best, this third-generation coffee plantation is located high upcountry in Keauhou *mauka*, but their retail operation is conveniently located in downtown Kailua-Kona. Country Samurai produces only 100 percent Kona coffee of the better grades: Fancy, Extra Fancy, Peaberry and Kona No. 1. By family tradition, they allow the trees to grow 15 to

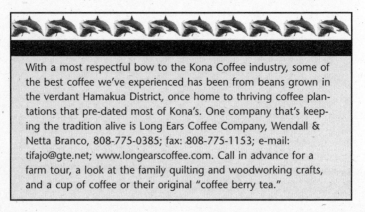

With a most respectful bow to the Kona Coffee industry, some of the best coffee we've experienced has been from beans grown in the verdant Hamakua District, once home to thriving coffee plantations that pre-dated most of Kona's. One company that's keeping the tradition alive is Long Ears Coffee Company, Wendall & Netta Branco, 808-775-0385; fax: 808-775-1153; e-mail: tifajo@gte.net; www.longearscoffee.com. Call in advance for a farm tour, a look at the family quilting and woodworking crafts, and a cup of coffee or their original "coffee berry tea."

20 feet tall, rather than keep them stunted for easy harvest, and age the beans for 1.5-2 years before processing. The result is a fragrant, buoyant coffee that elevates the spirits. Enjoy a cup of freshly brewed Kona coffee, learn about their history and coffee secrets (including how to make the perfect cup of coffee) and shop for *omiyage* (gifts). They pack and ship special orders to the mainland. *Kona Square, 75-5669 Ali'i Drive #1104A, Kailua-Kona HI 96740; 888-666-KONA; 808-331-1444; 808-322-0656; e-mail: kunitake@earthlink.net; www.countrysamurai.com.*

Ferrari Coffee Hawaiian Mountain Gold Visitors Center Ferrari now offers two Visitors Centers on Mamalahoa Highway in the Holualoa area just five miles south of the Palani Road/Highway 190 junction. Look for them across the street from the "pink hotel." You'll also find Ferrari in a couple of "mobile" coffee outlets along Ali'i Drive. *P.O. Box 390486, Kailua-Kona, HI 96739; 800-288-1542; phone/fax: 808-324-1542; www.ferraricoffee.com.*

Greenwell Farms Visitor tours of historic coffee estate orchards, processing facilities and the family's historic home (part of the Kona Historical Society); sample Greenwell Farms Private Reserve Kona Coffee. Open Monday through Friday 8 a.m. to 4:30 p.m., Saturday 8 a.m. to 3:30 p.m. *81-6560 Mamalahoa Highway, between 111 and 112 mile markers, P.O. Box 248, Kealakekua, HI 96750; 888-592-5662; 808-323-2275; fax: 808-323-2050; www.greenwellfarms.com.*

Holualoa Kona Coffee Co. Visit the Kona Le'a Plantation in Holualoa for a free coffee farm tour, and taste the finished product. Monday through Friday 8 a.m. to 4 p.m. *77-6261 Mamalahoa Highway in Holualoa, one mile north of 1-mile marker; 800-334-0348; 808-322-9937; www.konalea.com.*

Kona Blue Sky Coffee Company This is the family-run Twigg-Smith Estate located on 500 acres on the slopes of Mount Hualalai. They offer 100 percent Kona coffee; complimentary guided walking tours of the estate, and a gift shop in Holualoa. They also have an espresso bar and outlet shop at the Waikoloa Beach Marriott, Kohala Coast. *P.O. Box 470, Holualoa, HI 96725; 877-322-1700; 808-322-1700; www.konablueskycoffee.com.*

Kona Historical Society's Kona Coffee Living History Farm located in Captain Cook, this is an excellent opportunity to visit the past and present with coffee farm and mill tours, living-history programs, hands-on demonstrations and a retail shop on-site. Open daily; however, please call ahead for tour reservations. *808-323-2006; fax: 808-323-9576; www.konahistorical.org.*

Kona Joe Coffee Farm and Chocolate Company Just below Lanakila Church in Kainaliu. Retail shop, roastery, tastings and farm tours. Open Monday through Friday 9 a.m. to 5 p.m. Kona Joe

Coffee lovers should seek out the **Kona Coffee Country Driving Tour**, published by the County of Hawai'i and the Kona Coffee Cultural Festival. This brochure has a map and comprehensive listing of coffee farms, mills, shops and museums of the Kona Coast, including the history of Kona coffee and the annual cultural festival, how to get to the coffee farm areas and what to look for along the way. There are tips for buying and brewing coffee and even a recipe or two. It's a bright, colorful guide to a driving tour of Kona's famed coffee country. And, look for the Cultural Society's excellent *Kona Coffee Cookbook* in local bookstores. 808-326-7820; www.konacoffeefest.com.

grows his award-wining coffee on trellises, "like wine." *877-KONA-JOE; 808-322-2100; fax: 808-322-2770; www.konajoe.com.*

Kona Pacific Farmers Cooperative Look for the Pink Donkey to find this 300-farmer co-op building with historical displays, farm tours and farm-direct outlet store. Open Monday through Friday 7 a.m. to 4 p.m. Call ahead for tours. *82-5810 Napo'opo'o Road, Captain Cook; 808-328-2411; fax: 808-328-2414; www.kpfc.com.*

Ueshima Coffee (UCC Hawaii) Corp. Roastery and Coffee Bar open daily 9:30 a.m. to noon for tours and tastings. Or call ahead for the "Roastmaster Experience" and try your hand at your own private reserve coffee blend with your family photo on the label. *82-5810 Napo'opo'o Road, Captain Cook; 888-822-5662; 808-328-0604; fax: 808-328-5663; www.ucc-hawaii.com.*

FISHING

There are few places in the world that match the Kona Coast for the thrill and excitement of big-game fishing. In August, Kona is the site of the "grandfather of all big game fishing tournaments," the annual Hawaiian International Billfish Tournament, which for the past 46 years has attracted participants from around the world. HIBT, P.O. Box 4800, Kailua-Kona, HI 96745; 808-329-6155; www.konabillfish.com. Numerous other fishing tournaments are held throughout the year.

Kona harbors a large and diverse fleet of charter fishing boats that offers a complete range of full- and half-day arrangements (or longer if you like), from budget-minded small charters to top-of-the-line high-tech, high-dollar excursions. Prices vary depending on the size of the boat, how it is equipped (showers, beds, fully stocked galley) and number of passengers. Full-day charters start from around $200 per person with normally a four-person minimum/six-person maximum. Half-day charters might start at $125 per person. Whole-boat charters range in price from approximately $300 to $600. Generally a 50% deposit is required at time of booking. Night fishing, overnights and custom charters can be arranged. Usually non-fishing guests can ride along for a reduced charge. Most boats are only licensed to carry six anglers at a time and provide all fishing equipment and ice. Generally you must bring your own food and beverages as these are not included in charter rates. You are not required to have a fishing license; it is provided by the boat.

Please be aware that because of Hawai'i's generally low charter boat rates in comparison to other areas, the general policy among charter boat associations is that any fish caught belongs to the boat captain or owner, who sell it on the market to augment their fares. This is the reason for the policy. However, if you want to keep your catch, or part of it, request it from the captain in advance and avoid disappointment. In the case of good table fish such as mahimahi or ahi tuna, most captains will be more than happy to share the catch with the fishing party to enjoy a fresh fish dinner. For a fee, the chef at your hotel will most likely prepare your fish for dinner at your request.

Tipping is generally at the discretion of clients but about 15% is customary. Captains can arrange for your catch to be mounted and shipped home for you. Tag and release is a popular option for most boats, to conserve the marine population for future fishing trips.

And so what can you expect to catch, with a little traditional fishing luck? Kona's waters teem with a variety of Hawaiian game fish. Perhaps most popular is the Pacific blue marlin with an average size of 300-400 pounds, but with "granders" of 1,000 pounds entirely possible. Other average catches would be striped marlin, 50-100 pounds, black marlin, 200 pounds, sailfish, about 50 pounds or less. Swordfish are generally more difficult to catch but average 250 pounds when they are landed. The popular yellowfin tuna ranges up to 300 pounds, while mahimahi will be about 25 pounds. Other local fish you might encounter include *ono*, *aku* and *ulua*, and some captains go for tiger or other species of shark and barracuda.

All charter boats and boat captains must be licensed and certified by the U.S. Coast Guard. Best bet is to arrange your charter in advance through a booking agency such as the ones suggested below. Most agencies represent several boats and can give you complete information on how to book a charter, what to expect, and how to cater the experience to suit your group and maximize your deep-sea adventure.

Boat-chartering Agencies

Charter Desk This booking service offers charter deep-sea fishing from a large fleet of professional fishing boats. Watch the daily fish weigh-ins at 11 a.m. and 3 p.m. on the Honokohau Harbor docks from the free public viewing area. Deli, gas station, clothing store and general store also available; restaurant at the harbor. *74-381 Kealakehe Parkway, Honokohau Harbor, Kailua-Kona, HI 96740; 808-329-5735; 888-KONA4US; fax: 808-329-5747.*

Charter Locker This service specializes in fishing and boat charters, private or shared basis, full- or half-day. *Kealakehe Parkway, Honokohau Harbor, Kailua-Kona, HI 96740; 800-247-1484; 808-326-2553.*

★ **Kona Charter Skippers Association, Inc.** This professional operation provides complete, personalized booking service for Kona's charter fishing fleet, recreational, snorkel-diving cruises and related water sports and activities. *74-857 Iwalani Place, Kailua-Kona, HI 96740; 800-762-7546; 808-329-3600; e-mail: konafish@hawaii.rr.com; www.konabiggamefishing.com.*

A fisherman's tips on avoiding seasickness. Prescription Scopolamine patch (try before you leave home), OTC Bonine pill taken the night before your fishing trip, Sea-Band wrist bands that work with pressure-points, ginger raw, powdered, candied or as a pill. And don't forget to take it easy on dinner and alcohol the night before your voyage.

Kona Beach Activity Shack *Kona Pier on Ali'i Drive in front of the King Kamehameha's Kona Beach Hotel, Kailua-Kona; 808-329-7494.*

Kona Marina Sports Activities *74-425 Kealakehe Parkway, 3rd floor, Honokohau Harbor, Kailua-Kona, HI 96740; 808-329-1115; fax: 808-329-9104; e-mail: uki@ ilhawaii.net.*

★ **Ocean Sports-Waikoloa** *Located on 'Anaeho'omalu Beach in front of the Waikoloa Beach Marriott, An Outrigger Resort, 69-275 Waikoloa Beach Drive, Kohala Coast, HI 96743; 808-886-6666; 800-SAIL234; www.hawaiioceansports.com.*

★ **Red Sail Sports** *425 Waikoloa Beach Drive, Hilton Waikoloa Village, Kohala Coast, HI 96743, 877-RED-SAIL, 808-886-2876, fax: 808-886-4169; and Hapuna Beach Prince Hotel at Mauna Kea Resort, 808-880-1111; e-mail: redsailsport@yahoo.com, www.redsail.com.*

GARDENS

The Big Island is a botanical garden in and of itself, with diverse environments from desert-like rocky shoreline to lush forests where wild gingers and orchids grow along the roadside. State and county parks are free and provide many good examples of Hawaiian flora. Commercial botanical gardens are privately owned and may charge fees or donations, but if plants are your passion, they may be well worth the price. Some gardens focus exclusively on Hawaiian ethnobotany, while others take advantage of the climate to produce beautiful tropical flowers, trees and greenery from around the world. We'd also like to suggest visiting garden shops, florists and flower farms for less-formal lessons in the beautiful things that grow in Hawaii. For example, a stop by Akatsuka Orchids or the other excellent growers in the Volcano area guarantees a glimpse of at least one amazing specimen you haven't seen before. Chat with them about ordering cut flowers or shipping plants to the mainland. The following are among the Big Island's best botanical gardens. Contact them for specific hours and admission rates as these are sometimes seasonal.

★ **Amy B. H. Greenwell Ethnobotanical Garden**   This traditionally planted 15-acre garden has numerous native Hawaiian plants such as sweet potato, taro, breadfruit, sugar cane, banana and gourd, as well as Hawaiian medicinal plants and more. Learn about early Hawaiian horticulture and farming methods and how old Hawaiians used plants in their early subsistence lifestyle. Open Monday through Friday 8:30 a.m. to 5 p.m., guided tours Wednesday and Friday at 1 p.m. Admission: $4. *Located on Highway 11, at the 110-mile marker about 12 miles south of Kailua-Kona at Captain Cook. It's just a short distance north of the Manago Hotel. P.O. Box 1053, Captain Cook, HI 96704; 808-323-3318.*

Fuku-Bonsai Cultural Center & Hawaii State Bonsai Repository Located on the east side of the island near Kurtistown, the Bonsai Center is an amazing place full of tiny trees, carefully cultivated for aesthetic perfection on a miniature scale. Founder David W. Fukumoto promotes his "True Indoor Bonsai" as an offshoot of Japanese Bonsai and Chinese Penjing concepts, adding another level to this very interesting art form. The exhibit is open 8 a.m. to 4 p.m. Monday through Saturday, with free demonstrations on the second Saturday of each month. Admission by donation. Workshops, retail shop, free newsletter and extensive online plant store. (And be sure to ask about their "micro lobsters" too.) *Olaa Road, P.O. Box 6000, Kurtistown, HI 96760; 808-982-9880; fax: 808-982-9883; e-mail: sales@ fukubonsai.com; www.fukubonsai.com.*

Hawai'i Tropical Botanical Garden   This garden is located about 8.5 miles north of Hilo on the scenic four-mile drive on old Highway 19 to historic Onomea Bay. Nature trails cross streams and waterfalls and pass along the crashing surf of the ocean, meandering

through the rainforest and plantings of palm, heliconia, ginger, bromeliad and more, (some 2,000 species from around the tropical
world). Centuries-old mango, monkey and breadfruit trees tower
overhead, carefully preserved by the Garden's Lutkenhouse family.
Open daily 9:30 a.m. to 5 p.m. (last admission at 4 p.m.). Museum
and gift shop on-site; flowers are available for purchase online.
Admission: $15 adults, $5 children under 16, $35 1-year Family
Pass. *27-717 Old Mamalahoa Highway, P.O. Box 80, Papaikou, HI 96781;
808-964-5233; fax: 808-964-1338; e-mail: htbg@ilhawaii.net; www.hawaii
garden.com.*

Hawaiian Gardens This colorful garden is located on the
slopes of Mount Hualalai at 1,400-foot elevation above Kailua-Kona
town. The gardens have a variety of tropical plants and trees and are
also a full-service tropical garden center. It is marked by towering
trees, attractive landscaped grounds and numerous flowering and
ornamental plantings. Visitors can stroll the grounds and enjoy the
many plants. *Junction of Highway 190 and Highway 180, 3 miles north of
Kailua-Kona; 888-879-2485; 808-329-5702; e-mail: hawngard@gte.net.*

★ **Nani Mau Gardens** One of Hilo's most popular attractions,
20 acres of beautiful tropical flowers, orchids, anthuriums, native
Hawaiian plants, palms, pools, stream and waterfalls plus restaurant,
wedding gazebo and gift shop. Stroll the gardens on your own or
take a narrated tram ride of the grounds. Daily 8:30 a.m. to 5 p.m.
Admission: $10 adults, $5 children 4 to 10, children under 4 free.
Located 3 miles south of Hilo Airport on the Volcano Highway;
watch for turnoff at Makalika Street and the large floral "Aloha" sign.
*421 Makalika Street, Hilo, HI 96720; 808-959-3500; e-mail: garden@nani
mau.com; www.nanimau.com.*

Pua Mau Place A family-run, fun 15-acre tropical botanical
garden on the west side of the island above Kawaihae Harbor.
Unique features include a hibiscus maze with over 200 species, a
"magic circle" reminiscent of Stonehenge, an aviary where you can
feed the birds and fanciful metal sculptures of giant insects. There is
an admission charge. Their Pikake Gallery sells local arts and crafts
and live plants and flowers, soft drinks and snacks. Pavilion area
available for weddings, meetings and other functions. Open every
day 9 a.m. to 4 p.m. *P.O. Box 44555, 10 Ala Kahua, Kawaihae, HI 96743;
808-882-0888; www.puamau.com.*

World Botanical Gardens This 300-acre garden opened in
1995 and is lovingly planted with numerous species of ornamentals,
fruit trees and plants, flowers and more beautiful flora. Take a stroll
along Rainbow Walk, covered with hundreds of wild orchids and
100 species of bromeliad. The Rain Forest Walk follows a trail
through the forest and past native and introduced species to the fan-

tastic overlook at the 300-foot cascades of Umauma Falls. Free samples of fruit and juice in season. Open daily 9 a.m. to 5 p.m. Admission: $8.50 adults, $4.25 teens, $2 children 4 to 12, children under 5 free. Guided garden tours with lunch (featuring tropical fruits from the Gardens) are $40 adults, $30 teens, $20 children 5 to 12. *Located 16 miles north of Hilo at the 16-mile marker on Highway 19. P.O. Box 324, Honomu, HI 96728; 808-963-5427; fax: 808-934-9106; e-mail: info@wbgi.com; www.wbgi.com.*

GOLF

Heralded as the "golf capitol of Hawai'i," the Big Island hosts some of the finest golf courses in the world. From top-dollar resort courses with $200 green fees and near-perfect golf weather year-round to neighborly (if sometimes rainy) municipal courses upcountry where you can play for as little as $15, we have a golf experience for every player. The Kohala Coast resorts have established high-caliber, full-service golf facilities offering everything a quality club can provide: lessons, equipment rentals, fully stocked pro shops with restaurants and bars-even tournament planning. Advance  reservations are recommended, although different resorts have different policies protecting times for their hotel guests, particularly in the morning. You might not be able to reserve too far in advance, and some resorts may not take players who are not their guests. A little homework goes a long way in preventing disappointment. Most offer room and golf packages, and golf vacations can also be arranged through travel providers and golf specialists on the internet. Many courses also offer discounted twilight rates for afternoon play. Green fees usually include a shared cart but, again, ask first. Soft spikes are becoming a requirement on Hawai'i's golf courses, and pro shops can provide them for your shoes at a nominal fee.

If you're looking to just drive a few balls and have some fun, you might want to try **Swing Zone**, located at the corner of Makala and Kuakini Highway just opposite of the Old Kona Airport Park entry. They have a full driving range plus putting and chipping area along with a bunker. *74-5562 Makala Boulevard, Kailua-Kona, HI 96740; 808-329-6909.*

There is also **Menehune Country Club**, which is an all-grass putting course like mini-golf. They also have outdoor baseball batting cages. Open 8 a.m. to 9 p.m. daily. Driving range rates: 1 token/60 balls $6; Menehune course round $6; baseball batting cages/10 balls $1.

For something completely new and different, check out "Disc Golf" at **Hawaii Castaways Disc Club**. Formerly called "frisbee golf," the object of the game is familiar: tee off, reach your target in the fewest number of shots and continue around the course to the end. Only instead of aiming a little white ball at holes in the ground, disc golfers fling a plastic disc at hanging bamboo "bunkajins." Various specialized discs (priced far less than golf clubs at $7-20) are used to tee off, bank right or left or go for a curved shot. Organizers praise it as a family sport that's easy to learn and fun for all ages and abilities. Although there's no official course as such in Hawaii, temporary courses are set up for tournament play and special occasions. *For more information visit www.hcdc.us or call Mike Leitch, 808-968-7465.*

★ *Big Island Country Club*   This is one of the Big Island's best-kept secrets an 18-hole country club course with beautiful undulating fairways and well-set greens, designed by Pete and Perry Dye. Cooler temperatures of the upcountry setting make for pleasant play. Call for tee times. Rates: $99 mornings, $69 after 11 a.m. *Located about mid-way between Waimea and Kailua-Kona on Highway 190. P.O. Box 1690, Kailua-Kona, HI 96740; 808-325-5044.*

★ *Hamakua Country Club*   It's a nine-hole course laid out on very sloping terrain. Lovely views of Honoka'a and the ocean. Entrance is easy to miss, just off the highway and next to the Union 76 gas station. Rates: $15. *Highway 19 in Honoka'a on the Hamakua Coast about 40 miles north of Hilo. P.O. Box 751, Honoka'a, HI 96727; 808-775-7244.*

Hapuna Golf Course   This 18-hole championship links-style course, designed by Arnold Palmer and Ed Seay, is earning a reputation as one of the Big Island's best. Hapuna plays along natural contours from sea level to about 700 feet elevation, with stunning views of coastline, ocean and surrounding volcanic mountains. Fully stocked pro shop for all your golf attire, equipment and accessories, plus locker rooms, driving range, lessons, clinics, club and shoe rentals and refreshment cart on the course. Arnie's Clubhouse restaurant on premises. Rates: $115 guests, $145 off-property players, twilight rates available seasonally. *Hapuna Beach Prince Hotel, Mauna Kea Resort, 62-100 Kauna'oa Drive, Kohala Coast, HI 96743; 808-880-3000.*

Hilo Municipal Golf Course   This is a very nicely maintained 18-hole course operated by the County of Hawai'i. It gets a lot of use from local golfing cadres, especially on weekends. During Hilo's rainy periods the fairways can get pretty water-logged. There is a driving range lighted for night use. Rates: $29 weekdays, $34 weekends; cart $16. *340 Haihai Street, Hilo, HI 96720; 808-959-7711.*

Hilton Waikoloa Village   (See Waikoloa Beach Resort below.) Golfers enjoy 36 holes of great golf on two courses: the *Beach Course*, designed by Robert Trent Jones, Jr., or the *Kings Course*, designed by Tom Weiskopf and Jay Morrish. There's also an 18-hole Seaside Putting Course. Open to the public, but with preference given to guests. Book well in advance. Rates: $125 guests, $175 off-property players, $85 after 1 p.m. *425 Waikoloa Beach Drive, Kohala Coast, HI 96743; 808-886-1234.*

Hualalai Golf Club   A private resort course located within the Four Seasons Resort Hualalai, and reserved for the exclusive use of its guests and residents. The course was designed by Jack Nicklaus and is an 18-hole par-72, 7117 yards. If you're lucky enough to be invited, green fees are $190. *100 Kaupulehu Drive, Kaupulehu-Kona, HI 96740; 808-325-8481.*

★ **Kona Country Club**   This is actually two golf courses in one, reportedly offering a great day of golf with "no strong winds." The 18-hole championship course runs ocean-side and in the heart of the Keauhou resort condo area. The Mountain Course 18-hole layout runs upslope, providing spectacular ocean and coastline views. Complete pro shop with rental clubs, carts and instruction available. The Vista Restaurant & Lounge are on premises. Rates: $155 Ocean Course, $145 Mountain Course; twilight rates $99 and $89 after 1:00 p.m. Open daily, starting times required. Located six miles south of Kailua-Kona in the Keauhou resort area. *78-7000 Ali'i Drive, Kailua-Kona, HI 96740; 808-322-2595; www.konagolf.com.*

Makalei Hawai'i Country Club   Located about five miles above Kailua-Kona town on Highway 190 on the cool, breezy forested slopes of Mount Hualalai, with a pristine pastoral setting and spectacular views at 2,000 feet elevation. The 18-hole layout is a par-72 championship length of 7,100 yards. Most of the holes play downslope with undulating fairways and challenging greens. Rates: $110, $50 after 12 noon. Special $50 senior rate on Thursday and Friday. *72-3890 Mamalahoa Highway, Kailua-Kona, HI 96740; 808-325-6625.*

For something different, explore Ke'ano Kolepa (the "inner game of golf") with coach Darrin Gee. Clinics are based on relaxation, focus, balance, visualization and "pre-shot ritual" to improve your swing and lower your scores. Two-and-a-half-hour instruction includes range balls, clubs and refreshments. Seven-hour Clinic+18 holes adds cart, round and lunch. Scheduled for 8:30 and 11:30 a.m. Reservations and information 808-887-6800; www.spiritofgolfhawaii.com.

★ **Mauna Kea Golf Course**   Created by Robert Trent Jones, Sr., in 1965 from barren lava rock and brackish water, Mauna Kea set the bar very high for Hawai'i golf courses. Consistently ranked in

Golf Digest's Top 100, this championship golf course continues to win acclaim for its rewarding-yet-challenging play. Lush, mature landscaping enhances panoramic seascapes from almost every hole, and the over-the-ocean shot at the legendary third tee may be the most-photographed in Hawai'i. Friendly, experienced staff at the fully stocked pro shop assist with tee times, lessons, clinics, shoe and club rentals, golfing attire, equipment, gifts and accessories. Driving range, putting green, locker rooms, great food and libations at the 19th Hole Clubhouse, refreshment cart on the course. Soft spikes required. Call in advance for tee times. Rates: $135 guests, $195 off-property players, twilight rates available seasonally. *Mauna Kea Resort, 62-100 Mauna Kea Beach Drive, Kohala Coast, HI 96743; 808-882-5400.*

★ **Mauna Lani Resort Golf Course** The *Francis H. I'i Brown Golf Course* is a gorgeous and challenging 36-hole layout with two separate championship courses. There are several breathtaking holes and fairways carved out of raw lava rock that climb across the rugged coastline, providing every level of golfer with an extraordinary day of play. The links surround the Mauna Lani Bay Hotel, the Fairmont Orchid and condo complexes. The course has won wide acclaim from golf groups and the media and provides an incredibly beautiful golfing experience. Very nice pro shop with The Gallery restaurant and Knickers clubhouse bar. Call for tee time. Rates: $130 for guests, $195 off-property players, twilight (after 3 p.m.) $75. *Mauna Lani Resort. 68-1310 Mauna Lani Drive, Kohala Coast, HI 96743; 808-885-6655.*

Naniloa Country Club This is a short nine-hole, par-35 course. There is a pro shop with club and cart rentals available, instruction and driving range. Rates: $25 weekdays, $30 weekends. On hotel row along Hilo Bay. *120 Banyan Drive, Hilo, HI 96720; 808-935-3000.*

GOLF AID

If you're unable to book a tee time at the course of your choice or you want to check on rates, a golf booking service may be able to help on obtaining a tee time. Try **Stand-by Golf**. They can assist with guaranteed tee times and discounted rates. They charge a fee for their services. 888-645-2665. **Fins and Fairways Hawai'i** can arrange accommodations at hotels/condos along the Kona and Kohala coasts and book tee times at most of the major resort golf courses. Look for their free publication at concierge desks and tourist kiosks island-wide. It's loaded with information and discount coupons. P.O. Box 9014, Kailua-Kona, HI 96745; 800-367-8014; 808-325-6171; e-mail: golfkona@kona.net; www.golfkona.com.

Sea Mountain Golf Course This is a superb 18-hole championship course located in the peaceful southern coast area of the Big Island. The fairways are nicely landscaped with lots of greenery and flowering plants. The biggest factor are the strong coastal breezes. Rates: $46.50 weekdays, $49.50 weekends and holidays. Located in Punaluʻu in the Kaʻu District. *P.O. Box 190, Pahala, HI 96777; 808-928-6222.*

★ **Volcano Golf and Country Club** This is a lovely and lush 18-hole course set amidst the grandeur of the national park country. There is a pro shop with club and cart rental and the Volcano Country Club Restaurant is on premises. Rates: $62.50. Call for tee time. Located 1.5 miles west of entrance to Hawaiʻi Volcanoes National Park on Highway 11. *P.O. Box 46, Piʻi Mauna Road, Volcano, HI 96718; 808-967-7331.*

Waikoloa Beach Resort Located between the Waikoloa Beach Marriott and the Hilton Waikoloa Village at Waikoloa Resort, Kohala Coast are two highly rated golf courses, the *Beach Course* and the *King's Course,* each with a personality all its own and each offering a distinctive style of play. The Beach Course was designed by Robert Trent Jones, Jr., and set amidst the dramatic contrast of black lava flows and the blue Pacific Ocean. The King's Course is a par-72 championship layout, created out of barren lava desert by Tom Weiskopf and Jay Morrish, who were influenced by the famous open, windswept links of Scotland. The course features some of the most intimidating bunkers and sand traps of any Big Island course. The challenges to golfers come from Mother Nature the strong Waikoloa winds, lava rock formations, sand traps, bunkers and an occasional water hazard. Not an easy round, but an accomplishment even for the best golfers. Full-service pro shop, lessons, rentals and Beach Grill restaurant. Rates: $125 guests, $175 off-property players, $85 for everyone after 1 p.m. *1020 Keana Place, Waikoloa, HI 96738; 808-886-7888; 877-WAIKOLOA; www.waikoloagolf.com.*

★ **Waikoloa Village Golf Club** Robert Trent Jones, Jr., artfully designed this 6,791-yard, par-72 golf course to challenge the serious golfer and please the beginner as well. Reasonable green fees and consistent weather make it an exceptional value. Full-service pro shop, lessons, driving range, restaurant and lounge on-site. Call for tee times. Rates: $80, after 12 p.m. $65. Cart fee $20 additional. Located in the cool and breezy uplands between Highways 19 and 190. *P.O. Box 383910, 68-1792 Melia Street, Waikoloa Village, HI 96738; 808-883-9621.*

Waimea Country Club The 6,661-yard, par-72 layout is spread through former ranch pasturelands and takes in the natural undulating and rolling hill terrain. Stands of forest and pastures border the fairways along with strategic water hazards and sand traps. It can get breezy and foggy out in the fairways at times when low cloud fronts move through. Pro shop and snack bar on-site. Rates: $85 morning, after 12:30 p.m. $75. Located about two miles east of Kamuela on the Mamalahoa Highway in the heart of Parker Ranch country. *P.O. Box 2155, Kamuela, HI 96743; 808-885-8053.*

HEALTH AND FITNESS CENTERS (*See also* Spas)

To keep up with the demand for exercise equipment by visitors, almost every hotel and condo property now offers fitness centers with workout rooms. The larger facilities will also have saunas, locker rooms and a full menu of spa therapies and salon services, along with classes in yoga, aerobics, cycling and a variety of other work-out routines. If your hotel, condo or B&B doesn't have one and you want to keep up with your workout regimen, you might try any of the following health and fitness centers. They welcome the public on a walk-in basis and generally charge a fee for use of the exercise equipment, spa, pool, saunas and other facilities.

Curves for Women 6:30 a.m. to 2 p.m. and 3:15 to 7 p.m. Monday through Friday, 7 to 11 a.m. Saturday. *Locations in Waimea, 808-887-1217; Kona, 808-331-2286; and Kealakekua, 808-322-6188.*

Hawai'i Naniloa Resort Spa 6 a.m. to 9 p.m. Monday through Friday, 10 a.m. to 6 p.m. Saturday and Sunday. Rates: $15 per day. *Hawai'i Naniloa Hotel, 93 Banyan Drive, Hilo; 808-969-3333.*

Health Haven 6 a.m. to 7 p.m. Monday through Friday, 7 a.m. to noon Saturday. *Located in the old Kaikoo Mall in Hilo; 808-961-6989.*

Orchid Isle Fitness 4:45 a.m. to 9 p.m. Monday through Friday, 8 a.m. to 3 p.m. Saturday, 8 a.m. to 12 p.m. Sunday. *29 Shipman Street, Suite 104, Hilo; 808-961-0003.*

Mauna Lani Sports & Fitness Club Located within the Mauna Lani Bay Hotel property. Classes and equipment open to the public for $15 per day. *808-885-7765; www.maunalani.com.*

Pilates & Yoga Centre of Kona Small classes, private sessions, bodywork and massage. *Pottery Terrace, Kailua-Kona; www.konapilates.com.*

Spencer Health & Fitness Center 5 a.m. to 9 p.m. Monday through Friday, 5 a.m. to 3 p.m. Saturday. Rates: $10 per day, $25 per week. *197 Keawe Street, Hilo; 808-969-1511.*

The Club in Kona 5 a.m. to 10 p.m. Monday through Friday, 7 a.m. to 7 p.m. Saturday and Sunday. Rates: $15 per day. *Kona Sports Center, 75-5699 Kopiko Street, Kailua-Kona; 808-326-2582.*

Guided Tours/Outfitters

More and more commercial guided hiking tour operators and out-fitters are getting into the Big Island adventure business, leading guided walking tours through cultural and historical areas, various nature and wilderness hikes and other excursions into Big Island wilderness areas, national and state parks, and other interesting places. Below are a few suggestions, but keep in mind that many Big Island activity providers happily "cross-book" or make combination adventures with a variety of land, sea and air activities. If you don't find what you're looking for immediately, don't be afraid to ask.

Arnott's Lodge These people go the extra mile to provide backpackers and adventurers with a quality, affordable vacations. The lodge is located in the Keaukaha area of Hilo near the beach parks. They offer added services such as an around-the-island "Big Island Experience" with stops at important historical and cultural sites, and daily hiking excursions including Hawai'i Volcanoes National Park, Mauna Kea Summit, South Point, Hilo Waterfalls, and Puna on the Rift Zone as well as custom adventure expeditions. Free shuttle service from Hilo International Airport. *Apapane Road, Hilo, HI 96720; 808-969-7097; fax: 808-961-9638; e-mail: info@arnotts lodge.com; www.arnottslodge.com.*

Adventures in Paradise (See "Kayaking.") A one-stop shop for hikers, snorkelers, scuba divers, fisherpeople and other kinds of adventure-seekers. Hike tours or combo snorkel-and-hike tours offer something for all levels and a wide range of interests. Rates: Volcano Hike, including transportation from Kona, $159.95 adults, $129.95 children under 12; morning (8 to 11 a.m.) or afternoon (1 to 4 p.m.) Kealakekua Bay Snorkel/Hike, $59.95 adults; $49.95 children; the easy and enjoyable Blue Lagoon Hike (and a chance to swim), $59.95 adults, $49.95 children. Customized experiences are available to families. *81-6367 Mamalahoa Highway, Kealakekua, HI 96750; 888-371-6035; e-mail: kayakhawaii@verizon.net; www.bigislandkayak.com.*

★ *Hawai'i Forest & Trail* One of the most popular outfitters on the island, HFT offers eight unique guided nature adventures in unique island ecosystems: Valley Waterfall, $125 adults, $99 children 8 and up, is a three-mile loop that leads along a cliffside trail to the 300-foot Kapoloa Falls, where it passes behind the cascades. Kohala Country Waterfalls Adventure, $99/$89, crosses streams and bridges, meets seven waterfalls, and concludes with a cool-off swim in a mountain pool. Kilauea Volcano Adventure, $149/$115, is a 12-hour tour that crosses the island via Saddle Road then delves into Volcano National Park's amazing places with several short walks and a chance to see flowing lava, if conditions permit. Hualalai Volcano Summit, $99/$79, climbs by car to 6,000 feet above Kailua-Kona, then tours ancient volcanic features along a misty mountain trail. Mauna Kea Summit & Stars Adventure, $159 adults 16 and over only, includes dinner, parkas and gloves to help brave the chilly temperatures as you see sunset from the summit then gaze into the Hawaiian heavens by telescope. Rainforest & Dryforest Birding Adventure and the Hakalau Forest Wildlife Refuge Birding Adventure, each $155 ages 8 and up only, include binoculars to search for endangered rare birds like the red *akiapola'au*, *i'iwi* and *apepane* (among others). R&D crosses two completely different environments: a sub-alpine dryland forest on Pu'u La'au and a cloudforest habitat on the slopes of Mauna Loa. Hakalau is only offered 18 times annually because of the extreme sensitivity of the area. (Listen to the birdcalls on their website.) Excellent guides provide knowledgeable narration on background culture, natural history, local lore and much more. Reservations are essential. Hikes are fully equipped and serviced with transportation from selected locations, beverages, snacks, deli lunch, walking sticks, raingear and other things you might need, depending on the adventure and conditions that day. Hiking time varies and groups are limited to ten; hikers provide their own hiking/walking footwear. HFT also offers the award-winning Kohala Mule Trail Adventure, $95/75, a guided trailride that skirts the rim of scenic Pololu Valley. There's an outfitting store and information center at their Kona headquarters and wonderful monthly natural history essays by owner-operator Rob Pacheco on their website. Open 7 a.m. to 5 p.m. daily. *74-5035B Queen Ka'ahumanu Highway, Kailua-Kona, HI 96740; 808-331-8505; 800-464-1993; fax: 808-331-8704; e-mail: info@hawaii-forest.com; www.hawaii-forest.com.*

An excellent resource on hiking trails is www.hawaiitrails.org; 808-974-4217.

Hawaiian Walkways This hiking outfitter specializes in "informative walks to amazing places," in a variety of half- and full-day eco-tours of the Big Island's natural scenic secrets. Waipi'o Waterfall Adventure, $95, is a half-day exploration of timeless Waipi'o Valley, through rainforest and field, across footbridges and streams, including a cool plunge and swim, so bring your suit. Kilauea Volcano Discovery, $135, sets foot on fantastic terrain within the dynamic geology of Hawaii Volcanoes National Park. Choices vary from an easy "sampler" to a challenging 14-mile trek. Saddle Road Explorations, $135, are customized to suit, from one to nine miles between the two volcanic mountains of Mauna Kea and Mauna Loa, great for birders and photographers. Other exclusive charter routes are available by advance arrangement. *800-457-7759; 808-775-0372; e-mail: hiwalk@aloha.net; www.hawaiianwalkways.com.*

Hiking Resources

The **Kona Hiking Club** is an informal group that takes monthly day hikes to the Big Island's less accessible and private beaches, forests and backcountry areas. Most of these hikes are not difficult or long and require minimal gear or hiking experience. The group encourages family hiking outings. The club generally takes hikes on the first Saturday and third Thursday of each month. Membership is open to everyone. There are no dues or fees and visitors are welcome to participate. This is a good way to get to know some local folks and enjoy a Hawaiian outdoors experience. Watch the local Big Island newspapers community news files for hike announcements.

For maps and information on hiking the national park, contact: Superintendent, Hawai'i Volcanoes National Park, Volcano, HI 96718; 808-985-6000.

For information and maps relating to state forest reserve lands, contact: Forestry & Wildlife Division, Department of Land and Natural Resources, Island of Hawai'i, 75 Aupuni Street, Hilo, HI 96720; 808-974-4221.

For information on state parks, contact: Division of State Parks, Hawai'i District Office, Dept. of Land and Natural Resources, P.O. Box 936, Hilo, HI 96720; 808-974-6200.

For information on county beach parks, contact: Department of Parks and Recreation, County of Hawai'i, 25 Aupuni Street, Hilo, HI 96720; 808-961-8311.

Hiking Trails

The Big Island has a wide range of hiking trails through the varied ecosystems, terrain and climates of coastal beach, valley jungle, mountain rainforest, lava desert and alpine mountain summit. Trails are located in state forest reserves and parks, county parks, national park areas and remote coastal regions. Visitors can hike on their own or take a guided hiking adventure with an outfitter such as those listed in the previous section. For more information, see "Suggested Reading" at the end of the book.

Kona District **Kealakekua Bay and Captain Cook Monument** are reached by a moderately difficult hiking trail leading off from Highway 11 near Captain Cook town. This is a 2.5-mile, 3-hour round trip. To locate the trail, turn off Highway 11 at Napo'opo'o

Road to Kealakekua Bay. Just 100 yards from the turnoff is a dirt-gravel trail directly across from three big royal palm trees and running downslope between fence rows. Park along the road. This is the old wagon road leading to the former Ka'awaloa settlement on the bay. The trail varies from steep to level, rough rocky/loose gravel to solid footing.

The first several hundred yards of trail are under shade trees along the fence rows but the trail soon opens to the warm sun and lava fields, so take hat, sunscreen and water. As the road nears the bay, it passes through old stone foundations of the former village. The trail ends at the bay. There is a tall cement monument to Captain James Cook and a smaller plaque marking the spot where he was killed by Hawaiians in a skirmish in 1779.

Snorkel and dive cruise boats filled with tourists anchor in Kealakekua Bay daily to swim and frolic in the waters of the Kealakekua Bay Underwater Marine Reserve, with its varied and colorful marinelife. The hike back up is quite steep and tiring, so allow some extra time.

Kaloko-Honokohau National Historic Park Trail is a coastal trail still under development. The distances vary from 1-2 miles and 1-2 hours hiking time. It is three miles north of Kailua-Kona, opposite Kaloko Industrial Area on a rough access road and adjacent to Honokohau Boat Harbor. Hikers can access the park trail from the Honokohau Harbor side. Turn right from Kealakehe Parkway leading to the harbor and follow the road to the end. The trail to the park starts opposite of the large rock berm. There are 1100 acres that span two miles along the coast, encompassing several old Hawaiian settlements. Archaeological sites include house foundations, fishing shrines, canoe landings, and petroglyph rock carvings. There are tidal pools and wetlands that serve as a preserve for migrant water birds and marine life, along with nice sandy beaches and plant life native to this coastal ecosystem. Restrooms at Kaloko fishponds; no facilities otherwise. Take water, sun gear and snacks.

★ *Kohala Coast*   One of the best for a family outing, the **Puako Petroglyph Reserve Trail** is located next to Holoholokai Beach Park, fronting the Fairmont Orchid Hawai'i. The trailhead is marked by a sign next to the parking lot and is about one mile roundtrip passing through dry forest and brush areas before coming to open lava fields and hundreds of petroglyph rock carvings, which may date back as far as 400 AD. The many mysterious shapes carved into lava include human figures, a five-foot image of what may be a Big Island map, sailing canoes, animals, geometric designs and other interesting things, each with their own story to tell. This can be a very warm walk so take sunscreen, hat and water. (Note: Free guided Petroglyph Trail Walks are available at nearby Kings Shops. Stop by and check their weekly schedule.)

Ala Loa Trail (the King's Trail) and **Ala Kahakai Shoreline Trail** are part of an old Hawaiian trail system believed to have connected the coastal settlements in ancient times, possibly encircling the entire island. Parts of the trail system are still accessible for varying distances. You can find one easy access point at Spencer Beach Park, where parking is usually available, and trail exit points at Mauna Kea Beach, Hapuna Beach, Puako boat ramp, Mauna Lani Bay Hotel & Bungalows and Waikoloa Resort. (You might want to prearrange transportation back to Spencer Beach Park.) It's about five miles from Spencer to the Puako boat ramp, so remember water, a hat, good footwear and sunscreen. The rocky trail passes through the golf courses and petroglyph fields, and follows lava flows near the rugged coast, marked occasionally by interpretive signs. Some portions are remarkably scenic, such as the well-tended section from Kawaihae to Anaeho`omalu Bay, and rest stops at the beaches are

A WORD OF CAUTION

Hawaii's County, State and National Parks are awesome places full of wonders to explore and experience. But they can also be full of hazards and dangers for the uninformed and careless. Anybody can get lost, and we hate hearing about otherwise "happy campers" having to spend the night alone in the woods, or worse. When hiking in the parks, or anywhere on the Big Island, for that matter, be sure to take the following very important (and very simple) precautions:

- Take a buddy.
- Stay on the trail.
- Let someone know where you are going, how long you expect to be gone and where your starting point is. Check in with rangers if appropriate.
- Take more water than you think you will need, food, sunscreen, hat, simple first-aid items and any medication you need on a regular basis.
- Pack a poncho or large plastic trash bag for some protection in case you get caught in the rain.
- Take your cell phone and some way to signal rescuers in the air-a mirror, bright-colored tape, etc.
- In the unlikely and unfortunate event that you should have trouble, rescue teams advise you **stay put** so they can find you. Once you know you're lost, don't keep walking.

refreshing. (For more information on this and other hiking trails, visit www.hawaiitrails.org, 808-974-4217.)

Kiholo Bay is located about six miles south of Waikoloa Beach Resort on Highway 19. There are private housing developments around this bay and a private access road. However, the public can access the beach area and beautiful aquamarine lagoons and ponds via a moderate hiking trail from the highway. The trail is about a mile long, leading through open lava fields with some *kiawe* trees. There are no public facilities at Kiholo Bay but good swimming and snorkeling. Parking is along the highway. Watch for cars parked near the trailhead, which is about a mile north of a traffic turnoff and overlook for Kiholo Bay.

Waimea/Kamuela White Road is one of the Big Island's most scenic hiking trails and one of its best-kept secrets. Leaving Waimea town for the Hamakua Coast, look for White Road on the left, turn in and follow the road to its end and park along the right shoulder. The easy hiking trail leads through pastures and bamboo forest to the "bowl" at the top of Waipi'o Valley and an amazing scenic over-look. This trail is becoming more popular and you may encounter fellow hikers and their dogs out for some exercise. Note: Recent access issues have resulted in padlocks and "No Trespassing" signs, sometimes police-enforced. Hopefully this will be resolved, but if you find your path blocked, heed the signs and choose one of the other fabulous Big Island trails.

★ *Hamakua Coast* 'Akaka Falls State Park is a special place. The half-mile loop trail takes about 30 minutes, but allow time to enjoy this veritable Garden of Eden setting. Located 11 miles north of Hilo, turn off Highway 19 at Honomu to Highway 220 and go through the small country town and upslope about 3.5 miles. The road terminates at the park. This is a moderately difficult walk only because there are some steep but short sections to climb. The trail meanders through lush tropical rainforest of *hapu* ferns, red and white ginger, banana trees, birds-of-paradise, plumeria, and giant philodendrons. Handrails aid in areas where the paved trail is quite steep and tends to be slippery when wet. Crossing the first bridge, if you've taken the right-hand route from the trailhead, you'll pass under a towering stand of giant bamboo. Further along, at the point where the trail makes a sharp left turn, is a small lookout for Kahuna Falls, a tumbling cascade which rolls down the north side of the canyon. Follow the trail on up the ridge to the main attraction, the beautiful 420-foot 'Akaka Falls, which plummets down a sheer cliff-side in veiled mists to Kolekole Stream below. There is a rain shelter at this lookout, offering a nice place to pause and soak in all the tropical beauty and lushness of Hawai'i. Continue on the trail back to the parking lot.

Waipi'o Valley is on the Hamakua Coast just about 50 miles north of Hilo. Take Highway 19 to Honoka'a, about 40 miles, then Highway 240 north 9 miles to Kukuihaele and the Waipi'o Valley State Park Lookout, a picture-postcard view of the valley and beautiful beach below. The **Waipi'o Valley Trail** is actually a .75-mile paved, narrow and extremely steep 4WD road leading to the valley floor. At the bottom, the road turns right for another .75 mile on a narrow dirt (if wet, muddy and rutted) lane to the mouth of the valley and Wailoa Stream. The beach here is good for picnics and relaxing but most of it lies on the other side of Wailoa Stream. There is a waterfall trailing off the south wall near the beach area. Back at the junction, the road leads left into the valley, and follows the stream toward Hi'ilawe Falls and other waterfalls. The topside streams were created for and are still occasionally tapped for irrigation by landowners above, turning the waterfalls "off" unannounced. Since much of Waipi'o Valley is privately owned, it's best to stick to the main road, which crosses several streams and passes by many taro patches. You may see resident taro farmers hard at work. The valley is a wondrously lush green environment with uncountable trees and plants, including wild guava, papaya and bananas along the trail. However far you wander, remember that you still have to return to the junction at the base of the valley cliff road and it's still .75 mile up and out of the valley. Also note: if you cross the river early in the day, be aware you may have to swim back late in the day, so pack your gear accordingly.

Waipi'o and Waimanu Valley Trail (Muliwai) leads north out of Waipi'o Valley. This is a difficult two- to three-day wilderness backpacking trip for experienced hikers only. Even for experts, it's advisable only during the drier May-to-October period due to the several flood-prone streams that must be crossed. The trail is an 18-mile round trip from Waipi'o to Waimanu Valley. Access the trail at the north end of Waipi'o Valley beach after fording Wailoa Stream. The trail is 100 yards from the beach in a forest at the base of the north wall cliff. This is a switchback "Z" trail up the 1,200-foot cliff and reaches the high coastal plateau between the two valleys. The trail crosses some 14 gulches and streams along this rugged coastline, passing through dense coastal rainforest. It can be heavily overgrown in places and very muddy, rocky and slippery as well. There is a trail shelter suitable for picnicking and camping about two-thirds of the way to Waimanu. Be on the lookout for horses and pig-hunters who frequent the area. After an equally steep descent into

A WALK IN THE PARK

Banyan Drive and **Liliuokalani Park** is one of Hilo's favorite walking tours. About a half-mile walk, one hour or longer, depending on how long you pause to enjoy the stops along the way, the Banyan Drive stroll is a must-do. Begin near the Seaside Hotel and follow the loop around Waiakea Peninsula under the cool canopy of giant banyan trees. As you stroll by, notice the signs by each of the 46 trees, telling its personal story: the name of the celebrity who planted it and its "birthday." The first was planted in 1933 by Mr. & Mrs. Cecil B. DeMille, who were on-island filming *Four Frightened People*. Babe Ruth planted his tree two days later. Other VIP notables include President Franklin D. Roosevelt, Amelia Earhart, Fannie Hurst and King George V. There's even one planted by a then-aspiring politician named Richard Nixon.

The trees shade your way along Banyan Drive as it loops past the hotels and restaurants to Liliuokalani Park, a collection of various Asian-style footbridges, pathways and ponds overlooking peaceful Hilo Bay. We've heard the designer's intent was to provide a peaceful place for a meditative walk. You might try walking mindfully through the Gardens, reflecting on your walk through life. Take note of the "bridges," the transitions you encounter, the highs and lows and the choices you make. You might walk away with a new perspective.

Waimanu Valley, turn right toward the beach, ford the stream and locate a suitable camping spot on or near the beach. You need a camping permit from the State Forestry and Wildlife office. Any stream water used must be purified and/or boiled first.

Kalopa State Park in the Hamakua Forest Reserve is 42 miles north of Hilo on Highway 19, turning left at the Kalopa State Park sign just past the 39-mile marker. This state park has a 100-acre block of native Hawaiian rainforest that is kept preserved in its natural state as much as possible, i.e., limiting incursions of alien species, pigs, and other destructive animals. There are several enjoyable hiking trails throughout. The ★ **Kalopa Native Forest Nature Trail** is an easy .7-mile loop trail, 1-hour-long walk, through a true Hawaiian rainforest. Trails are well marked, as are a number of tree and plant species. Pick up a trail guide at the trailhead near the parking lot. The nature trail is just opposite the cabins and leads into dark forest under towering *ohia* trees. The forest here also has large tree ferns, *kolea*, *kopiko*, *olomea*, *pilo*, ground ferns and much more. The **Kalopa Gulch Rim Loop** is a 2.8-mile, 2-hour-long walk, suitable for all hikers. Pick up a trail guide at the parking lot display.

This walk is through a 1930s reforestation project that was planted to conserve land and soil that had been badly overgrazed and misused. Fast-growing non-native species were introduced, including blue gum, paper bark, silk oak, ironwood and swamp mahogany. This large standing forest is still thriving and a native Hawaiian forest is beginning to re-establish itself. The area has various trails linking to the main loop trail and is a pleasant walk in the woods.

Puna District Kaumana Trail is a .5-mile, 1-hour hike and connects with the Saddle Road at two points, 17.4 and 19.8 miles from Hilo. The trail is a remnant portion of the old Pu'u O'o–Kaumana Trail, which was used as an access route between Hilo and the saddle area between Mauna Kea and Mauna Loa. It extends along the 1855 lava flow from about 5,200 feet down to 4,800 feet. Vegetation on the lava flow is Pele's favored *ohia* tree and *hapu,* tree fern. Common native birds are readily sighted along the trail. It is suited for short nature hikes, and hikers can be dropped off at one end and picked up at the other.

★ **Lava Tree State Park** is one of the best easy hikes through a most unusual natural phenomenon. This easy .8-mile loop trail, 30-minute walk, is located about 25 miles from Hilo. Take Highway 11 south from Hilo, turn left at Kea'au to Highway 130 south to Pahoa and then left onto Highway 132 about 3 miles to the park entrance. A 1790 lava flow from Kilauea Volcano covered the present site, which was a forest of *ohia lehua* trees. The lava destroyed the *ohia* trees and left a number of tree-shaped lava shells as the rapidly flowing lava drained away. The resulting "stumps" are almost like abstract sculptures in lava rock but are completely natural. They provide some truly unusual and strange formations. The *ohia lehua* trees with puffy red or red and orange blossoms thrive in the park along with other ornamental trees, shrubs and flowering plants such as heliconia, lobster claw ginger, torch ginger, colorful crotons, bracken fern, tree ferns and others. This is an enjoyable, level stroll through a tropical botanical garden. The park has restrooms and picnic shelters but can have lots of mosquitoes as well; bug repellent is advised. We've learned that this remarkable park has undergone severe trimming in recent months as part of the *cocqui* frog eradication project. If the place looks defoliated when you visit, don't be alarmed.

Hawai'i Volcanoes National Park Hawai'i Volcanoes National Park has some of the Big Island's best hiking trails, from short and easy walks to intermediate hikes and long, challenging overnight and multiday backcountry treks. Hikers are best advised to contact the Superintendent, Hawai'i Volcanoes National Park, HI 96718, 808-985-6000, or stop at the park's Kilauea Visitor Center for a map and details on hiking the park. Hikers are required to register and obtain permits for backcountry overnight hikes.

Some National Park trails require you to sign in and out. Do not, under any circumstances, venture out onto lava flows and fields by yourself, and do stick to marked trails. What may appear to be solid ground is often a thin, brittle shell over deep cracks and crevasses. You could fall in and be badly injured or even lost in a remote area with little chance of rescue. Also, never hike across lava fields at night. Trails are extremely difficult to follow in the dark and the potential danger is great. Hike only in daylight hours. Don't take chances with the health and safety of yourself and your family. Listen to the rangers. Near the eruption site, conditions can change suddenly and frequently. Fumes can be dangerous to pregnant women and people with heart or respiratory conditions and other ailments. Pay attention, be smart and enjoy the most awe-inspiring natural show in Hawai'i. The following are some of the park's most popular hikes.

Kilauea Iki is a moderate four-mile, two- to three-hour loop hike. Begin from Crater Rim Trail or Crater Rim Drive east of Kilauea Crater. The trail leads through young rainforest on the rim of the crater, then down a 400-foot descent into Kilauea Iki Crater and across the lava floor. Watch footing on descent as some areas are loose gravel that can be slippery. The trail across the crater floor has stone cairns marking the way and steaming vents in the crater floor. As you cross, look for "Pele's hair," long slivers of olivine crystals that collect in the recesses and cracks. The views all around are imposing and alien-looking. The trail switchbacks up the opposite crater wall and leads back to the forest.

Devastation Trail is an easy, level, 1-mile, 30-minute walk on an asphalt-paved trail across the edge of Pu'u Pua'i cinder cone, formed by the 1959 eruption of Kilauea Iki. The trail links the parking lots of Kilauea Iki Overlook and Devastation Trailhead. The trail can be walked as a round trip or one way if a pickup is arranged at the other end. It follows along the edge of an *ohia* and tree fern forest, where it meets the open, barren cinder cone. The 1959 eruption destroyed much of the nearby forest downwind that was covered with cinders, ash and pumice. The forest is now making a regrowth comeback, but the area covered by the cinders is still stark, with numerous dead trees sticking up from the dark barren surroundings in surreal contrast.

★ **Thurston Lava Tube** is a .3-mile, 20-minute loop trail, and is one of the park's most fascinating and popular walks. Begin at the parking lot on Crater Rim Drive about two miles from Kilauea

Visitor Center. The trail is paved asphalt and has a couple of steep sections but there are steps and handrails. It's often damp and rainy here and the trail can be slippery, so use caution. The trail passes through a dense *ohia* and tree fern forest descending into the lava tube, created over 400 years ago when a flow formed an outer crust while the interior kept flowing. Once the lava drained away, the lava tube remained intact. The resulting tunnel is 1,494 feet long, up to 22 feet wide and 20 feet high in places. (Some areas are considerably lower, so watch your head.) The tube is lighted but a flashlight might be useful. Standing puddles in the tube are formed by percolation of rainwater from above, making a natural "air conditioning." This is an enjoyable short hike providing a close-up glimpse of the Hawaiian *ohia* and tree fern forest and a unique geological attraction.

Halema'uma'u Trail is a moderate, 3-mile one-way or 7-mile loop trail, 3-6 hours, to Halema'uma'u Crater in the Kilauea Caldera. The trail begins behind the Volcano House Hotel, descends 500 feet through forest into Kilauea Caldera and crosses the floor to the Halema'uma'u Crater Overlook. The wind is usually brisk across the caldera and the sulfur gas smell is strong, making breathing difficult at times. Those with breathing difficulties or related problems should not attempt the hike. There are panoramic vistas of the caldera, steaming vents and cracks, old lava flows and close-up views of still-steaming Halema'uma'u Crater. Those hiking one way can meet their pickup in the Halema'uma'u parking lot. Those doing the round-trip hike back to Volcano House Hotel can pick up the Byron Ledge Trail, which loops across the caldera and up to the Byron Ledge ridge then back to the Volcano House Hotel.

Crater Rim Trail is a challenging 11-mile, day-long trek on varying terrain from forest to open, hot and windy lava rock. This is for experienced hikers only. The trail passes through a wide variety of geological and biological environments, circling the summit of Kilauea Caldera, passing Hawaiian Volcano Observatory and Jaggar Museum, Halema'uma'u Crater, near Devastation Trailhead and Thurston Lava Tube. On this full-day hike, you will see a cross-section of the entire summit area, including its *ohia* and tree fern forests, dry scrubland and desert, open lava fields and recent flow areas. Bring water and food, and be prepared for rain along the way. Sulfur gas fumes will be strong in the downwind southeast rift zone and Halema'uma'u areas.

Pu'u Loa Petroglyphs Trail is a one-and-a-half-mile round-trip, one- to two-hour, moderate walk over level to rolling lava fields, generally smooth with some rough, rocky sections. The trail is about 20 miles southeast of Kilauea Visitor Center off the Chain of Craters

Road, near the coastal flatlands and a few miles from the end of the highway (closed due to lava flows). It leads to smooth *pahoehoe* lava mounds on which you'll see many different types of petroglyphs in varying shapes, sizes and designs. Petroglyphs are fragile so don't step on or damage these ancient artworks in any way. This is an open, very breezy lava field with no shade trees. It can get very hot, and this area is downwind of the eruption site just up the coast so volcanic sulfur fumes can be intense.

Mauna Iki/Footprints Trail is a moderate to difficult 8.8-mile, five- to six-hour hike through the rocky cinder trails of the Ka'u Desert. The trail begins off Highway 11 about 9 miles southwest of Kilauea Visitor Center, links with the Hilina Pali Road and Highway 11 and bisects the Ka'u Desert Trail, allowing hikers to cut distances to points of interest in the Ka'u Desert and Hilina Pali areas. Extensions are possible for overnight camping treks via Ka'u Desert Trail, Hilina Pali Trail and Halape Trail; camping permits from park visitors center required for these treks. The first .8 mile of the trail is an easy hike on sandy or cinder trails to the "Footprints" exhibit. History says the footprints, preserved under glass cases, are those of Hawaiian warriors who had gathered in the area in 1790 to battle with the forces of Kamehameha the Great for control of the island. When Halema'uma'u erupted, the warriors were overcome by fumes and volcanic dust and as they fled, their footprints were left to harden in the ash. The trail beyond the exhibit passes through the upper sections of the Ka'u Desert and unique desert ecosystem plants and volcanic formations. This is an area of extreme temperatures, sun and high winds; caution is advised and take hat, sunscreen, water and food.

★ **Kipuka Puaulu (Bird Park)** begins off Highway 11 on the Mauna Loa Strip Road about 2.5 miles west of the entrance to Hawai'i Volcanoes National Park. Kipuka Puaulu is about 1.5 miles in on the Strip Road. This is an easy 1-mile loop trail, through a special ecological preserve area and is one of the National Park's most enjoyable walks. The *kipuka* is an "island" of native forest and rare plants surrounded by fairly recent lava flows that isolated this forest. The trail meanders through dense old-growth forest and open meadowlands and there is some gentle slope and climb. Overall an easy walk, alive with Hawaiian birdlife fluttering among the trees. Best to visit early mornings or late afternoons to enjoy this tranquil, pleasantly cool and breezy place. Picnic tables and restrooms available.

Mauna Loa Summit Trail is at the end of Mauna Loa Strip Road (6,662-foot level) off Highway 11, about 2.5 miles west of the entrance to Hawai'i Volcanoes National Park. This is a challenging 36.6-mile, 4-day round-trip hike for experienced hikers only. It takes two days to climb the south rim of Mokuaweoweo Caldera at 13,250 feet. Hikers spend the first night in Red Hill Cabin (10,035 feet) and proceed to the summit shelter on the second day. It takes an additional half day to hike around the caldera to the true summit at 13,677 feet. Hikers are subjected to high winds, altitude sickness, snow and cold temperatures. A shorter but equally difficult 13-mile, 2-day round-trip hike begins at the Mauna Loa Weather Observatory at the 11,000-foot level on the north side, accessed via the Saddle Road. Before taking this trail, hikers are advised to spend the night in their cars at the end of the road near the observatory, since no accommodations are available, to acclimate their bodies to Mauna Loa's elevation. Good hikers can do the trail in one day, but it's better to spend the night at Mauna Loa. A backcountry camping permit is required for either trip; check with Kilauea Visitor Center rangers.

Ka'u District   Ka Lae (South Point) and **Green Sand Beach** is a moderate 6-mile round-trip, 2-hour, coastal trail hike through open grassy areas following jeep trails. The area is reached via South Point Road, which branches off Highway 11 about 6 miles west of Na'alehu town. South Point Road is a narrow asphalt lane winding 12 miles through open pasture country. It passes by the Kamao'a Wind Farm, a wind-powered electricity-generating facility using huge windmill-like turbines. Ka Lae is believed to be where the first Hawaiians landed, around 400 A.D., in their early migrations across the Pacific. There are old canoe mooring holes in the rocks and the ruins of a fishermen's *heiau*. Fishermen still use the area to moor their boats but they hoist them up and down the high cliffs to the calm water below. The road turns east through the remnants of a World War II communications station, terminating at a small boat-launching harbor about a mile east. This is the beginning of the coastal trailhead. It's 3 miles to Green Sand Beach through open rolling grasslands along the coast. Mahana Bay, where the beach is located, is marked by a high cliff promontory rising along the coast and is visible from a distance. A hazardous trail leads down to the beach. Rough waters and currents make it unsafe for water activities but it's a nice place to just picnic and relax. You can easily see how it gets its name, from the sparkling green olivine crystals in the sand. There are no trees or shade along this entire warm, breezy coastline so take hat, sunscreen, water and food. Permits are required to access Green Sand Beach across the private property of Hawaiian Home Lands; 4WD vehicle access may be restricted; there is no charge for the permit, which can be faxed to your hotel or condo. For permit, contact the Department of Hawaiian Home Lands, 160 Baker Avenue, Hilo, HI 96720, 808-974-4250.

Manuka Nature Trail is a moderate 2.25-mile, 2-hour walk at the southwest tip of the Big Island's Ka'u District, very near the South Kona District. Located at Manuka State Wayside off Highway 11 just west of the 81-mile marker, or 81 miles from Hilo, roughly 40 miles from Kailua-Kona. This is a nice botanical garden park with varied species of ornamental trees and shrubs and wide grassy areas, a picnic pavilion and restrooms. The nature trail is a loop walk that climbs into a forest of native *ohia lehua*, tree ferns and *pukiawe* plus *kukui*, guava and other introduced plants and trees. This is a hike through an upland dry forest ecosystem where you'll see and hear a lot of birdlife in their natural habitat.

HORSEBACK RIDING

For the would-be *paniolo* and *paniola*, stables and trail-ride operators offer a unique Hawai'i adventure on horseback, through the Big Island's cool, upcountry ranchlands. Experienced guides "talk story" about local lore and introduce visitors to unseen landscapes, high above the beaches, golf courses and more ordinary things. Prices vary but start at about $75 per person for a basic 1.5- to 2-hour trail ride; longer rides of 5 hours start at about $145 per person. In general, riders must be at least 8 years old and weigh under 250 pounds, so ask first and avoid disappointment. Some outfitters offer trailrides on donkeys and mules for a different take on the *paniolo* experience.

★ *Cowboys of Hawaii, LLC* operates the trail-riding concession on the vast pastures of Parker Ranch. This 150-year-old ranch began the *paniolo* legend in Hawaii and still operates today as one of the world's largest cattle ranches, with 175,000 acres. Two-hour Cowboy Talk & Parker Ranch Rides start at 8:15 a.m. and 12:15 p.m., and there's a Sunset Ride at 4 p.m. (ATV excursions too.) Riders must be at least 7 years old; please advise in advance if a rider is over 250 lbs. Rates: $79 per person. *808-885-5006; www.parkerranch.com.*

★ *DaHana Ranch* DaHana Ranch is home to the 1994 International World Cup champion roughriders. Longtime *paniolo* Harry Nakoa and his family specialize in open-range rides on American Quarterhorses, *paniolo*-style in the uplands of Waimea ranch country. They take first-time to experienced riders and encourage family adventures that include children as young as three. Open daily, rides at 9 and 11 a.m., 1 and 3 p.m. Rates: 1.5-hour Ranch Ride $60, 2-hour Advanced Ride, $100, 2.5-hour Range Station Ride (help move a herd of Brahman cattle), $130. Da Hana also offers 2-week to 90-day very active horsemanship camps, $1,500-$4,000, Harry's renowned

"Silent Thunder" horse training clinics, and the "Roughrider Getaway," a weekend of riding, camping and cowboy skills, scheduled several times throughout the year. Families and group retreats are welcome, and custom experiences can be arranged with notice. Or, bring the ranch to you with a "Paniolo Party" complete with mechanical bull, horseback rides, petting zoo, roping demos and other theme events. *P.O. Box 1293, Kamuela, HI 96743, 7.5 miles east of Waimea town on Old Mamalahoa Highway; 808-885-0057; e-mail: dahana@gte.net; www.dahanaranch.com.*

Donkey Tales of Hawai'i This is a fun and rewarding adventure for kids 7 to 12 years old, way down south in the Ka'u District. During the 3 day/2-night "Summer Camps with Donkeys" kids hike up to a rustic bunkhouse at the 4,000-foot elevation of historic Kapapala Ranch, learn to ride and take care of the animals, hike, play and talk story around the campfire. Rates: $250 including meals. Kids must be able to overnight without parents. Donkeys available for special events, parties, riding lessons and more. *P.O: Box 1768, Kea'au, HI 96749; 808-968-6585; www.kapapala.com.*

Giddy-Up Go Trail Rides This outfitter/operator offers trail-ride excursions in the upland forest and ranchlands of the Hamakua Coast region. They'll also take good care of kids. *P.O. Box 34, Papa'aloa, HI 96780; 808-962-6840.*

★ **Hawai'i Forest & Trail** (See "Hiking.") One of the best and most popular, this excellent outfitter/operator offers the award-winning Kohala Mule Trail Adventure, a guided trailride that skirts the rim of scenic Pololu Valley. Open 7 a.m. to 5 p.m. daily. Rates: $95 adults, $75 children. *74-5035B Queen Ka'ahumanu Highway, Kailua-Kona, HI 96740; 800-464-1993; 808-331-8505; fax: 808-331-8704; e-mail: info@hawaii-forest.com; www.hawaii-forest.com.*

Kahua Ranch See "Kohala Na'alapa Trail Rides" below. *www. kahuaranch.com.*

Kapapala Trails This outfitter/operator has various adventure activities available on Kapapala Ranch, a 30,000-acre working cattle ranch in the southern Ka'u District on the slopes of Mauna Loa. There are horseback ranch rides with an emphasis on eco-tourism and respect for the environment. Custom overnight camping trips can be arranged, as well as rental cottages at reasonable rates. Guests are encouraged to spend time on the ranch alongside the *paniolo* to share the lifestyle and gain hands-on experience. Bring your own horse or lease one of theirs. Rates start at $75. *P.O. Box 1768, Kea'au, HI 96749; 808-968-6585; e-mail: info@kapapala.com.*

King's Trail Rides O' Kona They offer horseback trail rides exploring the backcountry lands of 20,000-acre Kealakekua Ranch and

Kona Coast trail rides to beaches for a picnic lunch and a swim. Monday through Saturday 8:15 a.m. to 12:15 p.m. *Kealakekua, Kona; 808-323-2388.*

★ *Kohala Na'alapa Trail Rides* This operator offers open-range trail rides (not "nose-to-tail") through scenic Kahua Ranch in the Kohala Mountains, a 12,000-acre working cattle ranch with panoramic views of Mauna Kea, Hualalai and the Kohala Coast. Custom picnic rides available. Riders must be at least 8 years old and not more than 230 pounds. Rates: $85 morning, $65 afternoon, $73 Sunset Ride. *P.O. Box 992, Kamuela, HI 96743; 808-889-0022; e-mail: naalapa@ilhawaii.net; www.naalapastables.com.*

★ *Paniolo Riding Adventures* This operator offers trail rides on an 11,000-acre working ranch in the scenic Kohala Mountain country. Skilled, knowledgeable guides lead riders on trained horses through lush pasturelands with scenic vistas of the Kona and Kohala coastlines. There is a standard 2.5-hour morning or afternoon trail ride or a three-hour picnic ride with gourmet lunch included. *P.O. Box 2957, Kamuela, HI 96743; 808-889-5354; fax: 808-884-5577; www.panioloadventures.com.*

WAGON RIDES

★ **Kohala Carriages Ltd.** operates comfortable, cushioned wagon rides through historic Parker Ranch. A pair of gentle giant draft horses pull the covered wagon on its 45-minute route from the Visitor Center every hour on the hour, Tuesday through Saturday 10 a.m. to 2 p.m. Rates: $15 adults, $12 children 12 and under. Other tour locations and special events on request. Parker Ranch Shopping Center in Waimea; 808-889-5955; 808-885-5881; www.parkerranch.com. **Waipi'o Valley Wagon Tours** takes you "back in time" from the Last Chance Store in Kukuihaele town, down into unspoiled Waipi'o Valley. From there, you climb aboard an old-fashioned mule-drawn wagon, whose storyteller/drivers share Waipi'o's culture and history as you take in lush tropical foliage, cultivated taro patches, the mythic Hi'ilawe waterfall and much more. Cushioned seats, Amish springs and shock absorbers make for a comfortable ride through a quieter, less-complicated place. This is a tour for people with imagination and respect for authenticity. Weather permitting, 1.5-hour tours depart Monday through Saturday 9:30 a.m., 11:30 a.m., 1:30 p.m., 3:30 p.m. Rates: $45 adults, $22.50 children, kids under 3 free. P.O. Box 1340, Honoka'a, HI 96727; 808-775-9518; e-mail: wagonaloha@ hotmail.com; www.waipiovalleywagontour.com.

Parker Ranch   See "Cowboys of Hawaii, LLC" above. *www.park erranch.com.*

Waipi'o Na'alapa Trail Rides   Leisurely paced 2.5-hour trail ride through the lush beauty of the famous Waipi'o Valley on the Hamakua Coast, taking in waterfalls, jungle trails, freshwater steams, taro patches and breathtaking views. Riders must be at least 8 years old and not more than 230 pounds. Tours depart Monday through Saturday from Waipi'o Valley Artworks in Kukuihaele town at 9 a.m. and 12:30 p.m. Closed Sunday. Rates: $85. *P.O. Box 437185, Kamuela, HI 96743; 808-775-0419.*

★ **Waipi'o on Horseback and Taro Farm**   This outfitter takes riders down into the beautiful scenic Waipi'o Valley. Meet at the Last Chance Store in Kukuihaele, then delve into the valley and explore trails through the lush rainforest jungles. Cross streams, pass waterfalls, and visit a working old-fashioned Hawaiian taro farm. Rates: $75 adults, $65 kids 8 to 12; $240 for a longer "Mauka-Makai" adventure. (ATV rides too.) *P.O. Box 183, Honoka'a, HI 96727; 808-775-7291; http://waipio.homestead.com.*

Waipi'o Ridge Stables   They provide a 2.5-hour "Valley of the Kings" ride and a 5-hour "Hidden Waterfalls" ride above Waipi'o Valley. Rates: $145 for a 5-hour ride including lunch, $75 for a 2.5-hour ride with snacks. *Located at Kukuihaele near the Waipi'o Valley overlook; 808-775-1007; www.topofwaipio.com.*

HUNTING

Outdoors and hunting enthusiasts will enjoy the challenge of an expedition on the slopes of Mauna Kea or other Big Island hunting grounds. Game like wild boar, Mouflon sheep and mountain goat, and wild game birds like turkey, quail, pheasant, chukar or francolin partridge are available in season, which may vary annually. The following hunting guide services and outfitters can make all the arrangements.

Ginger Flower Charters   Fishing and hunting guide Kenny Llanes specializes in wild boar hunting on the Big Island's remote mountain and forest slopes. In addition, bird hunting for wild turkey, pheasant, quail, chukar and francolin is available November through January. Archery hunts are available for sheep and goat in season. *73-1277 Awakea, Kailua-Kona, HI 96740; 808-325-7600.*

Glenn Kokubun   This outfitter has various hunting tours available in the upland mountain areas, open grasslands and forest areas for all game. *15-1922 Naupaka, Kea'au, HI 96749; 808-982-7349; mahana@aol.com.*

Hawai'i Hunting Tours   Guide Eugene Ramos specializes in custom hunts for sheep, wild boar, goat and game birds on private hunting grounds on the slopes of Mauna Kea, Mauna Loa and Hua-lalai. Scenic 4WD tours through majestic backcountry are also available. *P.O. Box 58, Pa'auilo, Hamakua, HI 96776; 808-776-1666.*

Kealia Ranch This outfitter offers guided hunts and excursions for all game in the upland ranchlands and forest areas of the South Kona region above Honaunau and Kealakekua Bay. *Kealia Ranch c/o Post Office, Honaunau, HI 96726; 808-328-2662.*

Parker Ranch The Parker Ranch Hunt Club provides year-round opportunities for hunters of wild game and birds. Parker Ranch now offers skeet shooting clays, for a "guilt-free" hunting adventure. *For information, contact Patrick Fisher, 808-885-7311 or 808-960-4148; pfisher@parkerranch.com; www.parkerranch.com.*

KAYAKING (*See also* Sea Excursions; Snorkeling)

Kayaking is becoming an extremely popular ocean sport in Big Island waters. Easy to learn, inexpensive and readily available, kayaks are environmentally-friendly, peaceful vehicles for adventure, and a fun family activity for all ages. Many outfitters provide guided tours and instruction island-wide. Please note, at this time kayak tours of Kealakekua Bay are not permitted, although individual kayakers may go it alone.

Adventures in Paradise This complete kayak and snorkeling outfitter provides equipment plus morning and afternoon tours of several scenic Big Island sites such as Pauai Bay, Puako and along the Kona Coast. Kayaks and equipment available for rent as well. Rates: $59.99-$99.95 per person. (Adventures in Paradise also offers dolphin or whale watch and snorkel cruises, scuba and fishing charters and various hiking tours. *Located south of Kona between mile markers 111 and 110, 81-6367 Mamalahoa Highway, Kealakekua; 808-323-3005; 866-824-2337; www.bigislandkayak.com.*

Aloha Kayak Co. Guided kayak excursions and adventures. Located in old Honalo town, this outfitter provides guided kayak excursions and equipment rentals, including a special "window" kayak with a glass insert for undersea observation and you paddle. Rentals include car rack and life vests. $25 single, $45 double kayak per day. Tours are $65 for 4-hour tour, $99 for a 6-hour tour. Children any age are welcome with parents' OK. *808-331-8558; 79-7428 Mamalahoa Highway, Honalo, HI 96750; 877-322-1444, 808-322-2868, fax: 808-322-1444; e-mail: alohakayak@yahoo.com; www.alohakayak.com.*

Aquatic Perceptions Multi-Sports Tours (See "Biking.") This multi-sport outfitter provides kayak tours and equipment rentals (along with scuba gear, dives and instruction) for Big Island adventures at sea. Rates: $20 single, $25 double kayak (up to 4 hours); two-hour Hilo Bay Kayak Tour, $35. They also offer pedal boat rentals at Hilo Bay for $25 per hour for a 2-person boat and $30 per hour for a 4-person boat. *111 Banyan Drive, Hilo, HI 96720; 808-939-9997; 808-938-1228; e-mail: kayakscuba @aol.com; www.multi-sport-hawaii.com.*

Ehu & Kai Hawaiian cultural tours and kayaking in the Kealakekua Bay area. *808-328-8775; e-mail: kahauloa@earthlink.net.*

Hawai'i Pack & Paddle Tours This operator provides kayak, hiking and camping tours and multi-sport adventures along the Kona Coast and customized two- to five-day kayak outings around the Big Island. *87-3187 Holomoku Road H, Captain Cook, HI 96704; 808-328-8911; e-mail: gokayak@kona.net.*

Kahalu'u Bay Surf & Sea Convenient location for kayak rentals, "right on the beach" on Ali'i Drive. Also offering outrigger canoe rides, surfboard sales, lessons and rentals, snorkel gear, boogie-boards and more. Rates: $19 single, $24 double kayak. *78-6685 Ali'i Drive, Kailua-Kona, 96740; 808-322-4883; www.kahaluurent.com.*

★ **Kealakekua Bay Kayak Rentals** They offer a full line of ocean kayak rentals, including the Dagger Kayak, 4" wider and 11" longer for a more stable ride; guided tours are available. Also snorkel equipment, boogieboard and other rentals. *On Highway 11 in Keala-kekua, right next to McDonald's at 112-mile marker; 808-323-3329; e-mail: kayakkona@aol.com.*

★ **Kohala Mountain Kayak Cruise** "Flumin Da Ditch" is one of the Big Island's best adventures and a unique kayaking excursion that you won't find anywhere else. It's a three-mile, three-hour cruise by inflatable kayak through the old Kohala Ditch, a concrete water-way built in 1905 to irrigate the sugar plantations of the North Kohala District. Escorted groups of kayakers float down scenic waterways, tunnels and flumes of the original ditch, through rain-forest and mountain pastures with breathtaking panoramic views. The original 22.5-mile-long irrigation ditch was a major engineering feat in its time, spanning the rugged gorges and valleys to reach the old Kohala Sugar Plantation for 70 years until its demise in 1975. "Flumin Da Ditch" is an attempt to bring eco-tourism activities to North Kohala and help restore the ditch and highlight the unique cultural history of the area. Snacks and hot/cold drinks are included at the end of the cruise, and kayakers can visit a secluded rainforest water-fall and swimming hole for a dip. Morning and afternoon departures. Cruises start with a van ride from Kapa'au town to the ditch site. Rates: $98.96 adults, $67.71 children 5 to 18. (They also offer Humvee rainforest safaris, an island first, $119.78 adults, $67.71

children.) *Headquarters for this popular activity is Kapa'au town, at the intersection of Akoni Pule Highway and Hawi Road/Kohala Mountain Highway, behind the Nakahara Store Building; P.O. Box 190573, Hawi, HI 96719; 877-449-6922; 808-889-6922; fax: 808-889-6944; e-mail: res@flumindaditch.com; www.flumindaditch.com.*

Kona Boys Homegrown Adventures This operator's catch phrase is "you deserve a good paddling." They provide a variety of fun, local-style kayaking tours and excursions, including half- and full-day sea treks and overnight tours, plus surf and dive instruction. The shop offers all kinds of rentals including kayak and snorkel equipment, scuba gear, surfboards, *tabi* reefwalking shoes and more. Billed as "the only surf shop in South Kona," Kona Boys is staffed by lifelong watermen and women, who share their enjoyment of the ocean, along with a sense of respect and aloha.-Rates: $27 single, $47 double kayak, $79 clear-bottom kayak, 24 hours. Kealakekua Bay kayak tour with lunch, $135, sunset kayak/snorkel, $75, overnight trips (weather-conditional) $350 per couple includes equipment, camping gear and meals. Custom charter tours welcome. *Mamalahoa Highway, Kealakekua; 808-328-1234 or 808-322-3600; www.konaboys.com.*

Ocean Safari's Kayaks This operator offers varied ocean kayaking tours, excursions, equipment rentals and instruction. Rent your own, or join in Ocean Safari's 3.5-hour Keauhou Sea Cave Tour, $59; a 2-hour Early Riser Dolphin Quest Tour, $30; 4-hour Whale Watch, $75. Tours include snacks, drinks, snorkel gear and fun. (They also offer surf lessons, $65-$85 and board rentals, $25.) Kids 12 and under half-price. Kayak Rentals $25 single, $40 double. *P.O. Box 515, Kailua-Kona, HI 96745; 808-326-4699; fax: 808-322-3653; e-mail: kayakhi@gte.net; www.oceansafariskayaks.com.*

Pineapple Park Hostels A pleasant retreat on the Hilo side of the island, specializing in fun for adventurous guests, Pineapple Park maintains a fleet of over 100 kayaks designed for fun at sea at their Kona shop location. Rates: $19 single, $40 double kayak. *81-6363 Mamalahoa Highway, Kailua-Kona; 808-322-4166.*

LAND TOURS

The Big Island earned its name. It's big, bigger than the other islands put together. There's a lot of open space here, and a wide variety of scenic places to visit and enjoy. We're of the opinion that one of the Big Island's best pleasures is  driving, exercising the American custom of taking a ride. With basically only one road (two in some places) around the island, relatively light traffic, reliable weather and beautiful country to watch roll by, the island cruise is a delight. Don't be afraid to take a look at the "Driving" section of Chapter 1 and make your own adventure.

Guided tours, however, have their own charms and benefits, particularly for some of the more remote or harder to find places beyond the reach of rental cars. In addition to regular land tours of the island, this section lists some unique tours to places like Waipi'o Valley and the summit of Mauna Kea. These operators provide special insight on their respective attractions and areas of the Big Island and make sure you see what you came to see.

ATV Adventures Experience the amazing Green Sand Beach at Ka Lae, Ka'u on a 5-hour excursion by individual ATV (maybe the best way to get there, with competent local guides and no special permissions needed). Rates: $125. Lunch, snacks and drinks included. *Located at Bedrock Ranch just outside of Wai'ohinu. 808-929-8157; e-mail: atv@bedrockranchatv.com; www.bedrockranchatv.com.*

ATV Outfitters Hawai'i ATV riding adventures through private ranchlands and coastal areas of the North Kohala District of the Big Island. Take in scenic offroad mountain trails, visit historic sites, and cruise along beautiful seacliffs, waterfalls and old plantation roads. All equipment, including gloves, goggles, and a helmet, is provided, along with safety instructions. Riders must be at least 16 years old, 90 to 300 lbs., children 5 to 15, 45 to 120 lbs., are permitted to ride with one of the trail guides. Rates: 1.5-hour Ocean Seacliff Trail, $94 adults, $75 children; 2.5-hour Waterfall Adventure, $166 adults, $130 children; 3-hour Rainforest & Waterfall Tour, $239 adults, $125 children. Reservations recommended, and long pants and closed shoes are required. Rates: $90 per person. *Sakamoto Store Building, Kapa'au, North Kohala, HI 96755; 808-889-6000; www.outfittershawaii.com.*

Hawaiian Adventure Tours Operating out of two Kohala Coast locations at Kawaihae and Puako, Hawaiian Adventure Tours specializes in respectful land and sea eco-adventures, professionally guided and outfitted for maximum guest experience. Its 3.5-hour tours depart at 8:30 a.m., with free transportation to Waikoloa hotels. Rates: $59 adults, $35 children under 12. *800-659-3544; 808-889-0227; e-mail: advtours@aloha.net; www.hawaiianadventuretours.com.*

Hawaii AgVentures Hawaii AgVentures, a new enterprise of the Big Island Farm Bureau, offers a "Chocolate Treats & Tropical Temptations" excursion that gives visitors a close-up look at a coffee farm and the region famous for its smooth-tasting java. Rates: $79 per person. Other packages mix in trips to orchid farms, cattle ranches and a banana plantation. Customized trips are available. *800-660-6011; www.hawaiiagventures.com.*

★ *HMV Tours*   This tour operation is owned by the same folks who operate the Kohala Mountain Kayak Cruise. HMV Tours use a 4WD military-type Hummer vehicle to explore the deep jungle and rainforest of Kohala Mountain. Take an adventure-filled ride into the real offroad backcountry of the Big Island mountain forest. Rates: $119.78 adults, $67.71 children. Tours go twice daily. *Located at the intersection of Akoni Pule Highway and Hawi Road in Hawi, North Kohala; P.O. Box 190573, Hawi, HI 96719; 877-449-6922; 808-889-6922; fax: 808-889-6944; e-mail: res@hmvtours.com; www.hmvtours.com.*

Kukui ATV & Adventures   This operator provides 2.5-hour guided adventures aboard automatic, easy-to-handle all-terrain vehicles. Old sugarcane backroads lead through beautiful country with mountain streams, waterfalls and pools, eucalyptus groves and wild gardens of ginger and tropical plants. Rest stop with snacks and beverages included. Tours depart daily from Waipi'o Valley Artworks in Kukuihaele town at 9:30 a.m. and 1 p.m. Riders must be at least 16 years old, 100-300 pounds. Rates: $100 per person for a 2.5-hour tour, $145 for a 3.5-hour tour including picnic lunch by the waterfall. *P.O. Box 6368, Kamuela, HI 96743; 808-775-1701.*

★ *Polynesian Adventure Tours* This longtime Big Island tour company specializes in the deluxe "Grand Circle Island Tour," a complete 260-mile, ten-hour drive around the island. All the major sites and attractions are included. Daily departures from Kona and Kohala Coast hotels in spacious, deluxe "big window" mini-coaches or mini-buses are 6:45 a.m. to 8:30 a.m., with return at 6 p.m. to 6:30 p.m. They also offer a special "Hawai'i Volcano Adventure" from Hilo area hotels departing at 9 a.m. and returning between 5-6 p.m. daily. The tours take in the major attractions of the Big Island and Volcanoes National Park. Rates: Grand Circle Island Tour (varies by pickup location) $63-$70 adults, $45-$55 children 3-11; from Kona Airport Hawai'i Volcano Adventure (from Hilo only) $55 adults, $38 children 3-11. *73-4818 Kanalani Street, Kailua-Kona, HI 96740; 800-622-3011; 808-833-3000; fax: 808-531-1357; e-mail: sales@polyad.com; www.polyad.com.*

STARGAZING

Mauna Kea Summit Adventures are specialists in sunset and star-gazing tours via 4WD vehicle to the summit of Mauna Kea and the telescope observatory complex. Transportation provided from various resort locations for the daily tour departure at 3 p.m., returning about 10:30 p.m.; parkas and hot drinks included. A "peak" Big Island experience you're unlikely to find anywhere else. Rates: $175. P.O. Box 9027, Kailua-Kona, HI 96745; 888-322-2366; 808-322-2366; fax: 808-322-6507; e-mail: kaymaunakeasummit@msn.com; www.maunakea.com.

★ **Robert's Hawai'i Inc.** Mini-coach/motorcoach full-day "Grand Circle Island Tour" from Kona and Kohala Coast hotels, stopping at all the Big Island's major attractions and a "Volcano Special Tour" taking in the highlights of Hawai'i Volcanoes National Park. Rates: Circle Island Tour (price varies by pickup location) adults $57-$65, children under 12 $50-$55; Volcano Special Tour adults $48, children under 12 $38. *P.O. Box 579, Kailua-Kona, HI 96740; 800-831-5541; 808-966-5983; 808-329-1688; www.roberts-hawaii.com.*

Waipi'o Valley Shuttle & Tours These experienced guides take pride in comprehensive 4WD tours of the lush Waipi'o Valley and its history, culture and sense of place. Tours available Monday through Saturday at 9 a.m., 11 a.m., 1 p.m. and 3 p.m. Rates: $45 adults, $20 children under 12. *P.O. Box 5128, Kukuihaele, HI 96727; 808-775-7121.*

★ **Waipi'o Valley Wagon Tours** Adventure exploration in an old-fashioned mule-drawn wagon along the back lanes and across streams of the beautiful, hidden Waipi'o Valley. Fully narrated historical and cultural tour takes in majestic waterfalls, meandering streams, taro patches still being cultivated, lush tropical jungle rainforest and more. Cushioned seats and stable suspension provide a smooth and comfortable ride. The 1.5-hour tours depart several times daily from the Last Chance Store in Kukuihaele just before Waipi'o Valley. Two tours daily, weather permitting. Rates: $45 adults, $22.50 children, free kids under 3. *Honoka'a; 808-775-9518.*

MOTORCYCLE AND MOPED ADVENTURES

Adventure-seeking visitors can rent everything from humble mopeds to Harley Hogs, as long as you have a motorcycle driver's license from your state of residence. Some companies have a minimum age of 21 or 23 and passengers must be at least 7 years old; Hawaii does not require (although we do recommend) motorcycle helmets. Deposit from $350 or higher is generally required. Rates for motorcycles depend on the size of the bike and number of days, but in general range from $100 to $150 per day. Mopeds and scooters are in the $40-$50 per day range. Check for weekly rates, which can be less expensive.

★ **DJ's Rentals** One of Kona's best, DJ's rents Harley Heritage medium bikes at $145 per day, Harley Sportsters at $119-130 and the V-Rod for $75-90 half-day and $145 full-day. If you don't need quite that much horsepower try a cruiser-friendly moped at $25 per day. *Across from the King Kamehameha Hotel and Kona Pier, 75-5663 Palani Road, Kailua-Kona, HI 96740; 800-993-HOGS (4647); 808-329-1700; e-mail: rent@harleys.com; www.harleys.com.*

★ *Kona Harley Davidson*   A must-stop for Harley lovers for the Kona HD T-shirt, this motorcycle dealer has a full range of Harleys for rent. Rates: $80-$100 for 4 hours, $100-$125 for 8 hours and an additional $30 for 24 hours. Military discounts and weekly rates are available. *74-5615 Luhia, Suite E, Kailua-Kona, HI 96740; 808-326-9887; e-mail konahd@kona.net; www.konaharleydavidson.com.*

MUSEUMS

Big Island museums are small and personable. In the last 200 years, the island has radically changed from a subsistence farming and fishing society to a diverse and growing international tourist destination. The time invested exploring our museums captures the colorful culture and history of a truly unique and special place. You can visit restored Hawaiian villages and *heiau*, the last palace of the European-style monarchy and missionary homes of the 1800s and a tiny wayside building dedicated to Hawaii's unique rail system. Learn about the history of the sugar cane plantations, which dominated life in east Hawai'i, the coffee farms of Kona on the west side, and the *paniolo* culture on the huge ranches of Waimea and North Kohala. These museums introduce you to the diverse ethnic groups that immigrated here to work those industries, and details how their heritage, language and even food contribute to the Big Island's multicultural island style. There's a museum dedicated to tsunami, one perched on the edge of a volcanic crater and even one dedicated to space exploration. There's ample material for science projects and history reports but don't tell how much fun it is to learn on your Big Island adventure vacation.

Ellison S. Onizuka Space Center   Located at the Kona International Airport, this memorial museum of space flight and astronaut lore is dedicated to Hawai'i astronaut Ellison S. Onizuka, who was lost aboard the 1986 space shuttle disaster at Cape Canaveral. Colonel Onizuka was born and raised in Kona and grew up on his family's coffee farm. The museum features memorabilia from his career in space exploration and includes various hands-on exhibits and a piece of "moon rock" donated by NASA. Open daily 8:30 a.m. to 4:30 p.m. Admission: $3 adults, $1 children under 12. *P.O. Box 833, Kailua-Kona, HI 96745; 808-329-3441; www.onizukaspacecenter.org.*

★ *Hulihe'e Palace Museum*   This attractive and imposing beachside structure was built in 1838 and used as a summer residence by the ruling Hawaiian monarchs. The palace is maintained by the Daughters of Hawai'i as a historical showcase of Hawaiian heritage and culture. The palace has some beautiful antique Hawaiian furniture, original bedroom furnishings, and antique handmade Hawaiian quilts and other memorabilia from the days of Hawaiian royalty. Open Monday through Friday 9 a.m. to 4 p.m., Saturday and Sunday 10 a.m. to 4 p.m. Admission: $6 adults, $4 seniors and $1 children under 18. *75-5718 Ali'i Drive, Kailua-Kona, HI 96740; 808-329-1877.*

Isaacs Art Center Located in a historic schoolhouse building in Waimea, the Isaacs Art Center is home to the Hawaii Preparatory Academy art collection and showcases works by important Hawaii artists of the last century. A Preservation Honor Award recipient from the Historic Hawaii Foundation, the Center is open Tuesday through Saturday, 10 a.m. to 5 p.m. Free admission. *808-885-5884.*

Kamuela Museum This privately operated museum has a large collection of ancient Hawaiian weapons, World War II artifacts, furniture of Hawaiian royalty, and other art objects and antiques on display. Open daily 9 a.m. to 4 p.m. Admission: $5 adults, $2 children under 12. Call first. *At the intersection of Highways 19 and 250 (Kohala Mountain Road) just west of Waimea town. 808-885-4724.*

Kona Historical Society Museum Housed in the historic Greenwell Store, one half-mile south of Kealakekua town on Highway 11, this old stone country store maintains an extensive collection of historic manuscripts, photographs, maps and artifacts. It also houses displays and exhibits of early Kona ranching, coffee farming, related commercial activities and general lifestyle of the Big Island's Kona District. The museum is part of the old Greenwell Ranch. KHS also operates the **D. Uchida Farm**, 808-323-2006, as a "Living History Farm." This is a seven-acre working coffee and macadamia nut farm. The farm's educational tours and programs help bring the history of Kona's coffee farming community alive through the use of historic buildings, authentic landscapes, artifacts, costumed interpreters and guides, live animals, working machinery and equipment and producing orchards and fields. Coffee farm tours are $20 per person; tours held Tuesday and Thursday only, 8:30 a.m. and 10:30 a.m. Museum hours are 8 a.m. to 4 p.m. weekdays; closed holidays. *81-6351 Mamalahoa Highway, Kealakekua, HI 96704; 808-323-3222.*

Laupahoehoe Train Museum The museum preserves the Hamakua Coast's railroad heritage with historic displays and exhibits and welcomes visitors 9 a.m. to 4:30 p.m. Monday through Saturday and 10 a.m. to 2 p.m. Sunday. They're in progress on restoring some old train rolling stock and related displays. Located in Laupahoehoe town at the intersection of the main street and Highway 19. Admission $3 adults, $2 students and seniors. *P.O. Box 358, Laupahoehoe, HI 96764; 808-962-6300; fax: 808-962-2221; e-mail: ltmhawaii@aol.com.*

★ *Lyman Museum & Mission House* This is an early New England–style missionary home built in 1839 for Hilo missionaries Rev. David and Sarah Lyman. Next door to the original Lyman House is the modern museum building that holds a unique collection of memorabilia of early Hilo and Big Island lifestyles. Displays cover the pre-Western, old Hawaiian days, the missionary and Hawaiian monarchy era of the 1800s, and the vast changes brought by the 20th century. There are many cultural artifacts representing the various ethnic peoples, including Portuguese, Chinese, Japanese, Korean and Filipino, who immigrated to Hawai'i over the generations and made this their home. Tours offered daily, except Sunday, at 10 and 11 a.m. and 1, 2 and 3 p.m. Open daily 9:30 a.m. to 4:30 p.m. Admission: $7 adults, $5 seniors, $3 children 6 to 17, children under 6 free, $21 families. *276 Haili Street, Hilo, HI 96720; 808-935-5021; e-mail: info@lymanmuseum.org; www.lymanmuseum.org.*

Memories of Hawaii-Big Island A new little piece of island history preserved in the old Ebesu Flower Shop on Keawe Street in Hilo. Memorabilia from sports, plantation days, railroads and day-to-day life of times gone by. From their brochure: "Photos, balls and other stuff from sportsmen that visited the Big Island ... Babe Ruth, Billy Martin, Joe DiMaggio, Bill Dickey, Steve Reeves, and Jesse Owens, who raced against a horse at Honolulu Park in 1946 ... the horse won." Tuesday through Saturday 9 a.m. to 4 p.m. and Sunday 10 a.m. to 3 p.m. Admission: $6 adults, $5 seniors, $3 students. *301 Keawe Street, Hilo, HI 96720; 808-961-0024; e-mail: mohbi@yahoo.com.*

Mokupapapa Discovery Center A new, small-but-fascinating museum on Hilo's bayfront Kamehameha Avenue. Kids of all ages enjoy interactive displays, including a 2,500-gallon reef aquarium and submersible training station. Affiliated with the National Oceanic Atmospheric Administration and National Marine Sanctuaries. Admission free. Open Tuesday through Saturday 9 a.m. to 4 p.m. *308 Kamehameha Avenue, Suite 203, Hilo, HI 96720; 808-933-8195; e-mail: jef frey.kuwabara@noaa.gov; http://hawaiireef.noaa.gov.*

Onizuka Center for International Astronomy The Visitor Information Center, accessible by cars without four-wheel drive, has displays and a variety of programs about Mauna Kea and astronomy. Star-gazing lectures and hands-on telescope programs are conducted every evening from 6 to 10 p.m., weather permitting, using an 11-inch Celestron telescope. Mauna Kea summit day tours are conducted on Saturday and Sunday only at 1 p.m. These day tours depart from the visitors center in a vehicle convoy to the 13,796-foot mountain summit and the Mauna Kea Science Complex of observatories; 4WD vehicle required for summit tours. Families are encouraged to visit; however, participants must be at least 16 years old and in good health with no cardiac or breathing problems; pregnant women are not allowed. Visitors should dress for freezing conditions (30-40 degrees). For weather updates and snow and road conditions on Mauna Kea, call 808-935-6268. Visitors Center open daily, 9 a.m. to 10 p.m. Located at the 9,200-foot elevation level (6.5 miles up the Mauna Kea Summit Road) off the Saddle Road between Hilo and Waimea/Kohala, Highway 200 (about 1 hour from Waimea or Kohala Coast). *808-961-2180; www.ifa.hawaii.edu.ifo.vis.*

★ *Pacific Tsunami Museum*   This is one of the island's most unique and fascinating museums. It's located in the old First Hawaiian Bank along downtown Hilo's bayfront Kamehameha Avenue. Check the museum website for information and developments on current programs and displays. The museum serves as a repository of information and research for scholars on global tsunami and tidal wave phenomena and as an educational museum for the public. Museum displays and exhibits preserve the social and cultural history of the local community and serve as a living memorial to those who lost their lives in past tsunami in Hawai'i. Guided tours, movies of tsunami events, and interactive computer terminals are available, and there is a museum gift shop. Open Monday through Saturday 9 a.m. to 4 p.m. Admission: $5 per person. *130 Kamehameha Avenue, P.O. Box 806, Hilo, HI 96721; 808-935-0926; fax: 808-935-0842; www. tsunami.org.*

★ *Parker Ranch Visitor Center*   The center is located in the Parker Ranch Shopping Center on Highway 19 in the heart of Waimea town. A large-screen video presentation highlights the Ranch's fascinating contributions to Hawai'i's history, and a look at day-to-day ranch life. Enjoy browsing through the museum, which depicts the six generations of the Parker family through 150 years of ranching history. Open daily except Sunday, 9 a.m. to 4 p.m. Admission: $6.50 adults, $5.50 seniors, $5 children 4 to 11. *P.O. Box 458, Kamuela, HI 96743; 808-885-7655; www.parkerranch.com.*

Parker Ranch Historic Homes   Another Parker Ranch Visitor Center attraction is the historic Parker Ranch home complex one mile west of Waimea on Highway 190. Here visitors can tour through Mana, the quaint New England–style house built by John Palmer Parker I in 1847. The interior is made entirely of native Hawaiian *koa* wood. Pu'uopelu, built in 1862, is the main ranch residence, featuring an outstanding 8,000-square-foot art gallery with a remarkable collection of original Impressionist paintings, Chinese antiques and many other *objets d'art*. The art collection belonged to the previous owner of Parker Ranch, Richard Smart, and is lovingly maintained for public appreciation and private parties. Pu'uopelu and Mana are open daily except Sunday, 9 a.m. to 5 p.m. Admission: $8.50 adults, $7.50 seniors, $6 children 4 to 11. *808-885-5433.*

★ *Thomas A. Jaggar Museum*   One of the Big Island's best, this museum and working science observatory is about 3 miles from the park entrance and main visitors center. Visitors, along with vulcanologists on 24/7 duty, watch multiple seismograph readings from the island's four active and dormant volcanoes, as well as the 20-year old eruption at Kilauea. You can even create your own earthquake at one exhibit. There is an awesome view of Halema'uma'u Crater, where the emptiness marked by steaming vents makes you marvel at what the forces of nature have created. Educational displays explain the formation of volcanoes and related geology with samples of many different kinds of lava rock, olivine crystals, "Pele's hair" and other products of eruptions. As interesting in a completely different way are the interpretive displays of Hawaiian mythology and religious culture created around the volcano. Admission included with national park admission ($10 per vehicle). *P.O. Box 52, Hawai'i Volcanoes National Park, HI 96718-0052; 808-985-6000.*

SCUBA DIVING   *(See also* Sea Excursions; Snorkeling)

Aloha Dive Company   This family-owned and operated dive boat company accesses some of the more remote dive sites of Big Island waters all along the western coast from North Kohala to Na`alehu. Explore hidden lava tubes and colorful coral reef formations; see a myriad of marine animals, plants and unspoiled mysteries. Blue water dives and night dives (including manta ray dives) a specialty, with top-of-the-line equipment. Prices vary according to time and location. Rates: 1-tank dives $75, 2-tank dives $95-$175, 3-tank dives $200. *P.O. Box 4454, Kailua-Kona, HI 96745; 800-708-5662; phone/fax: 808-325-5560; www.alohadive.com.*

Blue Water Hunter   For something a little different, check out spearfishing with Captain Tad on a 21-foot Sea Ray custom boat. Their online dive shop offers the latest technology in spearguns and accessories, freediving and snorkel gear, knives and watches and specialized wet suits including Deep Thought and Xcel Camouflage wet suits. Blue Water Hunter also offers "breathtaking" freedive instruction and excursions with noted marine author Carlos Eyles. "Diving Free" rates vary. Contact Carlos at 808-326-1569, info@carlos eyles.com. Rates for a 5-7 hour spearfishing cruise (and you keep

your catch), $400. Blue Water Hunter is open Tuesday through
Saturday 10 a.m. to 5 p.m. *73-5577 Kauhola Street #1, Kailua-Kona, HI
96740; 800-826-7341; 808-331-2237; fax: 808-331-2013; e-mail:
info@bluewaterhunter.com; www.bluewaterhunter.com.*

Bottom Time   Located in Kailua-Kona, this full-service dive
shop and charter boat operator offers a wide range of options for
divers of all experience and interest levels, from intro dives to certifications, day, night, Nitrox and more. Rates: 2-tank day or night
dives $109.95, 3-tank long-range dive $175.95 (6-diver minimum),
3-day special $260.95, 5-day special $409.95. *866-463-4836; 808-331-
1858; fax: 808-331-1859; www.bottomtimehawaii.com.*

Dive Makai Charter   Personalized diving cruises and personal
service are the emphasis of this dive operator. Complete dive packages and equipment rentals are available. The basic 2-tank boat dive
is $95 per person, departing Honokohau Harbor at 7:15 a.m., return-
ing 1 p.m. *808-329-2025; www.divemakai.com.*

East Hawai'i Divers   This NAUI-certified outfitter specializes
in custom tours and certification classes, scuba tours, snorkel tours
and introductory dives, and offers a full range of equipment rentals.
Scuba tours begin at $45 person, snorkel tours at $30 person, introductory dives at $60. *P.O. Box 2001, Pahoa, HI 96778; 808-965-7840.*

★ Fair Wind   Snorkel/Scuba Cruises aboard *Fair Wind II*, a 60-
foot catamaran with 149-passenger capacity, depart daily from Keauhou Bay pier. Cruises include snorkel gear and instruction, floats
and water toys, with Snuba and custom videos as options. For
snorkelers and scuba divers, the Luncheon Cruise, 9 a.m. to 1:30
p.m., includes continental breakfast and burgers for lunch. The Afternoon Cruise, 2 p.m. to 5:30 p.m., includes soft drinks and snacks.
Snorkel rates: Luncheon Cruise $99 adults, $59 children 4 to 12,
$29 children 3 and under; Afternoon Cruise $65 adults, $39 children
4 to 12. Children 3 and under free. Scuba rates: $109-$115 for the
afternoon dive, $149-179 for a morning dive including breakfast and
lunch. *78-7130 Kaleiopapa Street, Keauhou Bay, Kona, HI 96740; 800-677-
9461; 808-322-2788; e-mail: snorkel@fair-wind.com; www.fair-wind.com.*

Honu Sports   Dive equipment rentals, one- and two-tank
morning dives, torpedo propulsion vehicles, night dives, instruction
and scuba-kayak adventures. Rates: $79-$139 charters including
equipment, snacks and cold drinks; torpedo $40 additional. *Located
on Ali'i Drive in downtown Kailua-Kona; 808-938-9795; 808-327-3483.*

Jack's Diving Locker   This dive operator offers special scuba
diving charters, night dives, instruction and certification, and complete diving equipment sales and rentals. Dive rates begin at $95 per
person for 2-tank day dives, $115 per person for night dives. *75-5819*

ASSORTED WATERSPORTS

Aloha Jet Ski is Kona's only jet ski company, renting Yamaha XL 700 Waverunners that handle up to three passengers at a time. Instruction and safety gear provided; must be 16 years old to rent and drive. Open daily 9 a.m. to 4 p.m. Rates: $85 for one hour, $55 for a half-hour. (Your time starts after the mandatory safety briefing.) Located at Kailua Pier; 808-329-2SKI; e-mail: jetski@ kona.net; www.mauiwatersports.com. **Torpedo Tours** is something interesting: a battery-powered "torpedo" tows snorkelers or scuba divers along at 2 mph to get you where you want to be in the sea. Dive and snorkel boat tours depart from Honokohau Marina daily. Rates: $59 to $300 depending on equipment needs. Instruction and specialty and private charters available. 808-938-0405; e-mail: torpedo@kona.net; www.torpedotours.com. The calmer waters of the Kailua Bay area are favorable for the exhilarating flights of parasailers. ★ **UFO Parasail of Kailua-Kona** provides adventure parasailing excursions high above the Kona Coast with departures from Kailua Pier. Take off from and land on a large powerboat that pulls the parasail through the sky for one or two passengers together. Exhilarating ride, panoramic views of the Kona Coast and something called optional "simulated free-fall" offered at no extra charge. Rates: "Atmospheric" travel $47 for 7 minutes at 400 feet, "Stratospheric travel" $57 for 10 minutes at 800 feet. P.O. Box 5438, Kailua-Kona, HI 96745; 808-325-5UFO; 808-325-5836; 800-FLY-4UFO; fax: 808-331-2440; www.ufoparasail.com.

Ali'i Drive, Coconut Grove MarketPlace, Kailua-Kona, HI 96740; 808-329-7585; 800-345-4807; e-mail: divejdl@gte.net.

Kohala Divers Ltd. This shop offers a full range of professional diving services, equipment sales and rentals, and dive charters along the Kohala Coast. Open daily 8 a.m. to 6 p.m. Basic 2-tank, half-day boat dive is $109. *Kawaihae Shopping Center, Kawaihae, HI 96743; 808-882-7774; www.kohaladivers.com.*

★ **Kona Coast Divers** They offer diving charters and a full range of sales/service/rentals on professional diving equipment plus dive certification classes. Basic 2-tank half-day dives are $80 per person, departing 8 a.m. and returning 1 p.m. Night manta ray dives are $65-$99, also good for snorkelers. Children allowed if certified. Multi-dive discounts available. Open daily 7 a.m. to 6 p.m. *75-5614 Palani Road, Kailua-Kona, HI 96740; 800-KOA-DIVE; 808-329-8802; e-mail: divekona@ilhawaii.net; www.konacoastdivers.com.*

Kona Honu Divers Complete menu of one-, two- and even three-tank day and night dives, instruction, gear rentals, seasonal whale watching, kayaking and snorkel adventures. PADI and specialty certification courses offered in Nitrox, night and deep diving, underwater photography and videography and more. A "family-friendly" company, welcoming kids ten years and up who are confident in the water. Rates: $64.95-$164.95 for boat dives, $55 whale or dolphin cruise, $129.95-$474.95 instruction courses; $59.95 for snorkel cruise. *Honokohau Small Boat Harbor, Kailua-Kona; 808-324-4668; www.konahonudivers.com.*

★ **Live/Dive Pacific Inc.** This is part of the international Aggressor Fleet of high-quality dive boat operations with dives out of Truk, Palau, Tahiti, Costa Rica, the Galapagos Islands, Honduras, Belize, Cayman Islands, Turks and Caicos, Fiji and of course Kona. The Kona dive operation features one-week trips with unlimited diving. Up to 12 guests live aboard an 80-foot luxurious full-service diving yacht. There are private state rooms with bath and hot showers, gourmet galley meals, an onboard photo processing lab, hot tub and a sundeck. Dive up to five times a day, go for special certifications, work with pro photographers or go along for a fabulous ride. This is the ultimate in diving luxury. The *Kona Aggressor* is a Handicapped Scuba Association–approved barrier-free vessel. Occasional special dive programs are also coordinated with Jean-Michel Cousteau Expeditions, which are led by famed international diver Jean-Michel himself. The Kona cruise includes all meals and bar beverages. Custom dive charters are available at special rates. Cruises depart Kailua Pier each Saturday. Kona Rates range from $1,895-$2,195 per person for a week of cruising and diving. Reservations are suggested 30 days in advance. *74-5588 Pawai Place, Building F, Kailua-Kona, HI 96740; 800-344-5662; 808-329-8182; fax: 808-329-2628; e-mail: info@livedivepacific.com; www.pac-gressor.com.*

Manta Ray Dives of Hawai'i This operator features the 14-passenger glass-bottom dive boat *Rainbow Diver II* and offers multi-dive packages and PADI certifications. Night-time dives for manta rays are a specialty, "90% reliable on any given night." Rates: $69 snorkel, $85 dive, $35 ride-along on the boat. *800-982-6747; 808-325-1687; e-mail: rainbow@rainbowdiver.com; www.mantaraydiveshawaii.com.*

Mauna Kea Divers Conveniently located near Kohala Coast resorts at Kawaihae Harbor, near the Blue Dolphin restaurant, a family aquatic and activity center. Complete diving packages, underwater tours, charters and equipment rentals and other fun things are available. Also offers PADI scuba certification, seasonal whale watching, personalized private charters and full-service dive shop. Open Monday through Saturday, 9 a.m. to 5 p.m. *63-3616 Kawaihae Road, Kawaihae, HI 96743-9721; 808-882-1544.*

★ *Nautilus Dive Center Inc.* This shop features complete sales/service/rentals of professional diving equipment. They also provide PADI dive instruction and have a five-day certification program. Scuba charters along the East Hawai'i coast are available. Open Monday through Saturday 9 a.m. to 4 p.m. *382 Kamehameha Avenue, Hilo, HI 96720; 808-935-6939.*

★ *Ocean Eco Tours* Full menu of beach and boat dives, instruction and certification, equipment rentals and private charters. Rates: $85 shore dive, $95 boat dive, $125 intro dive. They also run a surf school; see listing later in this chapter. *Honokohau Small Boat Harbor; 808-324-7873; www.oceanecotours.com.*

Pacific Rim Divers This operator has daily charters for up to six divers, plus they offer manta ray dives, introductory dives and full PADI certifications. Basic 2-tank daytime boat dives are $98, night dives $110. departing Honokohau Harbor at 8 a.m., returning at 1 p.m. *P.O. Box 4602, Kailua-Kona, HI 96745; 808-334-1750; www.pacificrimdivers.com.*

★ *Red Sail Sports* A longstanding, reputable company offering a wide range of ocean activity (see "Sea Excursions-Sailing-Cruises"), Red Sails runs a Scuba School, including a Junior Divers program for kids in the 10- 11- and 12-14-year-old age brackets. Variety of organized dives from Refresher, $49 per person, to Advanced, $650 per person. They also offer value-added dive packages including all equipment, daily diving, a sunset sail, T-shirt and personalized service. Rates: $355 for a 3-day, $640 for a 6-day package plus $95 for additional days. *425 Waikoloa Beach Drive, Hilton Waikoloa Village, Kohala Coast, HI 96743; 877-RED-SAIL, 808-886-2876, fax: 808-886-4169; and Hapuna Beach Prince Hotel at Mauna Kea Resort, 808-880-1111, e-mail: redsailsport@yahoo.com, www.redsail.com.*

★ *Sandwich Isle Divers* One of Kona's most reputable family-run dive operations (and really nice people), this shop provides small charters, up to six passengers, with a fun, personable Big Island ocean experience. Captain Steve Myklebust has over 20 years of experience, 10,000 dives in Kona waters, a degree in marine biology and a great sense of humor. Daily scuba, snorkel and fishing cruises along the Kona Coast customized to your age group, interest and level of expertise for optimal pleasure in seeing lava tubes, coral reefs and tropical fish. Snorkel, scuba and boogieboard rentals, air fills, repairs and instruction, too. Open 8 a.m. to 8 p.m. daily. Basic 2-tank day dives are $90 ($105 with all gear included), departing Honokohau Harbor at 9 a.m., returning at 1:30 p.m.; 2-tank twilight dives $99/$115; 1-tank night dives $65/$75 per person. *75-5729 Ali'i Drive, Kona Marketplace, Kailua-Kona, HI 96740; 888-743-3483; 808-329-9188; fax: 808-326-5652; e-mail: sandive@aloha.net; www.sandwichisledivers.com.*

Sea Paradise Scuba This shop offers a full range of morning, afternoon and night dives as well as beginner dives and snorkeling outings on dive cruises, along with special charters, champagne sunset sails and a manta ray night snorkel. A complete line of equipment rentals is available. Rates: 2-tank morning dive $105, beginner "Try Scuba" two-dive non-certified experience, $140, DVP dive $149. Dive certifications $250-$400. Cruises depart from Keauhou Bay dock. *78-7128 Kaleiopapa Road, Kailua-Kona, HI 96740; 800-322-5662; 808-322-2500; www.seaparadise.com.*

SEA EXCURSIONS, SAILING, CRUISES (*See also* Scuba Diving; Snorkeling; Whale Watching)

The Big Island is big on boats. A playground for all kinds of water sports, it offers everything from deep-sea fishing charters to sunset cocktail and dinner sails, glass-bottom boat excursions, rubber raft adventures, scuba, snuba and snorkel cruises, Hawaiian sailing canoe voyages, and even a submarine dive. Most are concentrated in the Kailua-Kona area, or at the Kohala Coast resorts.

What's the difference between a pleasure cruise and a snorkel cruise? Not much! Thanks to the Big Island's fine fleet of activity craft, most boats can offer a visiting family as much, or as little, adventure and participation as they choose. Generally, basic recreational sightseeing or snorkel cruises sail along the Kona Coast, taking in historic sites such as Kealakekua Bay State Historical & Underwater Parks, the Captain Cook Monument, and Pu'uhonua o Honaunau National Historic Park at Honaunau. Half-day cruises with morning departures are customary,

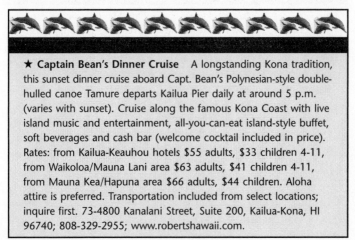

★ **Captain Bean's Dinner Cruise** A longstanding Kona tradition, this sunset dinner cruise aboard Capt. Bean's Polynesian-style double-hulled canoe Tamure departs Kailua Pier daily at around 5 p.m. (varies with sunset). Cruise along the famous Kona Coast with live island music and entertainment, all-you-can-eat island-style buffet, soft beverages and cash bar (welcome cocktail included in price). Rates: from Kailua-Keauhou hotels $55 adults, $33 children 4-11, from Waikoloa/Mauna Lani area $63 adults, $41 children 4-11, from Mauna Kea/Hapuna area $66 adults, $44 children. Aloha attire is preferred. Transportation included from select locations; inquire first. 73-4800 Kanalani Street, Suite 200, Kailua-Kona, HI 96740; 808-329-2955; www.robertshawaii.com.

and include snorkel equipment and towels along with refreshments—from light snacks to full lunch with open bar. Prices vary accordingly, and it's a good policy to ask what's included. Whale-watching adventures are seasonal from about December to March, when humpbacks visit the warm, protected Hawaiian waters to bear their young. Some whale species can be spotted year-round, along with schools of colorful tropical fish, sea turtles and dolphins. If your idea of an idyllic day on the ocean is relaxing on the sun deck while the kids snorkel and Uncle Harry hooks a sportfish, you can do that too. Many of the listings here are cross-referenced under more than one category, and if you don't see what you're looking for, we invite you to ask the reservationists, who we've found to be knowledgeable and friendly.

Big Island Water Sports   Offering something for ocean-lovers of all ages, Big Island Water Sports provides a full range of snorkel, kayak, scuba, seasonal whale watching and private charters. They're also the franchised operator for "Snuba Big Island," an easy-to-learn activity that allows you to dive up to 25 feet from the boat where your breathing apparatus is located. Kids must be 8 to snuba. Snorkel tours include equipment, instruction and underwater guide. Underwater cameras and digital video are available. Rates: $29-$70 snorkel, $90-$165 scuba, $60 (seasonal) whale watch, $95 kayaking, $120-$145 snuba ($79 from beach), $95-$120 "Snuba Doo" for kids 4 to 8 years old. Located on the beach at Honokohau Harbor. *P.O. Box 390430, Keahou, HI 96739; 808-324-1650; fax: 808-324-4719; e-mail: fun@bigislandwatersports.com; www.bigislandwatersports.com.*

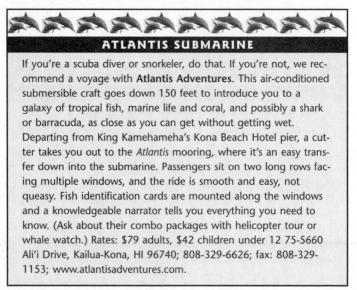

ATLANTIS SUBMARINE

If you're a scuba diver or snorkeler, do that. If you're not, we recommend a voyage with **Atlantis Adventures**. This air-conditioned submersible craft goes down 150 feet to introduce you to a galaxy of tropical fish, marine life and coral, and possibly a shark or barracuda, as close as you can get without getting wet. Departing from King Kamehameha's Kona Beach Hotel pier, a cutter takes you out to the *Atlantis* mooring, where it's an easy transfer down into the submarine. Passengers sit on two long rows facing multiple windows, and the ride is smooth and easy, not queasy. Fish identification cards are mounted along the windows and a knowledgeable narrator tells you everything you need to know. (Ask about their combo packages with helicopter tour or whale watch.) Rates: $79 adults, $42 children under 12 75-5660 Ali'i Drive, Kailua-Kona, HI 96740; 808-329-6626; fax: 808-329-1153; www.atlantisadventures.com.

★ **Captain Zodiac** Daily expeditions in motorized 24-foot rigid hull inflatable zodiac vessels along the Kona Coast. Explore sea caves and old Hawaiian village sites, and snorkel in Kealakekua Bay marine reserve on a four-hour cruise. Snorkel equipment and tropical snacks included. Two cruises daily at 8 a.m. and 1 p.m. Rates: $82 adults, $67 children under 12. They also offer seasonal whale watch excursions for $62/$54. *74-425 Kealakehe Parkway, Honokohau Harbor, Kailua-Kona, HI 96740; 800-422-7824; 808-329-3199; fax: 329-7590; e-mail: seakona@interpac.net; www.captainzodiac.com.*

Dolphin Discoveries This operator does small-group (6-12 people) whale and dolphin watching tours plus snorkeling excursions with a 28-foot rigid hull inflatable; snorkel gear is provided. Tours by dedicated marine mammal naturalists focus on respect for and education about whales and dolphins and Hawaii's underwater world. Explorations of Kona Coast lava tubes, sea caves and beautiful coral reefs along Kealakekua Bay and Honaunau Bay are unforgettable. Morning cruise 8 a.m. to 12:15 p.m. includes refreshments; afternoon cruise 12:15 p.m. to 3:30 p.m. Departures from Keauhou Bay, just south of Kailua-Kona. Rates: $83 adults, $62 children under 12. *77-116 Queen Kalama, Kailua-Kona, HI 96740; 808-322-8000; e-mail: dolphindiscoveries@aloha.net; www.dolphindiscoveries.com.*

Dolphin Journeys Captain Nancy Sweatt guides half-day or full-day excursions to encounter dolphins and ocean scenery along the Kona coast. Rates: $165 half-day, $280 full-day adventures. Her unique approach to the experience also includes "Family Camp," a multi-day experience for all ages including lodging, some meals, "talk story" time, games, dolphin swims, beach parties, island activities and more. Captain Nancy can customize Camp for family reunions, single parents, "kids over 35" or people with disabilities. Just ask. *75-5822 Pelekila Place, Kailua-Kona, HI 96740; 808-329-3030; e-mail: new@aloha.net; www.dolphinjourneys.com.*

Dream Cruises A "barefoot fun cruise," sailing along the Kona coastline for swimming, snorkeling or relaxing on the sundeck while the kids enjoy a water trampoline, kick boards, "water noodles" and other toys. Continental breakfast, deli lunch and soft drinks are included with no-host bar on board. Daily sails 9 a.m. to 1 p.m. Rates: $83.95 adults, $45.95 children 4 to 12. Dream Cruises also offers the Island Grill dinner cruise nightly 5:30 p.m. to 7:30 p.m. with a fresh gourmet menu, welcome mai tai, live entertainment and no-host bar aboard the trimaran *Kona Dream*. Rates: $54.95 adults, $34.95 children 4 to 12. *808-326-6000; 800-400-7300; fax: 808-592-5214; e-mail: aloha@dream-cruise.com; www.dream-cruises.com.*

Hawai'i Sailing Company Inc. This operator offers a variety of sailings and cruises including half-day and weekly cruises, picnic sails, whale watching and snorkeling. Departures from Honokohau Harbor. *44-2050 Ka'apahu Road, Pa'auilo, HI 96776; 808-776-1505.*

Honu Sail Charters Half-day, full-day and sunset sails out of Honokohau Small Boat Harbor. *808-896-HONU.*

In to Spirit, Inc. Two-hour marine mammal ocean adventures departing daily from Honokohau Harbor just north of Kailua-Kona. The vessel *Lilikoi* accommodates up to 16 "fun-filled" passengers on a search for seasonal humpback whales, Hawaiian spinner, spotted and bottlenose dolphins, pilot whales, sea turtles and their neighbors. Certified marine mammal naturalist provides narration; light snacks/beverages provided. Rates: 8 a.m. to 12 p.m. adults $75, children $50; Afternoon whale watching 1 p.m. to 3:30 p.m. (seasonal) adults $55, children $30. *808-936-1470; www.dolphinshawaii.com.*

★ **Kailua Bay Charter Co.** *Marian*, a 36-foot glass-bottom tour boat, accommodates 32 passengers on hour-long cruises around Kailua Bay to observe the underwater coral reefs and marine life. Expert guided narration highlights what you see. Daily cruises at 10 a.m., 11 a.m. and 1 p.m., or by demand, and depart from Kailua Pier. Rates: adults $25, children 7 to 12 $10, kids 4 and under free. *P.O. Box 112, Holualoa, HI 96725; 808-324-1749; fax: 808-324-0413; e-mail: info@konaglassbottomboat.com; www.glassbottomboat.com.*

Kale Kai 3.5-hour half-day and 6-hour full-day sailing charters plus 2-3-hour champagne sunset sails aboard a 42-foot Morgan racing sloop. Six-person maximum. *Honokohau Small Boat Harbor, slip J48, P.O. Box 1084, Kailua-Kona, HI 96745; 808-960-3367.*

Maile Charters One of the most familiar boats in Kawaihae Harbor, this long-standing operator with 20 years of sailing experience offers a variety of special adventure cruises aboard the 50-foot Gulfstar sloop *Maile*, including overnight and interisland outings, whale watching, snorkeling and scuba diving explorations along the Kohala Coast, ecology tours, fishing, sunset sails and private custom cruises from half a day to five days including food and soft drinks. With advance notice, *Maile's* experienced crew is happy

BOAT RENTALS

Captain Cruise Boat Rental rents "mini yachts," pontoon boats fully outfitted with ice chest, propane barbecue, CD player, cellphone, maps, fishing and snorkel gear for up to six people. No license or experience necessary to enjoy the feel of your own boat in Kona's friendly waters. Rates $49 per hour, $180 half day, $350 full day. In Kailua-Kona; 808-329-4977; www.captain-cruise.net. With **Kona Boat Rentals** you take your own boat out to sightsee, fish or snorkel without a license or a crowd. Fishing and snorkel gear, maps and more. Rates: $285 4-hour rental, $385 for a 7-hour rental. 808-326-9155; 800-311-9189.

to cater to your individual dining and alcoholic beverage requests
(additional costs may apply). Rates: $590 half-day for 6 passengers,
$990 full day for 6 (additional charge for additional passengers).
Longer charters have a 4-person maximum. Rates: $1,500 for 24-hour
charter, $2,500 2-day, $3,400 3-day, $4,200 4-day and $5,000 for a 5-
day charter. *P.O. Box 44335, Kamuela, HI 96743; 800-726-SAIL; 808-326-
5174; fax: 808-882-7689; e-mail: sailing@adventuresailing.com; www.
adventuresailing.com.*

★ **Ocean Sports-Waikoloa**   One of the Big Island's best, Ocean
Sports specializes in making the most of anybody's ocean experience
with champagne sunset sails, guaranteed (seasonal) whale watching
with marine naturalist, scuba lessons, one- and two-tank dives,
snorkel/picnic sails, exclusive deep-sea fishing charters, and awesome fully narrated glass-bottom boat cruises over coral gardens
(departures at 9, 9:45 and 10:30 a.m.). On the beach, rent wind-
surfers, kayaks, boogieboards, hydro-bikes and other fun stuff.
Instruction available. Don't miss their Hawaiian Humpback Whale
Center located at the Waikoloa Beach Marriott, open 8 a.m. to 5 p.m.
daily, admission free. Picnic/Snorkel Sail $84 adults, $48 children
under 12; Kayak Adventure $85 adults, $42 children; (seasonal)
whale watching $64 adults, $44 children; Glass-bottom Boat $19
adults, $9 children; Champagne Sunset Sail $69 adults, $39 chil-
dren; Scuba $119-$129. Private charters welcomed. *Located on
'Anaeho'omalu Beach in front of the Waikoloa Beach Marriott, 69-275
Waikoloa Beach Drive, Kohala Coast, HI 96743; 808-886-6666; 800-
SAIL234; www.hawaiioceansports.com.*

★ **Red Sail Sports**   Everything from luxury catamaran cruises
aboard the 50-foot *Noa Noa* to deluxe snorkel and scuba sails aboard
the 38-foot Delta dive boat *Lani Kai.* Sunset cocktail sails, seasonal
whale watching and a complete line of water sports equipment and
toy rentals plus Zodiac raft/snorkel adventure, Paniolo Cycle adventure, kayak excursion and bike rentals. Transportation provided
from nearby hotels. Families should ask about their "SASY" (sup-
plied air snorkeling for youth) tours for kids 6 and up, "Bubble-
maker" program for kids 8 through 11 and "all-inclusive family
watersports packages" for unlimited use of beach toys. Snorkel
Cruise $68 adults, $34 children 3-11; Sunset Sail $53-$59 adults,
$26.50-$29.50 children 3-11; Dinner Sail $68 adults, $39 children 3-
11; Whale Watch $59 adults, $29.50 children 3-11. (See their listing
under "Scuba Diving.") *425 Waikoloa Beach Drive, Hilton Waikoloa
Village, Kohala Coast, HI 96743; 877-RED-SAIL, 808-886-2876; fax: 808-
886-4169; and Hapuna Beach Prince Hotel at Mauna Kea Resort, 808-880-
1111; e-mail: redsailsport@yahoo.com, www.redsail.com.*

SKIING

Believe it or not, lucky Big Island visitors can surf in the morning and snow ski in the afternoon if the conditions are right on the slopes of Mauna Kea. Strictly a seasonal activity, and totally dependent on the whims of snow goddess Poliahu (although she's been generous the last several years), the nearly 14,000-foot summit of Mauna Kea can be covered with snow for limited periods between November and March (sometimes as late as May). When conditions are just right, skiers can enjoy some incredible downhill runs on the treeless slopes. The experience is one of a kind, but not without its negatives. The run is rocky and deceptive; weather conditions on the mountain change suddenly and there are no ski lifts, lodge, restrooms, medical help, emergency phone or any facilities whatsoever on the summit. A 4WD vehicle is almost always required. (Please be aware of the dangers of high-altitude activity and use caution if you have respiratory or cardiac issues. Very young children and pregnant women should probably find other amusements.)

One ski tour operator specializes in Mauna Kea ski tours. **Ski Guides Hawai'i** offers complete package tours to Mauna Kea on snow days, including 4WD transportation, skiing equipment and lunch. Snowboard rentals available too. *P.O. Box 1954, Kamuela, HI 96743; 808-885-4188; www.skihawaii.com.*

SNORKELING

Body Glove Cruises This 55-foot trimaran offers daily morning and afternoon Snorkel-Dolphin Sails along the Kona Coast to Pawai Bay. Departures from Kailua Pier at 9 a.m. and 2 p.m. Continental breakfast, deli lunch and premium bar included in the morning sail (4.5 hours); snacks and premium bar in the afternoon (3 hours). Snorkel adventures include exploration of caves and sea arches to meet Hawai'i's rich marine life, dolphins, manta rays and turtles. Snorkel gear and instruction, flotation and water toys (including a 15-foot water slide) included. Upgrade to Scuba Diving available morning and afternoon. Transportation available from nearby hotels ($20 adults, $16 children from Kohala Coast resorts). Rates: morning $94 adults, $54 children 6 to 12; afternoon $59 adults, $39 children 6 to 12; seasonal whale watching $59 adults, $39 children 6 to 12. Children 5 and under free. Upgrade to Scuba, $43-$63 per person. *P.O. Box 4523, Kailua-Kona, HI 96745; 800-551-8911; 808-326-7122; fax: 808-326-7123; e-mail: bcruises@gte.net; www.bodyglovehawaii.com.*

★ ***Kamanu*** This is a beautiful 36-foot catamaran offering two daily snorkeling cruises along the Kona Coast. Each 3.5-hour cruise includes ninety minutes of snorkeling time plus all gear, instruction,

WATERSPORTS RENTALS

Miller Surf & Sport rents all types of watersports and beach equipment including masks, snorkels, fins, flotation vests, beach chairs, boogieboards, viewing boards, picnic coolers, umbrellas and surfboards by the day or the week. Open daily 8 a.m.-5 p.m. 76-6246 Ali'i Drive #102, three miles south of Kailua-Kona at the Kona Bali Kai Condo; 808-326-1771; fax: 808-326-1772. In Kahalu'u, **Kahalu'u Beach Snorkel Rental Depot** offers all kinds of snorkeling and beach equipment at reasonable prices; 808-937-7460. Just about anything you'd ever want to get wet is available from local legend **Snorkel Bob**, who's been in the business (and the water) almost forever. Check out his "Budget Crunch Special," $9/week for mask, fins, snorkel, net bag, fish ID card, No-Fog Goop and "the Legend of Snorkel Bob." A good source too for wetsuits, flotation vests and "Looky Boogie" boards with viewing windows. He offers a free inter-island return policy and also books boat trips, bike and helicopter tours and more. His clever website is informative and fun to read, with a nice on-line store featuring his books and videos. 75-5831 Kahakai Road, Kailua-Kona, HI 96740; 808-329-0770; www.snorkelbobs.com.

drinks and a light tropical lunch. Good for beginning snorkelers, novices or experts to enjoy the colorful fish at Pawai Bay. Cruises depart daily from Honokohau Harbor at 9 a.m. and 1:30 p.m. Rates: $75 adults, $45 children under 12. *P.O. Box 2021, 74-425 Kealakehe Parkway #16, Kailua-Kona, HI 96745; 800-348-3091; 808-329-2021; fax: 808-329-7590; e-mail: info@kamanu.com; www.kamanu.com.*

★ *Sea Quest Rafting Adventure* This operator offers snorkeling cruises with inflatable boats taking in the remote areas from Keauhou Bay to Honaunau. The cruises take in sea caves, lava tubes, Captain Cook's Monument at Kealakekua Bay and the Pu'uhonua o Honaunau National Historic Park at Honaunau, with diving time allowed. Cruises include morning (8 a.m. to noon.) or afternoon (1 to 4 p.m.) adventures; rates include snacks, beverages and snorkel gear. Rates: morning, $83.34 adults, $75 kids 12 and under; afternoon, $62.50 adults, $56.25 kids 12 and under. *P.O. Box 390292, Kailua-Kona, HI 96739; 888-SEA-CAVE; 808-329-7238; www.seaquesthawaii.com.*

SNUBA (*See also* Scuba Diving; Sea Excursions; Snorkeling)

Snuba provides a way for the novice to experience the sensation of diving without restrictive equipment or lengthy instruction. Air supply is contained on a flotation device, with a 25-foot air hose and regulator. Easy to learn and fun to play with, snuba is an interesting option for underwater adventure, offered by local ocean activity companies for divers 8 years old and up.

Snuba Big Island A location on the beach at Honokohau Harbor. Snuba Beach Dives daily at 9 a.m., 11 a.m., 1 p.m. and 3 p.m.; Boat Snuba Dives 9 a.m. to 1:30 p.m. Beach Dives $79; Boat Dives $120-$125, "Snuba Doo" for kids 4-8 years old $95-$120. *P.O. Box 9020, Kailua-Kona, HI 96745; 808-326-7446, fax: 808-324-4719; www.snubabigisland.com.*

SPAS AND HEALTH RETREATS

For a soulful experience of a physical nature, consider a relaxing day of soothing massage and body therapies in tranquil, mindful environments. The Big Island is home to some truly excellent spas, most concentrated in the Kohala Coast resorts. Spa therapies include some Hawaiian options like traditional *lomi lomi* massage, heated stone relaxation, tropical aromatherapy, or exotic body wraps and scrubs using Hawaiian herbs, aloe, ti leaf, sea salt or seaweed, even poi and Kona coffee. The facilities are generally excellent and some offer beautiful, private outdoor massage locations near the ocean or a wooded waterfall. Policies change, and although the spas are designed for resort guests, they are usually open to the public for a nominal day charge.

Whether you're staying in one of these luxury properties or not, we invite you to experience a "day of beauty" as a very special indulgence during your stay. As always, please call in advance and avoid disappointment.

Kohala Sports Club & Spa This 25,000-square-foot facility has everything from whirlpools, free weights, Life Cycles, treadmills, bikes and a "treadwall" rock climbing machine, saunas and steam baths to classes in aerobics, yoga, tai chi and more. There's a full-service beauty salon and a delightful variety of massage therapies and body treatments including a Cosmopro Hydrotherapy Tub for underwater massage. Nice online store for their bath, skin care and aromatherapy products. Alternative therapies include astrology and I Ching consultations, behavioral health programs, naturopathic medicine, nutritional education, physical enhancement programs and a healthy breakfast and lunch menu at the Kohala Spa Café. *Hilton Waikoloa Village, Kohala Coast; 808-886-2828; www.kohalaspa.com.*

Spa Without Walls The Spa Without Walls, one of the best healing facilities on the island, has undergone an extensive renovation and enhancement to its Hawaiian-inspired spa facilities. They now offer ten individual massage *hale* (houses) in tropical outdoor settings, six indoor treatment rooms, steam room and dry sauna. Many treatments incorporate Hawai'i's therapeutic natural environment and ancient healing arts, such as *lomi lomi* massage, aloe vera wraps, Big Island coffee and vanilla exfoliation and other wonderful things. Spa Without Walls also employs unique practices such as ayurvedic facial treatments and the "BodyTalk System" of self-healing and synchronization, along with more familiar options such as yoga and meditation sessions, and soothing aromatherapies with local products. *Fairmont Orchid, Kohala Coast; 808-887-7540; www.fairmont.com/orchid.*

Mauna Lani Spa Mauna Lani Spa offers spa treatments in a quaint indoor/outdoor setting designed to resemble a Hawaiian village, with nine individual thatched *hale* (huts), two of which accommodate couples for tandem treatments. Features include a lava-sauna, Vichy shower, healing herb and fragrance garden, a selection of massage styles, body therapies, yoga, meditation, consultations and more. The 25,000-square-foot indoor facility offers nine treatment rooms including four wet rooms, fitness center, aerobics classroom and excellent retail shop (or shop online at www.maunalanistore.com). Admission to the spa is $25, or complimentary with a scheduled spa treatment. *Mauna Lani Resort, Kohala Coast; 808-881-7922; www.maunalani.com.*

Ho'ola Spa Located at the newly reopened Sheraton Keauhou Bay Resort & Spa, Ho'ola ("to heal") is designed to work with the local environment to promote physical wellness. Still "evolving" as of this writing, the spa offers a range of therapeutic massage techniques (including a Hapai Massage for pregnant women), wraps, facials and hair, skin and nail salon services. Spa Packages provide value-added treatment combinations to maximize your spa experience. One in particular, the "Tranquility Package" is designed to soothe away stress for a soon-to-be Bride or Groom. More to come. *Sheraton Keauhou Bay Resort & Spa, 78-128 Ehukai Street, Kailua-Kona, HI 96740; 808-930-4900; www.sheratonkeauhou.com.*

Hualalai Sports Club & Spa Exclusively for use of its guests and residents, the Four Seasons' facility is one of the best on the island. If you're lucky enough to visit, you'll enjoy state-of-the-art exercise equipment, expert fitness classes from yoga to kickboxing, an eight-court tennis club (four lighted), open-air gym with new Resistance and Strength Studio, 25-meter lap pool, basketball and volleyball courts, saunas and steam rooms, and nine individual *hale* for an eclectic range of massage therapies and body treatments. Ask about island-style practices such as a Hawaiian sandalwood or hibiscus wrap, macadamia nut oil and *lehua* honey scrub or spirulina body mask. The Kalona Salon's long, enticing menu of skin, hair and nail treatments surely has something for every beauty or beast. *Four Seasons Resort Hualalai, Kaupulehu-Kona; 808-325-8440.*

If a luxury day spa is not in your budget, don't worry—there are numerous licensed massage therapists in almost every neighborhood. We refer you to your hotel or condo concierge desk or the Yellow Pages. Please note that "adult" massage service is not at all common here, so you can call advertised massage services with confidence.

You might also contact the following:

Big Island Academy of Massage   *201 Kino'ole Street, Hilo; 808-935-1405.*

Hawaiian Islands School of Body Therapy   *81-6587 Mamalahoa Highway, Captain Cook; 808-323-3800; e-mail: massages@gte.net; www. hawaiianmassageschool.com.*

On a slightly different level, the Big Island has earned a new nickname in recent years: the "Healing Island." This is not only due to the increasing variety of alternative healing therapies available, but to some very sound, state-of-the-art Western medicine as well. Because of the diverse ethnic population, as well as the mid-Pacific geographic location, the Big Island can bring together Eastern and Western practices in a nearly perfect climate for healing work of many different kinds. The **North Hawai'i Community Hospital** in Waimea incorporates not only Eastern practices such as acupuncture and massage into its everyday operation, but alternative therapies like "healing touch" energy work and specially designed architecture, natural lighting and custom-written house music. *808-885-4444; www.northhawaiicommunityhospital.org.*

In line with that, groups such as **Five Mountain Medical** work to promote the island as a special healing destination, encouraging health professionals not only to visit but to meet, work and research here in the unique environment. Many doctors have already begun projects that bridge the gap between high-tech machines and low-tech cultural healing practices. *808-887-1280; www.fivemtn.org (click link to Ke Kukui, www.kekui.net, for extensive information on all categories of common and uncommon health resources).*

SURFING, WINDSURFING, KITE SURFING

The Big Island is not world-famous for surfing like the North Shore of Oahu, or for aerial windsurfing like Ho'okipa Point on Maui. Easygoing tradewinds and gentler ocean conditions prevail most of the year, although in winter months the western shores might see the 10- to 15-foot sets surfers wait for all year long. On all Big Island beaches, generally speaking, conditions are favorable year-round for boogie-

boarding, body surfing, sailing and wind-
surfing-depending on the mood of
Mother Nature. The Kona and Kohala
areas have more availability of facilities and
rentals for these activities, as well as more
consistent sunshine, but keep an eye on the
weather and don't rule out the Hilo side and its
share of great beaches, too.

Hawai'i Life Guard Surf Instructors This operator features
trained and certified professional life guards who provide safe surfing instruction for beginner or advanced. Family groups are encouraged to come out and try the waves. Kids under six are permitted if
they show they can handle the board. Lessons are usually held in the
Kona area. Rates: $69.99 for 1-hour, $114 for 2-hour, $165 for 2-
hour tandem or private surf lessons. *P.O. Box 390664, Keauhou, HI
96739; 808-324-0442; cell 808-936-SURF; e-mail: surflessons@yahoo.com;
www.surflessonshawaii.com.*

Ocean Eco Tours "Kona's #1 surf school" says they have surfa-
ble surf about 300 days every year, and love to share it with visitors
of all ages and skill levels. Rates: $95 private, $150 group surf lessons, $250 multi-day. Equipment rentals available too. *Honokohau
Small Boat Harbor; 808-324-7873; www.oceanecotours.com.*

Ocean Safari's Kayaks This operator has group or private surfing lessons and board rentals. Surf lessons: $65 group, $85 private.
Board rental $25. Ask about their 7 a.m. "early riser" class. *P.O. Box
515, Kailua-Kona, HI 96745; 808-326-4699; fax: 808-322-3653; e-mail:
kayakhi@gte.net; www.oceansafariskayaks.com.*

Ocean Sports A large general-service provider, Ocean Sports
has the exclusive windsurf concession on the Kohala Coast (along
with a lot of other fun things). Windsurfing equipment rentals and
instruction available year-round, conditions permitting. *P.O. Box
383699, 69-275 Waikoloa Beach Drive, Waikoloa, HI 96738; 888-SAIL-
234; 808-886-6666; fax: 808-886-9407; e-mail: information@hawaiiocean
sports.com; www.hawaiioceansports.com.*

SWIMMING POOLS

The County of Hawai'i maintains seven free public swimming pools
around the island. These facilities are generally excellent and include
full programs of swimming and aquatics instruction, adult lap swimming, and open recreational swimming hours daily and weekly. For
specific daily and weekly schedules of activities contact the individual pools listed.

Kona District   Kona Community Aquatic Center, Old Kona Airport Park complex, 808-327-3500; and Kona Swimming Pool, Konawaena High School, Kealakekua, 808-323-3252

Kohala Coast   Kohala Swimming Pool, Kamehameha Park in Kapaʻau; 808-889-6933

Hamakua Coast   Honokaʻa Swimming Pool, Honokaʻa High School, 808-775-0650; and Laupahoehoe Swimming Pool, Laupahoehoe High School, 808-962-6993

Hilo   (Instruction only.) Kawamoto Swim Stadium, at Hoʻolulu Stadium Complex, 808-961-8698; and NAS Swimming Pool, which stands for Naval Air Station, is a remnant of Hilo's World War II military airfield, at the old Hilo Airport Terminal, 808-961-8697

Puna District   Puna Pahoa Swimming Pool, Pahoa; 808-965-2700

Kaʻu District   Pahala Swimming Pool, Kaʻu High School, Pahala; 808-928-8177

TENNIS

Public Courts

The County of Hawaiʻi maintains a number of tennis courts at county parks and locations around the island. Some are lighted for evening use and are basically on a first-come, first-served basis.

For a map detailing public tennis court locations around the island contact the Department of Parks and Recreation, County of Hawaiʻi, 25 Aupuni Street, Hilo, HI 96720; 808-961-8311.

The following is a listing of the public tennis court facilities around the island.

Kona District   Greenwell Park in Captain Cook; **Higashihara Park** in Keauhou; **Kailua Park** at Old Kona Airport; **Kailua Playground** on Kuakini Highway near town.

Kohala Coast   Kamehameha Park in Kapaʻau town; **Waimea Park** in Waimea-Kamuela town.

Hamakua Coast   Honokaʻa Park in Honokaʻa town; **Papaʻaloa Park** in Papaʻaloa Village.

Hilo   Edith Kanakaole Tennis Stadium has 3 indoor lighted courts and 5 outdoor courts. Reservations suggested. Rates: $2 per hour for indoor courts 9 a.m. to 4 p.m., $4 per hour 4 p.m. to 10 p.m. Corner of Piʻilani and Kalanikoa streets; 808-961-8720. There are also **Ainaola Park, Hakalau Park, Lincoln Park, Lokahi Park, Malama Park, Mohouli Park** and **Panaewa Park** (most of these are right in the Hilo town area).

Puna District   Kurtistown Park on the highway in Kurtistown; **Shipman Park** at junction of Volcano and Pahoa highways in Keaʻau.

Ka'u District   Na'alehu Park on the highway through Na'alehu town; Pahala School Grounds at the school in Pahala Village.

Private Tennis Courts Open to the Public

While tennis is currently not enjoying the same boom as golf, this is good news for the recreational player who wants to take advantage of Hawai'i's great weather to play a few sets. Court times are generally easy to book and relatively inexpensive. The following are mostly hotel/resort private courts that are open to the public on a user-fee basis. Many offer a game-matching service, locker rooms and rentals, but may have a dress code, so please ask first.

Fairmont Orchid Hawai'i   The Tennis Pavilion has ten hard-surface courts, seven lighted for night play, a stadium court, and full-service pro shop. Daily clinics, instruction, ball machine rental. Rates: $15 per day for guests, $18 off-property players, unlimited play. *1 North Kaniku Drive, Kohala Coast; 808-885-2000.*

Hilton Waikoloa Village   Kohala Tennis Shop features eight plexi-cushion courts and a tournament stadium. Full-service pro shop, equipment rentals and sales, ball machine and instruction available. Rates: $25 per person for ninety minutes of court time. *425 Waikoloa Beach Drive, Kohala Coast; 808-886-1234.*

Seaside Tennis Club at Mauna Kea   One of the largest tennis facilities in the state, with 11 plexi-pave tennis courts stretched along breathtaking oceanfront property. Quality pro shop arranges court times, matching, lessons and clinics, ball machine, video lessons, racquet stringing and rentals. Great line of tennis attire, accessories and gear. Air-conditioned locker rooms, shaded refreshment lanai. Rates: $12.50 per person per day, unlimited play. *Mauna Kea Resort, 62-100 Mauna Kea Beach Drive, Kohala Coast; 808-882-5420.*

Mauna Lani Bay Hotel & Bungalows   Mauna Lani offers two separate tennis facilities: the Tennis Garden with ten hard-surface courts, and the Racquet Club with six hard-surface courts (three lighted for night play) and a stadium court. Full-service pro shop, instruction, rental equipment and sales on-site. Rates: $12.50 per person per day. *68-1400 Mauna Lani Drive, Kohala Coast; 808-885-6622.*

Royal Kona Resort   The Tennis Club has four hard-surface courts, three lighted for night play; pro shop available. Rates: $10 for one person all day, $15 for two people all day. *75-5852 Ali'i Drive, Kailua-Kona; 808-329-3111.*

Waikoloa Beach Marriott, An Outrigger Resort   The Tennis Club has six hard-surface courts, full-service pro shop, private and group instruction available, equipment rentals and sales. Rates: $10 per hour. *69-275 Waikoloa Beach Drive, Kohala Coast; 808-886-6789.*

Movie Theaters

There are a number of movie theaters around the island that show first-run movies on a regular daily schedule. Theaters in Hilo and Kailua-Kona are modern, stadium-style facilities with multiple screens and snack bars. More out-of-the way theaters have personalities of their own, with movies on weekends and live music, dance and theater performances at other times. Aloha Theatre in Kainaliu is connected to an outstanding restaurant; Peoples Theater in Honoka'a brings jazz and classical music greats to its annual Hamakua Music Festival, and Kahilu Theatre mounts a full season of eclectic productions from Hawaii's best hula and music concerts to unique global performers. Check local newspapers.

Aloha Theatre Not just for movies, this restored classic offers live performances on occasion and the added benefit of a great restaurant, the Aloha Angel Café. 79-7384 Mamalahoa Highway, Kainaliu town; 808-322-2323; www.alohatheatre.com

Honoka'a Peoples Theater Honoka'a Town, Hamakua Coast; 808-775-0000

Hualalai Cinemas Kuakini Highway and Hualalai Road, Kailua-Kona; 808-329-5900.

Kahilu Theatre Parker Ranch Center, Waimea town; 808-887-6368; www.kahilutheatre.org

Kress Cinemas 174 Kamehameha Avenue, downtown Hilo; 808-961-3456

Makalapua Stadium Cinemas Makalapua Shopping Center, Kailua-Kona; 808-327-0444

Na'alehu Theatre Na'alehu, South Kona; 808-929-9133

Prince Kuhio Stadium Cinemas Prince Kuhio Shopping Plaza, Hilo; 808-959-4595

Regal Keauhou Stadium 7 Cinemas Keauhou Shopping Center, Keauhou, Kona; 808-324-7200

Stage Productions/Performances

For information on stage productions, hula performances, band, choral and orchestra concerts and other shows, contact any of the following community theaters for details. A community production, especially as part of one of the cultural festivals, can make a great memory for your Big Island vacation. Please call for schedule and ticket information.

Hilo Community Players 141 Kalakaua, Hilo; 808-935-9155

Kahilu Theatre The Big Island's best facility for live performances, Kahilu was established by the late Richard Smart of the Parker Ranch *ohana* (family) to bring elements of culture to the Waimea community, and create an avenue for his own off-Broadway talents. A full season of varied international concerts and dance performances is presented, along with youth theater workshops, "circus camp," first-run movies and annual appearances by Hawai'i's celebrated Cazimero Brothers and the Honolulu Symphony. *Parker Ranch Center, P.O. Box 549, Kamuela, HI 96743; 808-885-6868; www.kahilutheatre.org.*

Aloha Performing Arts Company Kainaliu town; 808-322-9924.

University of Hawai'i-Hilo Theater 200 West Kawili Street, Hilo, HI 96720; 808-974-7310.

Waimea Community Chorus and Theater Uilani Plaza in Waimea town; 808-885-5818; www.waimeacommunitytheatre.org.

WALKING TOURS

★ *Downtown Hilo Walking Tours* Free guided walking tours are conducted the third Saturday of each month and are 1-2 hours long. Tours begin at the museum and include sites like Kalakaua Park (originally conceived as a civic center by King Kalakaua), Niolopa, the old and new library buildings, the old federal building, Lyman Museum and others. As an alternative, call the museum or stop by and pick up a free map to do the walking tour on your own. Sponsored by Lyman Museum and the American Association of University Women. *For reservations contact Lyman Museum, 276 Haili Street, Hilo, HI 96720; 808-935-5021.*

★ *Kona Historical Tours* The Kona Historical Society Museum conducts two guided walking tours in the Kona area. There is a walking tour of historic Kailua Village and a walking tour of the Uchida Coffee Farm. Both provide insight into the colorful history and culture of early-day Kona and the coffee farming community. The 1.5-hour Kailua Village tour is Tuesday through Saturday mornings at 9:30 a.m. and per person cost is $10. A special Friday afternoon tour at 1:30 p.m. is $14 per person and includes a visit to the Hulihee Palace. The 1.5-hour Uchida Coffee Farm tour is Tuesday and Thursday only at 8:30 a.m. and 10:30 a.m. and is $20 per person. Tours depart from the Kona Historical Society Museum on Highway 11 near Kealakekua. The Society also conducts special tours by appointment for groups, including a Captain Cook at Kealakekua Bay and Keauhou Archaeological Tour. Call for details and reservations. *P.O. Box 398, 81-6551 Mamalahoa Highway, Captain Cook, HI 96704; 808-323-3222; www.konahistorical.org.*

WHALE WATCHING (*See also* Sea Excursions; Snorkeling)

If you visit between November and May, you have to go whale watching. Although you can see whales from the shore as they breach and splash in the water, there is nothing like being out at sea with them. Just so you know, hundreds of humpback whales travel to Hawai'i's warm waters annually from Alaska to give birth to their young, mate and return. Poor mamas. They swim all that way with nothing to eat, give birth, feed the young hundreds of gallons of milk a day, *then* as Mother Nature's little joke, they go into heat and have to struggle with competitive males while trying to care for their babies. There's a whole lot of whale activity going on, and it's incredible to watch.

From the boat, you spot a distant spout, a plume of sea spray that is the whale's breath, and as you get closer you see different-sized spouts for mothers and babies. You may see males competing for female attention by slapping the water with their fins or tails, bobbing their massive heads out of the water, or leaping completely airborne with a gigantic crashing splash. Most boats have knowledgeable guides on board to explain what you're watching and answer questions. Some have an underwater microphone they lower to eavesdrop on the whales' unusual song. Most offer refreshments and a photo service.

The humpback is a protected species and boats of any kind are prohibited from moving towards a whale any closer than 100 feet. There are no "swim with the whales" programs or any closer encounters, and anyone who sells you one is breaking the law. Reputable whale watching operations are respectful of the ocean and these major mammals and take care to pass that on to their passengers.

Once again, we warn you about photos (and the crew will back us up). The chance of your getting the supreme shot of a whale flying over the ocean is remote. The chance of your getting a roll full of splashes after the fact is very good. We'd encourage you to buy a postcard, leave the camera, and enjoy the view.

Kona Outdoor Circle Whale Watch/John Keawe Floating Concert Cruises A limited edition that keeps coming back by popular demand. A volunteer nature and beautification society, Kona Outdoor Circle sponsors an annual schedule of special cruises during the winter months for *kama`aina* (residents) to enjoy. Award-winning slack key guitarist John Keawe entertains while whale-watchers cruise onboard Captain Bean's giant double-hulled canoe *Tamure*. The cruise and concert includes *pupus* and soft drinks, no-host bar, music and informative whale talk-story with Hawaii Marine Mammal Consortium. Select afternoons, 1:30 to 3 p.m. departing from Kailua Pier. $50 adults, *keiki* 6 and under free. Contact the Kona Outdoor Circle for dates. *808-329-7286; e-mail: ionaoutdoorcircle@ konacoast.com; www.konaoutdoorcircle.org/whalewatchinfo.htm.*

Dolphin Quest provides a chance to encounter bottlenose dolphins on a supervised swim with them in a saltwater pool during a dolphin-training session, a twilight camp or a family program. Much has been written about the physical and mental benefits of the experience, and it is one of the most popular, unique and exciting adventures on the island. Dolphin Quest gives priority to resort guests, but they do permit outside reservations up to two months in advance. Rates: A variety of customized programs include a 4-hour Animal Training Adventure for ages 13 and up, $320; 1.5-hour Dolphin Discovery for kids 5-12, $130; 30-minute Adult Dolphin Encounter for ages 13 and up, $160; 1-hour Dolphin Adventure Encounter for ages 13 and up, $180; and 4-hour Dolphin Twilight Camp for kids 5-12, $105 for the first child, $85 each additional child. There's also a fun group experience, Dolphin Family and Friends Encounter, for anyone 5 years or older, priced at $740 for a group of five people. 808-886-2875; fax: 808-886-7030; e-mail: dqhawaii@dolphinquest.org; www.dolphinquest.org.

★ *Living Ocean Adventures*   In the whale business since 1977, Captain Tom Bottrell runs a real classic 31-foot Bertram fishing boat equipped to handle just six whale watchers. With BS degrees in meteorology and oceanography and a master's in ecology, Captain Tom has a wealth of information to share on his 3.5-hour cruises. Sight humpbacks, sperm, false killer, melon-headed and pilot whales plus four species of dolphins that frequent the Kona Coast, while you troll for game fish for dinner. Daily cruises 8 a.m. to 11:30 a.m. Rates: $70 adults, $55 children under 12; entire boat for 6 people $350. Exclusive charters available. *P.O. Box 1622, Kailua-Kona, HI 96745; 808-325-5556.*

Ocean Sports   A large general-service provider, Ocean Sports operates an educational Whale Center at the Waikoloa Beach Marriott (in the tennis complex) year-round. Free admission, lots of photos and information plus souvenirs for sale. Seasonal whale watch excursions depart morning and afternoon, with a marine biologist onboard, refreshments served and sightings guaranteed. Hint: take the evening cruise and enjoy a spectacular sunset at sea. *P.O. Box 383699, 69-275 Waikoloa Beach Drive, Waikoloa, HI 96738; 888-SAIL-234; 808-886-6666; fax: 808-886-9407; e-mail: information@hawaiiocean sports.com; www.hawaiioceansports.com.*

★ *Whale Watching Adventures*   One of the best, this 30-year veteran Kona marine biologist and whale researcher, Captain Dan

McSweeney guarantees a whale sighting. Whale watchers board the 40-foot *Lady Ann*, a 42-passenger U.S. Coast Guard–approved vessel, fully equipped, including underwater hydrophone for listening to Hawai'i's various species of whales year-round. Three-hour cruises depart at 7:30 a.m. and 12 p.m. from Honokohau Harbor just north of Kailua-Kona, and include snacks, cold drinks and an 8x10 photo to commemorate your cruise. Captain Dan has been in Kona since 1969 and earned a reputation as an expert, contributing to the Wild Whale Research Foundation through his business. Ask about the "Whale Adoption" program when you make a reservation. Rates: $59.50 adults, $39.50 children 11 and under. *P.O. Box 139, Holualoa, HI 96725; 800-WHALES-6; 808-322-0028; e-mail: konawhales@net scape.net; www.ilovewhales.com.*

Suggested Reading

With thanks to Basically Books in Hilo (www.basicallybooks.com) for their assistance and suggestions.

FOR CHILDREN

A Is for Aloha, Stephanie Feeney
Discover Hawai'i series, Katherine Orr
Goodnight Gecko, Gill McBarnet
Hawai'i Is a Rainbow, Stephanie Feeney
Iki, the Littlest Opihi, Tammy Yee
Kapono and the Honu, Edie Bikle
Keiki's First Books series, Wren/Maile
Ki'i and Li'i: A Story from the Stones, Jeremiah Gruenberg
Lehua, A Tale of Ancient Hawaii, Dietrich Varez
Luka's Quilt, Georgia Guback
The Stowaway Fairy series, Mary Koski
The Musubi Man, Sandi Takayama
S Went Surfing, Ruth Moen Cabanting

FOR ADULTS

Hawaii, James Michener (historical fiction). If you only have time to read one book, really this is it. And/or watch the 1966 film starring Julie Andrews, Max Von Sydow and Richard Harris.
Trouble Free Travel with Children, by Vicki Lansky

History

A Concise History of the Hawaiian Islands, Dr. Phil Barnes
Exalted Sits the Chief, Ancient History of Hawaii Island, Ross Cordy
Hawaiian Antiquities, David Malo
Hawaiian Sovereignty: Do the Facts Matter?, Thurston Twigg-Smith
Hawaii's Story by Hawaii's Queen, Queen Liliuokalani
Letters from Hawaii, Mark Twain (also *Roughing it in the Sandwich Islands, Mark Twain in Hawaii*).
Loyal to the Land: The Legendary Parker Ranch, 750-1950, Dr. Billy Bergin
Memories of the Old Plantation, Frank Hustace
Shoal of Time, Gavan Daws
Six Months in the Sandwich Islands, Isabella L. Bird

Trivia & Humor

Hawaii to da Max, Peppo
Hawaii This & That, LaRue Piercy

Language

Instant Hawaiian Immersion (CD-ROM or 8CD Audio)

Learn Hawaiian at Home, Kahikahealani Wright (book and cassette tapes)

New Pocket Hawaiian Dictionary, Mary Kawena Pukui

Pocket Place Names of Hawaii, Mary Kawena Pukui

Mythology and Folklore

Hawai'i Island Legends, Mary Kawena Pukui

Hawaiian Legends of Tricksters, Vivian L. Thompson

Hawaiian Legends of Volcanoes, William D. Westervelt

Hawaiian Mythology, Martha Beckwith

Hilo Legends, Francis Reed

Hina, the Goddess, Dietrich Varez

Water of Kane and other Legends, Mary Kawena Pukui

Spirituality/Hawaiian Culture

Change We Must, Nana Veary

Chicken Soup from the Soul of Hawai'i: Stories of Aloha to Create Paradise Wherever You Are, HCI, 2003

Hawaiian Herbal Medicine, June Gutmanis

Ka Po'e Kahiki, The People of Old, Samuel Kamakau

Nana I Ke Kumu (Look to the Source) I and II, Mary Kawena Pukui, E.W. Haertig, MD and Catherine A Lee

Powerstones, Letters to a Goddess, Linda Ching

Secrets & Mysteries of Hawaii, Pila

Island Adventuring, Special Interests and Sports

50 Thrifty Big Island Restaurants: Dining on a Budget, Island Style, Jessica Ferracane

101 Fishing Tips, Mike Sakamoto

Beaches of the Big Island and *Hawaii's Best Beaches,* John Clark

Camping Hawaii, Richard McMahon

Fishing Hawai'i Style, Volumes 1-3, Jim Rizutto

Hawai'i Trails: Walks, Strolls and Treks on the Big Island, Kathy Morey

The Hawaiian Spa, Sophia Schweitzer

Healing Vacations in Hawaii: A Travel Guide to Retreats, Alternative Healers and Spas (Big Island Edition), Susanne Sims

Hiking Hawaii, the Big Island, Robert Smith

Petroglyphs of Hawaii, Likeke R. McBride

Pocket Guide to Hawaii's Beautiful Birds and *Pocket Guide to Hawaii's Trees and Shrubs,* Douglas Pratt

Pocket Guide to Underwater Paradise, John Hoover

Roadside Geology of Hawai'i, Richard W. Hazlett

Stars Over Hawaii, E.H. Bryan, Jr.

Surfers Guide to Hawaii, Greg Ambrose
An Underwater Guide to Hawai'i, Ann Fielding and Ed Robinson
Wave-Finder, Larry Blair and Buzzy Kerbox (www.wave-finder.com)

Fiction

Potluck: Stories That Taste Like Hawai'i, Catherine Bridges Tarleton
Shark Dialogues, Kiana Davenport
Red Wind, Ian MacMillan

MUSIC

Hawaiian music has been in the national and international arenas for decades, recently made "official" in 2005 when a Grammy Award was created to acknowledge this remarkable genre. The nominated albums were

The Brothers Cazimero, "Some Call It Aloha…Don't Tell," Mountain Apple Company
Ho'okena, "Cool Elevation," Ho'omau Inc.
Willie K and Amy HanaiAli'i Gilliom, "Amy & Willie Live," Blind Man Sound
Various Artists, "Slack Key Guitar Volume 2," Palm Records (Grammy winner)
KeAli'i Reichel, "Ke'alaokamaile," Punahele Productions

And we can't talk about Hawaiian music without remembering the late Bradda Iz, whose rendition of "Over the Rainbow" touched millions of TV and movie-viewers in *ER*, *Meet Joe Black*, *Finding Forrester*, *50 First Dates* and others. Enjoy listening to Israel Kamakawiwo'ole, "Alone in IZ World" and others from Mountain Apple Company.

MOVIES

For your pre-trip movie night, the following suggestions might give you a sneak preview of the scenery and a taste of Hawai'i history and culture.

Hawai'i, James Michener's epic novel adapted for the screen by Dalton Trumbo, this 1966 film starring Julie Andrews, Richard Harris and Max von Sydow is long (170 minutes) but is a well-told story of the drastic impact of Christian missionaries in the early 19th century. The scenics are beautiful; the local characters are perhaps more interesting than the *haole* and a lot of history is presented in digestible narrative form. A good "orientation" for travellers of all ages, but parents should be aware that some scenes show bare breasts and brief violence. A learning guide is available from www.teachwithmovies.org.

Lilo & Stitch, a Walt Disney animation set in Hawai'i, teaches a few new words ("Ohana means family") and gives a nice sense of aloha and local life in a sci-fi-meets-comedy family movie that's fun to watch.

Picture Bride, a 1994 independent movie about a young Japanese woman who travels to the alien island of Hawai'i for an arranged marriage with a man she's never met. Beautifully filmed in the islands, it is a vivid portrait of the difficult sugar-cane plantation lifestyle circa 1920. Dramatic and maybe a little sad for young children.

Paniolo O Hawai'i, Cowboys of the Far West is an excellent, entertaining documentary by independent Hawai'i filmmaker Edgy Lee. It may be hard to find in mainland video stores, but should be available here. It is the detailed, remarkable story of the tough yet colorful *paniolo* history and culture, from the first cows arriving on the Big Island to present-day ranch life.

Rapa Nui is about Easter Island, not Hawai'i, and it's been criticized for cutting a wide swath of poetic license out of actual history. That aside, the story of an aboriginal island people's relationship to, and eventual destruction of, their sustaining natural environment draws some interesting parallels and asks important questions—just don't make this the *only* movie you watch. Some violence and intensity may be a little tough for young children.

Volcanoscapes, like *Paniolo O Hawai'i*, may not be easy to find on the mainland, but it is the best volcano cinematography out there. A series of amazing videos shot over years of up-close-and-personal encounters, *Volcanoscapes* is an education in truly awesome visuals.

Whale Rider, an independent film released in 2002, is set in New Zealand. However, the similarity between the Maori and Hawai'ian people and environment is so strong that this film was shown in classrooms all over Hawai'i as soon as it became available. It is a wonderful story of a young girl's struggle to maintain family and cultural values, and an innate connection with nature, as she assumes her own role in a shifting modern world. That's a heavy way of saying that Pai wants to learn Maori martial arts but her grandfather stonewalls her because she's a girl. She ends up finding her own way to fight for herself, her people and the whale. Actress Keisha Castle-Hughes was nominated for an Academy Award for her role as Pai.

Index

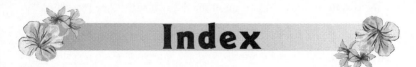

Lodging Index

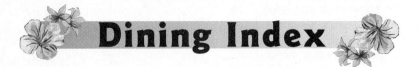

Dining Index

Dining Index by Cuisine

Paradise Family Guides

Ideal for families traveling with kids of any age—toddlers to teen-agers—Paradise Family Guides offer a blend of travel information unlike any other guides to the Hawaiian islands. With vacation ideas and tropical adventures that are sure to satisfy both action-hungry youngsters and relaxation-seeking parents, these guides meet the specific needs of each and every family member.

Hidden Guides

Adventure travel or a relaxing vacation?—"Hidden" guidebooks are the only travel books in the business to provide detailed information on both. Aimed at environmentally aware travelers, our motto is "Where Vacations Meet Adventures." These books combine details on unique hotels, restaurants and sightseeing with information on camping, sports and hiking for the outdoor enthusiast.

Ulysses Press books are available at bookstores everywhere. If any of the following titles are unavailable at your local book-store, ask the bookseller to order them.

You can also order books directly from Ulysses Press
P.O. Box 3440, Berkeley, CA 94703
800-377-2542 or 510-601-8301
fax: 510-601-8307
www.ulyssespress.com
e-mail: ulysses@ulyssespress.com

PARADISE FAMILY GUIDES

___ Paradise Family Guides: Kaua'i, $16.95   ___ Paradise Family Guides: Big Island of
___ Paradise Family Guides: Maui, $17.95   Hawai'i, $16.95

HIDDEN GUIDEBOOKS

___ Hidden Arizona, $16.95
___ Hidden Bahamas, $14.95
___ Hidden Baja, $14.95
___ Hidden Belize, $15.95
___ Hidden Big Island of Hawaii, $13.95
___ Hidden Boston & Cape Cod, $14.95
___ Hidden British Columbia, $18.95
___ Hidden Cancún & the Yucatán, $16.95
___ Hidden Carolinas, $17.95
___ Hidden Coast of California, $18.95
___ Hidden Colorado, $15.95
___ Hidden Disneyland, $13.95
___ Hidden Florida, $18.95
___ Hidden Florida Keys & Everglades, $12.95
___ Hidden Georgia, $16.95
___ Hidden Guatemala, $16.95
___ Hidden Hawaii, $18.95
___ Hidden Idaho, $14.95

___ Hidden Kauai, $13.95
___ Hidden Maui, $13.95
___ Hidden Montana, $15.95
___ Hidden New England, $18.95
___ Hidden New Mexico, $15.95
___ Hidden Oahu, $13.95
___ Hidden Oregon, $15.95
___ Hidden Pacific Northwest, $18.95
___ Hidden Salt Lake City, $14.95
___ Hidden San Francisco & Northern California, $18.95
___ Hidden Southern California, $18.95
___ Hidden Southwest, $19.95
___ Hidden Tahiti, $17.95
___ Hidden Tennessee, $16.95
___ Hidden Utah, $16.95
___ Hidden Walt Disney World, $13.95
___ Hidden Washington, $15.95
___ Hidden Wine Country, $13.95
___ Hidden Wyoming, $15.95

Mark the book(s) you're ordering and enter the total cost here ⇨ [_____]

California residents add 8.75% sales tax here ⇨ [_____]

Shipping, check box for preferred method and enter cost here ⇨ [_____]

❑ Book Rate (free)   ❑ Priority Mail/UPS Ground (call for rates)
❑ UPS Overnight or 2-Day Air (call for rates)

Billing, enter total amt. due here and check payment method ⇨ [_____]

❑ Check   ❑ Money Order

❑ VISA/MasterCard_____Exp. Date_____

Name_____Phone_____

Address_____

City_____ State_____ Zip_____

MONEY-BACK GUARANTEE ON DIRECT ORDERS PLACED THROUGH ULYSSES PRESS.

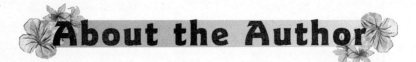

About the Author

CATHERINE BRIDGES TARLETON, a freelance writer, is the author of the 8th and 9th editions of *Paradise Family Guides: Big Island of Hawai'i*; a narrative biography, *Mr. Mauna Kea*; and a collection of short fiction, *Potluck: Stories That Taste Like Hawai'i*. Her writings have appeared in *Hawaiian Style, Honolulu* and *Aloha* magazines, *Bamboo Ridge, North Hawaii News, Hawaii Tribune-Herald* and *Waimea Gazette*. She also writes web content for the Big Island Visitors Bureau pages on www.gohawaii.com and works with fellow writers to edit and polish their manuscripts for publication. Originally from Gloucester, Virginia, "aloha capitol of the South," Tarleton came to Hawai'i for the first time in 1978 and fell in love with the islands at first sight. She and husband Dwight "immigrated" permanently to the Big Island in 1989. They reside in Waikoloa, along with a family of tri-lingual blue and gold macaws who speak a few words of English, Hawaiian and Klingon.